The Lyric Opera Companion

THE LYRIC OPERA
Companion

The History, Lore, and Stories of the World's Greatest Operas

LYRIC OPERA OF CHICAGO

ANDREWS AND MCMEEL

A Universal Press Syndicate Company, Kansas City

The Lyric Opera Companion:
The History, Lore, and Stories of the World's Greatest Operas
copyright © 1991 by Lyric Opera of Chicago.

For information write
Andrews and McMeel, 4900 Main Street, Kansas City, Missouri 64112.

Library of Congress Cataloging-in-Publication Data

The Lyric Opera companion : the history, lore, and stories of the world's greatest operas /
    Lyric Opera of Chicago.
        p.   cm.
    Includes index.
    ISBN 0-8362-6221-2 : $24.95. — ISBN 0-8362-6218-2 (pbk.) : $14.95
    1. Operas—Stories, plots, etc.   2. Opera.   I. Lyric Opera of Chicago.
MT95.L97   1991
782.1'026'9—dc20   91-18146
                                                                         CIP
                                                                          MN

Cover photo of Frederica von Stade and Claudio Desderi in the 1989 Lyric Opera of
Chicago production of *The Barber of Seville*

Photo by Tony Romano

Editor: Alfred Glasser

Book design by Cameron Poulter

Attention: Schools and Businesses
Andrews and McMeel books are available at quantity discounts
with bulk purchase for educational, business, or sales promotional use.
For information,
please write to: Special Sales Department,
Andrews and McMeel, 4900 Main Street, Kansas City, Missouri 64112.

Contents

ix   Preface by Ardis Krainik

1   *Abduction from the Seraglio* (MOZART) by Thomas Willis

6   *Aïda* (VERDI) by Stephanie von Buchau

12   *Alceste* (GLUCK) by Dorothy Samachson

17   *Andrea Chénier* (GIORDANO) by Jonathan Abarbanel

22   *Anna Bolena* (DONIZETTI) by Karen Monson

27   *Arabella* (RICHARD STRAUSS) by Karen Monson

32   *Ariadne auf Naxos* (RICHARD STRAUSS) by Dorothy Samachson

35   *Attila* (VERDI) by Peter P. Jacobi

40   *The Barber of Seville* (ROSSINI) by Jonathan Abarbanel

49   *La Bohème* (PUCCINI) by Dorothy Samachson

54   *Boris Godunov* (MUSSORGSKY) by Dorothy Samachson

58   *I Capuleti e i Montecchi* (BELLINI) by Philip Gossett

64   *Carmen* (BIZET) by Alfred Glasser

70   *La Cenerentola* (ROSSINI) by Arthur Kaplan

76   *La clemenza di Tito* (MOZART) by Thomas Willis

82   *Così fan tutte* (MOZART) by Maxine R. Kanter

88   *Don Giovanni* (MOZART) by Thomas Willis

93   *Don Pasquale* (DONIZETTI) by Frederick Walter

96   *Don Quixote* (MASSENET) by Jonathan Abarbanel

101   *I due Foscari* (VERDI) by John Clarke Adams

104   *Elektra* (RICHARD STRAUSS) by Frederick Walter

107   *The Elixir of Love* (DONIZETTI) by Stephanie von Buchau

111   *Ernani* (VERDI) by Peter P. Jacobi

118   *Eugene Onegin* (TCHAIKOVSKY) by Dorothy Samachson

124   *Falstaff* (VERDI) by Maxine R. Kanter

129   *Faust* (GOUNOD) by Dale Harris

134   *La favorita* (DONIZETTI) by Stephanie von Buchau

138   *Fidelio* (BEETHOVEN) by Peter P. Jacobi

143   *Die Fledermaus* (JOHANN STRAUSS II) by Stephanie von Buchau

148   *The Flying Dutchman* (WAGNER) by Stephanie von Buchau

153   *La forza del destino* (VERDI) by Peter P. Jacobi

159   *Die Frau ohne Schatten* (RICHARD STRAUSS) by Stephanie von Buchau

166   *La Gioconda* (PONCHIELLI) by Jonathan Abarbanel

170   *Girl of the Golden West* (PUCCINI) by Peter P. Jacobi

175   *Götterdämmerung* (WAGNER) by Speight Jenkins

179   *Hamlet* (THOMAS) by Jonathan Abarbanel

184   *Idomeneo* (MOZART) by Alfred Glasser

187   *The Italian Girl in Algiers* (ROSSINI) by Karen Monson

191   *Katya Kabanova* (JANÁČEK) by Lilias Wagner Circle

198   *Khovanshchina* (MOUSSORGSKY) by Dorothy Samachson

202   *Lady Macbeth of Mtsensk* (SHOSTAKOVICH) by Dorothy Samachson

207   *Lakmé* (DELIBES) by Jonathan Abarbanel

211   *Lohengrin* (WAGNER) by Speight Jenkins

215   *The Love for Three Oranges* (PROKOFIEV) by Jonathan Abarbanel

220   *Lucia di Lammermoor* (DONIZETTI) by Jonathan Abarbanel

225   *Luisa Miller* (VERDI) by Peter P. Jacobi

231   *Lulu* (BERG) by Karen Monson

237   *Macbeth* (VERDI) by Stephanie von Buchau

241   *Madama Butterfly* (PUCCINI) by Peter P. Jacobi

246   *The Magic Flute* (MOZART) by Thomas Willis

252   *Manon* (MASSENET) by Thomas Willis

257   *Manon Lescaut* (PUCCINI) by Peter P. Jacobi

261   *Maria Stuarda* (DONIZETTI) by Speight Jenkins

265   *The Marriage of Figaro* (MOZART) by Jonathan Abarbanel

272   *A Masked Ball* (VERDI) by Karen Monson

277   *The Mastersingers of Nuremberg* (WAGNER) by Stephanie von Buchau

284   *The Mikado* (GILBERT AND SULLIVAN) by Alfred Glasser

287   *Orfeo ed Euridice* (GLUCK) by Jonathan Abarbanel

292   *Orlando* (HANDEL) by Nancy Peponis

295   *Otello* (VERDI) by Peter P. Jacobi

301   *I pagliacci* (LEONCAVALLO) by Roger Dettmer

303   *Paradise Lost* (PENDERECKI) by Speight Jenkins

307 The Making of *Paradise Lost* (PENDERECKI) by Gregory Speck

311 *Parsifal* (WAGNER) by Stephanie von Buchau

318 *Pelléas et Mélisande* (DEBUSSY) by Ernest Ansermet

320 *Peter Grimes* (BRITTEN) by Dorothy Samachson

324 *Rigoletto* (VERDI) by Speight Jenkins

329 *Roméo et Juliette* (GOUNOD) by Speight Jenkins

332 *La rondine* (PUCCINI) by Roger Dettmer

339 *Der Rosenkavalier* (RICHARD STRAUSS) by Dorothy Samachson

344 *Salome* (RICHARD STRAUSS) by Dorothy Samachson

350 *Samson* (HANDEL) by Thomas Willis

358 *Samson et Dalila* (SAINT-SAËNS) by Alfred Glasser

364 *Satyagraha* (GLASS) by Thomas Willis

369 *Simon Boccanegra* (VERDI) by Peter P. Jacobi

374 *La sonnambula* (BELLINI) by Jonathan Abarbanel

379 *The Tales of Hoffmann* (OFFENBACH) by Speight Jenkins

384 *Tancredi* (ROSSINI) by Alfred Glasser

388 *Tannhäuser* (WAGNER) by Lilias Wagner Circle

391 *Tosca* (PUCCINI) by Stephanie von Buchau

396 *La traviata* (VERDI) by Jonathan Abarbanel

403 *Tristan und Isolde* (WAGNER) by Speight Jenkins

408 *Il trovatore* (VERDI) by Stephanie von Buchau

413 *Turandot* (PUCCINI) by William Weaver

417 *La Voix humaine* (POULENC) by Jonathan Abarbanel

423 *The Voyage of Edgar Allan Poe* (ARGENTO) by Charles Nolte

431 *Werther* (MASSENET) by Thomas Willis

435 *Wozzeck* (BERG) by John W. Freeman

439 Index

PREFACE
by Ardis Krainik

If you have chosen to peruse this book, I am assuming that you are an opera fan. Perhaps you avidly attend every performance where you live, listen to recordings constantly, and tune in to opera programs on radio and television on a regular basis. Then again, maybe you are just starting to get the opera "bug."

After spending most of my life in this fascinating business, I feel that I can safely say this about opera aficionados: The more they know about opera, the more they want to know about it; and the more they know about it, the more they love it!

This international art form has been written about—praised, condemned, and criticized—in all the languages of the Western world during the four centuries that have elapsed since those Florentine intellectuals who called themselves the "Camerata" ("roomful") set the whole, marvelous phenomenon in motion.

Some books simply give the plot of various operas; others are couched in such "high falutin'" terms that advanced degrees in music theory are prerequisites to reading them; still others strongly resemble cryptograms from one expert to another!

I can assure you that *The Lyric Opera Companion* is none of these!

Contained in a few brief pages is just the information you need about each opera to provide you with a well-informed evening in the opera house. Happily, these facts are not presented in the dry manner of a scholarly tome, but rather in an entertaining fashion that is actually fun to read. Do you know, for example, which of the four "Ring" operas Wagner wrote first? Can you define a "Gesamtkunstwerk"? Do you know why Mascagni decided to write *Cavalleria rusticana*? Or which Shakespeare play was Verdi's favorite? Or why Leoncavallo hated Puccini? Or where Sir William Gilbert dug up the name of Yum-Yum's sister, Pitti-Sing? These are but a few of the myriad questions that are answered in *The Lyric Opera Companion*.

You will also find that these articles are written in a delightful variety of styles that derives from the fact that they have been contributed by a consortium of writers including critics, musicologists, impresarios, and conductors.

The Lyric Opera Companion is an anthology of the best of the specially commissioned background articles that have appeared in Lyric Opera of Chicago programs since these features began in 1970. Whether you enjoy live performances, opera recordings, or videos, I believe this book will help you to increase your enjoyment of what—for me—is the most exciting art form in the world!

Ardis Krainik
General Director
Lyric Opera of Chicago

The Lyric Opera Companion

MOZART'S *Abduction from the Seraglio*
by Thomas Willis

Mozart's first imperial operatic commission had a stormy time during rehearsal. There had been all kinds of intrigue behind the scenes—spats between jealous and temperamental singers, disparaging comments from Vienna's reactionary musical establishment, and back stabbing by established composers who feared competition from the gifted twenty-six year old just up from provincial Salzburg. When the first performance of *Die Entführung aus dem Serail* finally took place on July 16, 1782, the old Burgtheater became the scene of a lively audience demonstration, complete with hisses, whistles, shouts, and an attempt to create a disturbance during the performance itself. According to Mozart, the second night was no better. "Could you have imagined," he wrote to his father, "that there would be an even noisier cabal yesterday than on the first evening? The whole first act was hissed. But they could not prevent the loud cries of bravo for the arias."

A celebrated interchange is supposed to have taken place immediately thereafter at a court affair. Encountering the young composer, the emperor, Joseph II, took it upon himself to review the new opera: "Too beautiful for our ears, and monstrous many notes, my dear Mozart." To which the intrepid newcomer answered, "Exactly as many as necessary, your Majesty." Scholars have been debating the anecdote's accuracy for years, a fact that did not keep Peter Shaffer from giving it new life in *Amadeus*. True or not, it affords a valuable insight into this first opera of Mozart's dramatic maturity and the commanding genius who brought it into being.

Even before the premiere, *The Abduction* was creating a stir. The poster outside the theater on opening night read "Comic Singspiel in three acts. Text by Christoph Friedrich Bretzner, revised by Gottlieb Stephanie the younger." True as far as it goes. Bretzner, a Leipzig businessman and prolific author of German-language stories and adaptations, had written a libretto entitled "Belmont and Constanze" for the composer Johann André; it was performed in Berlin in 1781. Taking advantage of the lack of copyright protection in eighteenth-century Europe, Stephanie and Mozart pirated the text and used it as the basis for their new opera. Bretzner was not amused. A notice in the *Leipziger Zeitung* swiftly appeared: "A certain person in Vienna by the name of Mozart has taken the liberty of misusing my drama 'Belmont and Constanze' as an opera libretto. I hereby solemnly protest against this violation of my rights, and propose to take further action. Bretzner." Apparently he thought better of his threat; in 1794 he made a German translation of *Così fan tutte*.

Had he chosen to pursue his plagiarism case, Bretzner would have had a difficult time. "Turkish" operas and plays were so common as to make them public property in mid-eighteenth-century Europe. They had their basis in historical reality; the Ottoman Empire remained a threat to central Europe until 1683, when an unsuccessful siege of Vienna put an end to the Turks' western expansion. By the 1720s, history had given way to fantasy. From north to south, playbills burst forth with titillating titles: *The Liberated Slave, The Pilgrims of Mecca, Caravan to Cairo, The Pasha of Tunis, The Sultan, Or a Peep into the Seraglio,* and the like. Mozart himself had been working on a similar subject shortly before *The Abduction;* his unfinished comic opera, *Zaide,* is based on a libretto entitled "The Seraglio, Or the Unexpected Encounter in Slavery of Father, Daughter, and Son," whose plot is similar in many respects to the one claimed by Bretzner.

Whether comic or tragic, these "Turkish" theater works shared a common thread: cruelty. Stereotypes still familiar today were already in place. A turban-clad sultan, or pasha, ruled in barbarous omniscience. Standard punishments included beating the soles of feet, boiling in oil, or roasting on a spit. Women of many lands were sequestered in the harem, or seraglio, with eunuchs for guards. Seen at a comfortable distance, these characters and situations had an ambivalent attraction similar to those in contemporary motion pictures, where extreme violence can arouse both fear and laughter.

The plots of these "Turkish" works were exercises in sentimentality not unlike our current daytime soap operas. A French writer of the period characterized the category succinctly: "I understand by the comedy of sentiment . . . one that places before the eyes of the spectator characters who are virtuous and persecuted; as well as an interesting situation in which passion struggles against duty, or honor triumphs over self-interest; one, finally, that instructs us without boring us, moves us without saddening us, and causes gentle tears to fall, the first requirement of a sensitive heart." Humor, when present, is included for contrast and is generally relegated to nonfeeling characters such as harem guards or overseers of the slave detail, both of whom can provide comic relief by exaggerating their villainy to ridiculous lengths. Unlike soap operas, their endings had to be happy.

Bretzner's libretto conformed precisely to specifications. There are two serious characters, Constanze and Belmonte, whose happiness is threatened by the Pasha. A lively subplot is created by the servants, Pedrillo and Blonde (an English captive named for the color of her hair). The comic role is allotted to the harem guard, Osmin. At the end, the Pasha recognizes Belmonte as his long-lost son and gives up Constanze to promote family tranquility.

However accurately it conformed to its sentimental roots, Mozart quickly perceived the libretto's inadequacies for the Vienna of Joseph II and the National Singspiel Company which he had founded in 1778. Intended to promote German culture in a city where the pervading atmosphere was French, the company of musicians and actors was to be "a reflection of the German nation" at its best. The company had had a hard time finding successful material, and many of the song plays that had been well received were German adaptations of foreign works. The German works that had succeeded were mostly trivial collections of popular tunes, dialect jokes, homespun proverbs, and the inevitably sentimental plots. Mozart realized that a better solution was at hand. Seizing upon the Enlightenment currents of thought that were swirling about the imperial court, he insisted that Stephanie revise Bretzner's libretto according to the humanitarian principles that were attracting the liberal, educated Viennese patrons.

Instead of the clumsy discovery of a long-lost son, the Mozart-Stephanie *Abduction* gives us a truly generous Pasha, intellectually akin to Rousseau's "noble savage." He releases Constanze because she cannot find it in her heart to love him. Morever, he gives her to Belmonte, who has now become the son of his archenemy, a tyrant who once robbed the Pasha of his birthright and drove him from his homeland. He is the prototype of the enlightened ruler, whose virtue is innate rather than acquired through Christian civilization. One thinks of Voltaire's *Candide* or *Zadig,* the latter dedicated to an imaginary Turkish sultan of whom the author said, "You neither say nor do evil, in spite of the prodigious facility you would have for it." Selim becomes a study in passionless purity of vision, a spiritual progenitor to *The Magic Flute*'s Sarastro. As befitting his elevated role, he speaks rather than sings.

In the dualistic world of the Enlightenment, absolute good must have its evil alter ego. The Mozart-Stephanie Osmin has his roots in an eighteenth-century comic stereotype, the raging infidel. Cruelty, vengeance, and unreasoning passion make him the idealized opposite of his employer, the Pasha. Borrowing from his first operatic love, the Italian opera buffa, composer and librettist move forward from there, creating a fleshed-out, believable archreprobate who bears more than a little similarity to Shakespeare's Falstaff, with some of Caliban added. We see him variously as a homey character gathering figs, a pathetic old lover losing his battle with a young woman, a loyal servant, and a raging anti-Christian whose fury sustains itself to the very end of the opera, continuing even as the liberated lovers praise their benefactor's mercy. Moreover, in some remarkable way attributable only to the Mozart genius, we believe in him as in no one else onstage.

Mozart spent a great deal of his composer's energy on Osmin. The singer for whom he was writing was Karl Ludwig Fischer, the pre-eminent German bass of his day. He had a range from bottom C to baritone high A and a florid technique that from all accounts was unexcelled. "He has an excellent voice," Mozart wrote to his father, "and we must take advantage of it, particularly since he has the whole Viennese public on his side. In the original libretto Osmin has only this short song and nothing else to sing, except in the Trio and the Finale; so he has been given an Aria in Act I, and he is to have another in Act II." Mozart was in the midst of composing *The Abduction* when he wrote the letter. As it turned out, Osmin was given no fewer than six arias and duets to round out his musical character, a fact that contributed greatly, then as now, to the opera's continuing success.

This letter, written on September 26, 1781, is one of the most valuable in the Mozart legacy. More than any other source, it reveals the process of his composition, his conscientious attention to detail, and the certainty of his dramatic instinct. From the start, it is Osmin who occupies his thoughts:

> I have explained to Stephanie the words I require for his opening aria in Act I—indeed I had finished composing most of the music before Stephanie knew anything whatever about it. . . . Osmin's rage is rendered comical by the accompaniment of the Turkish music. In working out the aria, I have given full scope now and then to Fischer's beautiful deep notes. The passage *Drum beim Barte des Propheten* ("Therefore, by the beard of the prophet") is indeed in the same tempo, but with quick notes; but as Osmin's rage gradually increases, there comes (just when the aria seems to be at an end) the *allegro assai,* which is in a totally different measure and in a different key; this is bound to be very effective. For just as a man in such a towering rage oversteps all the bounds of order, moderation, and propriety, and completely forgets himself, so must the music too forget itself. But since passions, whether violent or not, must never be expressed in such a way as to excite disgust, and since music, even in the most terrible situations, must never offend the ear, but must please the hearer, or in other words must never cease to be music, I have gone from F (the key in which the aria is written) not into a remote key, but into a related one, not, however, into its nearest relative, D minor, but into the more remote A minor.

The "Turkish music" that Mozart was referring to is more often called "Janissary music." Popularly associated with Turkey in the eighteenth century, it necessitated the noisy application of triangle, cymbals, and bass drum, plus lively flourishes for piccolo, and lots of repeated chords. (Many piano students have become familiar with the style by playing the "Rondo alla turca" from Mozart's A Major Piano Sonata, K. 331. Added to the quickening pulse of the notes and the sudden, unexpected change of key, the clangor creates a vivid, humorous impression of a man whose passion has transgressed the bounds of reason. Most important of all, the aria achieves its effect without offending the ear. A true child of his time, he had no trouble with the assertion "Music . . . must never cease to be music."

If Osmin inhabits the *Marriage of Figaro* world of opera buffa, the serious young lovers, Constanze and Belmonte, are drawn from the musical environment of opera seria, where interior feelings and psychic affections reign supreme. Their trials—Pasha Selim's threatening of Constanze, the couple's first confusion over faithfulness, and their unsuccessful abduction attempt— trace a familiar emotional path from sorrow and pain to joy and bliss, with the music in control. In *Idomeneo,* the serious opera composed for Munich a year previously, Mozart had demonstrated his capability in this highly stylized realm, where virtuoso singing collided with dramatic veracity. With expert vocalists in the *Entführung* cast, he had the resources for melding genres in a novel combination. Once again, his letter shows the process:

Let me now turn to Belmonte's aria, *O wie ängstlich, o wie feurig* ("Oh, how eagerly, Oh, how ardently"). Would you like to know how I have expressed it—and even indicated his throbbing heart? By the two violins playing octaves. This is the favorite aria of all those who have heard it, and it is mine also. I wrote it expressly to suit Adamberger's voice. You feel the trembling—the faltering—you see how his throbbing breast begins to swell; this I have expressed by a crescendo. You hear the whispering and the sighing—which I have indicated by the first violins with mutes and a flute playing in unison. . . . I have sacrificed Constanze's aria to the flexible throat of Mlle. Cavalieri, but I have tried to express her feelings as far as an Italian bravura aria will allow it.

The bravura aria he refers to is the famous *Martern aller Arten* (Torture of every kind), which stops the action at the midpoint of the opera with a lengthy orchestral introduction featuring four solo instruments: flute, oboe, violin, and cello. The subsequent interchange between the singer and the instruments provides a vivid musical description of Constanze's feelings as she moves from fear to courage, entreaty to resolve, and finally, resignation in the face of death. Mozart's purpose is clear—we are asked in no uncertain terms to take his central characters as living, emotion-filled characters in a humanized musical drama. When, near the end of the opera, the couple is united in adversity, this element of feeling rises to a climax as they contemplate the bliss of death together. Once again, the music has a beating heart, this time expressed with unison strings and bassoon and impassioned coloratura. Separation has been replaced by togetherness, and Mozart has led us to the realization in a way all his own.

However intensely Mozart concentrated on characterization and feeling, he remained a canny, pragmatic professional. Describing the trio that closes Act I of *Entführung,* he notes: "It opens quite abruptly—and because the words lend themselves to it, I have made it a fairly respectable piece of real three part writing. Then the major key begins at once *pianissimo*—it must go very quickly—and wind up with a great deal of noise, which is always appropriate at the end of an act. The more noise the better, and the shorter the better, so that the audience may not have time to cool down with their applause." The previously mentioned pseudo-Turkish music, also present in the overture, Act I's welcoming chorus, and the finale, was guaranteed to please the crowd. So, in all likelihood, did the sight of Blonde, the liberty-loving English serving maid, and the sound of Pedrillo's pseudo-Spanish "Im Mohrenland." Having the Pasha's chief eunuch sung by the deepest bass in Austria is low comedy in more than one way. Pairing him with the highest soprano in a duet emphasizes the joke still more.

The emperor's comment notwithstanding, *Die Entführung* found its public at once. It was performed repeatedly in and out of Vienna, and during Mozart's lifetime remained his most popular opera. Gluck had a performance given at his special request and invited the composer to supper afterward. It reached Prague within a few months of the premiere and became an important factor in the formation of a Mozart-loving cult there. Although it has been performed uninterruptedly in German-speaking opera houses, Die Entführung's reputation began to wane during the nineteenth century. Its plot was regarded as mere childish entertainment, its characters as inferior precursors of those in Magic Flute. As the knowledge of Mozart's earliest operas has grown, The Abduction's place in Mozart's creative output has been secured. Relationships have been established not only with the earlier Zaide and the later Flute but also with Bastien und Bastienne, his first attempt at Singspiel, and La finta giardiniera, which also pits serious against comic roles.

Today we recognize Die Entführung aus dem Serail for what it has been all along—a turning point in the history of the musical theater. It freed the German song play from the limitations of its antecedents, opening the road that Beethoven was later to take in Fidelio and Weber in Der Freischütz. Mozart accomplished this intuitively, drawing freely on his knowledge of Italian opera, both serious and comic. His orchestrations were buoyant examples of the newest advances in instrumentation, with unequaled wind ensembles setting off the latest novelties, the clarinets. Amid the diversity of convention, tradition, styles, and attitudes he found what he needed to become Mozart, developing a wholly personal, immediately recognizable musical language. In the process, he changed and enlarged our thinking about the purpose, human dimension, and seriousness of vernacular musical comedies.

VERDI'S *Aïda*
by Stephanie von Buchau

By its very nature, opera is prone to legend. Opera lovers want to believe the most extravagant, romantic stories about this "exotic and irrational entertainment." No operatic legend is more romantic or irrational than the still-prevalent notion that Giuseppe Verdi's Aïda was commissioned and performed to inaugurate Cairo's new opera house during festivities commemorating the opening of the Suez Canal in 1869.

The legend is entirely false, but it wasn't until Verdi scholars such as Hans Busch and Julian Budden unearthed reams of documentation that one began to see how the legend had got started in the first place. Here are the facts, long available in any reputable opera encyclopedia but ignored by legend mongers: on November 1, 1869, the Cairo Opera House, commissioned by Ismail Pasha, khedive (viceroy) of Egypt, at a cost of 2 million Egyptian pounds and built in less than six months by Italian architects and engineers, opened with a performance of Verdi's Rigoletto, then eighteen years old. The canal, brainchild of

French engineer Ferdinand de Lesseps, opened officially to water traffic on November 17.

Ismail Pasha, through Paul Drancht, intendant of the new opera house, had asked Verdi, as the world's most important living composer, to write an ode in honor of the occasion, but the composer had declined. Budden, in the third volume of his monumental work on the complete Verdi oeuvre, suggests that this invitation may be the source of the continuing myth that Verdi wrote the anonymous instrumental march that "served until recently as the Egyptian national anthem . . . many Egyptians believe it to this day."

Ismail Pasha did not give up his dream of securing an opera from Verdi, especially one with an Egyptian theme. In this desire he was enthusiastically seconded by the celebrated Egyptologist Auguste Mariette, commonly known by his Turkish honorific, Mariette Bey. Mariette had been a French schoolteacher whose passion for hieroglyphics led him to study Egyptian language, history, and mythology. As a minor functionary in the Egyptian antiquities department of the Louvre museum, Mariette was finally sent to Egypt in 1850 to acquire Coptic manuscripts.

Instead, he applied himself to archæological digs, discovering the tombs of the Apis bulls, the temples and tombs of the pharaohs at Giza, Abydos, Sakkara, and Thebes. Eventually, working in hardship and pain (five of his eleven children and his wife perished in the cholera epidemic), Mariette secured the patronage of Ismail Pasha and the friendship of de Lesseps and was able to discover the great temple at Luxor and create an antiquities museum at Boulaq near Cairo, where he died in 1881.

At the time of the Suez opening, Mariette conceived an original outline for the plot of *Aïda*. The waters are a tad muddy, and not all experts agree on exactly *how* original this plot is. Charles Osborne *(The Complete Operas of Verdi)* suggests that the composer's friend and collaborator, Camille du Locle, fleshed out Mariette's original ideas with blatant cribs from Metastasio and Racine, while Budden counters that the love triangles in those works are generic and similarities to *Aïda* are merely coincidental. Mariette's younger brother, Edouard, claimed after Mariette's death that Auguste had stolen the plot from Edouard's own unpublished novel, *La fiancée du Nil*.

Amid these counter claims, what is documented is a lengthy, cordial correspondence between Verdi and du Locle, a librettist and impresario who represented the avant garde in his position as director of Paris's resurgent Opéra-Comique. Du Locle had inherited the job of finishing the libretto for Verdi's five-act grand opera *Don Carlos* after the death of Joseph Méry and had become a close friend of the composer. *Don Carlos,* though we revere it today, had not been a success at its 1867 Paris premiere, and du Locle spent time and energy trying to persuade Verdi to try again, especially to write something for the Comique.

Du Locle's suggestions included plays by Victorien Sardou (remembered today as the author of Giacomo Puccini's *Tosca*), *Le Cid* (set by Jules Massenet in 1885), *Adrienne Lecouvreur* (set in 1902 by Francesco Cilea), *Froufrou* (by Jacques Offenbach's librettists, Meilhac and Halévy), Molière's *Tartuffe* (!), and even an opera on the subject of Nero (later to become the intractable, unfinished project of Arrigo Boito, librettist of *Otello* and *Falstaff*). But nothing seemed to interest the composer, who was having a bad time personally.

In 1867 both his real father and his surrogate father and patron, Antonio Barezzi, died in old age, while his friend the librettist Francesco Piave suffered a debilitating stroke. Verdi's scheme to perform a requiem to commemorate the death of Rossini (in 1868), each section written by a different composer, fell through. Verdi's colleagues in this project are forgotten, but his selection, the "Libera me," was recycled in 1874 for the "Manzoni" Requiem which some, including his wife Giuseppina, thought of as "Verdi's greatest opera." (Verdi blamed the Rossini Requiem debacle on conductor Angelo Mariani, who at that time was engaged to soprano Teresa Stolz, later to become the composer's favorite Aïda.)

Early in 1868, du Locle made a trip to Egypt where Mariette Bey acted as his guide. (Possibly, they had already discussed plans for an Egyptian opera when Mariette visited Paris in 1867 to display some of his archaeological findings at the Paris Exposition.) In any case, on his return, du Locle broached the subject to Verdi—perhaps during an 1870 visit to the composer's pied-à-terre in Genoa, where Verdi and Giuseppina avoided the damp winters of their Po Valley estate, Sant'Agata. (Note the date. The Cairo Opera House had already opened when the *Aïda* project was first suggested to Verdi; ergo, the opera couldn't have been commissioned for that occasion.)

At first Verdi refused du Locle's suggestion; he was still looking for a lighter subject. Mariette, seeing the project as a way to get free transportation to Paris (his employer, Ismail Pasha, kept him on short rations), sent an outline of his story to du Locle in April of 1870, along with a wheedling letter assuring the impresario that the khedive had approved the subject, that du Locle should write the libretto and feel free to "change, turn around, and improve as you see fit," and that he (Mariette) hoped that du Locle would claim that the subject was so "archaeologically Egyptian and Egyptological that you cannot write a libretto without an advisor at your side . . . and that my presence in Paris is indispensable for the sets and costumes."

Du Locle sent the anonymous outline to the composer, and Verdi rose to the bait. How could he not? Although *Aïda* has an old-fashioned plot with characters (except for Amneris) who operate as tidy, abstract symbols rather than as messy, breathing organisms, its outline displays classical proportions and themes—among them a father-daughter conflict and a duty-vs-love conflict—that were catnip to Verdi's moral and theatrical biases.

Once the composer had agreed, the project speeded forward. In July, 1870, Verdi contracted with the khedive to produce the work in six months. His 150,000 franc fee was four times what he had received for *Don Carlos,* but the khedive was a big spender, anxious to make Egypt part of the European community. (As a result of his grandiose ideas, Ismail Pasha bankrupted his country and died in exile.) Du Locle visited Sant'Agata, Verdi's home, to write a prose libretto in French, which Verdi and Giuseppina then enlarged and translated into Italian. Finally the poet Antonio Ghislanzoni (translator of *Don Carlos* and author of the 1869 revision of *La forza del destino*) turned it into Italian verse.

This latter task was something of a joke; correspondence between Verdi and Ghislanzoni shows the composer dictating every meter, every psychological turn, and even writing his own verses when he can't get exactly what he wants from the librettist. One of Verdi's favorite maxims, according to Budden, was the sly "In the interests of good theater, poets and composers should show a talent for writing neither poetry nor music." As if to demonstrate, Verdi asks Ghislanzoni for "something sweet, ethereal . . . a farewell to life," for *Aïda*'s final scene. He sketches some verses to show the librettist what he means, but when Ghislanzoni's lines arrive, Verdi writes: "I received your verses. They are beautiful but they aren't quite right for my purpose . . . in order to save time I have already composed the music to the monstrous verses I sent you." Those "monstrous verses," of course, are the moving, simple stanzas of the duet "O terra addio."

The Egyptian premiere of *Aïda,* supposed to take place in January, 1871, had to be postponed until the following winter season, not because the score wasn't ready—it was—but because the Franco-Prussian War, which had broken out in July, had culminated in the grueling Siege of Paris. Not only was the unlucky Mariette Bey detained in the French capital that winter, but, more importantly to Verdi, so were his "historically authentic" sets and costumes.

It is worth noting that the "historical accuracy" of *Aïda* doesn't bear much scrutiny. Although Mariette was a scholar, he also tended to be careless and off-hand. In one of his first letters to du Locle, he remarks casually that technically, the heroine's name should be "Aita." Other solecisms include naming Radamès general of the army (the pharaohs always commanded their own troops); the worship of Vulcan (a Roman god, and not a warlike one at that); the planned surprise attack through the gorges of Napata (the Egyptians did not attack by surprise); and the use of ceremonial trumpets (another Roman custom).

Verdi's contract with the khedive gave him permission to perform *Aïda,* after a six-month grace period, if the Cairo premiere should have to be postponed, but Draneht Bey persuaded Verdi, by appealing to the composer's "loyalty, tact and sense of delicacy," to defer the planned La Scala performances until after the Cairo premiere was rescheduled in December, 1871. Verdi graciously agreed, partly because the extra time allowed him to refine the score and to finesse better casts for both Egyptian and Italian premieres.

The Cairo performance on Christmas Eve 1871 starred Antonietta Anastasi-Pozzoni *(Aïda),* Eleonora Grossi (Amneris), Pietro Mongini (Radamès), and Francesco Steller (Amonasro), and was conducted by Giovanni Bottesini. It was a predictable success and earned the composer the title of commendatore of the

Ottoman Order. But it was the La Scala premiere the following February that proved consequential in the composer's personal and artistic life. Here the female stars were Teresa Stolz (Aïda) and Maria Waldmann (Amneris).

Throughout his career, Verdi was attracted to the artistic temperament of Austro-Hungarian singers such as Stolz and Waldmann. Since we know him as an ardent nationalist, this preference may seem strange, but to see what might have fueled Verdi's bias, one need only recall that a pair of our era's most passionately appealing sopranos—Leonie Rysanek and Sena Jurinac—came from that same tradition. Waldmann and Stolz were such expressive singers that the composer chose them to create the mezzo and soprano roles in his "Manzoni" Requiem. He was crushed when Waldmann ended her career at age thirty-four to marry into the Italian aristocracy.

Stolz was neither as young nor as beautiful as Waldmann (a point not lost on Verdi's jealous wife), but something about her excited the fifty-eight-year-old composer's ardor. Biographers and well-meaning partisans have spent nearly a century trying to obscure the facts, but it appears that when the soprano first visited Sant'Agata in September, 1870, to coach the title role with the composer, Giuseppina's antenna switched on. After the La Scala premiere of Aïda, we find Signora Verdi metaphorically gritting her teeth in letters and diaries as she remarks on how often her husband traveled to Milan to hear his new opera. Verdi's normal procedure was to hear the first three performances of a work and then dismiss it. Not, apparently, when La Stolz was singing.

Frank Walker, in his sensible The Man Verdi, concludes that "beyond all doubt he [Verdi] was in love with Teresa Stolz. But to fall in love is no crime; everything depends on how one behaves in that predicament." Unfortunately, we have evidence that Verdi treated Giuseppina badly; he was a well-known domestic tyrant, terrorizing servants and wife alike, and at one point, when Giuseppina objected to Stolz's extended presence in the villa, the composer suggested that Giuseppina leave instead, which apparently she did. As unpleasant as this is to contemplate, such correctives to the usual hagiography that follows the death of great artists are probably all to the good.

If the personal consequences of the La Scala Aïda premiere infuriated Giuseppina, the artistic consequences infuriated the composer and nearly cost posterity Otello and Falstaff. Audiences loved Aïda, as they do today, but the critics tempered their praise with complaints about "Wagnerism" and comments on the opera's supposed "coldness" and lack of "Futurism" (i.e., progress). The "coldness" charge is dismissed by Budden who remarks astutely that Aïda is perfect, and "as Proust observes, there is often something rather disappointing about perfection . . . [Aïda] is the work of Verdi the classicist. If Don Carlos is his Don Giovanni, Aïda is his Così fan tutte."

The "Wagnerism" charge rankled particularly because though Verdi was aware of his contemporary colleague, he wasn't that familiar with Wagner's music. He had only heard Lohengrin a few weeks before the Aïda premiere, traveling to Bologna to hear Mariani (Stolz's ex-lover) conduct the work's first

Italian performance. He liked much of it, but found the action slow. (Years later, Arturo Toscanini assessed *Tristan*'s second act thus: "If the lovers were Italian, they'd be married and have children by the end of the act, but they're German so they are still talking about it.")

Verdi was never comfortable with criticism, even if it was favorable, but the attacks on *Aïda* for being "old-fashioned" infuriated him. He wrote to his publisher Tito Ricordi in 1873 about "stupid criticisms and even more stupid praise . . . and at the back of it all, a certain sense of grudge as though I had committed a crime in writing *Aïda* . . . ." True, *Aïda* is not a "progressive" opera, something the Zeitgeist of the late nineteenth century seemed to demand, but it is one of those works of perfect proportion, reconciliation, and refinement in which an experienced, creative composer does not try to dazzle or startle his listeners. Instead, using the most mundane materials, he creates subtle and original musical and emotional effects which resonate with universal appeal. Johann Sebastian Bach was such a composer, and in *Aïda*, Verdi comes very near the Leipzig master's mastery of economy.

Still, *Aïda* is not be sneezed at. For instance, it is the first grand opera from which not one note can be removed. Grand opera, a hybrid form spawned in Paris by Gioacchino Rossini with his virtually unperformable *Guillaume Tell* (1829) and continued (I don't think "developed" is an appropriate word) by Giacomo Meyerbeer with behemoths such as *Robert le Diable, Le Prophète,* and *L'Africaine,* witnessed its first viable masterpiece with Verdi's 1867 French version of *Don Carlos.* This sprawling, uneven, but passionately realized work contains a marvelous ballet, "La Peregrina," the same music used in this century by George Balanchine for his radiant "Ballo della Regina." The ballet was a custom required by Parisian aficionados in mid-nineteenth-century grand opera, yet even a superior example of the genre such as "La Peregrina" can be removed from *Don Carlos* without damaging the opera's musical integrity. The two ballets in *Aïda,* however, are so organically integrated that removing them would leave ugly surgical scars and spoil Verdi's carefully calibrated "Egyptian" atmosphere.

Finally, though *Aïda* contains all the requisite elements of grand opera—the ballet, the massive choruses, the spectacular processionals, even room for a pachyderm or two—it is essentially a very confidential piece. Each of its important scenes—with the exception of the Triumphal sequence—depends on two or three singers voicing intimate, personal concerns. Yet this is done, as Budden points out, within the traditional "number opera" format, in which formal arias, duets, dances, and ensembles are embedded in a continuous musical texture. This is, of course, the opposite of "Wagnerism." No wonder the uncomprehending critics infuriated the composer to the point where he threatened to retire from the operatic lists. They had committed the cardinal critical error of attacking him for what he hadn't done, while ignoring what he had so carefully created.

And what did Verdi create in *Aïda?* A perfect opera, yes, but one that recently has enjoyed less than its former unquestioned popularity. Budden suggests that this faint decline may be due to our increasing suspicion of authority. It is difficult to sympathize with a party functionary such as Radamès who, after all, doesn't resist the totalitarianism of the Egyptian regime but dumbly submits to its oppressive power. I am suspicious of psychological explanations for the vagaries of musical fashion. Just as reasonable is the point that in today's precarious operatic economy, Aïda is a budget buster. Furthermore, we are in a strange cycle right now where weighty Italianate voices are in short supply.

Therefore, it is wise for a responsible impresario to plan judiciously before scheduling Aïda. The days when Verdi's twenty-fourth opera could be performed casually every season for fifteen years, as it was at the Metropolitan Opera between 1951 and 1965, are gone forever. Maybe this is for the best, because familiarity *can* breed contempt. (How else to explain why someone would question Radamès's political savvy?) If we are deprived of Verdi's prodigious score except on special occasions, we may never again undervalue its wonders.

GLUCK'S *Alceste*
by Dorothy Samachson

Although Christoph Willibald Gluck's talents earned him his place in the galaxy of musical immortals, one must also credit the two "virtuous women above price" who played significant roles in his striking mid-life evolution from facile composer of shallow operas to musical revolutionary. His declaration of war on the meretricious displays being paraded as *opera seria* on European stages started an artistic revolution that irrevocably altered the future course of the lyric theater.

Gluck's first "virtuous woman" was Marianne Pergin, whom he married in 1750 after a frustratingly long courtship due to her wealthy father's opposition. An accomplished, cultivated woman, she brought him personal happiness, intellectual companionship, and—equally important—a large inheritance. Although Gluck was already a well-known, respected composer, this new-found financial independence helped liberate him from total dependence on royal patrons and enabled him to begin striking out for musical independence as well.

The other "virtuous woman," Alceste, was even more directly responsible for his ascent into the ranks of the immortals. She was the mythological heroine of the 1767 opera in which he incorporated his principles about unifying music and text in "beautiful simplicity" and gave them and her life.

Alceste is the crown jewel of Gluck's creativity, but actually it wasn't the first in which he had tested his reformist philosophy. Several years earlier, he had composed *Orfeo ed Euridice* with an equally reformist-minded librettist, Raniero de' Calzabigi. However, the Philistine Viennese audience didn't, at first, appreciate the work and its many moments of incredible beauty, forcing Gluck to return to the composition of the pot-boilers that were profitable.

In *Alceste,* Gluck and Calzabigi brought their fully developed principles to the stage, and lest there be misunderstanding about their artistic aims, they issued a remarkable preface, written in the form of a dedication to the grand duke of Tuscany, the future Emperor Leopold II, and signed by Gluck alone.

This manifesto explained how, in *Alceste,* he had resolved to divest Italian opera of the abuses that had made "the most splendid and beautiful of spectacles the most ridiculous and wearisome." He stipulated that the overture should acquaint "spectators with the nature of the action to be represented, and to speak its arguments"—to be thematically consistent with the music of the opera itself. He declared that music must serve poetry through its expressiveness and that displays of florid vocalism inserted solely to show off the singers should be abolished. The same restrictions should apply to ballet divertissements that disrupt the plot's clarity.

"There is no musical rule that I have not willingly sacrificed to dramatic effect" in order to "animate the figures without altering their contours." In conclusion, he restated his credo: "Simplicity, truth, and naturalness are the great principles of beauty in all artistic manifestations."

Although Gluck was not the only one to question the disreputable state of Italian opera seria, he was the one who codified the principles of reform. In *Alceste* he showed that these precepts, when applied, could be an emotionally stirring and meaningful experience.

In theory, Gluck's monumental manifesto had a powerful effect on many composers—from Mozart through Berlioz to Wagner—who recognized it as a dramatic ideal to aspire to. In practice, it was not always observed. Still, as Romain Rolland has noted, "Gluck had the highly unique privilege of directly influencing the three great musical schools of Europe all together and leaving his imprint upon them . . . the melody of the Italians, the declamation of the French, the lied of Germany, the simplicity of the Latin style, the naturalness of opera comique, the fine gravity of German thought . . . . If Gluck's melodic vein is exquisite, it is not very abundant . . . we must measure this master by the matchless quality of his works, and not by their quantity."

Yet nothing in Gluck's antecedents suggests that he would be a musician, let alone a musical revolutionary. He was born in 1714, to a Bavarian family that for generations had been in service to various noble landowners as gamekeepers and gun bearers. His parents were so poor that in midwinter, he and his brother went into the snowy forest barefoot and hatless.

Since he was expected to follow the tradition, his father managed to send him to a Jesuit seminary when he was twelve, for some education to prepare him for service. It was there that he was fortuitously introduced to music—learning to sing and to play the violin, cello, and organ so well that he played for church services, which helped him earn his keep.

In Prague six years later, he supported himself by giving music lessons, playing in churches and at village festivals. He was more frequently paid in eggs than in cash, but the die had been cast. He knew that making music, not carrying guns for some nobleman, would be his life's work.

He made his way to Vienna on his own, where luck was with him, and he was engaged as resident musician by a Count Melzi, who took Gluck to Milan, where he studied with Giovanni Battista Sammartini, a celebrated composer of the period, and where he composed his first opera, *Artaserse*. That initial success led to other commissions and invitations from England, Denmark, Rome, and Vienna. Yet despite his growing international fame and support from patrons, he continued to lead a precarious itinerant existence until his marriage.

However, since he was not only enterprising but also extremely intelligent, those sometimes harsh experiences opened his mind to the cultural, intellectual forces of the era. They shaped his thought, his burgeoning artistry, and his independent, frequently testy, and gruff personality. He was unsentimental, undemonstrative, had a violent temper, and paid little attention to the niceties of social behavior. This plebeian, so dependent on the aristocracy for favors, was fiercely independent, in spirit a democrat who could not bow to anyone— regardless of lineage—whom he didn't respect, and he could be openly rude to them. In short, he was just the man to rebel against the artificialities so prevalent in opera. During his long professional career, Gluck composed 119 operas and ballets—a mind-boggling example of musical fecundity. Actually, the number was not that extraordinary. Most opera composers of the Baroque era had to be prolific to survive. Niccola Piccinni, for example, composed some 300. Operas were written to order for noble patrons' courts and for theater managers, who constantly demanded novelty for the avid opera public.

Most of the operas of the time, including Gluck's, were almost barefaced imitations of each other and were soon consigned to the vast dustbin of deservedly forgotten operas. In later life he accused himself of wasting thirty-five years of his life in imitation—composing works that were, in fact, indistinguishable from the works he was now attacking. However, he was unfair to the many composers who bastardized their talents in order to survive the superficial, dog-eat-dog operatic world. He was also unfair to himself, for even in those years his art was constantly refining itself and maturing, and the seeds of his rebellion continued to germinate.

He put those seeds to work in ballet a year before *Orfeo* with a score for *Don Juan* that illuminated the choreography with a dramatic power hitherto unheard in ballet music. The ballet is still occasionally rechoreographed, because the music is such a gorgeous example of eighteenth-century ballet music and lends itself so effectively to movement.

In the century and a half since the Florentine amateurs—the Camerata—had invented opera in the delusion that they were restoring ancient Greek drama and music, opera had first matured and then degenerated into empty lavish spectacles, devoid of aesthetic artistry. The singers—male, female, and castrati—ruled the roost. They earned fortunes, subverting the music with endless florid trills and whatever vocal tricks they could get away with. One story, probably apocryphal, had a furious Handel—when he was still composing Italian opera—dangling a soprano out of a window until she agreed to sing his music as he had written it.

Composer André Grétry's satiric description of the atmosphere in eighteenth-century Roman theater goes far to explain the revulsion that anyone of musical taste must have felt at a performance: "When anybody went there, it was to hear this or that singer; but when the latter was no longer on the stage, everyone retired into his box to play cards and eat ices, while the pit yawned." Another keen observer reported: "Chess is an excellent pastime for filling the void in these long recitatives, and music equally excellent for interrupting one's too great passion for chess."

The Baroque era was now coming to its inevitable end, as the Age of Enlightenment, exemplified in music by classicism, pushed it toward oblivion. Gluck bridged the two eras, and his music for *Alceste,* which revealed his prodigious talent, fit naturally into the Classic ideal of flowing melody and individuality of expression.

Gluck and Calzabigi were well matched as collaborators. Both were openminded, well-read intellectuals, dissatisfied with the shabby condition of opera, and eager to experiment. In their personal lives, however, they were utterly unlike each other. While Gluck, a happily married man, led a stable life, subject only to the vagaries of royal patrons, Calzabigi, born the same year, was an adventurer with a notorious reputation. Although a distinguished poet and critic, he led a life marked by scandal. He was admiringly described by his friend Casanova as "a great conniver, familiar with financial dealings, a poet and great lover of women." In Paris, Calzabigi had lived under the protection of Mme. de Pompadour, the powerful mistress of King Louis XV. When Calzabigi's shady dealings were on the verge of catching up with him, he fled to Vienna and the meeting with Gluck that led to *Orfeo.* Eventually, he had to depart from that city, too.

For their magnum opus, they chose the myth of Alceste, which had already served other opera composers. Alceste (Alkestis in the Greek) was a mortal, the daughter of King Pelias and the wife of Admetus, king of Therae, who had won her when his devoted friend the god Apollo substituted for him in yoking bears and lions together in a carriage as her father demanded.

She was celebrated, however, because she was the noblest wife of all. When Admetus was condemned to death by the goddess Artemis, whom he had offended by forgetting to offer her a suitable sacrifice, Apollo interceded for him, and the vengeful goddess agreed to rescind her dire order if another would volunteer to die in his place. Unhappily, the only taker in the entire kingdom for this signal honor was Alceste, his wife.

When all seemed lost, Hercules, mythology's favorite strong man and another friend of Admetus's, tore her from the arms of Thanatos, the god of death, and returned her alive to her joyful husband.

In 438 B.C., Euripides immortalized her in a play that, with remarkable psychological sensitivity, contrasted her heroism with the craven characters of her husband, willing to accept his wife's supreme sacrifice, and of his aged parents who enjoy life too much to save their own son.

Although many mythological characters are better known, Alceste remains a unique paragon of womanhood, and her virtues were frequently extolled. Plato called her "a monument to all Hellas." Homer praised her as the "loveliest of Pelias's daughters," and Milton and other poets alluded to her virtues.

The opera, which the authors called a *Tragedia in Musica,* was based on Euripides but diverged in its emphasis. All characters extraneous to the final happy ending, including the parents, were dropped. Admetus became a hero—so devoted a friend to Hercules and Apollo that they rush to help him—and a loving husband, unaware of whose death will save his life. *Alceste* was now a drama of conjugal love, permeated by the dread fate that looms over the pair.

For Vienna's conservative audience, the authors replaced the rowdy, drunken Hercules as rescuer with the more dignified Apollo. Calzabigi reintroduced the Greek chorus which acquainted the audience with the details of the unfolding plot. He gave poignant mystery to the scene where Admetus learns the identity of the substitute. Above all, he presented the pathos of Alceste's desperate situation with psychological sensitivity. But it was Gluck's music that imbued the entire work with compassion, humanity, and soaring beauty.

His dramatic overture was revolutionary for the manner in which it introduced the opera's somber theme. The Greek chorus had an awesome, almost supernatural quality, and the music Gluck wrote for Alceste's fearful, yet exalted, plea to the gods—"Divinités du Styx"—is heartbreaking in its poignancy. Even the usually boring recitatives had a new-found musical flow. Alceste's poetic and musical unity and purity were triumphant vindication of Gluck's revolutionary message.

The premiere in Vienna, on December 16, 1767, was hardly a smashing success. Some complained about the gloomy subject, and one critic asked "what pleasure one could find in the jeremiads of an idiot who died for her husband." He turned out to be shortsighted, for audiences soon found so much pleasure in Alceste's suffering that the opera enjoyed a two-year run.

However, that did not end Gluck's involvement with Alceste. He recomposed a good part of the opera for Paris, since the French translation of Calzabigi's Italian text did not work well with his original score. Gluck's translator, Le Blanc du Roullet, a diplomat, however, went still further and made a number of dramatic changes in the libretto—introducing swashbuckling Hercules as Alceste's savior and relegating Apollo to the role of benevolent commentator. Gluck, who stubbornly refused to make this change, was by now back in Vienna for the funeral of his niece, whom he and his wife had adopted. He was too preoccupied with his family tragedy to fight the issue, so the Opéra's managers simply went ahead on their own and commissioned François-Joseph Gossec, a young French composer, to write music for that segment.

The Paris premiere, like Vienna's, was a fiasco. However, Gluck, who numbered Queen Marie Antoinette—his former vocal student—among his admirers, soon won the public over, and the French *Alceste,* which remains the accepted version in the international repertory, triumphed. Much of influential Paris went mad over him, and the City of Light was quickly divided between Gluckists and anti-Gluckists. His ardent fans commissioned a bust by the sculptor Jean-Antoine Houdon, inscribed with words that translate into the passion that ruled Gluck's life: "He preferred the Muses to the Sirens." If, after a time, *Alceste* faded from attention, its recent welcome return to the lyric theater confirms that noble sentiment.

GIORDANO'S *Andrea Chénier*
by Jonathan Abarbanel

Italy of 1889 was a nation enjoying the confidence and pride of a burgeoning nationalism, a nation gloriously unified less than twenty years before under the constitutional monarchy of Vittorio Emanuele. It was an idealistic and socially progressive nation in many ways (passing, for example, workmen's compensation and pension acts in the 1890s), the imperialistic tendencies of which were still nascent and untroublesome.

Nowhere was the spirit of nationalism and independence more fervently expressed than in the music of the nation; and the music of Italy was opera. Indeed, opera dominated the cultural life of Italy as did theater in England and orchestral composition in Germany (until the acceptance of Wagner). As the world knew, opera and nationalism met in the person of Giuseppe Verdi, who personified the genius of the former and the highest principles of the latter. Indeed, his very name had come to be a political slogan. During the struggle for unification, the graffito "Viva Verdi" was an acronym for the political slogan "Viva Vittorio Emanuele, *Re D'Italia.*"

Imagine, then, the void that was felt when, after *Aïda* in 1871 (a year after unification), the maestro went sixteen years before producing another opera, his astounding *Otello* of 1887. He then fell silent again, many assumed forever because of his advanced age. No one could foresee his brilliant last fling, the *Falstaff* of 1893.

Thus, in 1889, Italy's cultural pride was at stake. The search for the heir apparent to Verdi had been on for over a decade, with no one emerging. Add to this heated state of cultural affairs a rivalry—that between the two great music publishing houses of Ricordi and Sonzogno—and you have the setting for the famous contest of 1889. Sonzogno offered a large cash prize plus contracts for the best one-act opera in Italian. Scores of scores poured in. As every opera goer knows, the contest was won by Pietro Mascagni for *Cavalleria rusticana.* It made him rich and famous and began the brief movement in opera known as verismo.

But, wait now. What has all this to do with *Andrea Chénier,* about which not a word has yet been mentioned, eh? Well, it all has to do with that contest and a twenty-two-year-old student at the Royal College of Music in Naples whose opera—entitled *Marina*—didn't win the contest. It didn't win a prize at all, but it *did* place sixth, impressing Sonzogno enough to offer the young student-composer a stipend of 300 lire a month and a contract for a full-length opera. The young southerner, who was born in 1867 across the mountains in Foggia, was Umberto Giordano.

Quick cut to five years and two operas later. Giordano has seen his first full-length opera, *Mala vita* (1892), score a limited success, arousing people more for its lurid dramaturgy than for its music. His second opera, *Regina Diaz* (1894), was produced only in Naples, where it failed. Meanwhile, Sonzogno has published Ruggiero Leoncavallo's *Pagliacci* (1892) which equals *Cavalleria* in acclaim and rewards for its composer. Giordano is twenty-eight, frustrated, hungry. He is still collecting 300 lire a month from Sonzogno, and the old tune-plugger wants something for his money.

"My boy," Sonzogno says, "tempus fugit, money spent, nose to the composition tablet, make the grade. Oh, by the way, shake hands with Luigi Illica. Librettist. Experienced. A real pro. Worked with Catalani and Franchetti and Puccini, who wants him back again. Make hay, expect great things, you can do it, so long."

Illica and Giordano kicked around several ideas for subjects, including Victorien Sardou's hit play *Fedora,* which Giordano was to set several years later. Also, works by Turgenev and George Sand. Illica, too, was busy completing *La Bohème* with Puccini and colibrettist Giuseppe Giacosa. Finally, composer and Baron Alberto Franchetti tossed the idea of an opera about André Chénier the way of young Umberto. Franchetti and Illica had done some preliminary work on the subject, but Franchetti felt Giordano's talents might be more conducive to a successful setting of the story. So he let Illica take it to his new collaborator.

In November of 1894, Illica completed a libretto for *Andrea Chénier.* Giordano began composing early the next year, and he moved to Milan from Naples to be near his collaborator, renting a studio in a bizarre warehouse filled with funerary sculpture. He composed much of the score in Switzerland, where he played some of the work in progress for Massenet, who had befriended him. Giordano appears to have worked steadily and with ease, with complete confidence in his own abilities and his subject matter. Indeed, throughout his career, Giordano seems to have exhibited little self-doubt or elements of melancholic introspection. He took life as it came and enjoyed it or dealt with it.

Giordano's collaborative life with Illica seems to have been open, respectful, and lively. Their only serious argument was over Illica's wish to expand the role of Bersi, Maddalena's maid (a role that was to be sung by a particular friend of Illica's, aha!). Critic Harvey E. Phillips reports that Giordano was not successful in dissuading Illica by letter and finally went into action: "He confronted Illica not only with his conviction but with a gun. Petrified, Illica conceded the issue and was able to laugh when the composer showed him that the weapon was nothing more than a toy."

When the opera was submitted to Sonzogno in the fall of 1895, one of the senior editorial advisors said it was worthless. Giordano had to persuade his friend Mascagni to intercede on his behalf with Sonzogno personally, who accepted the score and set it for production at the end of the Scala season. *Andrea Chénier* opened at La Scala on March 28, 1896 (on a double bill with Tchaikovsky's *Sleeping Beauty* ballet!), and was an instantaneous success, a triumph. It was given eleven performances that season and eleven more the next. Every major opera house soon programmed it, and *Chénier* quickly became a vehicle for some of the outstanding opera singers of the era. Sonzogno signed Giordano to a more favorable contract (after rival Ricordi made overtures), and Giordano was able to marry the woman he loved. The day of his wedding, he was made a Cavaliere della Corona, and while he was still on his honeymoon, *Andrea Chénier* had its triumphant American premiere at the New York Academy of Music (November 13, 1896).

Happy ending, right? Well, yes and no. *Andrea Chénier* made Giordano rich and famous all right, and he enjoyed his good fortune the rest of his life (as mentioned above, he was not an introspective type). But, as with his friend Mascagni and *Cavalleria, Andrea Chénier* was Giordano's great early success which he never was able to top or, indeed, to equal. Actually, Giordano did better than most in an era filled with "one-opera composers"—Ponchielli, Mascagni, Leoncavallo, Boito (as composer, not librettist), Wolf-Ferrari, even Bizet and Charpentier. Giordano had a success with his next opera, the aforementioned *Fedora,* which premiered in 1898. It still holds the stage in Italy and is revived on rare occasions elsewhere. In all, Giordano composed ten operas. His work is uneven but certainly better than that of most of his contemporaries. His principal sin as an opera composer seems to have been that he was not so good as Puccini.

Andrea Chénier alone of his operas clings tenaciously to the edge of the international repertory, beloved of audiences and often roundly damned by fashionable critics who dislike its blatant emotionalism or its musical excesses and lack of subtlety. Understated it isn't. *Chénier* is a robust, highly charged, muscular drama with a profusion of melody. It sweeps its audience along with a broadstroke musical and dramatic portrait of a tumultuous era, the French Revolution. Four of its arias are firmly entrenched in the standard singer's repertory: the tenor arias "Un dì all'azzurro spazio" (Act I) and "Come un bel dì di maggio" (Act IV), the soprano aria "La mamma morta" (Act III), and the baritone aria "Nemico della patria" (Act III).

Who Was André-Marie de Chénier?

The real André Chénier was the son of a bourgeois French career diplomat who aspired to the petty nobility and almost made it. The family, in any case, called themselves "de Chénier" which was a pretension of nobility. André-Marie was born in Constantinople, where his father was posted, in 1762, moving with his mother and siblings to Paris in 1773. His mother was a woman of education and culture, descended from a well-to-do Greek family. From her, André developed both an understanding and an appreciation of the classical tradition in literature and philosophy. Though not wealthy, she conducted a weekly salon which attracted an unusual number of artists of distinction, including the painter Jacques-Louis David, who was to become a close friend of young André.

For his education, André's parents were able to enroll him in the Collège de Navarre, an institution operated on the most enlightened educational principles of the day, and one usually open only to aristocrats. As a student, André became a fine Greek scholar and first began to write verse. All his poetry, in fact, was strictly classical in form. Also at school, André befriended many members of the nobility who encouraged him greatly in his writing. A number of them became lifelong friends, too, giving André substantial financial support from time to time. Thus, the young poet grew up with the tastes of the aristocracy to which he did not belong. He also grew up with their essentially conservative political viewpoint.

During the 1780s he had a short fling as a gentleman-cadet in the army, traveled extensively in Italy and Switzerland (at the expense of his noble friends), and served several years as a secretary in the French Embassy in London. He wrote much of his major poetry during this period but never published any of it. In fact, he wasn't even known as a poet except by his circle of friends.

The Revolution drew him back to Paris permanently in 1791, though he had published his first political essay a year before. He wrote twenty-seven articles and essays in all, and these, not the two poems published in his lifetime, were the basis of his reputation during the French Revolution.

Politically, Chénier was a staunch moderate. He supported the first phase of the Revolution (the Tennis Court Oath and all that) which was a revolt of the middle classes calling for a representative legislature and a constitutional monarchy. He abhorred the increasing violence and anarchy of the Revolution as the second phase (the Reign of Terror) approached. He was a fierce patriot, and the idea of Frenchmen spilling the blood of other Frenchmen was anathema to him. His articles became increasingly anti-Jacobin as that faction became increasingly bloody.

In 1792 he withdrew in disgust from participating actively in any party politics. It was best, also, for him to be out of Paris at that time, so he traveled a bit. There are hints, but no proof, that he may have been involved in certain anti-Jacobin and promonarchist activities while "in hiding." It is clear, however, that he helped prepare the defense for the trial of King Louis XVI. It must be noted that none of this activity was in any way illegal; even his defense of the king was not the reason for which he was executed.

Chénier was arrested by mistake in March, 1794, while visiting some aristocratic friends near Paris. The officers were after his hostess, but had no warrant for him. The Revolution held him for four months, trying to figure out what to do with him, while his father and brother (a well-placed Jacobin) made efforts to secure his release. They didn't help. Chénier, who certainly *did* participate in Revolutionary activities for which he might have been tried, was condemned by stool pigeons for participating in a plot with which he had utterly no association. Ironically, he was also confused with yet another brother, Louis, who was imprisoned at the same time.

Chénier was hauled before the Revolutionary Tribunal on July 25, 1794, condemned to death, and guillotined the same day. He rode a tumbril to execution shared by a fellow poet, Roucher (also a character in the opera). According to legend, on that last journey they loudly recited verses from Act I of Racine's *Andromaque*.

While in prison, Chénier met, briefly, Aimée de Coigny, the Maddalena of the opera. They never were lovers. His most famous poem, "La Jeune Captive" (The Young Captive), was written *about* her, but not *for* her. She was for him a feminine ideal and nothing more. In real life, Aimée de Coigny, the Duchess of Fleury, had several husbands, a scandalous number of lovers, and bribed her way out of prison for one hundred louis.

Chénier's poetry was first published in a collected edition in 1819 and became the instantaneous rage of the burgeoning Romantic Movement in art and literature. His tragically short life, the irony of his death at thirty-two, the myth of his prison romance, the confusion of those revolutionary times—all created a legend of the ill-fated young poet which the Romantics clasped to their collective bosom. Philosophically, Chénier was a student of Montesquieu, Voltaire, and Rousseau and, thus, forward-thinking. His ardent love of country and patriotism obscured the fact that politically he was quite conservative. And the Romantics simply ignored the fact that in terms of form he was the last great neoclassicist, looking back towards Racine, and not a precursor of their own innovations.

Thus, Chénier, in yet another posthumous irony, came to influence Alfred de Vigny, Victor Hugo, Charles Augustin Sainte-Beuve, Alfred de Musset, and other writers of the nineteenth century. Chénier became a character for fictional treatment, being a subject of de Vigny's novel *Stello,* a novel by Méry, plays by Jules Barbier and Ernest Renan, all of which were sources for opera librettist Illica.

Illica clearly also studied carefully Chénier's verse, as two of the great tenor arias of the opera directly paraphrase two of Chénier's most important poems. Witness "Hymne à la justice," 1787 (prose reduction): "I have seen beggers in villages, the image of misery . . . peasants trampled at the feet of the great, discouraged . . . salt taxes, forced labor, extorters, a thousand ruffians decked with the holy name of prince saddening a province and arguing over its brokenhearted members." Compare this to the opera's Act I aria:

> "I cross the entrance of a humble cottage.
> There a blaspheming man maligned
> the soil that barely satisfies his taxes,
> and against God and man
> he hurled the tears of his children!
> In such misery,
> what do the ranks of the nobility do?"

Chenier's last poem was written in prison, no more than two or three days before his death. It became the model for the great Act IV tenor aria.

> "Comme un dernier rayon . . ." (1794)
> As a last ray of light, as a last balmy breeze
> Livens the end of a beautiful day,
> At the scaffold's foot I again strike my lyre.
> Perhaps before long the place will be mine . . .
> The sleep of the coffin will press my eyelid
> Before I end this verse which now I chant. . . .

And from Act IV of the opera:

> "Just as a beautiful day in May
> that, with the kiss of the breeze
> and the caress of the sun's rays,
> dies out in the sky,
> I, with the kiss of rhyme . . .
> climb the highest peak
> of my existence. . . .
> and perhaps before the last
> of my stanzas is completed,
> the executioner will announce to me
> the end of my life."

DONIZETTI's *Anna Bolena*

by Karen Monson

More than four hundred and fifty years have passed since Anne Boleyn died by the blade in the Tower of London on May 19. As queen of England, the second wife of Henry VIII, she was granted the privilege of being executed by a swordsman brought in especially from Calais for the occasion; lesser mortals died by the ax. "I heard say the executioner is very good, and I have a little neck," Anne is said to have reasoned.

The next day, May 20, 1536, the king took Jane Seymour, Anne's lady in waiting, as his third wife. He lived in the constant, albeit ultimately fruitless, hope of leaving a male heir who would ascend to the throne and supplant the birthright of little Elizabeth, whom Anne had borne him a few months after their wedding. Recent scholarship has strongly suggested that Henry deserves neither pity nor empathy; the boorish, even villainous parts of his personality, which history once identified with his declining years, were apparently well cultivated throughout his lifetime. It is, however, not true that the wedding festivities for Henry and Jane began even before poor Anne was decapitated. That, gentle listener, is operatic license—although who would put it past this king to begin prenuptial festivities as his wife walked to meet the swordsman?

In fact, Henry would probably have had plenty of company at a celebrative banquet away from the Tower on that fateful day in May, for Anne was by no means a popular queen. Although contemporary engravings portray her not at all unflatteringly, a writer from the period described her as "not one of the handsomest women in the world; she is of middling stature, swarthy complexion, long neck, wide mouth, bosom not much raised, and in fact has nothing but the English King's great appetite, and her eyes which are black and beautiful." Her neck was long but small. Other accounts spoke of her sickly complexion. She is said to have had an extra fingernail on her right hand. But whatever she had—or didn't have—it was enough to lure Henry VIII.

However, once Anne was England's queen, the defense rose in favor of Catherine of Aragon, Henry's first wife, who died only months before Anne was executed. Charles V, Catherine's nephew, convinced the pope to deny Henry's divorce, and Charles threatened invasion. The public believed, perhaps with some accuracy, that it was the influence of the Protestant Anne that led to violence against churchmen, plundering of monasteries, and turmoil both religious and social within the palace. History has put the actual plotting against Anne on the shoulders of Thomas Cromwell, who recognized the crucial importance of an alliance between France and England and concluded that Anne's mere existence was the primary impediment. So then it was perhaps Cromwell who engineered Anne's demise.

Revisionists have not concentrated on the issue of Anne herself, so she is often portrayed as a nagging shrew, a hysteric who did not hesitate to offend her husband, and a woman who had decided that the one thing in life that she wanted was to be the queen of England. When she was seventeen, she had fallen in love with Percy, the son of the earl of Northumberland, but the king and Cardinal Wolsey saw that such a match would not take place. Anne was banished to the countryside, then was brought back to court three years later, when she allowed the king to be only one of several suitors for six years, after which coy course she relented and found herself pregnant.

Marriage was, of course, necessary, though the union would last only three years (and through several disheartening miscarriages). The details of Anne's demise as they have come down to us over four centuries of history written and rewritten seem to include more sordid elements than would ever fit into an opera: incest (allegedly with her own brother, since she had been alone with him for several hours), adultery, calculated bitchiness have been suggested but never proved. "If any man will meddle with my cause, I pray you to judge the best," Anne said as she went to her death.

The questions behind the lady herself tend only to add interest to Gaetano Donizetti's *Anna Bolena,* though there is no doubt that the composer and his librettist, Felice Romani, honored Anne's request and judged her the best in their 1830 opera about her demise. To be sure, the creators took liberties with history, committing sins of omission as well as those of commission. Percy, for example, was actually one of twenty-six peers who voted to condemn Anne to death; his punishment for having loved Anne had been a pallid marriage, not exile. And, of course, the opera's Anne appears to be a strong woman and even hysterical in the final scene, but she is hardly portrayed as the shrew or wench she is said to have been.

But this was a case in which even the fanciful world of opera could not swallow all of the vagaries that life had brought to bear upon the royal household, so when Romani prepared his libretto, he pared extraneous intrigues, all but eliminated the political factors, aimed for dramatic clarity, and made it clear that he believed in Anne's innocence. (It must be noted that he also used the Italianate versions of the names; for the sake of simplicity and, I hope, intelligibility, I have used the original versions. Giovanna di Seymour seems a bit much for English-speaking readers to be asked to digest, when Jane Seymour is so much easier.)

Although the dramatic sources for this particular libretto remain a mystery (some say the idea may have come from a French play of the 1820s), Romani apparently ended the first version of the libretto with Anne's being beheaded on-stage. Whether for fear of the censors' pencils or just in the name of good taste, the final curtain of the final version finds Anne only in a faint, though the arch of the musical lines and the colors of the score depict death.

It would be tidy to be able to say that Romani and Donizetti produced *Anna Bolena* with a larger project in mind, specifically, what has come to be called the "Tudor trilogy" or the *Tudor Ring: Anna Bolena* (1830), *Maria Stuarda* (1834), and *Roberto Devereux* (1837). But such was far from the case. Though the thirty-three-year-old composer was well aware of the vogue of the novels of Sir Walter Scott when he received the libretto for *Anna Bolena* (and also for the previous year's *Elisabetta al Castello di Kenilworth*), he entertained no particular interest for the history of the British throne. And of the three texts for these operas which have become so grouped together in our minds, Romani produced only one, *Anna Bolena.* He sent it to Donizetti during the first part of November, 1830. Donizetti did what any ambitious young Italian opera composer of the period would have done: he took the libretto and set it to music in time for the new opera to go into rehearsal for a premiere on December 26, to open Milan's newly formed rebel Teatro Carcano. When you have a cast, a theater, and an opening date, you write fast. But Donizetti was used to that; he produced as many as five operas in a year.

Although Donizetti might not have realized it when he sat down to compose the score to Romani's *Anna Bolena,* he was at a turning point in his career, a turning point which seems in large part to have been brought on by a combination of circumstances and text. First, Romani knew that the cast for the premiere of the new opera would include four of the era's greatest singers: Giuditta Pasta, Elisa Orlandi, Giovanni Rubini, and Filippo Galli. With such resources, Romani said, "the poet can throw away the pale melodramatic rubbish known as 'librettos' and soar to the heights of lyric tragedy; the composer can leave in his desk his worn-out stock of routine phrases and everlasting cabalettas and rise to dramatic truth and the music of passion."

With this realization, Romani gave Donizetti a text that demanded much more music and, therefore, performance time than those to which audiences of the time were accustomed. (It should probably be noted nevertheless that the first performance of *Anna Bolena* was accompanied by a five-act ballet, *La vedova,* choreographed by Luigi Henry. It is amazing that the performance is not still going on, even as we speak.)

And the writer filled those hours with implication-filled dialogue—nothing oversimplified, but everything packed with viable emotion and suggestion. The speed with which the plot moves and the subtleties that are suggested look forward to Verdi. In the 1830s, it was common for a libretto to be printed with brackets marking the lines of text that the composer saw fit not to set; the idea was apparently that the bracketed lines would complete the listeners' understanding of the plot. In *Anna Bolena* there were virtually no lines of the original text which were not committed to music. Although Donizetti made minor changes in the libretto to satisfy his desire for verbal economy and musical flow, the words were set to music virtually as they stood in the libretto which he received six weeks before the first performance.

It is impossible to say whether Romani's work was the source of inspiration or whether Donizetti had reached the point in his creative life at which he was determined to break the traditional stride and accomplish new musico-dramatic feats. Whichever, *Anna Bolena* saw significant changes in the composer's techniques. (For details on these issues, interested readers must consult *"Anna Bolena" and the Artistic Maturity of Gaetano Donizetti* by the University of Chicago's Professor Philip Gossett, published by Oxford University Press.)

Donizetti seemed to thrive on the possibility of extended dialogue recitative, none of which has been thrown away or written as a mere prelude to the trend-setting arias. In another break with tradition, he wrote out the ornaments in the repeated lines of set pieces, so instead of simply inscribing his score with such commands as "repeat from A to B," from which suggestion the singers would have assumed that ornamentation was in order, he composed variations on both melodies and accompaniments. Obviously the composer as well as the librettist took heart from the talents of the principal singers set for the cast of the premiere of *Anna Bolena,* and neither Donizetti nor Romani found reason for compromise. With less than a month to spare before the first performance, Donizetti felt perfectly comfortable writing "Al dolce guidami castel natio" and "A miei lunghi spasimi" (after "Home, Sweet Home") in the final mad scene, then taking his leading lady directly into the double series of trills in the cabaletta "Coppia iniqua." The modern listener can hardly wonder at Anne's having passed out before her actual execution.

The Teatro Carcano in Milan existed for only one season, but its place in history has been secured by its presentations not only of the premiere of *Anna Bolena* but also of Vincenzo Bellini's *La sonnambula,* about three months later. And the fate of the impresarios who held a grudge against La Scala was not ruined by *Anna Bolena.* On the contrary, Donizetti wrote to his wife Virginia, whom he had sent to her family in Rome while he composed his newest opera, that the premiere was "a triumphal success, delirium, it seemed as though the public had gone mad. Everyone said that they could not remember having been present at such a triumph."

The triumph of *Anna Bolena* was to become Donizetti's calling card in both Paris and London, and it attracted such stars as the sopranos Giulia Grisi, Caroline Unger, and Therese Tietjens and the basso Luigi Lablache as Henry VIII. The success and longevity of the presentations seems to have depended on the ladies, and all of the sopranos who espoused the role of Anna are said to have been able to take over the stage with the combination of delicacy, energy, and vocal fire that are necessary for Donizetti's heroine. So although the triumph of *Anna Bolena* made a big difference in Donizetti's international reputation during his short lifetime (he died in 1848 at the age of 51), the opera held the stage for a mere fifty years and then was consigned to obscurity.

The revivals of *Anna Bolena* have depended no less on the casting than did its initial successes. All but forgotten since the 1870s, the opera was revived in Donizetti's native Bergamo in 1956, then brought to La Scala in Milan in a production by Luchino Visconti with Maria Callas in the title role in 1957. A concert performance followed in New York, with productions at Wexford, Glyndebourne (the reasons for interest on the part of British audiences are evident), Santa Fe, Dallas, Barcelona, and Düsseldorf, among other towns and cities.

Anna Bolena quite simply does not exist without an Anne Boleyn, and the fact that the mid twentieth century has been able to boast the presence not only of Callas but also of Dame Joan Sutherland and Beverly Sills has attracted new attention to this masterwork. This is not to say that the opera is simply a vehicle for the soprano. It has much more to recommend it not just to scholars but also to lovers of grand opera. But like *Lucia* and *Norma* of the same period, it needs a leading lady to carry its impact. And like music of all types and all periods, it will be in and out of the repertory depending on the availability and temperaments of those ladies or those proponents.

The question of version must always arise regarding operas of this period, but in *Anna Bolena* the issue is relatively uncomplicated. This tightly conceived score was designed for the virtuosi whom Donizetti came to expect on his stages. He made a few cuts and additions during his lifetime for different singers in specific performances, but those emendations did not change the fabric of the opera significantly.

It may be argued that no one audience will ever hear the entire score for *Anna Bolena,* but this point seems meaningless when one considers the fact that the composer himself never intended all of the music to be performed in a single evening—he intended to substitute one scena or aria for another in what was already a long music drama. Rather than quibble with the historians and literalists, we must insist only that the score keep the proportions of Romani's drama as Donizetti set it to music, so that the scale of the opera remains noble and gentle and gracious and suggestive of drastic intrigue on a scale worthy of its heroine who is acquitted through her music.

RICHARD STRAUSS'S *Arabella*
by Karen Monson

"Romanticism in a vanishing world. . . ." That was the way Hans Meyer referred to *Arabella* and its setting in Vienna of the 1860s. His description, though unduly apocalyptic, was not entirely inappropriate.

"What is vital is to find the right atmosphere for the whole thing, a certain general atmosphere in which the whole piece lives," the librettist Hugo von Hofmannsthal wrote to the composer Richard Strauss in July, 1928. "The atmosphere of *Arabella,* again, differs greatly from that of *Rosenkavalier.* In both cases it is Vienna, but what a difference between them—a whole century! Vienna under Maria Theresa—and the Vienna of 1866! By means of the (incidentally quite imaginary) idiom, I steeped the Vienna of the 18th century in an atmosphere at the same time pompous and cozy—the atmosphere of *Arabella,* quite close to our own time as it is, is more ordinary, less glamorous, more vulgar." The "unhackneyed" era of the sixties was ready for theatrical revival.

Strauss had doubts about an opera that would take place in Vienna two years after he had been born. Hofmannsthal's letter, the composer wrote a week later, "hasn't made the somewhat rotten setting of Vienna in 1866 any more palatable to me. To keep up this style throughout three acts a man would almost need the levity and the talent of the composer of *Fledermaus.* True, in *Rosenkavalier* I managed a few corrupt episodes for Ochs von Lerchenau, but whether I shall now be able to feign dissolute naivete for three whole acts has yet to be seen. The true dramatist, of course, ought to be able to do it—but will I have the patience?"

It had, indeed, been Strauss's impatience that had goaded Hofmannsthal into drafting the first act of *Arabella* almost a year earlier. "Now I've got no more work to do: totally cleaned out! So please, write something. It could even be a second *Rosenkavalier,* if nothing better occurs to you." The composer and librettist had nearly finished their work on *Die Ägyptische Helena,* and Strauss, for one, was tired of mythology and ready to repeat the success he had enjoyed during the last decade with the Marschallin, Octavian, Baron Ochs, and Sophie. A "Lyrical Comedy" was in order.

"Yes, *Rosenkavalier,"* responded Hofmannsthal. "But even lighter, even more French, if I may put it that way—still further removed from Wagner." A few weeks later, the author was able to promise something "even better than *Rosenkavalier,"* and he would soon be ready to send the composer an outline of the plot with a detailed first act. Strauss agreed to set the opera in what Hofmannsthal called "a rather vulgar and dangerous . . . pleasure-seeking, frivolous, debt-creating Vienna" in what finally ended up to be the year 1860. The composer did not find this picture especially attractive, but he evidently had to concede that *Arabella* would make no sense in the silky opulence of *Rosenkavalier,* and that a tinge of seediness, however unpleasant to his tastes, was a necessary part of the hotel in which the Waldners ensconced themselves for the purpose of marrying off their beautiful elder daughter, thereby restoring their fiscal solvency at the time of the Coachmen's (we would say Cabbies') Mardi Gras Ball.

The beginnings of *Arabella,* the sixth and final masterpiece which Strauss and Hofmannsthal created during their quarter-century of collaboration, are meticulously documented in voluminous correspondence. Composer and librettist rarely met, even when they were in the same city or attending the opera on the same night. Hofmannsthal almost always addressed his "Dear Dr. Strauss," while, in response, Strauss's moods took him from "Dear Herr Hofmannsthal" to "My Dear Friend." The letters were obviously intended for posterity, but even if they had been scribbled and relegated to the fire, one has to believe that they would have been no less formal and businesslike. What many believe to be the century's most inspired pairing of composer and librettist was not born of Viennese *Gemütlichkeit.*

So when Strauss saw his partner's early sketches for the new opera, he had no qualms about expressing his displeasure. He could envision parallels between Arabella and the Marschallin, between Zdenka and Octavian, between Mandryka and Ochs, even between the historically inspired Fiakermilli and the Italian Tenor of their beloved *Rosenkavalier* —but he didn't find the inspiration he needed in Hofmannsthal's words. "The new piece, so far as I can judge at this stage, lacks a genuinely interesting female character," Strauss wrote, immediately identifying the one element of an opera, however grand, that was his touchstone.

The composer did like the idea of Mandryka, and he headed to the library to get out "four splendid volumes of South Slav folk-songs and dances from which not only a colossal ballet could be knocked together for our second act, but which might even yield the most enchanting songs for our Croatian, possibly with highly characteristic *original* words." Hofmannsthal approved of the "South Slav folk-songs" (which, in various adaptations, have come to form some of the most beautiful and memorable parts of the opera), vetoed the notion of the "colossal ballet," and stood by his idea of Mandryka—while Strauss went on to call the character a "cardboard hero" with "almost imbecilic good nature." It is a wonder that the marriage of composer and librettist survived the twenty-year mark.

But there is nothing to prove that either harbored a thought of giving up on *Arabella*. The librettist honed both his poetry and his formal outline while defending the integrity of his characterizations. He held to the ideals of

—the "courageous and self-reliant Arabella" who, "having looked too deeply into certain aspects of life, has been slightly wounded by cynicism and resignation";

—the "touchingly impulsive Zdenka";

—"the three Counts in frivolous pursuit of all skirts," especially Arabella's;

—the "cashiered cavalry captain" Waldner and his "whole shady milieu";

—Waldner's wife Adelaide, whom Strauss had once wanted to turn into another Marschallin;

—the innocent and well-meaning Matteo, who will have Zdenka's hand now that two weddings can be paid for;

—and, especially, Mandryka, who motivates *Arabella,* as Ochs motivates *Rosenkavalier.*

"For Mandryka," Hofmannsthal wrote, "this pleasure-seeking, frivolous Vienna, where everybody lives on tick, is the foil; he is steeped in his world of unspoilt villages, his oak forests untouched by axe, his ancient folk-songs. With him the wide open spaces of the vast half-Slav Austria enter Viennese comedy and carry into it a breath of fresh, totally different air."

The discussions continued. Should Arabella seem to be more enamored of Matteo? Should Mandryka have a passionate love scene with Fiakermilli? Should the Counts turn their attentions to the still-beautiful Adelaide? Should Mandryka and Waldner jump ship and go off partying by themselves? Should the "Lyrical Comedy" end up tragic? The creators even debated the opera's beautiful conclusion, when Arabella presents Mandryka with the glass of pure water. Strauss wondered whether the liquid might better be wine. Hofmannsthal defended water as a betrothal ritual of the Slavs. (But did they drink and break the water glass?) "I do not think I shall find anything more attractive and at the same time so simple for the quiet, lyrical ending. . . . For it must be something which happens in the village and can be copied on the hotel staircase. . . ," the librettist wrote. The possibilities were infinite, but the composer held fast on some points: Act II, as he saw it in its early forms, was mere "lyrical gurgling."

Hofmannsthal encouraged his collaborator "to reach a 'less-of-music,' to reach a point where the lead, the melody would be given rather more to the voice, where the orchestra would accompany (at least over lengthy passages) and would be subordinated to the singers. . . . I am not so foolish as to imagine it feasible to *resuscitate* simpler and more unsophisticated forms of art. . . . No—but if it were possible to escape, half way, or even two-thirds, from that German *professorial* concept of music, that something, that 'too-muchness' in German music which made Piccini say of Gluck: *puzza di musica* —it reeks of music. Oh, if only it were possible for the master, in the mature assurance of his power, somehow to leap over his own shadow, his German 19th-century shadow, his time-bound prejudices (even that word is already too clumsy, for this is the subtlest of the subtle), if that were possible, perhaps then the gain would indeed be magical, so enchanting that all the Korngolds and Beckmessers would start off by calling it treason, monstrosity, bankruptcy, fraud, impudence—and these would be names of honour to accompany our child on its way across the world amid the cheers of the public."

"As for your fundamental warnings concerning the musical matter," Strauss responded, "I understand you entirely. What's more, you're quite right! but you forget that ever since *Intermezzo* I have been pursuing the goal you suggest with unflinching persistence, and that in the case of *Arabella* I shall try even more to leap over my own shadow. But for all that a German can never become an Italian—even Goethe and Mozart knew that!"

In November of 1928, Strauss began to try to put notes to paper, but "the thing doesn't even begin to come to music and, to be frank, the characters don't interest me in the least." The revisions continued until, finally, the composer had to confess that he would be unable to accomplish anything until he had the finished libretto in front of him. Both men went through periods of ill health; Hofmannsthal, especially, was badly affected by Austria's *Foehn*, the wind from the south that is said to bring on afflictions. On July 6, 1929, Strauss wrote to ask that the end of Act I belong to Arabella, the end of Act II to Mandryka, and the end of Act III to the two together. On July 10, Hofmannsthal replied that such had been his intent, at least in part. On July 13 Hofmanns-thal's elder son, Franz, committed suicide. On July 15, moments before his son's funeral, Hugo von Hofmannsthal died at the age of fifty-five.

Strauss had written nothing; in his mind *Arabella* was not ready to be composed. But the word of his colleague's death spurred him to action, and within two months he had sketches for the first act, perhaps including the melting F-Major duet for Arabella and Zdenka, *"Aber der Richtige, wenn's einen gibt auf dieser Welt. . ."* (But the right man—if there is one for me. . .). The composer made changes to his own tastes and whims; these are clear from the version of *Arabella* published with the complete works of Hofmannsthal and from the various alternatives allowed to operatic producers. But it is also clear that, despite procrastination (including taking comfort in the crafting of a new version of Mozart's *Idomeneo*), Strauss had been sold on *Arabella*.

His solutions to old problems added up to a conversational, ensemble approach, with the moderate-sized orchestra acting as a "chamber music" accompanist to the voices. There is much to remind the listener of *Der Rosenkavalier,* but there is also much in *Arabella* that refers to *Don Juan* and *Till Eulenspiegel.* Folk song is never forgotten, and whether Strauss is actually quoting the Slavonic intonations or just imitating them, they provide the unifying, accessible threads for the opera. Analysts have worried over whether these nationalistic traits and the waltz and polka rhythms degraded *Arabella,* made it a "lesser" work. Audiences have rarely had the same dire concerns.

The new work had been promised to the Dresden Opera, and at the prodding of that house's intendant, Strauss promised, "I'll get it together all right, even if I pass seventy." That he did, well in advance of his anniversary. He drew the final barline on the score on October 12, 1932, and declared his labors past on November 27 of the same year.

But as Hitler was coming into power, both the Generalmusikdirektor and the intendant of the Dresden State Opera were evicted from office, and what would have been the sixth Strauss premiere at that theater was postponed. The composer wanted to put the opera "back in the drawer," but he consented to a first performance on July 1, 1933, at the Semper Opera House in Dresden, with Clemens Krauss conducting. Strauss had hoped to have Lotte Lehmann sing the title role, but Krauss lobbied for his wife, Viorica Ursuleac, and won. Eva Plaschke-von der Osten, the first Octavian, was the artistic advisor. *Arabella* was a "gigantic theatrical success," much to the composer's surprise, since he had come to have little faith in his "new *Rosenkavalier.*" Strauss continued to worry that audiences would not be able to catch the subtleties of the quickly passing conversations. (He wanted the house lights always to be left bright enough for patrons to be able to read.) He wondered, too, whether the critics who said that his work was aging, less inspired than it used to be, weren't better judges than the cheering, charmed public.

Arabella moved from Dresden to Berlin, with Wilhelm Furtwaengler conducting, then to Vienna, again with Krauss, but this time with the title role sung by Lehmann (who was later to write that *Arabella* was not her cup o' tea anyway . . .). The American premiere took place at the Metropolitan Opera in New York in February, 1955, sixteen years after Strauss's death: it was presented in English, and despite the obvious problems and cultural gap, the composer would probably have approved of the use of the vernacular. Eleanor Steber sang the title role, with Rudolf Kempe conducting. The initial response was lukewarm. It took subsequent performances with the lovely Lisa Della Casa to establish Arabella and *Arabella,* the romantic but fragile "Lyrical Comedy," in this country and around the world.

RICHARD STRAUSS'S *Ariadne auf Naxos*

by Dorothy Samachson

Richard Strauss had barely allowed himself time to savor *Der Rosenkavalier*'s triumphant reception in 1911, before he began to urge Hugo von Hofmannsthal, his 'dear poet,' to start work on a new subject. "Don't forget," he wrote. "I've still no work for the summer. Writing symphonies doesn't amuse me at all any longer."

He was, as a matter of fact, working haphazardly on an orchestral work that would take shape, years later, as the Alpine Symphony. But, he jokingly complained, it amused him "even less than chasing cockroaches." It's doubtful whether Strauss, by now a wealthy man from royalties and conducting fees, ever saw a cockroach. He and his singer wife, Pauline, lived in an impressive villa in the Bavarian Alps, and it's unlikely that any annoying insect would have the temerity to invade the premises and risk the rage of caustic-tongued, house-proud Pauline.

Strauss continued to importune Hofmannsthal for a libretto, even slyly hinting that Gabriele D'Annunzio had contacted him about possible collaboration. But this was largely empty talk, for Strauss would not desert the partner he had so assiduously courted when, in 1906, he had worked with Hofmannsthal for the first time—setting his powerful play, *Elektra,* as an opera.

"We were meant for one another and are certain to do fine things together if you remain faithful to me," Strauss, like an infatuated school boy, had written to Hofmannsthal. He had sensed an artistic affinity with the writer and was eager to establish a permanent partnership.

Although Hofmannsthal is remembered today primarily as Strauss's librettist, he was, during that era, as well known for his lyric poetry, symbolist plays, and probing essays as Strauss was for his music. A member of a wealthy family of part Jewish, Italian, and Austrian descent, Hofmannsthal was a complex personality—reserved, shy, and interested in every area of human behavior. Together with Max Reinhardt, he founded the Salzburg Festival, where his play *Everyman (Jedermann)* is still presented annually.

However, despite all his other activities, he was as eager to collaborate with Strauss as Strauss was with him. It was flattering to be wooed by the foremost composer of the period, but more important to Hofmannsthal was the opportunity to place his personal stamp on opera, and make music and text true equals.

If left to his own devices, Strauss would probably have preferred to stay with intensely melodramatic, pathologic subjects like *Elektra* and *Salome.* Early in their relationship, he had shown his predilection for blood and sex by asking Hofmannsthal for "an entertaining renaissance subject for me. A really wild Cesare Borgia or Savonarola would be the answer to my prayers."

Hofmannsthal had simply ignored the request. In response, he presented Strauss with *Der Rosenkavalier,* a bittersweet Viennese comedy set in the eighteenth century, which Strauss would fondly call his Mozart opera.

But now, in 1911, Strauss again returned to gore, suggesting Georg Büchner's *Danton's Death* and Victorien Sardou's *Ninth Thermidor,* violent dramas about the French Revolution, and Pedro Calderón de la Barca's *Semiramis,* dealing with a legendary Assyrian queen, as fabled for her sexual adventures as for her military exploits. Hofmannsthal turned them all down.

Instead, Hofmannsthal proposed a short "interim work to make myself still more familiar with music, especially your music." Entitled *Ariadne auf Naxos,* it could, Hofmannsthal promised, "turn into something most charming, a new genre which to all appearances reaches back to a much earlier one. . . ."

Hofmannsthal was referring to the lavish opera productions on heroic mythologic subjects that wealthy aristocrats presented in their palaces. However, since both host and guest frequently tired of the lofty, cerebral, serious operas, it became the custom to introduce an intermezzo between the acts. This was light, popular entertainment consisting of music, dancing, comedy, and even juggling, performed, as a rule, by itinerant commedia dell'arte players, and had no connection at all with the serious opera.

It was this milieu and performance that Hofmannsthal wanted to re-create but from his sophisticated, twentieth-century outlook. Ariadne would be the heroine of the serious opera, while Zerbinetta of the commedia dell'arte would be the star of the intermezzo. However, in his entertainment, both would be performed simultaneously in what he, himself, described as a "bizarre mixture of the heroic with the buffo elements."

Although Strauss had serious doubts about the plot, which he frankly admitted he didn't quite understand, he agreed to the project. Since *Ariadne* was intended as a short work, it shouldn't take him too long to compose the score, and it would please Hofmannsthal, who would then devote himself to *Die Frau ohne Schatten,* the major opera they were planning.

To create the seventeenth-century atmosphere, Hofmannsthal needed a framework for this curious divertissement, and he found it in Molière's comedy *Le Bourgeois Gentilhomme* (The Would-Be Gentleman), first produced in 1670, about the attempts of a parvenu to break into high society.

As it happened, Hofmannsthal and Strauss had been planning to do a Molière play for Reinhardt to show their gratitude for his invaluable, but uncredited, staging of *Rosenkavalier.* Now, Reinhardt would have a double premiere—a play and an opera, all in one.

Hofmannsthal completely rewrote the play in German and created a final scene that would serve to introduce *Ariadne auf Naxos.* In this version, the Amateur Gentleman, nervous about pleasing his important guests, orders that both opera and intermezzo shall be presented at the same time.

On hearing of this grotesque notion, the opera's composer, the diva, and the commedia dell'arte players argue about how the changes will affect them personally, and the quibbling reveals their character traits. The young composer is most sympathetically limned, for he represents the creative artist, like Strauss and Hofmannsthal themselves.

Strauss's incidental music for *Le Bourgeois Gentilhomme* was soon completed and was such a delight that he later set it as a suite, independent of the play. But *Ariadne auf Naxos* created problems and led to such serious disagreements between composer and librettist that they threatened their future relationship. Finally, each gave a little—Strauss more than Hofmannsthal—which was to be the pattern of their more than twenty years together.

It was a curious relationship, in which Hofmannsthal, younger by ten years, led the composer, and Strauss followed. Unlike the traditional composer-librettist partnership, in which the librettist might propose a subject and the composer would either accept or reject on his own terms, Hofmannsthal set the terms, as he did with *Ariadne*. He followed his own artistic vision, and Strauss invariably surrendered.

With *Ariadne,* there was complete misunderstanding. Strauss envisioned the opera as a minor, if charming, divertissement. Hofmannsthal saw it as a profound psychologic, philosophic statement about fidelity in love. To him, Ariadne and Zerbinetta were paradigms of two totally divergent elements of womanhood, representing "two spiritual worlds . . . in the end ironically brought together in the only way in which they can be brought together: in noncomprehension."

Ariadne was a mythic Cretan princess who led Theseus safely through the labyrinth where he slew the Minotaur. They escaped, but he then marooned her on the barren island of Naxos. Despite the cruel desertion, Ariadne continued to love him and yearned only for death until she was rescued by the god Bacchus, who married her.

Ariadne was Hofmannsthal's spirit of true love, as he explained to Strauss: "The wife or mistress of one man only just as she can only be one man's widow. . . . One thing, however, is still left even for her: the miracle, the god."

Zerbinetta, on the other hand, was "frivolous . . . in her element drifting out of the arms of one man into the arms of another."

Whether he understood Hofmannsthal's thesis or not, Strauss composed music that most beautifully developed character and beguiled the ear. For Ariadne's Lament, he wrote an exquisitely moving expression of grief-stricken love. For Zerbinetta, whom he made a coloratura, he composed one of the most dazzling, demanding arias in all the operatic repertory. "Grossmächtige Prinzessin" is not only a brilliant exposition of the coloratura art; it is also a practical, if cynical, lesson in love to the oblivious, unhappy Ariadne. The role is also a tour de force of clowning, dancing, and flirtation.

The opera concludes with an exalted, ecstatic duet for Ariadne and Bacchus. While she believes she is welcoming the god of death, he is reawakening her to life, and the sweep of their voices with Strauss's orchestration is unutterably rhapsodic.

For a text he said he couldn't understand, Strauss succeeded masterfully. Even the minor characters—the three nymphs and Zerbinetta's ribald clown companions—are delineated with musical imagination and wit, and Hofmannsthal's transcendental message of love made its point, mainly because of Strauss's music.

The premiere was finally given October 25, 1913. The little 'interim' half-hour divertissement had grown to an hour. Performed with the play, however, it was a long evening, and not a total success. As Strauss put it later, "The playgoing public had no wish to listen to opera and vice versa."

Nevertheless, the two were presented a number of times in Germany and elsewhere. However, two casts—actors and singers—proved too expensive for most theater managers. Besides, the partners now realized they should make the work a full-length opera and substitute a vocal prologue for the play.

Hofmannsthal took the final dressing-room scene of the play and rewrote it, adding richer characterizations to the backstage bickering and explaining why the opera seria and the commedia dell'arte were being performed simultaneously.

Now, Strauss had one of his happiest ideas—he made the Composer a soprano, like Octavian in *Rosenkavalier* or Cherubino in *Le nozze di Figaro*. Hofmannsthal wrote an eloquent poetic text, extolling the joys and pains of the artist, and Strauss wrote one of his most beautifully moving arias for the Composer.

The second version of *Ariadne* made its debut October 4, 1916. This so-called minor work had occupied Strauss much longer than he had anticipated. Lotte Lehmann made her major operatic debut as the Composer. She later sang Ariadne also. But as she put it: "I have always loved this role. . . . When I sang Ariadne, I always used to stand backstage during the entire prologue, listening to the Composer with longing in my heart and wishing that I could sing both roles at once."

Strauss also loved this opera, despite the trials and tribulations while working on it, which "is so attractive in form and content that I cannot believe that a more cultured public than exists today will not sometime appreciate its value more fully." The world renown *Ariadne auf Naxos* has garnered since Strauss penned those words is proof that the cultured public does appreciate what Edward Sackville West called "the most nearly perfect work of art Strauss and Hofmannsthal achieved."

VERDI'S *Attila*
by Peter P. Jacobi

Factual sources reveal that Attila, the "Scourge of God," died in 453, having served for nineteen years, first as co-ruler with his brother (whom he murdered) and then as sole ruler of the Huns. With an army of half a million Huns he invaded Gaul but was defeated by the Roman general Aetius; he then invaded northern Italy but abandoned a plan to take Rome, due *not* to the legendary diplomacy of Pope Leo I but because his troops were short of provisions and because an outbreak of pestilence had decimated them. He was a harsh man but a just ruler of his own people; he encouraged learned Romans at his court so that their manner and knowledge might set an example for those around him. His death, following a feast for the last of his several marriages, was the result of a burst blood vessel, not murder as legend would have it.

The early-nineteenth-century German Romanticist playwright Zacharias Werner built upon these facts, a few intrigues, and considerable fable (by then Attila had made his way into the Nibelungen saga and other cloudy versions of history) in his 1808 drama, *Attila, King of the Huns.* Werner called it a romantic drama, and indeed, the play melds fact and fantasy to make the Attila story something for the romantic imagination to savor. The play covers Attila's march to Rome, his acquiescence to the Pope, and his ultimate murder by the woman he has just wed. Along the way Werner offers motifs that Goethe and, later, Wagner would seek—redemption, betrayal, and pure love. The seeming cast of thousands includes two armies, Druids, and a delicious lady villain named Hildegonde who, along with her band of warrior maidens, urges Attila to commit ever-greater deeds of violence; she wants his soul destroyed as part of her bargain with the legions of hell. It is interesting to compare this elaborate story to the much-leaner plot Verdi ended up with for his opera.

Werner was intrigued with the notion of fate. Beethoven had considered writing an opera based on the Werner play. With him and his great interest in fate and Godly heroism, the opera undoubtedly would have taken different turns. Verdi was attracted to simpler matters. He saw another opportunity to express his patriotism and to use that patriotism, he hoped, to sell the public on his opera. He was, after all, a pragmatist. Writing to his oft-time collaborator Francesco Piave, he said:

> I should like to make it into a prologue and three acts. We must let the curtain rise on a view of Aquileia in flames with a chorus of townspeople and a chorus of Huns; the people are praying, the Huns threatening and so forth, then Hildegonde's entrance, then Attila's and so on.
>
> I would begin Act I in Rome and I would have the banquet behind the scenes instead of on the stage, and have Azzio (Aetius) on stage pensive and meditating on the various events, etc. / etc. then finish the first act at the point where Hildegonde warns Attila about the poisoned cup, which Attila thinks she's done for love of him when in fact it's only to keep for herself the pleasure of avenging in person the deaths of her father, brothers, etc.
>
> The whole of the scene in Act III with Leo on the Aventine and all that fighting down below would be magnificent.

This story stimulated Verdi's compositional Muse; he wasn't always so drawn to work during those years of the mid 1840s. These were his "days in the galley," as he used to term them, days of contractual servitude that forced him to produce operas for quick deadlines. He had just bombed with public and press; his opera *Alzira,* which some scholars rate as Verdi's worst and which the composer himself called dreadful, had caused some to wonder whether Verdi was hovering at an artistic impasse. *Alzira,* a failure. He had achieved public success with *Giovanna d'Arco* but without breaking new musical ground. Shortly before that, *I due Foscari* had been a public failure, even though the composer considered it a step forward in his development.

So, here he was, producing, chained to his galley, creating under conditions he considered detrimental to health and personal progress. But *Attila* inspired him, raised his spirit to a rare optimism, submerged some of the usual gloom, though the course of the project was anything but straight and untroubled. Quite the contrary, he was beset by delay, libretto problems, and the usual wranglings over cast and production. However, he did not lose his enthusiasm; he liked what he was doing.

The opera was scheduled for introduction at the Teatro la Fenice in Venice for the 1845–46 season. The libretto assignment went to Temistocle Solera, a bendable sort of fellow inclined to give in to Verdi's arguments; he had served the maestro as collaborator in three previous projects, all winners: *Nabucco, I Lombardi,* and *Giovanna d'Arco.*

Solera proceeded to cut the Werner play to pieces, keeping only selected elements and scenes. It is the way of opera, of course, to require play reductions and simplification. Solera went beyond mere trimming: he cut freely, and Verdi agreed with the general direction, if not the details. Verdi may have been attracted to the romance of the original, but he realized that his public was anxious about the need for independence and enhanced personal freedoms and that patriotic and nationalistic aspects of the story were the required focus.

Both Solera and Verdi felt the pulse of the moment historically. The 1848 revolts were still to come, yet the atmosphere in various parts of Europe, and certainly in Italy, suggested disquiet and discontent. The winds of change were present and building toward storm. (An actual storm was to play a significant part in this latest Verdi opera.) Characters took on more Italianate characteristics. A scene was added to the Prologue dealing with the founding of a new Rome, this one at the edge of the Adriatic (à la Venice).

Solera may have been a pliant sort and he may have shared story goals with his composer, but all that did not prevent conflict during the opera's gestation. For one thing, Solera dawdled while Verdi fumed. Verdi's confidant and pupil, Emanuele Muzio, noted at one point that Verdi was ready to collect his libretto "from which he will make his most beautiful opera, but that lazy dog of a poet hasn't done a thing." Then Solera fumed when Verdi went to another of his librettists, Piave, and asked him to supply verses for the final act. Verdi sent Solera the Piave contributions, advised him that he could make changes, but then added, "I warn you I've already composed the music for the most important passages." Solera called that "a shattering blow," and as a result, *Attila* turned out to be their last collaboration.

Verdi had his periods of slothfulness and doubt as well. After all, as he wrote to a friend: "I look forward to the passing of the next three years. I have six operas to write, and then farewell to everything." It was not to be farewell after those six operas, but the expression of weary resignation is telling. His mood alternated rockily, so that one day he could say to a friend: "*Attila* keeps me busy. What a wonderful, wonderful subject." Soon after, he wrote:

> Thanks . . . for remembering your poor friend, condemned continually to scribble musical notes. God save the ears of every good Christian from having to listen to them. Accursed notes! How am I physically and spiritually? Physically I am well, but my mind is black, always black, and will be so until I have finished with this career that I abhor.

Muzio was concerned for him. He recognized that the spasmodic physical breakdowns Verdi suffered in those years were tied to the pressure of work, work that included not only meeting contractual obligations for new operas but also rehearsing and conducting. Muzio offers this graphic picture of his mentor:

> I go to the rehearsals with Signor Maestro, and it makes me sorry to see him tiring himself out; he shouts as if in desperation; he stamps his feet so much that he seems to be playing an organ with pedals; he sweats so much that drops fall on the score.

And sure enough, at one point during the work on *Attila,* Verdi became ill, delaying completion of the project. He wrote his impresario:

> I am immensely sorry to have to advise you that my illness is not a trifling affair, as you believe; tincture of wormwood is useless in my case.
>
> As for the excitability of Vesuvius, I assure you that is not what I need to get all my functions working again; I have need of quiet and rest.

The impresario doubted the illness, hinting that Verdi just wanted more time to compose and to assure that he might get Eugenia Tadolini for his cast. Tadolini, then awaiting childbirth, was a dramatic singer much to Verdi's taste. Scheming may well have been a part of the situation, but the illness was fact: a gastric fever.

Verdi's actions were much watched and commented on by that time. He was a celebrity, a state that always bothered the shy composer. Why, he wondered, would the papers waste space reporting when he appeared in a restaurant or on the balcony of Mme. Tadolini's apartment or wore brown shoes, "trifles" that should not concern the journalists in a great city. All that added to his burdens.

But of course, Verdi managed to finish the opera despite "the most deplorable physical condition." The state of his health and disposition did not diminish the fervor of his working hours. When he composed, he composed feverishly, and the opera remained very much on his mind almost constantly. He even sought authenticity, asking a colleague in Rome to do some research:

> May I ask a big favor of you—I know there is in the Vatican either tapestries or frescoes by Raphael showing the meeting of Attila and Saint Leo. I want to know about Attila's appearance. Do me a couple of pen drawings and give me a verbal description of his costume and its colors; above all his head dress. If you can do this for me, you will have my sincerest thanks.

On March 17, 1846 (without Tadolini in the cast; she was still recuperating), *Attila* was introduced. The press was cool; the public not so. An account noted that "with flowers, bands and torchlight they (the Venetians) accompanied him home." The work became part of the repertory during the years that followed. Italians embraced its patriotic sentiments. At each performance when the Roman general Ezio shouted out, "Avrai tu l'universo, resti l'Italia a me," the people stood and stamped and shouted, for he was speaking for them. "You may have the universe, but let Italy remain mine" was his message. It was as purely patriotic Verdi as the Hebrew slaves in *Nabucco* singing "Va pensiero sull'ali dorate" (Fly, o thought, on golden wings). That the Austrian censors, who so often gave Verdi fits, passed the scene was a blundered-into miracle.

When the historic factors that had given wing to *Attila* disappeared, the opera ceased to be heard. Opera-house managements generally preferred other operas from Verdi's bounteous repertory. But in recent years, musicologists and then the public have become attracted to the musical wealth of these lesser-known works. *Attila* has its share of moments. Yes, it has some of the hurdy-gurdy oom-pa-pa spirit of all these pre-*Rigoletto*, pre-*Il trovatore* (surely a hurdy-gurdy favorite) operas. Yet it has more.

The orchestration shifts for the first time to an occasional languid use of strings that becomes the essence of *La traviata*'s mood. There are instrumental evocations of nature, too, which Verdi was to improve and perfect for *Rigoletto, Un ballo in maschera,* and *Otello* (*Attila* is unique in having a plot that takes place entirely out-of-doors). As yet there is less subtlety of emotion in the orchestral coloring than one finds in later operas, but there's a beginning to the arrest of muscular boom-boom brass and percussions.

The opera has a low male voice at center stage, which simply was not conventional but which Verdi chose to do again in *Simon Boccanegra* and *Falstaff* (by then the bass-baritone had turned pure baritone, but the tenor, at least, was demoted).

For those who like multivoiced finales, *Attila* offers its share. There's the composer's marvelous grasp of human voices, his ability to show contrasts of low and high, of male and female, by combining them in adventurous musical lines and counterpoint. He knew how to create vocal excitement, and *Attila* amply demonstrates that talent.

From the largo, dark prelude to the beautifully effective second scene of the

Prologue in which all the action and patriotism are grounded and in which one can hear an early promise of beloved later Verdi, there is considerable listening enjoyment—in the banquet scene, in an unaccompanied chorus in Act II, in a haunting trio in the final act, and in each aria and ensemble.

ROSSINI'S *The Barber of Seville*
by Jonathan Abarbanel

Music lovers all of us, we carry Gioacchino Rossini in our hearts. But we carry Pierre Augustin Caron de Beaumarchais on our wrists and in our pockets.

We honor Rossini because of the immutable genius of his music. And Beaumarchais? Do we honor him as a great man of the arts? No. Mostly we regard him only as the fellow who wrote those Figaro plays, which Mozart and Rossini turned into operas. It's an unjust evaluation of a man who burned for justice so passionately that, at times, he may have been the only Frenchman of his era who was incorruptible in pursuit of it. Beaumarchais was a great man of letters in his own right, and much more besides. It is an irony indeed that his popular fame rests upon his having been an indirect supplier to a couple of composers.

Had Beaumarchais never written *Le Barbier de Séville* and *Le Mariage de Figaro,* Rossini and Mozart still would have been composers of renown, whose operas are heard the world over. It's just that we, perhaps, would not be hearing them; for had Beaumarchais not written his plays, there might not have been a United States of America or even a you and me! Beaumarchais's multiple careers as playwright, politician, and polemicist were so intricately linked that if his legions of enemies had been successful in permanently stopping him in any one, the others would have given way as well. If his career had been interrupted before writing *Le Barbier de Séville,* the American colonies would have lost the *single* voice that persuaded young King Louis XVI and his foreign minister to aid them.

As it turned out, Beaumarchais *was* a lost man time and time again. Imprisoned in London, Vienna, and Paris, his goods and fortune impounded more than once, pursued through courts and parlements by enemies of the highest rank, Beaumarchais always bounced back and won the day.

Beaumarchais never met Rossini, for he died in 1799 when young Gioacchino was just seven. No doubt they would have been friends, particularly if they had met in salon society, of which both men were connoisseurs and past masters. Beaumarchais might have despaired of Rossini's apolitical attitudes and basically bourgeois nature, but there still would have been sufficient mucilage to cement a friendship.

In most regards, the two were as different as night and day, yet their lives had a number of superficial congruities. Both Beaumarchais and Rossini were sons of the working class. Young Pierre-Augustin was the son of a clock maker, while Gioacchino was born to a horn player and a singer. Both learned music initially from their parents. Both men achieved local renown by the age of twenty and were internationally celebrated by thirty. Both men were acclaimed for their wit and amiable good humor, but Beaumarchais also for his bite. While both men loved "le bon mot," Beaumarchais also treasured—and used most effectively—"le mot juste."

More congruities: both men were known for their amorous adventures, though the Frenchman probably outstripped (pardon the expression) the Italian in sheer quantity. They both "abused Venus" (in the quaint medical parlance of the era) and paid for it with bouts of gonorrhea. Both entered long-term live-in relationships with mistresses who, eventually, became their wives. Olympe Pélissier became Rossini's second wife in 1846 after living with him for fifteen years, while Marie-Thérèse Willermawlaz lived with Beaumarchais for ten years and had a daughter by him before becoming the third Madame Beaumarchais in 1784. I don't know about Rossini, but marriage never slowed up Beaumarchais, who continued to have numerous affairs—sometimes for reasons of state—until the end of his life.

Additional congruities: both men loved Paris and made it the center of their lives. Beaumarchais was born, lived, and died there. Rossini called Paris home for six crucial years during his opera-composing career and again for the last thirteen years of his life. While they never met, they *did* reside for a time at the same address: Père Lachaise, the celebrity-riddled Parisian cemetery. Beaumarchais originally was buried in the garden of his own great Paris mansion and was moved to Père Lachaise twenty-three years later. Rossini was placed there in 1868 and was reinterred in Florence in 1887, after the death of his wife.

Final congruity: the first performance of *Le Barbier de Séville* in Paris, 1775, and the first performance of *Il barbiere di Siviglia* in Rome, 1816, were both magnificent disasters.

So, little quirks of fate aside, let's get on with the opera, eh? It would be wonderful to tell you that Rossini treasured the work of Beaumarchais; that he was drawn to the subject because of his profound understanding of the characters and author's intent; that his labors on *Il barbiere di Siviglia* consciously embodied and defined his musical theories and advanced his aesthetic credo for all the world to see. I'd love to tell you that, but unfortunately, I can't.

The writing and composing of Rossini's *Barbiere* was, to characterize it most bluntly, a typical piece of nineteenth-century operatic hack work. As is well known, it was written in less than three weeks, under pressure, to satisfy a contract Rossini had signed just a few weeks earlier. This was the way opera worked in those days. There were dozens of opera houses and scores of young composers like Rossini. Most operas ran for just a few performances at worst, or a few weeks at best. The composers and librettists were paid a single fee for the work. There was no copyright law and, therefore, there were no royalties (but in France there *was* a copyright law, thanks to Beaumarchais!). Rossini already was regarded as several cuts above most other composers, and he was paid an above-average fee, but he still was not universally hailed as Italy's master composer (as he was a few years later), the true successor to Domenico Cimarosa and Giovanni Paisiello.

Obviously, however, things clicked. Rossini was *not* just another hack; he was a composer of genius. The old Beaumarchais play (it had been around for forty-one years) inspired him. His librettist was as quick as he was and suited for the task. In all of his thirty-seven operas, Rossini had only two or three really good librettos, and *Il barbiere di Siviglia* was one of them.

While Rossini didn't speak French (he learned it in Paris eight years later) and therefore couldn't read the original play, it is quite possible he had seen it or read it in translation. Also, of course, he would have known it indirectly through the opera of the same name by Paisiello. While nearly forgotten now, Paisiello wrote over a hundred operas and was regarded as the preeminent Italian composer of his day. His *Barbiere,* written in 1782, was an international success and held the stage until bumped off by Rossini's version.

The fiasco of Rossini's opening night was probably due as much to factionalism as anything else: the audience punished him for daring to treat the same subject matter as the esteemed Paisiello. They shouldn't have, of course: at least six other composers—both before and after Rossini—also used *Le Barbier de Séville* as the basis of an opera.

And why not? After all, the entertainment industry wasn't much different from what it is now. Today, best-selling books or hit plays become movies; back then, they became operas. The point is that back then, with no copyright restrictions, every composer and librettist was free to choose the best. And *Le Barbier de Séville,* the play, *was* the best. Which brings us back, at least for a little bit, to Beaumarchais and why we carry him in our pocket and on our wrist.

This peripatetic and altogether remarkable man was born in 1732 as Pierre-Augustin Caron. His father, a clock maker, was a French Protestant who underwent conversion to Roman Catholicism in 1721. Under the laws of the time, French Protestants had no legal rights. They weren't permitted to join guilds and practice a trade. Their marriages weren't recognized. Their children were regarded as illegitimate. No wonder the father decided to throw it all over. He never was a good Catholic, however, and neither was his son, who well understood the hypocrisy upon which his legitimacy was based. Beaumarchais's passion for tolerance and social justice was intimately connected with his own birth.

Pierre-Augustin grew up in an exceptional family circle. No ordinary tradesman, Caron *père* saw to it that Pierre-Augustin learned English and music. He became accomplished on harp and flute. Together, the family (there were also five daughters) would read poetry, novels, and plays and would compose their own dramas and music.

At age fourteen, much against his will, young Caron became apprenticed to his father. By the age of twenty, *"fils* Caron" was the greatest clock maker in France and, probably, the world. He invented a regulator which kept clocks and watches synchronized. That is to say, your watch and mine would keep the same time and would agree with our clock on the wall. We take this for granted. In 1753, they didn't because no one had been able to pull off that particular trick before. In fact, the regulator young Caron invented still is the one used in clocks and watches today. Thus, we carry Beaumarchais on our wrists and in our pockets.

But he was not yet Beaumarchais. The royal clock maker attempted to present the new regulating mechanism as his own. Young Caron appealed to the Royal Academy of Sciences, after gaining the attention of the public in an effective polemic letter in the leading newspaper of the day. The academy, having to decide between one of its most distinguished members and an upstart apprentice, judged in favor of the apprentice! The young man argued his own case before the academy, presenting the truth with clarity, wit, and reason. Throughout his long career and many legal adventures, this remained the hallmark of Beaumarchais's style: effective public polemics first, followed by comprehensive, lucid pleading.

Louis XV himself was first in line for a new watch, and Pierre-Augustin used this entrée into Versailles to build a career. First, he became the royal clock maker. Next, he purchased a minor royal office (overseeing the king's meat). Then, he married a rich court widow some twelve years his senior, who died ten months later. Her money went elsewhere, but she left Our Hero a name. She owned a small wooded property, a "bois marchés." Soon, it became Beaumarchais. Pierre-Augustin now called himself Caron de Beaumarchais, landed gentleman and court official.

He lived by his wits and charm at Versailles. By 1759 he was giving harp lessons to the four unlovely, unwed daughters of Louis XV, organizing court concerts and entertainments, and entering a business association with an elderly world-class royal banker named Joseph Duverney. The powerful old man, a surrogate father, taught the young man business and politics, while the young man supplied mobility, persuasiveness, lucidity, gallantry, and a prodigious capacity for hard work.

Within a few years, Caron de Beaumarchais was very rich. In 1761 he purchased a royal secretaryship, an office that carried with it formal entry into the nobility. He was now just plain Beaumarchais. Cost: 55,000 francs. He set himself up in fine Parisian quarters, taking his old father and several unmarried sisters under wing. Not bad for a man not yet thirty. Naturally, a great many people in high places resented the parvenu.

In May, 1764, Beaumarchais began an extended visit to Madrid, ostensibly to save his sister's honor in the face of a Spanish gentleman who reneged on a marriage proposal. While he was there, Beaumarchais engaged in extensive business for himself and Paris-Duverney, conducted secret diplomacy for King Louis, collected his father's debts, set his brother-in-law up in business, initiated a fourteen-year correspondence with Voltaire, engaged in a major love affair, and collected Spanish folk songs . . . just a relaxing Iberian holiday. The

Spanish music and local color turned up in *Barbier* and *Mariage,* complete with detailed costume notes. Beaumarchais shamelessly promoted his sister's affair into an international scandal with himself as hero and the hapless Spanish gentleman bureaucrat as the villain. It became the subject of three plays, including one by Goethe, and *Eugénie,* Beaumarchais's own first play, produced at the Comédie-Française in 1767.

In 1770, Paris-Duverney died, plunging Beaumarchais into the greatest fight of his life with the old man's executor. The money involved was not all that much. The real test was over aristocratic privilege, truth versus slander, and a mercenary judiciary. The legal proceedings took eight years and were international news. Beaumarchais went through three appeals and was sued for libel by one of his judges. His name and reputation were viciously degraded in masterful slander campaigns, he was reprimanded by Parlement, imprisoned, his property and fortune seized, his rights as a citizen stripped away. He fought back with incredible endurance and tenacity, with wit and incontrovertible logic, with a series of four brilliant polemic *Mémoires* which galvanized literate public opinion worldwide and won the hearts of the people of Paris. When, at long last, it was all over, Beaumarchais was vindicated. He had exposed a corrupt judiciary, confirmed the rights of the individual citizen, brought down a sitting parliament, and had all his rights and property restored. He indirectly had won major battles against the absolutism of the monarchy, though the king remained neutral in what was, officially, a private matter.

While all this was going on, this amazing fellow Beaumarchais *also* made another business fortune, supported his father and sisters, married again, and continued to be an intimate advisor both to old King Louis XV and young King Louis XVI and their ministers. He traveled abroad widely on many delicate ambassadorial and spy missions for the crown, swayed French foreign policy in support of the American War of Independence, masterminded the gun-running operation which supplied our forefathers with millions of francs' worth of arms, and slept with a truly extraordinary number of women. Oh, yes, he also had another play produced in 1775, *Le Barbier de Séville.*

Beaumarchais's original concept of the piece was an opera buffa, and so he wrote it. He composed the music himself, drawing on the Spanish popular songs he had collected. It probably was akin to an English ballad opera or German Singspiel. In any case, the Comédie-Italien rejected it, so Beaumarchais reset it as a play. He offered it to the Comédie-Française, which said yes, in 1773. The day before the scheduled production, Beaumarchais landed in jail. Play canceled. It was two years before the theater deemed it politic to offer the work, which premiered in five acts on February 23, 1775 (almost the same date as the opera premiere, forty-one years later). It was met with universal derision. Undaunted, Beaumarchais heavily revised the play overnight. Two days later, it was offered again in its present four-act form. It was a complete triumph and has remained in the repertory of the Comédie-Française ever since. Within a year, it had been translated into most European languages.

Today, the work seems a pleasant, mild comedy with stock characters; but the original audiences recognized the political undertones. The corruptible Don Bazile (Basilio in the opera) was none other than Beaumarchais's corrupt judge, complete with his great speech on calumny. Figaro, clearly, was Beaumarchais himself, bouncing back from every misfortune, goring his literary and political opponents. The opera's "Largo al factotum" replaces quite a different speech in the original, containing very thinly disguised references to Beaumarchais's situation. The wit and blitheness of Figaro are the same in both works, however. Numerous scholars have pointed out that eighteenth-century French pronunciation made "fils, Caron" come out as "fi', Caro'" . . . Figaro!

Our time is past due for turning from the Beaumarchais play to the Rossini opera. A few more words about Beaumarchais's astounding life seem essential, however. He wrote several more plays, most notably the 1784 *Le Mariage de Figaro*. There was no mistaking the revolutionary nature of this work, in which Figaro, the common man, triumphs over Count Almaviva, his aristocratic employer. Louis XVI initially forbade its production. A sequel to the first two Figaro plays was produced in 1792, *La Mère coupable,* but was not a success. Beaumarchais also wrote an opera of some note, *Tarare* (1787), with music by Antonio Salieri. Beginning in 1778, Beaumarchais spent twenty years and much of his own money to publish the first edition of the complete works of Voltaire. He also founded the French Society of Dramatic Authors, which continues in existence today.

His political life continued up and down as he slipped in and out of favor but always managed to serve his nation and liberty well. Louis XVI almost made him a minister. Louis didn't, which probably enabled Beaumarchais to survive the Reign of Terror and later serve the Committee of Public Safety as a commissioner of the republic. Nevertheless, the French Revolution seized his property, jailed his family, and sent him into two years of exile where he became friends with fellow exile Talleyrand.

Beaumarchais was restored to his nation, city, family, and remaining property in time to spend his last two years or so in relative quiet. He was consulted as an elder statesman but was left behind the hurly-burly of daily events. When he died in 1799, he left a grand mansion in Paris, a few other properties, and about 200,000 francs. The United States of America owed him 3 million francs. It was not until 1886, when French archives were opened, that the extent of his influence on French and American history became known.

A titanic life, to be sure. But now we must turn our attention once again, in a not very graceful transition, to a titanic composer. When we last saw him, we left Rossini in an operatic lurch. Let's pick up the story.

Rossini was not yet twenty-four when he wrote *Il barbiere*. Only five years out of the Bologna Liceo Musicale, he already was the composer of sixteen operas, including *Il signor Bruschino, Tancredi, L'italiana in Algeri,* and *Elisabetta, regina d'Inghilterra*. His name already had appeared on the bill at La Scala, La Fenice, and Teatro San Carlo. Yet, most of his greatest works still lay ahead, including his *Otello, La Cenerentola, La gazza ladra, Semiramide, Le Siège de Corinthe,* and *Guillaume Tell* (composed when he was thirty-seven, and after which he never again wrote for the lyric stage, even though he lived another thirty-eight years). He was, surely, as precocious in the musical sphere as Beaumarchais was in the sphere of mechanics.

In 1815, Rossini began an eight-year tenure as musical director of the opera houses of Naples, including Teatro San Carlo. Biographers regard the Neapolitan years, 1815–23, as Rossini's great and fertile middle period, during which he abandoned opera buffa and wrote his finest opere serie. He had in Naples the luxury of writing over an extended period of time for a specific company of singers and musicians. The forte of this artistic family—which included Rossini's first wife, the Spanish soprano Isabella Colbran—was drama rather than comedy; so drama he gave them.

However, Rossini's Naples contract gave him freedom to accept commissions in other cities. No sooner had his first Naples opera premiered in October, 1815, than he was off to Rome on just such a freelance job. He was to write an opera to open the carnival season at Teatro Valle. His assigned librettist was Cesare Sterbini, a thirty-two-year-old Roman poet and treasury secretary. Their collaboration, *Torvaldo e Dorliska,* opened December 26, 1815.

Meanwhile, Rossini had been approached by Duke Francesco Cesare-Sforza, impresario of Rome's rival Teatro Argentina and scion of the Milanese Sforza duke who had been Leonardo da Vinci's great patron. Cesare-Sforza wanted an opera buffa to *close* the carnival season.

December 15, 1815—Rossini signs a contract for an opera to premiere on or about February 5, 1816. He agrees to set any libretto that management selects, direct musical rehearsals, and conduct the first three performances from the keyboard. Rossini is to receive 400 Roman scudi (an above-average $1,250) and housing for the duration of the contract. His house mate is baritone Luigi Zamboni, who soon will be the first Rossini Figaro.

December 26, 1815—*Torvaldo e Dorliska* opens, one of the most dismal flops of Rossini's career; an opera so bad that even today it hasn't been resuscitated.

January 1, 1816—carnival season in full swing. No libretto from Duke Cesare-Sforza.

January 15, 1816—no libretto. The good duke has sent his first-choice librettist packing. He and Rossini call in Sterbini, of all people. Sterbini is reluctant, but Rossini persuades him. Rossini *wants* to work with him again. Who knows why.

But wait! Could there be an ace up some sleeve? Perhaps the Beaumarchais play already has been discussed as a possible subject, and Rossini knows that Sterbini is fluent in French? He can, therefore, work directly from the original play.

January 17, 1816—Sterbini signs on the dotted line.

January 18, 1816—Sterbini sets to work, completing the entire libretto in twelve days.

January 25, 1816—Sterbini delivers Act I to Rossini and Cesare-Sforza.

January 29, 1816—Sterbini delivers a completed Act II.

February 6, 1816—Rossini delivers his Act I to the musical copyists, to be copied overnight so that rehearsals can begin the next day.

Night of February 6–7, 1816—oops! The Good Duke dies of a stroke. He's forty-four.

February 7, 1816—mourning.

February 8, 1816—funeral.

February 9–19, 1816—O.K., kids, back to work. There's a contract to fulfill, an opera house to save, and a widow and children to feed.

Rossini is worried. Busy, but worried. He's worried about Paisiello and Paisiellists. The old man is still alive (though seventy-five and sick) and living in Naples. His supporters will be outraged to learn that young Rossini has dared to "compete" with the hero of Italian opera by setting the same play. This was a serious concern. We cannot begin to imagine today the power of musical factionalism in the era of bel canto. That old-timer and his loyalists could ruin Rossini. What to do?

The libretto to the opera, as was then customary, was published the day before the opening. Rossini attached to it a brief letter, swearing his devotion to Maestro Paisiello, disclaiming any merits for his own inferior work, disavowing any rivalry, and stating that he and Sterbini used the original play, rather than Paisiello's libretto, in order *not* to copy any scenes or situations from the earlier, revered opera. Further, to avoid confusion the new piece would *not* be called *Il barbiere di Siviglia,* but *Almaviva, ossia l'inutile precauzione* (*Almaviva, or the Useless Precaution,* the same subtitle used by Beaumarchais).

Years later, Rossini also claimed to have written a personal letter to Paisiello, seeking the latter's permission and approval. Rossini said Paisiello wrote back, wishing him well. Stendahl, Rossini's first biographer whose *Life of Rossini* appeared in 1824, also mentions this correspondence. But no one has ever turned up the letters. Keep this situation in mind; it has a mirror image.

February 20, 1816—first performance of *Almaviva, ossia L'inutile precauzio-ne,* at Teatro Argentina, Maestro Rossini conducting. Boos, hisses, whistles, catcalls. The curtain is rung down in the middle of the second act. Rossini calmly applauds his cast to the jeers of the audience, then goes home and goes to sleep.

February 21, 1816—Rossini pretends to be ill. He makes extremely minor changes in the piece, which is performed that night with great success.

February 22, 1816—third performance, resounding cheers. The opera is off and running on its international career.

February 29, 1816—Rossini, a leap-year baby, celebrates his *sixth* birthday.

Footnote—the overture used for the first performance was an original employing Spanish melodies and themes. The "standard" overture we know was added later the same season, Rossini having used it for at least two (and possibly three) earlier operas.

Footnote—Giovanni Paisiello died in June, 1816.

Footnote—the next staging of the opera was in September, in Bologna. Here, for the first time, the work was called *Il barbiere di Siviglia.*

Rossini's new opera was produced in London in 1818 and in New York the year after. It was first performed in Beaumarchais's Paris in October, 1819. A month later, Paisiello's *Barbiere* was also staged to offer audiences a side-by-side comparison. The older version was withdrawn after two performances.

Remember the letter that Rossini claimed to have written the dying Paisiello? Here's the mirror image. As Rossini lay dying of cancer in 1868, he received a letter from his old home city of Bologna. A twenty-six-year-old composer and conductor had written a new setting of Sterbini's libretto and wanted permission to dedicate the new *Barbiere* to Rossini. Here is Rossini's reply:

> . . . Although your name was not unknown to me, given that some time back there reached me the widespread report of the brilliant success that you had obtained with your opera *I due orsi,* it is nonetheless dear to me to see that you (a daring young man, by your own words!) hold me in some esteem, . . . I certainly did not consider myself daring when I set to music (in twelve days) after Padre Paisiello the very charming comedy of Beaumarchais. Why should you be so, coming after half a century and more, and with new styles, in setting a *Barbiere* to music?
>
> Not long ago, Paisiello's was performed in a Paris theater; being, as it is, a gem of spontaneous melodies, of theatrical spirit, it won a very happy and well-merited success. Many polemics, many disputes have risen and always exist between old and new music lovers; you should take to heart (I advise you) the old proverb that says *between two contending parties, the third party benefits.* You may be certain that I do not wish that third to be the winner.
>
> May, then, your new *Barbiere* join your opera *I due orsi* ["The Two Bears"] as a big bear to form a musical triumvirate and assure you, as its creator, and our common century imperishable glory. These are the warm good wishes offered you by the old Pesarese who has the name Rossini.
>
> P.S. Confirming the above, I shall be happy to accept the dedication of your new work. Please accept in anticipation the most heartfelt thanks.

Since the second performance of the Beaumarchais play and the second performance of the Rossini opera, the jury of public opinion has acclaimed *Le Barbier/Il barbiere.* The musical establishment, too, has always treasured the work. Stendahl wrote in 1824, "Rossini had imagined himself to be writing for a Roman audience; but it turned out in the end that what he had created was to be the greatest masterpiece of *French* music." The great German conductor Hans von Bülow called it a "model comic opera" which pleases public and musicians "as much, furthermore, as *Die Zauberflöte* or *Die Meistersinger.* Eternal youth lives in this opera." And a final word from Verdi, writing in 1898:

"You may say many things about Rossini . . . but I confess that I cannot help believing *Il barbiere di Siviglia,* for abundance of ideas, for comic verve, and for truth of declamation, the most beautiful 'opera buffa' in existence."

PUCCINI'S *La Bohème*
by Dorothy Samachson

La Bohème has been called Giacomo Puccini's "most nearly perfect opera . . . a work of consummate operatic craftsmanship, applied with a sureness of touch and exhilarating vigor. Above all, however, there is its charm and warmth, gaiety and genuine pathos . . . deriving from a peculiar authority, and the infectious youthfulness of music."

These sentiments, so eloquently expressed by British musicologist Spike Hughes, have been echoed for almost a century by the hundreds of thousands who are everlastingly captivated by its bittersweet, yet comic musical portrayal of poverty-stricken young artists, struggling to live, laugh, love, and create important works in the Latin Quarter of mid-nineteenth-century Paris.

One key to *La Bohème*'s allure is its authenticity, for Rodolfo, Mimi, Marcello and Musetta, and their gay companions actually existed, and their adventures were true incidents. It was Puccini's musical genius that imbued them with extraordinary tenderness, humor, and poignancy and made them immortal.

Yet, long before Puccini and his lyricists, Giuseppe Giacosa and Luigi Illica, Italianized the characters' names and introduced them to the non-French-speaking world, they had achieved a sort of literary immortality as *Scènes de la vie de Bohème.* They first appeared in 1845 in a Parisian periodical, *Le Corsaire,* as a series of thinly disguised autobiographical vignettes by Henri Murger, a hungry, unpublished poet of twenty-three, and appeared on and off for several years. Murger, who wrote them out of poverty-stricken necessity, received the munificent sum of 15 francs for each. "But," he wrote a friend, "I've tossed a dozen or so incidents into *Le Corsaire*'s mail box and I'll enjoy seeing them in print."

Murger, whose father had entertained the futile hope that his son would become a coat maker, managed to keep body and soul together with minor literary odd jobs. He wrote articles for a millinery trade paper, served for a time as a sort of amanuensis for a Count Tolstoy, informing him on French literature for the edification of the tsar. Murger's poetry did not see the light of day on a printed page, although it was eventually published to mixed critical reviews.

Murger's entertaining pieces told about the bone-chilling cold he and his friends suffered in their garret; the almost constant gnawing hunger; and their desperate, frequently comic attempts to earn money through their writing, their music, their paintings, and especially their wits. He had a remarkable ability to find the humor and absurdity in their physical hardships, as well as the pathos and tragedy in the thwarted and doomed relationships.

But more important, Murger wrote of the warm companionship and protective affection his "four musketeers" felt for one another, and of course, he wrote about love, for he was young, ardent, and Gallic.

The collected stories remain a delight to read. In one humorous episode, he tells how he and a friend shared one pair of wearable trousers. When one friend went out, the other was forced to remain in bed. He is particularly amusing in the group's witty attempts to outwit their angry landlord—an incident that Puccini and his librettists translated perfectly into music in a comic scene with M. Benoit in the opera's first act.

In his stories, Murger became Rodolphe, and he was candid enough to describe himself accurately as unprepossessing-looking, heavily bearded, and balding. Balding? What self-respecting lyric tenor would accept such an image for the stage? None that I know of.

Schaunard was based on Alexandre Schanne—a painter and musician who was to achieve fortune as a toy manufacturer. In the book, he composes on an out-of-tune piano and is the central character in a hilarious story about a parrot that Schaunard has been paid to kill by endlessly playing the piano.

That fee is what has made the opera's first-act feast possible, and he tells the story in great musical style. Since there is no piano in the opera, Schaunard tootles a trumpet in the Café Momus scene. And yes, there was a Café Momus, where the musketeers congregated and rarely paid their bills.

Colline is a composite of Jean Wallon, a theology student, and a strange character, Trapadoux, who is a "hyperphysical philosopher who earns a living teaching subjects that end in 'ics,' like mathematics, etc."

Although Schaunard and Colline are equally important characters in the book, where they have their own loves, they play supporting roles in the opera. However, Colline does sing a moving farewell to his prized overcoat in the final act, as he prepares to sell it for medicine for the dying Mimi. In the book, he always wore a capacious coat, its pockets crammed with books.

Murger's Marcel is another composite of several painters. One, a certain Tabar, was constantly reworking an enormous painting—altering the subject, from Biblical to historic, to mythic—depending on which possible customer he might find. He is also Musetta's on-and-off lover in the book. In the opera he plays a principal role—suffering the pangs of love, along with Rodolfo, although his relationship with Musetta is volatile and mainly comic, balancing beautifully with Rodolfo's tender-tragic feelings for Mimi.

Musetta is also a composite—based largely on Marie Roux, a model and singer, nicknamed "Mademoiselle Bagpipe" because she sang loudly and off key. She was high-spirited, luxury-loving, and flirtatious in the book as well as in the opera. One delicious story tells of a great party she threw for her friends in the courtyard of the building from which she was being evicted. Another is the party she gives the night before her marriage—to be dedicated to carousing and loving Marcel. It is a farewell to her former free life and a prelude to respectable wifehood. Sort of like a bridegroom's stag party, except that Murger has made it the bride's, and it all reads very reasonably. In real life, she drowned when the ship she was on sank.

Mimi, the fragile heroine of book and opera, was also a composite of several of Murger's lovers, all of whom he called Mimi. At least three died of consumption—the disease of the ill-fed, ill-housed, and overworked poor. In the book, however, she is not the gentle young girl, but is rapacious, greedy, and faithless.

But the young women weren't the only ones to sicken and die. Many men also spent time in and out of hospitals and died. When Murger's stories were published in a single volume, the Goncourt brothers, noted critics, said it was "a triumph of Socialism." An ironic tribute, indeed; for Murger's dearest wish was to leave Bohemia behind and to lead a comfortable bourgeois life. He referred to his Bohemian years as "this gay, terrible life."

Murger did achieve a well-to-do life style and public recognition, too, in 1849, after he and the playwright Théodore Barrière adapted the stories for the stage as *La Vie de Bohème*. The play, with incidental music, was a huge success, as was the profitable publication of the collected stories. He did very well and moved to the Right Bank of Paris where he and his final love lived a respectable, respected life. He enjoyed a successful literary career and was awarded the Legion of Honor.

As a highly regarded member of French artistic and bourgeois society, he returned often to the subject of Bohemian life with the same ironic wit and affection for his characters, but now he wrote from a different perspective— warning against the excesses and suffering of that life, which destroyed many creative young people through drink, hunger, and disease. (Murger's own drink of choice was coffee. It was cheap, warmed him in the cold garret, and kept him awake while writing.) His excessive use of coffee was even blamed for his early death in 1862, when he was only thirty-nine; but it's much more likely that the years of deprivation had damaged his constitution. His last words were: "No music, no noise, no Bohemia."

However, that was a futile, belated cry, for Murger was undoubtedly responsible for the influx of young writers, musicians, and painters who, for many decades, flocked to the Latin Quarter, bedazzled by Murger's stories. He had made no attempt to glamorize the conditions of life, but the friendships, love affairs, and even the desperate situations he described struck a responsive chord in the hearts and minds of many. And who can blame them? To be young, to paint, compose, or write poetry, and to be in love in Paris is a dream many still share.

Scenes from Bohemian Life has been hailed by writers such as D.B. Wyndham Lewis, who called it "a classic . . . woven out of the gossamer stuff of youth, careless, happy, defiant youth, so precious and fleeting." Others have praised it as "pure nectar." The students of the Latin Quarter recognized Murger as their spokesman, and for many years, they blanketed his bust in Luxembourg Gardens with roses on his birthday. Whether that delightful custom persists, I don't know, but it was an honest tribute to the man who added the word Bohemian to the international vocabularly; gave it a home: Paris; and a neighborhood: the Latin Quarter. The Quarter was so called because the Sorbonne students for centuries spoke only Latin. Today, the Quarter is synonymous with the exuberance of youth, art, and carefree behavior—the transient period before adult responsibilities take over.

Murger was not the first to use the term Bohemian (George Sand, Honoré de Balzac, and others used it), but he linked it irrevocably with the artistic life, instead of the purely raffish vagabondage of those who had no creative purpose. The word derived from Bohemia, the purported home of the gypsies.

In his own youthful student days in Milan, Puccini also lived a Bohemian life as a struggling, poverty-stricken musician, but he was already honored, recognized, and financially secure when the subject of *La Bohème* loomed on his horizon.

Puccini had achieved a stunning triumph with *Manon Lescaut* in 1893. No longer merely promising, he was now being hailed around the civilized world as Verdi's successor. But now, the thirty-five-year-old composer faced another serious problem—how to follow that success with an equally powerful one.

This was a problem that worried him throughout his career. He once admitted, "I am a passionate hunter of fowl, women and libretti." With *La Bohème* that passion led to bitter enmity and public acrimony between him and Ruggiero Leoncavallo, the composer of *I pagliacci,* who wrote libretti as well as music.

Some time previous, Leoncavallo had sent Puccini a draft of a libretto for a proposed opera based on Murger's *Scènes,* and Puccini had returned it. Later, they happened to meet, and Puccini casually mentioned that he was composing a *La Bohème.* Leoncavallo was outraged, accused Puccini of having stolen it from him, insisted that he had proprietary rights to the subject and was composing the opera himself. Leoncavallo immediately sent a furious report to a newspaper, to which Puccini responded in another newspaper. Puccini stated that, first of all, he didn't remember ever seeing Leoncavallo's script and that, second, he had returned it.

Puccini may have told the truth. On the other hand, he wasn't always scrupulous about the methods he used to acquire the rights to a subject. Several years later he eagerly entered into a plot with his publisher, Ricordi, to dissuade Alberto Franchetti from writing *Tosca* as being too sordid for the lyric theater. As soon as Franchetti rejected the idea, Puccini snapped it up for himself.

But by now, ethics should not concern us, for Puccini's *La Bohème* is unquestionably a masterpiece of delicate youth, impeccable taste, and poignant beauty that has captured the enduring love of the public.

Once Puccini became involved in a subject, he worked rapidly, but he had many conflicts with his collaborators. Giacosa was a well-known poetic playwright, while Illica was a gifted librettist; but Puccini was also an intuitive man of the theater, and the arguments went on for several years.

They worked various stories from the collection to form a more unified whole and to create a brilliant balance between comic badinage and sentimentality. They studied not only Murger's stories but also the play. They merged Mimi with Francine, the tragic heroine of a separate story in the book.

It was this story that gave Puccini the touching meeting between Mimi and Rodolfo—the candle and key—that set the love story in motion. However, Rodolfo had no connection with Francine. Her lover was a young sculptor who gave the muff to warm her chilled fingers as she lay dying.

The discussions and arguments went on and on, with Ricordi trying to act as mediator and get the work finished and on the stage. There were profits to be made.

Puccini was very moved by the music he wrote for Mimi's death in the last scene: "I had to get up in the middle of the night and, standing by the study, alone in the silence of the night, I began to weep like a child. It was as though I had seen my own child die." He was an emotional man, and he admitted it openly. "They have accused me of being sentimental, saying that sentimentality is a sign of weakness. Well, I prefer it that way . . . I am incapable of creating anything that doesn't come from the heart."

And certainly, *La Bohème* came from the heart. Even the lively, raucous Café Momus–Act II came from the heart—the heart that enjoyed lively company, high-spirited gaiety, and colorful atmosphere.

Finally, the opera was ready for its premiere in the same Teatro Regio in Turin where *Manon Lescaut* had had such a spectacular success. The young Arturo Toscanini conducted that February 1, 1896, and a very distinguished audience was present, eager to cheer. But the reception was a cool one; not necessarily hostile, but there were few cheers. The audience was bewildered. This was hardly an opera of larger-than-life proportions, of elaborate period costumes, of heroic, historic, or literary characters. And then, too, this was an opera without a villain, only one dead heroine—one who died too quietly— after which the curtain rang down.

Puccini, who always suffered doubts while working on an opera, was bitterly hurt by the adverse comments. Only one critic had the acumen to realize that Puccini had taken a giant step forward musically since *Lescaut*. But Puccini wasn't consoled: "I, who put into *Bohème* all my soul and love it boundlessly and love its creatures more than I can say, returned to my hotel completely heartbroken. I passed a most miserable night. And in the morning I was greeted with the spiteful salute of the critics."

As so often happens, the general public had more sense and taste than the critics and the elite opening-night audience. The public understood and responded wholeheartedly to Puccini's characters and to the exquisite lyrical music in which he had clothed them. Those audiences laughed, wept, and cheered them. During that first month the opera was performed twenty-four times to sold-out houses, and then it continued its triumphant tour to other cities and countries.

La Bohème made its way to Paris in 1898, and Murger's own city also hailed Puccini. Claude Debussy was deeply impressed; he told Manuel de Falla: "If one did not keep a grip on oneself, one would be swept away by the sheer verve of the music. I know of no one who has described the Paris of that time as well as Puccini in *La Bohème*."

Today, the millions who never knew Murger's Paris find it in Puccini's Latin Quarter, where they laugh along with the "four musketeers" and are deeply moved by Rodolfo and Mimi and the sad end of their love. No matter how often one makes that journey, the magical visit is always fresh, always loved, and a lyrical joy for the human spirit.

MUSSORGSKY'S *Boris Godunov*

by Dorothy Samachson

Modest Mussorgsky's *Boris Godunov* occupies a unique place in the musical theater. It cannot be compared with any other work in the entire repertory, nor can it be pigeonholed into any comfortable category.

Boris is the first operatic work in which the ordinary people—their hopes and fears, their earthy humor, their unrest and misery—play an active role on stage. It is also a profoundly moving and perceptive psychological study of Boris, the enigmatic, ambitious, superstitious, and finally, conscience-stricken tsar. *Boris* is also a stunning theatrical spectacle; above all, it is a musical work of such extraordinary originality, power, and emotional depth that many, led by prominent music biographer M.D. Calvocoressi, have hailed it as the "most soul-stirring lyric drama ever written."

Yet precisely because *Boris Godunov* is so extraordinary an achievement, so advanced in Mussorgsky's innovative use of new harmonies, rhythmic structures, and speech patterns, it continues to be the subject of controversy. In the 106 years since *Boris* was premiered in St. Petersburg, it has suffered many vicissitudes and interferences, primarily because Mussorgsky's monumental step into the next century was neither understood nor appreciated.

Had Mussorgsky been alive when the mangling began, he might well have said, "I can defend myself against my enemies, but defend me from my friends." Those friends kept the real *Boris* hidden from public sight and sound for many years.

It started in 1896 when his closest friend, Nicholas Rimsky-Korsakov, reorchestrated, smoothed out harmonies, and rearranged the dramatic structure of whatever he considered "crude" in Mussorgsky's opera, fifteen years after the composer's death. Rimsky-Korsakov had already done a similar service for Mussorgsky's *Khovanshchina,* which Mussorgsky had never quite finished or orchestrated during his lifetime.

Boris, on the other hand, was a fully orchestrated work which had already been performed in public; it did not deserve such "kindness." However, Rimsky-Korsakov's version was so richly orchestrated that it was much more accessible to the public, and it gained acceptance rapidly. In the process he lost sight of Mussorgsky's revolutionary musical breakthrough. In 1908, Rimsky "improved" on his own version, followed by a long line of other musicians who wanted to "clarify" Mussorgsky's ideas. Anatol Liadov, Michael Ippolitov-Ivanov, Nikolai Cherepnin, Boris Asafiev, Dmitri Shostakovich, and Karl Rathaus—all have added their own touches. Some have made extensive amputations, while others, like Shostakovich, had such respect for the original that they were more modestly helpful.

Reorchestration was not the only indignity *Boris* suffered over the years. Depending upon the conductor or stage director, scenes have been ruthlessly lopped off or shifted from one place to another in performance, all done with the best of intentions, each feeling he understood better than Mussorgsky what the opera should be. *Boris* has been sung in English, Italian, and German while the principal sang in Russian, which hardly added to the performance's credibility. Of course, *Boris* demands a great artist in the title role, so one should have been grateful for the star's presence, even in such a polyglot version.

As a result of all these various versions and the bowdlerizations the work has been subjected to, there is such confusion about the opera that the frustrated opera goer might well ask, "Will the real Boris please stand up?" In the Lyric Opera of Chicago's production, the rightful *Boris Godunov*—Mussorgsky's own—at last stands up and takes its true place on stage, giving the audience its first opportunity to understand why, despite all the changes and "improvements," *Boris* has not only survived but, like the fabled Phoenix, has risen triumphant from the ashes of its destruction. The opera is sung in Russian, which also allows the full flavor of Mussorgsky's musical imagination to be heard in all its authentic richness. Will it quiet the argument? Probably not, for although this is Mussorgsky's official, definitive work, it is not the only one he wrote.

In the autumn of 1868, Modest Mussorgsky, then twenty-nine years old, began *Boris Godunov.* Earlier that year he had finished the first act of *The Marriage,* an opera based on Nikolai Gogol's comedy in which Mussorgsky had, for the first time, applied his theories about rendering "straightforward expression of thoughts and feelings as it occurs in ordinary speech." He never completed *The Marriage.* It had served his purpose, showing him how to turn speech into musical imagery. In a letter to a friend, he explained: "I have now crossed the Rubicon. . . . What I should like to do is to make my characters speak on the stage exactly as people speak in everyday life, without exaggeration or distortion, and yet write music which will be totally artistic. As for *The Marriage,* it is not in keeping with my chosen path . . . it contains too little of big, simple-hearted Mother Russia."

When Vladimir Nikolsky, a professor of literature at the university, suggested that Alexander Pushkin's poetic tragedy *Boris Godunov* might be a worthy subject for an opera, Mussorgsky knew immediately that here was the epic theme in which he could represent Mother Russia in all her suffering and grandeur, forever harried and buffeted by the whims of her rulers. In Boris himself he had the towering figure of an enigmatic man whose presence and death had ominous portent for the Russian people. Apart from its glorious language and psychological insights into Boris's personality, what made Pushkin's drama so vital was that it, like Shakespeare's chronicle plays, dealt with actual historic persons.

Boris Godunov was elected tsar in 1598. He had been the guardian of Ivan the Terrible's young son, Dimitri, who had died mysteriously in 1591—a death rumored to have been Boris's doing. It is equally true that a pretender, calling himself Dimitri, miraculously alive, did appear (Antonín Dvořák would later compose an opera, *Dimitri,* on this subject) who, with the aid of a Polish army and rebellious peasants, marched on Moscow. Amidst this turmoil Boris died suddenly of a heart attack, which is where Pushkin ended his tragedy.

Actually, the turmoil had just begun. It was "The Time of Troubles," during which Dimitri, a dupe of the treacherous Prince Shuisky, was killed. Shuisky seized the throne, only to be faced by invasions of both Polish and Swedish troops. By the time the invaders and rival factions were cleared out and a new tsar, Michael Romanov, was elected, the land was ravaged and desolate.

Mussorgsky knew his history well, but he merely hinted at the future in his own opera. The canvas that Pushkin had created was vast enough for him. Pushkin's play consisted of twenty-four scenes, not divided into acts—one of the reasons it is so unplayable. Furthermore, the scenes were presented as separate episodes, almost like a historic pageant.

With *Boris,* Mussorgsky could truly express his artistic credo: "Life, wherever it is shown; Truth, however bitter. Speaking out boldly, frankly . . . that is my aim. The artistic presentation of beauty alone is sheer childishness. To trace the finer characteristic of human nature and of the mass of mankind . . . that is the mission of the artist. My business is to portray the soul of man in all its profundity."

He got down to his business wholeheartedly. It was probably the happiest time of his all-too-short life. His alcoholism was under control, as was his "nervous" disorder (posthumously and tentatively diagnosed as epilepsy). His financial situation, desperate ever since the liberation of the serfs had impoverished his family, forced him to work at a dull, time-consuming, mind-stultifying clerical job. But his spirits were high, and he worked at *Boris* steadily.

He condensed Pushkin's twenty-four scenes into seven and wrote his own libretto, combining sections of Pushkin's text with his own words. He also added original scenes, and retained the episodic pattern of the Pushkin work in order to present a panoramic picture of the turmoil within Boris's soul and of the political and social turbulence that surrounded him.

Mussorgsky completed the work, including orchestration, within a year and submitted it to the Maryinsky Theatre for approval. It was rejected in February, 1871. The judges objected to an opera without a prima donna, without a ballet, without arias, and without at least one love scene. They were repelled by the work's unrelenting, stark somberness, and they simply didn't understand Mussorgsky's unusual harmonies and rhythmic structures. Furthermore, the theater committee must have been uneasy about how the tsarist censors would respond to a work in which the common people take an active role and cheer a pretender to the throne.

Although Mussorgsky was disappointed by the rejection, he wasn't devastated, and he quickly began his revisions. He shifted some scenes, cut others, and added the Polish act, which included a polonaise and a love duet for the pretender and Marina, the Polish princess. The scene, with a different dramatic emphasis, had been in Pushkin's drama.

Again *Boris* was rejected, although several scenes had already received public performances to great praise. But never underestimate the power of a woman. Julia Platonova, a leading soprano at the Maryinsky, threatened not to renew her contract unless she was given a full production to sing the role of Marina. The management surrendered, and *Boris* was finally performed February 8, 1874. It was a public triumph but a critical disaster. Only one critic recognized Mussorgsky's audacious genius.

Boris was sung ten times that year, fewer in succeeding seasons, and disappeared completely from the repertory after 1881, the year of Mussorgsky's death. *Boris* was first presented to western European audiences in 1908 by Serge Diaghilev in the Rimsky-Korsakov version, and it was a sensational success. Yet, Diaghilev himself was not too happy with Rimsky's work, because it wasn't unorthodox enough. Still, it was Rimsky's version that held the stage, and still does, in many theaters.

Mussorgsky's own *Boris* finally reemerged in the 1920s, again to sharply divided argument, this time about which of Mussorgsky's own versions was stronger and whether his orchestration and progressive ideas were valid expressions of his innate genius.

The Polish act, for example, has been the object of sharp criticism by some because the music is not Russian in character. But why should it have been? Poland was a European, not a Russian, nation, and Mussorgsky rightfully represented it as such. Even the ecstatically beautiful love duet between Marina and the false Dimitri has been attacked for its very beauty, as not belonging in this otherwise socially conscious work. What such critics overlooked, however, is that the passionate duet expresses, not romantic love, but the desire for political power.

The problem in accepting Mussorgsky's work for its own wonderful qualities can be traced back to his relationships with his closest friends—the coterie of musicians called the Five, including Rimsky-Korsakov, Alexander Borodin, César Cui, and Mili Balakirev. They recognized Mussorgsky's prodigious talents, but they neither approved nor understood them. Despite their very genuine affection for him, they were also disturbed by Mussorgsky's disordered personal life, with its frequent bouts of alcoholism. Mussorgsky was considered a dilettante; his ideas about realism in art and his vast sympathy for the peasantry were further examples of aberration. Balakirev, although very fond of him, called him an idiot.

Actually, Mussorgsky was a cultivated, witty, well mannered, charming member of the upper classes; he had originally trained as a military officer, at which time alcohol first laid its grip on him. He left the army to devote his life to music at just about the time his family lost its money, and he had to take menial jobs to keep body and soul together.

If Mussorgsky was misunderstood and denigrated in his own time, posterity has recognized his remarkable originality and his towering accomplishment. Claude Debussy and Maurice Ravel were strongly influenced by the harmonies that Mussorgsky's contemporaries could not understand, and many twentieth-century younger composers are studying his *Boris Godunov* and his wonderful, evocative songs.

The Lyric Opera of Chicago's production has given our more accepting hearts, minds, ears, and eyes the rare privilege of gaining a true understanding, not only of Mussorgsky's genius, but of the tsar, destroyed by his own conscience, and of his nation, which has, somehow, survived all the bloody chapters in its history.

BELLINI'S *I Capuleti e i Montecchi*
by Philip Gossett

Of Vincenzo Bellini's major operas, *I Capuleti e i Montecchi* has fared worst in modern times. Invoking the sacred name of Shakespeare, critics lambaste Felice Romani's libretto on totally inappropriate grounds. Deploring the convention by which a mezzo-soprano sings Romeo, conductors revise the role for tenor, upsetting Bellini's entire conception. Disturbed by the genesis of the opera and its melodic borrowings from Bellini's only fiasco, *Zaira,* scholars question its respectability. Yet *I Capuleti e i Montecchi* is one of Bellini's great achievements, a masterful blend of passionate declamation and exquisite lyricism in the service of dramatic truth. The composer of *Norma* stands here before us fully mature.

Fresh from his apprenticeship in Naples, Bellini conquered northern Italy with two extraordinary premieres at the Teatro alla Scala of Milan *(Il pirata* on

October 27, 1827, and *La straniera* on February 14, 1829). These immediately identified him as a luminary of the post-Rossini generation, but unlike Gaetano Donizetti, Giovanni Pacini, or Saverio Mercadante, Bellini refused to plunge into the vortex of Italian operatic custom. Bellini kept aloof. Consciously molding his image to differentiate himself from other composers, he imagined himself the object of their envy and hate. Insisting on his unique talent, he normally composed but one opera per year, accepting commissions only under satisfactory financial arrangements (and his demands, by contemporary standards, were exorbitant).

Only once did Bellini compose two operas in rapid succession, with disastrous results. A new theater was to open in Parma during the spring of 1829. When Rossini, occupied in Paris, proved unavailable to accept a commission for the inaugural opera, the contract went to Bellini. Immediately after the premiere of *La straniera,* the composer departed for Parma. For reasons both serious (the subject of the libretto was in dispute) and comic (special dispensation from the grand duchess was required for the librettist Romani to keep his "too-liberal" moustache unshaven), there were constant annoyances. Finally performed on May 16, 1829, *Zaira* failed miserably.

Having taken consolation in the arms of his mistress, Giuditta Turina, at her country villa, Bellini returned to Milan. That summer Giuseppe Crivelli, impresario of the Teatro la Fenice of Venice, invited Bellini to stage *Il pirata* during the next carnival (the theatrical season beginning December 26 and continuing through Lent). He may also have proposed that Bellini write a new opera during a future season but could not offer him a commission that year since other composers had already been approached. Yet there was reason to believe that conditions might suddenly change. One commission had gone to Giovanni Pacini, a composer towards whom Bellini exhibits in his correspondence practically a paranoid distrust. But Pacini was simultaneously scheduled to write for Turin in that same carnival. Were Pacini consequently unable to satisfy his Venetian obligations, Crivelli wanted Bellini present to fill the gap. Bellini was, in any case, ambivalent about Venice, as he wrote his uncle, Vincenzo Ferlito: "Perhaps it's better this way, since Romani has so many libretti to write that it would be difficult for him to make me a good one: in Venice there are not such good singers as in Milan." After his earlier exertions that year, Bellini was content without a new commission.

With Pacini still officially engaged for La Fenice, Bellini departed Milan for Venice on December 12 to supervise the production of *Il pirata*. A new work by Giuseppe Persiani, *Costantino in Arles,* opened the season on December 26. *Il pirata* followed on January 16, with Bellini making significant alterations in the score to adapt it to the particular capabilities of the performers, Giuditta Grisi, Lorenzo Bonfigli, and Giulio Pellegrini. But nothing was heard from Pacini. On January 5 Bellini signed an agreement with the management: if Pacini did not make clear his intention to fulfill his contract by January 14, Bellini was to write an opera on the libretto *Giulietta Capellio* of Romani. Contractually, no more than a month and a half was to separate the moment he received the libretto from Romani and the day of the first performance. When severe weather interrupted communications between Venice and the mainland, Pacini's deadline was extended to January 20. When nothing was heard then, Bellini's contract took effect.

Surviving letters demonstrate that Bellini accepted this commission with reservations. As he wrote to Gaetano Cantú, brother of Giuditta Turina, on January 15: "The government and practically all of Venice has entreated me that, should Pacini not come to write the new opera, I must do it in only one month; they have all beseeched me to do this as a favor for Venice, which will be content with what I write in such a brief time. To win the public's heart I accepted, and thus if that anti-gentleman Maestro Pacini does not come, all this toil will fall to me, and who knows how much unpleasantness with it." To his friend Francesco Florimo, librarian of the Naples Conservatory Library, he called the enterprise "a most perilous undertaking."

As early as January 5, then, the Romeo and Juliet theme was settled, presumably by common consent between Romani and Bellini, though in her memoirs Emilia Branca, Romani's wife, claims the idea came from Giuditta Grisi, who had long wanted to interpret Romeo. The libretto was not new. Romani had prepared it five years earlier for Nicola Vaccaj's *Giulietta e Romeo,* but he now revised it extensively. Large portions are cut, details of the plot are altered, and many verses or entire scenes are completely rewritten. In the printed preface to the Bellini libretto, Romani explains that they felt "constrained by the pressure of time to an extreme brevity and [were] persuaded to omit many recitative scenes which would have justified the continuity of the drama." But Bellini and Romani made a virtue of this necessity, for the greatest strengths of the libretto of *I Capuleti e i Montecchi* are its single-mindedness of direction and its unity of action. Nothing is permitted to distract us from the plight of the lovers and their warring families.

Although for many years the literary source for Romani's libretto was not known, one thing should have been apparent: it has nothing whatsoever to do with Shakespeare. Emilia Branca suggests the source is the ninth novella of part 2 of Matteo Bandello's *Le novelle* (1554), a collection frequently reprinted in Italy during the early nineteenth century. Her remark that Romani derived the libretto "della narrazione d'una pietosa istoria che in Verona al tempo del signor Bartolomeo Scala avvenne" ("from the narration of a pitiable story which happened in Verona at the time of Bartolomeo Scala") is a direct quote from Bandello's preface to this novella. And yet Romani's version—in which Romeo has killed Capellio's son, Tebaldo is betrothed to Giulietta, and Lorenzo is a doctor rather than a priest—shows no sign of being derived directly from Bandello or from Luigi da Porto's *Istoria novellamente ritrovata di due nobili amanti* (c. 1530) or from Girolamo dalla Corte's *Dell'istorie della città di Verona* (1594–96). Although Romani may have consulted several different sources, it seems clear that his principal source was a tragedy by the Italian playwright Luigi Scevola, *Giulietta e Romeo,* published in Milan in 1818. Most of the dramatic structure of Bellini's opera follows the outlines of Scevola's treatment of the well-known story.

Romani arrived in Venice on January 19, and work on the opera began immediately. By January 26, two pieces had been written and orchestrated. As Bellini wrote to Giuditta Turina: "I work from morning to evening and it will be a miracle if I emerge from this without some sickness: with these awful chills I have caught a chest cold that refuses to leave me." He suffered terribly from the severe winter, but he continued work, regularly reporting his progress to Giuditta. After the premiere of the third opera of the season on February 20 (*Maria di Brabante* by Albert Guillon), Bellini's score went into rehearsal. As late as March 3 he had not completed the opera, as he informed Giuditta: "I must still compose a scene of the second act. This morning the first act was rehearsed with full orchestra, and it seems it will make its effect." *I Capuleti e i Montecchi* had its premiere on March 11, 1830, and the Venetians were delirious in their enthusiasm.

The apparent rapidity of the composition of *I Capuleti e i Montecchi,* together with Bellini's utilization in the opera of many themes from the failed *Zaira,* have tended to influence negatively critical judgments about the opera. But both of these "problems" are largely illusory. Although Bellini prepared only one opera a year, it did not require a year to write an opera. *La sonnambula,* his next work, was conceived, composed, and mounted in two months, scarcely longer than *I Capuleti e i Montecchi.* And Bellini, just like Rossini and Donizetti, constantly drew thematic inspiration from failed or lesser-known operas, while practically never reusing material from a successful work. *Norma* borrows ideas from *Adelson e Salvini, Bianca e Fernando,* and *Zaira,* as well as the *Ernani* sketches. For *I Capuleti e i Montecchi,* themes from *Zaira* are used, but never entire compositions, and practically everywhere the themes are recast. Indeed, in the score the only number borrowed intact is Giulietta's cavatina, "Oh! quante volte," taken with some alterations from Bellini's student opera, *Adelson e Salvini.* In short, neither in terms of the time of composition nor in the use of borrowed material does *I Capuleti e i Montecchi* differ significantly from Bellini's normal procedures.

Bellini gave appropriate credit for the success of his opera to the singers, mezzo-soprano Giuditta Grisi as Romeo, soprano Rosalbina Carradori-Allan as Giulietta, and tenor Lorenzo Bonfigli as Tebaldo. (That the parts of Capellio and Lorenzo are comparatively small is surely a function of the singers available in Venice.) So many vocal effects are calculated for these particular timbres: the magnificent cabaletta of the Act I finale, where from opposite sides of the stage Giulietta and Romeo sing in unison, "Se ogni speme è a noi rapita," accompanied below by men's voices alone, or the interplay of the women's voices in the tomb scene, particularly after "Un solo accento ancor." As Bellini reported to his friend Alessandro Lamperi on March 16: "Not I nor any one else could desire better actor-singers, for these act and sing in ways it would be impossible to achieve with even the most celebrated performers. Grisi, with her beautiful and extended voice, whose most sympathetic chords I have struck, has excited enthusiasm, also as an actress. Carradori in the part of Giulietta is sublime both for her ingenuous appearance and for her singing and spontaneity of action. The tenor Bonfigli has surpassed himself and the public's expectation, for he had earlier made himself so antipathetic to all that no one would look him in the face any more."

Listening to *I Capuleti e i Montecchi* today, we are struck first by the remarkable balance Bellini achieves between the declamatory style with which he experimented in *La straniera* and that style of ornamented melody, subtle, delicate, and flexible, he was to make his own. It is seen best in the cantabile sections, "Ah! crudel, d'onor ragioni" from the Giulietta-Romeo duet and "Morte io non temo il sai," the primo tempo of Giulietta's Act II aria. These melodies move almost exclusively by step, but rhythmic patterns and details shift kaleidoscopically. Giulietta's melodies all arise from the same rhythmic gesture, yet the tunes have such different effects: the languid, minor-keyed "Oh! quante volte, oh! quante"; the more assertive "Morte io non temo il sai," with its continually rising line; and the practically monotone melody "Ah! non poss'io partire," which she sings after drinking the potion. But Bellini's melodies are certainly not monochromatic: witness the *marziale* cabaletta of Romeo's cavatina, "La tremenda ultrice spada," with its exciting accompaniment for horns, or the abandon of the cabaletta in the Romeo-Tebaldo duet, "Svena, ah! svena un disperato," with its interplay of voices and harmonic progressions weaving through major and minor modes.

The drama is articulated in a series of closed numbers, arias, duets, and the two finales. As in Rossini's Neapolitan operas, which Bellini knew well, these numbers are not purely lyrical; they also encompass much dramatic action. Bellini goes quite far indeed in introducing diverse characters and events within the context of an aria, particularly in Giulietta's of Act II, where Capellio, Lorenzo, and the chorus all have significant roles. Some of the most beautiful moments, however, lie outside these formal numbers, in the instrumental solos introducing scenas that precede formal compositions: the horn solo before Giulietta's cavatina, the cello solo preceding her aria, or the clarinet solo introducing the Romeo-Tebaldo duet. Throughout the opera, Bellini embodies the emotional content of his score in these dark instrumental sounds. The concluding tomb scene is characterized by a rich blend of flute and clarinet, together with some magnificent writing for the horns (particularly at "Sorgi, mio ben").

Although in *I Capuleti e i Montecchi* Bellini rarely introduces full melodic periods within the recitative (an exception being Romeo's "Lieto del pari" preceding his cavatina), the freer approach to form that such periods represent finds its most profound expression, perhaps in all Bellini, in the tomb scene. There is only one full melodic period in the entire scene, Romeo's "Deh! tu, deh! tu, bell'anima." Otherwise Bellini depends on inspired declamation and short melodic fragments. The recitative, chromatic, even painful, in its use of dissonance, follows with enormous sensitivity each detail of the situation and text. Even after Romeo and Giulietta achieve a more continuous musical texture at "Ah! crudel! che mai facesti!" Bellini allows them no rest. The lyrical "Vivi, e vien talora sul mio sasso a lagrimar" is barely touched before the composer sets the voices in rapid alternation, bringing them closer and closer until for the briefest moment they sing together once again before Romeo collapses.

Fate has been unkind to Bellini's opera, and tampering with the score has been inexplicably foolish. The composer himself was compelled to adapt the work for performance at La Scala to open the season on December 26, 1830, since his cast included two mezzo-sopranos, Giuditta Grisi, who again sang Romeo, and Amalia Schütz, who portrayed Giulietta. Bellini lamented in a letter: "The opera made half the effect on me it did in Venice; perhaps because the theatre is larger, or because Rolla [first violinist and conductor] set such slow tempos, or because in all the ensembles the voices of the two women go poorly together since both are mezzo-sopranos. In any case I no longer hear the *Capuleti* of Venice." For this version he added a beautiful melodic phrase for Giulietta just before she drinks the potion in her Act II aria, "Morir dovessi ancora."

Worse was to come. The great Maria Malibran, singing Romeo at the Teatro Comunale of Bologna in October, 1832, decided to replace Bellini's finale with that of Vaccaj's opera. While this shares much of the text of Bellini's final scene, Vaccaj wrote much more conventional music, totally lacking the emotional depths of Bellini's score. Unfortunately, the practice persisted, and in one edition, Ricordi even printed the Vaccaj finale with the infuriating instruction: "To be substituted, if desired, as generally done, for the last piece of Bellini's opera." The modern sin of using a tenor for Romeo is hardly less offensive, since it completely distorts the vocal scoring.

But there is a wonderful letter of June 18, 1834, from the great singer Giuseppina Ronzi-De Begnis, written from Florence, where she was portraying Romeo. It should be taken to heart by every conductor who feels the urge to manipulate an operatic score and by every singer who demands alterations in her part. Ronzi wrote:

The third act (i.e., the tomb scene) was supposed to fail but did not fail. Here they had been saying that Vaccaj's is better, and they wanted Ronzi to do the *pasticcio alla Malibran;* but I replied:—if I make a fiasco, at least it will be all Bellini—I assure you that I was trembling, as the Florentines have the vice of not listening; and you know that in this third act there are no things that flatter the ear, and that to enjoy the beauties, whether of music or of declamation, there must be religious silence. I obtained that, and once the audience had seen me, they remained as if unable to move. In short, to make the matter brief, it gave great pleasure, and after it we were all called out.

Things seem to me to be going well; I really am content. To tell you the truth, I would have been very unhappy if this opera had failed; and I am the more content because it is all Bellini's work. There were people to say: how does Malibran happen to change the third act? It seems to me that, as a singer who is said to be such an actress, she should be content. Does this seem to you a small triumph?

For Bellini it was a great one.

BIZET'S *Carmen*
by Alfred Glasser

March 3, 1875, was a big day for Georges Bizet. That morning he was named a *chevalier de la Légion d'honneur.* That evening the opera that was to win him immortality, *Carmen,* premiered at the Opéra-Comique. But it was not a happy day for the composer. He had devoted two years to the composition of an opera with which he hoped to revolutionize the staid formulas of the opéra comique. He knew this was the best music he had ever written, and he longed for a triumph, which did not materialize. True, the entr'acte before Act II was encored; Escamillo's couplets in Act II received enthusiastic applause, as did Micaëla's aria in Act III. The rest of the opera, however, met a stony silence. No curtain calls. No torch-light procession to a gala supper. Nothing. Deeply depressed, the thirty-seven-year-old composer went home and sought solace a few days later in Bougival, a quiet town on the Seine where he had a country retreat. His thoughts were of the future. He signed a contract for a production of *Carmen* in Vienna that autumn. Tragically, he did not live to see *Carmen's* success in the Austrian capital, nor the triumphant march across Europe that followed immediately afterward. A chronic throat ailment from which he had suffered most of his life flared up and claimed his life on June 3, his sixth wedding anniversary and three months to the day of the fateful Paris premiere.

Although he wrote instrumental works and songs, Bizet was attracted to the lyric stage from the outset of his career. While still in his teens he achieved recognition with a delightful one-act operetta, *Le Docteur Miracle,* which won a prize and a production at Offenbach's theater, the Bouffes-Parisiens. (The Lyric Opera Center for American Artists presented its Chicago premiere in 1979.) At the Paris Conservatory, where his remarkable talent and the lobbying of his musical parents gained him enrollment well before he had reached the minimum age, he studied with men of the theater. His professor of composition was Fromental Halévy, who later became his father-in-law. Charles Gounod frequently gave the young Bizet his counterpoint lessons when the eminent but elderly Pierre Zimmerman was unable to keep his appointments. At nineteen Bizet won the coveted Prix de Rome and scandalized the committee by submitting a comic opera instead of a sacred composition when the time came for his first formal envoi. (This two-act opera buffa, *Don Procopio*, written to an Italian text, was premiered in Monte Carlo in 1906.)

After the three years in Italy, which turned out to be the happiest in his life because of the combination of the mild climate and freedom from financial worries, Bizet returned to Paris where he quickly learned he could not earn a living by composition alone. He considered teaching at the conservatory, but turned instead to all kinds of musical odd jobs to make ends meet. He played the piano at rehearsals, arranged piano reductions of orchestral scores, even worked on dance music and accepted piano pupils. The strenuous work schedule was a drain on his less-than-robust health and left little time for composition. Yet he persevered. He made plans for operas and wrote sketches for many. Some projects mentioned in his correspondence were probably never begun; others were left unfinished. Seven of his stage works were produced during his lifetime. Except for *Le Docteur Miracle,* not one of them was successful initially. His first serious opera, which still occupies a niche in the international repertory, was *Les Pêcheurs de perles,* which the Lyric Opera of Chicago staged in 1966. Those critics who did not call it a "fortissimo in three acts" dealt with it in a patronizing manner. Only Hector Berlioz, the music critic of *Le Journal des débats,* praised those elements of the score that were original and stated that the opera was a credit to Bizet. The public did not rally to its support, and *Les Pêcheurs de perles* closed after eighteen performances. Over two decades elapsed before it was revived in 1886.

La Jolie Fille de Perth, based on a novel by Sir Walter Scott, was produced by the Théâtre Lyrique at the end of 1867. The critical press received it warmly; but the public did not, and it closed after eighteen performances.

In the one-act oriental fantasy *Djamileh,* Bizet seems to have assimilated those Gounod and Meyerbeer influences that his critics assailed and molded them into an intensely personal style all his own. *Djamileh* was written swiftly under great pressure to a libretto by Louis Gallet based on Alfred de Musset's *Namouna.* The exotic setting showcased Bizet's unique flair for creating a landscape in sound; but not even Bizet's talent could outweigh the libretto's theatrical weaknesses. The premiere at the Opéra-Comique was lavishly produced but poorly cast. The audience was not prepared for the harmonic originality of the score, which drew from the critics the "Wagnerism" charges they applied to any music they did not like or understand. After eleven performances *Djamileh* disappeared from the repertory. In honor of the Bizet centenary in 1938 it was revived, but it remains a fascinating curiosity rather than a viable work for the stage.

The music for which Bizet is remembered was written during the brief period 1871–75, the pinnacle of his creative powers so abruptly silenced by his untimely death. The *Jeux d'enfants,* a masterful set of pieces for piano duet, was orchestrated and expanded into the *Petite Suite d'orchestre,* which has been a concert-hall favorite since its first performance in 1873. Léon Carvalho, a prominent Parisian impresario and admirer of Bizet's music, sought the composer's assistance in an attempt to revive the once popular form of the *mélodrame* at the Théâtre du Vaudeville. (A *mélodrame* was a play with incidental music; crucial moments of dialogue were spoken over musical passages often only a few measures long, and extended musical numbers served as prelude, entr'actes, and interpolated songs and dances.) The play was Alphonse Daudet's *L'Arlésienne,* which opened on October 1, 1872, and closed less than three weeks later. Although the musical press did not condescend to review the premiere of such a hybrid work, the distinguished composer-critic Ernest Reyer attended a later performance and hailed Bizet as a genius whose work should be studied by all aspiring musicians. The *Arlésienne Suite,* an expanded version for full orchestra that Bizet arranged from four of the movements, triumphed at a concert conducted by Jules Pasdeloup on November 10. (A second suite, arranged posthumously by Bizet's friend Ernest Guiraud, never attained the popularity of the first.)

Despite the failure of *Djamileh,* Camille du Locle, the director of the Opéra-Comique, commissioned a new opera from Bizet and secured the services of Henri Meilhac and Ludovic Halévy (the latter was a cousin of Bizet's wife) to write the libretto. By hiring the two most celebrated word smiths in Paris, the versifiers of Offenbach's *La Belle Hélène* and *La Vie parisienne,* du Locle sought to avoid the dramatic pitfalls that had plagued *Djamileh.* Bizet upset the apple cart by choosing, not a brilliant satirical comedy that would have been grist for the poets' mills, but *Carmen,* Prosper Mérimée's naturalistic novella that had become a classic in the years following its 1845 *succès de scandal.* The Andalusian setting gave Bizet opportunities to conjure a tonal picture of Spain along the lines of his Arabian and Provençal tours de force in *Djamileh* and *L'Arlésienne.* Instead of the two-dimensional cartoons who populated the plots of the opéra comique, he had flesh-and-blood characters with strong personalities that prompted equally strong musical characterizations. The plot was not a series of stage conventions, but was a conflict that derives from the characters themselves and builds to a climax through a sequence of more and more exciting incidents.

Although the novella is short, it is rich in episodes that the librettists adroitly manage to pare down to operatic proportions. They invent the character of Micaëla to dramatize the choice José must make between two irreconcilable ways of life. Since it is impossible to include all the twists of the plot, the librettists eliminate wherever possible the more unsavory ones. They omit Carmen's husband and the violent deaths of Dancaïre and Remendado. Escamillo, the matador, is a glamorization of Mérimée's lowly picador named Lucas, whose brief amorous interlude with Carmen provokes José's ultimatum. What works in a prose narrative does not always work on the stage; the theatrical instincts of Meilhac and Halévy lead them to transpose the death of Carmen from a lonely country road to the empty street outside the bullring. The spoken dialogue includes many direct quotes from Mérimée and deftly informs of incidents that there is no time to act out. Bizet played an active role in the shaping of the libretto. Indeed, the words to the "Habañera" are his own, a substitution for more conventionally literary lines not in keeping with the character and less effective for Carmen's all-important first utterance.

The music for *Carmen* was written swiftly. The composition was spread over a two-year period because of other projects that intervened: a revival of his friend Gounod's *Roméo et Juliette,* for which he handled all the negotiations, and work on a five-act grand opera, *Don Rodrigue,* for the Opéra, which was left unfinished and never produced. (The manuscript is in the collection of the Paris Conservatory. Jules Massenet's *Le Cid* of 1885 utilized the same libretto.) Act I was finished by the summer of 1873; by the end of the year, after a number of singers had been offered the part, Marie Galli-Marié agreed to create the title role. The opera was finished by the summer of 1874, and the orchestration took two more months. Rehearsals were delayed by the management of the Opéra-Comique, largely because of the attitude of Adolphe de Leuven, the codirector. He had been appalled by the choice of *Carmen* at the outset and had badgered the librettists, with some success, to tone down the text. When it came to changing the ending to avoid the final murder, Bizet flatly refused, and de Leuven resigned.

This was not mere prudishness on de Leuven's part. He was concerned for the future of the Opéra-Comique, which was in an unusually shaky financial position. Above all he did not want to alienate the middle-class audience that kept the Opéra-Comique afloat. The theater's repertory had always been of an anodyne nature suitable for family evenings. Immorality and violence on this stage were unprecedented.

When the rehearsals finally began, Bizet received complaints from the orchestra and vocalists alike that his music was unperformable. Meilhac and Halévy accused Galli-Marié, whose realistically sensual interpretation of her role delighted Bizet, of portraying Mérimée's Carmen, perhaps, but certainly not theirs. By the time the stormy preparation had been completed, however, the performers had been convinced of the validity and the beauty of Bizet's score.

The first production ran for forty-eight performances, which looks at first glance like a successful opening. However, box-office receipts were so poor that *Carmen* was nearly withdrawn after the first few nights. Toward the end of the run, most of the audience held complimentary tickets. The dismal reviews in the press did nothing to stimulate sales. Some of the critics seem to have wanted a Wagnerian music drama from Bizet and accused him of pandering to popular tastes with the melodious set numbers; others could hear no melodies at all and reproached him for abandoning the glorious French traditions laid down by Daniel Auber and François Boieldieu. Within months, however, the more honest reviewers admitted their initial misjudgment, while a few maintained they had praised the work from the start.

The critical about-face was triggered by the *Carmen* furor that swept Europe after the brilliant success of the Vienna production, which was presented in German with recitatives by Ernest Guiraud substituted for the spoken dialogue. Guiraud, a close friend of Bizet's since their days as Prix de Rome pensioners in Italy, did such a remarkable job that this version supplanted Bizet's original concept nearly everywhere. It was the version with recitatives that was presented at the Opéra. For that house a balletic divertissement was also required; this began the unfortunate tradition of inserting the *Arlésienne Suite* as a ballet immediately after the opening choruses of Act IV. This prolongs an already complete evening and dissipates much of the tension before the dénouement.

Bizet had sold the score to the publisher Choudens (for 25,000 francs) three months before the premiere, but he did not live to oversee the edition, which appeared with modifications—insertions and cuts—he had not authorized. In 1964 Fritz Oesel's critical edition separated the real Bizet from the traditional and restored deleted measures. Since Oesel's work has been available, producers of *Carmen* have tended to favor the original version more and more. Admiration for Guiraud's recitatives has not been universal. When Camille Saint-Saëns heard them, he denounced them as inappropriate and a distortion of the opéra comique spirit in which Bizet had conceived the piece.

Bizet wrote a French opera in a French form. His superbly realized intention is to conjure a romantic vision of Spain, not to recreate ethnic Iberian music. He resisted suggestions to visit Spain and absorb the folklore.

The prelude to Act I opens with a rousing theme, brilliantly orchestrated with drums, cymbals, and brass, that evokes the bullring. A lively, less sumptuous secondary theme intervenes before the march that identifies Escamillo is heard. The prelude ends with the fate motif on the cellos under a shimmering tremolo on the violins. All of these themes recur in the opera.

The opening chorus is about as Spanish as a cheese soufflé and certainly as delicious. Micaëla's innate diffidence is captured in the theme in triplets on the violins that marks her entrance. Her arch repetition of Moralès's phrases as she declines his invitation reveals the strength of a character that goes beyond treacly demureness, preparing credibility for her courageous meeting with the smugglers in Act III. Carmen's entrance to a rhythmic variant of the fate motif is a master stroke. The tune of the "Habañera" is borrowed from a song, "El Arreglito," by the Spanish-American composer Sebastián Yradier. The melody of her impudent refusal to answer Zuniga's questions about the stabbing in the cigarette factory is an authentic Spanish folk tune; the words "coupe-moi, brûle-moi" are genuine Mérimée, but not from his *Carmen*. They are quoted from his translation of a narrative poem by Alexander Pushkin, "The Gypsies."

The entr'acte that precedes Act II is an angular tune, sung later in the act by Don José as he enters Lillas Pastia's tavern. This is an indelible contrast to the

sensuous gypsy song, sung by Carmen, heard as the curtain rises. The jux-
taposition of the pieces palpably expresses the essential mismatching of José
and Carmen. Their mutual infatuation has blinded them both. Escamillo's
couplets are an irresistible crowd pleaser. Escamillo, of all the principals in
Carmen, comes closest to a traditional opéra comique personnage—charismatic and witty, suavely confident that Carmen cannot help but succumb to his
charm eventually. The mercurial quintet both delights the ear and advances the
plot. This is the first suggestion that José should be brought into the band of
smugglers. Carmen's song to José demonstrates that Bizet's counterpoint lessons were not in vain; once the horns start to sound the retreat, it blossoms into
an ingenious two-part invention. The melody to José's "Flower Song," one of
the finest Bizet ever penned, is both a showpiece for the tenor and an admirable
revelation of character. It starts quietly and builds in intensity, showing that
José has a gentle nature but is capable of violent passion; but it ends pianissimo,
showing he is not yet confident that his love is returned. The tragic fate that
brought José and Carmen together in the first place now returns in the person
of Zuniga. His encounter with José prevents the young soldier from turning
back. The trio sung by Carmen and the smugglers to the bound Zuniga is
impertinence set to music.

The entr'acte for flute and strings before Act III is enigmatic. Is it perhaps a
nostalgic reminiscence of the serenity of José's life before Carmen entered it?
The imminent appearance of Micaëla lends a flimsy support to this idea.
Perhaps it is a musical description of the rugged, pure mountains of Andalusia,
about to be polluted by the infamous smugglers. The furtive movements of the
smugglers are consummately and melodiously mirrored in the stealthy music of
the opening chorus of Act III. Carmen's discovery of her death and José's in the
infallible cards is dramatized by the girlish glee of Frasquita and Mercédès who
turn the scene into a trio. Micaëla's haunting aria may indeed hold up the
action, but it is worth it; and the soprano who sings the role obviously needs
more than the Act I duet to earn her fee. The José-Escamillo duct and duel adds
action and excitement. Micaëla's news that José's mother is dying is imparted
to the same music that described her in the first act. Few acts in opera end as
dramatically as this one: the distant voice of Escamillo restates the jealous
tension of the moment, while the orchestra reiterates unresolved statements of
the fate motif up to the abrupt final cadence.

The entr'acte before Act IV is based on another authentic Spanish melody, a
polo from a *tonadilla* by the celebrated singer Manuel García. The opening
choruses are a recapitulation of the beginning of the prelude to Act I, except
that Bizet superimposes a counter melody for the vocalists over the stirring
bullring music; the children's chorus takes up the secondary theme. The brief
scene where Frasquita and Mercédès warn Carmen that José is in the crowd
brings the listener back from the pomp and spectacle to the intimate drama
about to conclude. The prosaic "C'est toi?"—"C'est moi" that sets the final
duet in motion is a masterpiece of understatement. The changes of mood in

José's part, from supplication to threat to violence and to final remorse are drawn with exquisite moderation: any shorter, the scene would be perfunctory; any longer, an ignoble harangue. Carmen's courage and her sense of fatalism are brought out in her reaction to this confrontation. She has a strong nobility as she submits to destiny. A strumpet would merely have left town.

Carmen is a crowning achievement to Bizet's career. It also represents the apogee of the form in which it is written, the opéra comique.

ROSSINI's *La Cenerentola*
by Arthur Kaplan

Cinderella. The name alone of this most popular of fairy tales conjures up a world of enchantment. According to Funk and Wagnalls' *Standard Dictionary of Folklore, Mythology and Legend,* in its prototypical form the story of Cinderella tells of an "Ash Girl who, with the aid of an animal or dead mother, appears at a dance, festival or in later versions at church, disguised as a grand lady, wins the admiration of the prince, is discovered by a ring or a slipper test and marries the prince."

The origins of the legend remain unknown, though they are most likely oriental. The earliest written version comes from ninth-century China, and an Eastern provenance would account for one of the essential features of the tale, the heroine's tiny feet, which denote extraordinary distinction of virtue and beauty. There are over five hundred variants of the story in Europe alone, and from Europe it was carried to Indonesia, the Philippines, and North and South America.

The first European version in print is *La gatta Cenerentola* (Cat Cinderella) by Giovanni Battista Basile, published in 1634. It is the sixth diversion of *Pentamerone,* modeled after Giovanni Boccaccio's famous *Decamerone.* Fifty tales, including the first printed *Rapunzel* and *Snow White* are told in Neapolitan dialect to a prince and his bride over a five-day period. Zezolla, the heroine of *La gatta Cenerentola,* has not one but two stepmothers. The first is an evil woman whom Zezolla kills by slamming the lid of a heavy chest down on her head upon the advice of her beloved governess. Once her father has married the governess, the new stepmother introduces her previously concealed six daughters. Zezolla is reduced to doing the kitchen drudgery and becomes "Cat Cinderella." The remainder of the story follows the general outlines as they later appear in *Aschenputtel* by the Brothers Grimm, except that there is no sibling rivalry in Basile, nor any mistreatment of Cinderella by her stepsisters. Basile's version is unusual in that the heroine's early debasement is clearly the consequence of her killing the first stepmother; in most other versions, Cinderella is completely innocent of any wrongdoing and in no way merits her degradation. It was Basile's version that established the basic features of the story in the occidental tradition.

Charles Perrault (1628–1703), a poet, critic, and artistic advisor during the régime of Louis XIV, wrote *Histoires et contes du temps passé, avec des moralités* (1697), claiming to have transcribed stories told to him by his ten-year-old son Pierre, whose name appears on the first edition of the eight Mother Goose tales (in addition to *Cinderella,* the collection includes *Sleeping Beauty, Little Red Riding Hood, Puss and Boots, Blue Beard, and Tom Thumb*). Pierre was alleged to have learned the tales by rote from his nurse, a woman steeped in French folklore.

It was Perrault's version of *Cinderella* that Walt Disney and team used in 1950 to create their magical animated cartoon adaptation seen by millions of movie goers throughout the world. The full-length film has inevitably influenced the modern perception of this beloved children's story.

Cendrillon, ou la petite pantoufle de verre (Cinderella, or the Little Glass Slipper), begins with the traditional "Il était une fois" (Once upon a time) and includes all of the elements familiar to us since childhood that were invented by Perrault and enhanced by Disney and team: the fairy godmother; her wand-waving transformation of a pumpkin into an elegant coach, six live mice into a team of horses, a rat into a mustachioed coachman, and six lizards into liveried lackeys; her admonition to return home before the stroke of midnight; and the slipper made of glass. Although Perrault did not distort the legend by these alterations, he did substantially change its tone.

In his version, the story ends with two morals: (1) Beauty is a rare gift, but grace is more valuable and priceless. To win someone's heart, grace is the true gift of the fairies. Without it you can't do anything; with it you can do everything. (2) All the gifts and advantages you possess will be of no avail unless you have a godfather or godmother to bring out their true value.

The tacked-on moral lessons are proof of the anodyne nature of Perrault's achievement in sugar-coating and sanitizing the Cinderella story. As the noted child psychologist Bruno Bettelheim points out in *The Uses of Enchantment: The Meaning and Importance of Fairy Tales* (1976), by making the heroine insipidly good and lacking in initiative (it is the fairy godmother who tells Cinderella that she wishes to go to the ball, and from then on Cinderella is entirely under her command), Perrault reduces the story to "a nice fantasy with no implications for ourselves."

Perrault's *Cendrillon,* no doubt because of its greater charm, physical attractiveness, and classical refinement, has remained the most widely popular version of the Cinderella story, far eclipsing the Brothers Grimm's account, which is considerably more sordid and sadistic. In their *Aschenputtel,* one finds such grisly events as the cruel stepsisters' attempts to fit into the slipper by cutting off parts of their feet with a knife supplied by the stepmother and the unmasking of this deception by two pigeons, who draw attention to the blood in the stepsisters' slippers and later punish them for their wickedness and falsehood by pecking out their eyes.

Nicolo Isouard, the Maltese composer of the first successful operatic version of the Cinderella story, which had its premiere at the Opéra-Comique in Paris on February 22, 1810, shared the rose-colored, sentimental view of the legend with Perrault. Charles-Guillaume Étienne's libretto for this *opéra-féerie* presents an idealized fairy-tale heroine, innocent, ingenuous, loving, and humble (the work's most popular number was Cinderella's romance, "Je suis modeste et soumise" [I am modest and obedient]).

In Isouard's version, the physical transformation from vestimentary rags to riches occurs during the first intermission, after Cinderella has fallen asleep by the hearth. At the beginning of Act II, she awakens, bedecked like a princess. She is then given a magic rose so that she may remain incognita at the ball, even to her stepfather and stepsisters. The story line follows the principal events in Perrault, including the happy ending where Cinderella rushes into her stepfather's arms and forgives her stepsisters.

According to Rossini scholar Giuseppe Radiciotti, *Cendrillon* owed its tremendous success to the dazzle of the spectacular effects, the beauty of the staging, and especially to the presence of two immensely popular singing actresses, Mlle. Saint-Aubin (Cendrillon) and Mlle. Regnault (Tisbé). Radiciotti deemed the music pleasant, facile, and often sentimental but lacking in any real originality, with trite harmonies and uninteresting and unvaried orchestration.

The popularity of Isouard's work was such that it gave rise to a spate of imitations and strongly influenced the two most celebrated Cinderella operas, Rossini's *Cenerentola* (1817) and Massenet's *Cendrillon* (1899). Whereas the French composer and his librettist took the tone and general feeling of the more romantic French style from the earlier *Cendrillon,* the Italian maestro and his librettist took the names of all the characters and certain of the unique plot devices and scenes from the *opéra-féerie,* which predates *La Cenerentola* by less than seven years.

Such wholesale borrowing—not to say plagiarism—would be unthinkable today, but in the early nineteenth century, when both copyright laws and the Romantic notion of creative individuality were all but nonexistent, it was common practice. The librettos of Pietro Metastasio were used over and over again by numerous eighteenth-century composers, and those of Felice Romani, the most famous librettist of the bel canto period, often served more than one composer. Musically speaking, Rossini himself borrowed unabashedly from his own unsuccessful works in creating new operas for the various Italian theaters.

Furthermore, due to the vicissitudes of scheduling and to Rossini's proverbial laziness, *La Cenerentola* proved to be a last-minute effort. The composer had signed a contract with the Teatro Valle in Rome to furnish a comic opera to a libretto provided by the management for the opening of the carnival season on December 26, 1816. Rossini then left for Naples, where he was engaged to write two operas, one comic and one serious. The famous Teatro San Carlo had just burned down, and the maestro was in no hurry to begin work. *La Gazzetta, ossia il matrimonio per concorso* opened at the Teatro dei Fiorentini on September 26 and was a total flop (Rossini salvaged the overture for *La Cenerentola*); *Otello, ossia il Moro di Venezia,* although considerably more successful, did not receive its premiere at the temporary home of the San Carlo company, the Teatro del Fondo, until December 4.

By the time Rossini returned to Rome in mid December, Cartoni, the impresario of the Teatro Valle, had already decided to produce the maestro's new work as the season's second offering, rather than the opener. *Ninetta alla corte,* a libretto adapted by Rossi from a French play, had been selected but was rejected by the papal censor as too immoral. The poet Jacopo Ferretti, who had earned a reputation as a doctor of plays, was called in by Cartoni to attempt an accommodation with the censor. However, the demanded alterations would have completely denatured the spirit of the comedy, so an impasse ensued. A disconsolate Rossini implored Ferretti, who had ironically been passed over as the poet of *Il barbiere di Siviglia* scarcely a year before, to supply him with a new libretto.

Here is Ferretti's own account of the subsequent events:

> On that freezing cold evening [December 23] we were reduced to drinking tea at Cartoni's house. I proposed 20 or 30 melodramma subjects; but this one was thought too serious, and in Rome of that day, at least at Carnival time, people wanted to laugh; that one too complicated, another too expensive for the impresario . . . and another finally not suited to the artists who were to perform. Weary from making suggestions and nearly dropping from sleep, I whistled out in the middle of a yawn: Cinderella. Rossini, who the better to concentrate had lain down on the bed, sat up . . . and said to me: "Would you have the courage to write me a Cinderella?" And I shot back: "And you to set it to music?" and he: "When can you have the scenario?" and I: "In spite of sleep, tomorrow morning."

With such a deadline in mind, is it any wonder that Ferretti cribbed so heavily from Isouard's *Cendrillon* (in large measure via its Italian imitator, *Agatina, ossia la virtù premiata,* music by Steffano Pavesi and text by Felice Romani, which had been produced at La Scala in 1814)? The librettist claims it took him twenty-two days to write the verses (unlike *Cendrillon* and *Agatina,* which have long sections of prose—dialogue in the former, recitative in the latter—*La Cenerentola* is rhymed throughout) and Rossini twenty-four days to write the music. The opera was first entitled *Angiolina, ossia la bontà in trionfo,* but the censors objected, suspecting an allusion to a notorious lady by that name who was then breaking hearts all over Rome. So *La Cenerentola* it became. In the preface to the original libretto, Ferretti declared that one of the main reasons for proposing the Cinderella story was "that air of ingenuous goodness, which was one of the distinguishing traits of the good Madame (Righetti-)Giorgi," who portrayed the title role.

The cast of characters in *Cendrillon* and *La Cenerentola* is identical, down to the very names. In Isouard, besides Cinderella and her two stepsisters, Clorinde and Tisbé, there is a cruel stepfather, the Baron de Montefiascone; a godfather type named Alidor, who is tutor and counselor to Prince Ramir; and a supercilious servant, Dandini, with whom the prince exchanges identities so that he can find out whether he is loved for himself or for his title and wealth.

The opening scenes of the two works are virtually identical, with the chattering, chastising stepsisters ordering Cinderella around while she sings a dreamy ballad. (In the French work, it is merely a pastoral folk song of no intrinsic significance; in *Cenerentola,* borrowing an idea from *Agatina,* the words constitute a résumé of the action to come.) Then Alidor, disguised as a beggar, appears at the door asking for a piece of bread. He is pitied and protected by Cinderella, vilified and banished by the stepsisters. The din awakens the baron, who enters in his nightclothes. He has been aroused from the loveliest of dreams. (Ferretti, taking his cue from Romani, seizes the occasion to furnish the text from the first of Don Magnifico's magnificent buffo arias "Miei rampolli femminini"; there is no corresponding dream *récit* in *Cendrillon.*) When the prince enters, Cinderella becomes confused and tongue-tied in her attempt to explain her position in the household and her kinship to the baron and his daughters.

Other parallel scenes, also found in *Agatina,* involve the comic character Dandini. While masquerading as the prince, he names Cinderella's stepfather his cellar master because of the baron's propensity for the grape (Baron de Montefiascone translates 'Baron of Mountflagon'). Later, still impersonating Prince Ramir, he simultaneously woos Clorinde and Tisbé, flitting from one to the other with vows of eternal devotion.

Lastly, just before the final happily-ever-after chorus of jubilation which brings down the curtain on both Cinderella operas, it is the wise Alidor who points up the moral of the story. In *Cendrillon,* he says, addressing the heroine: "Vous avez un bon coeur, tout vous réussira;/Le ciel vous récompensera" (You have a good heart, everything will go well for you;/The heavens will reward you). And in *Cenerentola:* "Giusto ciel! ti ringrazio! I voti miei/Non han più che sperar. L'orgoglio è oppresso,/Sarà felice il caro alunno. In trono/Trionfa la bontà" (Righteous Heaven! I thank you! My wishes/Have nothing more to hope for./Pride has been humbled,/My dear pupil will be happy. Upon the throne/Goodness triumphs).

Despite these obvious similarities, Isouard's *Cendrillon* and Rossini's *Cenerentola* are very different works. The former is clearly within the tradition of French *opéra comique*; the latter within the tradition of Italian *opera buffa*.

Written during the Napoleonic period, when moral tales exalting virtue and condemning evil were nearly de rigueur in the theater, the *Cendrillon* libretto by Étienne, not so coincidentally the head of the censorship office under the Empire, extols goodness, honesty, sincerity, and humility. It is essentially a sentimental comedy with music, continuing in the line of the *comédies à ariettes* and opéras comiques of the eighteenth century, with a dash of fairy-tale fantasy for added appeal.

Interspersed amidst the spoken dialogue, there are seventeen musical numbers spread out over three acts: two choruses, eleven ensemble numbers, and only four solos, although short solo passages appear in the act finales. Of these four, there are a romance for both Cinderella and her prince, a vengeance number for Tisbé, and in the only piece so designated in the libretto, an aria of moral character for Alidor.

The "précepteur et grand astrologue" plays a major role in the French work (and in *Agatina*) as opposed to his secondary status in *Cenerentola*. There are several reasons for this disparity. In *Cendrillon* the moral tone, as exemplified by Alidor, is paramount. It is not by accident that his aria is at the center of the work, for it contains the thematic homily of the opera: "Make sure you preserve your goodness, / That fortunate gift of Nature. / Never change, through deceit / That endearing simplicity: / The most elegant of adornments / Is goodness."

In Rossini's opera, especially in the original 1817 version, for which a second-rate composer (Luca Agolini) furnished a second-rate aria ("Vasto teatro è il mondo") for a second-rate bass (Zenobio Vitarelli), Alidoro's role is played down. It was enhanced somewhat during the revival of *La Cenerentola* for the 1820–21 carnival season in Rome, when Rossini substituted a new aria, "Là del cielo nell'arcano profondo," for the excellent bass Gioacchino Moncada. Ferretti relates in his memoirs: "I wrote for him an important moral aria, for which Rossini created a musical masterpiece, thunderously applauded, but which was never again sung in this *melodramma* because the other Alidoros never went beyond the very discouraging limits of mediocrity, and that aria is not for the mediocre."

Another significant reason for Alidoro's relative lack of importance compared to his French counterpart lies in the nature of opera buffa. The roles of the two male buffo characters, Don Magnifico and Dandini, had to be expanded to meet the expectations of the genre and the talents of the much-admired Andrea Verni and Giuseppe de Begnis. In *Cendrillon,* the stepfather and valet were speaking roles, their interpreters called upon to sing only in the finales. It is the stepfather who has the least important male role and the tutor who has the most important one in Isouard; in Rossini it is just the opposite.

Perhaps because of de Begnis's stature or to differentiate more clearly between the two buffo characters. Dandini is much less a witless oaf in *Cenerentola* than in *Cendrillon* or *Agatina*. He is more a friend and accomplice of the prince, especially in Act II, than a fatuous and bumbling dummy. The audience laughs with him as well as at him. On the other hand, the baron, who is merely a silly and somewhat sadistic stepfather in Isouard, becomes a full-blown buffoon in the best Italian tradition—more clownish than cruel—in Rossini.

The great Act II duet for Don Magnifico and Dandini, "Un segreto d'importanza," was literally written at the eleventh hour on the night before the premiere. With the text lifted virtually verbatim from *Agatina* (it is the sole example of word-for-word plagiarism from Romani's libretto), Rossini rehearsed it with Verni and de Begnis the next morning and once again during the actual performance, in the interval between the first and second acts.

In fact, it is the buffo roles that give *La Cenerentola* much of its relief, rather than the sentimental figures of Cinderella and Prince Ramiro, despite their attractive music. Since Rossini was given neither to sentimentality nor to magic, there is only one duet for the lovers and no abracadabra transformation scenes whatsoever. In this respect *La Cenerentola* parts company with *Agatina,* which retains the magic rose from *Cendrillon* and goes its French source one better by including the two transformation scenes in the stage action.

Curiously, both *Agatina* and *La Cenerentola* omit one of the key features of the Cinderella legend, the slipper test. In Pavesi's work, Cinderella is recognized by claiming the magic rose she had discarded upon fleeing the ball; in Rossini, the slipper is replaced with a bracelet. When a French critic dared suggest that Mme. Righetti-Giorgi probably had a more attractive wrist than foot, the singer herself responded in print: "In the theaters of Rome, performers are not permitted the same freedom of movement as in France. It was thought that the use of a slipper might somehow offend decency, and since it was a musical work, a bracelet could easily be substituted."

Despite its initial failure at the Teatro Valle on January 25, 1817, due primarily to insufficient rehearsal time and inadequate performances in all but the title role, *La Cenerentola* went on to become an immense favorite with nineteenth-century audiences, rivaling even *Il barbiere* in popularity. Now, after years of neglect, Rossini's *dramma giocoso* has returned to public favor, due jointly to the emergence of such exemplars in the coloratura mezzo-soprano repertory as Agnes Baltsa, Teresa Berganza, Marilyn Horne, Lucia Valentini-Terrani, and Frederica von Stade to do justice to the title role, and to the rediscovery of the wealth and sparkle of comic invention which permeates the score.

MOZART'S *La clemenza di Tito*
by Thomas Willis

If we are to believe the chroniclers of ancient Rome, something remarkable happened to Titus Flavius Sabinus Vespasianus on his way to becoming emperor. A military man who saw duty in Germany and Britain, he joined his father Vespasian in suppressing the Jewish rebellion in A.D. 70. The eastern Mediterranean apparently had an effect on him. He brought back to Rome a harem household of dancers and eunuchs as well as Berniece, his Jewish mistress. "Both as private citizen and later as his father's colleague," the historian Suetonius notes, "Titus had been not only unpopular but venomously loathed." Others saw him as a latter-day Nero.

Titus's reign was short—two years, two months, and twenty days, we are told—but hardly uneventful. Mount Vesuvius erupted two months after he was declared emperor, destroying the cities of Pompeii and Herculaneum. A year later, fire and plague ravaged Rome itself. But when Titus died at the age of forty-two in A.D. 81, he had changed his image completely. He was described as "graceful and dignified, both muscular and handsome, except for a certain paunchiness. He had a phenomenal memory and displayed a natural aptitude alike for the arts of war and peace; handled arms and rode a horse as well as any man living; could compose speeches and verses in Greek or Latin with equal ease, and was something of a musician."

Above all, posthumous reports tell us, he was a man of clemency. During the disasters, he offered support to the suffering and financed a rebuilding program from the emperor's private coffers. He was lavish in his distribution of gifts to the populace and produced numerous festivals and gladiatorial games. He suspended executions, pardoned those who conspired to do him in, and once arranged a splendid wedding for the daughter of a former enemy—even providing her dowry and trousseau. So determined was his pursuit of virtue, the account concludes, that "one evening at dinner, realizing he had done no good deed since the previous night, he spoke these memorable words, 'My friends, I have wasted a day.'"

The more skeptical among us—including more than one contemporary stage director for Mozart's last opera, *La clemenza di Tito* —may question this wimpish "born again" antique cameo, but the eighteenth-century court poet, Pietro Metastasio, was not about to be critical. His patron, the Holy Roman Emperor Charles VI, had commissioned an opera libretto for his name day, November 4, 1734. Praising Charles's skill on the battlefield would be a mistake in timing; he and his troops had suffered a decisive defeat the preceding July during the Wars of Polish Succession. Clemency, praised by philosophers from Seneca onward as the most esteemed imperial virtue, was just the subject. The opera seria that resulted was in the customary form of the time: three acts of alternating recitatives and arias—twenty-five in all—with the choruses at the four climax points. Marriage desires and an assassination conspiracy provided the necessary framework for the orderly dramatic progression. In the setting by Antonio Caldara, the first performance was a resounding success at the Vienna Court Theater.

That was only the beginning for the libretto. It quickly became recognized as an ideal court opera, noble in purpose and politically harmless. Partisans of Italian opera in France echoed Voltaire, who termed it "an eternal lesson to all kings and a delight to all mankind" and compared the poetry to that of Corneille and Racine. Others saw its central character as the very model of a modern, enlightened absolute monarch. Between 1734 and 1839 the text was adapted and set at least forty-five times, by composers as diverse as Hasse, Gluck, Galuppi, and Haydn's impresario J.P. Salomon.

So it was hardly surprising that when they finally got around to planning the coronation festivities for Leopold II in Prague, scheduled for September, 1791, the Bohemian committee-in-charge mentioned *Tito* as a possible libretto. They were hoping for a new text, to be sure, but it was already July 8 when they signed a contract with the theater manager and impresario, Domenico Guardasoni. And Metastasio's subject was made to order for Leopold's self-image; during his twenty-five years as ruler of the Italian province of Tuscany he had endeavored to create an enlightened modern state, abolishing torture and the death penalty, moderating the sentences decreed by criminal law, and remaining neutral when the peace was threatened.

The contract for the coronation opera required that Guardasoni secure an internationally known Italian castrato and prima donna, to present new costumes and two new changes of scenery, and to provide the National Theater with festive illumination and floral tributes. The choice of composer was not important and was to be left up to the impresario.

Moving quickly, Guardasoni selected Caterino Mazzolà, who had just replaced Mozart's friend and former librettist Lorenzo da Ponte as Leopold's official court poet, to adapt and shorten the Metastasio libretto. And although he had discussed an opera with Mozart two years previously, the impresario prudently offered the composition commission to the current court Kapellmeister and Mozart rival, Antonio Salieri. Salieri turned out to be otherwise occupied—substituting for Haydn during other festivities at Esterházy palace—and Mozart, known and respected in Prague, was the second choice. Although he was in ill health and already at work on *The Magic Flute* and the Requiem, he accepted. The 200 ducats plus travel expenses—a little more than $4,000 in today's American currency—doubtless had something to do with it. But it may also have been that Mozart, ever interested in new musical challenges, wanted to try his hand at a modern opera seria.

Mazzolà cut Metastasio's text by about a third, removed almost all of the second act and an accompanying subplot, and broke the monotonous procession of recitatives and arias with ensembles; the final result contains eleven arias, three duets, three trios, a quintet, a sextet, and five choruses. This variety tightens up the action, gives the main characters clearer profiles, and allows the composer to delineate the work's emotional life by playing the musical characters off against one another. He also focused the action of the opera with an impressive and spectacular finale for each of the two acts. For his part, Mozart eliminated much of the excess weight in the traditional opera seria. The lengthy introductions to the arias have all but disappeared, and the arias themselves are radically simplified. Accompanied recitatives—so important in *Don Giovanni* and *Idomeneo*—occur at only four points when a character is going through a crisis. Instrumental textures are as transparent as in his symphonic works, and the orchestra for the most part serves as accompaniment. There are only two independent compositions—the overture and a march. And the two arias with instrumental obbligatos—for clarinet and basset horn—were composed especially for Mozart's virtuoso friend Anton Stadler, who was a member of the orchestra for the Prague performances.

Such adaptations of traditional serious operas were being created in Italy by composers such as Domenico Cimarosa, Giovanni Paisiello, and Giuseppe Sarti. Long after Mozart's death, when *Tito* was performed in Milan for the carnival of 1816–17, the printed libretto described it as follows: "Serious musical drama in two acts by Pietro Metastasio, adapted for modern theatrical usage with music by Amadeus Mozart." Daniel Heartz, the distinguished Mozart scholar, concludes that *Tito,* far from being a relic of a vanishing genre, was in fact the "most modishly up-to-date work he left."

Mozart's first two biographers, Franz Niemetschek and Georg Nissen, insisted that work on *Tito* began "in his travelling coach *en route* from Vienna to Prague, and he finished it in eighteen days." Few modern scholars have accepted the figure, and one, Alan Tyson, has done some fascinating musicological detective work to disprove it. In 1975, he analyzed the music paper that Mozart used. Most of the opera, it turns out, was written on north-Italian papers preferred in Vienna; only Titus's second aria, the instrumental items, and some of the accompanied recitatives were composed on paper purchased in Prague. Furthermore, some of the early sketches for the opera were made on sheets he also used for *The Magic Flute.* In some of these, the part of Sextus is set for a tenor; but very soon the composer switches the role to soprano castrato. The first items to be written were the three duets, two of the trios, the choruses, an aria or part of one for Sextus, and almost all of Titus's solo music. Piecing this and other evidence together, we get a surprisingly clear picture of the way Mozart proceeded on what proved to be his final large-scale project.

It is remarkably similar to the way George Gershwin, Cole Porter, or Leonard Bernstein created during the heyday of Broadway musicals, when everyone worked around the clock until just before opening-night curtain. Here is a short chronology, drawn in part from H.C. Robbins Landon's *1791: Mozart's Last Year.*

Around July 15: On his way to Bologna to hire his stars, Guardasoni firms up arrangements with Mazzolà and Mozart. They confer on and off. Mozart suggests incorporating a previously composed scene into Act II; it is done and is later to be a particular success.

July 15–August 15: The libretto is gradually completed. Without hearing the singers, Mozart cannot compose their arias. He can, however, compose the choruses and most of the ensembles. One voice, the tenor who is to sing Titus, is known to Mozart. He is Antonio Baglioni, who had sung the first Don Ottavio in the 1787 Prague *Don Giovanni.* Mozart composes almost all of his music. He is presumed to have asked his pupil Franz Süssmayr to set the recitatives.

August 16–25: Guardasoni returns to Vienna with contracts for his guest stars and descriptions of the cast. Mozart starts work on some of their solo music.

August 25: Mozart and his wife, Constanze, leave behind their sixth child, the month-old Franz Xavier Wolfgang, and together with Süssmayr board the fast mail coach for the three night and four day trip to Prague, a distance of 150 miles. No doubt he used the time on the stagecoach to compose the missing numbers in his head. As they were boarding the coach, the mysterious messenger who had commissioned the requiem materialized "like a ghost" (wrote Niemetschek and Nissen) and plucked the hem of Constanze's traveling cloak. "And what is going to happen with the Requiem?" Mozart apologizes, says that the trip is necessary and that the work will be his first order of business when he returns.

August 28: Ten days before the premiere, Mozart arrives in Prague to continue composing, start rehearsals, and supervise the copying of the parts. The city is awash in precoronation entertainment. In addition to the opera company, there was a theatrical troupe, a "Persian Fair" which needed one hundred twenty pairs of children, many adults, and over a hundred horses, some disguised as camels. A circus, a magic show with automatons, fireworks, and chemical experiments were to be found elsewhere. The aristocracy held banquets, garden parties, masked balls, and musical soirées.

September 2: Mozart finds time to attend a performance of his *Don Giovanni*. According to Nissen, he also occasionally visited a coffee house to distract himself by playing billiards. "For some days it was noticed that as he played he sang a motif softly to himself. Several times when his opponent was playing his shot, [Mozart] took a book out of his pocket, glanced quickly at it, and went on playing. Later, he played to his friends the beautiful quintet from *The Magic Flute* between Tamino, Papageno, and the Three Ladies, which begins with just that same motif that occupied him while he was playing billiards."

September 5: According to one account, possibly exaggerated: "Messenger after messenger was sent out by the orchestra for the missing [*Tito*] overture. Mozart paced up and down in the room, answering the repeated injunctions with 'Not a single idea will come.' Finally, as the concertmaster himself approached, a friend shouted at him, 'then for heaven's sake begin it with the calvary march!' Whereupon Mozart flew to his spinet and finished the overture. Parts were hastily copied and the messengers hurried off with the sheets, still wet."

September 6: Coronation day. In the Cathedral of St. Vitus, Leopold was crowned King of Bohemia. Some of the sacred music that Salieri conducted was by Mozart. *Tito* took place that evening. The royal couple arrived late for the ticket-only, free performance. The official coronation journal notes that "the composition is by the famous Mozart, and is an honour to him, although he had not much time for writing it, and moreover fell ill as he was in the process of finishing the last part."

Although it was not written until three years afterward, Niemetschek provided the best review:

> *Tito* was given at the time of the coronation, and then given several more times; but as fate willed it, a miserable castrato and a *prima donna* who sang more with her hands than in her throat, and whom one had to consider a lunatic, sang the principal parts; since the subject is too simple to be able to interest the mass of people busy with coronation festivities, balls, and illuminations; and since it is—shame on our age—a serious opera, it pleased less in general than its really heavenly music deserved. There is a certain Grecian simplicity, a still sublimity, which strike a sensitive heart gently but none the less profoundly—which fit admirably to the character of *Titus,* the times and the entire subject, and also reflect honor on Mozart's delicate taste and his sense of characterization. The vocal parts, let it be said, are throughout, but especially in the andantes, of a heavenly sweetness, full of emotion and expression; the choruses are full of pomp and dignity; in short, Gluck's dignity is united to Mozart's original art, his flowing sense of emotion and his wholly magnificent harmonies.

After Mozart's death, Constanze became *Tito*'s most enthusiastic exponent, arranging benefit concert performances to aid herself and her son. The first Viennese performance in 1794 was followed by similar events in Graz, Hamburg, Dresden, Budapest, and Kassel. Staged versions followed throughout Europe in the early decades of the nineteenth century, but romantic music critics and other commentators effectively buried the work as they re-created Mozart in their own distorting mirrors. Wagner further consigned the work to obscurity, using it as evidence of Mozart's "carefree lack of discrimination" when it came to aesthetic considerations. Later generations of scholars and critics dismissed the opera as a speedy hack job, done in haste and with little thought by a mortally ill composer whose inspiration had temporarily deserted him.

The situation began to change in the late 1960s with the revival of interest in productions of opera seria. Critical editions of *Idomeneo* and *Tito* brought out in the early 1970s prompted reevaluation and further study. The late Jean-Pierre Ponnelle was particularly influential, staging a series of productions that began in Cologne in 1969 which took the opera out of its ancient Roman setting and placed it in the eighteenth century. Renewed interest in Mozart, who is now the most popular classical composer, has further stimulated the opera community—producers, performers, and audiences—to award it a respected place in the repertory. As the composer's bicentennial approached, Mozart's masterly musical hybrid finally came into its own.

MOZART'S *Così fan tutte*

by Maxine R. Kanter

In January, 1790, Wolfgang Amadeus Mozart entered the following in his personal catalogue: "Così fan tutte: o sia la scuola degli amanti. Opera Buffa in 2 Atti" (So do they all, or the School for Lovers. Comic opera in two acts). Exactly who are *they,* and what is it *that they all do?* The answers to these tantalizing questions not only provide the story line for this most delectable of all Mozart's operas but also offer us a choice insight into the regard that eighteenth-century upper-class European society had for the female of our species. *They* were women—*all* women—and they were vain and irresponsible, fickle and flirtatious, and incapable of depth of feeling or constancy in matters of the heart. In short, they might have been adorable featherbrains, but men continued to succumb to their charms and, eventually, to excuse or overlook their shortcomings.

However, nineteenth- and early-twentieth-century moralistic points of view could not countenance such shallow and frivolous portrayals, and the plot of *Così fan tutte* was considered to be "trashy." Even such eminent Mozart admirers as Ludwig von Beethoven and Richard Wagner expressed their disapproval of the subject matter.

In any event, despite the sexist overtones generated by the opera and its many critics, it has survived. No work of Mozart's has experienced such opposition and led to so many attempts to "redeem" it as *Così,* and it has entered the standard opera repertory only since the 1950s.

Così fan tutte, composed only two years after *Don Giovanni* (1787), was the last of the great trio of operas written in partnership with Lorenzo da Ponte. Although it is obvious from Mozart's correspondence that opera seria and the newly emerging German opera occupied his principal interest at the time, the demand for buffa opera at the Viennese court theater obliged him to move in the direction of Italian comic opera, and he soon sought a librettist to provide him with appropriate texts. After looking at dozens of opera librettos, all of them unsuitable—merely rehashes of commedia dell'arte characters and situations—he engaged da Ponte, one of the staff court poets, who was already deeply involved with writing for a number of popular composers in Vienna but who, nevertheless, agreed to collaborate with him. Mozart undoubtedly had observed that da Ponte had been successful with opera librettos based on French plays about real characters rather than the stock figures found in commedia dell'arte and that he meticulously set his librettos to the musical style of each composer.

Da Ponte himself was a colorful yet brilliant eccentric whose own life story could provide the plot for a romantic novel, if not an opera libretto.

At the start of their association (in 1785), however, da Ponte was taking a chance on success; for all the friendliness and good will of the emperor, Mozart had powerful rivals in Vienna: Salieri, Paisiello, Sarti, and Martín y Soler. All enjoyed fine reputations, while Mozart, the local talent, was, for all his experience in the field of opera, acknowledged to have produced only one opera, *Die Entführung aus dem Serail,* and that, moreover, was in German. Realizing that he was operating with a number of odds against him and desperately eager to make a "big splash" to really show what he could do in this arena, Mozart wisely put aside an earlier idea for a comic opera and chose *Le Mariage de Figaro,* the sequel to Beaumarchais's play *Le Barbier de Séville.*

Work was begun on *Figaro* sometime in the latter part of 1785 with da Ponte being regularly prodded by the composer. In da Ponte's *Memoirs,* he reports that "as fast as I wrote the words, Mozart set them to music."

Figaro was premiered on May 1, 1786, and had a moderate success. A later production of the opera by an Italian opera company in Prague was very well received and became immensely popular, drawing large and appreciative audiences. The city went "*Figaro*-mad," and one heard its music played, whistled, or sung everywhere.

Much encouraged by his success, Mozart agreed to write a new opera for the Prague company; this was to be *Don Giovanni,* and da Ponte was expected to be the librettist again, repeating the triumph of his collaboration with Mozart on *Figaro.*

If little is known about the genesis of *Don Giovanni,* even less is known about that of *Così fan tutte.* What has been well remembered and oft repeated is the disappointment and frustration that Mozart was forced to endure at this period of his life. It is, alas, all too true that the late 1780s were lean years for the composer. The year following the 1787 premiere of *Don Giovanni* was a dismal one for him: there were no commissions; he had few pupils, a sickly wife, and as always for him, not enough money to cover his mounting expenses. During the summer of 1788 he wrote three symphonies, Nos. 39, 40, and 41, his last and greatest in this genre, but the series of concerts at which they were to be performed did not materialize and had to be canceled. The small post at court brought in only a fraction of what he needed and what he deserved, yet he was determined to succeed in Vienna, and he repeatedly turned down offers of employment elsewhere. (One is tempted to speculate what benefits such a relocation might have had on Mozart's health, wealth, and happiness.)

In July, 1789, Emperor Joseph II ordered a revival of *Figaro,* a welcome change of heart, as he had attempted to suspend all Italian opera in Vienna earlier that year. (Happily da Ponte devised a subscription procedure which convinced the emperor not to disband his opera troupe.) The success of this new *Figaro* production led to the commission of another comic opera by Mozart and da Ponte. Rumor in Vienna had it that the emperor himself had proposed the subject, a comedy involving two young couples in which the men are persuaded to test the fidelities of their fiancées by disguising themselves, switching their intended wives, and then moving full-speed ahead for a complete and victorious seduction. Perhaps Joseph had heard the story related as having been an actual happening, inasmuch as it was a current topic of gossip in Vienna.

Da Ponte also must have heard such a tale whispered about, although he claimed he had created the plot "out of his own head" (by the time he published his *Memoirs* in 1826, he took credit for everything possible). How truly remarkable it is, then, that the basic plot and cast of characters could so easily fit an idea Mozart had for an opera buffa many years before. In the same letter to his father (May 7, 1783) in which he passionately declares his eagerness to "show what I can do in an Italian opera," he expresses his thoughts about the matter:

> The most essential thing is that, on the whole, the story should be really *comic;* and, if possible, he [the librettist] ought to introduce *two equally good female parts,* one of these *seria,* and the other *mezzo carattere,* but both parts equal *in importance and excellence.* The third female *character,* however, may be entirely buffa, and so may all the male ones, if necessary.

The above plan could very well serve as the blueprint for *Così fan tutte.* Did Mozart, musing about his scheme for a sensational opera buffa for over six and a half years, find or just happen upon the right story match for his music, or did the scenario develop as a vehicle for a trim and sophisticated comic opera to fit characters already real to the composer?

Così has the pair of female singers; Fiordiligi, high-minded and intense, whose music could be straight out of opera seria (just as the Queen of the Night's two dramatic coloratura arias are in *Die Zauberflöte*), and her sister, Dorabella, temperamental, weaker of will, and more easily enticed.

The two sisters are described as coming from Ferrara, though living now in Naples (all of the action of the opera takes place in Naples), but since ladies from Ferrara were said to have questionable reputations, this may have been a sly bit of mischief on da Ponte's part as Adriana Ferrarese del Bene (from Ferrara) was da Ponte's current mistress.

Signora Adriana, for whom the part of Fiordiligi was written, possessed an extensive vocal range in which she took great pride. The composer, who did not like the lady, nevertheless provided her with abundant opportunity to demonstrate this specialty. Her first act aria, "Come scoglio," is the grand vocal spectacle of the whole opera and was so designed by Mozart for his prima donna. It begins with a solemnity typically found in opera seria and proceeds to parody the older style with a display of treacherous intervals, monumental arpeggios, and giant vocal leaps.

Dorabella's great aria, "Smanie implacabili," introduces us to the other side of her lively personality. She is in a highly charged emotional state, reminiscent of, and possibly parodying, Donna Anna's famous aria "Or sai, chi l'onore," at the beginning of *Don Giovanni.* Overly dramatizing her situation, she exaggerates her grief in short, breathless phrases that resemble sobbing, alternating with moments of desperate rage at being separated from her sweetheart. (One is justified in thinking that the lady protests too much.)

Mozart has written her aria in the key of E-flat major, a "serious" key in his music and one that is known to be the key for Masonic music. This key and its symbolism take on additional and important meaning in Mozart's last opera, *Die Zauberflöte.*

The third female role is that of the saucy and wily chambermaid, Despina, based on one of the standard figures in both commedia dell'arte and opera buffa, and is kin to Susanna, Zerlina, and Blondchen from other, earlier Mozart operas. Despina provides much of the comedy in *Così* with her wit and determination, her peasantlike common sense, and her gift for mimicry and impersonation. She is the exact opposite of her naive young ladies and has no illusions about her "place" or her future. To her, people are either simpletons or charlatans, and she will side with one or the other as long as it is in her best interests to do so.

The three male roles nicely balance the plot: they are the two young soldiers, Ferrando (tenor) and Guglielmo (baritone), and an elderly bachelor, the philosopher Don Alfonso (bass-baritone), whose cynical attitudes about the faithfulness of women prompt the wager that generates the subsequent story action.

Inasmuch as the opera is about couples, there is a high proportion of ensemble music, an area in which Mozart is the consummate master, and he generously lavishes his genius for combining vocal textures and tone colors throughout the entire work. As for a brief résumé of the story of *Così,* it could be said that it is about a soprano who is in love with a baritone, and a mezzo-soprano who is in love with a tenor. (Originally written for soprano, Dorabella is now given to a mezzo-soprano.) There is, lastly, the "odd couple," Despina (soprano) and Don Alfonso (bass-baritone), who, together, engineer most of the comic situations.

After all the possible permutations and vocal combinations have been spun out in finest detail, the "swapping" takes place, and the romantic duets change to soprano-tenor and mezzo-baritone. Perhaps the composer preferred this musical arrangement (as do I), for at the conclusion of the opera there is no indication that the two pairs of lovers should examine their feelings or simply revert to their original partners. The audience is left to come to its own conclusions.

(In truth, there would have been no time for any soul-searching, because according to a custom of the time, all the story action was to take place in a twenty-four-hour period. This is not unlike the sitcoms of today's radio and television programs which are packaged in unchanging blocks of time and must reach their dénouement at the stroke of the studio clock.)

The concept of wife (or partner) swapping was not new. In fact, it was a standard *lazzo,* or situation farce, that was a mainstay of Italian opera. From ancient times the use of disguise to test the faithfulness of a wife or beloved occurs in literature. We can find it in the myth of Cephalus and Procris in Ovid's *Metamorphoses* and, many centuries later, in Shakespeare's *A Midsummer Night's Dream*. In all cases, the implied rubric is "love must always be a pleasure and never a burden."

We know practically nothing about the performance preparation or premiere of *Così fan tutte* compared with the other operas of Mozart. The unusually (for Mozart) ample period for its composition came about as he had so little work to do. Things had gone from bad to worse; indeed, his was a falling star. The only composition dating from this time is the Clarinet Quintet (K. 581) from which Mozart "borrowed" the finale, reworking and developing it into the tenor's Act II aria, "Ah, lo veggio quell' anima bella."

From early September, 1789, when Mozart began to sketch the scenario together with da Ponte, until the end of December, when he invited his staunch friend and generous supporter Baron Puchberg and Franz Joseph Haydn to his home to hear a run-through of the opera, Mozart had sufficient time to confer with his librettist, to shape and polish the text, and to develop the characters to his musical satisfaction. As a result of this double-edged gift of time—and his own growing maturity—there is no evidence of hurried craftsmanship or other constraints; it is, quite simply, a succession of glorious music: arias and vocal ensembles and, from the sparkling overture to the scintillating finale, sophisticated and witty orchestral accompaniment.

In spite of the limitations of the plot—after all, it is meant to be a comedy and only an evening's entertainment at that—Mozart's music breathes life into the characters on stage. His genius for characterizations in music, his knowledge of human emotions, and his ability to explore the psychological profile of each personality transform what is essentially an opera buffa into a profound human comedy.

Sometime in December, 1789, Mozart must have given the cast (who were, luckily, in Vienna at the time) their parts so they could be prepared for the rehearsal to take place on New Year's Eve. The singers, several of whom had been on Mozart's "ideal" cast list and had their parts written especially for them, were all operatic stars in the city. The orchestral parts were not finished until sometime in January, and the first rehearsal with the orchestra took place at the Burgtheater (later renamed the Imperial and Royal National Court Theatre) in Vienna on January 21, 1790, with Puchberg and Haydn again in attendance. The premiere of *Così* took place on January 26, the eve of Mozart's thirty-fourth birthday.

Although there are no descriptions of the rehearsals and only a few reviews of the first performance, Mozart confides in a letter that "Salieri was plotting against *Così fan tutte,* but his plots are being undermined," thus refuting the thesis that Mozart was an innocent and simple-minded wimp as portrayed in Peter Shaffer's fanciful play *Amadeus,* particularly in his relationship with Salieri.

After the premiere, the opera was performed only ten times between January and August, 1790. After that it disappeared from the Viennese stage and was not revived again until long after the composer's death. During his lifetime only the overture and some half-dozen numbers in the piece were printed as a piano score.

Considering that the opera came into being in 1789–90, it is curious that there is not the faintest whiff of the incendiary and ominous heaviness in the air which threatened to—and finally did—change the entire structure of European society. *Così* was written while the Bastille was being attacked, yet Mozart and da Ponte maintained the prerevolution theater customs and directed their entertainment to the aristocracy, the Austrian counterparts of the French ancien régime. It was as if nothing of importance had happened: they were depicting the upper classes easing their lives of idleness and boredom by playing elaborate parlor games and practical jokes.

(Mozart came close to acknowledging the reality of the French Revolution in his occasional use of a triadic motive very similar to that of the first few notes of the *Marseillaise*.)

Out of the ashes of the revolution a new woman emerged. This one, often modeled on the central figure in true events of rescue and salvation, was noble and self-sacrificing, loyal and brave. She would be epitomized by a Leonora, and she was a closer relative to the heroines of mediaeval literature than to the vain and frivolous image so dear to the hearts of the Viennese. It was totally inconceivable that this paragon of virtue would want to—or be allowed to— view her sacred promises so lightly, and as for trading lovers, even the suggestion of such behavior was shameless. Women in the Romantic Era were placed on a pedestal and worshipped for their goodness, whereas men were still exempt from the rules. Undeniably, there was a double standard in effect long before the term was invented.

For a while *Così* survived, carried along by the sheer beauty of its music and for its dazzling, effervescent entertainment value. Even so, throughout the nineteenth century, when it was presented, it was always in its altered, whitewashed—and consequently mutilated—form. (One of the thorniest problems had to do with Don Alfonso's lines at the end of the opera, where he justifies the behavior of the two sisters with the words "Così fan tutte" [They all do it]. He then orders the two disillusioned young men to repeat the words after him, instructing them to no longer expect women to be less fallible than men.)

It was not until 1809 that a performance of the opera was given in France, albeit with apologies for the tastelessness of its story. The adapter of the libretto confesses that he does not know if there is any truth contained in the story; he explains:

> I do know that a few malicious and less-intelligent women cause other intelligent women extreme injustice. They dare to give them a bad reputation as though they were little butterflies which anyone can catch.

London saw its first *Così fan tutte* in May, 1811, when it was presented in Italian at the Haymarket Theatre, and again in July, 1828, in an English version entitled *Tit for Tat, or the Tables Turned.* It was only when we were well into the twentieth century that *Così* appeared again in its original form.

There is no mention of the opera's having been produced in the United States before the Metropolitan Opera presented it on March 22, 1922. By that time, it was not considered necessary to make either adaptations or apologies for the work. Clearly, the twentieth-century woman was not the flighty, doll-like figure of the eighteenth century, nor was she the nearly deified, but just as artificial, creature of the nineteenth. This modern woman was—and is— concerned with sexual equality, freedom of expression, and liberation from stereotyping. Granting her the vote was only the beginning!

This last great effort of Mozart's in the field of Italian comic opera has finally and firmly come into its own. As opera historian William Mann has written:

> He [Mozart] most nearly approached the discovery of music's Grail in the unsacred but totally human and all-perceiving *Così fan tutte,* in which he penetrates human nature while mocking it. *Così* is gloriously comic, yet unfathomably profound, the whole story of the attraction between women and men, a subject which deserved and was granted the most captivating music ever composed.

MOZART'S *Don Giovanni*
by Thomas Willis

George Bernard Shaw regarded *Don Giovanni* as the greatest opera ever composed, "eminent in virtue of its uncommon share of wisdom, beauty, and humor." The Danish philosopher Søren Kierkegaard found the moral issues it raised sufficiently noteworthy to make the opera's performance the subject of one of his most important treatises. E.T.A. Hoffmann called it the quintessential romantic opera, "reflecting the eternal presence of the demonic in human life." Nineteenth-century Germans viewed it through Faust-colored glasses. Freudian psychologists attributed the Don's 2,065 female conquests to his faulty mother love. Taking a still-different psychological tack, the German psychoanalyst Otto Rank proclaimed the mighty Giovanni to represent "an ancient fertility god or demigod, whom the Christian ideal of continence and sense of guilt have changed into a mere gross sensualist."

Surely no opera has occasioned so much discussion as Wolfgang Amadeus Mozart's towering masterwork. The ambiguities of its construction and of Lorenzo da Ponte's brilliant but hastily assembled libretto provoke weighty arguments among scholars and tempt stage directors to extreme solutions. For example: the time frame. There is some indication that all of the action was conceived as taking place within twenty-four hours—the final day in the life of an anti-hero. But if so, how did that equestrian statue of the Commendatore appear within hours of his murder? Probably the worthy gentleman had it constructed in advance, as was the custom in seventeenth-century Spain and Italy, leaving only the date of demise to be chiseled in when fate determined.

And what about dear Donna Anna, the first of the Don's conquests to appear on stage and the one whose outcries initiate the series of actions that form the opera's plot? Did Don Giovanni manage to seduce her before she discovered her mistake and chased him away? To put it bluntly, did she make a mistake at all, or was she enraged when he loved her and left her? The first of the Dons to make his appearance in modern form, Don Juan Tenorio in Gabriel Tellez's seventeenth-century Spanish play, admitted he had failed to seduce Donna Anna. Most of the other playwrights and librettists who treated the popular subject in the years preceding da Ponte and Mozart's 1787 version went along with that conclusion. After all, it made for such dramatic consistency; despite his reputation and international catalogue of amatory successes, Don Giovanni appears to be entirely unsuccessful in his advances during the rest of the opera—at least on stage. True, we never learn *exactly* what happens in the private room to which he leads Zerlina during the Act I finale, when three orchestras are distracting our attention. Maybe the wily country girl also screamed after the fact. And we are never told what takes place with Donna Elvira's maidservant, to whom Don Giovanni sings the ravishingly beautiful serenade "Deh, vieni alla finestra," or to Leporello's girl friend, who is a dim but clearly identified presence, or to the other town and country lasses whom he approaches casually during the opera's crowd scenes.

Should you tire of these and other ambiguities and ambivalences in the libretto construction, you can move onward to Mozart's score. *Don Giovanni* was composed for Prague, where *The Marriage of Figaro* had had such outstanding success the previous year. It was to be played and sung by substantially the same personnel who were involved in that opera. Looking at the manuscript for that performance, you can see the correspondence in vocal and personal requirements for the singers—Count Almaviva in *Figaro* with Don Giovanni, Countess Almaviva with Donna Elvira, Susanna with Zerlina, and so on. But things changed when *Don Giovanni* finally arrived in Vienna in May, 1788. Both singers and public in the musical metropolis were making different demands. Arias were added and subtracted, a comic scene was inserted, the epilogue was deleted. Among the additions were Don Ottavio's "Dalla sua pace," composed to replace the more difficult "Il mio tesoro," which the Vienna tenor could not manage. Today, few would countenance the omission of either. Nor would we, or today's sopranos, look kindly upon the cutting of Elvira's magnificent "Mi tradì," also a Viennese addition. Once you decide to keep the best of the Mozartean additions, where do you insert them without destroying the dramatic continuity? No solution is entirely successful;

hence the arguments in a time when fidelity to the composer's intentions is an important artistic issue.

Like most works of absolute genius, *Don Giovanni* is a mutant, a sport. Mozart could not help being attracted to the subject when da Ponte proposed it. Neither man was willing to accept the story of "The Libertine Punished, or the Stone Guest" as he found it, of course. Both realized that this was no mere opera buffa, full of patter songs, slapstick caperings, and frivolous musical fun. Nor did the story allow for the full opera seria treatment accorded to lofty, noble subjects enmeshed in tragic and heroic undertakings. This must be a *dramma giocoso*—a blend of serious and comic elements, an attempt to capture and take the measure of humanity in all theatrical and musical ways. Although the original title was *Il dissoluto punito, ossia il Don Giovanni* (The Libertine Punished, or Don Giovanni), the idea of retribution was only part of the subject matter. Da Ponte was familiar with both audiences and the ever-present scissors of the censors of the day. Very, very carefully he adapted and fashioned words that would suggest, rather than proclaim. In this, he not only was playing safe; he was also relying on his composer and collaborator for the fleshing-out which only music can supply.

And what a perfect subject for music to exert its power upon! A protagonist who is emphatically not a hero of fiction or the cardboard conventions of the old-fashioned operatic stage. One who savors all the pleasures of living, who exerts his magnetic attraction upon all women, who has the curiosity of an encyclopedist of love, and who, confronted with the choice of repentance or instant damnation, chooses to neither repent nor retract. Mozart's Don Giovanni was born from the same imaginative womb as Count Almaviva—he is an aristocrat accustomed to having his way with equals and subordinates alike. He is avaricious and without scruple in attaining his ends, but he also is brave, handsome, spirited, and courteous, a figure of appeal to both men and women. What man does not wish to attract all objects of affection to himself? What woman does not wish to be the object of true, uncomplicated adoration?

Remember, Don Giovanni is not a rapist or a traitor who moves merely to defy the social order. He is a seducer—one whose entire object in amatory adventure is to lead his would-be partners to willing acceptance of his suit. It is partly a game, of course; what courtship is not? It is also the display of a miracle fact of the human condition: the frank, unsentimental amorous attraction which can come into existence between two receptive partners, whatever the external circumstances of their existence. Such an attraction is irrational and difficult to put into words, for all the attempts of the poets and dramatists through the ages. But music, embedded as it is in both our psyches and our societies, can move in this mysterious realm without difficulty. Like Don Giovanni himself, it can charm, magnetize, and yes, seduce us in ways that defy coherent explanation. The genius of Mozart here, as in his other late operas, lies in his ability to create vibrant musical characters and place them in truly human contexts which we instantly recognize.

These characters in the opera, who or what are they? Each is a satellite to the Don. All the women in the cast are in love with him; all the men are in conflict with him. Even Leporello, whose musical character most closely resembles the stereotypes of classic comedy from Greek times to the present, acts as a sort of checkrein or conscience at times. Although he admires and is attracted by Don Giovanni and wishes he could equal him in ability, he is not without ethical spine. Like Figaro, who is much more than a barber, Leporello is more than a servant-clown.

The two Donnas are polarized, both by their words and by the music Mozart provides for them. Donna Anna, for whatever cause, is obsessed by vengeance, by her desire to even the score. "Now you know who sought to steal my honor," she sings in her great aria, "Or sai chi l'onore," and the word "vendetta" arches into the vocal upper altitudes time and time again. But she is not single-minded despite her obsession. A true Spanish temperament, she alternates from one mood to the other, shapes the truth to her own ends, and cannot always keep her stories straight. Donna Elvira is less complex. Although a singer who can do justice to the vocalism of the role is hardly likely to be in her teens, she is described as a *fanciulla,* a young girl. She resembles in many ways a character in another *Don Giovanni* offshoot, Tatiana in Pushkin's *Eugene Onegin.* Both are awkward, credulous, naive, stiff-necked, uncompromising, unworldly, and very vulnerable. In her continuing love for Don Giovanni and her ever-present willingness to forgive him, she is more than a little ridiculous. But both she and Donna Anna arouse our sympathy, for they are sad figures continually visible in daily life.

Like *Figaro*'s Susanna and *Così fan tutte*'s Despina, Zerlina is an ingénue only on the surface. R.B. Moberly, who has some stimulating and controversial ideas about all three operas, suggests she was blonde and probably a dairy-maid—doesn't the Don tell her that her fingers are as soft as junket? She also has more than a little of Despina's "gather ye rosebuds while ye may" philosophy. She knows exactly what the Don wants, and she is tempted. She also is aware that there is no future in this kind of liaison and decides on a safe, secure marriage to her "rough young plowboy," Masetto. Mozart suggests in his music that in matters of love, at least, she is marrying considerably beneath her station. Her cajoling "Batti, batti" is every bit as seductive as anything Don Giovanni sings. Masetto, on the other hand, emerges in the score and text as a self-pitying, rough-cut baby who has little to recommend him. Zerlina, Moberly suggests, "will be a valuable property; an energetic mother and house-wife, a wife and general molly-coddler. Perhaps he will be prudent enough not to damage the property except when drunk."

If Zerlina is in some ways a female counterpart to Don Giovanni, Don Ottavio is his direct opposite. Where Masetto instantly detests Don Giovanni and immediately engages him in a contest of wits, will power, and force, Don Ottavio is a puppet, a correct gentleman who is a stranger among men of strong character. He professes to love Donna Anna, and an arranged marriage has been contracted with her. In his original aria, "Il mio tesoro," Mozart fashions a brilliantly exaggerated parody of conventional tenor love. For all its supple bel canto and breath-requiring passage work, it is music undisturbed by sincerity or passion. He is above all else a dandy, a showoff. "Admire me," the aria says. "Admire my voice. Admire my technique. Admire my breath control." But no one who listens can admire his character or his actions. He is marvelously insufferable, humorless, thick-skinned, and vain.

Only one figure in the drama remains, the Commendatore. Originally the role was doubled by the singer who sang Masetto. Of all the characters, he has the least to do and sing. But his role as protector and supernatural visitor gives rise to fascinating speculation. As protector of his daughter Donna Anna's honor, he is commendable on the side of conventional behavior, of Right and Decency, of the established order. But when he seeks to protect her, he is killed by the Don. Only after the Commendatore has gone to his grave is he armed with sufficient power to accomplish his aim. Without supernatural intervention, the story suggests, the Don Juans of the world will prevail. It was this implication of the centuries-old story which gave rise to the Faustian interpretations, to the link with Satan myths and other identifications with nonhuman sources of evil.

Remember, though, that Don Giovanni is not punished for his amorous prowess but for his insulting of the dead, traditionally a grave (the pun is irresistible) impiety. Mere womanizing is not what the Don Juan legend is made of. As Anthony Burgess has noted in a trenchant introduction to one of the libretto translations, "Don Juan has his place in the mythology of the West because of the manner of his blasphemy and his subsequent end. He kills a high hidalgo, who happens to be the father of one of his amatory victims. A statue is erected in honor of the great man, and Don Juan sneers at it. The statue comes to life (a very ancient, indeed classical, fabular device) and there is a supper invitation. In the opera, it is Don Giovanni who invites the Commendatore; in the older versions it is the Commendatore who invites Don Juan. The latter version is the more terrible and the more characteristic, since Don Juan is foolhardy enough to go to a graveyard where adders and other inedibles are served, and, as a *bonne bouche,* is dragged down to the city of the dead which lies beneath the gravestones. Da Ponte and Mozart were not really in search of terror, except in a Pickwickian sense. To them the legend is material for a kind of black comedy which is a new, and original, variant of *opera buffa.*"

For the creator of *A Clockwork Orange* to term *Don Giovanni* a new breed of black comedy is not surprising. Whether you agree with him or not depends to a large extent on your understanding of the opera's closing moments. In Vienna, now as in Mozart's time, the opera is usually ended as the Don is dragged to hell in what can only be termed a tragic finale. As originally conceived for Prague, there is the epilogue. The five principals enter accompanied by "ministers of justice" to arrest Don Giovanni. Leporello, somewhat incoherently, describes what has happened. One by one, the characters describe what they intend to do, now that "heaven has avenged us all." Elvira will take the veil. Don Ottavio still thinks of marriage. Donna Anna bids him cool his well-mannered ardor for a year, and Masetto and Zerlina decide to go home and have dinner. The opera concludes with a suitably sanctimonious moral: "This is the end of the wrongdoer; his death is as ugly as his life."

One school of thought holds with Paul Henry Lang that "with the death of the Don the moral order of the world has been re-established; any further discussion of his demise, no matter how beautiful the music, can only weaken the drama." Burgess, along with most contemporaries, sees more irony at work: "The final ensemble proclaims the essentially *buffo* character of a work that some, incredibly, would like to take for a serious morality play. It is a wonder of pseudo-profundity, a civilized grotesquerie to match its words: 'let the scoundrel remain below with Proserpine and Pluto.' The rogue must dwell between Pluto and his queen forever. Not the Christian inferno after all, but the stock classical Hades: three in a bed, Don Giovanni in the middle, but Pluto probably awake all the time. It is a pleasant conceit and a fitting punishment."

Whichever you choose, the fact of Mozart's immortal music remains. Not merely the surface delights—the trombones borrowed from Gluck's *Alceste* to lend somber religiosity to the Commendatore's utterances, the multiple orchestras, the glitter of the paired woodwinds in the arias and ensembles, the overall chamber-music quality of the score—but the deep, abiding sense of purpose which informs each measure, the clarity with which each character emerges in melody and harmonic vocabulary from the rest of the tonal fabric, and the apparently inexhaustible inspiration which charms our ears as certainly as Don Giovanni beguiled his ladies. Not for once, as was the Don's custom, but again and again, with growing affection, concern, and abiding joy. For Don Giovanni, it was a question of conquest; for Mozart and music, it is a matter of love.

DONIZETTI'S *Don Pasquale*
by Frederick Walter

It's an odd thing, but many commentaries on operatic comedy analyze and appraise everything but the comic elements. Consider, for example, three recognized masterworks of the genre—Verdi's *Falstaff,* Mozart's *Nozze di Figaro,* and Wagner's *Meistersinger.* Analysis usually centers on some musical distinction: Verdi's scoring, Mozart's ensemble writing, Wagner's polyphony and leitmotif development. Additional space is then given over to thematic concerns: *Meistersinger,* we learn, presents the struggle between tradition and innovation in the arts; *Figaro* asserts the sublimity of forgiveness; *Falstaff* is colored by an autumnal sadness—the emotion, in B.H. Haggin's phrase, "of a man nearing the end of his life." Now unquestionably these observations are accurate, yet one issue scarcely figures in the discussion: why are these works, for all their serious underpinnings, actually *funny*?

Certainly it is puritanism to insist that comedy is not worthy unless it is textured with Deeper Significance. Gaetano Donizetti, for one, brought no solemnity to the composition of *Don Pasquale*. Historians and scholars are unclear as to details, but the story of its inception is a simple one. The premise for the libretto came from that of an earlier opera, *Ser Marc' Antonio,* a work ascribed by some sources to one Stefano Pavesi, or, by others, to a Salvatore Cammarano; the controversy seems unimportant. Donizetti collaborated on the book with his friend Giacomo Ruffini (Giovanni Ruffini, according to the Colombo piano score). He dashed off the music in little more than two weeks and saw the work staged on January 3, 1843, in Paris. His delight at its opening-night success was simple and uncomplicated: "I was called to the stage at the end of Acts II and III," he wrote to a friend, "and no piece . . . passed without some sort of applause." Apparently, that was enough for him.

But it has not been quite enough for others. Confronted with good-natured music and simple, stylized characters, some listeners have nevertheless searched the score for the subtleties of Mozart, Wagner, and Verdi, missing its different but very genuine values. Even sensitive observers have fallen into this trap. C.J. Luten, for example, seeks for taut motivations and rounded characterizations—and appears to find them. "Each character," Luten writes, "behaves in a believable, convincing manner. None loses his basic humanity." Donald Grout's classic textbook, on the other hand, senses profundities beneath the comedy: "It is also touched with deeper feeling and thus lifted above the level of mere amusement."

These are excellent thoughts, yet the approach seems wrong. Is mere amusement so despicable? And after all, what kind of drama is *Don Pasquale*? It is farce, pure and simple. Don't be misled by the period mannerisms, the presentational style, the asides and other ancient theatrical conventions. This is unashamed situation comedy; its conspiracy-plot is no more pretentious than *Barefoot in the Park.* Granted, there is a trumpery moral at the end: "Old men who marry are begging for trouble." But this is hardly worth a plaque over the mantlepiece.

Most crucially, the characters are well-tried theatrical types. Pasquale, for instance, is the jealous, miserly, self-deluding old-man-with-a-young-wife. Long before Donizetti, his kind was familiar from the comedies of Molière and Goldoni. Ernesto is simply the conventional juvenile lead. Malatesta has little character at all: he is a functionary of the plot, a mechanism for advancing and developing the conspiracy. Even Norina, the most varied and interesting personality, adheres to the stereotype of the tough little minx.

Nor does Donizetti's music give additional dimension to the creatures of the libretto. Ernesto's Act II cantilena, "Cercherò lontana terra," is a completely serious lament, free of ironic overtones. Were Mozart the composer, a few incredulous snorts from the woodwinds would put this self-pity in larger perspective.

Donizetti's purpose, then, was the simple yet wholly estimable one of charming and amusing an audience. It is therefore appropriate to assess this opera solely on the grounds of its effectiveness as comic entertainment. Focusing on Donizetti's own achievement and ignoring the later contributions of specific stage-production schemes, one asks: How funny is *Don Pasquale*?

At the outset, the libretto is a good, sound specimen of its sort. And happily, it remains thoroughly comprehensible to a modern audience: there are no topical issues, no outdated customs, no need for footnotes. As for the pattern of the plot, it simply records the good-humored conspiracy of Norina and Ernesto, assisted by Malatesta, to trick old Pasquale into condoning and financing their marriage. Every event relates rigorously to this main design. There are no subplots, no irrelevancies. The action is as straight and clear as a line of tracks.

A number of fine comic possibilities evolve naturally from this conspiracy. There is an impersonation, a fraudulent wedding ceremony, a drastic character change for the heroine, a planted love note to arouse the victim's jealousy, and (always good theater) a battle of the sexes. Within these larger events there are passing niceties, such as Norina's simpery play-acting or Pasquale's virility problems. All in all, a libretto of considerable comic promise.

How does Donizetti's music address these possibilities? In the first place his musical vocabulary is ideal. Conventions that seem arbitrary and misapplied in his tragic operas are here most apt. If not funny in themselves, his chirping staccatto accompaniments, silky melodies, and air of wholesome extroversion are well adapted to the comic mood.

But funny in themselves are certain details of conception and scoring. One pet device is mock tragedy: Malatesta mentions the forthcoming arrival of Pasquale's bride (Act I, scene 1: "Fra poco qui verrà"), and a grim chord tolls in the orchestra while Pasquale wonders if he still has it in him. Note, too, the ominous string tremolos as, in Act II, Pasquale first woos that bride (compare Siegmund winning the sword in Wagner's *Walküre*). Or consider the woeful cadences and coloration of Pasquale's "È finita" (Act III, scene 1) while the old man ponders suicide as the alternative to his wife's overspending. In each of these instances Donizetti has clothed a trifling situation in a comically disproportionate scale of emotions.

Too, there are entire sections of the score where even the vocal and instrumental sonority makes for effective comedy. Donizetti has frequent resort to patter-writing—sequences of scurrying polysyllables whose very sound (as distinct from meaning) is humorous. An instance is the "gabbling" quartet in Act II, where Malatesta hastily brings Ernesto up to date on the conspiracy. A variation, whose comedy depends on a grotesque marriage of word and note, is the subsequent "Et cetera" sequence, where Donizetti sets a legal document to music.

But for a stretch of music whose whole structure is comic, the finale of Act II is unparalleled to that point. With "Di servitù novella," Norina commences her program of abuse against Pasquale. Here the orchestra launches a mischievous little rotary-motion figure in the strings, often repeated, instantly hummable, amusing in itself. The busy little tune accelerates with the action till Pasquale can take no more. The old man then erupts ("Son tradito") in a frenzy of gibbering Italian consonants that would make the finale of the act humorous even to one who did not understand Italian.

Act III, scene 1, repeats the patter-writing to good effect in the vengeance duet of Pasquale and Malatesta, capped by "ha ha's" of fiendish glee, funny by virtue of their perfect timing. But the most succulent comic invention of all is Ernesto's serenade in Act III, scene 2. It is the culmination of the conspiracy: Ernesto and Norina have staged a fake assignation in the garden for Pasquale to witness from the shrubbery. Donizetti's conception is gorgeous hokum: a parody serenade, complete with guitar, tamborines, and—crowning improbability—a chorus in the bushes. For similar reasons, certain Hollywood musicals have been funny without intending to be. Donizetti, however, knew perfectly what he was doing.

Don Pasquale is, then, the stuff of successful comedy. Within its farce framework it boasts a well-knit plot whose potential is well realized by Donizetti's musical sense of humor. But has the score other virtues besides comic ones? Of course. Like any theatrical or musical component, humor can wear itself out through overemphasis, and an audience must rest on occasion. Yet *Don Pasquale* demonstrates that there need not always be a pill beneath the sugar-coating. There are those who insist that an artistic experience be Good for You, and who accordingly plumb that experience for spiritual and sociological values. They forget one thing: laughter, too, is good for you.

MASSENET'S *Don Quixote*
by Jonathan Abarbanel

Don Miguel de Cervantes Saavedra, author of *Don Quixote de La Mancha,* and Jules-Émile Frédéric Massenet, composer of *Don Quichotte,* were both born—almost three centuries apart—into family conditions of genteel poverty. And there virtually all similarity ends, except for their common ability as men of creative authority.

For Massenet, success came early and almost easily. He spent the greater part of his seventy earthly years in extreme material comfort, publicly honored and privately content. For poor Cervantes, life was a desperate struggle, bringing little honor or recognition until very late. It is not surprising that the lives of both artists are reflected in their work, as if in the blade of a double-edged sword: sometimes their work transcended their lives, but sometimes their lives limited their work.

Cervantes's life is the very stuff of opera. He was born near Madrid in 1547, living in an age during which the monumental façade of Spanish economic and military power—never more than a façade, really—began to crack. Cervantes was just over forty in 1588, the year the "Invincible Armada" suffered defeat at the hands of English nautical sagacity and stormy North Sea weather. It was, nonetheless, a golden age for Spanish arts, the flowering of the Renaissance in Iberia. Cervantes's contemporaries included the painters El Greco, Velasquez, Ribera, Murillo, and writers such as St. John of the Cross, Calderón, and Lope de Vega.

Cervantes was born into poverty, the son of a struggling apothecary surgeon. With few opportunities open to him, he opted for a career in the army. He fought in Naples and Tunisia. He lost the use of his left hand through injuries suffered in the Battle of Lepanto against the Turks. On the way home, his galley was attacked by Barbary pirates, and Cervantes was sold into slavery in Algiers. He bungled numerous escape attempts before being ransomed.

At home once more, he spent more than twenty years as a completely toothless literary lion. He achieved no critical acclaim whatsoever and was imprisoned for debt. At age fifty, this threadbare man—bruised and battered by a lifetime of failure and prepared at last to acknowledge his own mediocrity—sat down to write an amusing short story which would burlesque the exalted, impossible chivalric codes then so popular in literature.

Something happened. Cervantes's burlesque transcended itself. The book which emerged, *Don Quixote de La Mancha,* became one of the greatest masterpieces of Spanish literature. Even today it is the book which has been reprinted more often than any other except the Bible. Who can say how much of Cervantes's tale of the Knight of the Woeful Countenance is satire and how much is autobiography? For Cervantes, a man sustained for half a century on dreams and ideals, created a hero half-mad with ideals. The illusions about romantic codes of behavior which fill the head of Don Quixote surely are the illusions with which the young Don Miguel de Cervantes marched off to war and which were knocked out of him at Lepanto and in Algiers.

And yet, there stands gaunt old Don Quixote, so hopeful and so spotlessly pure that all society seems corrupt and polluted by comparison. Transcendence occurs: the burlesque about an impossibly honorable old knight errant suddenly becomes a satire about the whole of society, against which he stands alone. We are not sure whether Cervantes is ridiculing idealism or praising it; whether he is mocking his dreaming hero or us.

In counterpoint to Don Quixote, Cervantes created his eminently pragmatic and materialistic squire, Sancho Panza. Some say that Quixote and Panza represent the two poles of Spanish temperament. Other critics say that in his classic odd couple Cervantes was painting a picture of the balance of forces necessary for a healthy mind: in short, an abstract of every human soul.

In any case, Cervantes created a genuinely universal character in Don Quixote. Whether we read Cervantes's intentions correctly or not—is he *really* an idealist or is he *really* world weary—his work continues to invigorate readers and excite the imagination of artists. Perhaps no other work has inspired so many treatments by other artists. Daumier and Picasso—and hundreds of lesser lights—have painted or etched the knight and his squire. Musically and theatrically, Cervantes's tale has been turned into suites, ballets, symphonic variations, and musicals by Telemann, Oscar Espla, Richard Strauss, Roberto Gerhavel, and the team of Dale Wasserman, Mitch Leigh, and Joe Darion, who are responsible for the most popular manifestation of all, *Man of La Mancha*.

In 1904, a French playwright named Jacques Le Lorrain took a crack at the great work, creating a verse drama which took Paris by storm. Le Lorrain, a poverty-stricken combination poet-shoemaker (shades of Hans Sachs!) strongly identified with the character of Don Quixote. He took virtually all of Quixote's foolhardiness and eccentricity and exaggerated them, and he threw out almost all of Cervantes's plot and sense of burlesque. What he kept was the Don, Sancho Panza, the episode with the windmills, and a heroine named Dulcinea, though her station in the world was elevated. Everything else, characters and plot, he made up. It was the Le Lorrain play, entitled *Don Quichotte,* which became the basis of the Massenet opera. But poor Le Lorrain was more hapless even than Cervantes. Desperately ill when the play opened, he dragged himself to Paris against doctor's orders to see it, lapsing into a three-day coma on arrival. He regained consciousness long enough to view his play, and then he died.

Also viewing a performance of the play was Raoul Gunsbourg, boulevardier and the inventive, irrepressible producer of the Opéra, Monte Carlo. Gunsbourg had befriended Massenet two years before, producing the premiere of his *Le Jongleur de Notre-Dame* at Monte Carlo. It became one of Massenet's greatest successes, with over 350 performances "under its belt" by the outbreak of World War II. After *Le Jongleur,* Monte Carlo became a yearly winter stop of Monsieur and Madame Massenet. In the last ten years of his life, Massenet saw five of his operas staged in Monaco. One of these was *Don Quichotte,* suggested by Gunsbourg to Massenet and his frequent librettist, Henri Cain. It was Massenet's twenty-first produced opera (out of twenty-two written), and was a triumph in his sixty-eighth year.

The road to the glitter of Monte Carlo—where he was decorated by His Serene Highness Prince Albert I—was not as long as it might seem for the poor boy that Jules Massenet once had been. He was born into a poor but proper family on August 12, 1842. His grandfather had been a professor, and his father had been a student at the polytechnic school. His father served as an officer under Napoleon but left the army when the Bourbon monarchy was restored. Falling back on his education, he became a master founder, and through the craft of metallurgy he eked out an extremely modest living for his eight children by two wives (four by each). Young Jules-Émile Frédéric was a son of the second marriage. Curiously, none of the first four children had any musical abilities, while all of the second four did.

The family moved to Paris in 1847, where Madame Massenet gave piano lessons to supplement the family income. It was from his mother that Jules took his first lessons, beginning specifically on February 24, 1848, as he later recorded in an autobiographical article. At the age of eleven, he entered the Paris Conservatory, where he remained for most of the next ten years, studying piano with Adolphe Laurent, harmony with Napoléon-Henri Reber, and composition with Ambroise Thomas. A star pupil, Massenet took many prizes, culminating with the 1863 Prix de Rome. Thomas himself had won it, also Halévy, Gounod, Berlioz, and Bizet. The government scholarship for three years of study in Rome and northern Europe gave Massenet the opportunity to travel, broaden himself, and mix with the large, lively artistic community living at the Villa Medici in Rome on French government stipends. Ever after, Massenet treasured Italy.

In Rome, Massenet met Liszt, who asked Massenet to give piano lessons to a young Frenchwoman of quality, Constance de Sainte-Marie. Massenet gave her lessons in piano, and they gave each other lessons in love. After overcoming the customary family concerns as to his choice of livelihood (or lack of same), Jules and Constance were married in Paris on October 8, 1866. Soon, he was able to support her.

His successes at the conservatory and his Prix de Rome had left him quite well connected in the Parisian musical establishment. This alone, however, was not enough to ensure a career. Bizet had the same advantages but died without gaining an unalloyed success. Temperament and musical politics played a part: did you despise Wagner, or love Gounod? Massenet, besides being a prodigiously hard worker all his life, also was extremely amiable. He avoided most artistic quarrels, was generously supportive of fellow composers, and managed to be called both "la fille de Gounod" and a champion of Wagner. Is it any wonder that such a clever diplomat and genuinely talented composer saw his first opera, a trifle called *La Grand'tante,* a success at L'Opéra-Comique in 1867? Massenet was just twenty-five.

That success unleashed a prodigal flow of music which extended even beyond Massenet's death in 1912. Fully four major works were given posthumous premieres in the decade after he died. Rarely did two years go by without a major new piece from the pen of Massenet: twenty-five operas, three ballets, four oratorios, incidental music to over a dozen plays, two dozen orchestral works, eight major song cycles (still beautiful and among his most important works), plus choral and religious works. He became wealthy and was honored above all his contemporaries in the world of the arts, even above Saint-Saëns. He came not only to dominate but also to personify French opera in the decades just before and after the century mark. And his competition was first rate: Debussy, Dukas, Ravel, Chabrier, d'Indy.

Massenet's genuine musical influence—as opposed to his mere public acceptance—was very great also. Along with most of his operas, the modern public forgets the caliber of respect and influence he achieved. In 1878 he was appointed professor of composition at the Paris Conservatory. His students included Gustave Charpentier and a host of other later well-known composers. His students won more Prix de Rome than the students of any other teacher, and he was terribly proud of this fact. By all accounts, he was an open and generous teacher, preferring to encourage the individual strengths of each student rather than imposing any doctrinaire ideas of his own. Such an attitude was quite unusual—downright modern, in fact—in the stodgy conservatory world.

Massenet helped to popularize the musical ideas of Wagner, subtly and gracefully introducing leitmotif, heavier use of brass, dramatico-literary techniques into his own works, but never so radically as to offend his audiences. He even went to Bayreuth. His influence on composers as far afield as Tchaikovsky and Puccini was very real and very direct.

Compare Massenet, then, at age fifty to hapless old Don Miguel de Cervantes in his tattered cloak. Massenet premiered *Werther* that year, as well as a ballet and a toccata. He ruled the musical roost of France. During the "cinq à sept" each night, he'd receive one and all in a room at his publisher's, with a kind word to each: singers who wished to meet him, anxious composers seeking advice, journalists looking for a word on the next "big one." Just months before his fiftieth birthday, he was inducted into the Union Vélocipédique de France, riding his bicycle around the table at his initiation banquet!

That's not simply an obscure fact; it's a character note. Bicycles in the 1890s were all the rage of the upper middle class. In America, for example, Lillian Russell and Diamond Jim Brady could be found pedaling. It is characteristic of Massenet that he should be swept up in the bicycle boom, for his great and long success was due entirely to the fact that he perfectly captured the middle-class taste in music and story. While he may have admired Wagner, he never risked sacrificing his own popularity by too much innovation. An evaluation in *Grove's Dictionary of Music and Musicians* states: "Like Puccini and Richard Strauss, Massenet enjoyed a popularity and a corresponding financial success that reveal how faithfully his music reflected the ideas, prejudices, anxieties and preoccupations of his contemporaries." Massenet's muse was fertile, rather than original or self-critical.

None of this should be interpreted as pejorative. It is no mean feat to remain at the very top of one's profession for twenty-five years. Most of Massenet's operas were effective in their day, and all exhibited a mastery of musical pastiche, as well as a gift for nearly divine, languid, suave, luxurious melody which delights us today. A critic of his own era referred to his gift as the "phrase massenétique with its feline and sensual inflections."

If the public today knows Massenet principally for only two operas, *Manon* and *Werther,* surely that is gift enough. But at least two other operas cling to the margins of the standard repertory. Both were written to showcase stellar voices in the title roles. One is *Thaïs,* written for American soprano Sibyl Sanderson. The other is *Don Quichotte,* the only starring role that Massenet ever wrote for a bass. Both operas are revived from time to time to fit the talents of a great singer. In our own time, we may treasure the famous interpretation of Don Quichotte by Nicolai Ghiaurov.

The opera originally was written for the immortal Fyodor Chaliapin, who wept and embraced Massenet when the composer played the score for him. Less than a year before, Massenet had suffered one of his rare, crushing failures with the opera *Bacchus,* which had premiered and been instantly entombed in Paris. *Don Quichotte,* then, was a bounce-back work; something to prove that the sly old opera master could still produce the real goods. He wrote the score under trying circumstances, wracked with the pain of severe rheumatism and confined to his bed for weeks. Nonetheless he completed it on time, composing without the aid of a piano as usual, and having the entire score printed before rehearsals ever began.

Don Quichotte opened at Monte Carlo on February 24, 1910. It was a triumph for Massenet, for Chaliapin, for Raoul Gunsbourg. Clever producer that he was, Gunsbourg made use at this very early date of film sequences to cover several scene changes of Massenet's "comédie-lyrique en cinque actes." Critics praised the refinement and dramatically distilled simplicity of Massenet's orchestrations and melody lines. The broad shoulders of Miguel Cervantes's *Don Quixote* had "done it again" for another great artist in another era. From the poverty and disappointment of Cervantes's life came gold for many. Eventually, even aural gold for all of us.

VERDI's *I due Foscari*
by John Clarke Adams

I due Foscari marks the first significant advance in Giuseppe Verdi's development into becoming Italian opera's greatest dramatist since Claudio Monteverdi. In this work, Verdi took a wide step toward personal, intimate, believable characterization.

By the time he began to compose operas, libretto writing, which a century before had attracted such illustrious poets as Pietro Metastasio, had become hack work turned out by uninspired and plagiarizing rhymesters concerned almost solely with the problems of ending acts with rousing finales and giving each principal singer the proper number of opportunities to display his virtuosity. Thus the most famous librettists of the day, Eugène Scribe in Paris and Felice Romani in Milan, produced their work by formula, in accordance with established and rigid patterns. One could not expect powerful, tradition-ridden hacks such as these to keep pace with the innovating musicians of the Romantic Movement, who sought to discard the arid stylization of the opera seria of the preceding century and to individualize their principal characters. In desperation such different composers as Donizetti, Berlioz, and Wagner became their own librettists. Verdi continually tormented his librettists; knowing intuitively what he sought, he fretted, fulminated, cajoled until he got it.

The librettists of Verdi's first operas—Romani for *Un giorno di regno* and Temistocle Solera, either alone or in collaboration, for the others (*Oberto, Nabucco,* and *I Lombardi*)—were too prominent and too sure of themselves to learn new tricks. The libretto for Verdi's fifth opera, *Ernani,* was not much better. Again, as in *Nabucco* and *I Lombardi,* Verdi won the acclaim of the Italian public with the exuberance and passion of his music and with the dramatic intensity and verity of some of the scenes, but the characters he portrayed were stereotypes and puppets, with whom neither composer nor the public could feel more than sporadically involved.

Like all great creative artists, however, Verdi was never content to repeat himself. Each new opera was an attempt to take a step forward to create the future, rather than to re-create the past. Rarely has a composer taken so large a step as the one that separates *Ernani* from Verdi's next opera, *I due Foscari,* or one that opened such vast horizons.

For his sixth opera Verdi turned again to the librettist of *Ernani.* Francesco Maria Piave—an urban Jew of bohemian tastes, struggling to support a family on his facility for writing poetry only slightly above doggerel, on his intimate knowledge of the Venetian theatrical milieu, and on a highly developed and frequently exploited proclivity toward accommodation—was in many respects the antithesis of Verdi. Yet the men were ever friends, and at the end, Verdi's generosity was instrumental in keeping Piave from the fate of a pauper.

It was in collaboration with this unlikely companion that Verdi made his greatest initial strides in the direction of that form of opera which the composer was destined to perfect—drama in which music is the principal vehicle of communication. It is immaterial whether the ideas were all Verdi's or whether Piave contributed significantly in the development. Perhaps Piave's share in the glory is limited to his attitude toward Verdi, which combined unstinted respect and admiration for the artist with unswerving loyalty to the man.

Piave's second libretto for Verdi, *I due Foscari,* was based on a play by Byron. It remained in the tradition of the period in that the setting was a noble court and called for historical costuming and ample pageantry. It broke from the pattern of the five previous Verdi librettos in that for the first time it gave Verdi the opportunity to focus his attention on life-size human beings, their sorrows and suffering within the intimacy of their family relations. A peculiarity of this libretto is that the three characters represented—a father, a son, and a daughter-in-law—are uniformly good; yet two of them die, and one is left prostrate as the result of an external and only superficially explained political agitation that serves as *satana ex machina.* Musically, each of the principals has a "tag" theme that recurs in the orchestra during the course of the opera.

Francesco Foscari, Doge and father, torn between patriotic duty and paternal love, is Verdi's first great tragic character. The opera depends on him to a degree that no previous Italian opera had depended on a baritone, and its initial success was due in good part to the spectacular singing and stage presence of Achille de Bassini. The final scene, in which the Doge dies at the shock of losing his son and then being forced from the throne, is a broad and effective musical conception of moving power; shortly before, when he pleads for the return of his son, we cannot help thinking ahead to the eloquence of Rigoletto, bereft of his daughter by the "vile courtiers" of Mantua.

Jacopo Foscari (tenor), the Doge's ill-fated son, is a less fully developed character. Like Florestan in *Fidelio,* he is the victim of forces quite beyond his control. We see him only in moments of affliction, a defeated man. It is Verdi's ability to express Jacopo Foscari's love for his fatherland (though it rejects him) and for his family (though he must leave them behind) that makes him an object of compassion rather than just pity.

Lucrezia Contarini (dramatic soprano), Jacopo's wife, is one of the finest-drawn of Verdi's noble matrons, a woman whose high-minded courage and devotion to her husband are reminiscent of Beethoven's Leonore. When Lucrezia sings, often with taxing coloratura, her melodies show intensity and purpose—as when she begs the Venetian senate for her husband's acquittal from unjust charges of treason. At the end of Act II, Verdi and Piave introduce a scene in which Lucrezia brings her children to try to soften the hearts of her oppressors, and the resulting ensemble is one of the opera's high points.

There are other fine, fully developed episodes in the score, such as the Doge's duet with Lucrezia in the Act I finale, which marks an important advance over the earlier Abigaille-Nabucco duets and makes us think ahead to the great father-daughter scenes in *Rigoletto, Simon Boccanegra, Aïda,* and (essentially) in *La traviata.* At the time of composing *I due Foscari,* however, Verdi had not freed himself from the tradition of including dramatically unconvincing and musically often unrewarding cabalettas or strettos at the close of major scenes.

Perhaps the most striking feature of *I due Foscari,* however, is the failure to bring to life the evil Jacopo Loredano. By the time Verdi wrote *Otello* he had become a master of portraying wickedness, but the villain of *I due Foscari* is scarcely more than a comprimario. His few solo utterances, occurring mostly when he makes a strong demand (Jacopo Foscari's exile, the Doge's abdication), are cast in stentorian style, with repeated notes and octave jumps. This manner, adapted from the Statue in *Don Giovanni,* was developed to far greater effect in the character of Monterone in *Rigoletto.* There is a glimmer of macabre gaiety in Loredano's invitation to a barcarolle toward the start of Act III, but nowhere even the germ of an aria or monologue in which he can explain to us, or even state, his vengeful motivation. His only musical function is to turn the Act II trio into a quartet by adding his voice; elsewhere he merely doubles the bass line of the chorus.

Whether by design or accident it is difficult to say, but in *I due Foscari,* Verdi concentrated exclusively on a family tragedy. Had he gone out of the family circle to include Loredano among the three-dimensional characters, he would have written a quite different opera, one that would perhaps have been more significant in his own development. For Verdi to learn to write a human drama, however, it may have been important to start with an intimate drama. In later and greater operas, Verdi portrayed far-more-complex characters, but in the black-and-white setting of *I due Foscari* he was able for the first time to concentrate on character delineation and on the expression of the loves and anxieties of a family inexorably oppressed by the world outside.

RICHARD STRAUSS'S *Elektra*
by Frederick Walter

Richard Strauss's *Elektra* is about a woman who unsexes herself.

"I am breeding a vulture in my womb," the heroine says. Only hatred, only "curses and despair," only the energy for revenge can issue from her body. Elektra is a hag: she cannot love; she cannot procreate. Her organs and functions are consecrated to her father's memory, and they have rotted away. She is not a woman. She is barely a person.

The usual gruesome Greek myth? Well, not exactly.

This is an old story. It was told by Aeschylus, Sophocles, and Euripides in ancient times. It has been retold by Eugene O'Neill, Jean Giraudoux, Darius Milhaud, Jean Paul Sartre, and Jack Richardson in our time. But none of these presents Elektra as per above. That, with the approval of Richard Strauss, was the doing of his librettist Hugo von Hofmannsthal.

The story? It goes as follows: Agamemnon, returning from the Trojan War, is murdered by his wife Klytämnestra. Their son Orestes, the gods decree, must return home to avenge the crime, and his sister Elektra waits hungrily for this day of reckoning. After many years Orestes does return; with his sister's help, son murders mother. There it is, short but not sweet.

Hofmannsthal, a famous Austrian playwright, cast the myth first as a work for the legitimate stage. His model for the sequence of events was Sophocles, whose version uses mild-mannered Chrysothemis as a foil to her ferocious sister. Successfully produced in 1905, the play attracted Strauss's attention. Four years later the opera *Elektra*, in text almost identical to the play, was staged in Dresden.

Hofmannsthal invented new horrors for the old story. Overall there is a violence, tension, and gory detail that exceeds all earlier versions, even the one by Euripides. But the German playwright's main inventions are these:

1. Elektra is characterized as a compulsive, each day recalling the murder that was, each day rehearsing the vengeance to come.

2. Elektra is made to recall the murder in vivid circumstantial detail. An ugly new implication is drawn from the myth: she was, as a girl, an eyewitness.

3. The murder weapon, an axe, is stolen by Elektra, presumably from the

scene of the crime. It is kept in readiness as the appropriate instrument of vengeance.

4. Once the vengeance is accomplished, Elektra dies. *This is contrary to all earlier versions.*

5. There is a new thematic undercurrent. Elektra's vendetta is here rendered as a disease, a psychosis that strangles basic womanly functions (i.e., lover, wife, mother).

It is No. 5 that is the most distinctive part of the Hofmannsthal reworking. The implication, once again, is that Elektra actually *saw* her mother kill her father: no pompous psychiatric paragraph can overrate the force of that experience. So, for the rest of her days, Elektra is dominated by the memory of Agamemnon. In her opening monologue she says that each night he comes "like a shadow in the corner of the wall" to console her. Further on, she tells Orestes that "the dead are jealous; he gave me hate, hollow-eyed hate, as a bridegroom." In short, while her father's spirit is near, she can never mate.

Here, then, is the unsexing of her.

Other women—the palace maids, her sister Chrysothemis—are the vessels of life and creation. Elektra has become a disembowelled engine of destruction.

This polar opposition Hofmannsthal works with throughout the action. At the outset we see Elektra's hatred for women who are still women. To the maids she screams, "Go sleep with your men!" When Chrysothemis says she wants most to marry and have children, Elektra mocks her. Yet in a later scene we find Elektra envying her sister: "You are full of strength," she says. "You are lovely, you are like a fruit on the day it has ripened." Yes, she needs Chrysothemis as an accomplice; but it means something that Elektra, in exchange, then offers to serve her sister *as duenna and midwife.* This, maybe, is the only substitute for what she has lost.

Still later she tells Orestes the story of that loss: "I think that I was beautiful. . . . I felt it when the moonbeams bathed the white nakedness of my body. . . . And my hair was such that men would tremble at it—this hair that now is disheveled, filthy and beastlike. You understand, brother? I had to give up all that I was. I have sacrificed my womanly modesty. . . . I had to sacrifice it to our father." The tale is crucial to her. Hofmannsthal has her so engrossed in its telling that she makes a giant mistake in her revenge scheme—she forgets to give Orestes the axe.

Afterwards she dies. Her passing could be metaphorical, could be metaphysical: we never learn its medical cause. But essentially she has no further reason for being, and Strauss himself makes the connection clear. At her death the orchestra plays music associated with Agamemnon.

Daughter loves father, hates mother: that's the famous Elektra Complex. This same myth, once only the source for a handy label, is here converted into a case history of the condition.

For Hofmannsthal had been reading *Studies in Hysteria* by Josef Breuer and Sigmund Freud.

It is Elektra's loss of womanhood which draws from Richard Strauss an attitude very, very rare from him: real sympathy.

Now, his work in *Salome* shows that Strauss was fully equal to the grislier aspects of the myth. No other composer deals so efficiently with the abnormal and the depraved: Salome's final arioso may be the most authentically *evil* music ever written.

On one level this myth is simply a horror story. There Strauss's standard procedures do wonderfully well. The busy textures, the feverish modulations, the cynical woodwinds, the sickly-sweet strings—these, used in a framework of leitmotifs and Wagnerian declamation, provide the perfect queasy atmosphere. Thus, when the murderess Klytämnestra appears, the composer basks in the sheer ugliness of the scene—in the woman's hypochondria, her nightmares, the decay of her whole being. Wagner himself was too healthy for this, Mahler too saintly; Strauss copes easily.

But the surprise is his sensitivity.

Sympathy, sensitivity: they are words seldom used in discussing Richard Strauss. *Salome,* the story of a teen-age sex criminal, fascinates its composer, but no more; the music is all thrills, chills, and sensationalism. *Elektra* has that, yet it has a poignancy too. "Alone! Alas, I'm all alone!" says the heroine in her opening monologue. The vocal line and its accompaniment both betray a sincere and unusual concern on the composer's part.

One element, not much emphasized in Hofmannsthal's text, arouses these feelings in Strauss. It is the resonance of the past, the contrast between was and is, between things lost and things remaining. The murdered Agamemnon stands here for that past, for those days of the Family, for those days before the changes wrought by the murder. "Father," sings Elektra near the start, "I want to see you." And from the orchestra rises the longest, shapeliest motif in the score, a true melody, delicate, painful, and lovely.

That motif is Strauss's emblem for what is gone. It returns to shade the words of Chrysothemis and Orestes. It even returns as a flicker of pity for the unspeakable Klytämnestra. Elektra praises her, and the latter says, "It seems . . . like something I had forgotten from long, long ago." Then along comes the motif, reminding us of her better days as wife and mother.

But mostly Strauss's sympathy is directed toward the heroine and her loss. In her great confession to Orestes (quoted earlier), Elektra compares her former and present selves. Deployed at length, as in the development section of a symphony, this one motif is the connective tissue of the accompaniment. Here, if anywhere, Strauss makes sublime music.

Yet the text does not ask for any of this, and so the composer has added a dimension. Hofmannsthal shows us, clinically, the spectacle of a woman isolated, insane, dehumanized. Strauss adds a simple comment: this is a condition that deserves compassion.

Elektra is horrible. Amazingly enough, it is also humane.

DONIZETTI'S *The Elixir of Love*

by Stephanie von Buchau

There seems to be some confusion about the classification of Gaetano Donizetti's *L'elisir d'amore*. Many writers on operatic subjects refer to it as an opera buffa—and often go on to criticize it for lacking theatrical, emotional, or musical substance. Donizetti called it an *opera comica*. Herbert Weinstock, in his definitive biography of the composer, calls it an *opera giocosa,* perhaps to elevate it above the coarse wit of the typical opera buffa.

On the title page of my Ricordi score is printed: *Melodramma in due atti di* Felice Romani. In Italian, the word *melodramma* does not have the pejorative meaning of exaggerated sensationalism; it means simply a play to be performed with music. Although the Ricordi score is no more than listing a simple fact (that is, Romani's play with Donizetti's music), the neutral term *melodramma* is an excellent descriptive word for *L'elisir,* an opera that is too often dismissed as a charming trifle, a work that survives in the repertory, in the words of one scoffer, because "tenors like to sing 'Una furtiva lagrima.'"

Far from being a one-aria opera, *L'elisir* is one of the most nearly flawless blends in all theater of sidesplitting comedy and heart-wrenching pathos. (Pardon me if I exclude Mozart, but there is little about his comedies that is sidesplitting; in them, complex psychological penetration precludes much light-hearted laughter.) The most perfect performance of an opera I have ever heard or seen was a *L'elisir* in which the director, cast, and conductor collaborated in keeping the exact balance between the sun and the shade of Donizetti's work.

At the same time that Belcore, the arrogant *sergente,* was hissing "Va via, buffone" and cracking up the audience, poor Nemorino, begging his sweetheart ("Adina, credimi") to wait one more day before she committed herself, was bringing us perilously close to tears. Act I ended with the audience not knowing whether to laugh or cry; all we could do was stand up and cheer. Act II proceeded along the same narrowly wavering line between sentiment and hilarity ("Una furtiva lagrima" becoming psychologically almost unbearable in this context rather than the star turn it sometimes is), and I was left with a glowing memory of poignancy, sweetness, and effervescence which, many years later, has not dimmed one iota from that magic night.

The oft-repeated story of the haste and impossible conditions under which *L'elisir* was composed hardly prepares the auditor for the wealth of natural invention and canny theatricality with which Donizetti invested his score. In contemplating the two weeks which the composer supposedly spent setting Romani's libretto, one tends to forget that he had had an intensive apprenticeship before he created this first of his several operas that would remain regular repertory pieces for the next century and a half. Donizetti was born in 1797 in Bergamo, and he studied music with the composer Simone Mayr, who remained his lifelong friend. (The Bavarian Mayr wrote nearly seventy operas, of which only one, *Medea in Corinto,* is ever performed today.) Donizetti's first opera to be produced was *Enrico di Borgogna* (1818), but it wasn't until his thirty-fifth work, twelve years later, that his style became personal and recognizable. This opera, *Anna Bolena* (1830), was a huge success and is still heard today, often as part of a trilogy of Donizetti works about British queens which Beverly Sills has made popular. (*Maria Stuarda* and *Roberto Devereux* are the other two operas in the trilogy.)

L'elisir d'amore, his fortieth opera, followed in 1832. It can hardly be said that Donizetti didn't know what he was doing by this time; he had certainly had enough practice. The impresario of the Teatro della Cannobiana in Milan had asked Donizetti for a piece in a hurry. The story goes that a work by an unknown composer had been commissioned, and when it failed to be delivered, the Cannobiana management turned to Donizetti for last-minute help—but this is possibly apocryphal. Throughout his career Donizetti liked to embroider on the theme of his celebrated facility.

In any case, the following conversation has been reported between Donizetti and his librettist: "I'm obliged to set a poem to music in fourteen days. I give you one week to prepare it for me. We have a German prima donna, a tenor who stammers, a buffo with the voice of a goat, a French basso who isn't worth much—and still we must do them honor. Dear Romani, *coraggio,* march on."

Felice Romani, the most important librettist of his day, wrote works for Mayr, Bellini, Rossini, and Meyerbeer and created ten librettos for Donizetti, including *Anna Bolena, Lucrezia Borgia,* and *L'elisir.* For the last of these, it appears that he merely translated and adapted a play by Eugène Scribe called *Le Philtre,* which had already been set as an opera by Daniel Auber in 1831. Auber seems to have had the same rotten luck with it that he had with Scribe's *Le Bal masqué.* (That is, Auber's may have been first, but another composer's version is remembered today.)

Donizetti made the deadline, apparently not even breathing hard, and *L'elisir* was rushed into rehearsal for a premiere at the Cannobiana on May 12, 1832. It was an instant success, running for thirty-two performances, one of which was attended by Hector Berlioz, who remarked upon having to strain to hear the music over the din in the theater: "People talk, gamble, sup and succeed in drowning out the orchestra." Earlier, on a visit to Naples where he heard Donizetti's *Le convenienze teatrali* (usually performed in the United States as *Viva la mamma*), Berlioz had warmer words for Italian theaters: "*Opera buffa* is performed with such fire, spirit and brio as to raise it above almost every other theater of its sort."

After the premiere, Francesco Pezzi, music critic of the *Gazzetta privilegiata,* made the following insights into Donizetti's score (which should be taken note of by those who still consider *L'elisir* a piece of fluff): "The musical style of this score is lively, brilliant, truly of the *buffo* genre. The shading from *buffo* to *serio* can be observed taking place with surprising gradations and the emotional is treated with that musical passion for which the composer of *Anna Bolena* is famous." Donizetti, surprisingly modest on occasion, commented to Mayr that the *Gazzetta* praised him "Too well . . . too well."

After its success in Milan, *L'elisir* was quickly exported to other theaters. It was a disaster in Rome in 1834, apparently because of an inadequate cast and production, but a success in Naples and Berlin (1834), Vienna (1835 in Italian; 1838 in German where, as *Der Liebestrank,* it is still performed in German-speaking countries), and Paris (1839). It reached London in 1836 and America (in English) in 1838. The Metropolitan Opera staged it in 1904 with Enrico Caruso as Nemorino; it was one of his favorite roles, the one he was singing in 1920 at the Brooklyn Academy when he suffered the first of the attacks of pleurisy which killed him the following year.

Donizetti was as unlucky as Caruso. It is ironic that the composer of such sunny works as *L'elisir, Don Pasquale,* and *La Fille du régiment* should have had such a short, tragic life. Perhaps some of the poignancy of *L'elisir,* especially Nemorino's feeling that love is slipping away from him, had something to do with Donizetti's love affair with Virginia Vasselli whom he married in 1828. One after the other, their three children died in infancy, and in 1837, his wife followed. Donizetti never forgot her, though he was often physically involved with other women. (He dedicated *L'elisir* to "the Milanese fair sex . . . who better than they know how to dispense it?")

One of his mistresses is supposed to have been Giuseppina Strepponi, a soprano who appeared often in Donizetti operas, including the role of Adina in *L'elisir.* The composer created his *Adelia* (1841) for her. There is some suspicion that her supposed relationship with Donizetti aroused the wrath of the young Verdi (Strepponi lived with Verdi for twelve years and finally married him in 1859), for when Verdi was approached to contribute to the celebration of the Donizetti centenary, he refused to take part on the grounds of his advanced age. But his comment in an earlier letter makes it seem that his refusal was more his customary dislike of fuss than any lingering sexual jealousy against the older composer: "Donizetti knew how to create with his own hands such a monument that the composers who succeeded him will not know how to raise a bigger one to him."

Strepponi, when asked to contribute to a memorial volume, wrote the following encomium: "I nearly always sang in the operas of the great composer of *Lucia* and *Lucrezia Borgia.* Later, Maestro Donizetti wrote *Adelia* for me . . . it was then that I knew him personally and was able to admire—beyond his genius, familiar to all—his spirit, which joined his goodness and his vast culture to form the whole of a truly superior artist and gentleman."

What few knew about this superior artist and gentleman—and indeed it is still hushed over in biographies—is that sometime in the 1820s, Donizetti had contracted syphilis. By the time he fell afoul of the Neapolitan censor over the opera *Poliuto* (1839) and fled to Paris, he was beginning to feel the symptoms of the disease. It was said that he suffered from headaches, migraines that could have had some other origin than that of a ravaging venereal infection. Franco Abbiati, in a suspect and highly colored account of the composer's career, recounts the following gossip: "It was said that Donizetti invariably came to grips with headaches—and they allowed themselves to guess the unfortunate origin of these— every time he had to compose a new opera. And they made it clear that the periodic sufferings nevertheless resulted in some notable benefits, generating happy music if they seized him on the left side, serious music if they seized him on the right."

In Paris, Donizetti supervised a production of *L'elisir,* for which he wrote some new music, produced *Poliuto* as *Les Martyrs* (it was only a succès d'estime), and wrote his last important serious work which, in its Italian incarnation as *La favorita,* retains a precarious toehold on the repertory (although it should be better thought of, for its last act contains Donizetti's greatest music). His last important comic opera, *Don Pasquale,* followed in 1843. Thereafter, Donizetti maintained close connections with the French capital, returning to Naples only for *Caterina Cornaro* in 1844. It is from Paris that we have the famous, horrifying daguerreotype of 1847, showing Andrea Donizetti (the composer's nephew) sitting with a shapeless lump of former humanity, the eyes unfocused, the mouth slack. It is the composer in the last stages of paresis, nine months before his death.

But the tragedy of Donizetti's life need not destroy our enjoyment of his delicious operatic comedy—it serves only to remind us that *L'elisir,* like everything else in life that is worth considering seriously, is made of equal parts of joy and sadness. Even a brief examination of the score shows us how cunningly these opposites are combined, with what finesse Donizetti moves us from laughter to lumps in the throat and back again. The prelude offers two melodies—a bittersweet larghetto and an allegro of cheerful, mindless froth which becomes the opening chorus.

When the curtain rises, Adina is seen reading about the love potion of Tristan and Isolde. Too much shouldn't be made of this plot device. I've actually read that *L'elisir* was intended as a parody of *Tristan,* which ignores the fact that Wagner's opera wasn't written until 1865. (However, in 1866, W.S. Gilbert did write a parody of *L'elisir,* called *Dulcamara; or The Little Duck and the Great Quack.*) The clever harpsichordist who accompanies the secco recitatives often has some fun throwing in the famous *Tristan* chords when Nemorino asks Dulcamara about "Queen Isotta's potion," but the listener should realize that the joke is modern, not Donizetti's.

Nemorino's "Quanto è bella, quanto è cara" is tender; Adina's waltz is frivolous. Belcore's arrival is completely buffo, but minutes later Nemorino and Adina are singing the gorgeously limpid duet "Chiedi all'aura." With the entry of Dulcamara, the opera threatens to become a romp—bassos and stage directors are tempted to overplay the comedy in non-Italian-speaking countries. Yet the Nemorino-Dulcamara duet, with its repeated "Obbligatos," is musical wit at its most scintillating. I've already discussed the finale. Properly sung by a tenor who understands the pathos inherent in Nemorino's character—and who keeps this side of the lacrymose—"Adina, credimi" is one of the most touching things in bel canto literature. But then the hysteria takes over again, and as one writer has observed, "the act ends like some mechanical toy that smashes itself by winding up instead of down."

The second act is long on bumptiousness, but artists with style can make it endearing bumptiousness. The Dulcamara-Adina barcarolle and the Nemorino-Belcore duet are clever examples of characterization through vocal melody and word setting. In the following Adina-Dulcamara duet, the confusion surrounding the elixir is cleared up, and Adina realizes that she loves Nemorino after all. Then there is that most famous, most difficult to sing of all lyric-tenor arias—except perhaps for Mozart's "Un'aura amorosa." It requires a perfectly equalized scale, stupendous breath, elegant *messa di voce,* beautiful head tone; and all this technique must be steered by a musical intelligence that can make emotional sense out of what threatens to become an overwhelming technical exercise.

"Una furtiva lagrima," with its guitarlike arpeggios and bassoon obbligato, has a magical effect on audiences. The instant the introduction begins, the audience draws in its collective breath, as if to help the tenor. And invariably, unless he has butchered it beyond repair, Nemorino gets an ovation when it is over. But when it is sung really well, as Caruso sang it and as Alfredo Kraus and Luciano Pavarotti sing it today, it seems almost sacrilegious to applaud, to break the sympathetic spell that the composer and singer have cast over this simple country boy who wants only to love and live in peace.

Adina's capitulation can seem a little drawn out after this moment of magic, unless the soprano is as good as the tenor at matching technique with emotional penetration. After countless trills, roulades, *fioriture,* and other flourishes, Adina throws herself into Nemorino's arms, and all ends happily with Dulcamara doing a roaring business selling his elixir, alias Bordeaux. (I've often thought that the local wine-growers' association in an operatic town should be glad to finance a production of the opera which promises such spectacular results from their humble product.)

The sun finally prevails over the shadow in this wonderful example of bel canto chiaroscuro, as it never did in Donizetti's life. We are the richer for it. Call it an *opera buffa, comica, melodramma,* or whatever you will. It is really an elixir of love.

VERDI'S *Ernani*
by Peter P. Jacobi

Here are the basics.

Giuseppe Verdi had two hits to his credit, *Nabucco* and *I Lombardi.* Suddenly he was sought after, and among those who sought was the president of

Venice's prestigious Gran Teatro la Fenice, one Marquis Nanni Mocenigo. The marquis wanted a new opera for presentation during carnival and Lent in 1844.

Verdi accepted his blandishments, over those of competitors, and after a wide search for a story, focused on Victor Hugo's *Hernani,* which Italianized became *Ernani.*

The librettist was Francesco Maria Piave. The opera was to be their first of a number of collaborations.

The composer composed swiftly, more swiftly than his writer wrote. Verdi started the music some time before the end of September, 1843. By the first of November he had completed three acts. The final act awaited only Piave's words. Apparently Verdi finished his work before plunging into December rehearsals at La Fenice for the season-opening production of his *I Lombardi* on December 26.

Arduous preparation for the *Ernani* premiere followed in January and February. "If I have a fiasco," he told a friend, "I shall blow my brains out."

It's unlikely he would have. But he didn't have to.

The first performance on March 9, although not a spectacular success, proved triumph enough. The opera itself was more positively evaluated than the performance, which unfortunately included some out-of-tune vocalizing.

Verdi's benefactor and father-in-law, Antonio Barezzi, received a report from his son about the premiere. "Here's why [Carlo] Guasco had no voice," he wrote. "It was eight o'clock and time to begin and nothing was ready. Guasco continued shouting for an hour, and hence his hoarseness. Two sets were missing, the costumes were missing, and there were some ridiculous ones." With repetitions, however, the performance quality improved, and each time the opera was heard, it was wildly applauded.

Within months, requests came from virtually every opera house in Italy, plus Paris, Vienna, and London, for permission to produce it. And not only that, but to get Verdi contracted for a next opera. His devoted student Emanuele Muzio noted: "The Maestro is driving music publishers crazy; literally crazy."

A career was most definitely on the rise.

The basics tell one little.

The filler tells much more.

About his thoughts. About his methods. About his professional habits.

So, let's fill in.

Verdi and Impresarios

Although Verdi during his early composing years considered himself like a galley slave, chained to contractual obligations, he did not hesitate to let those who commissioned his works know what terms he would and would not accept. The managers might control purse strings and rule opera houses, but Verdi intended to control the creative process and rule the opera being staged.

And so, when Mocenigo sent the *Ernani* contract, Verdi more than perused it. He responded with terms accepted and terms not accepted. "I have received the contract," he wrote. "I seem to find in it some points that could raise questions, and since surely neither you nor I wants to quarrel, I am thus making some changes, which, of course, you may accept or reject."

And then he begins the incisions:

> I cannot agree . . . to article 2 of the contract, because the Presidenza might reject the first and the second libretto, etc., and thus we would never reach the end. The Presidenza can rest assured that I will try to have a libretto written for me that I can feel, and hence set to music in the best possible way. If the Presidenza does not have faith in me, then it can have the libretto written at my expense: provided always that this expense is within my possibilities.

"Stay out of the libretto process," in other words.

He also wouldn't have the full score by a requested date because "it is my rule to make orchestration during the piano rehearsals, and the score is never entirely finished until the rehearsal before the dress rehearsal."

"I'm going to do it my way," in other words.

As for being paid in full after the third performance, no, "because the third performance might not take place for a thousand reasons."

"Pay me before opening night," in other words (actually one-third on his arrival in Venice, one-third at the first orchestral rehearsal, and one-third after the dress rehearsal).

And yes, the composer planned to produce the opera around the end of January, *but* "provided that there have been all the rehearsals necessary for a good performance" and that the artists "chosen by the Maestro himself from the list of the company" are available.

"I'll meet your terms if you meet mine," in other words. And as it happened, the premiere fell, not in January, but in March because the chosen Ernani, tenor Carlo Guasco, was not immediately available. Mocenigo had suggested a substitute. Verdi wanted to hear him in Verona and reported, "I have heard Vitali, and I don't like him. With time perhaps he'll develop into a fairly good tenor, but at present he's nothing and his voice gets tired and half-way through the opera he tends to go flat." The premiere was delayed.

Verdi and Operatic Subjects

Always the search.

The search for a good story that also lent itself to treatment as libretto.

Verdi didn't always succeed, but one must say he always tried. He had a sense of theater and generally sensed what stories would (1) touch his audience and (2) be treatable in the compressed form that setting scenes and characters to music requires.

Faced with the Fenice commission, his first for that theater, in fact his first for any other than Milan's La Scala, for whom he'd written his first four operas, Verdi needed a story.

Somewhere in his mind, as usual, were singers—available singers. The man was pragmatic almost above all. What sense writing an opera, he would tell himself, if the appropriate singers weren't available?

For instance, *King Lear*. How he wanted to set that great tragedy to music! Now and in later years. But in 1843 La Fenice had no top-quality baritone or bass, and Lear, of course, just had to be baritone or bass.

What else could he turn to? Well, what about Byron's *The Corsair*? Again, no baritone. What about Catherine Howard as subject, she Henry VIII's fifth queen consort? Verdi didn't like the characters. What about Cola di Rienzi, the Roman hero, a subject of interest to Wagner too? Verdi called it a "magnificent subject" but judged that "even if much toned down, the police would probably forbid it." He was taken by the fall of the Longobards, but such an opera would require too sizeable a cast for Venice to supply in quality. He considered a second Byron subject, *The Two Foscari*. It's "Venetian and ought to arouse great interest," he said to Mocenigo, but the impresario discovered that the censors would start tampering with it. Victor Hugo's *Cromwell* occurred to them next. Again, too many characters. Then the story of Allan Cameron, pretender to the British throne when Charles II was about to ascend it. Verdi thought the story might weary his public.

And so, through trial and weeding, he came up with Hugo's *Hernani,* the author's call to romanticism. The idea, introduced by Mocenigo, set a spark in the composer. "Oh, if only we could do *Hernani,*" he wrote, "that would be tremendous."

Finally, after several months of searching, a subject had been found, one that dealt with liberalism, which enthused the composer, and one with a struggle for power at its heart, which intrigued him (as it had and would with *Nabucco, Simon Boccanegra,* and *Don Carlos*).

Verdi and Librettists

"A libretto! A libretto, and the opera is made," he once wrote to his French publisher.

That's why, although he trusted versifiers to handle the versifying for his operas, he didn't trust them far enough to leave them alone.

He offered scenarios. He offered guidance. He offered words of his own. He offered revisions. He offered interference. And he offered much criticism as the process of creation was carried forth.

Francesco Maria Piave, his new librettist, was inexperienced at the task when Verdi agreed to work with him on *Ernani*. Their collaboration would last through nine operas.

Correspondence shows that the composer never fully trusted his colleague. Letters are filled with statements of concern and dissatisfaction. Piave remained always the suppliant. He complied, and he supplied. "Throughout their relationship," writes Verdi specialist Julian Budden, "he treated the poet sometimes with affection, sometimes with impatience—and with no respect for his judgment whatsoever." Verdi wasn't to change that feeling toward his poets until he collaborated with Arrigo Boito on *Otello* and *Falstaff,* and then only grudgingly.

Piave outwardly was good-natured about it, remarking on a number of occasions, "That's how the Maestro wants it."

In the midst of the *Ernani* project, Verdi wrote to an officer of La Fenice:

> Sig. Piave has never written for the theater and is naturally deficient in these things. In fact, find me a soprano willing to sing, in succession, a big cavatina, a duet that ends in a trio, and a whole finale such as Piave has written in this first act of *Ernani*!
>
> Sig. Piave will have his own good reasons, but I have mine, and I reply that the lungs would not stand this strain. . . .
>
> You, who have been so kind to me, please make Piave understand these things and persuade him . . . I have seen for myself that many compositions would not have failed if there had been a better distribution of the numbers, if the effects had been better calculated, if the musical forms had been clearer . . . in short, if there had been greater experience both in the poet and in the composer. Often an overlong recitative, a phrase, a sentence which would be beautiful in a book, and even spoken in a play, makes you laugh in a sung drama.

There were numerous letters to Piave with suggestions about dramatic structure and verses. Read one: "I cannot understand why you make a change of scene in the third act. I am not convinced . . . because it prolongs the action, a useless chorus has to be made in the throne room, and the scenic effect is diminished. It seems to me that the moment Carlo appears and surprises the conspirators the action must proceed rapidly to the end of the act."

With *Ernani,* as with so many of the other works, Verdi created virtually all of the opera except for the actual text, and even in that he had his hand. He sometimes fit his music to Piave's words, but more often he forced the librettist to fit words to situations and even music that the maestro already had given him.

That was Verdi's way.

Verdi on Quickness and Composition

Verdi wrote swiftly. *Ernani* was composed in a matter of weeks.

He tended to compose music more swiftly than his librettist composed words, giving his impatient mind and personality more time to hassle and dominate a servile Piave.

Verdi wrote almost without stopping, the melodies having already formed in his mind, the instrumentation—although not always put immediately on paper—also very much formulated. A friend said: "To see him writing the instrumental score, you would think he was copying music. It takes him only the time needed to jot down the notes on paper."

The music seemed to be there even as he began to plan a work, before the librettist began his task.

This facility enabled Verdi to meet all his obligations on time. He met his deadlines—a habit that was appreciated.

Verdi and Singers

Rossini would cater to certain whims of his singers, though he spent a career fighting for the composer's right to control the musical substance of an opera.

Verdi insisted on control. Singers would do his bidding or get out.

He kept a professional distance from his singers, save those few who became lifelong friends (such as Teresa Stoltz) and lifelong companions (such as his mistress, then beloved wife, Giuseppina Strepponi). The others were necessary nuisances. Too many of them were difficult.

Among the difficult, by reputation, was his Elvira, Sophie Loewe, who also was signed to sing in I Lombardi.

During rehearsals for I Lombardi Verdi kept his distance. He was polite, no more. And he wrote to a friend that the two "exchanged a few complimentary words and that was the end of it. I haven't been to pay her a single visit yet, nor do I intend to unless it should be necessary. In all, I can only speak well of her, for she does her duty very conscientiously, without the slightest shadow of caprice."

But Loewe, flustered by the poor reception of I Lombardi, a result of the cast's less-than-satisfactory singing, sought to tamper with Verdi's new opera. She insisted that the opera end, not with a trio, as Verdi intended, but with a solo rondo for her. She ordered Piave to write the words, which he did. Verdi ordered those words destroyed.

Loewe did not get her aria. She *did* sing in the trio. Not with total gusto, apparently, or fidelity. "It is impossible to flat worse than Loewe did last night," he reported.

She sang better on following nights, but Verdi did not forget. When he left Venice, he did not make the customary good-bye call. He merely left a card.

They would work together later, forgiving slights but not forgetting them. But to him, singers would be singers. And Verdi was Verdi. Boss.

Verdi and Audiences

Verdi feared audience boredom. It was on his mind while working on *Ernani.*

He noted: "In this type of composition there is no effect unless there is action, so therefore let's have as few words as possible."

He noted: "I caution you that I do not like slow tempi; it is better to err on the side of liveliness than to drag."

He noted: "I do go to the theater all year long and pay great attention."

For him the audience was all.

A literary note is in order.

Victor Hugo disliked the opera because it cut his drama so severely that most of the context, the history, disappeared. His drama had been a revolutionary call to artistic battle for young writers and thinkers. Classicism was dead, it said. Long live a new age, of romanticism, of emotions taking control of history, of passion and unbridled action filling novels, ruling poetry, and dominating the stage.

All that, thought Hugo, was gone in an opera of admittedly rousing but statically designed music.

But surely his shocking spectacle would speak to a longer future than Verdi's latest opera, a caricature of the original, a desecration.

And still he must have thought that way more than thirty years later when he saw Sarah Bernhardt as the heroine Doña Sol (Elvira). Her characterization so affected him that on the following morning he had delivered to her a small box with a note attached: "Madame, you were great and charming; you moved me, me the old warrior, and, at a certain moment when the public, touched and enchanted by you, applauded, I wept. This tear which you caused me to shed is yours. I place it at your feet, Victor Hugo."

The "tear" was a diamond drop hanging from a gold chain bracelet.

Not too many years later, Bernard Shaw was to comment that "the chief glory of Victor Hugo as a stage poet was to have provided libretti for Verdi."

Today that drama for the ages is a curiosity, even in France. Today that muddled opera which Hugo so objected to still holds the stage.

Ah, the vagaries of history and the unaccountability of taste and convention.

In case you want to know about the music—just listen to it.

Ernani has been called a drama of individuals. The story—as dramatized— concentrates on each of the major characters. That permits Verdi to delineate those feelings of love and hate and sacrifice and longing which give his music such an indelible and singular flavor.

It is the music that carries the drama, rather than the drama itself. Movement, action, tension reside in Verdi's notes. The scenes are close to immobile, panoramas that come alive only in song. Music gives this opera life. Its words and stage structure could not stand alone.

Charles Osborne in his *Complete Operas of Verdi* comments: "The weak pages in *Ernani* are relatively few. What is most impressive is the opera's wealth of beautiful and gloriously singable tunes."

Agreed.

Ernani holds youthful vigor and gushes of emotionalism.

From the opening, when the adagio presages the melody that at opera's end calls Ernani to his death, to that ending in the form of a brilliant trio, the opera is brimfull with tunes. That trio, by the way, brought praise from the Viennese critic Eduard Hanslick. Critiquing *Tristan und Isolde,* the anti-Wagnerian Hanslick asked why Tristan should require an hour to die when Ernani efficiently does so "in a few modest bars?"

Along the way you get Elvira's popular "Ernani, involami," a finely crafted scene that became one of Verdi's first to achieve concert status.

And a well-constructed first-act finale inaugurated by Silva's superbly evocative bass aria "Infelice!" and concluded by a series of ensemblematic exclamations.

And the second-act trio for Elvira, Ernani, and Silva, with its beautiful love duet and considerable musical action (Verdi knows how to keep a listener attentive, happy, and just slightly off balance with shifts of mood and tempo and style).

And a wealth of vocal material in Act III, perhaps the strongest in the opera, including one of Verdi's exciting conspiratorial scenes, another of the composer's patriotic choruses, "Si ridesti il Leon di Castiglia" (Let the Lion of Castile Awake), and a trio completed by an "All honor and glory to Charles V" outburst involving chorus and orchestra, a joyous moment announcing the marriage of Ernani and Elvira but underscored with ominous sounds of Silva's vengeance.

Verdi didn't want his audience to be bored, so the music is ever melodious and always uninhibitedly theatrical.

Ernani looks to Verdi's future, a future during which increasingly he managed to clarify personalities in his musical outpourings. He wrote better operas, of course (Boito considered *Ernani* a descent from *Nabucco*). But he didn't write a lot that were more tuneful or that provided more vocal meat for virtuoso singers.

TCHAIKOVSKY'S *Eugene Onegin*

by Dorothy Samachson

Rarely in the history of opera has a composer become so emotionally involved with a character he is limning in music that he falls "absolutely in love with her," as Peter Ilyich Tchaikovsky did with Tatiana, the heroine of his opera *Eugene Onegin*. Other composers have been sentimentally touched by their own creations—notably Giacomo Puccini, who admitted that he wept while composing the music for Madama Butterfly, the little geisha betrayed by her love for an unworthy man.

But Puccini could put his score down, no matter how great his inspiration, and conduct his own life and loves. Tchaikovsky became so deeply wrapped in his heroine's unhappiness that "she had become for me a living person in living surroundings. I loved Tatiana, and was terribly indignant with Onegin, who seemed to me a cold heartless coxcomb."

Were he still alive when Tchaikovsky's *Onegin* was given its premiere in Moscow's Maly Theatre in 1879, Alexander Pushkin, the author of the original novel in verse *Eugene Onegin,* which was Tchaikovsky's source and inspiration, would have been surprised by Tchaikovsky's opera. He would have discovered that his ironic portrait of Russian society had been transformed into a touchingly beautiful tragedy of unfulfilled love. Tchaikovsky was faithful to Pushkin's plot—wealthy city man meets country girl and rejects her, only to be rejected by her years later when she is also part of his world. He used many of Pushkin's verses in the libretto, in which he was assisted by K.S. Shilovsky; however, the two masterpieces are totally different in intellectual and emotional thrust.

The poet and the composer were separated by half a century, and their portrayals of Russian life were products of their own cultures, of their social milieux, and, especially, of their own personalities.

Pushkin (1799–1837), acclaimed by all Russians as the "supreme embodiment of the national genius who shaped the literary language and fathered its literature," is ranked along with Shakespeare for the beauty of his language, his psychological and social insights into upper-class Russian behavior, and the mastery with which he wrote lyric and narrative verse, prose, and dramatic works. He has been a treasure house of inspiration for many Russian composers and choreographers.

In his extensive and fascinating analysis of Pushkin's *Onegin,* V.C. Belinsky, a distinguished nineteenth-century Russian critic, noted that "*Onegin* is a poetical picture of Russian society . . . a historical poem—the first and brilliant attempt to be undertaken in Russian, although it does not contain a single historical personage. Pushkin here is not simply and only a poet, but a representative of a newly awakened social consciousness."

Unfortunately, Pushkin is still little-known here, partly because it has been claimed that his poetry doesn't translate too well and because many American readers were simply not familiar with his works or the facts of his turbulent life, which are dramatic enough to serve as inspiration for novels, plays, or films.

A member of Russia's aristocracy, Pushkin was descended on his mother's side from a captured Ethiopian prince who was freed and raised to the nobility by Peter the Great. His father's family was one of Russia's oldest, and the handsome, gifted, and intelligent young man started out as a favorite in the tsarist court. He was also reckless, witty, and scornful of official backwardness. Like Byron, his English Romantic contemporary with whom he's frequently compared, Pushkin's private life was often undisciplined—he drank, gambled, dueled, and had numerous affairs with women. (He supposedly admitted to having had 113 loves.)

He was also peripherally involved with the officers known as the Decembrists, who were later sentenced to death or Siberia for their unsuccessful plot against the oppresive tsar.

Pushkin was sent into inner exile for his sympathy to liberal ideas, expressed in his *Ode to Liberty,* an irreverent, atheistic piece.

Eventually, he was pardoned and returned to the court, always under the scrutiny of the tsar's agents. When he was thirty, he fell in love with and married a beautiful sixteen year old, whose extravagances forced him into debt and whose scandalous liaisons so humiliated Pushkin that he fought a duel for her dubious honor. The duel may have been contrived to rid the government of his troublesome spirit, and it did.

Pushkin's *Onegin* was written over a period of eight years and was released to the public piecemeal, from 1825 to 1833, much like a serial. His Onegin bears many similarities to his own personality. Both were sophisticated men about town, cynical and bored by society's shallowness. Yet, Pushkin separated himself from Onegin by using a narrator who periodically interjects himself into the poem to add his own sardonic comments on the behavior of the characters—including Onegin himself. But he goes further, adding ironic opinions of society's mores, morals, tastes, and empty lives.

Pushkin was exasperated with those critics who called him a Romantic, and he was sharp with one critic, complaining, "He expected romanticism from me and found satire and cynicism." For that matter, a number of his readers were also offended by his objective ironic comments. Perhaps they recognized themselves and didn't like what they saw.

However, despite his disavowal of romanticism, Pushkin was a Romantic poet—the vital romanticism of revolt that emerged after the American and French revolutions, in its literature, music, and art, reflected the new spirit of the era.

Tchaikovsky, on the other hand, was a Late Romantic, when the movement was on the verge of expiring. His romanticism was much more personal and subjective, and in a letter, he wrote, "Where the heart is not touched, there can't be any music." Tchaikovsky's *Onegin* is a touchingly beautiful drama of unfulfilled love. Born in 1840, three years after Pushkin's death, Tchaikovsky, the son of middle-class parents, was hypersensitive, shy, neurotic, and a hypochondriac who, throughout his life, suffered from frequent bursts of emotional and psychological insecurity.

He was also homosexual, tormented by fears of exposure, and a very sentimental man who desperately yearned to lead what he considered a normal life as a husband and father—most unrealistic fantasies that were to lead to disaster when he was composing *Eugene Onegin*.

Tchaikovsky began his formal music training comparatively late—when he was in his twenties and working for the Ministry of Justice—a job he resigned in order to concentrate on music. His talents were recognized early on, but he earned very little as either composer or professor at the Moscow Conservatory. Not until Mme. Nadezhda von Meck, an equally neurotic wealthy widow became his patron, did he enjoy any financial security. Their relationship was a strange one. They never met, but for years they conducted a correspondence in which they confided to each other their most intimate thoughts. However, Tchaikovsky never mentioned his sexuality to her.

In 1877, while Tchaikovsky was working on his Fourth Symphony, he was also seeking a subject for a new opera. Although Tchaikovsky is best known as a composer of symphonic, instrumental, and chamber-music works, he wrote eleven operas, and he yearned for success on the operatic stage.

He had very ambivalent feelings about opera, to which he had been introduced as a schoolboy, attending performances in St. Petersburg. "To refrain from writing operas is, in its way, heroism. I don't possess this heroism, and the stage with all its tawdry brilliance none the less attracts me." Whether he really believed this, or was being politic in agreeing with Mme. von Meck, who thought opera a "false art," is open to question. For on the other hand, he also said, "There's something irrepressible that attracts all composers . . . opera and opera alone makes you friends with people, makes your music familiar to the real public, makes you the property, with luck, of the whole nation."

Furthermore, "An opera may be given forty times in one season, a symphony once in ten years." This was a very important consideration, for operatic performance and publishing fees would have eased his precarious financial situation.

In 1877 Tchaikovsky had already composed four operas that had hardly set the operatic public or critical fraternity on fire. He was honest with himself; he even burned a couple of scores because he was dissatisfied with them. One, *Undine,* which was never produced, he said was "atrocious." Yet, he did use some of *Undine*'s music as the enchanting White Swan pas de deux in *Swan Lake,* and one can't help wondering what the rest of the score would have been like if he hadn't tossed it into the fire.

One evening, a few months after his fourth opera, *Vakula the Smith,* had been presented, Tchaikovsky attended a party at the home of Elizaveta Lavrovskaya, the soprano who had given the first public performance of his song "None but the Lonely Heart." The hostess, during the conversation, suggested that he compose an opera on Pushkin's *Eugene Onegin.* Tchaikovsky rejected the idea out of hand as being utterly ridiculous.

Onegin, as he remembered, didn't have a dramatic plot strong enough to build a theater piece. It was a poem, not a play, and it was a narrative that wandered in time and place, developing characters, rather than action.

Nevertheless, later that evening it didn't seem such a crazy idea, and he managed to find a copy. He spent the rest of the night reading and falling in love, not only with the entire work, but also with Pushkin's heroine, Tatiana. By morning, he had already prepared a rough scenario.

The first piece he set to music was Tatiana's Letter Scene, in which the innocent, ardent seventeen-year-old girl opens her heart to Onegin in a letter and confesses that she loves him with all her passion and power.

This aria is vividly described by Konstantin Stanislavsky and Pavel Rumyantsev in their book *Stanislavsky on Opera:* "It would be difficult to find in any opera anywhere a scene of such profound passionate feeling and tenderness, one with such rich musical coloring, so penetrating in the revelations of thoughts, feeling, doubts, sufferings and joys of a young girl's first love as this scene."

Musically, the Letter Scene is as much a brilliant example of Tchaikovsky's mastery of the orchestra as it is of his understanding of the human voice. The oboes, clarinets, and harp, impetuously running up and down chromatically, have the fevered quality of her racing pen. The music flows and ebbs as Tatiana revels in her confession, as she stops to reflect on what her discovery of love means, and on how Onegin will respond. Throughout the aria, the music returns again and again to her theme, first heard in the short orchestra introduction to the opera. Orchestra and voice are equal partners in the aria, and they build such tension that the listener identifies with Tatiana's emotional agitation and exaltation.

And now life, in its ironic way, imitated art. During his work on *Onegin*, Tchaikovsky had been receiving love letters from a student at the conservatory. He barely knew the young woman, Antonina Miliukova, who was emotionally unstable and untalented.

Although he at first disregarded her letters, he was soon touched by what he saw as a parallel with Tatiana's letter and her rejection by Onegin. Since he had for years deluded himself with the belief that he wanted a normal family life and, perhaps, to still any gossip about his own sexual preferences, he wrote back, in the naive conviction that this might possibly be his one chance to fit into society comfortably.

Somehow he didn't stop to think about her own needs or to recognize that she didn't even share his cultural interests. When he did stop to think, it was already too late. He told her that normal husband-wife sexual relations would be impossible. Either she didn't listen, or she suffered from her own delusions about the future.

Still, nothing discouraged her, and after she threatened suicide, which should have given Tchaikovsky some warning of her mental state, he proposed. He would not be an Onegin and spurn the one who offered him her love so wholeheartedly.

However, Antonina was not Tatiana. Tchaikovsky was no Onegin, and the ghastly sham of a marriage lasted all of nine weeks, ended only by Tchaikovsky's utter mental and physical collapse. They never divorced, and Tchaikovsky, probably feeling guilty and responsible for the disaster, supported her until his death in 1893.

Neither life nor history has dealt kindly with Antonina. Granted that she was mentally disturbed even before the marriage, it is possible that her later, more severe mental disability, her numerous affairs in her quest for love, and the illegitimate children she bore might perhaps be traced back to Tchaikovsky's rejection. She spent the last twenty-one years of her life in an asylum.

Although Tchaikovsky had written about two-thirds of *Onegin* before his disastrous marriage, he couldn't work on anything during that traumatic period. When he had regained his health, he returned to it with his affections for the characters intact, and work proceeded swiftly.

Tatiana was the central character, and Dostoyevsky later said that Tchaikovsky should have renamed the opera Tatiana. Tchaikovsky himself had difficulty calling it an opera. He described it as "lyric scenes," but of course it is an opera. A number of years ago the late Dimitri Mitropoulos, at a rehearsal of *Onegin* he was conducting at the Metropolitan Opera, spoke of the work, which he dearly loved, as more a "psychological study of a small circle of people." Mitropoulos was right; for the music that Tchaikovsky wrote for each individual was colored by his understanding of all of them.

The music for the old nurse and for Madame Larina, the girls' mother, is nostalgic and more earthy and folklike Russian in character. The four central characters—Tatiana, Olga, Lensky, and Onegin—are sensitively drawn, and their music delineates them perfectly.

Tatiana is, at first, a shy, dreamy, innocent provincial seventeen year old, who lives through the books she loves, and in the last act, she is a mature, responsible, still-passionate noblewoman. Her music grows along with her.

Olga, her sixteen-year-old sister, is lighthearted, flirtatious, and rather empty-headed. She will never suffer from serious lifelong love pangs. Her carefree pursuit of pleasure unwittingly leads to the tragedy of Lensky's death. Her first-act aria describes her very aptly.

Lensky, the eighteen-year-old poet, Olga's fiery, truly romantic fiancé, has music that hints of Tchaikovsky's identification with his spirit. Lensky's duet with Olga is a lilting, charming expression of youthful ardor, while his famous aria before the duel—one of the most touchingly exquisite in all opera—is a heartbreaking, poignantly lyric expression of love and youth, doomed to early extinction.

In the last act, Tchaikovsky introduced Prince Gremin, Tatiana's husband to whom Pushkin had never given a name. For Gremin, Tchaikovsky composed one of the most tender and moving evocations of an older man's warm love for a young wife in an aria that any woman would be proud to claim for herself.

And finally, there is Onegin—Pushkin's and Tchaikovsky's anti-hero. Is he a villain? Hardly. He is a wealthy member of society, suffering from a severe case of ennui, bored by high society, and equally bored by the country life. If he causes Tatiana pain by his cool, avuncular lecture when he rejects her love, he believes he is being kind in advising her on why a young maid should behave more circumspectly. After all, he's a twenty-one-year-old man of the world, and she's an unsophisticated country girl. And if he deliberately flirts with Olga, it's not out of desire for her or out of hatred for Lensky, but out of petty pique. He blames Lensky for creating the embarrassing meeting with Tatiana, and he's irritated by the behavior of the provincial guests and neighbors at Tatiana's party. Onegin has no intention of creating a dangerous situation that will lead the jealous Lensky to challenge him to a duel.

Ah, that duel! A meaningless end to a life that has barely begun. But then we must remember also that in Pushkin's time and class, one defended one's putative honor through duels. A further touch of irony is known to the theater audience, for Pushkin himself was a victim of that "honor system" and fell to a duelist's weapon over the "honor" of an unworthy woman.

Tchaikovsky, rarely an ironist in his music, proves himself one in the final scene of the opera. When Onegin pleads his love for Tatiana, his music is a transfigured echo of Tatiana's passionate declaration of love for him in her letter. It is Tatiana who remains constant—honest and unwavering in her love for Onegin, but faithful to her marital vows and her sense of duty to her husband. Tchaikovsky had clothed her in music of such haunting tenderness and beauty that she remains in our hearts, much as she remains in the hearts of all who have met her as the very model of a warm, loving, generous-spirited woman.

Tchaikovsky worried about how his characters would be interpreted on stage. "Where," he asked, "shall I find the Tatiana whom Pushkin imagined and whom I have tried to picture in music?" The answer is on any stage where Tatiana, Onegin, Lensky, and Olga stir our emotions with the shimmer of enchanting music and the pulsating hearts of those who are suffering the trials and tribulations of young love.

VERDI'S *Falstaff*
by Maxine R. Kanter

Whoever first coined the phrase "You're not getting older, you're just getting better!" might well have had Giuseppe Verdi in mind, for his *Falstaff* was not only a remarkable achievement for an octogenarian, it was a superb finale to a long, fruitful, and incomparable career.

With the production of *Aïda* (1871), the fifty-eight-year-old composer was at the peak of his profession: he was recognized as the master of Italian opera; the entire nation idolized him; he was financially secure and internationally famous. Had he never written another note, his eminent position in the history of opera would have been assured.

Nonetheless, Verdi did not feel inspired to continue, and he began to sense that his active life as a composer was over. He was further depressed by the political and musical situations in Italy around 1880, and while he was not envious of Wagner's success, he feared that Wagnerian music and philosophy threatened the very heart of Italian artistic values and ideology. For over a decade, Verdi retired to his magnificent estate at Sant'Agata, where he spent his days primarily editing and revising previous works and living the life of a gentleman farmer. It was only a reading of Boito's splendid new libretto based on Shakespeare's *Othello* that aroused Verdi's interest and helped to dispel his anxieties about his creative powers and his fear of public failure. Arrigo Boito (1842–1918) was an Italian poet and composer in his own right, having provided both the text and the music for the operas *Mefistofele* (produced at La Scala in 1868) and *Nerone,* completed and edited by Arturo Toscanini and presented—also at La Scala—in 1924. Boito's first work did not please his Milanese audiences, who were fond only of Italian or French styles, and as he was perceived as being "too modern" (always a handy put-down), he incited the wrath of the anti-Wagnerians to the extent that the opera had to be withdrawn after the second performance. Although Boito was considered to be a leader among the more forward-looking Italian composers, he is best remembered today as the librettist for Verdi's last two operas, *Otello* and *Falstaff,* the latter acknowledged to be Boito's masterpiece.

The choice of texts based on Shakespeare's works was a shrewd one, for the English poet and playwright had long been Verdi's favorite dramatist. Moreover, Boito appeared to be the ideal, if not the only possible, partner for Verdi in this project. Of all Shakespeare's dramas, *Othello* is the best constructed and the most intensely and eloquently theatrical. Verdi was hooked, and in March of 1884 the seventy-year-old composer began to set Boito's book to music.

A misunderstanding between the two colleagues caused Verdi—who was oversensitive and easily depressed—to abandon this venture temporarily, and it was only after he was mollified by Boito's assurances and explanations that he resumed composing. It was December, 1886, before Verdi was able to write to Boito that he had sent off the last pages of *Otello* to the publishing firm of Ricordi.

The La Scala premiere took place on February 5, 1887, amidst a general atmosphere of excitement and keen anticipation. It was, after all, the first new opera by the master in over fifteen years! The results were overwhelming: his public adored him, and the Piazza della Scala was overrun with delighted admirers shouting "Viva Verdi! Viva Verdi!" *Otello* had not only vindicated Verdi's most deep-seated and serious apprehensions of failure; it took its place as the greatest Italian tragic opera of the nineteenth century and the triumphant refutation of German dominance in music by that of the Italian genius.

Verdi was immediately urged to write another opera; there was even a rumor that he was already working on a subject, but in fact, he was in no hurry to do so and had returned to Sant'Agata and busied himself with the affairs of his farm and community. Amongst these was a new hospital he had built at nearby Villanova. In his usual take-charge manner, he was largely responsible for designing its simple architecture, he carefully supervised the construction of the building, hired the medical staff, and together with his wife, Giuseppina, he chose all the furniture, linen, and interior necessities.

Although his mind was not occupied with thoughts of music, he was tantalized by a synopsis of a proposed libretto to be called *Falstaff,* which Boito sent him in July, 1889. Verdi longed to try comedy again. (One of his earliest pieces had been a comic opera called *Un giorno di regno* [1840], which had not been a success.) He must have thought this proposal by Boito was just what the doctor ordered, for he joyously and promptly replied to the poet:

> Excellent! Excellent! Before reading your sketch I wanted to re-read *The Merry Wives,* the two parts of *Henry IV,* and *Henry V,* and I can only repeat: Excellent, for no one could have done it better than you have done.

Some time after this letter was sent, Verdi had second thoughts about his age and health and the possibilities of his not being able to complete the work. Boito responded sagely with two major arguments: he suggested that "there is only one way of ending your career more effectively than with *Otello,* and that is to conclude victoriously with *Falstaff.*" He added: "I don't think you will find writing a comic opera fatiguing. A tragedy makes its composer really suffer. His mind dwells on grief, and his nerves become unhealthily agitated. But the jests and laughter of comedy exhilarate both mind and body." (Boito seems to anticipate Norman Cousins's theories regarding the therapeutic benefits of repeated and frequent doses of comedy—especially that which produces "belly laughter"—in the treatment of disease.) Furthermore—and this was probably meant to do away with any pressure that might be directed toward the composer—Boito advised that they should "promise to maintain the most scrupulous secrecy. I've told nobody about it. If we can work in secret we can work in peace."

Once again Boito's lure had worked; Verdi needed no further convincing. He immediately wrote to Boito:

> Amen, and so be it! Let us then do *Falstaff.* Let's not think now of the obstacles, my age and illnesses! But I want to keep it the deepest *secret:* a word I underline three times to tell you that no one must know anything of it.

He enthusiastically urged Boito to commence writing the libretto at once, and a few weeks later, Verdi wrote again—evidently very pleased with him-self—that he had actually started to compose. "I'm amusing myself by writing fugues! Yes, sir, a fugue: and a *comic* fugue which would be suitable for *Falstaff*!" Clearly the image of the elderly fat knight had tickled Verdi's imagination in a very special way, and he was enjoying composing, thus proving Boito's theories correct.

Boito wrote his libretto, and Verdi accepted it with few criticisms or changes and began the musical setting. It has been said that if Boito had succeeded brilliantly in adapting *Othello,* he performed an absolute and unqualified miracle with one of Shakespeare's lesser works, *The Merry Wives of Windsor.*

A tradition, first recorded by John Dennis in 1702, holds that this comedy was written in about two weeks at the request of Queen Elizabeth, who professed a desire to see the character Falstaff in love. This theory is, in part, confirmed by the choice of Windsor as the scene of action, the flattering references to the court, and the numerous passages in prose which would suggest a composition written in haste.

Undoubtedly, the *Merry Wives* followed *Henry IV,* and, perhaps, *Henry V* as well, although scholars are not in agreement over the latter point. What is more certain, however, is that the play's name appears on the Stationers' Register in 1602 and so was probably written in 1599 or 1600. In Boito's version— considered to be much superior to the original—the poor jokes are discarded, the awkward prose is replaced by excellent verse, and the ungainly, excessively large cast is reduced to just nine characters. The libretto is evidence of both the literary ability and the excellent judgment of a man of the theater with the keenly sensitive understanding of the poet for the working methods and style of his musical partner. Verdi, who had reread not only *The Merry Wives of Windsor* but the other two plays in which Falstaff figures *(Henry IV* and *Henry V),* was intent on portraying Sir John—not only as the key personage in his drama—but also as a buffo character whose immense persona matched that of his physical size. There certainly were precedents for such roles in many comic operas, including the sultans and pashas and slave masters in the works of both Mozart and Rossini. A clue to Verdi's paradigm for *Falstaff* may be derived from a comment he made concerning Rossini: "I can't help thinking that, for abundance of real musical ideas, for comic verve, and truthful declamation, *Il barbiere di Siviglia* is the finest *opera buffa* in existence."

When Shakespeare introduced Falstaff in the "Henry" plays, he was the dissipated companion of the prince of Wales, the Prince Hal who was to become Henry V. Falstaff's cronies were no better than he was—rogues, rascals, and mischief makers such as Bardolph, Pistol, Gadshill, and Mistress Quickly, hostess of a tavern in Eastcheap. Boito eliminates some characters and condenses others. (For example, Sir Hugh Evans, Justice Shallow, Slender, and Dr. Caius become one—Dr. Caius.) Anne Page becomes Nannetta Ford, and she has one unwelcome suitor, not two. The number of episodes in which Falstaff is tricked by the wives is two, not three, and the social position of Mistress Quickly has improved considerably, that is, if we agree that it is better to be a "friendly neighbor of the Wives," rather than the proprietress of a tavern.

Boito adapts several Falstaff episodes from *Henry IV,* most importantly that from Act V, scene 1, in which Falstaff gives us his interpretation of honor, concluding with: "Honor is a mere scutcheon; and so ends my catechism." In the opera it becomes a key passage, Falstaff's *Credo,* if you will; and since it appears early on (Act I, scene 1), his "Honor Monologue" acquaints us with the attitudes and character of the key figure of the story.

Although the opening monologue of Act III was chosen from a similar segment in *The Merry Wives,* most of the words were taken from the *Henry IV* plays. Curiously, the many references to social status that are threaded throughout Shakespeare's play were merely implied in the opera. On the other hand, there are situations in *Falstaff* that do not occur in either *The Merry Wives* or the *Henry IV* plays. It was the librettist's fancy to place the lovers Fenton and Nannetta behind a screen in Act I, scene 2, and then have them discovered there; also, most of Fenton's sonnet and Nannetta's song in Act III, scene 2, were Boito's invention.

However, the addition of a concluding fugue, that scintillating, bravura ensemble which sparked Verdi's musical initiation as a true buffa composer, was his alone and represents not only Verdi's mastery of that "learned" form, but also that *Falstaff* is a worthy successor to *Le nozze di Figaro*. Composing without a deadline, with no interruptions or demands from publishers, agents, or producers—in effect, writing for himself alone—Verdi was having fun! "Certain passages," he wrote, "are so droll that the music has often made me laugh while writing it."

The plots of his previous works (except for *Un giorno di regno*) had not only all been *serious,* they had been filled with gloom and violence. His earlier operas, in particular, belong to the genre of blood-and-thunder romantic melodrama and portray events requiring strong passions and vivid contrasts. Three Verdi operas immediately come to mind as examples in this style: *Ernani, Rigoletto,* and *Il trovatore.* Furthermore, they were written in a "set" style: that is, each character or group of characters had an aria, ensemble, or portion that was distinct and separate. There was a definite beginning, middle, and end.

Falstaff was different. Melody follows melody in a continuous stream of music; they practically topple over one another in a scurry to be heard. While still remaining a "singers' opera," the orchestra takes a greater role in the musical development, and the orchestration has grown more expert and original. It does not, however, have the symphonic importance or the polyphonic texture one finds in Wagner, nor is there any significant use of the leitmotif, although there are repetitions or short melodic fragments belonging to a phrase of text. (For instance, when Falstaff is informed that Ford, the husband of his ladylove, will be absent from home "dalle due alle tre," each time Ford or some other character repeats these words, it is to the same series of intervals.)

There are numerous instrumental effects that add to the humor and sophistication of Verdi's last opera: the piccolo doubling the cello at a four-octave interval in Act I as Sir John sings "Se Falstaff s'assottiglia," fantasizing Mistress Alice's admiration of his magnificent and noble figure. Where he further imagines her saying "Io son di Sir John Falstaff," Verdi employs an age-old buffo tactic of male falsetto. Then there is the scintillating perpetual motion of the strings in Act II, scene 2, as the maddened, jealous Ford rummages through the house searching for the hidden Falstaff.

The sounds of musical laughter permeate the entire opera, with a fast rhythm in a 6/8 meter associated with the women's playful teasing. One critic has observed: "If they themselves are too well-bred to laugh like Wagner's Valkyries, oboes, clarinets, horns and strings are ready to do so for them."

It is, however, in the last scene of *Falstaff,* in Windsor Park at midnight, that Verdi lavishes the listener with the most gorgeous sounds, spinning a web of magical and ethereal beauty. Enchantment fills the air as Nannetta, now the Queen of the Fairies, calls to her attendants, who gather together to the muted accompaniment of woodwinds and strings in a series of staccato effects, suggesting the twittering and fluttering of small birds. As an example of orchestral genius it not only rivals similar "fairy" tone painting in Berlioz and Mendelssohn, it represents the distance that Verdi has traveled from his early "oom-pa-pa" orchestral writing to this, his last opera. From every vantage point we can appreciate Verdi's admission that *Falstaff* was his most carefully written work.

After his energetic and enthusiastic beginning in mid March, 1890, Verdi's composition of the opera was repeatedly interrupted by illness, self-doubt, and depression, evils that had plagued him many times previously and to which he was sadly susceptible. In between these bouts he composed, and by September, 1891, he had begun to orchestrate and revise what he had finished; meantime, after more than a year, word had leaked out about his new project, and the long process of casting the first performance had begun.

Verdi completed the orchestral score in the autumn of 1892, and by the beginning of 1893 he and Giuseppina had arrived in Milan, and Verdi had begun to rehearse *Falstaff,* some of the sessions lasting for eight hours. Clearly Verdi was leaving nothing to chance; the proof copy contains many notes and directions concerning the production.

As we might expect, the premiere, on February 9, 1893, was the victory that both Boito and Verdi had privately expected, and it was attended by royalty, political leaders, and many figures from the world of the arts and the press. The reviews were excellent and mentioned that several excerpts were encored.

Poor old Sir John had survived the wives' plotting and scheming and was none the worse for all his humiliating adventures. The fugue that had inspired and delighted Verdi finds its true place in the final ensemble, where Falstaff begins "Tutto nel mondo è burla" (All the world is a joke), continuing: "L'uomo è nato burlone" (Man is born a joker). As they all join in, the message emerges "Man is born to be made a fool of," but what it really means is that humor can be our greatest gift, along with the courage to love and to hope.

GOUNOD'S *Faust*

by Dale Harris

The phenomenal success of Carl Maria von Weber's *Der Freischütz,* first performed in Berlin in 1821 and within four years seen in every corner of the musical world from St. Petersburg to New York, inaugurated a vogue in opera for the occult, especially for the demonic manifestations of occultism. That vogue and its counterpart in ballet (launched by *La Sylphide* in 1832 and brought to a climax nine years later with *Giselle*) satisfied the widespread need that showed itself in the early part of the nineteenth century for immersion in the irrational, for a confrontation with the darker side of human nature.

Recognition of these universal occult powers was long overdue. During a large part of the eighteenth century the forces of rationality, which dominated the thinking of the age, had kept the monsters of instinct at bay, though there were signs of psychic restiveness in the second half of the century—as witness the success of the so-called Gothic novel, such as Horace Walpole's *The Castle of Otranto* (1764), which was designed to inspire readers with feelings of awe, fear, and disorientation. Even Mozart, the most characteristic musical genius of the Age of Enlightenment, in *Don Giovanni* (1787) brought upon the stage the ghost of a murdered man seeking revenge, and in the penultimate scene of the opera showed the guilty man actually being dragged down to hell by, so to speak, real-life demons. Yet the essential point of *Don Giovanni,* no less than that of Gluck's *Orfeo ed Euridice* (1762), with its scenes of underworld horror, is the restoration of order, of sanity, of equilibrium.

But the sensibilities of the age were about to change to what a later generation was to call romanticism. Within two years of the premiere of *Don Giovanni* the French Revolution, destined in due course to overthrow the entire social order of continental Europe, broke out, giving a tremendous impetus to the age's as-yet-unfulfilled need to acknowledge openly the instinctual energies of the universe.

Like *Don Giovanni, Der Freischütz* condemns evil but, unlike it, grants evil a necessary educative role in life. It is through the unspeakable horrors they experience that Agathe and Max, the hero and heroine of Weber's opera, are brought to a state of moral awareness. The same is true of most of the demon operas that followed in its wake: Robert and Isabella in Meyerbeer's *Robert le diable* (1831) and Rodolphe and Agnès in Gounod's *La Nonne sanglante* (1854) are all ultimately blessed by the fearful tribulations they undergo.

But by the 1850s the impetus of romanticism had begun to slacken. *La Nonne sanglante,* adapted from Matthew Lewis's Gothic novel *The Monk* (1796) and featuring an avenging ghost, a spectral wedding in a ruined castle, and a finale in which a newly pardoned murderer is seen ascending to heaven, was quickly judged too absurd to be endured, and after only a few performances, it disappeared forever. Gounod's next opera, composed not long after he had recovered from a nervous breakdown, was the very different *Le Médecin malgré lui* (1858), a work which, dominated as it is by playfulness and wit—and by the sanity of Molière, from whom it was adapted—may be said to have restored Gounod to full health. With this, his third opera—his first was *Sapho* (1851)—he gave every indication of having at last found his true voice as a theatrical composer: graceful, sensuous, elegantly charming.

Yet within a year he had produced something very different again—*Faust,* a large-scale opera, adapted from Goethe, serious, moral in intention, tragic in its implications. Moreover, with *Faust* Gounod reverted once more to the mode of High Romanticism in which *La Nonne sanglante* had been couched, delivering himself not only of another demon opera, but this time of one in which the Devil himself appears and takes a leading role.

Faust, however, is hardly a return to the theatrical shock tactics of the previous generation. Although in many respects Gounod's subject may be seen as quintessentially Romantic, his music sought to achieve quite different ends from those of *La Nonne sanglante,* which were frankly sensationalist in character. What Gounod was after was not a return to the easy thrills of the past. In *Faust* he brought something new to French music: a sweet and earnest sublimity, exciting but, even more important, elevating. This he achieved by effecting a fusion between Gallic grace and Germanic seriousness.

As an artist Gounod was decisively affected by his youthful studies in Rome. Having in 1839, at the age of twenty-one, been awarded the annual prize given to a pupil at the Conservatoire in Paris for the composition of a cantata for voice and orchestra, he was able to spend nearly two and a half years at the expense of the French government in the Académie de France in Rome. At that time the Académie, housed in the Villa Medici, was headed by the great painter Jean Auguste Dominique Ingres, who had a passion for music in general and for German music in particular. For Gounod, trained according to Italianate principles at the Conservatoire, then led by the distinguished Florentine composer Luigi Cherubini, Ingres's enthusiasm for German music came as a salutary shock.

An even more potent influence was Fanny Hensel, the talented sister of Mendelssohn, then living in Rome with her painter husband, Wilhelm Hensel. It was Fanny who gave Gounod his first systematic introduction to German culture—to the writings of Goethe and, especially, to the music of Bach and Beethoven. After leaving the Villa Medici, Gounod traveled to Vienna, where he settled down for a year, immersing himself in the musical life of the city and writing a requiem. After Vienna and then Berlin, he went to Leipzig, where he visited, and was encouraged in his work by, Mendelssohn. By the time Gounod returned to Paris in 1845, his tastes were set. As Fanny had written not long after first meeting him in Rome: "The revelation of German music to him is like a bomb falling on a house, and it is possible that it may cause him serious damage."

When, nearly twenty years later, that revelation made itself fully evident for the first time in his operatic music, the results were by no means instantly appreciated. The critical reception of the first performance of *Faust,* given at the Théâtre Lyrique in Paris on March 19, 1859, was anything but encouraging. Only Berlioz—out of step with his contemporaries, as was so often the case—praised the work wholeheartedly, calling it "the greatest opera on the Faust legend." By one major critic, Pietro Scudo of the *Revue des deux mondes,* Gounod was denied the gift of melody, no doubt because of the greater importance accorded to the orchestra than was usual in contemporary French opera and also, no doubt, because of the work's equally unusual harmonic daring.

It was for the latter reason that accusations of "Wagnerism" were leveled against him both in France and in England, in which latter country the anonymous critic of the *Illustrated London News* accused him of being to all intents and purposes a German composer. Like Wagner, the writer continued, Gounod "sets at nought the time-honoured laws of musical art and indulges in (so-called) harmony and modulations which would drive Mozart or Cimarosa crazy, and are no small trial to the nerves, even at the present day." The London *Times* called the introduction "too vague, and in its harmony too much after the manner of Wagner to please the lovers of unadulterated music," and referred to the modulation at the end of the Garden Scene as "a piece of unmitigated Wagnerism." Frederick Gye, the manager of Covent Garden and the head of the Royal Italian Opera, turned the work down decisively, finding nothing in it to enjoy but the Soldiers' Chorus.

But the public thought otherwise. In Paris the opera achieved fifty-seven performances by the end of the year. In the French provinces during the following spring it was a great box-office success. So it was in Germany a year later. When in 1863, through the enterprise of Colonel Henry Mapleson, *Faust* finally arrived in London at Her Majesty's Theater, it enjoyed so decided a triumph with the public that Gye, realizing his mistake, immediately staged a rival production at Covent Garden—in Italian as *Faust e Margherita*—where the opera was subsequently featured every season for the next forty-eight years. In the same year as its English debut, *Faust* arrived in the United States at New York's Academy of Music, also in Italian, and quickly established itself as a favorite with audiences. It was, of course, the work with which the old Met opened its doors for the very first time in October, 1883, and by the nineties, when the company finally reverted to the original French and could muster casts led by Nellie Melba (or Emma Eames), Jean and Edouard de Reszke, Jean Lassalle, and Pol Plançon, it was performed so often and with so much popular approbation that W.J. Henderson, then chief music critic of the *New York Times,* in a celebrated bon mot, called the Met the "Faust-spielhaus." By 1890 George Bernard Shaw was jocularly complaining in the London *World:* "Something had better be done. . . . I have heard Gounod's *Faust* not less than ninety times within the last ten or fifteen years and I have had enough of it."

The reasons for the opera's immense popularity in the latter part of the nineteenth century are, I think, easy to understand. Initially the work was not a Grand Opera but an Opéra Comique—that is, like the ur-*Carmen,* it originally consisted of separate numbers linked by spoken dialogue—and within the first year of its life was given musical continuity by the composer. Other amplifications followed in due course. In 1864 Gounod added Valentine's aria "Even Bravest Heart" (later translated as "Avant de quitter ces lieux") for Sir Charles Santley, when the great British baritone appeared in an English-language version of *Faust* at Her Majesty's. Five years later, when *Faust* was seen for the first time at the Paris Opéra, Gounod added an extended ballet sequence to Act V, soon among the best-known sections of the score.

By the 1890s *Faust,* thus transformed, had come to seem to many music lovers the quintessential Grand Opera, a stirring large-scale spectacle, full of action and strong situations, a brilliant mixture of the exciting and the inspiring. For one thing, the well-beloved features of Romantic diabolism were still very much in evidence: the initial appearance through a trap door, accompanied by a flash of crimson light, of the Arch Fiend, dressed in red silk tights and with green spangles on his eyelids; his ability to conjure up visions out of thin air (as he does of Marguerite in Act I); his magical powers, against which ordinary mortals are helpless (until, that is, they confront him with the sign of the cross).

All this was the very stuff of early-nineteenth-century popular theater as well as of High Romantic opera. Yet whereas in *La Nonne sanglante* Gounod made the mistake of simply trying to extend the life of theatrical diabolism into an age that no longer needed to be filled so unambiguously with dread of the unknown, in *Faust* he added a new and striking element: the piety of pathos. Ordinary piety, it is true, had always been a component of High Romantic opera. In *Der Freischütz* Agathe's first solo passage (in Act II) is a prayer, and in the opera's finale only the intercession of a holy hermit guarantees a happy outcome for the young lovers, who are assured of conjugal bliss after a year's probation. What is different about *Faust* is the unequal way in which sinfulness is punished, the element of what one might call female victimization.

In *Faust* Marguerite is first seen on her way home from church, but for her there is no happy ending. Not, at any rate, on earth. Her reward, as we are shown on stage, is among the angels above. At the shining vision of Marguerite's heavenward progression Méphistophélès is sorely discomforted. Curiously enough, the reactions of Faust himself—after all, the opera's nominal protagonist—are left somewhat vague, especially in matters of detail. Yet what ultimately becomes of him is unambiguously clear. Last observed on his knees while watching the ascension of Marguerite, he is plainly absolved by her sanctity from complicity in the crime he has undoubtedly committed against her and thus is freed from the clutches of the Devil.

Like Verdi's Violetta of six years earlier, Marguerite is the sacrificial victim in a relationship unblessed by society. Unlike Violetta, however, Marguerite is endowed with redemptive powers. Her death, we are forced to conclude, redresses the balance of the world's morality. In *Traviata* Alfredo is left to mourn the loss of his beloved, whose untimely passing benefits none but the shadowy guardians of public morality, personified by the stern but understanding figure of Alfredo's father. In *Faust* the hero offers up a silent prayer of thanksgiving for Marguerite's salvation and thus for his own absolution from guilt. The German-speaking countries, which refuse to think of the opera by Gounod's title on the grounds that he made use of only one element in Goethe's complex masterpiece, have a point beyond the one they are ostensibly making: in naming the opera *Margarethe* they are actually drawing attention to its fundamental subject. To chart the treatment of the heroine in the operas of Weber, Verdi, and finally Gounod is to chart the gradual change from High Romanticism to High Victorianism.

To Gounod's vision of woman as simultaneously the pathetic victim of man and his saintly redeemer, the later-nineteenth-century audience responded with, on the whole, unshrinking admiration. Despite what the first critics said, for most people it needed only a hearing or two in order to absorb the work's "Wagnerian" elements and revel in the pleasures of Gounod's melody: the tenor's cavatina, for example, the Act III love duet, the Valentine aria added for Santley, the universally familiar Soldiers' Chorus.

Another feature that ensured the work's speedy acceptance was its elegance, the infusion into a colorfully passionate tale of the grace and charm that are so characteristic a part of nineteenth-century French music and that show themselves most beguilingly perhaps in the Kermesse scene of Act II, when Faust and Marguerite first meet against a background of sinuous waltz music. Méphistophélès, moreover, is not the heavy villain of early-nineteenth-century opera but is an elegant cynic, polished, sophisticated, almost a man about town . Like Edgar in *King Lear,* Gounod and his librettists, Jules Barbier and Michel Carré, obviously believed that "the prince of darkness is a gentleman"—something with which Weber would never have agreed.

No wonder, then, that George Bernard Shaw, while complaining of overexposure to *Faust,* always insisted not only that it was "a true musical creation" but that, above everything else, it was "seraphically soothing."

DONIZETTI'S *La favorita*
by Stephanie von Buchau

The history of *La favorita* started in 1838, when Gaetano Donizetti left Naples in disgust over the censoring of his new opera, *Poliuto.* The kingdom of Ferdinando II was having nothing to do with Christian martyrs, even as far removed as the Roman era. (This same blind censorship was to plague Verdi's *Un ballo in maschera* twenty years later.) Rightly assuming that *Poliuto* would be more welcome to the people from whose literature he had borrowed the story (it is based on Corneille's *Polyeucte*), Donizetti moved his base of operations to Paris.

Lucia di Lammermoor had previously been familiar to the public of the Théâtre-Italien, but the years 1838–40 saw a veritable explosion of Donizettian activity in the French capital. There were performances of *Lucia, L'elisir d'amore, Roberto Devereux, Les Martyrs* (as *Poliuto* was known in its French rewrite). The Bergamese composer began a work for the Opéra *(Le Duc d'Albe)* and wrote an opera specifically for the Opéra-Comique: the lively, Gallic *La Fille du régiment* which received a successful run of fifty performances in little less than a year. He also began a new work in three acts entitled *L'Ange de Nisida* for the Théâtre de la Renaissance, but when negotiations with that house fell through (the management went bankrupt), Donizetti was persuaded to recast the work for the Opéra as *La Favorite* (The King's Mistress).

A work for the Opéra had to conform to several unwritten rules (which we are familiar with from the difficulties Wagner and Verdi had with that house over *Tannhäuser* and *Les Vêpres siciliennes*). The opera should be in at least four acts (preferably five)—presumably to allow the ladies more intermissions in which to show off their *grandes toilettes*. There had to be a ballet in the second act (to give the fashionably late Jockey Club members an opportunity to ogle their favorite opera dancers), and the work should contain several spectacular ensembles for principals and full chorus. Donizetti, who was much less concerned with the sanctity of the artist than were his later colleagues (though that made him no less concerned with the sanctity of *art,* if you follow the distinction), agreed to the conditions and set about rapidly transforming *L'Ange de Nisida* with the help of Alphonse Royer and Gustave Vaëz, who had translated *Lucia* into French. (Eugène Scribe is sometimes given credit for the text of the fourth act.)

Many stories are extant about Donizetti's speed of composition and his casual attitude toward inspiration, but none is so apocryphal as the legend that he wrote *La Favorite*'s superb fourth act in five hours. After dining with friends, he supposedly sent them on to the theater while he remained behind to rapidly sketch the music to the opera's most tightly constructed act; he was found comfortably snoring on a couch by the fire when his friends returned. Herbert Weinstock, whose Donizetti is the standard, exhaustive work on the composer in English, scorns the legend; and William Ashbrook, also author of a biography, says that internal evidence from autograph scores proves that *La Favorite*'s fourth act is a direct adaptation from *L'Ange de Nisida*. In any case, speed of composition is not as important as the excellence of the final results, even if the composer did borrow one aria, the tenor's "Ange si pur" ("Spirto gentil"), from the now discarded *Le Duc d'Albe*.

As we have said, *La Favorite* was not an outstanding success at its premiere (December 2, 1840), although the mezzo Rosine Stoltz (mistress of the Opéra's director) was applauded for her work in the title role. But within weeks the work caught on and by the turn of the century had received more than 650 performances at the Opéra alone. In 1841 it was heard in Brussels, Germany, the Hague, and Vienna. In 1843 it was sung in French in New Orleans and in English at the Drury Lane Theatre in London. It reached New York, also in French, in 1845. The first Italian-language performance was in Padua in 1842 with a libretto translated by Francesco Jannetti, and it is the Italian version which holds the stage today.

The difficulty of performing opera in a language that is neither its original nor native to the audience is obvious. And the problem of translating *anything* from French without destroying the work's musical character seems insurmountable. Witness how the brittle, tart *La Fille du régiment* is distinguished from the softer, more sentimental *La figlia del reggimento*. But for some reason, of all the French operas commonly translated into Italian *(Les Huguenots, Don Carlos, Guillaume Tell, La Fille du régiment)*, *La Favorite* suffers the least stylistic damage. This is probably, despite Donizetti's adherence to the edicts of the Opéra, because the intimate story, with its Spanish background, falls more into the class of Italian melodrama than that of French grand opera.

La favorita (as we shall henceforward call it) is not like anything else Donizetti ever wrote. Harmonically the music is not particularly pioneering, but in its dramatic tone and its lack of extraneous coloratura display, it is possible to see ahead to later Verdian works, especially those with Spanish subjects. With its formal arias, its romanzas for the tenor, its short recitatives, the constantly flowing arioso that joins them, and the two grand ensembles that end the middle acts, much of *La favorita* represents Donizetti in his most assured dramatic vein—a summation of his efforts as a serious composer. *La favorita* is, in fact, the last familiar opera the composer produced, with the exception of that sweet-and-sour little comic masterpiece *Don Pasquale* (1842). By 1840 Donizetti was already suffering from the syphilitic infection that was to end his active career, though he hung on in paretic imbecility until 1848.

The overture, which begins quietly, explores first in the woodwinds and then with full orchestral panoply a stirring melody that Donizetti prodigally never refers to again. The first scene opens in the monastery of Saint James of Compostela. Almost immediately, as in Verdi's *Aïda,* the tenor sings a difficult romanza, "Una vergine, un angel di Dio," in which he describes how he first saw a beautiful woman, whom he now loves, praying next to him in church.

The second scene of the first act takes place on the island of St. Leon where Leonora di Gusman, mistress of King Alfonso XI of Castile, is installed in splendid isolation. After her companion Ines finishes a conventional two-part aria, Leonora has Fernando brought in blindfolded. They sing their first duet, "Ah, mio bene," which advances the plot. (He asks her to marry him; she refuses, without revealing her reasons.) The words "Fia vero? lasciarti?" introduce an affecting lyric theme, and after a unison passage, the duet ends the act with the first of Leonora's optional high notes. (Sometimes this role is sung by a soprano, but the meaty part of it lies best for a mezzo though she should have a high extension to bring the role brilliance. Noted Leonoras of the past have included, besides Rosine Stoltz, the premiere executrix, Giulia Grisi, who was a soprano, Ebe Stignani, Fedora Barbieri, and Giulietta Simionato.)

The second act discovers King Alfonso in the garden of the Alcazar, musing on how he will take his mistress, Leonora, as his queen, "defying Hell itself." (Historically, he was married to Marie of Portgual.) His formal aria, "Vien, Leonora," with its flute interpolations, consists of a languorous cantabile section followed by a showy cabaletta, "De' nemici tuoi lo sdegno." Leonora enters and the arioso-dialogue style which is so prevalent in this opera asserts itself as they argue. She has one line, "È la bella del re!" which particularly displays the mezzo's sultry lower register. At the words "Ah! l'alto ardor," they sing together in thirds and sixths.

At this point, Donizetti inserted the ballet required by the Opéra. It consists of four *entrées* for soloists and small corps. After the ballet, the plot advances again when the monk Baldassarre curses the King for desiring to set aside his lawful Queen and make a harlot his wife. The ensuing ensemble is remarkable, not in the later Verdian style of individual characterization, but because of its effective part-writing for voices and because it is topped with a memorable tune first voiced by Baldassarre. It falls into three sections, each divided by the monk's mounting anger and curses. (There is some confusion in Italian librettos which refer to Baldassarre as the father of Fernando and Alfonso's queen. It is common for a monk and novice to call each other "padre" and "figlio," but when both refer to a "suora" [sister], the audience becomes thoroughly bewildered. The confusion arose from the grafting of *L'Ange de Nisida,* which did contain a family relationship, to *La favorita*'s Italian version. There are no such references in *La Favorite*'s French text.)

If the first two acts are straightforward in their construction, the third resembles the bustle of O'Hare Airport at Thanksgiving. Fernando, Leonora, and the King make no fewer than five entrances and exits each in the course of the act. After the King has ironically given Fernando and Leonora permission to marry, she is left alone for her big aria, which leads from the larghetto "O mio Fernando!" to its brisk cabaletta, "Scritto è in cielo." This music, with its dramatic emphasis on the middle part of the mezzo's voice, its legato demands, and the vigorous declamation of its conclusion, helps explain *La favorita*'s relative neglect. Only once in a generation does a singer come along who can do justice to its vocal and histrionic demands.

Up to this point in the opera, Fernando has been little more than a cipher, a love-struck novice, putty in Leonora's hands, grateful and subservient to the King. Now his character exerts itself as Gasparo and the courtiers mock him for his marriage to Alfonso's mistress. He tries to shake hands, only to be told that he has forfeited his honor. The confused Fernando is finally told the truth by Baldassarre (who has a habit of showing up in time to further the plot), and the heretofore sanguine young man turns into a paragon of outraged manhood. The historical Spanish preoccupations with honor, virginity, and adultery are too well known to require further comment; Fernando's remorse and rage at Leonora and the King's deception is perfectly in character.

He insults Alfonso who, remarkably, sympathizes with the angry young man. Leonora is bewildered, thinking (until Gasparo enlightens her) that Ines had told Fernando the truth before the wedding. Fernando flings back the King's recently conferred orders and denies his titles of Count of Zamora and Marquis of Montreal. He even snaps his sword in half and throws the pieces at the King's feet. The first part of this fine ensemble, led by Alfonso, is in a style similar to the sextet in *Lucia,* though the melody is not so distinguished, while the fast section that concludes the act is a driving march tune.

After the court spectacles of the two middle acts, the famous fourth act reverts to the quiet intimacy of the first scene. Back at the monastery, Baldassarre and the monks are praying for the departed soul of the rightful Queen. Fernando sings the opera's most celebrated number, "Spirto gentil" (the "Ange si pur" which was borrowed from the unfinished *Le Duc d'Albe*). "Spirto gentil" has been a favorite of tenors for over a century, though few of them sing it well. Despite its deceptively simple melody, it requires all the technique for which bel canto is famous: *messa di voce* (the ability to swell and diminish the tone on a single note), endless breath control, seamless legato, and a voice strong enough to cope with the aria's *tessitura,* which lies dangerously on the *passaggio,* the break between the head and chest registers.

Leonora, suffering from exhaustion and illness, enters and sings a long recitative-cum-arioso. With Fernando and the monks singing off-stage, this piece looks ahead to the "Miserere" in Verdi's *Il trovatore.* The lovers are reunited for the last time in a long and stirring duet which begins with supplication on her part and disdain on his. Leonora exerts her power until the tenor cannot resist. Fernando at last cries "Io t'amo!" and launches into his big tune, "Vieni, ah, vien!" urging her to flee with him. She sings a verse, and their voices join in unison. But it is too late; she is dying. Thanking him for his forgiveness, Leonora whispers "Addio, addio" and dies, leaving the distraught Fernando to cry "È spenta!" In older versions of the opera, Baldassarre comes back to utter a few platitudes, but today, sensibly, the tenor is given his optional climactic high C with which to bring down the curtain.

BEETHOVEN'S *Fidelio*
by Peter P. Jacobi

Leonard Bernstein in his *The Joy of Music* provides a playlet—both witty and perceptive—called "Bull Session in the Rockies." In it he converses with a man of the heart, of passion, someone labeled Lyric Poet. The fellow looks at the mountains and exclaims, "These hills are pure Beethoven."

Why does every hill remind every writer of music's great Ludwig? Well, says the poet: "These mountains have a quality of majesty and craggy exaltation that suggests Beethoven to me."

You might read Bernstein's imaginative excursion yourself; it's enjoyable. In compression, here's what happens. Bernstein plays devil's advocate as Lyric Poet exudes and exults about Beethoven's melody, harmony, rhythm, counterpoint, orchestration. For instance, Lyric Poet calls Beethoven the harmonist "the radical, the arch-revolutionary." To which Lenny responds: "And yet the pages of the Fifth Symphony stream on with the old three chords chasing each other about until you wonder what more he can possibly wring out of them."

Eventually, rather quickly, Lyric Poet becomes enraged: "There he lies, a mediocre melodist, a homely harmonist, an itinerant riveter of a rhythmist, an ordinary orchestrator, a commonplace contrapuntist. It is impossible. . . ."

At that point Bernstein agrees. And he admits that he "worships the name." Why? Because Ludwig van Beethoven had *"the inexplicable ability to know what the next note has to be.* Beethoven had this gift in a degree that leaves them all panting in the rear guard. When he did it . . . he produced an entity that always seems to me to have previously been written in Heaven, and then merely dictated to him."

One need only take Florestan's heart-rending aria at the opening of Act II in *Fidelio.* It is music so appropriate for the moment, so exemplary of Bernstein's notion. The notes flow forth just exactly as they should to form a melody that evokes a tense blend of love and grief. And when, after cursing the darkness and silence that envelop him, Florestan holds thoughts of his Leonore to his heart ("I see, like an angel in golden mists coming to my side to console me, an angel so like Leonore, my wife, leading me to freedom in heavenly realms"), the melody seems to float, even to fly, along with his spirit. It is a glorious moment and, fortunately, just one of many that prove the Bernstein point and that lift the spirits of those of us who experience *Fidelio.*

As all the pundits have pointed out repetitively, it is not a perfect opera, or near it. There are jump cuts, missing steps, contradictions. My reaction to all that is, so what?

The opera is very special. And when one considers that it is Beethoven's first and only opera, then that which is special becomes miraculous. Never mind that the experts keep wanting to point out that *Fidelio* is an uncomfortable amalgam of operatic styles. Never mind that basically the story—even in its time a cliché melodrama of rescue and escape—is not worthy of its music. To Beethoven it obviously was considerably more.

He worked hard enough on it, leaving three versions which appeared between 1805 and 1814. Three versions and four overtures: the Leonore Number 1, which he prepared for a private performance just before the 1805 premiere; the Leonore Number 2, used at that premiere; the mighty Leonore Number 3, composed for an 1806 production (it now appears usually as the bridge between the scenes of Act II), and the *Fidelio* overture, written for the 1814 revision and now used with regularity as the curtain raiser. Next time conversation lulls at a cocktail party, just pose the question, "Hey, friends, what opera has four overtures?" Think of the sensation you'll create.

Fidelio may be Beethoven's one and only, but he wasn't immune to opera for the rest of his creative years. His father had been a singer. Young Ludwig played harpsichord in the theater in Bonn where his father sang. And as early as 1803 he was commissioned by Emanuel Schikaneder, the word smith for Mozart's *Magic Flute* who ran a thriving theater in Vienna, to write an opera. The commissioner even offered the commissionee room to work in the theater. But Beethoven turned down the space for being excessively noisy. He also turned down the libretto and gave up on the project. It was then he turned to *Fidelio,* which he first called *Leonore,* which was based on a libretto by a French poet named J.N. Bouilly, which was based on a historic incident during the Reign of Terror. And after Beethoven completed the first version, despite its lack of success and its withdrawal, he urged the Imperial Opera in Vienna to give him a contract to write an opera a year. That, obviously, never happened. And neither did such contemplated projects as stage works based on *Macbeth* and *Faust, Return of Ulysses,* and Scott's *Kenilworth.* Neither did something called *The Arrival of the Pennsylvanians in America.* Instead we gained more symphonies and late quartets, thank goodness.

The *Fidelio* story was in the atmosphere at the time. While Beethoven was working on it, so were two other composers—Simone Mayr and Ferdinando Paër. Beethoven was being practical. He had rejected a libretto from the German poet Johann Rocklitz, explaining in a letter to him: "If your opera had not been an opera with magic, I would have snatched it with both hands. But the public here is now as prejudiced against a subject of that kind as it formerly looked for and desired it." So he seems to have had practicality in mind.

The premiere, at the Theater an der Wien on November 20, 1805, was not successful. Length was a reason. Cast may have been a contributing factor. But the following year Beethoven began to revise and to shorten.

Josef Roeckel, the tenor to whom the part of Florestan would be entrusted in the 1806 reintroduction of the work, tells in his memoirs of efforts made by the composer's friends to force changes in the opera. He recreates an extended evening when friends listened to the opera and counseled a very sensitive composer to cut, cut, cut.

> The two initial acts, in which I played no part, were sung from the first to the last note. Eyes sought the clock, and Beethoven was importuned to drop some of the long-drawn sections of secondary importance. Yet he defended every measure, and did so with such nobility and artistic dignity that I was ready to kneel at his feet. But when he came to the chief point at issue itself, the notable cuts in the exposition which would make it possible to fuse the two acts into one, he was beside himself, shouted uninterruptedly "Not a note!" and tried to run off with his score. But the Princess [Lichnowsky] laid her hands, folded as though in prayer, on the sacred score entrusted to her, looked up with indescribable mildness at the angry genius and behold—his rage melted at her glance, and he once more resignedly resumed his place.

The session passed midnight, but Beethoven was unbending on the cuts. "Do not insist on them," he would say. "Not a single note must be missing." To which the princess responded, "Beethoven, must your great work then continue to be misunderstood and condemned?" Roeckel continues:

Then suddenly it seemed as though a stronger, more potent spirit entered into this delicate woman. Half kneeling and seizing his knees she cried to him as though inspired: "Beethoven! No—your greatest work, you yourself shall not cease to exist in this way! God who has implanted those tones of purest beauty in your soul forbids it: your mother's spirit, which at this moment pleads and warns you with my voice, forbids it! Beethoven, it must be! Give in! Do so in memory of your mother! Do so for me, who am only your best friend!"

The great man, with his head suggestive of Olympian sublimity, stood for many moments before the worshiper of his Muse, then brushed his long, falling curls from his face, as though an enchanting dream were passing through his soul, and, his glance turned heavenward full of emotion, cried amid sobs: "I will—yes, all—I will do all, for you—for my, your—for my mother's sake!"

The cuts and alterations did not make much difference with the audience. That second version did little better than the first. So Beethoven put the score away for some years, to suffer with deafness and personal loneliness, to write feverishly all sorts of other wonders. But in 1814 three singers from another Viennese theater, the Kärntnertor, asked that they be permitted to revive *Leonore*. Yes, he finally said, but not until he revised some more. And this he did, even calling in another librettist. On May 23 of that year the latest and last version of *Fidelio* was offered (minus the new overture which was late and minus some final changes in a couple of arias that were ready by the time the seventh performance came around). To version three audiences said yes, as they have ever since.

It's always dangerous, or at least presumptuous, to place meanings into works, to suggest motivations that might have guided a composer. And perhaps *Fidelio* was merely a practical solution to a commission offered, the setting to music of a simple story that Beethoven felt would be accepted by the Viennese public. But he worked too hard and too long to improve *Fidelio* for that to be the case. He was too much a man of tension and temperament to write just to write. And he did, after all, express strong feelings about human rights—later in the Ninth Symphony; earlier in the removal of Napoleon's name from the dedication space of his "Eroica." And he did, after all, express such strong longings not only for human companionship but also for female companionship. To his "unknown beloved" he wrote: "What tearful longings after you—you—my life—my all—farewell. Oh, continue to love me, never misjudge the faithful heart of your beloved Ludwig."

Beethoven lacked that tie to a woman. He searched a lifetime for one who would understand enough to put up with his eccentricities, with his gloominess, with his disorderliness, with his clumsiness, with his physical affliction. He searched and did not find.

Is it therefore too far-fetched to believe that in Leonore he placed all that love and all that loyalty which he hoped some woman sometime somewhere would shower on him? Is it too far-fetched to believe that Florestan is Beethoven as he saw himself, chained by circumstances of deafness and personality to an imprisoned life? Is it too far-fetched to think of Beethoven's dreaming—in this story—of his own escape through the devotion of a woman?

How else could he have written Florestan's marvelous aria of seeing an "angel in golden mists" to lift his thoughts to freedom?

And how can one ignore the undercurrent of freedom, which breaks forth first at that moment late in Act I when the prisoners of Pizarro's fortress are given, at Leonore's urgings, time out of their cells to see sunlight, and Beethoven's music soars skyward? The final scene, a foreshadowing of the "Ode to Joy," also holds what must be regarded as a vision of freedom, of brotherhood, of early-nineteenth-century belief that the future can only be good.

Beethoven the romantic infuses each part of his opera with emotion. Even when he adheres to classic form, such as in the canon "Mir Ist So Wunderbar" near the opera's beginning, he is the romantic. The singers hue to rhythm and meter and dignified musical predictability, but—as stage personages—they also express their own feelings.

One should note that his handling of ensembles is exemplary throughout, and highly charged as well. That's a particular strength of the opera. So is—as one might expect—his impassioned use of the orchestra. Not only do the voices break out in emotional fervor, but the Beethoven orchestra underscores each selected atmosphere.

Beethoven is way ahead of the era's other composers (Mozart, of course, was by then long gone) in establishing personality for his characters, not merely in words and stage actions but in the music as well. Leonore and Florestan are the grand characters, the heroic ones; their music reflects that stature, in form and in fervor. The others, like Marzelline and her father, remain in music what they are in mind and manner, much simpler, much smaller-scaled.

The range of Beethoven's music is astounding, from Rocco's little aria about his love of gold to Leonore's "Abscheulicher, wo eilst du hin?" her exclamation of hate and despair about Florestan's imprisonment (or death, since at that moment she does not know her beloved's fate) at the hands of Pizarro, followed by her "Komm, Hoffnung," in which she heatedly asks hope and faith to light her path.

Well, what gives me joy is that as Beethoven would have wanted it in life, so he has it happen on stage. Love triumphs. "Florestan is mine again," sings Leonore later on. And the chorus adds felicitously, "Never can we praise too much the wife who saved her husband's life."

When one gives oneself totally to *Fidelio,* an act made easy by the glorious music, one comes to understand that special quality which Leonard Bernstein wrote of, that "ability to know what the next note has to be." And one also understands Friedrich Nietzsche's observation: "Beethoven's music is music about music."

Absolutely. Definitely. Totally.

JOHANN STRAUSS II'S *Die Fledermaus*

by Stephanie von Buchau

If Richard Wagner and Giuseppe Verdi are the meat and pasta of nineteenth-century musical theater, operetta is the dessert. And like dessert, it is frowned on by musical nutritionists. For an operetta to be successful, it must be commercial and unpretentious. That, as operetta historian Richard Traubner has pointed out, "has always given operetta a bad name in the highest circles of musical art."

Sociologically, the musical calorie police have another reason for pooh-poohing operetta: this art form was never part of the elite, subsidized world of musical theater. It had to earn its own way. Archbishops, counts, and emperors supported Mozart, Beethoven, and Wagner. Shop girls, jockeys, bankers, and ladies of the night supported operetta—because they could go home singing the tunes.

Melody is the chief suspect in the operetta caper. Critics pretend to revile operettas for their inane librettos, their huge helpings of sugary sentiment, their adherence to rigid class structure, and their total unrelation to anything resembling reality. But the real, often unspoken, sticking point is operetta's abundant melody. For some unknown reason, twentieth-century musical aestheticians have decided that memorable, caloric melodies are suitable only for "pop" art; real music must do without.

I point to twentieth-century critics because the nineteenth century's most famous music critic, Eduard Hanslick, thought otherwise. The writer, pilloried by Wagner as "Beckmesser" in *Die Meistersinger,* opened his obituary of Johann Strauss II thus:

> When we buried Johann Strauss I fifty years ago, I remarked in an obituary that Vienna had lost its most talented composer. This was annoying to musicians and laymen alike. They refused to admit that a correct but characterless piece of concert or church music could reveal less talent, less in the way of natural resources, than a melodious, original waltz. I can only repeat this same plaint today, at the grave of the younger Johann Strauss [who died in Vienna on 3 June 1899]. Vienna has lost its most original musical talent.

Johann Strauss II's 1874 operetta, *Die Fledermaus,* holds the opera stage today better than many more "serious" works penned in the nineteenth century. It wasn't always an opera-house work, however; censorship in Vienna kept it out of the Hofoper for many years. Today, houses such as the Metropolitan Opera and London's Covent Garden are subjected to critical scrutiny when they dare mount the piece. There is, however, an excellent practical reason for performing *Fledermaus* in an operatic setting.

Although the "Waltz King" filled his operetta with his trademark, nonvocal dance music, its vocal melodies are equally memorable. (I think we should face the fact that practically all we remember about Offenbach, Strauss, Lehár, and Romberg—to mention just the crème of operetta composers—*is* melody.) These vocal tunes of Strauss, however, are very difficult to sing well, which is why *Fledermaus* in the opera house is preferable to *The Bat* on Broadway. Anyone who has ever squirmed as a summer-stock Rosalinde tried to warble the "Czardas" will instantly see the justice of this decree.

Die Fledermaus did not spring full-blown from Strauss's luxuriant head of hair. (Hanslick mentions the composer's "elastic figure, unbent by the years, with the full head of hair and the blazing eyes.") For a complete, engaging survey of the genre, you must read Traubner's *Operetta: A Theatrical History* (published by Doubleday). Here, the briefest exegesis will serve to place Strauss and his greatest dramatic work in a historical perspective. While operetta is mainly a French invention, it has roots in the comic-opera traditions of four European nations: Italy, England, France, and Germany. By the middle of the nineteenth century, these traditions had coalesced into an independent genre, which then became so codified that within two decades after World War I, it was dead—helped to the grave by jazz, moving pictures, and the social and economic realities that could no longer be squared with the Graustarkian frivolity of the typical operetta plot. (One of the reasons for *Fledermaus*'s continued success is its more-or-less realistic story.)

Italy, which never developed an operetta tradition of its own, contributed the "intermezzo" and "opera buffa" to the fledgling genre. The intermezzo (most celebrated example: Pergolesi's *La serva padrona*) was meant to relieve tedium between the lengthy acts of opera seria. We remember Pergolesi's intermezzo; we don't remember *Il prigionier superbo*, the opera it "interrupted." This is exactly the same dynamic that makes us remember Strauss's comic *Fledermaus* but not his serious *Ritter Pásmán*. The comic (or buffa) opera flourished under Gioacchino Rossini (*Il barbiere di Siviglia, L'italiana in Algeri, La Cenerentola*); the composer's permanent residence in Paris (for which he produced the witty, sophisticated *Le Comte Ory*) had a salutary effect on French light music.

In London, one of the light-music capitals of the world even today (remember Andrew Lloyd Webber?), operetta developed from the ballad opera (most notable example: John Gay's *The Beggar's Opera*) which drove Handel's Italian opera seria from the stage and caused that composer to turn his attention to the English oratorio. (Who says there isn't a divine plan at work in men's lives?) The ballad opera, when allied to the British music-hall tradition and the irresistible temptation to lampoon the hoarier aspects of serious foreign-language opera, led directly to the delightful Savoy operettas of Gilbert and Sullivan (*H.M.S. Pinafore, The Mikado, The Pirates of Penzance*). Unfortunately, these works are sui generis and had virtually no influence on the genre; but the British have an insatiable appetite for operetta and have imported many French and German works—often rewriting them to suit local tastes. *Fledermaus,* for instance, reached London only two years after its Viennese premiere.

In early-eighteenth-century France, a satirical form of music theater, called vaudeville, began to include spoken dialogues between its scabrous sung ditties, and thus opéra comique was born. (Technically, the musical play on which *Die Fledermaus* is based—Meilhac and Halévy's *Le Réveillon*—is a vaudeville, though an extremely sophisticated example of a once crude genre.) Opéra comique has many definitions, but it is a mistake to translate it literally as "comic opera." Subject matter alone does not define opéra comique. For example, Bizet's *Carmen* was originally an opéra comique, despite its sordid subject and tragic ending, because the music was interrupted by *spoken* dialogues. The dialogues were later replaced to make *Carmen* more "operatic."

Today, the best known of the *comic* opéras comiques are Daniel Auber's *Fra Diavolo* and Adolphe Charles Adam's *Le Postillon de Longjumeau*. Both were influenced by *Le Comte Ory,* produced in Paris in 1828. Encouraged by the mid-century economic and political situation—Napoleon III had established the luxurious Second Empire in 1852—a German-born cellist from the Opéra-Comique orchestra, named Jacques Offenbach, presented a series of comic-opera performances in Paris, first as an impresario to other composers, and then as producer of his own work. Offenbach's operettas—especially his masterworks, *Orpheus in the Underworld, La Périchole, La Belle Hélène,* and *La Grande Duchesse de Gérolstein* —combined the barest of plots (*Périchole* is the only one of the "big four" that has characters and situations you can actually care about) with ribald political satire (all of which goes over our heads today) and enchanting melodies, waltzes, and romances.

In no time, Offenbach was a worldwide household name. No place welcomed him more than the morally permissive, pleasure-seeking Austrian capital. By mid century, the Viennese popular theaters were looking directly to Paris for new ideas. They often mounted productions of Offenbach's early works without his permission. However, in 1861 he directed three of his operettas at the Karltheater and so overwhelmed the public (and critic Hanslick) that he was invited back later that same year with his own Bouffes-Parisiens company. A season of twenty performances consolidated his reputation—and coincidentally, made vast sums of money for the composer and the theater.

Thereafter he visited Vienna regularly. He was asked to write dance music, but he was reluctant to compete with Strauss, who at that time was the most established composer of waltzes the world had ever known. However, in 1863, both Offenbach and Strauss wrote waltzes for the carnival celebrations of the Concordia journalists' club. At that time, it is suggested that Offenbach urged Strauss to write an operetta.

Despite the popularity of the French form, Germanic music was not a fertile ground in which comic opera could grow. The operetta tradition of the German-speaking countries was confined to anonymous Singspiels and galumphing nationalistic works such as Gustav Albert Lortzing's *Zar und Zimmermann* and Carl Otto Ehrenfried Nicolai's *The Merry Wives of Windsor.* In Austria, a leap of faith was required to span the enormous gap between the comic operas of Mozart (technically Italian, but influenced by Viennese wit and sophistication) and the genuine operettas of Franz von Suppé and Strauss.

Yet Vienna had the bridge to that gap. It was the waltz, a dance form that grew "like Topsy" out of the late-eighteenth-century peasant dance, the *laendler.* (This form has more importance than just as a forerunner of the waltz; the scherzos of most of Gustav Mahler's symphonies are based on the *laendler.*) The waltz was a precursor of more than just music in 3/4 time; as the first dance in which the participants faced each other and the man held the woman closely, it was a precursor of a sexual revolution. This is not to say that eighteenth-century Vienna wasn't a ribald place, but the waltz caused the revolution to invade bourgeois society.

Johann Strauss II may have been the "Waltz King," but his father founded the Strauss Waltz Dynasty, which eventually consisted of Johann and his two brothers, Eduard and Joseph, and Johann III, son of Eduard, and Eduard II, nephew of Johann III. Johann I (1804–49) was a violinist who played in a quartet conducted by Joseph Lanner. In 1826, Johann I began to compose his own waltzes and formed a fourteen-piece orchestra that captivated the public in such Viennese suburbs as Rossau and Leopoldstadt. Chopin, Wagner, and Hanslick were all fans. Johann I became responsible for the music at court fêtes and dances and eventually toured Germany and England. He composed over 152 waltzes, but his best known composition is the "Radetzky March."

Johann I did not wish his sons to follow him in the music business, so Johann II (1825–99) became a bank clerk, and Joseph (1827–70) was an architect, while both secretly studied music. In 1844, Johann II formed his own orchestra of twenty-four and conducted waltzes by his father and by himself. When Johann I died, Johann II amalgamated the two orchestras and toured Austria, Poland, and Germany. For ten years he directed the summer concerts in St. Petersburg and led the Austrian court balls between 1863 and 1872. He visited Paris and London (1867) and the United States (1872) to great acclaim.

Johann II composed nearly four hundred waltzes, of which the most famous are probably "The Blue Danube," "Wine, Women and Song," "Emperor Waltz," "Roses from the South," "Tales of the Vienna Woods," and "Vienna Blood." Hanslick put his finger right on it when he wrote:

> One has only to sound the first three notes of the D-major triad [that opens "The Blue Danube"] and all cheeks instantly glow with enthusiasm. "The Blue Danube" not only enjoys unexampled popularity, it has also achieved a unique significance: that of a symbol for everything that is beautiful and pleasant and gay in Vienna. It is a kind of patriotic folk song without words.

Did Johann Strauss II, at the height of his wealth and celebrity, suddenly decide to write operettas because of a challenge from Offenbach? Traubner calls Strauss "an extremely self-conscious man, with 'the most musical brain in Europe,' according to Richard Wagner." Strauss had his personal eccentricities and own brand of egomania, yet Hanslick called him a "thoroughly lovable, forthright and well-disposed man." We probably will never know what the final goad was, but the fact remains that Johann Strauss II was forty-four years old before he began work on his first operetta, *The Merry Wives of Vienna*.

Despite the lack of a genuine Germanic operetta tradition, it is not as if Strauss had no Austrian models before Offenbach blew in from Paris. Strauss's predecessor (though they were almost contemporaries) in the field was Franz von Suppé, sometimes called "the father of Viennese operetta" (Traubner). Suppé is known today for the overtures to his operettas, rather than for the full works. His most enduring operetta is the one-act Pygmalion legend, *The Beautiful Galatea* (1865). But Suppé was busy all the time creating forty operettas and nearly two hundred other musical stage works—vaudevilles, farces, parodies, burlesques—many of them political. Traubner suggests that though Suppé began writing for the stage long before Strauss II did—Suppé's first farce was performed in 1841, when Johann was still a bank clerk—he wasn't able to surpass the Waltz King once Strauss had turned his attention to the genre. Suppé's most popular three-act works were *Fatinitza* (1876) and *Boccaccio* (1879), both composed after *Fledermaus*.

Strauss was no shoo-in, either. *The Merry Wives of Vienna* never did make it to the stage. His next try was *Indigo and the Forty Thieves* (1871), which despite a poor libretto was a popular success. Hanslick complained: "The transition to dramatic composition was not easy [for Strauss]. The strict waltz and polka rhythms had become too much a part of him. *Indigo* was not wanting in melodies, but it was plain that they were not born of the text."

During rehearsals for *Indigo,* Strauss apparently was already at work on his next operetta, *Carnival in Rome*. Based on Victorien Sardou's play *Piccolino,* it had already been made into two operettas, one with a score by Ernest Guiraud, the man who took the "comique" out of *Carmen* by composing recitatives to replace the spoken dialogue. *Carnival in Rome* was another heady success, opening during the 1873 Vienna Exhibition, but the Vienna stock-market crash in May curtailed most theatrical activity.

The 1872 vaudeville *Le Réveillon,* which we mentioned earlier, had been based by its French librettists on a Berlin farce by Roderich Benedix called *The Prison* (circa 1840). A *réveillon* is a Christmas or New Year's Eve supper party, and it forms the basis for Orlovsky's celebration in Act II, while the prison motif afforded Act III the now-famous drunken-jailer scene. *Die Fledermaus* corresponds to the original in many aspects; only the names—including the title—were changed. (It is interesting to note that most operettas got new names when they were translated to foreign shores; *Fledermaus* is seldom translated into English, however, possibly because *The Bat* has unpleasant connotations of vampirism in our culture. When the work appeared on Broadway many years ago, it was called *Rosalinda*.)

The publisher/agent Gustav Lewy thought Karl Haffner's German adaptation of *Le Réveillon* would make a good subject for Strauss's next stage work. The composer/conductor/librettist Richard Genée was signed to prepare a text at one hundred gulden an act. (He graciously gave Haffner credit.) Tradition holds that Strauss completed the score during six weeks' seclusion at his Hietzing villa. The premiere was held on Easter Sunday, 1874. Critical reaction was not warm, but the show ran for sixty-eight performances. Two months later it scored a bigger success in Berlin; that November, it was performed in German at a small New York theater.

It wasn't until the mid 1880s, though, that *Fledermaus* began to exert its spell, eventually becoming what Traubner calls, "*the* Viennese Golden Age operetta *in excelsis*." He explains the work's difficulty in gaining a foothold thus: "Unlike other Viennese and French operettas, it was in modern dress, which presumably made audiences, expecting costumed frivolity, a bit discomfited." (This odd reaction toward realism also led to the initial failure of Verdi's *La traviata*.)

Now, of course, Strauss's modern dress *is* costume; still, the plot to *Fledermaus,* while complicated and depending on improbable disguises, is very homey *(gemütlich)* and bourgeois. The only nobleman in the plot is the bored Orlovsky, and he's a caricature. Rosalinde and Eisenstein could be any well-to-do thirty-something couple. Adele and her sister Ida are exactly the kind of demimondaines who entertained men like Eisenstein, Falke, and Frank at parties like Orlovsky's.

While it is true that Strauss's second-best operetta score, *The Gypsy Baron* (1885), is virtually unproducible today because of its "nobleman-in-disguise" plot, nobody but a naif really thinks that *Die Fledermaus* survives because of its "realism." It survives—no, it *thrives*—because of its irrepressible music. With that immortal waltz and its fizzy, farcical, damn-the-consequences hedonism, *Die Fledermaus* remains the ne plus ultra of musical desserts.

WAGNER'S *The Flying Dutchman*
by Stephanie von Buchau

Legend has it that Richard Wagner conceived the idea for his fourth opera, *Der fliegende Holländer,* when he fled Riga and embarked on a sea journey from Pillau to London. The legend is wrong, of course, for there is ample evidence that Wagner had been considering a work based on the tale of the Flying Dutchman before he took the fateful sea voyage, but aspects of that trip were such that he may well have been artistically stimulated. We certainly hear the sea in the opera's overture and in its sailors' choruses.

Wagner had accepted a post as conductor at the German theater in Riga, the capital of Livonia (Latvia), as a method for mending his failing marriage to the actress Minna Planer. He was as yet an unknown composer with two operas, *Die Feen* and *Das Liebesverbot,* under his belt, who thought a more settled middle-class existence would pacify his embittered wife. He worked on his third opera, *Rienzi,* while situated in Riga, but his quarrelsome nature and financial chicanery soon made it imperative for him to leave the Baltic city. About the only lasting good to come out of the Riga experiment was Wagner's impression of the city's theater—the auditorium was very dark, the orchestra pit was low, and the orchestra seats were sharply raked upwards—all features later incorporated in the Festspielhaus at Bayreuth.

Because Wagner's debts were so pressing, he and Minna, with their New-foundland dog, Robber, were forced to sneak away from Riga and cross the Russo-Prussian border in the dead of night, within sight of sentries who had orders to shoot to kill. After an exhausting trip, during which their conveyance overturned and Minna may have suffered a miscarriage, the Wagners boarded a small cargo ship, *Thetis,* for what would normally be a one-week voyage to London. Instead, the trip took over three and one-half weeks, involving storms and hardships so violent that Wagner never went anywhere by sea again.

During the stormy journey, *Thetis* was forced to run to shelter in a Nor-wegian fjord, the bay at Sandvigen. Wagner was ecstatic over the scenic splendors of the fjord: "An inexpressible happiness seized hold of me when the echo of the immense granite walls threw back the shout of the crew as they dropped anchor. . . . The short rhythmic cries settled in me like a mightily comforting portent and soon formed into the theme of the sailors' song in my *Fliegende Holländer,* the idea of which I already carried with me." He also literally incorporated the fjord, for when Daland runs his ship into shelter from a storm, he exclaims: "Sandwike it is, well I know this bay!"

Wagner, wife, and dog finally landed in London, crossed the channel by steamer, and went directly to visit Giacomo Meyerbeer, the composer of *Robert le Diable* and *Les Huguenots.* This powerful and popular musician listened patiently to lengthy excerpts from *Rienzi* and wrote Wagner letters of recommendation. Later, he even tried to influence the intendant of the Berlin Court Opera on behalf of the now-finished *Fliegende Holländer.* Wagner, as usual, repaid Meyerbeer by describing him as a "pickpocket" in musical articles written from Paris under a pseudonym.

While in Paris, the Wagners nearly starved. Richard later referred to this time as "the worst of my life." At one point he was even thrown into debtor's prison. Their only pleasure was visits from friends in the artistic community. Wagner was introduced to Heinrich Heine and Franz Liszt. He continually sought advice from Meyerbeer on how to crack the indifference of the Paris Opéra, which he wanted to perform *Rienzi.* He published short articles on the city's musical life, and he attended concerts. He admired Hector Berlioz (the *Fan-tastique* was called "marvelous"), and a performance of Beethoven's *Ninth Symphony* at a Conservatoire rehearsal in 1839 so moved him that his musical uncertainty "fell away as it were into a deep abyss of shame and remorse." He immediately wrote the first movement of a projected *Faust* symphony.

Perhaps the most interesting product of Wagner's Paris years, besides the *Holländer* score, was a short story titled "An End in Paris," which as biographer Curt von Westernhagen has put it, was written "in revenge for all the shame he had endured." Heine exclaimed in admiration, "Hoffmann could never have written anything like this!" The story tells of the composer R, who falls victim to poverty, disillusionment, and consumption. Wagner sketches the painful struggle of a young artist to gain recognition in a Philistinistic society. The story ends with the credo, "I believe in God, Mozart, and Beethoven."

In 1841, living in abject penury in Meudon, outside Paris, Wagner began work on the prose sketch of *Der fliegende Holländer,* which he later sold, for 500 francs, to the Paris Opéra so that they could farm it out to one of their hack composers to be produced as *Le Vaisseau fantôme.* (This 1842 opera by Pierre-Louis Dietsch was an artistic failure, though it ran for ten performances.) Originally, *Holländer* had been proposed by Wagner to the Paris Opéra as a one-act curtain raiser for a ballet performance. Although the composer eventually cast the work in three acts, it was meant to be performed without break, a practice that has gained currency in recent years. It is no longer than *Das Rheingold,* and it gains immeasurably in sweep and conviction from being heard as the composer intended.

The original draft of *Holländer* took Wagner ten days in May, and when his piano arrived at Meudon in July, he apprehensively set to work on the score. Wagner reports in *Mein Leben* that the previous winter he had already composed "some of the lyric parts . . . the ballad of Senta, the song of the Norwegian sailors and the 'spectre song' of the Dutchman's crew. . . . When my piano arrived, I did not dare touch it for a whole day. I was terribly afraid lest I should discover my inspiration had left me." It hadn't. He sat down the next day, began composing in earnest, and in seven weeks the score of *Holländer,* except for the orchestration, was completed. At the end of the overture, written last, is the inscription: "Paris, 5 November 1841. Per aspera ad astra" (Through hardships to the stars).

The origins of the Flying Dutchman legend are unknown. Ernest Newman, in his informative *Wagner Nights,* lists the following antecedents to Wagner's opera. In 1821 there appeared in *Blackwood's Magazine* an anonymous short story entitled *Vanderdecken's Message Home; or the Tenacity of Natural Affection.* This story told of a vessel that encounters a mysterious ship carrying a Dutch sea captain named Vanderdecken, who had sworn many years before to round the Cape of Good Hope in spite of wind and weather "though I should beat about here until the Day of Judgement." The powers that be took him at his word, and he is still trying to round the cape. Periodically, he sends out his longboat with messages and mail for his family at home. The story's narrator is naturally horrified to discover that his family has been dead for seventy years.

The next English version of the Dutchman tale was a play produced at the

Adelphi Theatre in 1826 called *The Flying Dutchman, or the Phantom Ship.* It was at one time suggested that the poet and essayist Heinrich Heine, whose version of the legend was the direct inspiration for Wagner's opera, saw this play, but Newman discounts the theory on the grounds that the play was so farcical it couldn't have inspired a serious treatment such as Heine's. There is also a mention of the Dutchman legend in Thomas De Quincey's 1827 *Murder as a Fine Art.*

Captain Frederick Marryat's 1839 novel *The Phantom Ship* boasts a Dutchman named Vanderdecken. He is rescued from his blasphemy, not by the love of a faithful woman, but rather by the strenuous efforts of his son, Philip. The two perish together beneath the waves. It isn't until Heine's version of the legend that we come to the crucial point that inspired Wagner's interest: the redemptive powers of woman's love are a constant theme in Wagnerian opera, and from this viewpoint alone, the Flying Dutchman seems a natural for this composer.

In 1834, Heine published in his *Salon* a series of stories with the title *Memoirs of Herr von Schnabelewopski.* In one of these tales, the memoirist tells of attending a play in Amsterdam about the "dread Mynherr." The Dutch sea captain had sworn the usual oath to round the cape if he had to keep sailing until the Day of Judgment. The Devil takes him at his word and proposes that he sail until he is redeemed by the love of a faithful woman. The Devil, of course, means this as an eternal jest, since no woman in his opinion can ever be faithful. But the Dutchman meets Katharina, daughter of a Scottish skipper, and receives her promise to be true. The Dutchman generously warns Katharina of the doom that awaits her if she links her fate with his, but she jumps into the sea, and all aboard the spectral ship are engulfed by waves, the Dutchman redeemed at last.

When the prose sketch for the *Holländer* was published in 1933, it was discovered that Wagner had followed Heine more closely than had previously been realized. Wagner's action originally also took place on the Scottish coast. Erik was named George, and the heroine was called Anna. (In the French version of *Vaisseau fantôme,* the librettists called their heroine Minna, as she was possibly named in the original sketch after Wagner's own wife.) The name Senta seems to have been made up, perhaps from the Norwegian "tjenta" for maidservant.

In later years Wagner rewrote some of the *Holländer* score, purging bumptious brass and adding the redemption theme at the end of the overture. In 1878 Cosima, his second wife, noted that "Richard is thinking of revising *Der fliegende Holländer.*" We can consider ourselves lucky that he dropped the idea. Although the original *Holländer* has its youthful crudities, moments of overscoring and overexuberance, even moments of padding where the original one act becomes three acts, it is filled with such splendid tunes and such a vibrantly atmospheric orchestration that an overlay of sophistication would only spoil what is fresh and original about it.

Even so, Wagner had difficulty getting the work produced. As noted, Meyer-beer pushed it in Berlin, and Count Wilhelm von Redern, the intendant, finally accepted it for performance. But then Redern was replaced as head of the Berlin Opera by Theodor Küstner of Munich who had previously informed Wagner that his new opera was "unsuitable for Germany." Thus the honor of the first performance fell to Dresden, where on January 2, 1843, Wagner himself conducted the world premiere. Wilhelmine Schröder-Devrient, who had cre-ated Adriano in *Rienzi,* was the Senta. A fine dramatic singer who was also a close friend of Wagner's (she lent him money), she apparently gave a superlative performance. Wagner wrote of her: "The wealth, the power of her passion, the turbulence and force of her inner daemon, combined with such genuine femininity . . . our artistic collaboration was quite remarkable; a whole book could be written about us working on the part of Senta."

Except for Schröder-Devrient, *Holländer* might have been a failure, for its somber, naturalistic tone was foreign to an audience that expected the pomp and public posturing of *Rienzi*'s composer. Yet four performances were given to sold-out houses, and Wagner reported: "The second performance was yesterday and such was my triumph that enthusiasm mounted still further. Again I was twice called out with the singers. The first time I let the singers go out on their own, but the audience would not rest until I myself had gone out in their wake."

Dresden didn't revive *Fliegende Holländer* until 1865, but then it became so popular that the three-hundredth performance of the work took place there in 1910. In the meantime, the opera had spread to London, where it was given in Italian, at the Drury Lane Theatre in 1870 and at Covent Garden in 1877 (with Emma Albani and Victor Maurel). The first American performance, also in Italian, occurred at the Philadelphia Academy of Music in 1876. It was finally presented in German at its Metropolitan Opera debut in 1889. The Met dropped it for many years until the 1930 revival starring Friedrich Schorr and Maria Jeritza. In recent times, *Holländer* has been made popular by such lustrous Sentas as Leonie Rysanek and Anja Silja, both of whom share some-thing of Devrient's "inner daemon."

Up to the mid 1970s, productions of *Der fliegende Holländer* were usually realistic. Even the innovative Wieland Wagner couldn't do much to rescue the work from its awkward stage action. In 1975, Jean-Pierre Ponnelle, the brilliant French designer-director, unveiled a new one-act *Holländer* at San Francisco that was so audacious it left its auditors stunned, outraged, and overjoyed. At the premiere, after tumultuous applause (and isolated booing), the audience streamed into the main lobby and spent the next forty-five minutes vociferously arguing about what they had seen. Nobody wanted to go home, and sleep that night was impossible. It was as if *Fliegende Holländer* had been reborn.

Since that feverish premiere, it has become fashionable to criticize Ponnelle's efforts as part of the tyranny of the stage director that one critic has labeled "miscenation." It is pointed out, scornfully, that *Der fliegende Holländer* is

Senta's story and cannot become, as it does in Ponnelle's production, "the Steersman's dream." These literal-minded complainers forget that the opera already has an entirely supernatural bias and that far from doing it harm, the unifying device that Ponnelle adopts is perfectly consonant with the logic of the plot. Just because the Steersman is dreaming it doesn't mean that we suffer any less of a *frisson* when Senta, instead of jumping to her death, walks into the arms of the Dutchman and is swallowed up in his outsized cape. She is still sacrificed, and he is still redeemed.

As for the controversial single set—the steeply raked decks of Daland's ship on which even the spinning scene is played—Ponnelle is on record as not desiring to create only "aesthetic stage pictures." He is more interested in dramatic truth than in pictorial literalness. *Holländer* was staged for 132 years in literal, pictorial productions. Does anyone remember even one of them? Ponnelle's version, with its blood-red lighting and its grey-and-black costumes, creates a spectral, shivery atmosphere for what is, after all, a spectral, shivery opera. Too many productions of *Holländer* in the past have stressed the homespun values of Senta's exterior life. Ponnelle focuses on the tormented fantasies of her inner world.

However it is staged, *Der fliegende Holländer* remains a thrilling opera, flowing with romantic melodies, exuding the tang of salt air in its orchestration, making one literally want to sing along during its exciting choral episodes. The imaginative intensity of Senta's ballad and her long duet with the Dutchman are the first indication in Wagner's work that he would become one of music's great poets. Daland's gruff, practical outlook gives some hint of the realism that would flower much later in *Die Meistersinger*. In our ecstasy over the glories of the *Ring* and *Tristan*, we sometimes neglect the first opera that shows us Wagner's genius.

VERDI'S *La forza del destino*
by Peter P. Jacobi

The birth and early years of Giuseppe Verdi's *La forza del destino* can be told in and around documents of the time and around letters—letters that follow the opera's creator through both chronological time and the creative process.

It seems an appropriate method of telling how it came to be.

He had completed *Un ballo in maschera*. He had turned away from music. To his long-time collaborator, the librettist Francesco Maria Piave, he had written: "As you know, I am now the complete countryman. I hope I have bidden farewell to the muses and that I shall never again feel the temptation to take up my pen."

Giuseppina, Verdi's wife, wasn't at all sure, however, that he should remain idle. And she was pleased when the renowned singer Enrico Tamberlick sent Verdi a letter inviting him to write an opera for the Imperial Theatre of St. Petersburg. "You are quite free to choose the subject and the poet," Tamberlick wrote. "You can make your own conditions and the score will remain your property."

Well, Verdi bit, probably in part because of his wife's persuasive power. He wanted to set Victor Hugo's *Ruy Blas* to music. Tamberlick advised him that the censor said no. That was not the right response for a composer still disinclined to get back to work. "I've leafed through play after play without finding one which satisfies me completely," he wrote back. "I cannot and will not sign a contract before having found a subject suitable to the artists whom I would have at St. Petersburg and approved by the authorities."

That brought the great tenor's son to Italy to try diplomacy. In Giuseppina's words, he corrected "the mistake in the dispatch (Tamberlick's letter)" and declared "with the greatest calmness that Verdi could set to music *Ruy Blas* or anything he liked, since he himself had instructions to grant him all the conditions he could possibly require, apart from compelling Tsar Alexander to declare a republic in Russia."

The man's bend-over-backwards manner apparently softened Verdi, who began to downgrade *Ruy Blas*. Actually he had already been scouring the bookshops and had been mentally settling on a play by Spain's duke of Rivas, the romantic story of *Don Alvaro* or *La Fuerza del sino*. To the French impresario Léon Escudier, a long-time friend, Verdi wrote, "I like it very much." He called the play "powerful, singular, and truly vast."

Still, there were complications. Nonmusical. Nonagricultural. Political. These were years of turmoil for an Italy about to become Italy, years of French and Austrian oppression, of Giuseppe Garibaldi and Camillo Cavour.

It is 1859. Verdi's mind is on matters of country and patriotism. "I should not like to be thought of as a brave armchair soldier," he writes. "But what could I do, who am not capable of marching three miles, whose head can't stand the sun for five minutes, and who is sent to bed, sometimes for weeks, by a little wind or a little humidity? What a wretched nature I have. Good for nothing!"

It is a time of his life when health plays a larger role than it will for most of the remaining decades, of which there will be four. But health, or lack of it, will not keep him from getting politically involved. His name will be splattered across walls and fences, in double meaning: Italians honoring their favorite composer and Italians honoring in code their monarch-to-be, Vittorio Emanuele re d'Italia.

Verdi is not happy as a politician. But he tolerates his duties, even agrees to become a member of the first national assembly, this at the request of Cavour, whom he idolized. Consider Verdi's words to the statesman after the two had first met in that year of 1859:

I had desired for a long time to know personally the Prometheus of our people, and did not despair of finding an occasion to satisfy this great

desire of mine. What, however, I had not dared to hope for was the frank
and kindly reception with which Your Excellency deigned to honor me.
When I left you I felt deeply moved!

Cavour recognized in Verdi someone of tremendous importance to him and
his national cause. He therefore urged Verdi to participate in modern Italy's
first attempts at self-government.

Verdi quickly tired of legislative wranglings. He failed to enter the debates.
His votes echoed Cavour's. "That way I can be absolutely certain of not making
a mistake," he explained.

And just as politics was a likely source for his temporary withdrawal from
music, so just as likely politics brought him back. Facing the music (of *La forza
del destino*) came to be preferred to facing the endless speeches of the assembly.
Over the former he had control. Of the latter he could only be a bored victim.

When Cavour died in mid 1861, Verdi first grieved, then gradually switched
his attention from matters of state to matters of art.

The matters of art at this point involved *Forza*. He set to work in earnest,
jotting his musical notes, guiding his librettist Piave with a prose synopsis, and
prodding him with words like, "These lines are ugly . . . but you're a poet and
should be able to make them better." Lengthenings and shortenings of words
resulted, so that Verdi could write his music to a desired pace and length. And
refinements, too. "All the verses of the terzetto are quite bad," he told Piave.
Poor Piave. Verdi never seemed satisfied with his colleague's work. "For God's
sake, my dear Piave, let's think about this carefully. We can't go on like this: it's
absolutely impossible with this drama. The style must be tightened up. The
poetry can and must say all that the prose says, and in half the words. So far
you're not doing that."

The work continued. The work progressed, to a point where Verdi could
write Tamberlick:

Please advise the management of the theatre at St. Petersburg that . . .
besides the soprano, tenor and baritone, they will need:
(1) A soprano to do the gypsy woman, a very brilliant and important
role, like the Page in *Un ballo in maschera*.
(2) A basso profundo to do the role of the Father Superior.
(3) A comic baritone for the role of Fra Melitone, also a very important
role.

And Giuseppina made preparations for the trip. She ordered the wine to be
taken along: 100 bottles of ordinary Bordeaux, 20 bottles of better Bordeaux,
and 20 bottles of champagne for special affairs. The Verdis would be in St.
Petersburg from November through January. They'd take plenty of rice, macaroni, cheese, and salami. She told a friend: "The noodles and macaroni will
have to be very well-cooked to keep him in a good humour in the midst of all
the ice and furs!" And knowing her Verdi, she added: "For my part, to avoid

any trouble, I plan to let him be right in everything from the middle of October through January; for I know that while he is composing and rehearsing the opera is not the moment to persuade him that he may be wrong even once."

Nevertheless, the Verdis were impressed with St. Petersburg, its grandeur, its hospitable people. Although, of course, they missed home, they were prepared for their extended stay and were less than happy when that stay was cut short by a decision to delay the opera's premiere.

Giuseppina explained in a letter to another close family friend, Count Opprandino Arrivabene:

> Verdi will not give his new opera in Petersburg this year. Alas! Singers' voices are as fragile as . . . (I'll leave you to complete the phrase) and Mme. la Grua's voice, to her and Verdi's misfortune, is an appalling example. . . . Such being the case, lacking the prima donna for whom the part was written, and there being no other singer suitable for the role, Verdi asked to be released from his contract. To this request, he was given for answer a big "no," though preceded, followed, and seasoned with the fairest words in the world. So they have agreed to give the opera next winter.

Verdi and Piave still had some work to do when the decision came. Certain numbers were incomplete or missing. Verdi still had some instrumentation to finish. But now there was no hurry.

Instead, the Verdis did some sightseeing, then in February, 1862, headed rather indirectly for home. The composer wrote Tamberlick from Berlin:

> Here I am at Berlin after a trip without sinister events except the appalling cold from Dunaburg to Kovno. We traveled three or four miles in an uncovered train in 33 degrees of cold to join the train of a Grand Duke who had stopped at the fort. It is a terrible thing to be at the disposition of others, even a grand duke! Now I understand the meaning of *cold*.

They went on to London, via Paris, and participated in the celebration following the premiere of his *Inno delle nazioni* (Hymn of the Nations), done at Her Majesty's Theatre with a choir of two hundred and Therese Tietjens as soloist.

Eventually they returned to Sant'Agata, only to face a family tragedy of sorts. "Our Loulou, our poor little Loulou is dead!" Verdi wrote to Arrivabene. "Poor little animal! My sadness is great, but Peppina is absolutely desolate!" The dog was buried beneath a willow tree in the Verdi garden, and the headstone pronounced, "To the memory of one of my most faithful friends."

It was time to think of their return to St. Petersburg. Premiere time was nearing. Verdi completed his orchestration, and by October they were back in St. Petersburg for a November debut. And this time it happened.

The date: November 10, 1862. The critic of the St. Petersburg *Journal* commented:

It is midnight. We have just left the first performance of the new opera which Maestro Verdi has written expressly for the Italian Theatre of St. Petersburg. We should not want this issue of the paper to go to press without mentioning the brilliant success of this beautiful work.

We shall speak again at leisure about this magnificent score and about this evening's performance; but for the moment we wish to report the composer's victorious success and the ovations for the artists who, in order to comply with the insistent demands of the entire audience, had on several occasions to drag the celebrated composer onto the stage, to the sound of wild cheering and prolonged applause.

It is our opinion that *La forza del destino,* of all Verdi's works, is the most complete, both in terms of its inspiration and the rich abundance of its melodic invention, and in those of its musical development and orchestration.

Verdi was awarded the Order of St. Stanislas.

But his victory was not complete. Three Russian-language newspapers (the *Journal* served up its fare in French) reacted less enthusiastically, their critics considering the opera too long. And some pro-German opera enthusiasts demonstrated briefly during the third performance, though they were out-shouted, according to reports, by those supporting Verdi.

Verdi was dissatisfied with the original version of *Forza,* and almost immediately considered alterations for it. He permitted further performances of the original, however, in the months and years following the St. Petersburg premiere. Audiences in Vienna, New York, London, Buenos Aires, and Madrid responded with favor.

By 1864, although he was engaged in other operatic activities such as a major revision of *Macbeth,* he had Piave at work on *Forza.* And as usual, he was giving the poor fellow a hard time. "I have received your verses and, if I may say so, I don't like them," he wrote. "You talk to me about 100 syllables!! And it's obvious that 100 syllables aren't enough when you take 25 to say the sun is setting!!!" Considerably more follows in the way of advice. "Orders" would be a better word.

Verdi had history to make with *Don Carlo* in 1867. But *Forza* remained on his mind. La Scala wanted the work but would not get it unless and until the composer could perfect it. Now, suddenly, Verdi could no longer spit demands at Piave. In December, 1867, the gentle collaborator suffered a stroke which would leave him paralyzed for the eight remaining years of his life.

The task of completing the revision of *Forza* fell upon Antonio Ghislanzoni, a poet and journalist who later would collaborate with the composer on *Aïda.* The two men considered omissions, a new order of scenes, tightenings and additions, and a new ending. Everyone seemed to die in the first version. Verdi wanted the stage deaths trimmed and toned down. Verdi had told the publisher, Tito Ricordi, that he'd "adjust the catastrophe."

"It was necessary to reflect a lot," noted Ghislanzoni,

> before coming to a less-murderous solution that did not contradict the title of the opera, or rather the Spanish poet's predominating idea. Fatality required that Don Alvaro exterminate the entire Vargas family. . . . It was a matter then of letting fate fulfill its tremendous decree, and of sparing the spectators the sight of so many victims.

La Scala wanted *Forza* for 1869. Verdi and company would make that deadline. The composer, as usual, involved himself in details of production. "Urge the chorus master to make his singers learn the part so as to achieve real precision, and above all not to let them get away with a sloppy attack," he commanded.

> For massed voices attack is the most important thing. . . . We must at all costs arrange the voices and the effect of the female choruses in the camp scene. Contraltos on their own are intolerable and so are sopranos. So be sure and improve matters by adding some boys to the contraltos and finding some good solo voices among the sopranos.

He reminded Ricordi: "The success of our operas rests most of the time in the hands of the conductor. This person is as necessary as a tenor or a prima donna." Verdi disliked both the stick-wavers and the overly creative. "I do not admit the right either of singers or conductors to create," he once said.

And so, he told Ricordi: "I am coming myself to Milan to conduct what rehearsals I think necessary for *La forza del destino,* and I am changing the last finale and various other numbers here and there throughout the opera." Then he added: "I do not wish to have anything to do with the management of La Scala, I do not want my name put on the poster, and I shall not stay for the first performance, which cannot be given without my permission."

His revised *Forza* was a triumph. But by then Verdi had lost some of his interest. He'd already introduced his *Don Carlo,* an advanced work, an inspiration, he hoped, for the future.

Forza, with its extended musical scenes, also heralded some of that future, Verdi thought. But "it's a curious thing, and at the same time discouraging," he wrote Ricordi's agent in Venice. "While everyone cries out 'Reform,' 'Progress,' the public generally refrains from applause, and the singers only know how to be effective in arias, romances, and songs."

Critical reaction and audience reaction always bothered him, the latter even more so.

Verdi became perturbed when the critic of an Italian periodical judged Leonora's marvelous aria "Pace, pace mio dio" an imitation of the Schubert "Ave Maria." His reaction says much about Verdi's approach to life and music:

> . . . musically illiterate as I am I couldn't say how many years it has been since I heard Schubert's "Ave Maria." It would have been difficult for me, therefore, to copy it. Please don't think when I speak of my great musical ignorance that I'm simply exaggerating. It's the pure and simple truth. In

my house there is very little music. I have never gone to a music library or to a publisher to refer to a piece of music. I keep up with a few of our best modern operas not by studying them but by hearing them occasionally in the theatre. You will understand my purpose in all of this. So I repeat that, of all composers of past or present, I am the least erudite. Let us understand each other: I repeat, this is no modesty. I am referring to erudition, not to musical knowledge.

So what does one hear in *Forza*?

A work with glorious melody that begins with one of Verdi's best overtures (written for the revised version), an introduction that often stands alone in symphony concerts.

A work with marvelous solos and duets and trios and ensembles.

A work in which the singers, according to Verdi, "must have soul, and understand the words and express their meaning."

A work with major roles for major singers and major minor roles for major singers.

A work with scenes of humor and scenes of folk grandeur.

A work with stunning pianissimos as well as cascades of big sounds.

A work that some say made Mussorgsky's *Boris Godunov* possible.

A work of some fragmentation and unequal value, but with a glorious totality.

A work written when its composer was reaching the heights of his creative powers.

A work of considerable dimension.

A work with music to remember.

Verdi scholar William Weaver has called *Forza* "Verdi's boldest attempt to portray an entire, complex, contradictory world." The dramatic changes that Verdi and his librettists made between versions one and two may not have solved all stage problems; the opera remains one of pieces and scenes and situations. But the music of the final version is extraordinary, theatrical, devotional, rewarding. One may not always know or understand just what exactly is going on up there on stage (or even care), but the music indelibly presses into the mind and heart, searing one's emotions so that the characters on stage do assume a personality and a reality and an importance.

It is quite an opera.

RICHARD STRAUSS'S *Die Frau ohne Schatten*
by Stephanie von Buchau

In later years, Richard Strauss referred to his seventh opera, *Die Frau ohne Schatten,* as a "child of sorrow." This is because it was composed during World War I, when the librettist, Hugo von Hofmannsthal, was called up for active service (he eventually got a diplomatic post away from the front), and Strauss's twenty-one-year-old son, Franz, was inducted but then declared unfit because of a heart condition. The fact that the Germans lost the war might also have been a contributing factor to the composer's depression.

However, his rather naive assumption that wartime worries were "responsible for a certain nervous irritation in the score, especially halfway through the third act, which was to explode into melodrama," must be discounted. Certainly in the Strauss canon there are no scores more riddled with "nervous irritation" than *Elektra* (produced in 1909) and *Salome* (produced in 1905; about which the composer's musician father remarked: "It makes me feel as if my pants are full of maybugs"). *Die Frau ohne Schatten* (The Woman without a Shadow) is the opera that many musicians prefer to all other of Strauss's works. It also has its detractors; an examination of its gestation will partially explain this dichotomy.

Die Frau (which the composer playfully nicknamed "Frog" or, in German, "Fr-o-Sch") was conceived simultaneously with *Ariadne auf Naxos,* Strauss's sixth opera. The first hint of *Die Frau* comes from an entry in Hofmannsthal's notebook from early in 1911: "The Woman without a shadow, a fantastic play. The Empress, a fairy's daughter, is childless. She obtains a stranger's child. In the end she gives it back to its real mother. The second couple are Harlequin and Esmeraldina. She wants to remain beautiful. He is clumsy and good. She gives up her child to a wicked fairy."

This rough approximation of *Die Frau*'s eventual story line remains light, almost childlike. There is virtually no hint of the layers of psychology and symbolism that would eventually freight the libretto, layers that many listeners find impenetrable. Yet *Die Frau* is no more impenetrable than *Il trovatore;* you simply have to remember that it is an opera and requires occasional suspension of disbelief. The music makes it all quite clear, despite the spleen of commentators who pretend otherwise.

Romain Rolland, an admirer of Strauss but no lover of Hofmannsthal (was he jealous?), wrote in his *Journal:* "The poem of Hofmannsthal affirms the scenic incapacity of the writer. His obscurity of thought trails an icy shadow behind it. It weighs heavily upon any passion. Strauss suffers from this collaboration." Strauss "suffered" so much that he wrote six operas with Hofmannsthal, of which two *(Elektra* and *Rosenkavalier)* are immortal masterpieces, while two others *(Ariadne* and *Die Frau)* are twentieth-century chefsd'oeuvre.

In Hollywood, they will not make a film that cannot be reduced to a single sentence. Applying this crude yardstick to opera, we discover that the "obscure" *Frau ohne Schatten* is really the story "of a fairy who becomes a woman by learning her own desires are not worth hurting innocent people for." It is that simple. The otherworldly Empress becomes human (i.e., able to bear children) when she refuses to destroy the happiness of Barak by stealing his wife's shadow (i.e., the symbol of her as-yet-unborn progeny).

Because Strauss and Hofmannsthal were the last in a long line of thoroughly Germanic artists, however, they couldn't just leave it at that. The opera which its librettist originally insisted would stand "in general terms to *Zauberflöte* as *Rosenkavalier* does to *Figaro*" has virtually nothing Mozartean about it. Long after it was composed, Strauss was still talking about how Hofmannsthal had inspired a "lighter" touch in him for a change! In fact, they had produced what we now hear as the last Wagnerian opera, a grandiose work which follows most of the earlier Richard's precepts about *Gesamtkunstwerk,* endless melody, and music as drama.

All the lighter touches in Strauss's arsenal were expended on *Ariadne,* though in the original scheme for *Die Frau,* the composer had wanted to use a light "Ariadne orchestra" to accompany the Empress and the spirits of the upper world. Eventually he didn't follow this plan, but he carefully differentiated the three planes on which the opera takes place: the spirit world, ruled by Kei-kobad; the sordid and materialistic world of Barak, the dyer, and his discontented wife; and a kind of floating world between the two, where the Empress and her malevolent Nurse dwell while awaiting the outcome of the conflict.

Hofmannsthal based this conflict on a quote from Goethe's *Die Geheimnisse:*

> Von der Gewalt, die alle Wesen bindet / Befreit der Mensch sich, der sich überwindet (From the authority that binds all beings, / Man frees himself by transcending himself).

In other words, the Empress solves the problem of being bound by the laws of the spirit world when she chooses to become fully human. By refusing to drink from the golden fountain that will gain her the shadow of the Dyer's Wife, she transcends herself, placing the happiness of another above her own desires. (Forgive me for reiterating this concept, but it is the crux of the opera and, once understood, makes the so-called obscurity of the libretto melt away.)

Hofmannsthal wrote to Strauss in May of 1911: "The fact is that with so fine a subject as *Die Frau ohne Schatten,* the rich gift of a happy hour, with a subject so fit to become a vehicle of beautiful poetry and beautiful music, with a subject such as this all haste and hurry and forcing of oneself would be a crime. . . . Had you made me choose between producing this work on the spot, or doing without your music, I should have chosen the latter."

In other words, Strauss was going to have to possess his soul in patience for the next several years. Twelve months later Hofmannsthal notes: "I am writing to tell you that *Die Frau ohne Schatten* has now taken a powerful hold on my mind." Strauss answers joyfully, also commenting that their ballet *Josephs-legende,* which he was currently working on, is becoming "a hell of an effort. The chaste Joseph isn't at all up my street, and if a thing bores me, I find it difficult to set to music." This is a facer for those who later claimed that Strauss was bewildered by the *Frau* libretto; if that were even remotely true, then where did all that glorious music come from?

In 1913, Hofmannsthal is still promising that all the "details, twists and turns of dialogue, and transitions" are being worked out, "arousing in me a kind of envy for the composer who will have the chance of filling out with music what I must leave blank." He goes on in the same letter: "The profound meaning of the plot, the effortless symbolism of all the situations, its immensely rich humanity never fail to fill me with delight and astonishment." Hofmannsthal wanted desperately to be the literary successor to Goethe, who had himself desperately wanted to write an opera, and he quotes the master's definition of opera: "Significant situations in artificially arranged sequence. This is how he epitomizes the ideal in opera, and it is a phrase which has encouraged me immensely over *Die Frau ohne Schatten*."

Early in 1913, the collaborators made a short tour of Italy by car and must have intensively discussed the *Frau* project, because one of Hofmannsthal's next letters enthuses: "That was a brilliant idea you had in the moonlight between San Michele and Bozen, of accompanying the upper world with the *Ariadne* orchestra [an idea which we have already seen was later discarded]. In the upper sphere we shall have heroic recitative throughout (though much more rapid and flowing than in Wagner), while below there is real conversation such as only the Master of *Rosenkavalier* can compose." He proceeds to instruct Strauss—the century's greatest orchestrator—on how to manage the orchestral transition between the first and second scenes of Act I. The composer's reply is lost, or he held his tongue. Hofmannsthal, with his neurasthenic enthusiasms, was not the easiest person with whom to collaborate artistically.

Late in 1913, Hofmannsthal hits an impasse: "The serious hold-ups I have suffered in writing *Die Frau ohne Schatten* must have astonished you, for when we were in Rome I seemed to see it all so clearly before me. . . . The sections which take place in the realm of the fairies must be very simple; as I had them, they were too heavy in tone, too dark, too symbolic. . . . Perhaps the careful study of Wagner libretti which I made in May did me more harm than good. What depressed me at the time was . . . the inimitable excellence with which the way is prepared for the music [in Wagner]." Strauss, obviously putting the best face on it, assures Hofmannsthal that he can wait until the following Easter for the first act.

Yet Strauss had evidently seen part of the libretto by January of 1914, for Hofmannsthal speaks about the composer's making cuts to do away with dreaded exposition. He tries to soothe Strauss: "I believe that during the composition of these three acts, your road will be exactly like Dante's: from hell, through purgatory, into the heaven of the third act." (The soprano who sings the Empress may be forgiven for having exactly the same thoughts.) On April 4, 1914, Strauss is finally able to write: "The first act is simply wonderful: so compact and homogeneous that I cannot think of even a comma being deleted or altered." He then, of course, suggests numerous cuts and changes.

Hofmannsthal replies with a certain asperity: "I have no objection whatever to your firmly compressing the first half. Only one thing you must not, must never forget: the Empress is, for the spiritual meaning of the opera, the central figure, and her destiny the pivot of the whole action. The Dyer's Wife and the Dyer are, admittedly, the strongest figures, but it is not on them that the plot is focused; their fate is subordinate to the destiny of the Empress. . . . You should never lose sight of this, for otherwise the third act will become impossible."

The librettist here puts his finger right on *Die Frau*'s tenderest spot. The Dyer's Wife (who, incidentally, is never given a name) *is* the most interesting figure in the opera, just as Barak, the dyer, is the most human and appealing. Yet their story *must* be secondary if the point—that transcending one's self brings freedom—is to be made through the Empress's actions. If the remarkably beautiful and humane music of Act I that Strauss wrote for the simple Barak were the only great music in *Die Frau,* then we would have to account Hofmannsthal responsible for the failure of the rest of the opera.

Yet Strauss was able to follow the Austrian playwright into the lofty realms of Act III's spiritual world. The bourgeois Strauss, who was supposedly such a *lumpen* figure that all he cared about was beer, skat, and being bashed by his shrewish wife, was in fact perfectly capable of nobility and loftiness in music. Hofmannsthal's wish that Act III "lead us where music and poetry, without clipping each other's wings, and truly hand in hand for once, shall float lightly over the garden of paradise," may be couched in fulsome language, but the Empress's monologues in Act III and the jubilant C-major finale are powerful arguments on his side.

Pauline de Ahna Strauss, the composer's singer-wife, who was known to treat him roughly in public, was possibly the inspiration for the Dyer's Wife, a beautiful woman who is passionately in love with her husband but whose tormented mind and lacerating tongue keep her from experiencing true happiness. Strauss had some difficulty with this character, and Hofmannsthal delicately pointed out that he, of all people, should be able to understand her. "You have repeatedly expressed the desire to depict in music the capricious, flighty aspects of such a basically good woman." In fact, Strauss already had portrayed Pauline in the *Sinfonia Domestica* (1904) and would do so again in *Intermezzo,* his next opera, which is based on a true incident from his own marital life.

By the middle of 1915, Strauss was ready to begin work on Act III and was experiencing some pangs: "I have let Hülsen and Seebach read the first two acts. Both displayed total incomprehension, and Seebach understood only after I had orally explained the subject to him and played the first act on the piano. Everything tells me that the subject and theme are difficult to understand. . . . I ask you urgently therefore to recapitulate emphatically in act three (as Wagner often does) the decisive psychological processes so that nothing remains obscure. . . . Perhaps you have already done that, but I thought there would be no harm in drawing your attention to it again."

Yet when Strauss finally received the text, he reacted with his customary generosity: "Your third act is magnificent; words, structure, and content equally wonderful. Only in its quest for brevity it has become too sketchy. For all the lyrical moments I definitely need more text." (This may be the only instance in operatic history of a composer's asking for more instead of less.) Then, the obligatory gush out of the way, Strauss characteristically begins to dissect the act with minute attention to detail: "My greatest misgivings are about the character of the Empress who doesn't touch us closely enough on the human plane. Her remorse, her renunciation of happiness at the side of the Emperor . . . her vacillation between pity for the Dyer's Wife and her love for the Emperor—all these ought to emerge much more impressively." He never did sympathize with the Empress's apparent sacrifice; such altruism was a foreign concept to his earthy, pragmatic nature. "After all, the Empress, by declining to acquire the shadow through fraud or through wrecking the happiness of the Barak couple, sacrifices her own husband. This is somewhat unnatural and distasteful."

It is also the whole point of the story, and it is rather a pity that there is no reply from Hofmannsthal, since in April of that year the collaborators had one of their rare meetings. It is also unfortunate that performers and commentators appear to have taken Strauss's letters as a departure for their criticisms of the opera, rather than listening to the music itself. The third act of *Die Frau* is often cut to shreds in performance on the grounds that if the composer couldn't understand the theme, then why should the listener be forced to attempt to comprehend it?

This attitude underestimates the role of the subconscious or the unconscious in the creative process. Strauss may have thought that he didn't understand the Empress's dilemma, but the music he wrote belies his thoughts. A further letter exposes his determination to get the climax of the opera right. "'Ich will nicht' strikes me as rather empty and cold," he complains about the big scene in which the Empress refuses to drink from the tainted fountain. ("Ich will nicht," incidentally, does not mean "I will not," but rather "I don't want to.") "Surely there ought to be a big explosion here . . . something like the scream of a woman in childbirth."

Strauss pressed the childbirth theme on the reluctant librettist several times, but Hofmannsthal didn't see how he could amplify the scene. He heard part of the third act in 1916 and reported himself "somewhat oppressed and gloomy . . . exactly what one experiences when a piece of work has not quite come off. . . . It is a great relief to me to know that you intend to rescue the last part of this grave, sombre work with *secco* recitative." They had mutually decided that the Empress's scene could not be lyrically expanded.

What eventually resulted was what Strauss referred to as "melodrama," not what we call hysterical exaggeration, but an actual musical form in which orchestral passages unite with spoken dialogue. Beethoven uses melodrama to great effect in the prison scene of *Fidelio,* and Strauss resorted to it in *Die Frau's* penultimate scene. Is this because, as some critics have said, he just couldn't compose his way out of the scene, or because he genuinely thought the spoken words were more effective? When a great Empress such as Leonie Rysanek, who virtually owned the role for twenty years, cried "Ich will nicht!" it was far more shattering than any amount of coloratura flights or Wagnerian *melos* could have been.

Between 1911, when Hofmannsthal first conceived the idea of *Frau ohne Schatten,* and 1919, when the work had its world premiere at the Vienna Opera, Germany and Austria lived through a war that revolutionized their social structures. Lotte Lehmann, the first Dyer's Wife, tells in her book *Singing with Richard Strauss* how, despite the new social order, she was enchanted to meet royalty (the duke of Cumberland and the daughter of Kaiser Wilhelm II) at Gmunden in Upper Austria where she was on holiday.

It was here that she received a large parcel which turned out to be the piano score of *Frau ohne Schatten,* sent to her by her manager with the notation that the role of the Dyer's Wife had been written especially for her. (No mention of Lehmann's name is made by the collaborators during their work on the opera, however.) Maria Jeritza, who sang the Empress, later claimed that she had turned down the part of the Dyer's Wife, and Lehmann waspishly points out why: "The Dyer's Wife all but kills herself singing throughout every scene, while the Empress gradually unfolds not only her voice but her whole being in the second half of the opera, a situation which allows her to reap the lion's share of the laurels."

The cast of the world premiere, October 10, 1919, included Jeritza as the Empress, Lehmann as the Dyer's Wife, Karl Aagard Oestvig as the Emperor, and Richard Mayr as Barak. Franz Schalk was the conductor. Lehmann remarked about singing with Mayr: "He used to sing so divinely that I shall never cease regretting that it [the third act duet, "Mir anvertraut"] was not recorded and preserved for posterity. Our voices blended well and whenever I sang with him, I had the feeling that my voice was being carried by his on velvet wings." Mayr's talents notwithstanding, the role of Barak is one of the warmest and most human in all of opera; singing opposite such a saintly personage must automatically make the soprano feel good.

The Dyer's Wife, on the other hand, not only has to "sing herself into a state of near prostration" (Lehmann's words), but she has a tremendous acting job to do as well, for she appears unsympathetic and querulous throughout most of the opera. Lehmann, wondering what to do with herself during a long orchestral passage in Act I, encountered the following advice from the composer: "Do? Do absolutely nothing! Why must you be doing something? After all, in real life people don't keep running back and forth all the time, do they? Just stand there quietly and think yourself into the meaning of your role."

The received opinion that Hofmannsthal ruined the possible success of *Die Frau ohne Schatten* by overloading its libretto with symbolism has gradually given way to a more charitable view of the opera. The premiere may have been only a succès d'estime, and further German productions were insufficiently cast and/or mounted, but slowly the work gained international acclaim. San

Francisco mounted the first American performance in 1959, though it was heavily cut. The Metropolitan Opera's fantastic 1967 production ("Like Disneyland," an awed soprano reported) was one of the greatest hits of the new house at Lincoln Center. Both the Met and San Francisco Opera have frequently revived the work.

Hofmannsthal complained: "We have missed the lightness of touch." He was still yearning for that impossible Mozartean work, when Strauss had given him instead the final opera of Wagnerian psychology. As William Mann points out in his informative exegesis on the Strauss operas, "In *Die Frau ohne Schatten* Richard Strauss leaped by an extent that he had not suspected earlier. The characters of themselves are an *élite,* their music elect among all his other works."

PONCHIELLI's *La Gioconda*
by Jonathan Abarbanel

Music critic and composer Hugo Wolf, writing in 1884, said Amilcare Ponchielli's music for *La Gioconda* "lacks originality." He went on to elaborate: "His melodies, banal and flat, are really only patched together from the sediment of opera phrases by Gounod, Verdi, and Meyerbeer." George Bernard Shaw, wearing his music critic's cap in the late 1880s, said much the same thing, unfavorably comparing Ponchielli to Verdi. *La Gioconda,* Shaw suggested, was the sort of thing that came about when a composer attempted to imitate his betters. Shaw didn't even like the justly famous "Dance of the Hours" ballet from Act III. "I grant you that there are a few dance tunes that are worth listening to for their own sakes," he wrote in 1889, "but they are to be found neither in the *Gioconda* nor any other grand opera ballet."

If they strongly disliked the score by Ponchielli, they utterly condemned the libretto by Arrigo Boito (writing under the pen name of Tobia Gorrio). Wolf's review referred to "the infamous Arrigo Boito . . . this dull lunatic . . . this perverted Tobia Gorrio." He called the libretto a "book of horrors" and said of Boito's work, "His text for *La Gioconda,* trivial, dirty, cannibalistic as it may be in invention and execution, does not touch the monstrous, idiotic bombast of his *Mefistofele.*"

While Shaw and Wolf may have been particularly skillful and ostentatious in their invective, they certainly were not alone in their opinions. *La Gioconda* successfully premiered at La Scala in 1876. Within just a few years, it had conquered the opera capitals of Europe and America. Wherever it played outside of Italy, audiences loved it, while the most forward-thinking music critics loathed it. Critics had a field day. Outside of Italy, we must recall, they had crowned Richard Wagner king of opera, and his dramatico-musical concepts were rapidly becoming the lyric law of the land. The Wagnerite writers could not forgive the fact that *La Gioconda* looked backwards to Meyerbeer and the grand opera tradition of forty years earlier. To them, *La Gioconda* was a dramatically overblown, musically overstuffed, turgid, bombastic, thoroughly retrograde piece of Italianate trash.

Critics ever since have followed suit, almost universally damning *La Gioconda,* whatever the merits of an individual production might be. Even contemporary critics, mellowed towards the opera by a century of perspective, dislike it. Francis Robertson wrote in 1959 that "beside this cloak and dagger plot, *Trovatore* is a miracle of clarity." And even the judicious, scholarly, and essentially neutral *Grove's Dictionary* states that Boito's "libretto sacrifices clarity to scenes of undeniable effect." And yet one fact remains steadfast, to the eternal frustration of all the critics: *La Gioconda* remains the only non-Verdi Italian opera composed between the death of Donizetti (1848) and the premiere of *Cavalleria rusticana* (1890) to hold a place in the standard repertory.

La Gioconda is, of course, Italianate to the core; a triumph of display singing over text and drama. The purple passions of its plot are overwhelming and outrageous in the extreme. In the course of the opera's four acts, one encounters adultery, arson, kidnapping, lynching, poisoning, stabbing, suicide, terrible revenge, and a ballet. Everything you see on television every night (minus, of course, the ballet). If *La Gioconda* were being produced in contemporary terms, it would be a prime-time adult soap opera, or a four-part mini series with an international cast. No wonder audiences always have taken to it like a duck to water!

Like the grand operas of Meyerbeer, *La Gioconda* also is technically demanding, requiring lavish settings and special effects and summoning up all the artistic forces of orchestra, chorus, and corps de ballet. In short, it has a wide variety of appeal. To quote Francis Robertson, *La Gioconda* offers "sumptuous spectacle, ceremony, picturesque ballet, luscious arias and duets, and an almost unbroken pageant of violent and impassioned action."

It should be clear by now that the story of *La Gioconda* is, perhaps, the primary element that has redounded so negatively on the opera. Well, Arrigo Boito is not entirely to blame, for *La Gioconda* is based on a play by Victor Hugo, entitled *Angelo, Tyran de Padoue* ("Angelo, Tyrant of Padua"). Victor Hugo, the dominant man of letters in nineteenth-century France, "bestrode his narrow age like a colossus," dwarfing the literary achievements of Eugène Scribe and Victorien Sardou, Èmile Zola, and even of Alexandre Dumas, père *and* fils. The reforms in literary technique and subject matter which Hugo single-handedly brought about ushered in the French Romantic movement in literature and made possible the careers of all French writers who followed. The very syllables of his name have a solemn and lofty majesty. The appeal of Hugo's works for the opera stage was instantaneous. Composers by the dozens turned his works into scores of operas (most of which Hugo disowned). *Angelo, Tyran de Padoue* was set by Eugen d'Albert, César Cui, and Saverio Mercadante in addition to Ponchielli. But a great playwright Hugo wasn't.

Of Hugo's dramas, most written before he was thirty-five, *The Oxford Companion to Theatre* has this to say: "It has been said that they are masterpieces in all but their fitness for the stage. . . . All alike suffer from overloading, from a plethora of words and details. They are plays of youth—a young man and a young movement—and must be judged as such. Hugo's plays mark the entry of melodrama into the serious theatre. His plots come from the boulevards. The Romantic theatre carried in itself the germ of its decay, and its vogue was bound to be short."

Of all Hugo's plays, *Angelo, Tyran de Padoue* is the most excessive and ludicrously melodramatic, even granted the fact that it contains characters of Romantic passion and nobility, as well as a political "raison d'être" (as the title suggests) eliminated in the opera. Hugo Wolf said that *La Gioconda* has an "absurd libretto, brewed from leftovers of the cheapest, most banal, most brutal fustian," but *Grove's* more accurately observes that Boito "mirrors Hugo's flamboyant style with surprising faithfulness."

All those details—who is doing what to whom, and why?—*are* confusing, though, and they nearly got to Ponchielli. Working on *La Gioconda* in the summer of 1875, he wrote a friend: "More than a hundred times a day I am tempted to leave off. The reasons are many; the first of them is that I have no faith in the libretto . . . because of the frequent, too high-flown conceits, the verse and the involved expression in which I do not find the ideas that I want." Some lines later, in concluding the letter, Ponchielli continued in the same vein: "The public wants smooth, clear things, melody, simplicity; and all we do is shroud ourselves in confusion and complexities. Boito is forcing me in that direction. But I hope I'll have sufficient good sense to watch out for the abyss." This is the same Boito, we should keep in mind, who later wracked up operatic history in creating the sublimely compact and lucid librettos for *Otello* and *Falstaff.*

Boito, with deep and intentional irony, entitled the work "La gioconda," meaning "the joyous girl," a far cry from the young street singer we see, tormented by unrequited love and driven by vengeance. In sending the completed libretto to Ponchielli, Boito made a joke. "Che *La Gioconda* ci giocondi entrambi!" he wrote (May *The Joyous Girl* bring us both joy!). It did, assuming that Boito and Ponchielli were able to ignore the out-of-town reviews.

Whatever the abyss of the libretto may have been, Ponchielli attempted to compose his way out of it. And therein lies the glory of the work and its popular appeal. If it seems that up until now these notes have damned *La Gioconda,* we shall now issue a temporal indulgence and resurrect it. Even Hugo Wolf recognized the opera's one monumental strength and attempted to turn it against the work. "*La Gioconda* is composed solely for the singer," Wolf wrote, "and not for the public. Therein lies the severest criticism." But Wolf was wrong. Audiences absolutely adore singers' operas. Especially if they're Italian and nineteenth century.

In truth, *La Gioconda* has remained in the standard opera repertory not so much because the public clamors for it but because singers do. It is the type of opera, like *Don Carlos,* that can be carried only by artists of virtuosity and spark, peerless interpreters of the heroic Italian school. What's more, you've got to have a lot of them. Francis Robertson calls it a testament to the human voice, containing "six big fat parts, one to each of the six voice classifications."

And what wonderful numbers they all have to sing! (Yes, *La Gioconda* is an old-fashioned "number" opera; another reason the highbrow critics disliked it.) Act I offers "Voce di donna" for Gioconda's mother, La Cieca, as well as arias for Gioconda herself and the evil baritone Barnaba. It is full of wonderful opportunities for vocal display, too. Listen, for example, to Gioconda's high B-flat, pianissimo (if done properly) and sustained, as she leads her mother to the steps of the church singing "Come t'amo." Act II highlights include the tenor "Cielo e mar" (perhaps the most famous single aria from the opera) and Barnaba's song to the fishermen "Ah, pescator, affonda l'esca." Act III opens with a wonderful revenge aria for Alvise, the bass, before offering the "Dance of the Hours." It also contains highly dramatic scenes between Laura and Alvise and between Laura and Gioconda. Act IV, the culmination of all Gioconda's sufferings, is highlighted by her aria in contemplation of suicide, "Suicidio."

Throughout its length, *La Gioconda* reveals in both vocal and orchestral passages Ponchielli's great gifts for warmth of melody and highly effective orchestration. Technically, while the form of the opera may have looked backwards to Meyerbeerian grand opera, it pushed forward the role of the orchestra. Operas such as *La Gioconda* and *Carmen,* which premiered in Paris just a year before Ponchielli's work, greatly expanded the symphonic texture of the opera orchestra. In *La Gioconda,* that texture is rich, ample, and closely adapted to the rapidly shifting action of the text. Ponchielli may not have had "sufficient good sense to watch out for all the abyss" of Boito's libretto (Boito was, after all, a forceful personality while Ponchielli, by all accounts, was extremely amiable and even passive), but falling into that abyss brought out the very best in him musically. It is as if Ponchielli poured into his music for *La Gioconda* all the highly charged passions so conspicuously absent in his own life.

Whatever elements contributed to the success of *La Gioconda,* they were a combination that Ponchielli never found again. He enjoyed the fame and fortune of his one unequivocal triumph, however, for which he had paid with a long apprenticeship. Ponchielli was born in 1834 in the village of Paderno Fasolaro, near Cremona. His family's poverty did not compromise his musical education, which began with lessons from his father, the town organist. By the age of nine, little Amilcare was ready for the Milan Conservatory, where he remained until he was twenty. While still a student, he wrote an operetta with three fellow students. According to legend, on the day he graduated, Ponchielli called to another student, "My passions begin today!"

Passions or no, what began that day in earnest was the hard business of making a living in the precarious world of professional music. In the next two decades, Ponchielli held down a series of extremely modest posts: church organist, bandmaster of the Piacenza militia, leader of the Cremona town band. There were operas, too, six of them before *La Gioconda,* beginning with *I promessi sposi,* produced in Cremona in 1856 with little success. And so it went for twenty years; the journeyman composer paying his dues, making a slim living, receiving the occasional commission from a regional opera house, and building a reputation as a very pleasant and co-operative fellow.

Ponchielli's break came in 1872. Commissioned to write an opera for the opening of Teatro del Verme in Milan, he revised *I promessi sposi,* which was a resounding success. It became the first of his operas to travel the length of the land, and also to be produced outside Italy. A commission from La Scala followed, and *Le due gemelle* was well received there in 1873. After another opera in 1874 came the La Scala commission for *La Gioconda.* When it opened on April 8, 1876, it made Amilcare Ponchielli world-famous. Other operas followed, three new ones plus revisions of two earlier works, but none was a success outside Italy and none is remembered today. In his native land, however, they were well received, and their author was greatly honored. The town of his birth, little Paderno Fasolaro, today is called Paderno Ponchielli, after its most famous citizen.

As a result of the international triumph of *La Gioconda,* Ponchielli was appointed a professor of composition at the Milan Conservatory in 1883 (he had been a student there himself from the age of nine to age twenty). Before his premature death in 1886, Ponchielli taught Pietro Mascagni and Giacomo Puccini. Thus, he had a direct influence on two of the leading composers of the "verismo" school of opera composition, a school that drove the final nail into the coffin of musical obsolescence in which his own works were buried. Wagner may have made his works obsolete outside Italy, but "verismo" was the native-born killer. Perhaps he was *too* good a teacher!

Of Ponchielli's total output of ten operas, only *La Gioconda* remains on the boards today, sumptuous in its vulgarity and poison to the unremitting esthetes (to paraphrase a remark of Robert Lawrence's). Hugo Wolf may have found it "an uncommonly feeble product that, one hopes, will very soon and forever vanish from the repertoire," but his hope has not come true and is not likely to do so. "The esthetes may say what they please about *Gioconda,*" Francis Robertson observed. "It will come back again and again."

PUCCINI'S *Girl of the Golden West*
by Peter P. Jacobi

Giacomo Puccini referred to it as *mia* girl. My girl. *La fanciulla del West. The Girl of the Golden West.*

An opera born out of personal grief. An opera, no period piece but then harbinger of things to come. A Puccini opera that's gained less attention and deserves more. An opera surely not as good as a Puccini fanatic would have it be, but considerably better than lots of the musical pundits would make it.

Director Harold Prince has called it "an extremely well made musical—sophisticated in its naïveté" and "romantic as hell."

Prince seems totally smitten. Of *Fanciulla* he says:

> It's snobbery not to like the opera. Why, the whole thing is ingenious, disarming.
>
> Because it's Italian and based on something utterly American—that gives it an extra sweetness.
>
> It is not a horse opera. It's about mining, about a big country with few people, about isolation, loneliness.
>
> The melodies permit so much to go on internally, within the characters. Minnie, Dick, and the rest gain real life, and meaning, and depth, even though the story may for us TODAY seem totally unreal, even hoaky. That is our problem. Our loss.
>
> I believe in the characters and trust their motivations. Now that doesn't mean one should play it for reality. The original drama by itself is dated. It is the music that lifts the story to a kind of special reality, as the best of opera tends to do. Opera is not real; it's make-believe. But within that make-believe there is a sense of something one can believe, something of substance. And *Fanciulla* oozes such belief, such substance.
>
> And I like the happy ending. She deceives to win. That's charming.
>
> Something about this work, maybe its guilelessness, appeals to the kid in me. And I hope we can create the right atmosphere on the Lyric stage so that the opera appeals to the kid in everyone.

Puccini saw the play—David Belasco's *The Girl of the Golden West* —while visiting New York in 1907, this to attend the Metropolitan Opera premiere of his *Madama Butterfly*. And even though that grand success had been based on a Belasco story, Puccini was not immediately taken by *Girl*. He was at the time thinking of other operatic subjects, including one based on the life of Marie Antoinette. But the other subjects were discarded, one after another, and soon the composer focused on the Belasco play, which was easy enough to negotiate for, considering the triumph of *Butterfly*.

The story grew in his favor. As Puccini wrote to his publisher and friend Ricordi, he wanted a change from "*Boheme, Butterfly & Co.* Even I am sick of them." The frail, lovely heroines had been so much with him through *Manon Lescaut, Bohème,* and *Butterfly.* Only *Tosca* had been a departure, and now he wanted—no, needed—a change of pace again. That he had in this story which Belasco termed "a drama of love . . . against a dark and vast background of primitive characters and untrammeled nature."

Mosco Carner, the Puccini biographer, notes that "in a sense, it was Sardou's *Tosca* transplanted from Rome to the Cloudy Mountains of California." He points to a generally grim atmosphere in both stories (even though Puccini ultimately gives *Girl* a happy ending), as well as a love triangle, and even a Scarpia character, the sheriff, Rance.

Puccini undoubtedly also was tempted by the possibility of scoring another financial success in the American market; the story was, after all, American. And once again it would afford him the chance to create exotic effects, not the Far East this time, but the Far West.

Here was melodrama, too, a promising subject for Puccini music. Here was a heroine both pure and knowing (in the theater it was a rousing vehicle for Blanche Bates, back then an unrivaled actress on the American stage; in the opera house it would serve the great sopranos, Puccini thought). Here also was a story about men against the earth, a story of struggle and loneliness, something new for the composer.

Well, despite all that, the opera has not fared marvelously well. All that Puccini thought would make the stage quiver from sheer emotionalism turned rather quaint. Even the music was faulted as lesser Puccini or uninspired Puccini.

Today we can appreciate that rather than being lesser Puccini, *Fanciulla* was changing Puccini. It was the Puccini we would come to know briefly again in his last opera, *Turandot,* the work with musical sounds heralding a new direction that was not to be because death intervened.

Writing *Fanciulla* was a grievous battle. The period was bitter for Puccini. Family events turned terrible and constantly interrupted the peace that Puccini required for composing.

His marriage long had been troubled. Giacomo had a roving eye. Wife Elvira had a jealous one. Evidence suggests that she was considerably more jealous than he was amorous. And that capacity of hers to doubt his fidelity came to a dreadful peak during the *Fanciulla* period.

The tragic focus was Doria Manfredi, who at the age of sixteen had come to work for the Puccinis. Elvira became increasingly suspicious of the girl, now twenty-one and pretty. Eventually she charged the girl, despite incontrovertible evidence to the contrary, with engaging in "immoral conduct" with Giacomo. The seeds may have been planted by one of Elvira's relatives who disliked Puccini because he disliked them. Elvira came to accusing Doria around Torre del Lago, calling the girl a slut, a tart, a whore, her husband's mistress, to everyone's severe embarrassment and to the girl's torment.

Puccini himself wrote to a friend: "Life at Torre had become absolutely unbearable for me; I'm only telling you the truth when I say that I have often lovingly fingered my revolver."

In January, 1909, the crisis became a tragedy. Doria committed suicide.

The Manfredis, a respected local clan, sought retribution. An ensuing court trial proved ugly. Elvira was found guilty of defaming character, of libel, and of menacing another person's life and limb. There were appeals. And finally Puccini reached a settlement with the Manfredis. He offered them 12,000 lire; in return they withdrew legal action. The case was dropped.

That, of course, did not solve the unfortunate relationship between Elvira and Giacomo. Nor did it stop a gossipy press from running many inches of sordid material about the "Affaire Doria," the "Affaire Puccini." Nor did it silence the composer's enemies who found in this mess a certain satisfaction.

Puccini called it "the saddest time of my life."

And amidst it he sought to create *La fanciulla del West*. As usual he had libretto troubles. And he was obviously trying a new musical approach at a time when he was least able to handle it emotionally.

But somehow he got the work done. And on December 10, 1910, the opera was first performed, appropriately at an American opera house. The Metropolitan cast held Enrico Caruso as Johnson and Emmy Destinn as Minnie. Pasquale Amato was the villainous Rance. And in the pit: Arturo Toscanini. That premiere was an occasion and a triumph for Puccini, present to receive a crown of silver decorated with ribbons representing the national colors of Italy and the United States. There were fifty-two curtain calls. Never again would he have a comparable opening-night success. In fact, he hadn't had one like it since *Manon Lescaut*.

But after such an auspicious beginning and a first round of productions at major opera houses, Minnie and friends came to be pretty much ignored. The American market that Puccini hoped for didn't materialize. The world market didn't either.

Looking at and listening to this piece of musicalized fiction, one finds delights among the nonsense. It is a western as someone who hadn't the slightest notion of what the real West was like might envision it. As that, it's a pleasant diversion.

But it is based on events that actually took place. Belasco's father spent time in a mining camp and recalled a manhunt such as the one featured in the opera, as well as the dramatic moment of blood dripping from a loft to give the hunted man away, and a poker game with the prisoner's life at stake.

Puccini, with his sensitive ability to capture human emotions, colors the story with the warmth—nay, sometimes the heat—of his musical passions. He also strives to evoke atmosphere. And although sometimes what he accomplishes borders on the ludicrous (all those repetitions of "hello" and "all right" and "hip hooray" and "whisky per tutti"), the overall effect of the opera causes wonder. This because he understood what is dramatic. This because he understood what music can contribute to a dramatic situation.

Nary an opera has act endings any more effective than the three Puccini fashioned for *Fanciulla*.

Act I—Johnson consoles Minnie: "You are a creature with a good and pure soul, and you have the face of an angel." Fifteen tenors off-stage echo his thoughts. And Minnie, as if in a dream, repeats, "the face of an angel." Tough Minnie, ah really so soft, has had soft words spoken to her. A love story is under way. And all to an orchestra that diminishes away.

Act II—Minnie and Rance play poker for Johnson's life. She takes the first hand; he the second. Rance gets three kings the third time around, but Minnie cheats to trump him with aces. The sheriff, momentarily beaten, departs into the dark night as Minnie mixes laughter and weeping in exultant shouts of "He's mine! He's mine!"

Act III—Minnie and Johnson sing a monotonal fairwell, "Addio mia California," as the miners softly and sadly bid their beloved *fanciulla* goodbye. "You'll never come back," they sing. "Never more. Never more" (Mai più. Mai più). The same words first uttered so devastatingly in the glorious Nile scene of Verdi's *Aïda*. And the Puccini orchestra here is but a hush of strings, a touch of celeste, and a hint of bass drum.

Puccini leads to each conclusion with a sure sense of what will create attention. There's a harp with paper inserted among the strings to approximate the banjo. There are hints of ragtime and more than hints of folk songs. "The Old Dog Tray" and "Dooda Day." There's a balladeer. There is gun play. There are animals, be they horses or mules, but animals. There's Minnie reading psalms in a Bible class with those rough and doting miners of hers. There's the villain, a Scarpia type with a personality of his own. There are Indians and an Indian lullaby. There's a mob calling for blood or, more accurately, for Johnson's hanging. "We'll teach him to dance," they sing menacingly while considering the dangling corpse into which they'll be able to pump lead. There are longing and loneliness, gold miners thinking of distant family and home. There's mood, whether it's the miners pining for their wives or dawn breaking over the mountain; there's music to feed one's thoughts, music to express the moment.

And most of all there's a fetching romantic couple. Minnie with her heart of gold, who can sing of her beloved at one point, "You are the man who gave me my first kiss. You cannot die." And Johnson, who turns out to be a bit of Robin Hood in his banditry and who turns good for the love of a woman.

Listen, and you'll hear not only the familiar tenor aria, "Ch'ella mi creda libero." You'll hear Puccini music for men; for despite Minnie's importance, this is an opera also about men, rough men, down and out and yet spirited men. You'll hear much chorus. You'll hear Puccini experimentation with the orchestra, undoubtedly influenced somewhat by Debussy and Strauss, but also influenced by a maturing Puccini ready to test new areas of sound. You'll hear moments of tension and glorious moments of romance, and all imbued not only with the exoticism of a strange "Far West" but with the lyricism of Puccini's Italy.

"Viva Minnie," the miners sing. "La nostra Minnie." "Hooray for Minnie! Our Minnie!"

Perhaps we'll be ready to shout such praise after experiencing a revival of *The Girl of the Golden West*. Maybe as the lovers move off into sunrise or sunset or distance toward the joys of a new life, so this somewhat neglected Puccini gem will now gain new joys of acceptance.

After all, just consider this situation. Dick Johnson has been taken by Rance and faces the rope. He knows what Minnie chanced for him. He sings, "Ch'ella mi creda libero e lontano, sopra una nuova via di redenzione!"

> "Let her think I'm free and far away,
> On my way to a fresh start in life!
> She'll wait for me to return.
> And the days will crawl by, they'll crawl by
> And . . . well . . . I won't come back . . .
> Minnie, only flower of my life.
> Minnie, you who have loved me so dearly!
> Ah, you were the only flower in my life!"

Now there's romance, the sort we need more of.
We know Minnie is on her way. We know safety and happiness are ahead.
Romance, the sort we need more of.

WAGNER'S *Götterdämmerung*
by Speight Jenkins

Götterdämmerung. Look at the formidability of its very name. Not only does it have two umlauts, a strange German sign that seems more alien to Americans than Latin accents, but it adds up to a staggering number of letters. A cursory gambol through the works of popular composers finds only one competitor in length of one-word title, Mozart's *Schauspieldirektor,* but it is almost always known in America as *The Impresario* and is a chamber opera to boot. *Götterdämmerung* by name or in translation as *Dusk of the Gods* might also call to mind (to those over thirty-five) the blazing Wilhelmstrasse with a lunatic Hitler watching from his bunker.

Whatever the image *Götterdämmerung* evokes, it is always grand, never intimate nor small. Everything is on a huge scale in Wagner's final *Ring* opera, and the work is of such complexity, eclecticism, and individuality that it stands alone—not just in the composer's canon, but in opera. Its singularity stems from being both a grand opera and the embodiment of the most mature Wagnerian thoughts on the complete art work or music drama. *Tristan* is a music drama pure; nobody could confuse it with French or Italian grand opera. *Die Walküre* follows the principles of Wagner's 1851 book *Opera and Drama,* while *Die Meistersinger* is a nationalistic epic. But *Götterdämmerung* is the work in which Wagner in some ways shook off his own defensiveness and, while keeping his own style, took what he needed from French grand opera and from Italy to round his *Ring.*

Opera and Drama, the tract that served as the basis for *Das Rheingold, Die*

Walküre, and the first two acts of *Siegfried,* specifically condemns any ensemble: no duets, trios, quartets, or choruses. The music is supposed to come from the words, and nothing should blur the audience's understanding of the text. A deliberately archaic German was advocated to increase the mythic atmosphere (this continues in *Götterdämmerung*), and *Stabreim,* the hyper-alliterative prose that has so often been caricatured, was used to make the words sound the way the music does. Leitmotifs in these early *Ring* operas are open-ended, short, and easily comprehensible melodies that cue the audience in to the thoughts of the character. The tune detector can move swiftly through them, cataloging and classifying, working out a vast psychological scheme to amplify the music.

In *Götterdämmerung,* however, which was written from 1869 to 1874, more than a decade after the first two acts of *Siegfried,* almost all this is thrown out the window. By the second scene of the Prologue (another first for *Götterdämmerung*—can anyone think of a prologue with more than one scene? *Rheingold* cannot count because it's a whole opera), Siegfried and Brünnhilde are merrily singing away in a straightforward love duet, concluding on a high C for the soprano with the tenor a major third below. In the first scene of Act I the tenor and baritone join in the blood-brotherhood duet which has a long passage in thirds, much as does many a duet in Verdi, and the number of ensemble numbers would stack up with any Italian opera: a big choral scene, arias for the tenor and bass, two trios, one with obligato tenor accompaniment, and many others.

Inability to understand each word, always a problem, as Wagner correctly pointed out, any time more than one person sings, is exaggerated in this opera by the increase in volume of the orchestra. The scoring of *Das Rheingold* and *Die Walküre,* while not light, is softer, more penetrable than that of *Götterdämmerung.*

Even more radical, the whole use of the Wagner leitmotif has changed. The new ones are longer and far less easy to identify readily; the old ones are often developed symphonically and superimposed one on top of the other; and the original meanings are sometimes scrambled or discarded. Wagner's use of one leitmotif on another—a vertical sandwiching of themes that once were only used horizontally—has strong psychological sense: people are not two-dimensional and do not think that way. The "Curse" may affect someone simultaneously with thoughts on Wotan's power or rage or one's own love affair. It's just that this psychological reality defeats the goal of classifying every sound.

One might ask, who cares? And the answer is that audiences in general never have. Wagner was a supreme theater magician, and like one of his successors, Alban Berg, Wagner wanted people to enjoy his operas, not worry over what every note meant. Our grandfather scholars, however, took him and his theories, or at least his early theories, very, very seriously: he was Holy German Art personified. They studied very carefully and succeeded in writing justifications for the wildest symphonically developed motif.

What they really had to stretch to do was to explain the comic moments, when Wagner simply must have written in a tune because he liked it without regard to what it originally stood for. The funniest example, of course, takes place in the last act of *Siegfried,* composed just before *Götterdämmerung,* when the dragon motif comes in as Brünnhilde sings of her passion for Siegfried. But the later opera has its share: in the Prologue duet, Brünnhilde expresses her love for her horse, Grane, and the orchestra plays the love theme of Siegmund and Sieglinde from *Die Walküre;* she rides Grane into Siegfried's funeral pyre, and the orchestra thunders out the magic sleep motif from *Die Walküre.* One could argue in the latter case that her act is the logical outcome of Wotan's putting her into a magic sleep, or that she now is going into a magic (?) death, but both arguments appear completely artificial. At all times in *Götterdämmerung* Wagner's instinct for musical drama took over, and the music's contours fit what is sung, sometimes without regard to extramusical meaning.

Another addition to *Götterdämmerung* not found in the early *Ring* dramas is ornamentation characteristic of bel canto opera. Trills (the Wagner turn which he uses frequently in *Lohengrin* and the other romantic operas of his youth) and a general decoration of phrases crop up everywhere. In the "Vengeance" trio of Act II Brünnhilde combines both worlds in a typically Wagnerian yet bel canto influenced figure. On the word "Zauber" (magic) she sings in eighth notes an E-flat, E-natural, F, leaps to a high B-flat and holds it, then moves down to an E-flat again, the whole sung legato. It is a task for the soprano, very exciting and much more ornamental than what might occur in the first two *Ring* works.

How does this happen? Wagner's verbal explanation exists in two important essays published in 1870 and 1871, "On Beethoven" and "The Destiny of Opera." Always convinced that he was as great a theoretician and writer as he was a composer, Wagner had a strong characteristic that has been exhibited over the past two centuries by the United States Supreme Court and for the past twenty years by the Catholic Church. He never admitted that he had changed his mind, only that he had more carefully defined his point of view. No matter if a reasonable man could see that the new position was 180 degrees away from the earlier one; Wagner's prose still strove to prove that it was only a development of the first thought.

The whole concept of music coming out of words in *Opera and Drama* changed in these two essays. Now music is not secondary but is a full partner to drama. "A fixed, mimetic and musical improvisation" (how can an improvisation be fixed, as Robert Gutman has pointed out) is the key phrase, and by this Wagner meant that musical composition must be released from formal patterns and placed alongside—neither superior nor inferior to—the drama. The two serve each other's needs, and as Wagner said, "My dramas are acts of music become visible." The new definition freed the composer to write as he felt and to disobey any prior restrictions.

The evidence of *Götterdämmerung* shows the fruit of his theory. The music describes both the characters and their feelings with unerring skill; the great length of the work does not seem so, particularly if given uncut when the valleys balance the mountains; and Wagner allowed himself the right to bring in what he had learned in *Tristan* and *Die Meistersinger* to enrich his *Ring* music. The two earlier operas contribute the deceptive cadence (an incomplete stop in music; the melody does not come to an end but in fact continues into the next phrase) and suspension and anticipation within a chord (again the process of hearing an unending quality to music), plus a certain amount of chromaticism, which allows more tonal freedom; all give to the final *Ring* drama a plasticity and continuity unachieved by the other three.

Wagner's success in *Götterdämmerung* can also be judged by the richness of Brünnhilde. She is, of course, central to the whole *Ring*. The principal character in two of the dramas, she is the goal of the third. From a practical standpoint she is the focus of casting; audiences typically come to the *Ring* more because of the lead soprano than because of any other one reason. And *Götterdämmerung* is "her" opera. Hagen has wonderful music to sing; Siegfried develops maturity and is rewarded with a *tessitura* that demands formidable control and a role that requires power and stamina to a high degree. The other characters—Gunther and Gutrune, even Alberich, the Norns, and the Rhinemaidens—all have important moments.

But Brünnhilde in the final *Ring* work matters most because of her awe-inspiring humanity, brought about by all the components of Wagner's maturity. She is a great person—obviously not a goddess, but a larger-than-life individual. Her motif as a married woman, heard early in the Prologue and containing a graceful decoration, portrays her as surely as does the whole Prologue scene, with its eloquent duet as a fulfilled, happy woman. One might wonder in all good humor why someone as talented as she might want to spend all her time on that rock waiting for Siegfried to return, but obviously it doesn't bother her.

Happiness is still hers when in the final scene of Act I she is found contemplating Siegfried's love token to her, the ill-fated ring. Her reaction to her sister's plea to save the gods states musically and dramatically her boundless love for Siegfried. When the rape of the ring by the false Gunther follows, she shows her ability to turn events into metaphysical happenings. She knows that she is unique; consequently when a strange man breaks into her home, she blames the gods directly. That she is probably (though perhaps not totally) wrong only shows us more of her humanity.

In Act II Wagner goes one step further than with his first-act Isolde. In the Irish princess he has painted a woman in love, scorned and furious but at least not sexually betrayed. Brünnhilde finds herself about to be married to someone she does not know, with her own husband benignly looking on. When she then discovers—by looking at the ring on his finger—that he, disguised by a magic helmet, had won her for another, the limits of her rage almost put her into orbit. Only music can successfully convey such fury, and her repeated high As and Bs as well as the surging, violent Wagnerian orchestra convey the infinite nature of her anger just as surely as it limns her despair. Is there anything in opera more tragic than her cry, "Ah, Jammer! Jammer!" after her first temper has fled? She sits broken before us—perhaps a victim of hubris as she really thought she could control everything—without the least idea of what to do to win back her husband or her own self-respect.

The use then of a conventional conspirator's trio to plot the death of Siegfried has a dimension outside of its form: Brünnhilde can find neither magic explanation nor charm to solve her husband's actions, and so she falls back on treachery and deceit, two weapons available to far-lesser creatures than she. The music, by reverting to a vengeance trio, may well underline her own acceptance of the standard response.

The Immolation Scene, a direct descendant of the conclusion of *Norma,* sums everything up. First of all it glorifies the power of the intelligent, creative, active woman. Brünnhilde is any feminist's dream symbol, because she solves actively what no man was able to do. She realizes that she must end the gods, clean the ring, and start the world on a new life; and she does it all. The Rhinemaidens' whispering to her about Siegfried's potion only give her the bare facts; she is aware that the world is going bad, and she has the strength to save it. The musical climax of the Immolation Scene comes when she tells Wotan to rest, that she will give him peace. The use of the soprano's voice in a cello register, the quiet orchestra, the philosophical turn of phrase as she sings—all unite for a unique moment in the theater.

As Brünnhilde rides into the flames, the Rhine floods, Hagen is drowned, the ring is reclaimed by the maidens, and Valhalla burns, while the audience is treated to a symphonic review of many of the most important *Ring* motives. At the very end, in a stroke of sheer genius, Wagner brings in the motive associated with self-sacrificing love, first heard when Sieglinde thanks Brünnhilde for saving her so that she can bear Siegmund's child, in the third act of *Die Walküre.* Its rising, ornate theme pours out of the orchestra, and the whole purpose of Wagner's *Ring* is laid bare: man can only be saved by the redeeming, loyal, and intelligent woman, and the power of love conquers all. Could Cosima, the composer's wife and spiritual heir, have had a higher tribute?

THOMAS'S *Hamlet*
by Jonathan Abarbanel

Hamlet, the opera, has suffered the slings and arrows of outrageous fortune, as did its composer, Ambroise Thomas (pronounced "Toe-mah"). At its premiere at the Paris Opéra on March 9, 1868, *Hamlet* was declared (admittedly by chauvinistic Parisian critics) to be the finest new opera since Meyerbeer and Halévy. It followed by less than two years the premiere of Thomas's *Mignon* at the Opéra-Comique. The worldwide success of these works ensured Thomas's international reputation. Already a member of L'Académie française and the Légion d'honneur, and professor of composition at the Paris Conservatory, Thomas was appointed director of the conservatory in 1871 on the strength of the triumph of *Hamlet*. At the very pinnacle of his career, Thomas enjoyed a stature equal to that of Verdi, praised not only by the Italian master but also by Berlioz, Bizet, Gounod, and Massenet (who was a student of Thomas's at the conservatory). Indeed, Verdi abandoned his own thoughts of setting *Hamlet* out of deference to Thomas.

Unhappily, Thomas lived to see both his popularity with the public and his stature among musicians decline with almost brutal rapidity after 1870. In that year, France lost the brief Franco-Prussian War and saw the paper empire of Louis Napoléon collapse after an eighteen-year reign. The social order changed dramatically, and so did musical and theatrical tastes. Thomas found himself unable to relate to the musical efforts of younger moderns such as Bizet, Fauré, and Debussy, who increasingly turned away from opera in favor of instrumental music. In a famous incident, Thomas refused to appoint Fauré to the teaching staff of the conservatory.

Thomas was failing with the public, too. Of his last three operas, all written after 1870, only one was moderately successful. And while *Mignon* retained its astounding popularity—on the occasion of its one-thousandth performance in 1894, Thomas became the first composer to receive the Grand Cross of the Legion of Honor—his other works were performed less and less. Even *Hamlet,* which Thomas considered his masterpiece, received fewer than one-third the number of performances of *Mignon.*

Thomas died in 1896 at the age of eighty-four (he was two years older than Verdi), and most of his operas died with him. Today, *Mignon* still clings to the edges of the standard repertory—alone among Thomas's more than twenty operas—while *Hamlet* has been revived only as a specialty opera in the last decade, thanks to the attention of Sherrill Milnes.

Hamlet deserves better. It has come down to us with an undeservedly shabby reputation, as have so many other early- and mid-nineteenth-century works before they are "rediscovered." Wherever it has been revived, the critics have admitted their surprise at finding a work that is alive and fresh and dramatically effective.

First, one must consider the abilities of Thomas as a composer. His critics declare him a lightweight, most of whose work was written in the tradition of opéra comique rather than grand opera. This is true. It also is true that his music is not profound, as is the music of Mozart, Wagner, or the mature Verdi. Instead, Thomas was an archetypical composer of the French school: an absolutely brilliant orchestral colorist and a ravishing melodist whose music flows with a swift and seamless dramatic effectiveness. The critics say that

Thomas's talent was too slight for such a significant work as *Hamlet;* that Verdi should have done it just as Verdi should have done *King Lear.* Well, let them live on wishes. Verdi *didn't* do *Hamlet* or *King Lear.* Six composers did set *Hamlet,* however, and Thomas's work is the very best of the bunch.

What really upsets many of the critics is, not the score of Thomas, but the libretto by Jules Barbier and Michel Carré (which, of course, Thomas would have approved). You see, it's not completely and precisely the *Hamlet* of Shakespeare. For one thing, Hamlet lives to become king of Denmark. In the play, you will recall, Hamlet and almost everyone else die, leaving the kingdom to Fortinbras, the "mighty Pollack."

In the opera, Fortinbras isn't around at all. Neither are Rosencrantz and Guildenstern. The gravediggers make a brief appearance; but, alas, poor Yorick is gone, or at any rate, Hamlet's speech about him. Other famous speeches that are missing include: "Oh, what a rogue and peasant slave am I," "Oh, that this too, too solid flesh would melt," "What a piece of work is man," and "There is providence in the fall of a sparrow." "To be or not to be" is retained, although the score indicates that it is an optional cut. Among other characters, Polonius and his son, Laertes, are greatly reduced in size and importance (and Polonius is *not* killed by Hamlet), while Polonius's daughter, Ophelia, is greatly expanded in size and importance. Finally, the total body count is reduced from Shakespeare's eight to only two: Ophelia and Claudius, the king.

On the surface of things, it looks like Thomas and his collaborators have done considerable violence to the original play. In fact, their alterations are no greater than those made countless times by composers and librettists adapting novels or plays for the demands of the lyric stage. The only real difference is that *Hamlet,* the play, is so very familiar to us and is held to be sacred by some.

But it *wasn't* held to be sacred by the French (for whom Racine, Corneille, and Molière were/are sacred). Because Shakespeare rarely was performed in France at that time, and almost never in English, Barbier and Carré actually based their libretto on an 1847 adaptation of the play by Alexandre Dumas, *père,* and Paul Meurice. Even the British hardly were purists about Shakespeare; they bowdlerized him and changed his endings like crazy. It was the great British actor David Garrick, after all, who gave the world the *King Lear* with the happy ending and the *Romeo and Juliet* in which the lovers live (which version Berlioz used for his setting).

In any case, the critics of many English-speaking nations have carried a prejudice against the opera *Hamlet* for years because of the libretto. To this day, the British-edited *Grove's Dictionary of Music* reveals that prejudice in the pejorative language it uses in its analysis of the opera, describing Ophelia's mad scene as "floridly inconsequential" and the last act as "still more absurd" than the mad scene.

In fact, apart from the alterations cited, *Hamlet* is remarkably close to the play, following the play's act structure, its major plot devices, and the rudiments of the play's (of course, much more complex) intellectual thrust. Writing of the original production in the *Revue et gazette musicale de Paris* in 1868, Paul Bernard hit the nail on the head: "The libretto of the new opera remains perfectly within the atmosphere created by Shakespeare. The same passionate intensity (and) implacable fate. . . . The philosophic aspect alone is less developed; that was inevitable. One does not use melody to conduct a discussion."

What Thomas and his librettists created was a hybrid opera that looks back towards certain nineteenth-century conventions, on the one hand, and looks forward in its dramaturgy and advanced use of the orchestra, on the other hand. While Verdi, despite his profundity, still was writing traditional "number" operas, Thomas produced a work with very few set pieces, grand arias, or ensemble combinations. Those that exist in the work—you can number them on the fingers of one hand—are the conventions of the older tradition, in which Thomas was educated. There is a love duet in the first scene, a sparkling "brindisi," or drinking song, in the third scene (Act II, scene 1, in Thomas's original five-act plan), a trio in the fifth scene (Act III), and a ballet and mad scene in the sixth scene (Act IV). Beyond these few set pieces, the libretto is a tightly knit sequence of ariosos and ariettas, few of which run more than a dozen lines of verse. The verse itself is extremely direct; it is rhythmically similar to spoken French, at the specific insistence of Thomas. While the verse often is mundane, it never is cloying or overly ripe.

The orchestra is full-throated throughout and frequently is utilized in a surprisingly symphonic manner. Even the coloratura mad scene has a full orchestral accompaniment, not simply an obbligato part. Along the way, the score is full of surprising, unusual, even novel orchestral accents and details, such as the first use of the then-new saxophone in an opera orchestra. In all, it is clear that Thomas, Barbier, and Carré had a well developed and very astute understanding of theater and a modern—for that time—sense of integrated musico-dramatic composition.

The opera opens with a somber, moody prelude that segues into a grand march introducing the first scene, which establishes the pomp of the royal court in swift, bright strokes. The music soon turns melancholy, however, for the first entrance of Hamlet, whose brief meditation is drawn from the language of Shakespeare. Ophelia then enters for an arioso dialogue with Hamlet that gradually expands into a ravishing love duet. The love scene is *not* in Shakespeare, but it's gorgeous. Details include the flute obbligato, which underscores Ophelia's entrance, and the sweet solo oboe and horn lines of the duet. Laertes enters next with a brief, noble arietta. This is followed by the re-entry of the court on its way to a wedding banquet for Claudius and the Queen. The scene then ends on a quiet note. Typical of this opera, Thomas musically has gone through six complete shifts of mood and emotion in a brief establishing scene!

The second scene takes place on the castle battlements at midnight, where Hamlet speaks with the ghost of his father, murdered by Claudius (Hamlet's uncle). A highpoint of the opera, the scene's dramatic and grim prelude includes a fine cor anglais solo. Later in the scene, off-stage trumpets and cannon suggest the revelries of the wedding banquet, while woodwinds in their lowest registers provide an eerie mood for the ghost on stage. This scene follows Shakespeare with extreme fidelity and is both dramatically and musically superbly effective.

The third scene (Act II, scene 1) is, at first, a relatively uninteresting episode of character exposition, with a small display piece for Ophelia that's just a warm-up for her big mad scene. Towards the end, however, the traveling players arrive ("The play's the thing wherein I'll catch the conscience of the king!"), leading to Hamlet's drinking song, a famous highlight of the opera. "O vin, dissipe la tristesse" is more than a showpiece however: you will hear this melody again as a character theme for Hamlet and his feverish, perhaps lunatic, intensity.

The fourth scene (Act II, scene 2) is the play within the play. Listen for the saxophone solo as the pantomime begins, immediately after the brief, bright opening prelude. As the scene ends, one hears the orchestra and Hamlet reiterate snatches of the drinking song, which is repeated by the orchestra yet again in the opening bars of the fifth scene (Act III). Listen to the skitterish strings, reflecting Hamlet's feverish state of mind. As in the play, this scene is the emotional climax of the opera, in which Hamlet hesitates to kill Claudius in revenge because Claudius is at his prayers. Later, Hamlet confronts his mother, tightly paralleling Shakespeare's third act. Interpolated between these moments is a scene between Hamlet, his mother (the Queen), and Ophelia, which ends in a trio.

True to the conventions of French opera, Thomas opened the sixth scene (his Act IV) with a ballet to the suite of country dances, featuring another saxophone solo. The heart of the act is Ophelia's mad scene and death, a coloratura showcase that harkens back to the earlier era of bel canto. At the center of it is a haunting ballade, "Pâle et blonde," based on a Swedish melody. Thomas incorporated the tune into his opera at the request of twenty-four-year-old Christine Nilsson, the widely acclaimed first Ophelia. While *Hamlet* is set in Denmark, the inclusion of a Swedish melody was deemed a sufficiently authentic tip of the cap in the direction of Scandinavia. At the close of the scene, Ophelia dies to an off-stage chorus humming the Act I love duet.

The final scene is brief, highlighted by a robust and ironic tune for the two gravediggers, "Dame ou prince," and by a lovely and moving aria for Hamlet, "Comme une pâle fleur." Beyond these two items, the scene is musically ordinary, a functional act devoted to bringing the opera to a swift and dramatic conclusion in which the ghost appears one more time, the villain is killed, and Hamlet lives. Over the years, the ending has been altered several times. Thomas himself created an ending in which Hamlet kills Claudius and then himself. Called the "Covent Garden ending," it was performed in England to satisfy those who insisted that Hamlet must die. As recently as 1982, conductor and musicologist (or should that be muse ecologist?) Richard Bonynge created a third ending in which Laertes wounds Hamlet, who lasts long enough to kill Claudius before dying himself. While still quite different from the play, Bonynge's ending is the closest to Shakespeare.

MOZART'S *Idomeneo*
by Alfred Glasser

"A thing of beauty," wrote John Keats, "is a joy forever." Even as he penned the famous line in 1818, a thing of great beauty had been languishing for nearly four decades in almost total obscurity from which it did not begin to emerge until 1917. This was Wolfgang Amadeus Mozart's opera seria *Idomeneo,* commissioned by Karl Theodor, the Elector of Bavaria, for performance at the Munich Opera during the carnival season of 1781. The premiere, which had taken place two days after Mozart's twenty-fifth birthday, had been successful despite a less-than-exemplary cast. (Anton Raaff, the tenor who created the title role, was sixty-seven years old.) Yet, after the Munich production, Mozart heard his opera only once more at a private performance in Vienna a few years later.

Several factors contributed to this lamentable neglect of a masterpiece. One of them was the resounding success and popularity of each of the operas that flowed from Mozart's inexhaustible imagination during the following and final decade of his tragically short life. (At the premiere of *Le nozze di Figaro* in Vienna, the enraptured audience kept applauding until several numbers were repeated and others were performed three times. The disgruntled emperor spoiled the fun by forbidding encores after the first few performances.) Mozart in effect was competing with himself. And he was the greatest composer of his day, if not—as many claim—of all time.

Another factor was the lack of singers, suitable orchestra and theater for opera at the court of Hieronymus Colloredo, archbishop of Salzburg, to whose household Mozart was attached. Thus Mozart could not perform his operas at home and could not leave Salzburg to perform them elsewhere without first obtaining permission from his ungenerous "patron." Mozart finally left the Salzburg court without the security of another post to free himself to accept other commissions. While awaiting these and while applying in vain for court appointments, he supported himself by giving concerts and teaching.

The most important reason by far that *Idomeneo* had to wait so long to re-enter the repertory was the fact that it belonged to the tradition of opera seria. In theory, opera seria was an attempt to re-create the classic tragedies of the Greeks. The verses of the plays were declaimed on musical lines with instrumental accompaniment. By the beginning of the eighteenth century, the innovations of gifted composers to heighten the musical interest of opera by interrupting the flow of recitative with songs or arias had hardened into set, artificial rules. An opera seria was in three acts; the cast usually consisted of six characters, each of whom was given a fixed number of arias. The blending of voices into duets or larger ensembles was frowned upon. The use of chorus was extremely limited. This structured rigidity, which impeded dramatic action, was compounded by the performance practices of the baroque era. Composers left the ornamentation of the vocal line to the discretion of the singer. Singers soon discovered that their fees were in direct proportion to the applause they could generate. Those who were great artists as well as virtuosos wooed their audiences with a tasteful display of their skill that enhanced the dramatic dimension of their roles. Others, who too often succeeded, used any means whatever, however vulgar and dramatically inappropriate, to win the competition for applause. Opera seria degenerated into a series of *arie da capo* whose musical content strayed farther and farther afield from the words and emotions of the text. The reforms of Christoph Willibald Gluck were aimed at ridding opera of this artificiality and going back to the original concept of a drama in which the lines were sung rather than spoken and in which the dramatic problems were resolved musically as well as textually. Eventually, Gluck's ideas won out, and opera seria fell into disrepute. Mozart's opera seria, alas! suffered the same fate as those of Scarlatti, Vinci, and Salieri. Until the twentieth century. Mozart was at the height of his powers when he composed *Idomeneo*. Although he was only twenty-four when he began it, he had already written ten dramatic works which had been successfully staged. While these operas of his childhood and adolescence cannot compare with his later ones, they provided him with practical experience in handling dramatic problems musically. *Idomeneo* is not the work of a tyro.

Mozart, an admirer of *Orfeo ed Euridice,* followed many of Gluck's precepts in *Idomeneo*. It is an opera seria only in the strictest, technical sense. More meaningful is the fact that it is an opera seria by Mozart, whose contribution to the world is music, regardless of the form in which he chooses to express it. The forms prevalent in his era did not constitute a strait-jacket that checked his creativity; they formed the foundation upon which he built his lifework. He is acclaimed as a composer of operas and symphonies and concertos, yet he did not invent any of these. He simply wrote them better and filled them with more beauty and meaning than anyone had before.

Mozart's *Idomeneo* is missing none of the components of its genre. These components, however, successfully provide a musical characterization of the personages. The prescribed arias are differentiated as to the emotional states of the characters. The action, both psychological and physical, proceeds through the recitatives *and* arias. The latter do not interrupt the action; instead, they enhance it. Ilia's scene, which opens the first act, is exposition in that she reveals in it her conflict between love of country and love for Idamante, her country's foe. (Aïda's "Ritorna vincitor" performs the same function.) It also creates dramatic suspense, because she does not disclose how she plans to solve her dilemma. The next scene with Idamante seems to imply, by her coolness to his diffident declaration of love, that she rejects him. Electra enters to witness the freeing of the Trojan prisoners, and Mozart shows us through the agitation of her music that her admonition to Idamante is not motivated by a diplomatic concern for political consequences (which is all the text implies) but by far more personal reasons. When everyone rushes off to the site of the shipwreck to search for survivors, the text provides Electra with a soliloquy in which she reveals her fear that she has lost Idamante to Ilia if Idomeneo is no longer alive to support her cause. Mozart sets the lines to dramatic, accompanied recitative. The next section of her tirade expresses her desire for vengeance on her rival. Mozart now turns to the form of an aria, repeated in strict da capo fashion, to convey the nine lines of text. The emotion of the aria's music cannot be interpreted as anything other than what it is: unbridled fury. To proceed step by step in this fashion through *Idomeneo*'s three acts would be repetitious, since the point remains the same: there is dramatic, musical validity to the arias and recitatives throughout.

Mozart's problems with *Idomeneo* stemmed from his librettist, the chaplain of the Salzburg court, Giambattista Varesco. Mozart's letters to his father reveal that his requests for textual changes were arbitrarily rejected by Varesco, and Mozart had to take it upon himself to make numerous alterations without authorization. Varesco became enraged at Mozart's audacity and threatened to withdraw his libretto if any further changes were made without permission. Therefore, many verses were set that Mozart would have preferred to omit. Arias by secondary characters such as Arbace and the High Priest are usually cut in modern productions because they delay the action. Mozart, who had an innate sense of the theatrical, would probably agree with the deletions. Anyone familiar with Mozart's symphonies will concede that he was never long-winded when he worked without a librettist.

The libretto, however, is not without merit. It is also not entirely the work of Varesco, who by and large translated it from Antoine Danchet's French libretto for André Campra's *Idoménée*. Varesco ungraciously neglected to acknowledge his source. The tale, based on Greek history and legend, includes interesting, creative, and dramatically effective inventions. Homer never mentioned Electra's trip to Crete. Nor does Ilia rate any special attention among King Priam's progeny, who numbered fifty sons and fifty daughters, if we are to believe the ancient sources. Neptune's demand for a human sacrifice parallels Agamemnon's sacrifice of Iphigenia to Diana in exchange for a wind to sail his ships to Troy. Idamante's last-minute reprieve recalls the Old Testament account of the sacrifice demanded of Abraham but remitted once the patriarch's obedient piety had been proven. Neptune's clemency is of course a typical eighteenth-century deus ex machina; however, the sea god is moved to absolve Idomeneo of his promise by Ilia's selfless offer to take Idamante's place because of her love. This redemption through woman's love was a twist that Wagner would have praised wholeheartedly.

Idomeneo was revived in Karlsruhe in 1917 but was not professionally produced outside the German-speaking world until 1951, when the English premiere took place at Glyndebourne. In the British production, the castrato role of Idamante was revised for tenor instead of the more usual practice of making the part a *Hosenrolle* for mezzo-soprano. *Idomeneo* still does not enjoy a prominent position in the international repertory, but it is no longer the rarity it once was. Let us hope that Keats was right and that we may all, from time to time, have the joy of hearing *Idomeneo*.

ROSSINI'S *The Italian Girl in Algiers*
by Karen Monson

Now, please, remember this: *L'italiana in Algeri* is not a coffee opera. *Parsifal* may be a coffee opera, and *Die Meistersinger* might be a coffee opera, but *L'italiana* isn't.

And this is also not a martini opera. Save those potent potables for *Otello* or *Wozzeck*—they need them.

No. *L'italiana* is a champagne opera. When the lights go up for the single intermission, you head out for a glass of the bubbly to get your spirits aligned with those of Gioacchino Rossini and our friends Isabella, Elvira, Lindoro, Mustafà, Taddeo, Zulma, and Haly. Pretend it's New Year's Eve in Venice, a time to celebrate.

Everything is going to be okay, and after all, as Stendhal wrote in his *Life of Rossini,* the composer's "home was the delightful province of Venetia, the gayest land in all Italy, if not in all the world, and assuredly the least tainted with pedantry. The glittering reflection of the Venetian character falls across the texture of Venetian music; and musical Venice, rating lightness of heart above depth of passion, looks first and foremost for songs which entrance the ear. In *L'italiana,* the prayers of the people of Venice were abundantly granted; no race did ever witness an entertainment better suited to its own character; and, of all the operas which were ever composed, none was more truly destined to be the joy and delight of *Venice.*"

Please laugh. I know that giggling in the opera house sometimes seems like losing control in a house of worship. But this time it's different. You're not laughing *at* *L'italiana,* you're laughing *with* her, and with the composer, the librettist, and everyone else involved. If *L'italiana* doesn't strike the witness as funny, there's something dreadfully wrong, on one side of the footlights or the other.

Read the synopsis, but don't worry much about its details. You should be able to come up with a few sentences, beginning "Girl gets shipwrecked," and ending "Boy and girl sail off into the sunset." That's about enough. Again to quote Stendhal, who caught the spirit of the thing:

> I take the plot which the librettist has invented, and I require further from him one word, and *one only,* to give me the key to the mood of the scene. For example, I take Mustafà to be a man who is bored with his mistress and his own greatness, and yet, being a sovereign, not devoid of vanity. Now, it is not improbable that, if I were to follow the dialogue as a whole, this general impression would be ruined. So what is the remedy? Ideally, of course, the answer would be to have had Voltaire or Beaumarchais compose the *libretto;* in which case it would be as delightful as the music, and never a breath of disenchantment in the reading of it! But happily (since Voltaires are rare in our imperfect world), the delightful art which is our present study can well continue without the services of a great poet . . . provided always that one avoids the sinful indiscretion of reading the *libretto.* At Vincenza, I observed that, on the first night, it was customary to skim through it just sufficiently to gain some notion of the plot, glancing, as each new episode opened, at the first line, just so as to appreciate the emotion, or the shade of emotion, which the music was supposed to suggest. But not once, during all the forty performances which came after, did it occur to one single member of the audience to open that slim little volume with its gilt-paper binding.

Stendhal also noted, not so incidentally, that "there was not in all the audience a single head which held a notion of submitting sensual delight to the test of *critical judgment.*"

Rossini's biographer and friend was much too hard on *L'italiana*'s librettist, Angelo Anelli. Shakespeare this isn't, and Anelli was no Arrigo Boito. But the Italian girl, Isabella, who ends up in Algiers, does not pretend to be Otello; nor is she even Manon or Maria Stuarda. The words convey her spirit perfectly well: she needs to take only one look at a potentially awkward situation to know how she is going to get out of it to her own advantage (and those of her friends and lovers). She can play whatever role needs to be played; today's Isabellas must begin their studies by mastering the arts of dramatic deception and coquetry—the coloratura can wait, and so can the physical stamina and heft needed to get her through her final aria, a challenge that pits the coloratura mezzo-soprano against Wagner's Siegfried in its technical demands and its placement at the end of the evening.

This is not to say that the libretto is the work of a true and maligned master; not without reason is Anelli's name virtually forgotten today. But the text for *L'italiana* proved perfectly suited to Rossini's needs at the time, allowing and inspiring the composer speedily to arrive at what Stendhal called "un-reason organized and perfected." The year was 1813. The composer presented Venice with his new *Il Signor Bruschino* in January, then offered the same audiences *Tancredi* in February and *L'italiana* in May. (In December he would go on to

Milan with *Aureliano in Palmira*.) Rossini turned twenty-one that year—on February 29 (so he had no actual birthday, and perhaps we should say he was but five and one-fourth). *L'italiana* was his tenth (!) opera.

Already he was so much in demand that he had to "write hot!" in the apt words of the composer and critic Virgil Thomson. But keep in mind that Rossini's first nine operas had brought him only $1,650; he received no royalties and had no rights over future productions. He had no time to loll around waiting for the muse to perch on his shoulder. So *L'italiana* was written in either eighteen or twenty-seven days, depending on which source one chooses to believe (Rossini evidently claimed eighteen). Whichever, the opera benefits from its immediacy. There is hardly a spare note, and few works for the musical stage move with more economy. One might argue that some of the melodies and accompaniments sound a tad familiar. But so do many of the period, not only Rossini's, but also those of his rivals. It was a time when homage was "duly" paid to mentors and previous inspirations. Rossini idolized Mozart, and it should come as no surprise to hear references to "Dove sono" and "Voi che sapete." Years later, Stendhal asked Rossini his favorite opera; was it *Tancredi* or *L'italiana in Algeri*? Neither, answered the master, who had since retreated from opera. His favorite was Domenico Cimarosa's *Il matrimonio segreto*. Shades of that work are here, too.

But at the age of twenty-one, Rossini obviously had to have things on his mind other than meeting his obligations to the various operatic stages. One of those things was the opposite sex, and from the age of thirteen or fourteen he was romantically (and, it is said, sexually) linked with a series of well-known singers, many of whom resembled his mother, Anna Guidarini, a soprano whose career stayed chained to the provinces. Among his ladies was Marietta Marcolini, the mezzo with the agile voice and the gift for comedy for whom he evidently wrote the principal roles not only of *L'italiana in Algeri* but also of *Il barbiere di Siviglia* (with homage or apologies to Mozart, again) and *La Cenerentola*. Rossini did not have anything against knowing that his leading lady would be sympathetic to the music he gave to her. And then, perhaps, sympathetic to his own needs.

Then there was another important element in the existence of this musician (as of many others, even to this day): food. It is said that Rossini, asked for an opera, arrived to deliver his patron two fine sausages in the music's stead. Whether or not that story is true—and it could well be—there is no doubt that the composer appreciated his meals, and attractive as he was as a young man, he appears never to have been slim.

The conclusion of *L'italiana* must have appealed to him especially. Perhaps he had heard the friendly threat *pappataci!* (shut up and eat!) directed toward his own table. There seems to be no reason to doubt that he knew the potentially dire results of overindulgence in food and drink. It is also not impossible that during his travels, Rossini lost a lady as a result of such debauchery. It's the price a young man pays.

In light of this, it is not surprising that *L'italiana* is almost completely devoid of what we today would call operatic passion. (The obvious exception is Isabella's patriotic "Pensa alla patria," but even here the serious mood is quickly broken. There wasn't time for heartfelt effusions.) As a rule, Rossini's relationships with women did not exactly engage the emotions of either partner to great depth. And this is an opera to be delivered over a party table, not with a romantic dinner *à deux* in a private dining room with a comfortable couch—and certainly not in a somber, musicological seminar.

Rossini knew the stuff of his tenth opera. "I thought that after having heard my opera, the Venetians would treat me like a crazy man; they turned out to be crazier than I am," he is said to have reported on the morning after the premiere of *L'italiana.*

Many other audiences turned out to be "crazier" than Rossini, since *L'italiana* went on to become Rossini's first opera staged in German (Munich, 1816) and came to New York as early as 1832. Unfortunately, it was also his first opera to be heard in Paris (1817), and there it was a disaster, with cuts and an anti-Rossini clique which did its damage even before the music started.

In modern times, presenting *L'italiana* has become more difficult than the opera itself wants it to be; the performance should have a feeling of gleeful ease. But operatic styles of the late twentieth century have not nurtured the kind of vocal flexibility demanded by Rossini of virtually every member of this cast, and dramatic trends have encouraged robust realism at the expense of farcical finesse.

Nevertheless, *L'italiana* has delivered much pleasure to millions over its nearly 175 years of existence. So one returns to Stendhal, who found himself in a state of "strange delirium" at a fine performance of this opera and who put it best (albeit somewhat dyspeptically) when he discussed the merits of the Isabellas of his experience:

And indeed, it was for *la Marcolini,* for her ravishing contralto voice and for her magnificent gifts as a comic actress, that Rossini composed the superb comic role of the *Italian Girl in Algiers,* which we poor northerners have beheld so nobly distorted. There is a certain actress (yet, in deference to her beauty, she shall be nameless) who transforms this young creature with her southern temperament, this joyous, irresponsible, gay, passionate young woman, who, let it be admitted, has but the most fleeting regard for her reputation, into a solid, stolid Yorkshire miss, whose most deep-seated care, in every situation, is to merit the approbation of all the old wives in the parish, failing whose good opinion, she must be forever left high and dry without a husband. Is there *no* refuge, where a man may seek asylum from the furious pursuit of virtue? Do I patronize the *opera buffa* in order to enjoy the *noble prospect,* the monumental delineation of female perfection? I suppose I should be held guilty of "shocking the tone of our serious-minded generation," or of "offering flagrant insults to the laws of decency," etc., etc., if I dared suggest that, the more our manners and morals grow dingy, strait-laced and hypocritical, the better claim we have to some compensating debauch of *frivolity* in our entertainments!

Viva frivolity!

JANÁČEK'S *Katya Kabanova*
by Lilias Wagner Circle

An intimation of impending tragedy pervades the brief overture to *Katya Kabanova,* Leoš Janáček's 1921 opera based on a Russian play. From the first soft notes in the lower strings, which begin the overture, we know that there will be suffering; and the voice of doom in the timpani, which repeatedly occurs at key moments throughout the work, is one of its unifying elements. In these four minutes, the composer presents several other musical fragments which we shall identify repeatedly throughout the opera's three acts. This compactly constructed work provides an evocative picture of life in a provincial village on the Volga River, covering ten days in the life of Katya, a passive young wife, who briefly breaks out of her trap to find happiness in a doomed love affair. Her trap, however, includes not only her unempathetic family; she is equally enchained by her deep sense of sin. After confessing her guilt to her family during a violent storm, she plunges into the Volga.

It would be inaccurate to consider *Katya Kabanova* as merely a stark drama, however. In spite of the somber opening and the tragic end, it has, within its tightly written scenes, moments not only of lushly beautiful melodies and ravishing orchestration, reminiscent of Puccini, but also considerable charm and an ironic humor. Audiences today frequently approach twentieth-century opera—especially unfamiliar works—with a certain trepidation, but this one is quite accessible. When he selected the original play of *Katya Kabanova* as the basis for his libretto, Janáček reached back into nineteenth-century Russian literature, to a play by Nikolai Ostrovsky called *The Storm.* Consistent with its eastern-European origins both as play and opera, there are many mystic references to nature, which exerts a profound influence over the characters. The mighty Volga River frames the work, and the thunderstorm is the backdrop for the climax of the opera. This is entirely in keeping with the background of the opera's composer, Leoš Janáček.

Janáček was born in 1854 in Moravia, not far from the Polish border, into the large family of a village schoolmaster. Life in the neat, small village was centered on the Catholic Church and was influenced by the simple outdoor pleasures available to the villagers. But his home life also was filled with music:

his father started a local singing society which was often invited to sing mass at some of the larger nearby parishes, and the boy was given a thorough music grounding from age ten. Although his father died before the boy reached his teens, his tuition as a chorister in Brno was paid by his singing and playing. He completed his education in Prague while living in extreme poverty; then he returned to Moravia and founded the Brno Organ School in 1881, the same year that he married. The school (later a conservatory) was begun under very primitive circumstances, with the exalted intent of providing further education for professional musicians who would become the organists and choir masters in the parishes in Moravia. When Janáček retired more than forty years later, this conservatory had prospered, and since he appears to have inherited his father's teaching gifts, it remains one of his great achievements. Janáček supported himself through his teaching and by writing occasional criticism; he composed relatively few works until he was past forty. His marriage to a student twelve years his junior was a very rocky one, and the loss of both of their children only exacerbated a difficult situation.

Moravian folk music fascinated Janáček quite early in his career, and nearly twenty years before Béla Bartók and Zoltán Kodály began roaming eastern Europe, recording the folk music of the isolated villages, Janáček was doing the same thing in Moravia. He was so interested in these pithy songs that he would often ask a peasant to repeat a spoken phrase so that he could note it down in musical terms. His thorough study convinced him that language and music in the region were closely related, and this influenced forever his operatic style—a succinct, staccato thematic presentation of extraordinary expressive vigor. Since they relied so heavily on Czech language inflections, his operas were very difficult to translate and were consequently less accessible. However, the isolation of his locale also contributed to Janáček's long-delayed recognition, as did the diffuse character of twentieth-century opera. The expense of mounting any opera (especially one by a relatively obscure composer) further delayed the acclaim he finally achieved. Evidently he was also quite opinionated about the validity of his highly individual style, and he was not especially easy to work with.

Charles Mackerras, who conducted the only recording of the work, also indicates that Janáček's scores were very untidy and difficult to read. "He always composed straight into full orchestral score," Mackerras writes, "and then gave the score to a copyist, who wrote out the whole work, mistakes and all, into a neat score. Frequently Janáček added or scratched out things in the copy, sometimes correcting the copyist's misreading of his illegible manuscript and sometimes not."

Katya Kabanova is one of Janáček's later works. He was forty before he had his first modest success; the peasant opera *Jenůfa* was acclaimed in Brno. But acknowledgment of his talents outside Moravia did not come until *Jenůfa* was acclaimed in 1916 in Prague. The timing was most opportune; nationalism, which led to the formation of Czechoslovakia after World War I, was rising in the Czech provinces, and *Jenůfa*'s folk-style melodies fell on very receptive ears.

But once the world noticed him in 1916, Janáček was exhilarated. He worked feverishly during the last twelve years of his life, producing masterpieces almost too fast for the public to absorb them—including four remarkably varied operas (of which *Katya* is the second), the dazzling *Glagolithic Mass,* and the stunning *Sinfonietta.* During those last twelve years, Janáček was in love with a much-younger married woman, who evidently inspired him, providing him with the creative renewal that, coupled with his new success, spurred him on. The character of Katya was inspired by his love, as reflected in his letters to the lady, one Kamila Stoesslova. He wrote: "It was in the sunshine of summer. The sun-warmed slope of the hill where the flowers wilted. That was when the first thoughts about poor 'Katya Kabanova' and her great love came to my mind. She calls to the flowers, she calls to the birds—flowers to bow down to her, birds to sing to her the last song of love. My Katya grows in you, in Kamila! This will be the most gentle and tender of my works." In 1928, the year of his death, Janáček formally dedicated the opera to Kamila.

He appears to have been possessed of a fiery temperament, which could be visited not only upon his pupils and his family but also upon those unfortunate enough to be the targets of his musical criticism. One writer notes that Janáček was always right; yet inasmuch as his was a sensitive soul, he expected gentle treatment. The direct opposite was true, however, when he attacked someone else; then the other was expected to have the thickest possible skin and not be offended by what amounted to abuse.

The participants in the drama of *Katya Kabanova* may be roughly divided into three groups—Kabanikha and Dikoy, part of the village's ruling class and definitely the "old guard"; the younger, bolder generation, as represented by Barbara and Vanya; and Tikhon, Katya, and Boris, caught in a web from which they can see no escape. Katya's overbearing mother-in-law, Kabanikha, who is surely the model for all mother-in-law jokes, is not only one of the powerful rulers of the little town; but she is also bent upon humiliating her son and daughter-in-law. Her counterpart, the self-absorbed merchant Dikoy, has his foot on the neck of his nephew, Boris—the man to whom Katya is irresistibly drawn. Kabanikha is so absorbed in all of the conventional Russian rituals of the time and is so concerned about what people will think that she appears to have no soul. Dikoy indulges himself by baiting those beneath him, but he comes whining to Kabanikha after he's had a few drinks, since she seems to be his only equal. Nevertheless, Dikoy and Kabanikha observe all of the exterior rituals of the church as well as those of their society.

Barbara, Kabanikha's young foster daughter, and her boy friend, Vanya, see nothing wrong in carrying on a love affair outside of marriage—they have rather more "modern" ideas. Barbara and Vanya, who run off together to escape Kabanikha's carping, are often contrasted with Boris and Katya on the grounds that both are having love affairs outside marriage. Although this was looked down upon in the society in which they lived at the time and was very sternly denounced when the young couple was found out, neither Barbara nor Vanya was married to someone else. Granted that Barbara is portrayed as rather carefree (until Kabanikha gets wind of her foster daughter's love affair and locks Barbara in her room), Katya's love affair still has a different dimension, since Katya is, after all, a married woman. Barbara appears to be Katya's only confidant, and very early in the opera, she expresses sympathy for Katya.

But Katya's dull husband, Tikhon, seems unable to provide either warmth or understanding; so when Boris moves to town to live with his Uncle Dikoy and is smitten by Katya at their first meeting, the love triangle is joined. Boris watches her in church, attracted by her fresh beauty. And she, meanwhile, sensing some tenderness, is drawn to him as well. These three characters—the married couple, Tikhon and Katya, and her lover, Boris—all seem caught between the heartless older group and the more relaxed or amoral younger generation, in what some writers feel is a generation gap.

Janáček portrays the couples involved in distinctly different ways. Katya's gentle, sympathetic theme, which first appears in the overture, is lightly scored for oboe, flute, and violins. It also accompanies her first entrance, as Boris and Vanya watch the Kabanov family return from church. Katya's music tends to emphasize the high registers. As she is being corrected by her mother-in-law, she responds with the gentle (although probably untrue) assurance that she loves her mother-in-law like her own mother; and as Katya sings this line, an oboe delicately comments. The scoring for much of Katya's solo singing is generally very sparse, giving her music and character both clarity and vulnerability. Many operatic composers, depicting a heroine on the verge of madness, have been attracted to the dangerously high ranges of the soprano voice as she gradually loses her grip. Janáček is no exception; Katya's is the only high soprano voice in the opera, and frequently it soars from middle to very high range in a single leap—another characteristic of Janáček's writing, both for voice and for orchestra.

Katya's insensitive husband, Tikhon, has for his background music peasant-style rhythms with balalaikas, music that is introduced in the overture. When Barbara and Vanya play out their love scene in the second act, the music is also in folk style, rather playful and charming. These are also the most extended "tunes" in the opera. Boris, Katya's lover, does not appear to have great depth, and the music surrounding his statements is uncomplicated on the whole; but since he gives her the warmth she so desperately lacks at home, the music for their scenes together is passionate and frequently heavily scored, with middle and lower string voices, harp, and French horn.

While the scoring in the orchestra for Dikoy and Kabanikha is often rather lumbering and crude, they have no definite themes, suggesting to one critic that they have no souls to express, after all—hence, no themes. Early in the opera, as Kabanikha criticizes her son for loving his wife more than his mother, one of the brasses literally sneers as Kabanikha calls Tikhon a fool. When Dikoy is scolding his nephew Boris, a high string passage with uneven rhythm, first heard in the overture, is woven into the accompaniment.

Janáček had been fascinated by Russia from his initial visit in 1896, and his style in Katya seems to echo the breadth and the intensity of nineteenth-century Russian opera. He has, in fact, been called the Czech Mussorgsky, and critics cite not only his feel for the national folk music of his country, but also his semimelodic, conversational vocal writing, which approaches Mussorgsky's operatic style. While his use of leitmotifs is reminiscent of Wagner, Janáček is closer to Russian opera both technically and emotionally. He includes the orchestra as a full partner in the dramatic action; and while he frequently utilizes only a few instruments, his searing climaxes and burning lyrical passages—which reflect certain romantic roots—require a large modern orchestra. The organizing principle is rhythm. Key orientation as well as density of instrumentation may change very rapidly. This constant shifting of gears—from one key to another and from thin to full orchestration—has made Janáček's works somewhat difficult to understand on first hearing for some listeners.

As a music drama, *Katya Kabanova* is very focused; the seven characters play off one another with very little interruption from minor characters. The chorus appears only on the sidelines in the final act. They vocalize without words, symbolizing the Volga and adding to the confusion building in Katya's mind.

The general theme of *Katya Kabanova*—guilt—is at least as ancient as the Old Testament. Janáček's operas are filled with pity for human suffering, and although the subjects vary widely, they tend to deal with humanist topics. This is also common to many twentieth-century operas. However, contrasted with, say, some of the crisis scenes in Verdi, there are scenes which generally lack physical action, since so much of the conflict is interior.

There is, however, no lack of conflict, and Janáček goes to the heart of the matter very quickly, with both on-stage and orchestral expositions reflecting his economical and original style. The insistent timpani beat in the overture, which recurs at the end of Act I and reaches a deafening climax at the height of the storm and at the end of the opera, forces us to pay attention.

In the opera's first vocal utterance Vanya soliloquizes about the eternal quality of the river, but the young housemaid does not think it is very important. This is only the first of a multitude of contrasting views expressed throughout the opera. As the beginning of the overture paints an atmospheric picture of the Volga, so does the first spoken word remind us that the river is always with us.

Almost immediately, the overbearing Dikoy is heard in the distance, giving his nephew Boris a tongue-lashing. The agitated high string music from the overture serves as accompaniment, with uneven meter reflecting Dikoy's irritation. Boris explains to his new friend, Vanya, that he has come to live with this miserable man because he controls Boris's inheritance. Then Boris admits that he is falling in love with a married woman, and the Kabanovs enter, returning home from church. Tikhon is being reprimanded by his mother.

Kabanikha is quickly revealed as a highly skilled second-guesser; no matter what Tikhon and Katya do, there is something wrong with it. If Katya behaves with restraint in public, she is heartless; if she falls on her husband's neck as he leaves on his trip (and she does), she is a shameless hussy. Kabanikha, making up her own rules as she goes along, does not hesitate to correct her son and daughter-in-law in public. And finally, the opera's central conflict is presented, as Katya confides her interest in Boris to Barbara in the following scene.

The two young women, Barbara and Katya, are very different, as Janáček reminds us musically. What makes Katya work as a sympathetic character is the wonderful soaring music she is given to sing, especially in her long scene with Barbara, which is one of her two extended monologues in the opera. When Katya sits with her needlepoint in her lap, daydreaming about her simpler days as a young girl, wishing she could fly like a bird (to the twittering, rising accompaniment of the woodwinds), she reveals a sensitivity of spirit which makes her a character to care about. In a reverie about her rapturous spiritual experiences at church, shimmering strings, horn, and harp provide her accompaniment. Completely wrapped up in her ecstatic vision, she scarcely hears Barbara's comments. But reality returns as Katya confesses that she is in love with another man, and there is urgency in her voice. As she tells Barbara of her daydream of being held and loved, the music becomes infinitely tender and gentle. Barbara, while she cares about Katya, also acts as a temptress, urging Katya to meet her lover that night—in fact, Barbara provides Katya with a key to the gate so that she may sneak out undetected by the watchful Kabanikha. As Katya fearfully recoils for the moment from meeting him, Barbara coolly shrugs, "What of it?"

There are four love scenes in the opera, each carefully crafted to reveal the depth—or lack thereof—of emotional involvement between the characters who make up the four couples portrayed. In the first of these, Katya frantically appeals to Tikhon to take her with him on his trip, representing her final effort to save herself from disaster. For an instant, they sing a duet; but thanks to Tikhon's dense response, they end up completely at odds with one another. It will require a catastrophe to get his attention. Since Tikhon remains deaf to her pleas, he essentially delivers her into Boris's arms—unable to defend either himself or his troubled young wife against his mother's onslaughts, Tikhon looms as a worse villain than Kabanikha. He departs for his travels complete with sleigh bells and balalaika accompaniment.

The Act II love scene between Barbara and Vanya, played concurrently with the love scene between Boris and Katya, includes the most traditional romantic operatic writing in the opera. Vanya and Barbara sing lighthearted folk songs— his lively and tersely phrased like a Moravian folk song. Hers is a merry, rather uncomplex song. Then Boris arrives, and the orchestra echoes the thumping of Boris's heart as he awaits Katya's arrival. Their hesitant greetings soon give way to rapturously close harmony as they confess their love for one another. The settled harmonies give this scene a sense of repose and wholeness. In a neat piece of juxtaposed staging, Janáček has the couples change places—Katya and Boris, as they tremulously reach out to one another for the first time, are seen, while Barbara and Vanya have retreated to the summerhouse to be alone together. After they return, Katya and Boris take their turn at the summerhouse, and we hear them in the distance as they sing of their love. Confident that they won't be discovered, Vanya and Barbara continue their playful, earthy dialogue with only light pizzicato accompaniment—while the counter melody, ascending blissfully in the distance, accompanies Boris and Katya's confession, "You are my life."

One has the distinct feeling not only that Vanya and Barbara's love affair is more lighthearted but also that neither has done much hand-wringing about guilt or discovery. When they are discovered, it takes them only one uncomplicated moment to decide to run off to Moscow together. Boris and Katya, who will meet every night for the remaining nine days of Tikhon's trip, can never escape the shadow of her guilt.

The fourth love scene occurs inside Kabanikha's house during the same evening. Dikoy, who has been drinking, comes to Kabanikha looking for sympathy; they treat one another quite differently than they treat the people they browbeat, since they are equals. When she corrects him, it is in an almost friendly fashion. Both are so involved in concerns of money and position that they cannot have a close emotional alliance of any kind; but they rather respect one another. His clumsy effort to make a pass at Kabanikha is fully reflected in the accompanying music.

Each of the principal characters makes a final appearance during the third act, which begins in a ruined building whose walls reveal a mural about the descent of doomed souls into hell. Dikoy and Vanya discuss the storm that is approaching, beginning with a few tentative raindrops, the horns playing the delicate, agitated music which the flute and violins introduced in the overture. Barbara, fearing for Katya's sanity, rushes in to warn Boris that Katya is losing her grip since Tikhon has returned and is threatening to reveal their affair. The driving chromatic background throughout this final act adds to its urgency and reinforces each conflict. Restless as the river, building from distant thunder to more intense crashes, the storm charges onward, with deafening intensity, flowing, rolling music punctuated with fearful drum crashes.

As Katya insists upon confessing her sin, everyone has a comment. Dikoy and Kabanikha are unempathetic, of course, Kabanikha egging Katya on; while Barbara repeatedly tries to stop Katya and insists that the distraught woman doesn't know what she's saying. Tikhon finally makes a positive statement, also trying to stop his overwrought wife. But she is determined to tell them everything. Once Katya has confessed, everyone scatters, and the scene changes to the river bank. Her brief final meeting with Boris—of whom she has been thinking—seems almost to be a daydream; as they embrace, the music momentarily returns to the gentle harp and strings of their first night of love, with quiet solo strains in oboe and cello. But he must leave, and as her mind wanders, trying to remember her last instruction to him, insistent choral syllables grow in volume, snarling brass and ominous drums joining them. Her life has become a nightmare; she feels completely isolated; and now that Boris is gone, the Volga calls her. Briefly, she thinks of the birds and flowers around her grave (with fluttering music reminiscent of her early scene with Barbara), and then, to a huge drum crescendo and an alarm from the brasses, she plunges into the Volga. Shrieking high woodwinds and hacking music in the strings accompany the confusion of the people as they rush in. Tikhon finally turns on his mother, blaming her for Katya's death. Kabanikha, true to form and ritual to the end, turns and thanks the people for their kind services, bowing in all directions. But the river remains eternal; the choral voices and powerful timpani, in a throbbing crescendo, attest to that.

Katya Kabanova is an especially accessible, appealing work, a carefully constructed tale which is much more than a love triangle. It presents a clear picture of the culture of its time and place, combining romantic and twentieth-century music into a riveting drama. And throughout, there is the prevailing force of nature—in the violence of the storm, in the voice of the Volga, and in the gentle fluttering of birds, who are with Katya as she dies.

MUSSORGSKY'S *Khovanshchina*
by Dorothy Samachson

Khovanshchina! What a playful, diminutive sound the almost untranslatable word has. But it is a deceptive playfulness, for *Khovanshchina* is the scornful epithet with which Tsar Peter I, "The Great," dismissed Prince Ivan Khovansky's plot to usurp the Russian throne for himself and his son, Andrei, and freeze Russia into permanent feudal backwardness.

Khovanshchina is a grim and bloody reminder of a stormy, critical period at the close of the seventeenth century when Russia, ruled by Tsarevna Sophia as regent for Peter and his feeble-minded half brother, was being torn apart, not only by Khovansky's machinations, but by the revolt of the Streltsy, the crown's savage musketeers, who supported Khovansky, by palace intrigues of self-seeking nobles, and by the opposition of the Old Believers (Raskolniki), a schismatic mystic religious sect that rejected reform in church and state.

However, historic events, no matter how seminal, are forgotten as they slip into the past. If *Khovanshchina* is remembered today, it is because Modest Mussorgsky composed a lyric-theater work by that name—an unfinished masterpiece on which he worked during the last eight years of his life and which was completed after his death in 1881, as a labor of love, by Nicholas Rimsky-Korsakoff.

Not as well known in the United States as *Boris Godunov*, *Khovanshchina* is a striking panorama of visual splendor, set to some of Mussorgsky's most magnificent music. It has been compared with Shakespeare's chronicle plays for its portrayal of an epoch; it is a brilliant example of Mussorgsky's nationalist realism, of his artistic motto: "Not beauty alone, but truth wherever it be."

In the summer of 1872, while awaiting the Maryinsky Theater's verdict on *Boris* (it was again rejected for production), Mussorgsky was casting about for a new operatic theme. His friend Vladimir Stassov, a writer, suggested that the turbulent events surrounding Peter's accession to the throne might make a worthy successor to *Boris.*

Mussorgsky's imagination was immediately stirred by the epic magnitude of the subject, and the opportunity to again present "Big, simple-hearted Mother Russia in all her breadth," and he enthusiastically set forth on a period of historic research, first subtitling it, not *Opera,* but *A People's Musical Drama in Five Acts.*

In a letter to Stassov, to whom he dedicated the opera, Mussorgsky explained: "And what if Mussoryanin (his nickname for himself) dug into the raw black earth? It is not the first time (a reference to *Boris*). . . . And did they not dig Mother Russia at the end of the 17th Century with such a tool that she did not understand, and began to expire? . . . To put the past into the present—this is my task. As long as the people cannot examine with their eyes what is being done to them we shall remain where we were. . . . The people are groaning, and so as not to groan, they drink, and then groan the more."

The last may have been an oblique allusion to the uncontrollable alcoholism that was destroying him, but the statement reveals unusual perception of the society around him and sympathy for the Russian people.

Mussorgsky, a member of the landowning aristocracy, was the grandson of a serf woman, and although the liberation of the serfs in 1861 had impoverished his family, forcing him into ill-paid clerical jobs, he never lost his attachment for the peasantry.

They were, in his eyes, the true heroes of the nation's history. In *Khovanshchina,* as in *Boris,* he would show them—the innocent, confused pawns suffering and dying for the ambitions of power-hungry nobles.

He was, later, to make notes for a third opera, *Pugachevshchina,* based upon Pugachev's revolt against serfdom during Catherine the Great's reign. *Pugachevshchina* was to complete his historic trilogy, but it was never written.

For about a year, he immersed himself in history books, old documents, religious tracts, ancient liturgical chants, and folk song. By the time he ended his research, he had amassed enough material for several operas.

"I am swimming in information," he wrote. "My head feels like a boiler with a roaring fire underneath." He was certain that the opera must end with the Old Believer's self-immolation, but he had no firm notion of how to organize the rest of the work.

Rimsky-Korsakoff was to recall that "none of us knew the real plot or plan, and from Mussorgsky's very flamboyant, florid and complicated account—it was difficult to understand as a coherent whole."

When Mussorgsky began the actual composition, he still had not arranged his material into a cohesive plot, so he just pieced it together as he went along—which didn't help him achieve greater clarity.

He wrote scenes out of context, adding new scenes as he thought of them and cutting others. He shifted musical numbers from one act to the other, and he composed music he never wrote down. And he found himself slowing down, for the general structure of the opera was still unclear in his own mind.

For dramatic effect, Mussorgsky compressed time and altered historic events. When the opera opens, Peter is, presumably, only ten. By the last act, without the elapse of time, Peter has become an adult tsar. In real life, both Khovanskys were hanged by Sophia, and the Streltsy, far from being pardoned by Peter, were barbarously executed.

When Mussorgsky had written the libretto for *Boris,* he had had Pushkin's drama as a guide, and he had created the monumental figure of Boris, tormented by guilt and conscience, to give the national tragedy a powerful psychological focus.

In *Khovanshchina,* the central characters, all historic individuals, lacked that towering stature. The brutal, despotic Khovansky and his dissolute, doltish son represent "ancient, gloomy, fanatical, dense Russia." Prince Golitzin, representing those aristocrats who supported reform, is equally brutal and superstitious, while the crafty, murderous Shaklovity, whose denunciation spins the plot, combines genuinely patriotic feelings with self-seeking plots. (Shaklovity, the only survivor in the opera, actually was to lose his own head later.)

Dosifei, the leader of the Old Believers, is likewise unsuited to a heroic role. Patterned after a Prince Myzhetsky who had renounced his wealth, Dosifei is, despite his gentle saintly nature, also a fanatic.

Abhorring violence and corruption, he has, nevertheless, allied his congregation with Khovansky and the savage Streltsy against Peter, the "Anti-Christ." And Dosifei will march his followers into a suicidal funeral pyre as a final rejection of the future. The auto-da-fé that brings *Khovanshchina* to its awesome conclusion is based upon fact. The Old Believers were to continue this horrifying self-martyrdom for another hundred years.

They are tragic, doomed figures, but no heroes. However, Mussorgsky did create a most unusual heroine—Martha, Andrei's discarded mistress, now an Old Believer. Drawn from the life of a Princess Sitzkaya, Martha is a dramatic link to the other principals, but she is more than a theatrical contrivance for conventional love interest.

Martha is a fevered woman, her heart and spirit rent by the conflict between sensual passion and ecstatic religious fervor. Her true passion is for absolution through death. Oskar von Riesemann, in his analysis of *Khovanshchina,* suggests that Martha's eloquently beautiful "Confession" aria in Act II reflects Mussorgsky's own morbid attraction to death.

Emma, on the other hand, is a pallid counterfoil to Martha's passionate nature. She is introduced mainly to show the depravity of the two Khovanskys as they fight for her and to give Andrei a reason for a lyrical love song.

The protagonists, Peter and Sophia, never appear—either because the work was becoming too unwieldy or, more likely, because Mussorgsky was mindful of the proscription against representing the Romanov dynasty on stage.

And the Russian people—Mussorgsky's heroes? Divided and confused in their loyalties, they are skillfully characterized—the Moscow populace in its folklike music, the Streltsy and their wives in boisterous, quarrelsome song and recitative, and the Old Believers in the chanting of their prayers.

During the work on *Khovanshchina,* Mussorgsky began a study of human speech, which he called "The melody of life . . . well-thought-out, justified melody."

Khovanshchina contains many examples of this melodic recitative that are unmatched in their subtlety of characterization, whether in the comic delineation of the Scrivener, the brooding of Golitzin, the spiritual exaltation of Dosifei, or the lyricism of Martha's love for Andrei.

Mussorgsky's genius is also present in the orchestral section, even though Rimsky-Korsakoff did the orchestration from Mussorgsky's vocal score. The opera's prelude, "Dawn on the Moscow River," is a serene paean to nature and the land, which will survive all conspiracies, and the exquisite Dance of the Persian Slaves in Khovansky's palace is in jewellike contrast to Khovansky's murder that follows.

But Mussorgsky couldn't work consistently on *Khovanshchina,* and his lack of concentration cannot be traced wholly to the complexities of the opera. His own personal life was rapidly falling apart during those years.

The nervous disorder (probably incipient epileptic seizures aggravated by his drinking) that had plagued him for years was now appearing with frightening frequency, and his refuge was the oblivion of drunkenness. The once-elegant aristocrat often had to be dragged out of saloons a sodden wreck.

In 1874, Mussorgsky suspended work on *Khovanshchina* for a happier reason—the Maryinsky production of *Boris,* which was a public success and a critical failure.

Basically, Mussorgsky needed peace and quiet to concentrate on his music. Instead, he had to work at miserable jobs and return at night to his dismal rooms. Although he was now receiving more money in royalties and fees as an accompanist, life was a constant financial struggle.

In 1875, he suddenly began a comic opera, *The Fair at Sorochintsy,* as relief from *Khovanshchina,* and now a sad comedy of errors ended the possibility that either would be completed. A group of well-meaning friends offered him a monthly subsidy to finish *Khovanshchina,* while another group did the same for *The Fair.* The money went for liquor.

When Mussorgsky died at the age of forty-two, Rimsky-Korsakoff took the jumbled piano score of *Khovanshchina* and edited and orchestrated it for

production. In the process, he "smoothed" out many of Mussorgsky's innovative harmonies that he thought crude and unacceptable to the public, saying,
"If Mussorgsky's compositions are destined to live unfaded . . . such a musi-
cologically accurate edition will be possible. For the present there was a need of
an edition for . . . making his colossal talent known."

When Rimsky-Korsakoff presented the edited edition to the Maryinsky, it
was rejected on the grounds that "one radical opera *(Boris)* was enough."
Khovanshchina did not receive its Maryinsky premiere until 1911, when Chaliapin sang the role of Dosifei.

Rimsky-Korsakoff's orchestration and editing have been criticized for being
untrue to Mussorgsky. Other composers, including Stravinsky, Ravel, Shebalin,
and Asafiev, have attempted to reorchestrate the work in accordance with
Mussorgsky's intent. However, it is the Rimsky-Korsakoff version that prevails
on most operatic stages.

But no matter which edition, *Khovanshchina* is a monumental addition to
the operatic literature. As M.D. Calvocoressi describes it: "As in *Boris,* but to a
far greater extent, we are made to feel that the drama is one, not of persons, but
of a nation—torn by conflicting tendencies and confronted with an unknown
future." *Khovanshchina* is a powerful evocation of that drama, a living memorial to Mussorgsky's credo: "To be in keeping with historic truth and Russian
folk tradition."

SHOSTAKOVICH'S *Lady Macbeth of Mtsensk*

by Dorothy Samachson

"I will plan to write an operatic tetralogy about women—a Soviet *Ring of the
Nibelung*—the first such about women, of which *Lady Macbeth of Mtsensk*
will be *Rheingold*. The second will be built around Sofia Perofskaya, the
heroine of the People's Will Movement, who organized the assassination of
Tsar Alexander II, and was hanged along with her collaborators.

"The third will deal with a woman of our century, and finally, I will create
our Soviet heroine who will, in her character, combine the qualities of today
and tomorrow. This theme is the leitmotive of my daily thought, and will be for
the next ten years."

Thus Dmitri Shostakovich, still in his early twenties, announced a project of
epic proportions for the lyric theatre—a historic Marxist panorama that would
portray women's emotional, psychological, and political responses to the social
forces that molded them during various historic eras.

A bold, even an arrogant, announcement from such a young man? Perhaps,
but Shostakovich was not indulging in pretentious bluster. A loyal son of the
young Soviet Union, already making an impressive artistic mark as a composer,

Shostakovich believed that a composer had a specific role to play in building the new order. "I cannot conceive of my future creative program outside our Socialist enterprise, and my aim is to help in every way to enlighten our remarkable country."

The position of women certainly needed enlightenment in Russia. For centuries, they had survived in darkness, overworked, uneducated, and mistreated by men who themselves were for the most part treated as beasts of burden by the ruling powers. The 1917 Bolshevik Revolution and its slogans promised both men and women a bright new world.

Youthful Marxist ardor aside, Shostakovich had, from personal experience, gained insight into women's day-to-day travail. Growing up under the unbelievably harsh conditions of the postrevolutionary period, he observed how women struggled desperately to feed, house, clothe, and educate their children—often without husband and father to share the burdens.

Millions of Russian men had been killed in World War I; millions more during the civil war and foreign invasions. Still more men, women, and children had perished from famine and disease during those chaotic years.

Shostakovich's engineer father had died in 1922, while sixteen-year-old Dmitri was a student at the Petrograd (Leningrad) Conservatory, and the total responsibility for two daughters and a son fell upon his mother's shoulders. A former pianist, her office-job salary barely kept the family alive, and the three young people had to find work to help make ends meet. Dmitri's job as a pianist in a movie house didn't last long, however, for he would forget about playing when the movie became too interesting.

No matter how difficult life was, the Shostakovich home revolved around their resident genius who was a frail teen-ager suffering intermittent bouts from a form of tuberculosis. His condition required more nourishment than was provided by ration cards, and Alexander Glazunov, then director of the conservatory, came to the rescue with a special stipend for the student whose talents he compared favorably with those of Mozart.

Shostakovich didn't disappoint his mentor. His Symphony No. 1, composed for his graduation, was hailed tumultuously at home and abroad for its contagious gaiety and wit, buoyant humor, lyrical sweep, and highly individualistic orchestration. Here was proof that Russian music was alive and well despite the emigration of many composers during the turbulent times.

Despite the pleasing public acclaim, Shostakovich withdrew from composition for a year, explaining his creative silence as "I wanted to overhaul a great part of the musical baggage I had acquired." He concentrated on the piano, and he listened avidly to new music.

During the 1920s and early 1930s the Soviet Union was hailed as a beacon of light, and its major cities were hotbeds of intellectual, experimental ferment. Foreign avant-garde artists flocked there, assured of a warm welcome. Ernst Krenek, Paul Hindemith, and Alban Berg presented their works to enthusiastic audiences. Berg's *Wozzeck,* conducted by the composer, was a tremendous success, and Shostakovich responded wholeheartedly to the new, flirting for a while with atonality.

The first major composition after his recess was the Choral Symphony No. 2, dedicated to the October Revolution, and it did show some atonal influences. This work was sharply attacked for "formalist" and "constructivist" tendencies.

His first opera, *The Nose,* based on a story by Nikolai Gogol, with libretto by Shostakovich and Alexander Preis, didn't last long, either. *The Nose* dealt with a nose, accidentally separated from its owner's face at the barber's, that goes on to lead an independent life as a government bureaucrat. Cautiously advertised as an "experimental spectacle," it offended the Russian Association of Proletarian Composers, who dismissed it acrimoniously as "bourgeois decadence."

A similar fate befell his Choral Symphony No. 3, honoring May Day. It was also criticized for "Formalism and Constructivism," catchwords that were cropping up more and more frequently in official reviews of music, plays, poetry, and prose. As the Soviet government consolidated its power, the artistic experimentation that had formerly been encouraged was now increasingly frowned on. Was there fear in the country's leadership that cultural experimentation might lead to political experimentation and threaten the system itself?

Still, Shostakovich remained the Golden Boy of Soviet music, and his fertile creativity had few limits. He wrote ballets, piano pieces, incidental music for plays, movies, and even an orchestration of Vincent Youmans's *Tea for Two,* called *Tahiti Trot* in Russia. And although he must have been deeply hurt by the harsh criticisms of several of his works, he remained a loyal and devoted Soviet citizen and artist. "I am a Soviet composer and I see our epoch as something heroic, spirited and joyous. . . . There can be no music without ideology."

In *Lady Macbeth of Mtsensk,* based on a short story by Nikolai Leskov (1831–95), he would combine ideology and feminist insights with music, even though the story contained little of heroism or joy. "It is full of dramatic and social content," Shostakovich noted. "Perhaps there is not in Russian literature another work portraying the position of a Russian woman in prerevolutionary times more vividly."

Leskov, one of Russia's most popular tellers of tales, is not as well known as other nineteenth-century Russian writers, although translations are available. His earthy vigor, his sardonic view of provincial life, which frequently stressed the grotesque aspects of that society, and his original use of colloquialisms and funny plays on words give his stories a unique flavor.

During his lifetime Leskov was ignored by the influential critics. Neither a university graduate nor an outspoken radical, he was excluded from literary circles and thus prevented from gaining wider renown and the financial rewards that would have accompanied critical recognition. In later years, both Leo Tolstoy and Maxim Gorky were great admirers of Leskov's writing.

Although Shostakovich was impressed with Leskov's story, he was convinced that Leskov, as a prerevolutionary writer, could not interpret Katerina's personality correctly, so he made a number of changes in the plot. Leskov's Lady Macbeth was not a particularly sympathetic character, and the title of the story was a deliberately ironic reference to Shakespeare's powerful tragedy. The petty sexual passion that inflamed Leskov's provincial heroine had little to do with the fire that consumed those who killed to gain a nation.

Shostakovitch, who wrote extensively about his opera, explained his attempt to justify and acquit her to the operatic audience. "Yet," he wrote, "to call forth sympathy was not so simple. She commits several acts not compatible with ethics and morality, but she is a clever woman, talented and interesting, whose nightmarish surroundings have brought only dreariness. . . . She knows no joy . . . her crimes represented a protest against the life she was compelled to lead. . . . Apart from Katerina, there is no positive character or hero in this opera."

To further justify Katerina as a woman of potential destroyed by her stifling milieu, Shostakovich and Preis, his librettist, altered several incidents in the story and added others.

In the first act, Katerina tries to defend Aksinia, the cook, from the male workers who are brutalizing her, by singing about woman's exploitation by men, thus identifying herself with feminist insights.

In Leskov, she commits a third murder after disposing of her father-in-law and husband—their little nephew, guilty only of being heir to their estate which Sergei covets. Since killing a child for venal gain would have erased any sympathy for her, the incident was completely eliminated, as was the infant she bore Sergei in prison and indifferently gave away.

Although Boris, the father-in-law, was depicted as brutal and domineering in Leskov, Shostakovich and Preis added lechery. In his soliloquy that opens Act II, Boris is preparing to rape Katerina and betray his own son, Zinovy, a pallid, impotent shadow of his father, but mean-spirited. Their deaths don't arouse much sympathy.

Eliminating the child's murder freed Shostakovich to introduce a totally new plot twist—Katerina and Sergei's wedding, which occupies the entire third act. It also gave him the opportunity to create brilliant musical parodistic portraits of the village denizens at the wedding.

Musically this act builds enormous tension as the guilty pair await their wedding near the cellar where they've buried their victim. Yet, Shostakovich very cleverly contrasts their fears with the grotesquely comic song of the village drunk; the hypocritical guests, gossiping about Katerina in snatches of choral Russian folk music; the sycophantic priest; and the stupid, corrupt police. Vocally and orchestrally, the act is a masterpiece of satire. Musical ironies abound in the opera, as Shostakovich presented the false, fawning relationships of the servants to their masters when they praise Zinovy's virtues and their dependence on him in the first-act chorus. Katerina's exquisite lamentation on the death of Boris, whom she has killed, is a hypocritical gesture, yet it is extraordinarily moving, as is her superstitious fear when she sees his ghost.

Katerina is a complex heroine who has known no love, no gaiety, and no pleasure. A poor girl married off to a rich man, she is illiterate, is blamed for her barren condition, and is so lonely and sexually repressed that she is the perfect victim for Sergei. Her discovery of sexual passion releases her talents— but for evil—and her obsession with Sergei inevitably leads to her tragic end.

Sergei is her evil genius, and Shostakovich limned him in music that leaves us in little doubt that Sergei is an insincere, shallow opportunist, always ready to use his sexuality to gain any end. He wants wealth at any price—as long as he doesn't pay it.

Shostakovich drew all the characters with sure musical strokes. Katerina is the only purely lyrical voice in the entire work, although her music does change as her personality changes after the murders. The orchestral palette is rich, the harmonies are interesting, and the manner in which Shostakovich incorporated folk melodies demonstrated his masterly skill. The convicts' chorus in the last act is extraordinarily moving. Shostakovich's compassion for their wretched condition reminds one of Mussorgsky's choral passages in *Boris Godunov* where suffering Russia expressed its hopelessness.

One of Shostakovich's most unusual innovations was the way he connected the scenes in each act with orchestral entr'actes that continue the thematic structure of the opera while the sets are being changed.

The opera premiered in Leningrad on January 11, 1934, and was an enormous public and critical success. Hailed as the greatest opera created in the Soviet Union, it ran for about two years in repertory, was produced in Moscow, where it was equally popular, and reached the United States in 1935. At the Metropolitan Opera, the orchestral depiction of the seduction scene shocked some delicate souls, and one critic labeled it "pornophony."

True, the music is one of the most aurally graphic descriptions of the act of love, but its unbridled percussive beat, the incongruous sound of the trombone, and the relentless dissonances enable us to understand Katerina's wild abandon to passion.

When Shostakovich was working on Lady Macbeth from 1930 to 1932, his courtship of Nina Varzar was going badly because of family interference. It is likely that he released his own frustrations in this music which, by today's more permissive standards, doesn't raise a single scandalized eyebrow. By the time *Lady Macbeth* was premiered, he and Nina were married.

Lady Macbeth was still playing to full houses when, on January 28, 1936, a disaster struck in the form of an editorial in *Pravda,* the official newspaper of the Soviet government. Attacking the opera in unheard-of vitriolic terms under the heading of "Muddle Instead of Music," the article went on to call the music "quacks, grunts and growls," of "borrowing nervous, convulsive and spasmodic music from jazz," and of being "coarse, primitive and vulgar."

The vituperation continued with attacks on the critics who had praised the work and concluded with a further assault on Shostakovich as a representative of "Leftist" art that contained the "most negative features of Meyerholdism (a theatrical director of great innovative talents who was, a few years later, arrested and executed by Stalin's orders) infinitely multiplied."

Within a few days, *Lady Macbeth* disappeared from all stages, and Shostakovich came under further personal attack in letters to the editor and the Composers' Union. It was official that the state itself was stepping in to create what became known as "Socialist Realism" in art.

It was also the beginning of the end for the Soviet Union as a cultural beacon of light for the arts. Fear pervaded the intellectual community, and many prominent creative people began to disappear, not only from public life, but from life itself.

One might possibly understand the Soviet leadership's desire to present Russian life in a positive way and to create art that would attract the vast masses who did not relate to experimentation of any sort. But one can never understand or forgive the terror that became part and parcel of that drive. In our century only Hitlerite Germany and the Soviet Union, diametrically opposed in their politics, took similar reactionary positions. The Nazis removed all Jewish creations and those they considered Communist, while the Soviets removed all "cosmopolitan" works they considered "leftist" and reactionary.

Socialist Realism remains an active slogan in Russian life, and intellectual dissidents still face a most unhappy future, but some element of sanity has returned after years in which Soviet creativity was stifled by bureaucratic edicts. *Lady Macbeth,* now called *Katerina Ismailova,* has returned to the stage, although Shostakovich did make some minor changes to satisfy the authorities. Of course, he never completed his operatic tetralogy, which could have been one of the Soviet Union's most precious jewels, but fear is not a great impetus to free creativity. However, we must be grateful that he did give us *Lady Macbeth of Mtsensk,* one of the few masterpieces of our time.

DELIBES'S *Lakmé*
by Jonathan Abarbanel

French "opéra lyrique" flourished during the second half of the nineteenth century, building solidly upon the rich legacy of bel canto opera left to Paris by Cherubini, Donizetti, Rossini, and others during the first half. Opéra lyrique showered its adoring audiences, and posterity, with an overwhelming profusion of glorious melodies, lush orchestrations, and exotic stage spectacles. One may trace the progression of leading opéra lyrique composers in a succession of student-teacher relationships at the Paris Conservatory, from Cherubini (the

Italian composer who became director of the conservatory), through Ambroise Thomas, Gounod, Bizet, Massenet, Delibes, and Charpentier.

In the last quarter of the century, several of these composers produced a handful of works which mark the high point, as well as the twilight, of French opéra lyrique as it inevitably gave way to changing musical and dramatic tastes. *Lakmé* is one of these works, along with *Carmen, Manon, Louise,* and a select few others. In several important ways, *Lakmé* is the most characteristic opéra lyrique of the bunch. Written in 1883, *Lakmé* looked backwards to earlier glories of the genre, rather than towards the Wagner-influenced operatic future.

To understand the characteristic markings of *Lakmé* and to appreciate its importance to its first audiences, one must have a more specific idea of what is meant by "opéra lyrique," a term marked by inconsistency in its use. A brief overview of French opera in the nineteenth century will provide the essential framework.

When *Lakmé* was written, Paris had been the opera capital of the world for a century. Gluck had made it so when he chose Paris as his home in the 1770s, after the triumph of his great reform opera *Orfeo ed Euridice*. Thereafter, the greatest composers of the day and the most promising musical students congregated there. The quarter-century of the French Revolution (1789) and the First Empire (1804) interrupted the flow of opera production but ultimately had the most profound influence on opera composition and opera audiences. In the post-Napoleonic era of the restored Bourbon and Orléans monarchy, Paris was Mecca. The aforementioned bel canto Italians paid their respects and left their Paris operas, and later, Verdi did, too. The Germans were there as well, even poor, young, unknown Richard Wagner, copying out parts for Donizetti and proposing collaboration to Eugène Scribe, the greatest and most prolific librettist and playwright of the era. Above all, there was Meyerbeer.

If French opera—indeed, world opera—had a Colossus of Rhodes it was Berlin-born Jakob Liebmann Beer—Giacomo Meyerbeer. In partnership with Scribe as his librettist, Meyerbeer's theatrical genius and orchestral scope rewrote opera history. As no other composer before him, Meyerbeer dominated the stage, critical acclaim, and popular taste. The epic proportions of his five-act operas never before had been seen on a musical stage. It was for Meyerbeer that the term "grand opera" first was coined, and his works still define the genre: *Robert le diable* (1831), *Les Huguenots* (1836), *Le Prophète* (1849), and *L'Africaine* (posthumous, 1865). Technically, Meyerbeer was heir to the traditions of opera seria, but he infused the form with the full-blown wallop of Romanticism: stories of high tragedy, a huge cast and orchestra, passion, sweep, grandeur. Wagner and Verdi learned valuable lessons from Meyerbeer. And so did Léo Delibes, as a thirteen-year-old choir boy at the Madeleine, recruited to sing in the chorus at the premiere of *Le Prophète* at the Opéra in 1849. It was for the works of Meyerbeer and his successors that Louis Napoléon ordered the design and construction of the Palais Garnier, a home for grand opera on a scale to match the music.

The influence of Meyerbeer on all opera that followed cannot be under-estimated. In *Lakmé* it may be seen in many elements of music, staging, and exotic atmosphere, but most directly in the plot itself, which borrows from *L'Africaine.* Lakmé's father, Nilakantha, parallels the figure of Nelusko in *L'Africaine;* both are motivated by a desire for vengeance. Also, in both operas the heroines make use of native flora to do themselves in.

But if the Opéra was the shrine of grand opera, it was not the only opera house in town, nor did it present the only type of opera. Equally important to the world of nineteenth-century French opera, and especially to Léo Delibes, was the Opéra-Comique. The name of the theater defined the category of works performed there: not comic operas, but operas in which there was spoken dialogue. Initially, the term also indicated works with lighthearted subject matter or, at the very least, happy endings. Thus, technically, Beethoven's *Fidelio* is an "opéra comique" by French definition. Some composers were invited by management to work at both the Opéra and the Opéra-Comique (usually at the former only after proving their worth at the latter), but the Opéra-Comique also had a roster of composers exclusive to that institution, including François Adrien Boieldieu, Adolphe Adam (a principal teacher of Delibes's at the conservatory), and Jacques Offenbach. Delibes himself never had an opera of his produced at the Opéra (at least not in his lifetime), but he *did* cross the bridge with several ballets: *La Source* (1866, in collaboration with Louis Minkus), *Coppélia* (1870, along with *Lakmé* certainly his greatest claim to fame), and *Sylvie* (1876). It was the Opéra-Comique that saw the premieres of four Delibes operas, including *Lakmé* on April 14, 1883.

The focus on subject matter something less than high tragedy and the use of spoken dialogue combined to make opéra comique more directly responsive to the influences of popular drama and taste. It may also have given it a more diverse public appeal than grand opera, acting as the link between operetta and boulevard theater, on the one hand, and grand opera, on the other. Thus, French *pièces-en-vaudeville* and Italian opera buffa influenced the early years of opéra comique, while the principal nineteenth-century influence was French *mélodrame.*

It was *mélodrame* that served as the catalyst for the transition of opéra comique into opéra lyrique. *Mélodrame* itself had a long history and had undergone several transitions in character. By mid century it had left behind its lurid antecedents, which helped inflame Revolutionary mobs, and had taken on the refinement of the Second Empire. Public taste had changed. Rapid industrialization, plus large numbers of educated people coming out of the system of public schools and universities established by Napoléon, produced in France a large and growing middle class, a bourgeoisie. As in our own society today, they were the people who bought the bulk of the tickets, and their tastes dictated fashions in art.

What they wanted in theater was a new type of *mélodrame* which was sentimental and picturesque, usually a love story, and which reflected their stolid burgher values in matters of subject, piety, and morality. The lofty nobility of sentiment found in the greatest Romanticist works gave place to a more garden variety sentimentality.

The same demand was made of opéra comique. While retaining the technical device of spoken dialogue, it lost its specific focus on the lighthearted or comic. Drama was permitted, even unhappy endings; to wit, *Carmen,* arguably the greatest opéra comique. Eventually, the requirement for spoken dialogue was dropped also, as long as the work retained a strong, sentimental love interest.

The composers who emerged on the scene after 1850 didn't object to popular taste. On the contrary, we must remember that most of them were sons of the same middle class and shared the values of their Parisian audiences. While some such as Berlioz might have had loftier ideals, Bizet, Massenet, Delibes, and others were perfectly matched to the times. What they had to offer was a bottomless well of orchestration and melody: colorful, varied of line, sonorous, sensuous, suave, delicate, exotic, lush, rich, and graceful. This was opéra lyrique: exquisitely refined musical drama of sentimental romance, emerging from the tradition of opéra comique. *Lakmé* is an entirely characteristic opéra lyrique, having a sentimental love affair as its single important dramatic interest and having characters who are more like cameos than real-life people.

This essential shallowness of plot and character, typical of so very many nineteenth-century operas, continues to confound many critics and highbrows, who cannot reconcile the glories of the music with the vapidity of the librettos. *Lakmé* often is decried as merely a singer's opera. The critics of the time had no such troubles, however, giving *Lakmé* high praise at its premiere. If the troubled few in our own era simply would sit back, relax, and enjoy *Lakmé* as a popular work of musical theater, their problems would vanish. Many of us have the tendency, unfortunately, of applying the standards of grand opera to every kind of opera, without a proper understanding of the differences between various genres of opera or of the social and artistic forces that led to the development and popularity of each.

Genre aside, *Lakmé* has much to offer any audience. It is brushed with bel canto beauties, and not just in the fancy coloratura fireworks of "The Bell Song," but in more subtle ways such as the long, tricky tenor line in Act I's "Fantaisie aux divins mensonges." Concerted numbers, too, duets and trios of extraordinary beauty and skill, are intertwined throughout. And look at the highly theatrical and effective structure of the whole: a first act almost languorous in tempo and mood, followed by a brilliant, athletic second act, and a third act charged with drama and high emotion.

One realizes, of course, that *Lakmé* was written at a time when a new era of "verismo" and unified musical structure was sounding death knells for opéra comique and its lyrique off-shoot. The form tried to keep up with the times, with works such as Massenet's *Werther* supplying much greater psychological depth to the characters and with Charpentier's *Louise* offering a gritty look at

Paris itself. Basically, however, opéra lyrique was a conservative form, confined by its sentimental subject matter and rarely demanding a progressive musical style. Again, *Lakmé* fits the mold, looking back to the older tradition of a "number opera" design, rather than forward to a more integrated musical drama. If it is retrograde, however, it is endearingly so, even enchantingly so, which is one reason *Lakmé* has continued to beguile audiences for more than one hundred years.

WAGNER'S *Lohengrin*
by Speight Jenkins

The image of the knight in shining armor does not fade. Whether it is Richard Burton playing King Arthur in *Camelot* or the romantic heroes of Walter Scott, the knight embodies the ideal of manhood. Heroic, strong, true to his principles, even occasionally sensitive, the knight exists as a symbol of the code of ethics called chivalry. Although opera has more than its share of knights, none has the popularity or resonance of Lohengrin, and even in this era of on-stage extremes, Lohengrin is almost always treated traditionally, at least in his appearance. Not the stage world in which he exists—that can be and has been bizarre. But the knight himself is to my knowledge invariably clothed in bright raiment and acts his role in a straightforward romantic manner. His sweet farewell to his swan; his failure to kill his mortal enemy, Telramund, when he has beaten him in fair fight; his acclamation of Elsa just as they go into the church when he is sure she is faithful; even his leaving his sword, horn, and ring to the absent Gottfried—these are all the actions of the true and perfect knight.

But for all of Wagner's surface belief in romantic epics, his lead male characters, knights or no, were never the two-dimensional heroes of romantic legend. Beneath the glitter of Lohengrin's armor seethes a vastly complex character, one that resembles, in more than a casual way, Richard Wagner himself at the age of thirty-five.

In 1851, three years after completing *Lohengrin* and a year after the opera's premiere, Wagner wrote a *Communication to My Friends,* one of his prolix tracts which discusses his feelings about the opera. The tract was necessary because Wagner had been exiled from Germany for his part in the revolution of 1848, and he was not able even to attend the premiere of *Lohengrin* in Weimar in 1850. The communication would serve as a means of letting Wagner's fans— and there already were more than a few all over Germany—know his feelings about *Lohengrin,* the earlier composed *Tannhäuser,* and *Der fliegende Holländer,* and numerous other topics. Such a treatise was as necessary to Wagner as composing music; to him, his opinions on any subject—any at all—were so important that everyone must know them. In the *Communication* he relates his own nature to Lohengrin's, and however we might disagree with Wagner's conclusions, his thinking was never unimpressive. Indeed, it is amazing that all his ideas were penned decades before Freud and even before Henry James. In speaking of himself at the time, he wrote: "I was now so completely awoken to the utter *loneliness* [Wagner's italics] of my position as an artist, that the very feeling of this loneliness supplied me with the spur and the ability to address myself to my surroundings." He saw clearly that in his operas he was expressing his search for a woman—first the faithful-to-death Senta of *The Flying Dutchman,* then the pure and noble Elisabeth who showed Tannhäuser the way from the passions of Venus to heaven. When he reached Lohengrin, he found a hero who was seeking the woman who would "love him as he was" with an "unconditional love." And in a passage suggestive of some psychiatrist writing today, he tried to define Elsa as "the unconscious, the undeliberate in which Lohengrin's conscious, deliberate being yearns to be redeemed." He sets up the two as halves of the same being, then he suggests that Lohengrin aches to lose himself but cannot. Wagner is obviously moving toward *Tristan und Isolde,* still six years in the future. He doesn't complete the thought but makes instead a leap, characteristic of his writing: he sees Elsa as "the spirit of the folk for whose redeeming hand I, too, as artist-man was longing."

In his tract Wagner mentions that the idea of *Lohengrin,* though specifically suggested to him by a reference in Wolfram von Eschenbach's *Parzifal,* had more than a little connection to the myth of Zeus and Semele. Semele loved the god, who was invisible to her in his godly form. She begged him to appear as Zeus, and he did it sadly, knowing that she would die when she saw him. Although Wagner sees the connection to his Lohengrin as the desire of man (or woman) to experience a divine being totally, he does not point out the distinct difference in the two stories. Semele demanded to see Zeus, which had been forbidden her; Elsa was forbidden even to make an attempt to know more about Lohengrin. The onus lay on her to live up to his expectation or be rejected, and it is the unreasonable nature of Lohengrin's expectation that makes him a study of the Wagner who saw himself romantically isolated, Byronic in every way.

The composer's constant search for a woman who would love him without question until death runs through almost every opera he composed. Senta states the proposition in its simplest form: she will be loyal unto the Flying Dutchman until death, and she proves it by leaping to a watery grave when he thinks she has betrayed him. Elisabeth in *Tannhäuser* prays constantly to die so that she can help Tannhäuser in heaven, while Brünhilde sets the world on fire to prove her devotion and dedication to Siegfried. Isolde, too, chooses to join Tristan in death; and Kundry drags around after Parsifal with no hope that he may be her salvation. Elsa is the only faithless heroine in the Wagnerian canon, though she may be the most interesting. Elsa, unlike the women named above, is very human.

Rare would be the person not overwhelmed by a Lohengrin of either sex. First of all, he had appeared to Elsa in a dream; then after she prayed for him to save her, he appeared. That he is drawn by a swan adds to her (and our) wonder at his mystery. She is transfixed with the realization of her dream, a powerful situation to any psyche, and one that may happen once, or at the most twice, in the luckiest life. Lohengrin no sooner approaches her than he proposes marriage, rather a strange salutation but quite in keeping with Wagner's way in matters romantic. Then he charges her with the fateful questions: she must never ask his name, his father's name, or the name of his homeland. At that moment, even though Lohengrin repeats the charge, no one, least of all a young girl accused of being a murderer and a witch, could be expected to think deeply about such questions. Whatever her champion suggested would have been fine, and future consequences had to have been beyond her ability to think.

When she sees Lohengrin easily defeat Telramund (and Ortrud's magic), Elsa is not so much surprised as blissfully happy. It's all a fairy tale, and this may be why this act was the last that Wagner composed. Although the music is often stirring and lyrical, it is the least involved and least challenging to perform in the opera. That Lohengrin saves Telramund's life when he could have and should have slain him only fits his knightly image.

Among the hero's attributes, however, cannot be counted extrasensory perception. Although as the audience we are well aware of Ortrud's plotting and her use of Elsa as a foil, Lohengrin has not the least inkling that there is any danger until he is confronted by Telramund on his way to his wedding. Now we begin to get the measure of the man. Lohengrin steadfastly denies any obligation to tell his name or other information to anyone except Elsa, thus putting all responsibility on her, something for which she might well have been unprepared. When he sees that she is troubled by what has been said, he does not rush to give her sustenance, but instead prays to heaven to strengthen her, in effect to make her better and more what he needs. When he shortly thereafter sees the two evil ones around her, he strides over to her—here Wagner the stage director makes a rare mistake: he leaves too much time before Lohengrin sees them whispering to her—and questions her on her steadfastness. When she answers, "Far greater than the power of doubt will be my love for thee!" he hails her in a gloriously exciting phrase.

The opera's most crucial moments come in the Bridal Chamber Scene which opens Act III. After the wedding march—and how curious that music celebrating one of the least successful, shortest marriages in history should have been used by the great majority of those Americans married in a Protestant church in this century—Lohengrin continues for a while in a state of bliss. As Boris Goldovsky once pointed out in a perceptive article on the opera, the knight can be differentiated from all other extrahuman figures in such a situation because he obviously needs Elsa's love. The others enjoy the love of a mortal but are self-sufficient. When Elsa begins to waver, first because she simply wants to call her husband something, any name, Lohengrin tells her that she should be thankful that she won his confidence when she swore not to ask his name. And then in a cool, unsatisfying compliment—to very powerful, heroic music—he adds that if she lives up to his stricture, she will in his eyes stand above all women. Wagner the dramatist was growing at this point, because neither Senta nor Elisabeth, Elsa's predecessors, would have pursued the matter further. Both were so completely tied up in worship of the loved one that they had no thought of reality; Elsa sees beyond his words.

In the next breath Lohengrin makes a mistake by describing her love as the only reason he would ever desert the world from which he came, a fact that immediately makes Elsa wonder what he will do when he tires of her. Again this emphasizes Elsa's humanity. This is a thoughtful, not a hysterical, response, and it puts her ahead not only of Senta and Elisabeth but even of Isolde, who never imagines that the love the adored one feels might ever be diminished. The knight then makes it worse by saying, "Thy charm will never vanish whilst thou art free from doubt." This terrifies the girl, who at that moment is consumed by doubt. It is all over when her terror gives her a vision of the swan coming back for Lohengrin, and she blurts out the questions.

Lohengrin's actions from then on are not those of a considerate or loving person. First of all, Elsa alone was charged not to ask the questions, but when she did it, Lohengrin tells her that he will answer her before the king and court, about as embarrassing a situation as is possible to imagine. In this and all that follows, one can see Wagner's own attitude toward those who betrayed his commandments. One was either 100 percent with him, or one was cast into exile and publicly condemned. To the king, Lohengrin describes Elsa's actions as betrayal and then launches into "In fernem Land," a description of Montsalvat, the domain of the knights of the Grail. Where Wagner saw his hero as lonely, Lohengrin's description of Montsalvat suggests a self-imposed isolation: the Grail fellowship is too good for normal people. This suggests that Wagner saw himself as part of a higher, nobler order than that to which the common herd belonged: an order of the elect which cannot be understood by its inferiors.

Before all the people then, Lohengrin berates Elsa for failing in her charge and tells her that if she had waited only a year, she would have known all. It is not only unfair to tell her a time period after the fact, it is unkind, and all his additional talk about the return of her brother, Gottfried, passes over Elsa unheard. She is consumed with her failure and her loss of the man she worshipped, and though Wagner's music is passionate and sad, nowhere does Lohengrin express pity or sympathy; she disappointed him, and she must pay the price.

Wagner's knight is really Wagner himself, challenging Minna, his wife, and all the others not to question him in anything. His thinking, his politics, his prejudices, above all, his music, were sacrosanct, and he who questioned them might be humiliated and cast out of the Eden of Wagner's approval. Yet for this human "Lohengrin" there was a happy ending. When Wagner composed the opera, all may have been disappointing around him, but soon to come was Cosima. Here was an Elsa who followed Lohengrin's challenge to the end: what the master did was perfect, no questions, no thoughts contradictory. And after she appeared in his life some ten years after *Lohengrin*'s composition, she made the final fifteen years practically perfect for him personally.

Even if Wagner was to find his Elsa, the fascinating fact to us today is his self-portrait in 1848: unchallengeable and untouchable, a kind of man or woman not unknown in our time. Lonely and isolated because of his or her own demands, he or she lives alone, constantly decrying the unreliability and weaknesses of others. It may not make a pretty picture, but it shows *Lohengrin* to be far more than a fairy-tale opera: it is a serious work of alienation and a real tragedy, a portrait of the person who cannot be questioned, clothed in the most sublimely romantic music Wagner ever composed.

PROKOFIEV'S *The Love for Three Oranges*
by Jonathan Abarbanel

Opera has always been an eclectic art. Even in its purest incarnations—the Ring Cycle, say—it is a derivative art form, never able to escape its historical antecedents, always traceable backwards through the Italian Renaissance and, eventually, to the theaters of Rome and Greece. This is a truism.

Few works demonstrate the remarkable, healthy eclecticism of opera better than Sergei Prokofiev's Opus 33, *The Love for Three Oranges*. Here is a twentieth-century opera, based on an eighteenth-century Italian fable, commissioned in Chicago, composed in New York by a Russian musician, with an original libretto in French. Let's examine some of the constituent elements merged by Prokofiev in *The Love for Three Oranges*.

The opera was commissioned by the Chicago Opera Company in 1918 and was completed by Prokofiev (living in New York) by October, 1919 (when both piano and orchestra scores were delivered to Chicago Opera Company's director, Cleofonte Campanini). The idea for the work, however, dates back to 1913. Prokofiev, like most artists, had a number of ideas simmering on back burners, waiting for something (such as a commission) to bring them to a boil. In 1913, Vsevolod Meyerhold (1874–1943) first suggested to Prokofiev that an interesting opera might be fashioned from *L'amore delle tre melarancie,* a 1761 *fiabe*—dramatic fable—by Italian writer and dramatist Carlo Gozzi. Gozzi's work was an extension of the Italian commedia dell'arte.

Meyerhold himself was a Young Turk actor-director who had worked with Chekhov and Stanislavsky as a member of the Moscow Art Theatre from 1898 to 1902. He broke with them to pursue even more avant-garde notions of Symbolist drama, and he went on to have a distinguished career as the first great artist of post-Revolutionary Soviet theater. The Italian commedia dell'arte was attractive to the Symbolists because its stock characters and plot situations permitted directors to concentrate on symbolic and expressionistic motifs, rather than on character development. Carlo Gozzi's wit and imagination were particularly attractive, as was his strong penchant for satire. Meyerhold and his associates even published, sporadically, a journal which they called *The Love for Three Oranges,* and Meyerhold reworked and translated into Russian the original *fiabe.* It is this version which Prokofiev first saw in print, in 1914.

Commedia dell'arte was neither new nor unknown, even in Russia, at the time of World War I. Obviously, Gozzi's treatment of it was something special to arouse such interest and devotion. He merits some examination.

Carlo Gozzi (1720–1806) was a count, even though he was a younger son. Italy, as did France, permitted all the sons of a nobleman to inherit the titles. This produced an ever-larger, ever-more-impoverished nobility, who eventually had to marry into the bourgeois classes, trading titles for the daughters of monied merchants—a great stimulus to trade. But I digress. Gozzi was also a raging paranoid who, save for his title, may well have been certifiable. His battles of the pen with legions of enemies and rivals were multifarious and myriad. His greatest target of hate was Carlo Goldoni, the more enduring literary figure of eighteenth-century Italy. It was purely to spite Goldoni that Gozzi began writing plays. He chose a form he called *fiabe*—dramatic fables— which combined fairy tales of the most exotic sort with the farce elements of traditional Italian commedia dell'arte. In fact, commedia was the source of Gozzi's war with Goldoni.

By the 1750s, Italy's great improvisational theater style was over two hundred years old. Its influence had been spectacular (Shakespeare, Molière, and Beaumarchais—all so important to opera—were only three writers among many who were influenced by direct exposure to commedia performances), but the era of the greatest companies and actors had passed. The existing repertory had become debased: repetitive, corrupt, terribly licentious. Goldoni set out to reform Italian drama by eliminating improvisation and cleaning up the old plots. He wrote complete texts, with all roles and dialogue fully delineated. He brought to bear a keener sense of psychology and realism, thereby producing deeper character development.

Nothing would do but for Gozzi to preserve the old commedia ways, at least to some extent, in opposition to Goldoni. Gozzi's *fiabe* left room for some improvisation, while his fairy-tale plots gave the familiar playing styles new vigor. He retained many of the old commedia character names. For a while he had the upper hand, effacing Goldoni, but it didn't last. Although he extended the commedia form, his efforts were really the last gasp, permitting commedia dell'arte to make a graceful exit after 250 years of resounding success.

Posthumously, however, Gozzi one-upped Goldoni by having more than one of his works turned into an opera by more than one composer. In addition to *The Love for Three Oranges,* another Gozzi *fiabe* was *Turandot* (1762). Puccini, of course, turned it into an opera, as did at least six other composers. Can you imagine a season of nothing but *Turandot*s? Gozzi joined a very distinguished list of writers honored by multiple settings of their works: Shakespeare, Beaumarchais, Molière, Goethe, Schiller, Hugo (as dramatist, not novelist), Virgil, Sophocles, Pushkin, and a few more.

Now, what was it about Gozzi and *L'amore delle tre melarancie* that appealed to Meyerhold and Prokofiev? Gozzi was a literary lion in every sense. His *fiabe* operated on a satiric level and were his claws for savaging his life opponents. This satire combined with the fantasy of his plots to produce scenes of bizarreness and downright grotesquery. Meyerhold saw in them a vehicle to mock the stereotypes of romantic drama. Prokofiev also saw possibilities for both musical and literary mockery, as well as a considerable technical challenge: to write an opera with music that was amusing and capricious yet ironic.

Throughout his composing career, Prokofiev exhibited a keen relish for the grotesque and ironic, usually in the guise of sarcasm. Even his most lyrical pieces have it. In *Peter and the Wolf* a duck is swallowed alive and can be heard quacking about in the wolf's stomach. His score for Eisenstein's film *Alexander Nevsky* is heavy with sarcasm, especially in the treatment of the church. Even the delightful *Lieutenant Kije* (the suite was adapted from another film score of the same title) clearly exhibits the taste for satire, though in a much lighter, puckish vein.

In *The Love for Three Oranges,* the scenes of satire and the grotesque are numerous: the brisk literary satire of the Prologue, the treatment of the court doctors as dreary multisyllabic mumblers, the insipidity of all the romantic characters, the scoring of the Cook—a female role—for "hoarse bass," the deus ex machina ending, to list just a few.

Gozzi's *fiabe* also contained a strong Saracenic element: the Fata Morgana, devils, mysticism, magic, Cabalistic references, which appealed to Prokofiev. Perhaps it was some lingering trace of pre-Christian Russian blood in Sergei; perhaps it was a post-Revolutionary Soviet influence; both these reasons may explain the return to Saracenic themes found in other Prokofiev compositions throughout his career. In the case of *Oranges,* however, most likely it was the intellectual and psychological appeal of the Saracenic theme. In Freudian terms, Gozzi's fantastic vein anticipated the Pirandellian concern with myth and the workings of the subconscious (especially with respect to the reality/illusion conflict)—a concern that is increasingly sympathetic to our age. No doubt it was to Prokofiev as well.

One other literary-dramatic theme is developed in the opera, and that is the preposterous parody of the "quest motif" seen in the search of the Prince for his Three Oranges. It might be a slap at Wagner and the portentous quest of the Ring Cycle, or simply a burlesque of the picaresque tradition in literature, or both.

Musically, *The Love for Three Oranges* is vigorously, consciously, defiantly modernist. The use of dissonance is quite dominant; the absence of tunes (though not of melody in the technical sense) is striking; it is a noisy opera. The principal elements in Prokofiev's music have always been dynamism, lyricism, and sarcasm. Fortunately the dynamism remained a constant throughout his composing career. Lyricism and sarcasm, however, ebbed and flowed in relation to one another. Generally speaking, as Prokofiev matured, lyricism became stronger and stronger, while his sarcastic bent lessened.

The Love for Three Oranges, however, is a very youthful work. The Chicago Opera Company commission came when Prokofiev was just twenty-seven, and the opera was completed in his twenty-eighth year. He was only four years out of the St. Petersburg Conservatory and had composed only one work of major importance, his *Scythian Suite,* opus 20 (1914). (Note: in title and theme the *Scythian Suite* is a tribute to a Saracenic tribe of pre-Slavic Russia.) Prokofiev found compelling musical reasons, as well as dramatico-literary ones as discussed above, for giving his sarcasm full rein.

Partly, he was still being boyish and mischievous, an enfant terrible, scaring his old professors with novel devices and stimulating his youthful comrades in arms by his daring. His friendship with artists such as actor-director-producer Meyerhold is indication enough that Prokofiev, too, was a Young Turk. His St. Petersburg teachers had included Rimsky-Korsakov, Liadov, and Cherepnin. Prokofiev clearly wanted to demonstrate his break with the musical pedantry so recently left behind him, as well as put as much distance as possible between himself and any vestiges of romantic music. He accomplished both objectives quite well in *The Love for Three Oranges.*

Curiously, just a year before the opera commission, Prokofiev penned his Classical Symphony (1917), a work that adhered to classical form and classical tonality. His virtuosic mastery of contrasting musical forms and tonalities suggests that he was able to pick and choose his subjects and executional styles with intellectual dispassion. And indeed, his works have long been noted for their cerebral qualities, often over and above their emotional qualities.

In 1948, Prokofiev made the following statement in an interview with Olin Downes in the *New York Times:*

> I strive for greater simplicity and more melody. Of course I have used dissonance in my time, but there has been too much dissonance. . . . We want a simpler and more melodic style for music, a simpler, less complicated emotional state, and dissonance relegated once again to its proper place as one element in music, contingent principally upon the meeting of melodic lines. . . . Music, in other words, has definitely reached and passed the greatest degree of discord and of complexity that it is practicable for it to attain.

Of course, 1948 was the year of Prokofiev's shameful and barbaric censuring by the Central Committee of the Communist Party (what did they know about music?) for "formalism" (most of the leading contemporary Soviet composers were included on the censure list), so the above quotation from the *New York*

Times may be dismissed as a purely defensive statement by an ailing composer (he had suffered a stroke, though he continued to compose). But really, it should be taken as an accurate, though overstated, expression of Prokofiev's change in attitude in the thirty years since composing *The Love for Three Oranges*. The opera was an example of the dissonance he had used "in my time." One can hazard a guess that he even had it, more than any other of his works, in mind when he gave the above statement to the *Times,* a paper published in the city where he composed the opera and where a new English version was being prepared for production by the New York City Opera (premiered November 1, 1949). Clearly, too, *The Love for Three Oranges* was one of his most "Westernized" works.

Indeed, the original libretto, by Prokofiev himself, was in a Western language: French. It is distinguished by its triumph of style and vigorous forwarding of the action, rather than by any great flights of language, poetry, or romantic fancy. Prokofiev exhibits in it a very droll, sometimes dry, sense of humor, plus an ability to give most major characters a distinctive style of phrasing. The differences in style and word usage are perhaps most notable in the Prologue, during which literary cliques do battle with each other, espousing their individual literary loyalties.

Basically, however, it is a utilitarian libretto, explaining and advancing the action with leanness and speed. It is a libretto that does not suffer by translation, for there is little in the way of stanzaic structure or verse pattern to tamper with. Wagner would be pleased with it as a fully integrated musical drama.

The standard English translation was done for the 1949 New York City Opera production by Prokofiev's biographer Victor Seroff. Throughout, some strong liberties are taken with the French original, but nothing that substantially changes either tone or meaning. Most of the liberties are to clarify plot development through repetition or implanting of exposition or factual detail. In a complex plot based on an old commedia play, this is not an unwise thing to do, particularly when an opera is as unfamiliar as *The Love for Three Oranges*.

And that in itself is a curious fact: *The Love for Three Oranges* is one of the most popular unknown operas in the repertory. Its popularity rests almost entirely on the march from Act II—a little three-minute interlude so frequently anthologized by the likes of Arthur Fiedler. But how many opera goers know the whole opera? Indeed, it's not even easy to buy a recording of it. There is only one full-length stereophonic version available in record stores, and that is sung in Russian (an excellent recording by the chorus and orchestra of the Moscow Radio, Dzhemal Dalgat conducting, on the Angel/Melodiya Label).

One's access to the work is restricted, for *The Love for Three Oranges* is not much performed, at least not in the West. The production history of the opera is brief. The premiere was on December 30, 1921, at the Auditorium Theatre in Chicago. Prokofiev himself conducted. The premiere was delayed for over two years from the date upon which the score was completed and delivered, due to the death of Chicago Opera Company director Cleofonte Campanini and to subsequent reorganization of the company under the leadership of "directa" Mary Garden. It was a success in Chicago, as much, one imagines, for being a cultural "coup" as for its musical and dramatic qualities.

Apparently Prokofiev did not find the production all he had hoped it would be, although there are no indications of great discontent on his part. Still, annotator Karolynne Gee records the following anecdote. Prokofiev arrived in Chicago in October, 1921, to find rehearsals well under way. He jumped in immediately, involving himself in all aspects of the production with such alacrity that stage director Jack Coini demanded at one point, "Who is the boss here on stage? You or I?" Prokofiev replied firmly, in English, "You are, but merely to carry out my instructions."

Productions followed in New York (1922), Cologne (1925), Berlin (1926), and Leningrad (1926), where Prokofiev felt his real theatrical intentions were revealed and the opera was brought to life. It was done at La Scala in 1947 and was revived in New York in 1949 (with revisions and deletions). The Big Apple production was a real hit, and the work has remained in the repertory of the New York City Opera since that time. In more recent years, there have been productions at the Edinburgh Festival in 1962 and at Sadler's Wells in 1963.

The Love for Three Oranges is an opera buffa, though of a special kind. It is an extravaganza of dancing and mumming, of elaborate costumes and fantastic characters, of games, processions, and festivities. But don't get too carried away: Fata Morgana escapes at the end; she always does. She's lurking around the corner.

DONIZETTI'S *Lucia di Lammermoor*
by Jonathan Abarbanel

When Gaetano Donizetti died in 1848 (age fifty), he left over one thousand letters. Not one of them gives so much as a clue as to how or why he selected Sir Walter Scott's novel *The Bride of Lammermoor* as the subject for an opera. The year was 1835, and *Lucia di Lammermoor* was Donizetti's fiftieth opera in a career that had begun some nineteen years earlier.

Following an extended journeyman period during which he composed dozens of operas for dozens of Italian opera houses, Donizetti achieved international success with *Anna Bolena* in 1830. Other "hits" soon followed: *L'elisir d'amore* (1832), *Lucrezia Borgia* (1833), and *Maria Stuarda* (1834). Still to follow *Lucia* were twenty more operas, including *Roberto Devereux* (1837), *La Fille du régiment* (1840), *La favorita* (1839), and *Don Pasquale* (1842). With *Lucia,* Donizetti began to approach the very top of his compositional form and the zenith of his fame. He could not know in 1835 that the violent headaches he suffered during the composition of *Lucia* were the first signs of the tertiary syphilis that reduced him to mental idiocy and helpless physical paralysis two years before his death.

During the productive decade that still remained to him, Donizetti reigned supreme in the world of Italian opera, from Vienna to Paris to London to Italy itself. Rossini, the old king of opera composers, had retired from the scene in 1829 after *William Tell*. (Note: Actually, he did *not* retire; he had a commission for five operas in ten years as court composer to French King Charles X. The Revolution of 1830, however, put an end both to Charles X and to Rossini's commission, whereupon he retired.) Dozens of composers scrambled for the abandoned brass ring, writing more or less in the Rossini style, at the pinnacle of bel canto specialization. Two, Bellini and Donizetti, broke away from the pack after 1830, evolving personal composing styles and international reputations. The death of Bellini in 1835 (only thirty-three years of age) left Donizetti as the leading Italian opera composer until the emergence of the younger Verdi in 1842 with *Nabucco*.

So there was Donizetti in 1835, alone at the top. He was thirty-seven years old, known throughout the Continent, happily married, a dedicated musical craftsman, a hard worker, and wealthy (or on his way to becoming so). Like Rossini before him, Donizetti came from north central Italy, but he established himself in the bustling opera theaters of Naples, where he really solidified his reputation, career, and craft. From 1822 to 1839, Naples was home, though Donizetti traveled extensively throughout Italy, fulfilling commissions and staging his works. In Naples, honors came, including appointment as director of music of the Royal Theaters of Naples, maestro di camera to the prince of Salerno, and pro tempore professor of counterpoint and harmony at the Royal College of Music.

In 1834, Donizetti received a commission from Rossini, as director of the Théâtre-Italien in Paris, to compose an opera for the French capital. The result was the now-forgotten *Marin Faliero,* enough of a success in its day for French King Louis Philippe to name Donizetti chevalier of the Legion of Honor, in March, 1835.

It was with this acclaim that Donizetti returned to Naples in Italy, already having selected Scott's *The Bride of Lammermoor* as his next project. How or why he made the selection we still do not know, but at least we have placed the opera within the time line of Donizetti's career. It is probable that Donizetti knew the work through a French translation or a stage adaptation, possibly reinforced by his three-month working visit to Paris.

Donizetti himself appears to have chosen the story and proposed it to the management of the Teatro San Carlo. Salvatore Cammarano was selected as librettist. The thirty-four-year-old Cammarano was well established as an artist, scene painter, and stage manager at San Carlo, and he had begun to add the additional theatrical credits of playwright and librettist to his lengthening résumé. Cammarano's great success with *Lucia* led to seven other collaborations with Donizetti and to four later efforts with Verdi, including *Luisa Miller* and *Il trovatore*.

There is no mystery as to why Cammarano was selected for the libretto; he had a good deal to recommend him. What is mysterious is why Felice Romani was *not* selected. Romani was the leading librettist at that period, and he had worked with Donizetti on eight operas over a dozen years, including *Anna Bolena, Lucrezia Borgia,* and *L'elisir d'amore.* Donizetti and Romani had worked on no fewer than three operas together in 1833–34 alone, before Donizetti's Parisian project. Romani would appear to have been the natural first choice for a new work for a house as important as San Carlo.

As with important opera artists today, timing and schedules often impose themselves upon artistic decisions. Romani lived in Turin (where he was a newspaper editor), while Cammarano was right there in Naples with Donizetti. More importantly, Romani was in demand by all the leading composers (he provided librettos for Rossini, Mayr, Bellini, and Verdi, among many others), and he probably had made commitments while Donizetti sojourned in Paris. And so the choice—happily for the history of opera—was Cammarano.

There can be no doubt that both the composer and the librettist were well acquainted with Sir Walter Scott, who was ubiquitous at that time. Born in 1771, Scott had established his literary reputation firmly by 1810 with historical collections of Scottish folklore and ballads and with some of the most popular epic poetry ever written, notably *Lady of the Lake* (1810). He then turned his hand to writing novels, completing over two dozen between 1814 and his death in 1832. The runaway success of these novels, which were translated into all major European languages, made Scott the most widely read contemporary writer of the century, until the emergence of Dickens. Scott was the first British novelist to become a noted public figure, a popularity recognized by his being created a baronet in 1820. Curiously, until 1827 Scott published all his novels pseudonymously, though the educated reading public readily saw through the disguise.

Scott's novels not only were read in translation; they were freely and frequently adapted for both the dramatic and lyric stages, in that era of lax copyright law. In addition to his *Bride of Lammermoor,* at least three other Scott novels became operas. Donizetti himself turned *Kenilworth* into *Elisabetta al castello di Kenilworth* for Teatro San Carlo in 1829. Additionally, Bizet set *The Fair Maid of Perth* in 1867, and Sir Arthur Sullivan wrote his only so-called grand opera, *Ivanhoe,* in 1891 (which ran for a still-phenomenal 160 consecutive performances!).

The Bride of Lammermoor was written in 1819, a year in which Scott completed three novels, including *Ivanhoe.* Scott clearly worked with the same prolificness in his field as Donizetti, Rossini, and other composers of the time did in the musical sphere. We must remember that the opera stage and the popular press were the television of that era, spitting out new works at a frantic pace and chewing up talent at an awful rate to meet the constant need for new work. Today, television dispenses with writers and actors in the same manner, as television series come and go as quickly as did operas 150 years ago. In the pre-electric era, the public itself had a voracious appetite for the latest novel and the newest opera. The business of the arts demanded—and rewarded—the swift, sure craftsman.

Both Scott and Donizetti were swift and sure craftsmen to a fault, with the most compulsive and regular working habits (Scott preferred to write during predawn hours; Donizetti labored from just after an early breakfast through late afternoon). Critics often have pointed out that their constant work under deadline pressures often affected the quality of their art. This cannot be denied. The wonder is that both men were able under such high-pressure circumstances to produce anything of merit at all, let alone the abundancy of superb work each has given us.

It must be admitted, however, that were it not for *Lucia di Lammermoor,* Scott's novel would be little remembered. It is *not* generally held to be one of his superb works. Its transition to the operatic stage elevated and immortalized it. Scott wrote it under trying physical circumstances: he was heavily drugged to alleviate the agonizing pain of gallstones, which, combined with the powerful sedatives, made him nearly delirious. It is reported that Scott actually was incapable of writing *The Bride of Lammermoor* and that he dictated it to two secretaries. When the novel was published (June, 1819), Scott, his health recovered, read it with no memory of having composed it. Asked how he liked it by his publisher, Scott said, "As a whole I felt it monstrous, gross and grotesque, but still the worst of it made me laugh."

Whatever misgivings Scott had, the public had none, snapping up edition after edition all over Europe. There had been at least a dozen major dramatizations in New York, England, and Paris by 1828, and an opera version, *Le nozze di Lammermoor,* by Michele Carafa, was produced in Paris in 1829. Donizetti and Cammarano hardly could have missed the work, even if they had wanted to.

Donizetti and Cammarano most likely prepared their version based on a French dramatization of the novel. Cammarano pared the work down to the basic love plot between Lucy/Lucia and Edgar/Edgardo, eliminating the more elaborate complexities and subplots of the novel.

The Bride of Lammermoor was drawn from an actual case history that occurred in Scotland in the late 1680s. Scott used many of the real details, though he changed the locale, names, and time, setting his work during the reign of Queen Anne (1702–14). In the novel, Lucy is seventeen years old, and Edgar, master of Ravenswood, is twenty. In addition to the pale and guileless heroine and the dark, brooding, aloof hero, Scott's novel is filled with Jacobite politics, detailed descriptions of Scottish country-gentry life of the earlier period, and comical secondary characters written in thick, authentic Scottish dialect.

In the novel, as in the opera, Edgar is a high-minded but impoverished nobleman whose family has been stripped of its estates by the chicanery of Lucy's family, the Ashtons. The opera, however, leaves out the political background for this chain of events. Also gone are all the secondary characters and Scottish local color. *Lucia,* the opera, really could be in any country.

In the novel, Lucy's father is a major character, a well-placed court official who sees the political wisdom of making peace with young Edgar when the political winds shift in the hero's favor. Lucy's mother, however, a proud, disdainful termagant, drives a wedge between the lovers that seals their doom. In the opera, both the mother and the father are gone, and Lucia's brother, only a minor figure in the novel, is the driving force. This is a perfect example of Cammarano's skill at reduction and condensation, as it admirably suits the need of opera for swift and uncluttered plot lines (a need all too rarely met in that era).

The most radical differences between novel and opera are in the ending. In the novel, as in the real-life model, the bridegroom survives his nuptial-night injuries. Also, young Edgar doesn't commit suicide (though he loses the will to live), but is swallowed up by quicksand at the foot of his castle, Wolf's Crag, as he rides to meet Lucy's brother in a duel during which he has resolved to let himself be killed. The brother's challenge to the duel remains in the opera in the so-called Wolf's Crag scene (Act III, scene 1) which frequently is cut in performance as the action it sets up has no "payoff" in the subsequent denouement of the opera.

Other details of the novel cleverly are incorporated by Cammarano, though altered slightly in form or position. Scott has the lovers pledge their troth by breaking a gold coin in half; in the opera, the love tokens are rings. In the novel, Edgar sees the ghost by the fountain in the woods, late in the story; in the opera, the incident of the ghost becomes Lucia's first big aria, "Regnava nel silenzio," a few minutes into Act I. In the novel, Alice is a blind old retainer of the Ravenswood family, who cautions the lovers against their infatuation; while in the opera, Alisa has become Lucia's lady in waiting. And so on.

Cammarano also made the tale much more Italianate. A true Neapolitan, he found the work a story of family honor as much as of illicit romance. Indeed, the most frequent, and nearly constant, words in the libretto are "blood," "hatred," "revenge," "fury," "rage," and "kill," with much calling down of heaven in vows of anger and love. If you wish to find surviving details of Scott's novel, you will find most of them in Act II of the opera, a sequence of scenes heavy with plot, conveyed frequently in recitative, and climaxed by the justly exalted sextette.

Cammarano delivered to Donizetti a taut and passion-filled libretto that spurred the composer to write what some critics regard as the first Romantic Era opera. By degrees, since *Anna Bolena* in 1830, Donizetti had been escaping the ironclad formulas of bel canto opera seria, and in *Lucia di Lammermoor* he made further progress. Inspired as always with a rich outpouring of melody, Donizetti also was able to capture a sense of mood; at one moment languid and almost erotic, at another moment suggesting the somber brooding of the hero or the doomed fortune of the young lovers. The role of the orchestra was slightly more prominent than in earlier efforts. Shared musical themes were subtly employed (the opening chorus of the huntsmen is echoed, for example, in a portion of Edgardo's final aria). Even the abundant coloratura was not purely and simply decorative; it actually was somewhat sustained by dramatic action, especially in the "mad scene."

These small musicological advances may be dismissed by modern audiences, especially when compared to what Verdi and Wagner were achieving just twenty years later; nonetheless, they paved the way that Verdi and Wagner had to walk in order to reach their respective houses. It is in this light that *Lucia* is regarded as a foundation stone of musical romanticism.

The opera was written in a very short space of time, owing to administrative snafus at San Carlo. Cammarano didn't receive official permission from management to begin work until about June 1. Donizetti snatched the pages of text from him one by one, editing them first, and then composing with his usual rapidity. The opera was completed on July 6, as is noted in Donizetti's own hand on the autograph score, which still is preserved. Bureaucratic snarls (the San Carlo was having financial problems) delayed acceptance of the score until August 20, when the copyists finally went to work making individual parts. The opera went into rehearsal, under Donizetti's direction, but even as late as September 5, there were difficulties with salaries for the artists. All was made right, however, and *Lucia di Lammermoor* met the world on September 26, 1835, with a distinguished cast headed by Fanny Tacchinardi-Persiani as Lucia and French tenor Gilbert-Louis Duprez as Edgardo. It was an instant and tremendous success, catapulting the composer to new heights of fame and fortune.

The history of *Lucia di Lammermoor* has been one of success and sopranos ever since. Within eight years, it had been performed at every principal European and New World opera house, including Havana (1840), Mexico City (1841), and New York (1843). Adelina Patti made her debut with it in 1859 (aged sixteen!). Marcella Sembrich, Luisa Tetrazzini, Nellie Melba, Jenny Lind, Amelita Galli-Curci (American debut in Chicago), Lily Pons, Maria Callas, Joan Sutherland, Beverly Sills. We don't wish to slight the superstar tenors and baritones who have sung Edgardo and Ashton, but we will stop with a few of those who have sung the title role, in order to save these notes from closing merely as a catalogue of greatness.

Whatever his reasons for writing *Lucia di Lammermoor,* Donizetti gave us a lasting and enriching musical treasure and a vehicle made for stars. *Lucia di Lammermoor* may be the only mad woman we welcome back with open arms.

VERDI'S *Luisa Miller*
by Peter P. Jacobi

Giuseppe Verdi was lean of language when it came to writing. He didn't leave volumes of philosophical shavings and personal reflections behind.

Whoever heard of Verdi essays? His letters are closer to few than many. But what he said, when he put pen to paper, held meaning: about his music, about the course of his life, about how his music and his times intertwined. There's a lesson in every paragraph.

For instance, take two letters he wrote at the time that *Luisa Miller* was in gestation, the first to Vincenzo Flauto, who presided over the San Carlo in Naples, the commissioning theater of his new work:

> I would certainly be lying if I were to tell you I was satisfied with Naples last time: but, believe me, what disgusted me was not the outcome, but the endless petty wrangling that had nothing to do with any opera. Why attack me because I went to a popular café, or was seen on a balcony with Tadolini, or wore light-colored shoes instead of black, or a thousand other trifling matters which were certainly not worthy of a serious public or a big city?
>
> If you think that my presence will contribute to the success of the opera, you are wrong. I repeat what I told you from the beginning: I am a bit of a savage, and if the Neapolitans found so many defects in me the first time, they will not change their opinion now. True, I have been living for a year and a half in Paris (that city in which everything is said to acquire a certain polish), but, to be frank, I have become more of a bear than ever. I have now been writing operas and wandering from place to place for six years and I have never in the pursuit of success addressed a word to a journalist or asked a favor from a friend or paid court to a rich man. Never, never! I shall always despise this kind of thing. I write my operas as well as I can; then I let matters take their course without any effort to influence public opinion.

It is a letter filled with self-concern, with a plea for privacy (which he always sought, even when he was the most public of composers), and with his dislike for Naples and conditions there. It reflects strongly that he really wanted no part of the current project, and indeed, he told his librettist and friend Salvatore Cammarano that he was doing it only to help him out ("You, an honest man, father of a family and a distinguished artist, would be the victim of all these ignoble [Neapolitan] intrigues. I, protected by my contract, am able . . . to forget the whole business, but for your sake, *purely for your sake,* I shall write the opera for Naples next year").

The second letter of note Verdi sent to a friend in Paris. And to place it in perspective, Verdi left Busetto, his home, in early October of 1849 for Naples, where he would supervise the *Luisa Miller* production. With him was his beloved Antonio Barezzi, the father of his late wife. For two weeks the two were held up in Rome because of an anticholera quarantine. While there, Verdi wrote to his Parisian friend:

> The affairs of our country are desolating! Italy is no longer anything but a vast and beautiful prison. If only you could see this sky, so pure, this climate, so mild, this sea, these mountains, this city, so beautiful!! To the

eyes—a paradise: to the heart—an inferno!! The rule of your countrymen in Rome is no better than that of the rest of Italy. The French do
their best to win the favor of the Romans, but so far the latter are most
dignified and firm. One sees Frenchmen everywhere—parades, reviews,
military bands that torment the ears in every corner of the city, all the
time, but one never sees a Roman taking part. Whatever your newspapers may say, the demeanor of the Romans is most praiseworthy, but
. . . the French are in the right . . . they are the strongest!!!

Theatrical affairs are desolating: the management is about to go bankrupt! For my part I'm not at all unhappy about that, for I desire nothing
more than to retire to some corner of the earth, to blaspheme and to curse!

Verdi could not separate himself from the events that erupted around him,
the turmoil in his beloved Italy.

And 1849 was a critical year, a year first of hope, then later of despair,
particularly in Rome, where the year might be said to have started, not on
January 1, but on January 27. On that evening the latest work of the "Maestro
of the Italian Revolution," one Giuseppe Verdi, was introduced at Rome's
Teatro Argentina.

Already on dress-rehearsal night the huge crowd—in and out of the theater—had been vociferous and almost uncontrollable. But on opening night it
was delirium that occurred, no less. The opera on view was *La battaglia di
Legnano,* a full-length love song to Italy and its honor. The story concerned the
defeat in 1176 of the German king and Holy Roman Emperor Barbarossa by
the Lombard League cities at the battle of Legnano. But Verdi and Cammarano, his word smith, and everyone knew that the opera was really an
occasion piece, a work about *now,* mid-nineteenth-century Italy.

Giuseppe Garibaldi and Giuseppe Mazzini, the military and political patri-
ots of the prolonged Italian independence movement, had entered Rome. Pope
Pius IX had fled, and a republic was on the verge of being announced, a republic by and for Italians, without the foreign oppressors.

When in the opening chorus the men sang "Viva Italia! Sacro un patto tutti
stringe i figli suoi," the audience went wild. And why not? Those words meant,
"Long live Italy. A sacred pact binds all her sons." There were shouts of "Viva
Italia" as well as "Viva Verdi."

And at the end of the opera, the reaction was happy hysteria, so ceaseless that
the fourth act had to be repeated, as became the custom at performances that
followed. Italians traditionally showered a stage with tokens of pleasure—
roses, coins, gloves. But on this occasion one witnessing soldier, sitting way,
way up in the fourth tier, threw his sword, his coat, his epaulettes, even the
chairs around him.

La battaglia happens to be a decent Verdi opera, but if it had been pure junk,
the reaction is likely to have been the same. People were in a state of frenzy
which continued into early February when the Roman Republic was officially

proclaimed by a constituent assembly against the wishes of the pope who, from temporary exile, urged the Continent's Catholic powers (Austria, France, Spain, and Naples) to rescue Rome. That effort began almost immediately. Mazzini, Garibaldi, and company fought valiantly through early summer. But it was like a handful versus a legion. Vincent Sheean, in his stirring biography of Verdi called *Orpheus at Eighty,* has written:

> There was very fierce hand-to-hand fighting, far more savage, really, than the great clashes of armed millions who (as in contemporary warfare) so seldom even see each other. The stories of heroism in the final days of the Roman Republic are numerous, and although it is natural to suppose that some have been embellished by patriotic imaginations, most of them seem true. Italy and Europe watched with awe; this Garibaldi, with his few groups scattered here and there, seemed to be holding whole armies at bay. Finally, of course, the sheer weight of power was too much for him. He extricated himself and his followers from the city and executed a skillful and daring retreat.

That retreat signaled the end of the Roman Republic, the hibernation for some years of the Italian struggle for independence, and an end also to Verdi's close musical ties to historical events. He would remain the patriot and touch upon that grand emotion from time to time in his later operas, but he would become a different composer, one in whom music became the object of his service.

It began then.

It began with *Luisa Miller.*

They call it the first opera of his second period—the one that was to produce treasures from *Rigoletto* and *Traviata* to *Un ballo in maschera* and *La forza del destino.* Don't expect astounding differences in *Luisa Miller* from what you heard in *Nabucco, I due Foscari, Attila,* and *Macbeth,* other early operas by Verdi. There is the beginning of a more expressive sound in the orchestra and a more subdued expressiveness in the vocal line. It's a more intimate work than its predecessors. And in it Verdi begins to break away from the conventions of set arias and ensembles, those that begin just so and end just then. He's more willing to extend a mood or an interaction, and not end it for the customary applause.

He had thought about *Luisa Miller,* or rather, Friedrich Schiller's *Kabale und Liebe* (Intrigue and Love) earlier, though at this time—to fulfill his contractual obligation to Naples—he actually wanted to set another patriotic story to music, this on "The Siege of Florence." But the censors, increasingly touchy about Verdi's operas, would have none of it.

So Verdi, not in a mood to fight and perhaps satiated from a too heavy and now depressing political atmosphere, turned to Schiller. He admired the German playwright, having used his stories twice before: for *Giovanna d'Arco* and *I masnadieri.* Later he would turn *Don Carlos* into *Don Carlo.* And in his late years he would keep a volume of Schiller's plays by his bedside, along with his Shakespeare collection.

Cammarano's job came first. He had to reduce five acts of drama to three acts of words and music. Some have called him a butcher for it, but actually he carried out his editing with intelligence. What resulted may not have been true to Schiller, but it was true to opera. Most of the intrigue was cut, along with certain characters. Intrigue tends toward the complicated; opera thrives on simplicity. Therefore, hurray for love.

While the Schiller play deals with social issues—the curse of absolute government, the destruction of private lives by societal corruption and practices—the Cammarano version reduces the story to innocence destroyed by social conventions. Cammarano, who had collaborated with Donizetti on *Lucia di Lammermoor* and who would still do *Il trovatore* for Verdi, might have become Verdi's long-term teammate had he lived beyond 1852. Verdi liked him; he also liked his work and his flexible independence. Cammarano had ideas, but he also listened; that was ideal in a librettist, according to Verdi.

Verdi expressed satisfaction with the *Luisa* plan that Cammarano presented him in May of 1849. Satisfaction, yes, but not complete acceptance. As usual, the composer participated in the preparation of the libretto. Correspondence between the two men reveals the give-and-take. Verdi makes suggestions:

> It seems to me, however, that all that devilish intrigue between Walter and Wurm, which dominates the whole of the play, doesn't here have the color and force that it has in Schiller. Perhaps in verse it will be different, but in any case let me know yourself whether you think I am right or not. . . .
>
> Deal with these remarks of mine in any way you wish, but let me say that in the first act finale, I am against having a stretta or cabaletta. The situation doesn't require one, and a stretta would probably lose all its effect in this position. The beginning of the piece and the ensembles you can deal with as you wish, but at the end you should stick as closely as possible to Schiller. . . .
>
> In the second act, take great care with the duet between Wurm and Eloisa. Make a strong contrast between Eloisa's terror and desperation and Wurm's diabolic frigidity. It seems to me that if you can give to the character of Wurm a slightly comic touch, the situation will become even more terrifying. After the other duet between Walter and Wurm, are you having a quartet? I think you need one here for unaccompanied voices. . . .
>
> The third act is superb. Try to develop further the duet between father and daughter: make it a duet to bring tears to the eyes. The duet which follows is superb and tremendous, and I think it will be necessary to end with a trio with the father. . . .

Cammarano understood Verdi's need to influence the libretto. In fact, a letter to Verdi considers a path that Wagner already had decided on:

Did I not fear to be branded as an Utopian, I should be tempted to say that for an opera to obtain the maximum of perfection, one mind should be responsible for both text and music. From this it will be clear to you that when two authors are in question, I think that the least they can do is to collaborate with the greatest possible intimacy. Poetry should be neither the slave nor the tyrant of music.

Verdi's early work on *Luisa Miller* was done in Paris, where he and his beloved Giuseppina Strepponi were in residence. But the task was finished in Busetto. The two of them left for Italy in mid August. Had they been able to occupy the house on his newly acquired farm, Sant'Agata, perhaps some of the grief might have been prevented. But the place was being reconstructed, so the couple occupied a palazzo in the heart of town. Verdi and Strepponi, an alliance not yet legitimized by marriage, raised eyebrows and hackles. According to the folks of Busetto, their Verdi was living in sin and flaunting it by bringing this woman of the stage to live amongst them. Their reaction: to snub the woman. Not to suggest that the unpleasant atmosphere influenced heavily the composition of *Luisa Miller* (historians tend to read too much psychology into artists' work), but the mood in Busetto and the emotions kindled in Verdi and Strepponi seem to be reflected in the opera.

Later Verdi would write to Antonio Barezzi, who also had problems accepting the relationship:

. . . you live in a town where people have the bad habit of prying into other people's affairs and disapproving of everything that does not conform to their own ideas. It is my custom never to interfere, unless I am asked, in other people's business, and I expect others not to interfere in mine.

Verdi finished work in October, then reluctantly headed for Naples. His stay was not a happy one. He fought with the management over artistic policy and finances. He asked for three thousand ducats due him in advance of the premiere, and he threatened to leave unless payment were made. That caused the superintendent of the royal theaters to threaten invocation of a law which forbade an artist from leaving Naples without his approval. Verdi responded characteristically. He wasn't about to bow to such maneuvers. He simply announced he'd take his opera and depart by French frigate.

Matters were smoothed enough for rehearsals to begin. But they were stressful and not eased by the presence of an amateur composer who greatly admired Verdi but who—according to local superstition—possessed an "Evil Eye." The fellow had been around a few years earlier when Verdi's opera *Alzira* bombed. Now he was around again, and Verdi's friends feared the worst. The worst didn't happen. Still, when the Evil Eye managed to get around guards to enter the theater, a stage wing collapsed, barely missing Verdi.

As if Evil Eye and an antagonistic theater superintendent weren't enough, Verdi's stay in Naples also was marked by the effort of a local critic to be bribed. This miscreant came to the composer with two reviews, one approving, the other disapproving. Grease the palm, he suggested, and the review would be good. Verdi's response was brief: "Print whatever you like."

Luisa Miller had a successful opening night. But Verdi didn't linger in Naples to savor his triumph. He wanted to get out of there, and he did, vowing never to write another opera for the place. He didn't.

The opera, although at least reasonably popular in Italy through the years, did not gain great acceptance elsewhere until recently. But we live, fortunately, in a pro-Verdi era. He's come to be recognized for his stature, and that has led to revivals of all the works.

Luisa Miller turns out to be one of the better of the lesser known. From the well-constructed overture to the final trio in which conflicting emotions pour forth in luscious sound, the score is filled with Verdian melody. There are arias expressive of passions and pain. There are ensembles that permit each voice its due. The most famous moment is the tenor's, his Act II aria, "Quando le sere," about which Verdi's later collaborator, Arrigo Boito, said: "Ah, if only you knew what memories and excitements that heavenly song arouses in an Italian's heart—and above all in the heart of one who has sung it from his tenderest years! If only you knew!" Francis Toye, Verdi's critic and biographer, terms it "a perfect example of mood-painting in melody . . . a truly remarkable piece of music, worthy to rank among the best examples of the kind in operatic literature."

That second act also has, as Verdi requested of Cammarano, an unaccompanied quartet of high merit.

Act III, which really offers choicest evidence of the new Verdi, is a gem throughout, with an extended father-daughter scene that more than hints at the Violetta-Germont scene in *Traviata,* with a love-hate-love scene between Rodolfo and Luisa, and with the already mentioned final trio.

Luisa Miller is an opera to enjoy. It is one you'll probably want to hear again once you've been introduced to it, as those who already have been can tell you.

Let it unfold.

Let its beauties enfold you.

BERG'S *Lulu*

by Karen Monson

Even Arnold Schoenberg, the teacher and mentor, was surprised when, in 1928, Alban Berg began to fashion his second opera on Benjamin Franklin Wedekind's banned dramas *Earth Spirit* and *Pandora's Box,* which together were intended to form what the writer called "A Monster Tragedy in Five Acts."

It had been bad enough, Schoenberg later wrote, that Berg had already cast his fate with Georg Büchner's *Wozzeck:* "That is how surprised I was when this soft-hearted, timid young man had the courage to engage in a venture which seemed to invite misfortune: to compose *Wozzeck,* a drama of such extraordinary tragedy that seemed forbidding to music. And even more: it contained scenes of everyday life which were contrary to the concept of opera which still lives on stylized costumes and conventionalized characters."

But now, as Berg entered his forties, *Wozzeck* was bringing him international celebrity. Another opera was clearly in order, and after brief ruminations, the composer secured the rights to *Pandora's Box* from Tilly Newes Wedekind, the playwright's widow, who had played the role of Lulu in a performance Berg had seen in Vienna in 1905, when he was an impressionable twenty year old. The fascinating and beautiful form of the opera would come later. At first, Berg was struck by the subject.

On a self-destructive course toward despair, Wedekind traveled with a circus troupe, then became a balladeer in a literary cabaret in Munich. From a total infatuation with the works of the then-obscure Büchner, he produced his first published play, *Spring's Awakening,* indicting the ways in which adults hide sex from their naturally curious children, who then die at the hands of abortionists or by suicide, in shame and disgrace.

Late in his life, in the play *Death and the Devil,* Wedekind had the prostitute Lisiska describe what had happened to her as a result of the backstairs life the playwright had come to know so well:

> For God's sake, you must never trust my love! My duty here is to pretend at love. Consider for a moment what it means when suddenly the door is torn open, and all at once, you must scrape your love together. . . . To all who gather here, love is eternal torment, insatiable greed. . . . How long my dream of highest bliss has been a land of undisturbed, eternal rest!

Berg had undoubtedly read these lines, just as he read those of Casti-Piani, the romantic moralist who is a white-slave trader in several of the Wedekind dramas, including the *Lulu* plays:

> What is there left for me when sensual pleasure is only hellish human slaughter . . . like all the rest of the earth! So this is that ray of divine light that penetrates the dreadful midnight of our martyr's existence. I wish I had put a bullet through my head fifty years ago! Then I'd have been spared admitting this miserable bankruptcy of my swindling, stolen-together spirituality.

The "soft-hearted, timid" Berg saw himself in these words. He had already been married for nearly two decades to the former Helene Nahowski, who was widely rumored to be the illegitimate daughter of the Emperor Franz Josef. The Bergs had polished their roles as lord and lady of the manor, handing out candies to children on the street, dressing beyond their means, and being seen at all the right places, often with Berg's lesbian sister, Smaragda.

No less a Viennese luminary than Alma Schindler Mahler had put together a consortium to finance the initial publication of *Wozzeck*. And the same woman, in memory of whose daughter Berg was to spend the final months composing the Violin Concerto, had suggested that Berg stay with her wealthy sister-in-law, Hanna Fuchs-Robettin (the sister of Franz Werfel, Alma's third husband), when he went to Prague.

And so it was that Berg fell in love for what was probably the first, and certainly the last, time. The long-distance affair with Hanna lasted through the last decade of the composer's life and affected all of his music from that period. And much as Berg loved Hanna, he also prized her daughter and son (who, like their mother, are pictured in the Lyric Suite for string quartet). Berg and his wife were childless, but the composer had sired a daughter during his teen-age years, and he longed for knowledge of his only offspring.

Guilt hit, and Berg envisioned himself in Wedekind's strange and wonderful world. Lulu is not Hanna; Lulu, the irresistible, is instinct. She has no father, no mother, no real name; she is called Nellie, Mignon, Eve, and Lulu, and she doesn't know which is correct. She is at the same time pure, unspoiled nature and the ultimate in degeneracy—a murderess with no remorse, no morals, no feeling for right and wrong, good and evil. She is a snake who lurks, pulsing with venom, lacking any rational comprehension of her own lethal power. She is a naive, innocent, comely child, centuries old and newborn, with no past and no future. She is totally free and completely enslaved, victim and victimizer, always the same and always different. She lives for love, but she has no sense of love. She is the embodiment of irrationality and self-fulfillment. She is beauty; she says she wants to be like nothing else in the world, so she is the epitome of beauty in all its forms—transient, everlasting, delightful, saddening, destructive, and redeeming. There is nothing that can be done to her or about her. She is inevitable. It is not the flame's fault that the moth flies into it and is annihilated.

But Berg, during his years of loving Hanna but being married to Helene, saw himself as a "detached being." He wrote to Hanna that he was a man "separated" from his "real existence . . . who (only in order to characterize him in some way) might for a time be fulfilled with the joys of motoring, but could never manage to compose *Lulu*." Given these torments and the worsening political climate of Austria, it is not at all surprising that Berg jumped into the character of Alwa and turned the son of the newspaper publisher Schön into a composer so that he could sing of Lulu, "Someone could write an interesting opera about her."

(Were one to continue these kinds of associations between the stage and real life, one would have to wonder whether Ludwig Schön had been modeled on Hanna's industrialist husband. And it seems more than likely that the Countess Geschwitz mirrored Berg's sister Smaragda. But there it stops.)

The work on *Lulu* went slowly, partly because Berg was interrupted by attendances at performances of *Wozzeck,* partly because cutting the "Monster Tragedy" to operatic proportions was a time-consuming chore and, not incidentally, because Berg allowed himself to be distracted. Berg wrote *Der Wein* for soprano and orchestra as a kind of study for his planned second opera, as if to test himself and his coloraturas. He went to work on *Lulu;* then—because he needed the money—he accepted a commission from Louis Krasner to compose the Violin Concerto, which turned into a masterpiece in memory of Manon Gropius. In the late summer of 1935, he returned to work on his opera. He died just before Christmas of that year. Anna Mahler—the daughter of Alma and Gustav and the half-sister to Manon—took the death mask. *Lulu* was not quite finished.

And then the confusion began.

Over the years, as the stories go, Schoenberg, Anton von Webern, Alexander von Zemlinsky, Igor Stravinsky, Luigi Dallapiccola, and, probably, others were approached to do the final work on *Lulu.* They are said to have refused, for various reasons, most of which are probably spurious. The rights to Berg's works went to the widow Helene, of course; and *Lulu* received its first performance, in the truncated two-act version with just a tad of Act III serving as a finale, on June 2, 1937, in Zürich. If one is to believe some reports, Helene asked even after the premiere that the opera be completed by some competent and sympathetic composer. At a guess, however, she wanted no such thing.

By that time Helene knew the details of her late husband's affair with Hanna (thanks to Alma Mahler, who was never one for subtlety), but she also knew about the existence of his illegitimate daughter. She was not happy, but she did know her new role: she was a professional widow. And she would be damned if the world were to hear the whole of the opera her husband wrote with his mistress in mind.

The catch was, of course, that *Lulu* was virtually complete. Friedrich Cerha had no easy task when Universal Publishers assigned him to add the finishing touches to Berg's second opera; but his problems were far from insurmountable, and the handful of men who had been allowed to see the material in the Universal vaults had already made that fact known to the music world. Cerha had the complete libretto, a fair copy of the short score, including the "musical drift" from beginning to end, the sketches, large serial tables of the rows and their employments, a vocal score by Berg's assistant Erwin Stein of the whole third act, and other resources. So when he went to work on the completion of *Lulu,* the composer Cerha was in business.

But he was not allowed to go to work—at least not officially and openly—until after Helene's death on August 30, 1976. And even then there were snags, since the widow's will specified that *Lulu* not be completed. Helene, you see, believed that she had talked to Alban after his death (perhaps from the chair near the piano where she had left the ashtray with the butts of the cigarettes he had smoked just before his final illness). And from the grave, Alban had pleaded with her not to release the third act of *Lulu.*

By this time, you're saying, "Yeah, and there's this bridge I can buy." But it's true—the best, most gossipy tale of opera in the twentieth century, hanging onto this "soft-hearted, timid" man and his complex, lurid opus. No sooner was Helene dead than the Metropolitan Opera in New York offered to give *Lulu* its first complete performance, claiming to be ready to add the third act to the two already planned and prepared for the coming season. The Royal Opera House at Covent Garden, London, would have been similarly obliging. So would the Vienna State Opera, but Stefan G. Harpner, one of the directors at Universal, told the *New York Times,* "The devious methods of expression of any opera director in Vienna would not make it possible for him to express any desire directly."

Then a mysterious front-runner emerged. The soprano Teresa Stratas, who had been the Metropolitan Opera's choice to sing Berg's title role, had bowed out, evidently because another company had offered her the chance to sing the first performance of the complete work. Pierre Boulez, whose music was also published by Universal and who was then the music director of the New York Philharmonic, was said already to have put the finishing touches on Berg's score. Someone, it was rumored, had been led into the back room at Universal, had witnessed the ceremonious unlocking of the vault, and had been allowed to hold—but not to scrutinize—the complete *Lulu,* with the missing notes filled in by what was supposedly Boulez's hand.

And indeed, the winner for the world premiere of the three-act version of *Lulu* did turn out to be the Paris Opéra under the baton of Boulez, though it wasn't Boulez who actually filled in the blanks of the opera. Miss Stratas sang the title role, as she did when the complete *Lulu* finally came to the Metropolitan in the 1979–80 season. There were people who tried to stop the performances, but their energies were wasted. The world had all of *Lulu,* and that was right.

Now, with the wisdom of hindsight, we can look back and ask *not* whether *Lulu* should have been completed—which it has been, and grandly—but why the opera was never finished by its creator. Berg had plenty of time to finish this magnum opus, despite its serial complexities and its emotional demands. When he completed the Violin Concerto, he was left only with a mission of filling in the blanks of *Lulu.* It is true that with no practical prospects of the opera's being performed when Berg's works were proscribed throughout Germany (because they were too modern and he was thought to be Jewish), there was no drastic hurry. But Berg had always believed that his opera would receive its premiere in Germany, probably in Berlin, its spiritual home, with Kleiber conducting. And if he had really begun to lose interest in *Lulu* so late in the work's progress, would his instincts not have been to finish it quickly, rather than to linger over the all-but-completed score?

It could well be that Lulu and her circle had become too sordid and distressing, even for Berg, and that the two sides of his personality had entered into mortal conflict. Was the man who wanted nothing more than to be the respectable, good-looking, well-dressed, widely honored *grand seigneur* struggling with another part of himself, the part that would forever love a woman other than his wife, the part that was ineluctably drawn to the amoral heroine of Wedekind's drama?

Or perhaps Berg feared that in finishing *Lulu,* he would also be bringing to a close the time when he could freely wander in his heroine's dark and dreamlike world and would have to return to the realities of Vienna, the daily turmoil, the hypocrisy he saw around him, the political instability, the moral and economic decline. It took courage for Berg to compose *Lulu.* Perhaps, in the painful last days of his life, he was beginning to realize how much courage it had taken and how much he was going to lose once *Lulu* left him and went on her own in the world.

The Structure of *Lulu*

Wedekind wrote: "In the description of Lulu, I attached importance to the way in which the words she speaks paint the body of a woman. With each of her remarks I asked myself if it served to make her young and beautiful."

Such a young, beautiful woman begged for opera. Berg gave her arias, set pieces, duets, pauses in which applause may interrupt the action. *Lulu* and Lulu are old-fashioned. They beg for reaction, just as might the lion tamer and the tightrope walker in the center ring.

But in an opera derived from a 12-tone row, the basic set had to belong to Lulu, the woman from whom the whole drama flows. Her line of pitches (B-flat, D, E-flat, C, F, G, E, F-sharp, A, G-sharp, C-sharp, B) is first paraded by in full dress when she identifies herself "in the tempo of a pulse beat . . . in a determined, proud manner," in Act II. By subdividing Lulu's row into four groups of three, Berg settled upon the quartet of chords that would identify her portrait in the Pierrot costume. Melodies derived from the various voices in these "portrait chords" stand for Lulu in her relationship to the painter and his work, her innocent beauty and her destructive powers. These work neatly into singable, scalelike arcs.

By repeating Lulu's basic series and skipping first one, then two, then three notes, and so on, Berg charted the row that would be assigned to Dr. Schön. Repeating the series again and again and pulling out every seventh pitch, the composer assigned a row to Alwa. The countess's basic set, similarly derived, was worked into a pentatonic system (based on the interval of the fifth), which harks back to the musical traditions of ancient Greece and the Isle of Lesbos. By filling out the countess's chords into clusters of tones, Berg characterized the rowdy harshness of Geschwitz's opposite, the athlete Rodrigo. A creeping chromatic series, full of half steps and scored skeletally, would represent Schigolch. Every bit of the music, with the exception of a ballad by Wedekind, derives from Lulu's row in a manner that can be drawn in intricate charts that indicate symbolic relationships.

But beyond that, Berg arrived at a form for the opera that would explain his ramifications of the row, extending the characters themselves through the whole length of the drama, up until the very last bars in which Schigolch remains in a thinly scored chromatic scale, the dust from which everything comes and to which everything goes. Only Lulu herself is chameleon enough to be part of all of the sections of the opera's larger forms. She is strong enough, with her possession of the natal row, to be the queen of all of the permutations.

Dr. Schön's signature is the sonata, the most important formal product of Western musical tradition. Alwa is the rondo, whose theme/mind keeps returning to Lulu's beauty. And in working Wedekind's plays into a libretto, Berg constructed an alp, a kind of musical palindrome which rises, peaks at the *ostinato* interlude between the first and second scenes of Act II, and then goes into retrograde. Lulu's luck has reversed; it will soon run out.

It is not crucial that every listener know every link; indeed, not every link has been discovered. But the relationships hit the listener's unconscious, quite insidiously. And they are a major part of *Lulu,* from the moment the animal trainer introduces the circus acts—and those acts never stop parading by. The unity of the opera works on even the least tutored witness, much as Lulu worked on the souls of her victims. Without quite knowing why, though they sensed they were doomed, those victims could no sooner leave her than they could forget her.

VERDI'S *Macbeth*

by Stephanie von Buchau

When *Macbeth,* Giuseppe Verdi's tenth opera, was revived at Paris in 1865, one critic remarked that the composer did not know his Shakespeare. Verdi was furious. "It may be that I did not do *Macbeth* justice," he wrote to Léon Escudier, his French publisher, "but to say I do not know, do not understand, and do not feel Shachespeare [*sic*]—no, by God, no! He is my favorite poet. I have had him in my hands from earliest youth, and I read and reread him continually."

Although at various times in his career Verdi contemplated setting such Shakespearean works as *Hamlet, The Tempest, Antony and Cleopatra,* and especially *King Lear* (though he finally told Mascagni he gave it up because "the scene where Lear finds himself on the heath terrified me"), he eventually set three: *Macbeth* (1847), *Otello* (1887), and *Falstaff* (1893). The librettos for the last two masterworks were by the poet-composer Arrigo Boito, but *Macbeth*'s libretto had a more uncomfortable genesis. Verdi himself, suffering from stomach ailments and a psychosomatic sore throat which plagued him throughout his life, wrote a prose reduction of Shakespeare's play before farming it out to the librettist Francesco Maria Piave for versification.

This was in 1846, after the Italian public had taken the bellicose patriotism of *Attila* to its heart. The critics were not so friendly. "The scourge of God ought not to be the scourge of our nostrils," one paper remarked. *Attila* was lacking the psychological depth and ground-breaking musical effects that Verdi would apply to *Macbeth*. While his doctor ordered six months of rest, the composer mulled over new projects, among them Schiller's *Die Räuber* (which eventually became *I masnadieri*) and Grillparzer's *Die Ahnfrau,* which came to nothing, as well as the Shakespeare play. (It will be seen that all these sources were "foreign" to Italy, and in fact, critics of *Macbeth* later complained that Verdi did not choose national subjects, to which the composer replied that if Italian theater were to offer him plays equal to Shakespeare and Schiller, he would be glad to set them.)

In any case, having promised an opera to Alessandro Lanari, the manager of the Teatro della Pergola in Florence, Verdi set about securing the right singers. Since no tenor was available for the demanding part of Karl Moor in *Die Räuber,* Verdi put aside his work on that text and concentrated instead on *Macbeth.* He had already envisioned the title role as a baritone, and since the excellent Felice Varesi was available, negotiations with Lanari were finalized. Verdi wished Lady Macbeth to be sung by Sophie Loewe, but he was not upset when Marianna Barbieri-Nini was engaged in her place.

Varesi later went on to create the leading baritone roles in *Rigoletto* and *La traviata,* so we can assume that Verdi was satisfied with him, but we actually have a memoir from Mme. Barbieri-Nini about the composer's approval of her reading of the sleepwalking scene. She studied it for three months, earning a tremendous ovation at the *prima.* "I was standing in my dressing room, trembling and exhausted, when the door flew open and Verdi stood before me . . . I saw that his eyes were red. He squeezed my hand very tightly and rushed out. That moment of real feeling repaid me many times over for the months of hard work and continuous agitation." Among the "months of hard work" she notes 151 rehearsals of the first-act duet between Macbeth and his Lady.

Piave worked diligently on transforming the prose sketch that Verdi had given him, but the composer was never satisfied, and his abuse of his librettist makes rough reading even today. His favorite comment was "Poche parole" (fewer words): he was continually attacking the poet for being too prolix and not lofty enough. "This tragedy is one of the greatest creations of man. . . . If we can't make something great out of it, let us at least try to do something out of the ordinary." Piave complied with all the composer's requests, but in the end Verdi asked his friend Count Andrea Maffei to rewrite some of the text (including the entire sleepwalking scene), and Piave's name was left off the title page. (Piave, of course, was later restored to favor and created the texts to *Il corsaro, Stiffelio, Aroldo, Rigoletto, Simon Boccanegra,* and *La forza del destino.*)

The libretto to *Macbeth* is less than half the length of the play. Shakespeare's more than twenty characters are reduced to eight. The opera begins in the third scene of the play, with Macbeth and Banquo meeting the witches on the heath. Verdi specified that there should be three covens of at least six witches each, instead of three individuals, to create a fuller sound. (He also involved himself in the stage direction and costume design, complaining that the producer knew nothing of Scottish history and rattling off the names and dates of English kings contemporary with Macbeth.)

Duncan is a mime role in Verdi, as is Fleance, Banquo's son. Lady Macbeth's aria and cabaletta in the first act parallel her speeches. "Hie thee hither / That I may pour my spirits in thine ear" and "Come to my woman's breasts / And take my milk for gall, you murdering ministers." In many places, the text is an exact translation of Shakespeare, as in Macbeth's "The bell invites me. Hear it not Duncan, for it is a knell / That summons thee to heaven or to hell." Comic relief is dispensed with: Verdi in his Risorgimento mood wouldn't have cared for the pithy sayings of the roistering Porter.

The first scene of Act II in the opera corresponds to Shakespeare's Act III, scene 2, except that Lady Macbeth's "La luce langue" (added for the Paris revival, about which more in a minute) has no corresponding counterpart in the Shakespearean text. Banquo's soliloquy likewise is invented. Nor is there a drinking song in the play, though Verdi weaves his "Brindisi" skillfully into the scene where Banquo's ghost startles the guilty Macbeth. The opera's Act III equals the play's Act IV, scene 1. Verdi originally wished for a ballet at this point, after the apparition of the eight kings, but the opera was to be presented in Florence at carnival, and no dancing was permitted on stage during Lent. The ballet was eventually written and inserted in the 1865 Paris production, though it is often omitted from modern performances. In it, Hecate has a silent, nondancing role.

The subplot of Macduff's murdered family is crammed into one aria for the tenor, "A la paterna mano," and Ross's speech beginning "Alas, poor country! Almost afraid to know itself," is encompassed in the choral lament that opens Act IV, "Patria oppressa," which was nearly as effective a rallying cry to the Risorgimento as its counterpart in *Nabucco,* "Va, pensiero." The sleepwalking scene is a close parallel between the play and the opera, except that the poetry removed by the journeyman versifying is restored by Verdi's music, with its misterioso accompaniment, its sotto voce comments by the doctor and the maid, and its spooky ending, where the soprano rises, on *un fil di voce,* to a pianissimo high D-flat.

Much has been made of the kind of voice required to sing Lady Macbeth. A letter from the composer to Salvatore Cammarano (librettist of *Il trovatore*) at the time of *Macbeth*'s San Carlo premiere in 1848 is often quoted as evidence that Verdi did not wish Lady Macbeth to sound beautiful. "I would prefer that Lady [the Italians always refer to her this way, as if her title were her first name] didn't sing at all. Tadolini [the proposed Neapolitan Lady Macbeth] has a marvelous voice, clear, limpid and strong; and I would rather that Lady's voice

were rough, hollow, stifled. Tadolini's voice is angelic; Lady's should be devil-
ish." How literally we are to take this advice is moot. It is likely that Verdi was
overstating the case in order to correct some of the narcissistic abuses that then
existed in Italian opera—like the Banquo who refused to stay around for the
banquet scene because he "didn't have anything to sing." *Macbeth* was the first
opera in which Verdi vigorously attempted those theatrical reforms which
would become commonplace with his later masterpieces.

In order to clarify the ending of *Macbeth* it is necessary to discuss the Paris
revisions. In 1863, Carvalho, impresario of the Théâtre Lyrique, wished to
present *Macbeth*, and the composer, after looking over the sixteen-year-old
score, suggested to Escudier that the revision would require an aria for Lady
Macbeth in Act II ("La luce langue," which replaces a commonplace cabaletta
called "Trionfai!"), revision of the hallucination scene, and the addition of a
ballet (always a requirement in French productions, although we have seen that
Verdi originally intended a ballet), Macbeth's Act III aria rewritten (it was
eventually replaced by a duet for the Macbeths), revision of the exile's chorus,
and the composition of a new finale.

The finale was a problem, which still exists today as producers try to arrive
at the most felicitous arrangement of the existing material. Originally, Macbeth
had a soliloquy and then died on stage. In the Paris version, the death scene was
cut, although it is sometimes reintroduced into performances of the 1865
edition. Verdi makes his intentions clear in a letter to Escudier: "All the scenes
from the baritone's romanza ("Pietà, rispetto, amore") to the end are new, that
is the description of the battle and the final hymn of victory. You will laugh
when you see I have written a fugue for the battle. I, who detest everything that
smacks of theory!"

The important thing to remember about these changes is that the two scenes
that the composer felt were the heart of the opera—the Macbeths' first-act duet
and the sleepwalking scene—are from the 1847 version and were the original
inspirations of a thirty-four-year-old composer. It is true that parts of the score
are banal (the witches, Duncan's march) and that some scholars find the
revisions awkward, since they are so much more sophisticated than the 1847
original. But the fact is that *Macbeth* takes an enormous leap forward from the
operatic conventions of the time, towards the use of scoring and melody to
provide psychological depth rather than mere attractive display. *Macbeth* was,
in fact, music drama, and Verdi knew it. "The opera is a little more difficult
than my others, and its mise-en-scène is important. I confess I care for it more
than for the others and I should be sorry to see it fail."

It is the very stretching of conventions that accounted for *Macbeth*'s dubious
reception. The premiere, at the Pergola on March 14, 1847, was certainly a
success. Verdi took twenty-five curtain calls, but some felt that the calls were
for the composer, not for the opera. One critic referred to the new work as a
vera porcheria, which surely needs no translation. *Macbeth* traveled around the
world but it never attained the kind of popularity that even *Ernani* and

Nabucco enjoyed. It was always looked at as an "oddity," this Shakespearean subject with no love interest which an Italian thought he could set with impunity.

At the premiere of the Paris revision, April 19, 1865, the opera was even less successful than it had been in Florence. Verdi wrote to Escudier, "I thought I had done quite well with it . . . it appears I was mistaken." It wasn't until our century that the revised version became a repertory piece, the notable revivals being at La Scala in 1938 (with Gina Cigna), the Maggio Musicale in 1952 (with Maria Callas), and the Metropolitan Opera in 1959 (with Leonie Rysanek).

PUCCINI's *Madama Butterfly*

by Peter P. Jacobi

Event Number One: February 17, 1904

Earlier in the day, Giacomo Puccini had written the portrayer of his heroine, the lovely Rosina Storchio:

> My good wishes are not necessary. So true, so fine, so moving is your wonderful art that the public must succumb to it! . . . Until tonight, then—with confidence and much affection.

He wasn't often, but that evening he was jubilant, confident. He'd even invited his family, sisters and all, to attend, and that was a departure from custom. Preparation had been a joy. Stagehands often stopped their work to listen. Members of the orchestra rose to acclaim him after the dress rehearsal.

But when the La Scala curtain rose, silence. Through the early passages, silence. Storchio waited in the wings for her entrance, with Puccini at her side. The soprano's hands were ice cold. On cue, Storchio accomplished her stage entrance to those magical strains we now know so well. Silence. The composer's confidence turned to mere composure and then to nervous smoking. "Siam giunte," she sang.

"That's from *Bohème*!" someone shouted. His words became echoes. "Give us something new," someone else shouted, "We've heard that before."

Then, more quiet. Through to the end of the act, even through that love duet into which Puccini had poured so much emotional energy. At its conclusion the smattering of applause was awkwardly blended with hissing sounds.

Puccini was beyond consolation, so Tito Ricordi, his publisher and friend, turned to Storchio, attempting to calm her fears. "At the second act the reaction will set in," he said. "I swear to you that it will be a success."

But during that second act, early on, a quick movement by Storchio caused her kimono to billow. "Butterfly is pregnant," an ugly voice called out from the darkened theater, now seeming more and more to Puccini a tunnel filled with unknown enemies, terrifying beasts, and demons. Storchio broke into tears. She barely managed to negotiate "Un bel dì."

During the night vigil scene, performed that evening with curtain open while the orchestra played the Intermezzo, the crisis became disaster. The planned chirping of birds to mark the breaking of dawn brought unplanned, or at least unexpected, chirping from the audience, along with growls, groans, moos, and assorted farmyard noises.

Quiet did return, but the final curtain, after Cio-Cio-San's suicide, brought more laughter, more shouting, too little applause, and not a single curtain call.

"Puccini slunk home," notes his biographer, George Marek.

Event Number Two: May 28, 1904

In the wings of Brescia's jewel-box Teatro Grande, the soprano Salomea Krusceniski waited for her entrance as Butterfly.

The curtain had opened to applause. Krusceniski's moment came. Applause. After the love duet, applause; so much applause that the duet had to be repeated. After "Un bel dì," applause. Each ovation seemed to surpass the previous one.

When the heartbreaker ending concluded, numerous women—and not such a few men—were seen to be weeping, or at least wiping tears away. Applause blended with cheers, and happy screams of support enveloped cast and composer. Puccini was brought back to the stage apron again and again.

He did not slink home that night.

And just so you know: Rosina Storchio had her second chance in July. She appeared then as the heroine in the first production of the opera outside of Italy, this in Buenos Aires. Toscanini conducted. The audience found her and the opera stunning.

Before—Between—After

"There is no comparison between my love for the others and what I feel for her for whom I wrote music in the night," he said of this beloved work, on which he lavished some of his most inspired music.

He had not come to the subject easily, but then each decision leading to a new work seemed to be traumatic for Puccini, from first work to last.

His success with *Tosca* following *La Bohème* following *Manon Lescaut* prompted action. He wanted to get on with this blossoming, nay, this exploding career. Not really much of a reader, he now turned to reading for clues. The works of Alexandre Dumas and Honoré de Balzac and Victor Hugo. He considered a story by Gerhart Hauptmann. He had a chat with Émile Zola. He had another with Gabriele D'Annunzio. Edmond Rostand's *Cyrano de Bergerac* appealed. So, in quite a different way, did Feodor Dostoevsky's trenchant *House of the Dead*.

But Puccini kept looking. He kept thinking. He kept stewing. It was a time when things Far Eastern attracted artists, Puccini included. And one evening while in London he attended the theater. Its offering was a one-act tear-wrencher about a Japanese geisha and an ugly American who betrays her. Based on a short story by John Luther Long, first published in a U.S. magazine, it had been shaped for the stage and for actress Blanche Bates by the flamboyant director-writer-impresario David Belasco. Well, like almost everyone everywhere who was touched by the gooey, gushy drama, so was Puccini. Perhaps it was fortunate that he understood so little English, because the dialogue, particularly that given to the heroine, was dreadful. Poor Butterfly spoke in pidgin English. But as Puccini experienced it, the story evoked reaction. Here was one of those frail heroines who would continue to attract him. Here was a subject. Here was *the* subject for his next opera.

"The more I think of *Butterfly*," he wrote to Ricordi, "the more irresistibly am I attracted."

Cio-Cio-San was not the first East-versus-West-and-destroyed-by-the gulf-between heroine. Nor would she be the last. Consider Selika in Meyerbeer's *L'Africaine* and Lakmé in Delibes's opera. In our day, Gian Carlo Menotti's Chicago-premiered opera *Tamu Tamu* exploits that theme. And of course, so does *South Pacific*.

Puccini had his subject. Belasco was delighted to cooperate, though the periods and dotted *i*'s took some time to work out. Delighted Belasco should have been. His no-account little drama would be transformed by a master of music.

Puccini once commented: "Almighty God touched me with His little finger, and said: 'Write for the theatre.' I have obeyed the supreme command."

He certainly did with *Madama Butterfly*, on which he worked with diligence and with a passion for the subject. The work did not progress without interruption, however.

The first break: sadness and ceremony. His idol Verdi died early in 1901. Puccini broke all self-imposed schedules to attend the funeral as well as a memorial concert at La Scala as well as the observance one month later of Verdi's permanent burial in the cemetery of the Home for Musicians, which Verdi had founded in Milan. Melodies for a *Requiem* honoring Verdi began to form in Puccini's head, even though he wasn't to complete that score until several years later. With all that, his mind couldn't concentrate on *Butterfly*.

Delay came again in the form of slow agreement with Belasco over the uses of his play.

And then came libretto problems, as usual.

And then, an accident. On a fog-drenched night, Puccini's chauffeur-driven car skidded off a road, overturned, and crashed in a field. The composer's wife and son escaped with mere scratches; the chauffeur, with a thigh fracture. But Puccini was found trapped under the car, unconscious, nearly asphyxiated, and with his right shin broken. A doctor messed up the setting of that fracture, thus resulting in the need to break the bone again and a second setting.

Recovery took eight months, a period of at least partial inactivity. Not so incidentally, Puccini never lost the limp that even healing could not remove.

But of course, work on the opera did resume. Some orchestration here. Some composition there. In succession. In tandem. He finished the opera at 11:10 P.M., he noted, on December 27, 1902, about thirty months after first being intrigued by the play in London.

Preparations for the La Scala premiere began.

That ill-fated event, one of the most notorious failures in opera history, has never been adequately explained. Most likely it never will be. One problem was the length of the second act, which in Puccini's revision after the failure became today's acts II and III. Italians aren't fond of long acts. Verdi, aware of that foible, said his forty-two-minute first act of *Otello* was "two minutes more than necessary."

Most likely, however, the failure had little to do with the opera itself. The composer, though popular with the general opera-going public, was far from popular among artistic colleagues. First, he was a loner. Second, he had stepped on toes in the selection of *Manon Lescaut* as a subject matter, since the esteemed Jules Massenet had only a few years earlier entered his version *(Manon)* into the records. Third, he had more than stepped on Ruggiero Leoncavallo's toes in stealing story and thunder by writing *Bohème* in the full knowledge that Leoncavallo already was working away on his *Bohème*. Fourth, Puccini had angered Alberto Franchetti by talking him out of doing *Tosca,* only to turn around and do a Puccini version. Add jealousy on the part of others. And as in an Agatha Christie mystery, there were plenty of suspects for this musical murder. No proof has come to light, but the hints of and reasons for an engineered cabal are strong. One journalist wrote:

> Groans, explosions, lowing, laughter, shouting, snickering, the usual solitary cries of *bis* deliberately meant to enrage the spectators further; this, in synthesis, is the welcome of the Scala's audience to the new work of Maestro Giacomo Puccini. After this pandemonium the public left the theatre happy as can be, and never were such merry faces seen, so joyously content in their collective triumph.

Puccini termed the affair a lynching. He spoke of "cannibals" who "didn't listen to a single note" and of "a terrible orgy of madmen drunk with hate." But though he lost face, he did not lose faith. "My *Butterfly*," he said to a friend, "remains as it is: the most heartfelt and most expressive opera that I have conceived. I shall win in the end, you'll see." And to another friend, a priest, he wrote: "Never fear! *Butterfly* is alive and real, and will soon rise again."

Revisions and cuts were made, leading to the victory at Brescia and to victories ever after. Following the Brescia re-premiere, he wrote to his sister: "It was exactly as I had wished: a real and unqualified triumph. The success is greater every evening."

And What Do We Have

"A thread of smoke," according to Puccini.

A delicate work in which a character is developed from girl to heroine and in which the music has transformed treacle into tragedy. Yes, tragedy. Mosco Carner argues persuasively in his *Puccini: A Critical Biography:*

> Though couched in terms of a melodrama, it contains an element of true tragedy. The catastrophe is the inevitable corollary of the geisha's character; because she is what she is, she cannot act otherwise than she does. Faced by three alternatives—marriage to Prince Yamadori or resumption of her former profession or death—she makes the most courageous choice. Caught in a moral conflict, she solves it by self-annihilation and thus grows to a heroine in the true sense of the word.

We have a work of theater that would today be laughed off the stage as theater and yet, with Puccini's music, holds its theatricality, indeed enlarges upon it. A work that never ceases to cause even macho men to weep. A work that keeps Cio-Cio-San human-scaled and yet lifts her to legendary status. A work—and how unlike Italian opera—that's hard to take apart musically; only "Un bel dì" works alone, outside the web of relationships that Puccini created in and with his score. A work—and again how unlike Italian opera—in which the tenor has a lot and yet little that's memorable to do, in which he doesn't really have an aria to sing. A work that seems, because of tonal touches, to feel Japanese (the wife of the Japanese ambassador to Italy had provided Puccini with "native Japanese music") but that in essence is pure Puccini, meaning as Italian as music can be.

At this point, more than eighty years after its introduction, what can one say about the music of *Madama Butterfly* that hasn't been said before and that isn't known by everyone within the reach of this article?

Nothing, probably.

It's poignant, of course.

And plangent.

And melodic.

And evocative.

And with so many moments—some extended—in which the listener is transported into a timeless, spaceless dimension where emotion rules.

Puccini, as was his custom, prepared for the opera. He studied Japanese music and customs. He does, therefore, manage to imbue the opera with motives that suggest the world in which the story unfolds. His gift of orchestration, by then, had progressed significantly, permitting him to use woodwinds and bells, for instance, to approximate oriental sounds. Add to that certain harmonies of a twentieth-century nature with which he was experimenting, and we have a work, as music, more avant-garde than we're likely today to give it credit for being, meat-and-potatoes repertory piece that it has become. And just possibly, these at least slightly strange elements may have contributed to the alienation of that Scala audience. Doubtful, but just maybe.

You undoubtedly have your own "watch-out-fors" in *Butterfly*. But watch out for the haunting entrance of our heroine early in the first act.

And that most complicated Puccini love duet ever, which ends the act, with its seven sections, each with its own mood and purpose, but all one piece of music extending outward and upward toward an appropriate, ecstatic, love-propelled climax.

Aside from Butterfly's hope-in-despair cry, "Un bel dì," and the glorious Humming Chorus, the second act tends to be overlooked as a section of highlights. But that's only because it is one extended highlight. In it Puccini has so shrewdly woven his elements into a unified portrait of a woman, a woman too overcome with love to be overcome by the realities of her situation. The music is at every point a brush stroke within that portrait, adding color and depth. One may leave the opera house with other scenes and other tonal snatches in mind. But none of these would work without the portrait which is Act II.

In the final act we're led—no, driven—toward Butterfly's Farewell and a scene virtually unmatched in all opera, so captivating is it. The music is so telling that one could close one's eyes and, not knowing the story, know exactly what it is about.

A rapturous opera, this *Butterfly,* one that the opera devotee never ceases to take delight in, that the opera newcomer accepts easily, that a poor performance cannot destroy, and to which a good performance gives ever-renewed vigor.

MOZART'S *The Magic Flute*
by Thomas Willis

An estimable singer by the name of Cletis ("Sweet Man") Crowley once capsulized his lyric-theater experience in a song entitled "Opera Gives Me Cause to Sing the Blues." It began "Oh, a singer comes in from the left, / And a singer comes in from the right; / By the time they say hello / It's taken up half the night," and it continued with other examples of the difficulty of cross-cultural communication. Clearly, he was not speaking of *Die Zauberflöte*. Not only do the singers introduce themselves quickly, they present themselves in the nearly universal context of a fairy tale, play at dungeons and dragons, fall in love at first sight, struggle with temptation, tell dubious jokes, and view life as a battle between the Black Queen and the White King, one heading the forces of darkness and hypocrisy (although she is not *all* bad), and the other, a sunlit Valhalla where the brave and virtuous are rewarded with eternal beauty and wisdom. Today, as for nearly two centuries, there is something for nearly everyone. Above all other operas in the repertory, this enchanted hybrid has retained its ability to communicate with men and women throughout our global village, with the circus herald's "children of all ages."

Ingmar Bergman went part of the way in explaining why. His motion picture was placed in a quixotic, timeless Never-Never-Land, panning back and forth between the eighteenth-century court theater at Drottningholm and a variety of more modern locales with balloonist boys, body-suited modern dancers, and Brechtian signboards to underscore the underlying messages. During the intermission music we got backstage scenes of the actors making up, smoking under a "No Smoking" sign, and barely making an entrance on time. Again and again as his abridged and altered version of the opera progressed, we were returned to the audience area for a close-up of the director's wide-eyed daughter, listening attentively, laughing at the incongruities, frowning in innocent puzzlement. Ambivalent, ambiguous, and altogether human, the opera crackles in its multilevel assault upon the associative faculty of our minds. It is a happening to stir the most 1960s devotee, a jumble that defies logic on every hand, tempting to artists as different as Marc Chagall and David Hockney and to a line of stage directors that included Guenther Rennert, who termed it "inexhaustible." With astonishing directness *Die Zauberflöte* joins the Talking Heads in asking us to "stop making sense" and return to the synthetic, creative world of our childhood.

There is much more. Psychologists and students of mythology have noted the presence of a veritable Jungian lexicon of archetypes, *ur*-characters, and basic affective states: Pamina and Tamino demonstrate "the feeling of security resulting from true companionship, as in the man/woman bond—the noble pair." Tamino and the lovable rascal Papageno, like Don Quixote and Sancho Panza, illuminate the "brotherly comradeship between fellow travelers." There is "wise guidance from afar (Sarastro) and from close at hand (the Three Genii, the Priests) and friendly dumb animals. Feelings of harmony; all's right with the world in the end; driven to the precipice of death and night, life is beautiful; the good are also the mighty."

The opera has been likened to Shakespeare's *The Tempest,* Sarastro to Prospero, the Queen of the Night to Sycorax, Caliban to Monostatos, Ariel to the Three Boys, and, in each, a pair of young lovers whose quest for each other must be made difficult "lest too light winning make the prize light." Like so much else in the opera's history, the idea is tempting, but the fit is far from perfect. Then there is the fact that Mozart and his librettist, Emanuel Schikaneder, were both Freemasons; we are told that the pseudo-Zoroastrian rituals contain more than a little to suggest the goings on at Masonic lodge meetings. Goethe did not know this, but he was enamored of the *Zauberflöte* libretto. Believing that its "high meaning will not elude the initiated," he proceeded to write a second part (in which Monostatos wedded the Queen of the Night) in the manner of his *Faust,* but he was not able to find a musician to set it. Other commentators have pursued this line of thought. Stanley Sadie, the eminent Mozartean and editor of the *New Grove's Dictionary of Music,* finds that the music possesses, above all, serenity of spirit, "a quality that rises above the trivia and the naiveties it contains, and makes it ultimately—in the fullest and richest sense of the term—a religious work." Bruno Walter, peerless in his time as a Mozart conductor, put it more simply: "*Die Zauberflöte* is Mozart's spiritual testament."

Mozart and Schikaneder, an entrepreneurial actor whom he had first met during his Salzburg years, had nothing so pretentious in mind. For Mozart, the opportunity to compose a German-language opera was a continuation of the interest that began in 1777, when he wrote to his father from Munich: "I am very popular here. And how much more popular I should be if I could help forward the German national theater! And with my help it would certainly succeed. For when I heard the German *Singspiel,* I was simply itching to compose." This interest led in 1779 to *Zaide,* whose music has come to us only in fragments, in 1782 to *The Abduction from the Seraglio,* and in 1786, to a bit of exquisitely composed fluff, *The Impresario.* By 1785, he had all but given up on the imperial court theater as a place for vernacular opera: "It seems to me that the directors here are too thrifty and not sufficiently patriotically-minded. . . . Were there but one patriot in charge—the situation would immediately become different! But then perhaps the now-budding German national theater would start to flourish, and of course it would be an eternal shame for Germany if once we Germans seriously started thinking as Germans, speaking in German and, indeed, singing in German." In March, 1791, when Schikaneder first approached him about a new German opera, Mozart's financial situation was desperate. His wife, ill and pregnant, had departed to Baden for a rest cure. The composer respected Schikaneder as a pioneer producer of German-language plays and operas and was no doubt more than willing to spend the summer composing music for something called *Lulu, oder die Zauberflöte* despite its less-than-lofty subject.

Schikaneder, on his side, had in mind the customary objectives of the nonsubsidized impresario: to entertain the audience and fill the house. His theater stood in the Viennese suburb of Wieden, which translates to "Willows," near Prince Stahremberg's customs house, or Freihaus. He and his wife had rented the Freihaus Theater auf der Wieden in 1789. Where previously he had been presenting Shakespeare in translation and the new German dramatists, he now concentrated on German and Italian musical works: operas by Paisiello, Martin, Gluck, Haydn, and, above all, Mozart, who was represented in the repertory by productions of *The Abduction, The Marriage of Figaro, Don Giovanni,* and *Così fan tutte.* Second most important of Vienna's public theaters, the Freihaustheater seated 800, with two tiers of boxes, and had room in its pit for an orchestra of 35. The stage was 33 feet wide and 55 feet deep, with three trap doors and a full Baroque complement of overhead and side machinery for elaborate stage effects. Then as now, spectacle played an important part in popular theater, and Schikaneder was giving his expanding suburban audience full measure. When completed, *The Magic Flute* would require thirteen scenic transformations and illusions.

The libretto that made these multiple changes and their concomitant lavish decor necessary was a crazy-quilt combination of assemblage and invention. The basic narrative for the first act came from *Dschinnistan,* a 1789 collection of pseudo-oriental fairy tales. Written by Liebeskind, *Lulu, oder die Zauberflöte* tells of a prince who is sent by a good fairy to rescue her daughter from the clutches of an evil magician and who is equipped with a magic flute for the purpose. He has various adventures, including one in which he plays while the animals in the forest dance. He succeeds in his quest, falls in love with the princess, and they live happily ever after. The second act depends heavily on a much earlier French novel, *Sethos: Histoire ou vie tiré des monuments, anecdotes de l'ancien Egypte.* Published in 1731, it had supposedly been written by an ancient Greek but was soon discovered to be by the contemporary Abbé Jean Terrasson. In *Sethos* we encounter initiation ceremonies and ritual mysteries from ancient Egypt. The sun is a symbol of enlightenment, hence Zoroaster-Sarastro and the subterranean caverns and passages through the pyramids are seen as symbols of man's pathways through life to light. The third major element in Schikaneder's design for a popular hit was Papageno, the rascal clown, who traces his ancestry back through an ubiquitous Viennese comic figure, Kasperl, to the commedia dell'arte Truffaldino. *Papagei* is German for parrot, perfect for the man who can't keep his mouth shut.

Schikaneder had presented "magic operas" before. His theater had opened in 1789 with *Oberon,* based on the same tale that Carl Maria von Weber was to use in his romantic opera. This was followed by *Der Stein der Weisen,* which had music by one Benedict Schack, the company's principal tenor. Although he was an expert flutist, there was no flute in Schack's opera. In *The Magic Flute* he combined his singing and flute playing as the first Tamino. But the play that may have had the most influence on Schikaneder's libretto was not seen by him—if indeed he saw it at all—until it appeared on the stage of the rival Leopoldstadt theater in July, 1791. Also based on *Dschinnistan*'s Prince Lulu, it was entitled *Die Zauberzither, oder Kaspar der Fagottist.* Although its comic protagonist played bassoon instead of flute, the plot was similar to the one that Mozart and Schickaneder were in the process of writing. This sudden appearance of a competitor has been advanced by some scholars as an explanation of the plot and character shift that occurs just before the finale to Act I of *The Magic Flute,* which has puzzled and challenged producers and listeners alike. Faced by the possible accusation of plagiarism, the argument contends, Schikaneder hastily transformed his good fairy and her frolicking ladies into evil witches, and he advanced Sarastro from a "usurping kidnapper" to the ruler of an idealistic Egyptian sun kingdom, incomprehensibly leaving the evil slave Monostatos behind.

Was this indeed the case? Mozart's letters, so fascinating and full of detail on many points, give us no clue. "In order to cheer myself up, I hopped over to the Kasperle to see the new opera *The Bassoonist,*" he writes on June 12, 1791, "but it does not offer anything." Neither he nor Schikaneder attempted to explain the abrupt switch or remove the discrepancy. Nor has anyone since to our complete satisfaction. The "practical" explanation, with its hint of compromise and carelessness, makes us uneasy. An alternative conclusion, easier to accept today than in some times past, leads again into the fairy-tale world where evil often pretends to be good and where punishment and violence are present in even the most virtuous kingdoms. Still another points to the possible collaboration of Karl Ludwig Giesecke—an erudite member of Schikaneder's company who often assisted in text preparation—as contributor of the Egyptian-Masonic sections; the assumption here is that no one would mind if careless collaboration produced an inconsistency or two.

We know very little about *The Magic Flute*'s composition. On June 11, 1791, Mozart wrote to Constanze that "from sheer boredom I composed today an aria for my opera . . . I got up as early as half past four." Later in the same letter he quotes a phrase from the opera; clearly both must have been familiar with it. By July 2 he is asking Constanze to "please tell that idiotic fellow Sussmayr" (the same man who finished the *Requiem* after Mozart's death) "to send me my score of the first act from the introduction to the finale, so that I may orchestrate it." On July 4 he declared himself "weak for want of food." The next day he asks Sussmayr to "send me numbers 4 and 5 of my manuscript." On July 12 he writes an anguished note to his wife: "Even my work gives me no pleasure, because I am accustomed to stop working now and then in order to exchange a few words with you. Alas! This is no longer possible. If I go to the piano and sing something out of my opera I have to stop at once, for this stirs my emotions too deeply."

After that, there is only conjecture. Mozart had received and accepted two further commissions, one for an opera, *La clemenza di Tito,* to be presented in Prague for the early September coronation of Leopold II as King of Bohemia, and the other from Count Walsegg-Stuppach for a *Requiem* to be composed under conditions of secrecy, the count wishing to pose as the composer. In any case, the bulk of the *Flute* was finished by the last week of August, when the Mozarts set out with Sussmayr for Prague and *Tito*'s premiere on September 6. By mid September, they were back in Vienna, and Mozart, now in uncertain health, worked on *The Magic Flute,* the clarinet concerto, and some smaller works. The opera was finished on September 28 and had its premiere two days later.

The original program stated: "Today, Friday the 30th September, the players of the Imperial and Royal privileged Theater on the Wieden have the honor to perform for the first time *Die Zauberflöte,* a grand opera in two acts by Emanuel Schikaneder . . . the music is by Herr Wolfgang Amade Mozart, Kapellmeister, and actual I & R Chamber Composer. Herr Mozard [*sic*], out of respect for a gracious and honour-worthy public, and from friendship for the author of this piece, will today direct the orchestra in person." Mozart conducted only the first two performances, but he returned to the theater several times afterward. Reporting to his wife on the October 7 performance, he noted that "the opera was as full as ever . . . as usual the duet, *Mann und Weib* and Papageno's glockenspiel in act one had to be repeated, and also the trio of the boys in Act Two." He added that "what always gives me most pleasure is the *silent* approval . . . you can see how this opera is becoming more and more popular." The following evening he was back again, creating a diversion by playing the glockenspiel part for Papageno's bells and mistiming it with the gestures of the actor—Schikaneder himself! On the ninth of October, a correspondent for the *Berlin Musical Weekly* wrote the opera's only extant review: "The new machine comedy, *The Magic Flute,* with music by our Kapellmeister Mozart, has been presented at great expense and with much splendor of decoration, but is failing to find the hoped-for applause, because the content and diction of the piece are too poor." The anonymous critic was wrong in both short- and long-term estimation. By May 6, 1801, the theater had logged 226 performances, and *Die Zauberflöte* was unquestionably the most popular of all operas in German-speaking countries.

We who live in the waning twentieth century quite possibly have less trouble with *The Magic Flute*'s contradictions and inconsistencies than did our predecessors. The plays of Luigi Pirandello and the novels of Italo Calvino—to mention only two of many influences—have accustomed us to shifting views of reality. We can accept without difficulty the viewpoint of Janos Liebner, who in *Mozart on Stage* maintains that the whole first scene of *The Magic Flute* may be considered as a play within a play, directed by the Queen of the Night to gain Tamino's soul for her own purposes, and who further suggests that Tamino's journey from blind faith in the Queen to full allegiance to Sarastro is mirrored in the suspended disbelief of the audience. We can equally accept the divided loyalties of the Three Genii, who are sent out by the three ladies of the Queen's court but who end up espousing the plans of Sarastro, in the same way we accept *The Tempest*'s Ariel: all are amoral spirits who come to the aid of good causes regardless of auspices. And as for the inherent contradiction between lowbrow humor and lofty idealism, we have only to remember George Santayana's most Mozartean declaration: "Every phenomenon of existence is lyrical in its ideal essence, tragic in its fate, and comic in its form of appearance."

Mozart's music is the catalyst, traveling the centuries without difficulty and underscoring each image with his single-minded genius. The variety of forms employed in *The Magic Flute* is astonishing: nonacademic counterpoint in the Overture, hummable strophes for Papageno (and his Papagena), highfalutin Baroque heroics for the "star-blazing Queen," exquisite recitative for Tamino, the intimacy of "Ach, ich fuhl's" for Pamina, flute and timpani for the fire scene, combined brasses and woodwinds for the Masonic processions and invocations, solemn chords and choralelike melodies for the priestly choir. But equally astonishing is that every note is undeniably, unmistakably a product of the same mind and spirit.

With that fact in mind, we can forgive Peter Shaffer's *Amadeus* revisionism and Milos Foreman's excessive motion-picture extension. We simply do not need the "finger of God," "divine spark," or emotion-laden clichés to explain away the unexplainable. Nor should *The Magic Flute* be encapsulated in the vocabulary of a worn-out Enlightenment, words such as "humanity," "spiritual struggle," "truth," "mystery," and "perfection." Mozart's most recent biographer, the literary critic Wolfgang Hildesheimer, is quite right to assert that the work is "not something complete and successful within itself. . . . It would be an injustice to the greatest of all musical geniuses to declare *Die Zauberflöte*—a work that did not offer him this opportunity—the sum total of his creative work, or his earthly swan song. It is rather a final demonstration of his tremendous ability to objectify, the brilliant response to a last challenge; but it is not his last will and testament."

Such an assertion, of course, has no effect whatsoever on the opera's durability. As W.H. Auden reminded us in the "Metalogue" between the acts of NBC television's 1956 bicentennial production:

> Genius surpasses all things, even chic.
> We know how little—which is just as well—
> About the future can, at least, foretell,
> Whether they live in air-borne nylon cubes,
> Practice group marriage or are fed through tubes,
> That crowds, two centuries from now, will press
> (Absurd their hair, ridiculous their dress),
> And pay in currencies however weird
> To hear Sarastro booming through his beard. . . .

MASSENET'S *Manon*
by Thomas Willis

Who is she, anyway, this Manon? Is she the archetype, the mother of a new line of literary and operatic heroines, or is she a soap-opera teenybopper who never grows up? Is she a conqueror-victim in an ageless psychodrama, worthy of serious concern, or a glittering superficiality, invented by an author looking for fame and given musical existence by a shrewd composer who knew what his audience wanted?

A French literary historian has declared emphatically that "in her devotion and her caprices, she is a marvelous representation of the young Parisian who, in coming into the world, brings with her, as sole dowry, a great store of grace, beauty, lightheartedness, skepticism, and love!" Massenet's most recent biographer, an Englishman, dismisses her as "tender, superficial, and quite brainless. She embodies all the characteristics of the flirtatious girl who takes a healthy enjoyment as much in the sentimental as in the physical aspect of an affair. There is nothing degraded about her, and the wholehearted innocence she brings to the game accounts for much of her success with men."

Several commentators take an archetypal approach. Writing a century ago, Alfred de Musset referred to Manon as "a talking Sphinx, a Cleopatra in hoopskirts." Alexandre Dumas, whose Marguerite Gauthier became the Violetta of Verdi's *La traviata,* knew that his lady of the camellias was a relative of Manon's. He justified the borrowing by the "everybody's doing it," or generic, doctrine. With a glancing tribute to the omnipresent Industrial Revolution, he noted that "we all owe Manon monuments of gratitude; she is now exploited like steam or photography." Henri Murger, creator of *La Bohème*'s Mimi, would no doubt agree. All three girls have a genetic commitment to affection, sincerity, frailty, and amorality. Similar strong cases could be made for Goethe's Philine *(Wilhelm Meister),* Daudet's Sappho, and Du Maurier's Trilby, all characters in now-forgotten operas. Lulu is part Manon. So is Christopher Isherwood's Sally, most recently incarnated in Broadway's *Cabaret.* There are many more.

Manon's creator, Antoine-François Prévost d'Exiles (1697–1763), tried hard to relegate her to second place. When the novel was first published in Paris in 1731, it was entitled "The Adventures of the Chevalier des Grieux and Manon Lescaut." The lower priority accorded to Manon was reinforced in the author's preface to the subsequent Amsterdam edition, where he takes pains to emphasize the "moral significance" of his work, which by then had been banned in Paris and, possibly as a consequence, had attained enormous popular success.

"The public has read with great pleasure the adventures of the Chevalier des Grieux and of Manon Lescaut," he notes. "One sees therein a young man of brilliant and amiable qualities, who ensnared by a foolish passion for a young girl who appeals to him, prefers a libertine and vagabondish life to all the advantages which his talents and his station in life held out to him; an unhappy slave of love, who perceives the cause of his misery and has not the will power to take the proper measures to remove it; who feels his unhappiness profoundly, yet plunges more deeply in it and neglects the methods of procuring a more happy state of mind; in short, a young man at once sinful and virtuous, thinking good and doing evil, commendable in his sentiments, detestable in his actions. He is a most singular character."

And Manon? The author finds her even more complex: "She knows what virtue is, even respects it, and yet all her actions are scandalous. She loves the Chevalier des Grieux with a violent passion, and yet her desire for luxury and her wish to dazzle him cause her to betray him and take up with a rich financier. What art has been used to interest the reader and to inspire in him a compassion for the disgraces and fatalities which befall that corrupt girl!" That is all.

Prévost never gives us a description of Manon. Was she fair or dark, tall or short, plump or slender? We are never told. She lives only in her speech and her movements and in the effect she makes on those who enter her Never-Never-Land. It is des Grieux who keeps the plot pot bubbling and provides the heaviest grist for the morality mill. Manon has only to be herself, and we succumb.

The novelist paints a vivid picture of her seductive strength. Unlike Massenet and his librettist (or Puccini, who followed him with the Italianized *Manon Lescaut*), Prévost begins his story near the end. Manon appears in the inn at Pacy, sitting among the prostitutes, dirty, bedraggled, and chained like a criminal. But "her whole air and figure seemed so ill-suited to her present condition, that under other circumstances I should not have hesitated to pronounce her a person of high birth. Her excessive grief, and even the dirtiness of her linen, detracted so little from her surpassing beauty, that at first sight of her I was inspired with a mingled feeling of respect and pity. Even her first movement is an essential part of her character. She tried as well as the chain would permit her, to turn herself away, and hide her face from the rude gaze of the spectators. There was something so unaffected in the effort she made to escape observation, that it could have but sprung from natural and innate modesty alone."

In the courtyard at Amiens, where the opera opens, the seventeen-year-old des Grieux takes up the portrait painting: "She struck me as being so extremely beautiful that I, who had never before thought of the difference between the sexes, or looked on women with the slightest attention—I, whose conduct had hitherto been the theme of universal admiration, felt myself, on the instant, deprived of my reason and self-control. I had always been excessively timid, but now, instead of meeting with any impediments from this weakness, I advanced without reserve towards her, who had thus become, in a moment, the mistress of my heart." Love has conquered reason, with predictable consequences.

With reckless abandon, Manon and her complaisant lover flout the social order. During their flight to Paris, "we had not even the patience to reserve our caresses until we were alone. The postillions and innkeepers stared at us with wonder, and I remarked that they appeared surprised at such uncontrollable love in children of our age. Our project of marriage was forgotten at St. Denis; we defrauded the Church of her rights, and found ourselves united as man and wife without reflecting on the consequences. It is certain that with my easy and constant disposition, I should have been happy for my whole life if Manon had remained faithful to me."

Faithful Manon was not, as we all know. He envisions a happily-ever-after love nest, tea for two, and all the rest. She sings a different song, more like "I'll be faithful to you, darling, in my fashion." Diamonds are, indeed, this girl's best friend. And yet, she loves him to the bitter end.

Pragmatic, conventional souls may have a hard time believing this. Skeptics among us still find it difficult to imagine that a woman may love a man all her life and remain precisely eight days faithful to him. Her profession of attachment for her moping chevalier interfaces poorly with the open flouting of a lover's prerogatives. Underneath the high-flown language lurks an uneasy suspicion that we are dealing with a gullible namby-pamby and a passionless nymphomaniac. And yet, she loves him.

How do we know? We know because we know she is French and is an indisputable creature of her time and place, for all the connections she has with other seductresses around the world. To understand Manon's contradictions, we must understand something of the France of her time and Massenet's. Listen, for example, to Guy de Maupassant, author of the famous short stories.

"Here is Manon," he enthused in a preface to one edition of the *Adventures,* "more truly feminine than all the others, treacherous, loving, distracting, spiritual, formidable, and charming. In this figure, so full of seductiveness and instinctive perfidy, the writer seems to have embodied all that is most pleasing, the most tempting, and the most infamous of the creature woman! Manon is completely, entirely woman, as she always has been; as she is and as she will always be. No artistic creation has ever appealed more strongly to man's senses than this exquisite jade, whose subtle and malign charm seems to emanate from her like an indefinable perfume through all the pages of this extraordinary book."

However hyperbolic it may seem today, his estimate is revealing. Manon is not just woman; she is woman personified. Her words and actions arouse deep-seated feelings in Maupassant, as they did in Massenet and the well-off, decent men who came to the Opéra-Comique during the Third Republic. Without for a moment putting themselves in the position of des Grieux, they could embrace Manon's simple-minded libertarian beauty as a delectable, if unattainable, fantasy.

But there is more than fantasy to this exquisitely French Manon whom de Maupassant hymns: "This changeable girl, complex, variable, sincere, odious, and adorable, full of inexplicable sensations, incomprehensible sentiments, of whimsical calculation and criminal frankness—is she not admirably true to nature? How she differs from the models of vice or virtue presented to us, without complications, by sentimental romanticists who imagine invariable types without understanding what a many-sided being a woman is!"

That is the crux of it. For all her position in the male fantasy world of nineteenth-century Frenchmen, Manon is a fully believable human being. Prévost and, after him, Massenet have preserved the contradictions and inconsistencies that bring her to life. Long before psychiatrists were practicing, they understood that a lasting relationship can be based upon attachments and affections that are independent of current physical attachments.

To be sure, neither Prévost nor Massenet treated their men with equal understanding. Des Grieux, for all his passion, remains an emotional monochrome. By 1884, when Massenet and his librettists, Henri Meilhac and

Philippe Gille, were fashioning their opera, des Grieux became even less of a person. As Bernard Shaw acerbically pointed out in his review of the London *Manon* premiere, *Manon* dates from the first half of the eighteenth century, when society appears to have been so corrupt that a gentleman could preserve some self-respect under circumstances in which an Englishman would be expected nowadays to loathe himself. The librettists have kept the Sunday side of their hero well before the public and have suppressed the episodes in which his failings led him into actual disgrace. "To whitewash Manon," Shaw concludes, "would have been not only impossible, but bad policy in catering for a Parisian—perhaps no less so for a London—audience."

Certainly no one would think of whitewashing her today. Four generations of gifted operatic actresses have fleshed out her musical and dramatic character with memorable portrayals of their own. French opera, and Massenet in particular, is enjoying a welcome revival. The bustling ensembles, "antique" dances, and plangent melodies are especially welcome antidotes to noisy exaggerations, past and present. Her farewell to the table in their Parisian love nest, des Grieux's dream aria, the Gavotte, and the soaring orchestration of the final scene are as touching today as ever.

As for her character, one fact should be kept in view. Manon's feelings for des Grieux remain absolutely consistent in their self-centeredness from the start of the opera to the close. If he can accept this, so can we. The pleasure they find in themselves and in their love is amply sufficient to ensure our enjoyment as well as theirs.

In his *Souvenirs,* Massenet tells an anecdote that puts an evening spent with Manon into an appropriately Gallic perspective.

One day, it seems, the composer encountered a husband who complained of his wife's lack of interest in him.

"Here," said Massenet, "use these tickets and go with your wife to the Opéra Comique. Each time she cries, take her hand gently."

"But we're not on that sort of terms," the man insisted.

"Never mind," replied the composer, "try all the same. It won't cost you anything."

A little later he met the husband again, still in the depths of melancholy. "Didn't my little trick work?" he asked, "didn't you take your wife's hand at the sentimental moments?"

"Yes," came the lugubrious answer, "but when, during the third act, I tried to grab her hand, I found it was already held by the man in the seat next to hers."

"My friend," Massenet replied, "that merely proves that her neighbor was more of a musician than you!"

PUCCINI'S *Manon Lescaut*
by Peter P. Jacobi

Giacomo Antonio Domenico Michele Secondo Maria Puccini once described himself as "a mighty hunter of wild fowl, opera librettos, and attractive women."

Duck hunting was a passion. He much preferred it to work. Wife Elvira often had to chide and scold and tease and temper tantrum him back to composing chores.

Women were a passion. He much preferred them to being alone or monogamous. Elvira lived with that knowledge, not easily mind you, in fact sometimes with a frenzy that led her to following him disguised in men's clothing or counting on old wives' tale nostrums to reduce his sexual longings, but to no avail.

Librettos were a passion. He much preferred interfering with his writers to leaving them alone. Elvira is said to have told Puccini once, while he was in heated dispute with a librettist, to leave the words to others and concentrate on his melodies.

But that he could never do, any more than he could give up hunting ducks and women. He was driven to hunt for the right stories and the right dramatic approaches so that his emotional musical outpouring could freely pour.

And so it was with *Manon Lescaut,* a make-or-break opera. His previous work, *Edgar,* had failed, victim of an awful story and a just as awful libretto.

This time everything had to be right.

But it wouldn't come easily. It never seemed to for him, probably because he had such special notions about the musical stage and about the sort of tale and character he could write music for effectively.

Puccini wrote to publisher Giulio Ricordi sometime in 1889, "If you continue to have faith in me, and if you still want an opera from my pen, I have found the perfect subject."

It was an old story, a French one—that of Manon, "a heroine I believe in, and therefore it cannot fail to win the hearts of the public."

The Abbé Prévost had written his novel, *L'Histoire du Chevalier des Grieux et de Manon Lescaut,* in 1731. It already had served composer Daniel Auber. And it most assuredly served composer Jules Massenet, whose opera *Manon* premiered in 1884 and had since gained considerable allegiance from critics and public. So, here was Puccini six years later, seeking to make his mark with the same story.

Gall. Foolhardiness. One or the other or both. That was his way. Puccini's biographers suggest that Massenet's success led Puccini to try the same story, meaning that the story had gained public acceptance and therefore might do so again with Puccini's score. Meaning also that perhaps it was a dare; if Massenet could do it, Puccini could, too.

It would not be the last time he played games over librettos. For instance, *La Bohème* caused him to tangle with composer friend Ruggiero Leoncavallo. Puccini had rejected *Bohème* as a story, leading Leoncavallo to start an operatic version of his own. Puccini then changed his mind and announced that he would set the story to music. Leoncavallo finished first, but Puccini's was introduced first. Last or first, the Leoncavallo work never had a chance. Puccini lost a friend, needless to say, as the world gained a masterpiece.

There was nothing so underhanded with *Manon Lescaut,* but some controversy resulted in his choice of story. He seemed to relish that. He did not relish libretto trouble, of which he had plenty.

Puccini responded to the concern of friends that his work would be compared to Massenet's: "Why shouldn't there be two operas about her? A woman like Manon can have more than one lover."

Well, the search for a good libretto began with Leoncavallo, at that point still a friend. He was a good librettist; he had a way with words. Would he try setting the Prévost story for Puccini? Sure. But Puccini was dissatisfied with the results, and librettist number two was sought.

He wrote his sister: "I am working at *Manon Lescaut,* but I am desperate about the libretto, which I have had to get done over again. Even now there isn't a poet to be found who can write a good poem!"

He turned to Marco Praga, a playwright of some note who had never attempted libretto-fashioning. Praga set to work and soon handed Puccini a manuscript. "Things could not have been better," he later recounted, then added:

> But such a pleasant state of affairs was of short duration. A few months after, the composer was no longer satisfied with the plot or with the division of the acts. He could no longer feel that it was an *opéra comique.* He wished to eliminate the second act, substituting the third for it, and for the third finding a striking and dramatic situation. As a dramatist I did not approve of the change. Neither did I from my own point of view feel like changing the structure of the libretto. I declined the task, and handed over the whole matter to Domenico Oliva with complete liberty to change it as he thought fit.

Enter librettist three. The poet Oliva accepted Puccini's thoughts and totally revised the work's structure.

Would that be the end of it? Hardly.

Puccini studied Oliva's work, then sent Ricordi a detailed criticism. "True, there are some good things in it," he wrote, "but the quartet, for example, is hideous. I don't understand why here Oliva has discarded the original outline, which was so clear." And so forth, at some length.

It was Oliva's turn to become angry. He would not be Puccini's "galley slave." Another author was needed.

Ricordi turned to playwright Giuseppe Giacosa, a most literate fellow who said he would prepare a prose script. Someone else would have to provide the poetry, and that someone, he said, should be Luigi Illica. Thus, librettists four and five.

The Giacosa-Illica involvement was most important not merely for *Manon Lescaut* but also for the future. A Giacosa-Illica-Puccini partnership would result in *Bohème, Butterfly,* and *Tosca.*

Puccini's long-time friend and biographer Dante del Fiorentino called Illica the more important of the pair,

> not a man to be trifled with. Tall, slender, his long beard parted in two, stiff as a ramrod, Illica possessed an aggressive spirit. His steely blue eyes were the visible tokens of an extreme tenacity. He was a good poet, a prolific writer, a humorist, a gourmet and the owner of an enchanting castle not far from Firenzuola d'Adda, where he would receive his guests in a painted cart drawn by a horse named after an opera singer. He had a passion for rising early, and no one was ever able to sleep late in his castle, for he would go from door to door, shouting: "Get up, lazy ones! Work comes first!" And it was not surprising that his friends called him Signor Perpetuum Mobile.

Giacosa apparently served as intermediary and conciliator whenever necessary. For Illica a major difficulty was that Puccini already had composed some of the music. Thus, certain early scenes could no longer be changed. He worked mostly, therefore, on Act III. But Puccini did not find Illica's work satisfactory either. Thus, Giacosa was asked to do more than conciliate. He was asked to write. So Puccini had two authors laboring in his behalf.

No, not merely two. Four. Publisher Ricordi contributed significantly to the verbal package. A number of letters from him to Puccini give suggestions that were incorporated in the final version. And Puccini himself was a librettist, the seventh.

Not all the consumption of time can be blamed on shaping the libretto. Puccini himself wasted it, and this by hunting around Torre del Lago and spending too much time at a café which soon was to be named the Club Bohème. There he and a relaxed set of cronies ate and drank, told stories, and played cards.

Del Fiorentino recalled that Elvira would glower in the café's direction and mutter again and again, "Well, they're doing their best to ruin him." He writes:

> When Elvira taunted the bohemians for not letting her husband alone, they decided to make a peace offering—they found an upright piano, miserably out of tune, and promptly installed it in the café for Giacomo's benefit. So Giacomo played on the piano looking out over the lake, spent

most of his time joking with his companions, and lived on fish and wild-fowl, though occasionally a scrap of meat would be brought in by friends from Viareggio or Lucca. Giacomo was happy, or at least he gave the appearance of being happy, but Elvira probably summed up the situation correctly when she said, "Here we eat very little and Giacomo doesn't do a damned thing."

But he did create *Manon Lescaut*. He often wrote with a vengeance, a vigor. He knew how much was at stake for him.

At one point, after making sufficient progress, Puccini decided to vacation in Switzerland. He and Elvira found a small apartment in a hamlet called Vacallo. Stepping out on the balcony, Puccini saw a banner hanging from a nearby house, a banner with the outline of a clown.

It turned out that Leoncavallo was living there. The banner heralded his work of the moment, *I pagliacci*. Puccini, not to be outdone, decided on a banner of his own, with a gigantic hand on it, representing his work of the moment, *Manon*. In the Tuscan dialect the word for a large hand is *manon*.

A lot of talent was at work in that block.

When Puccini's opera finally was done in October, 1892, three years of work had gone into it. And only after that was it officially known as *Manon Lescaut*, thereby distinguishing it from Massenet's *Manon*.

It premiered at Turin's Teatro Regio on February 1, 1893. No lyricist-librettist was given credit. It was merely a "Lyric Drama in Four Acts, Music by Giacomo Puccini."

But not merely. The opera was a remarkable success, definitely the turn-around that Puccini needed in his career. A Milanese reporter wrote:

> A few moments ago Manon uttered her last indescribable, heart-rending cry. The curtain has just fallen, and Puccini and his interpreters have withdrawn again into the darkness of the wings after facing the glare of the footlights in answer to the wild shouts of an immense public, transported with enthusiasm. The echo of the last notes of the orchestra, epilogue to a drama of human suffering, has just died away, and I am here, confused, stunned, and wondering, and, what is of more impor-tance, profoundly moved: moved even to tears. And I am not alone in this. The public has wept with me, and even the Turin musical critics, known for their reserve and their coldness, confess that they were moved, and tomorrow they will say it themselves in their papers.

They did. So did critics from elsewhere. They spoke of the Italian quality of his vocal style, of his deft, modern handling of the orchestra, of his genius. And since the premiere occurred eight days before Verdi's last, *Falstaff*, the pundits and observers could refer to one man's glory ending to make way for a new hero, a successor in the long line of operatic composers stretching way back to Monteverdi.

The opera swiftly gained acceptance—throughout Italy and then elsewhere. London had its first *Manon Lescaut* in 1894. George Bernard Shaw was present and said it again: "Puccini looks to me more like the heir to Verdi than any of the others."

Now, even a Puccini biographer, Mosco Carner, considers Massenet's version of the story superior. But Massenet was a finished musician, considerably older, more mature when he set his setting. Puccini was the very young man, still studying his own capacities. And the result is a beautifully melodic work— a little bits-and-pieces in the story (no wonder with all the stops and starts and multitudinous contributions) but overflowing with themes and tunes and therefore thoroughly entertaining. No, he hadn't matured yet in *Manon Lescaut,* but he was fast maturing and was just a few steps away from *La Bohème.*

His approach? Puccini explained: "Massenet feels it as a Frenchman, with the powder and the minuets. I shall feel it as an Italian, with desperate passion."

The music is almost overwhelming because Puccini had so much of it in his head. The melodies tumbled out. Too many of them, if that's possible. Sometimes they're almost wasted. A tune is introduced, momentarily offered, only to be withdrawn for a fresh one. The composer hasn't yet the control to elaborate, to take those melodies most useful to the story and develop them. In the rousing love duet of Act II, for instance, the melodies pour forth like a flood, one into the next. But cohesion is lacking. Puccini sweeps one along, the listener wondering what will come next rather than becoming immersed in one musical act of love. No matter, we *are* swept along.

Manon's "In quelle trine morbide" and des Grieux's "Donna non vidi mai," their extended love duet, the lovely intermezzo, the almost Verdian ending to Act III, and the somber, heavily colored death scene—an eighteen-minute duet for the lovers. All these and so many more moments, little and big, make *Manon Lescaut* a pleasure.

In *Manon Lescaut* we get musical richness requiring vocal experts, all the melodic and harmonic clues for Puccini's later operas, and the first of his lovely, fragile heroines upon whom he lavished so much artistic love. *Manon Lescaut* is all energy and enthusiasm, Puccini passionately on the prowl for a place in opera history. With it he nudged himself toward that place.

DONIZETTI's *Maria Stuarda*
by Speight Jenkins

In mid September of 1834, bills were out on the streets of Naples advertising the premiere of *Maria Stuarda,* a new opera by Gaetano Donizetti; and inside, the San Carlo rehearsals were frantically proceeding. As did Bellini in *Norma,* Donizetti gave the limelight in his new opera to two sopranos, and unfortunately the two whom Donizetti had chosen—Giuseppina Ronzi-De Begnis (Maria) and Anna del Serre (Elisabetta)—despised each other. To make matters worse, as with Norma and Adalgisa, there's no question who is the real star of the show: Maria not only gets one whole aria-scene more than Elisabetta, she gets the final two scenes of the evening. Still, unlike *Norma,* the *seconda donna* is Queen Elizabeth, in any audience's mind a pretty memorable figure, and in the rehearsals in question Signorina del Serre was out to show the public that she was the star.

One notable afternoon a rehearsal was called of Act II—the famous meeting of the Queens—and the two launched into their confrontation with gusto. After del Serre had heaped insults on Ronzi's head according to the libretto, Ronzi, the furious Maria, denounced her rival as the libretto demanded. First she labeled her an obscene prostitute not fit for the throne; then in unmistakably clear Italian she called her a "vile bastard." Del Serre, utterly overcome with rage, smashed Ronzi in the face; Ronzi, not to be outdone, knocked del Serre down and started beating on her, while the whole theater echoed with their screams. Although the fight was broken up short of hospitalization of either party, feelings got even nastier; both sopranos kept on calling each other names, and both charged Donizetti with favoritism toward the other.

The ill will kept up until the dress rehearsal, given for an invited audience, including Queen Maria Cristina of Naples. According to William Ashbrook, an eminent biographer of Donizetti, the audience seemed to like the score, but the queen, perhaps overwhelmed by fears of what could happen to her, fainted in the midst of the third act—when Mary receives word that she is to be executed—and had to be carried back to the palace. The next day the king personally prohibited any performances of *Maria Stuarda.* The strange saga of Donizetti's forty-sixth opera had begun.

Strange is the word for *Stuarda,* because after its controversial early history it slept almost untouched for a century; then suddenly it sprang to life as a favorite piece of the four major bel canto sopranos of the post-Callas era. At this time, *Maria Stuarda* is the only bel canto opera that has served Montserrat Caballé, Leyla Gencer, Beverly Sills, and Joan Sutherland equally well, and all the ladies mentioned have scored flamboyant successes in it.

Perhaps the basic reason is the historical subject matter. Mary, Queen of Scots, has led a charmed life in romantic history ever since the headsman's axe felled her in Fotheringay Castle in 1587. She has been the subject of songs, poetry, novels, biographies (including the landmark best seller by Antonia Fraser), movies, and plays. The greatest of the latter is Friedrich Schiller's free retelling of her conflict with Elizabeth, important to Donizetti's opera because Giuseppe Bardari drew his libretto from it. Of course, as in Schiller, the fictional meeting between the two Queens serves as the center pole of the plot. Although the two should have met—and when one reads Miss Fraser's account of Mary's life, the feeling is inescapable that Mary would have been able to charm Elizabeth—they didn't, and this is only the most important of several glaring historical inaccuracies in the opera. In the opening pages, Elizabeth tries to get Leicester's jealousy aroused by talking of the Duke of Anjou as her prospective husband. In fact, ideas of a French marriage had been discarded some sixteen years before the action of the plot. For purposes of tenor-soprano relationships, Leicester and Mary seem to be in love; in fact there was nothing between them. And Talbot, a friend of Mary's, who was grieved at her death, was certainly no priest in courtier's clothes. Interesting also is that the good grey Cecil, Elizabeth's secretary of state for most of her reign, was not Mary's implacable foe; he only grudgingly agreed to her execution when he realized that Catholic plots inside England would never cease as long as she lived.

The original libretto was obviously out of the question after the king forbade any performance. So Donizetti, one of the most resourceful of opera composers, wheedled a good bit of money out of the San Carlo, and in a space of a few weeks he used all the music and the same cast of *Stuarda* for an opera about politics in renaissance Italy called *Buondelmonte*. As Donizetti laughingly related, he changed the big third-act prayer to a conspiracy scene, and he expanded the original six characters to ten. The opera bowed on October 18, 1834, and made little impression.

Donizetti then looked about Italy for a place for the opera as originally conceived and settled on La Scala in Milan. There, the Austrian censors passed the libretto with no words changed, and Donizetti set the premiere for December 28, 1835. The fascinating Maria Malibran was to enact the title role, with Giacinta Puzzi-Toso as Elisabetta.

Malibran deserves a paragraph to herself. The daughter of Manuel García (who along with his whole family introduced Italian opera to New York, in 1826), she was for the twelve short years of her career the great rival of Giuditta Pasta, the originator of Norma, and was a favorite of such disparate artists as Chopin, Liszt, Rossini, Bellini, and Henriette Sontag, a younger and much longer-lived soprano. Malibran apparently acted with greater enthusiasm and realism than did Pasta and most of her contemporaries, and Henry Pleasants in *The Great Singers* quotes Ernest Legouvé, a Parisian librettist of the time, as describing Malibran as "all spontaneity, inspiration and fermentation." Although there were those who felt she tore a passion to tatters—in one *Maria Stuarda* she reputedly ripped her handkerchief and even her gloves to shreds— she had a vociferous following.

The beginnings of *Stuarda,* however, may have been cursed by Malibran's inability to say no. The premiere, scheduled for December 28, was canceled due to her undisputed "voicelessness." With no physical improvement she sang the opera's premiere on the thirtieth, thereby avoiding a fine of some 3,000 francs but doing nothing for Donizetti's music. No one else saved the show, and the audience was not favorably impressed by her bravery. Then, to top off these problems, the censors stepped in and demanded changes in both the last two acts. Malibran refused to sing the changes, and the opera died at La Scala.

Now resurrected with great success in New York, San Francisco, Chicago, and all over Europe, *Maria Stuarda* represents bel canto opera at the full flower of its development. This is a somewhat later stage than Rossini's *Semiramide*. The difference between Rossini's writing and Donizetti's is considerable, as Rossini in *Semiramide* was writing for vocal display pure and simple, and it would be difficult for anyone to cite music in *Semiramide* that necessarily was describing the characters' words. Although Donizetti also wrote to show off the voice in *Maria Stuarda,* which comes from the period in his life when he composed *Lucia di Lammermoor, Roberto Devereux,* and *L'elisir d'amore,* his music and words were beginning to match. Very florid and always faithful to a formula of a slow aria followed by a fast aria for each major character (with two for the prima donna), a few duets, one or more concerted pieces, and a big ensemble to end Act II, Donizetti was still beginning to characterize with his music. So the definition of bel canto as it applies to Donizetti is that the voices come first, but more and more the melodies suit the words.

Look at the big double scene for Mary—the opera's conclusion. She receives the sentence of death in a noble yet feminine manner, for Donizetti faithfully renders the Scots' Queen as both strong and vulnerable. Then, in a melodious larghetto passage she recalls her early loves, remembering especially her second husband, Darnley. When Talbot, her confessor, asks her about her relations to Babington, a man who tried to lead the English Catholics against Elizabeth on Mary's behalf, she cries out her innocence of sexual misconduct with him in believable tones—"Lo giuro a Dio" (I swear before God).

Absolved and certain of death, she goes before her retainers, to whom Donizetti has given a beautiful chorus full of hushed timpani and soft foreboding. In her big prayer scene, Donizetti created a melody that perfectly conveys supplication—first the soprano and then the chorus sing the theme; after she soars over the chorus with the main theme, she sustains a long, long note while the chorus sings her theme, and finally she again rides over the chorus higher and higher. The whole sounds more and more like a hymn, and yet it never loses its meaning—a prayer of Mary's that God will gather her into His grace and protection. Interestingly enough, her next arioso, in which she asks that Elizabeth will not be punished for her death, has the technique of brilliant coloratura without the heart of the earlier prayer. Was Donizetti subtly suggesting that Maria might not really care as much what happened to Elizabeth? Under any condition, she is sincere as she bids farewell to Leicester and her servant Anna; at the end she seems more than ever a fragile flower preparing for the scythe.

The sweetness, no matter how wonderful, is not all there is to *Stuarda*. The passionate outburst in Act II that caused the battle between the first two interpreters of the roles is very important, not only for this opera, but for all Italian opera that followed. Superficially it suggests the battles between Gioconda and Laura, or Aïda and Amneris; and its style leads directly into Verdi. Elizabeth, who is characterized as a pretty unpleasant woman in Act I and an even less friendly creature in the beginning of this scene, now becomes sweetness and light as she rains insults on Maria's head. The first indication that Maria will not stand for Elizabeth's nastiness is in the phrase "E il soffrior?" (And I should suffer this?) when she animates her high voice and begins to forgo her prior abjectness.

As Elizabeth continues, Maria seems to rise in power, until finally she intones the great words "Figlia impura di Bolena" (Wanton daughter of Anne Boleyn) and becomes a she wolf. Her denunciation of Elizabeth, replete with blazing high notes, would do justice to the Norma of Act II or to the Act II Brünnhilde of *Götterdämmerung*. Elisabetta matches high note for high note as she calls for guards to arrest Maria, but the moment is the Scottish Queen's, and the sense of emotional commitment—the deepest feelings expressed by the emotional means of the voice—makes the confrontation in *Maria Stuarda* one of the greatest moments of Italian opera.

MOZART's *The Marriage of Figaro*
by Jonathan Abarbanel

It sounds like the start of a musical joke: "A Frenchman, an Italian and a German were walking down the street one day, when they decided to write an opera. One was a picaresque rogue, one was a peripatetic man of letters, and one was a brilliant composer." How else does one explain the wonderful twists of eighteenth-century history that brought together the artistry of Beaumarchais, da Ponte, and Mozart?

The joke also could begin like this: "A Protestant, a Catholic, and a Jew were walking down the street one day, when they happened to pass the opera house." For Beaumarchais was of French Protestant descent, and da Ponte was born Emmanuele Conegliano, an Italian Jew. Only Mozart was born into the church, though as an adult he was no more strict a Catholic than were his nominally observant collaborators.

Indeed, all three artists appear to have been faithful only to their art (and Beaumarchais to his politics as well). One wouldn't think, in fact, that three notorious philanderers, who strewed broken hearts across most of central and western Europe, would be the ideal candidates to create an enduring testament to conjugal devotion; but that is precisely the case with *Le nozze di Figaro*.

To begin with, they were men of similar socioeconomic backgrounds, modestly born sons of a clock maker (Beaumarchais), a leather worker (da Ponte), and a court musician (Mozart). Solidly bourgeois, they were raised in surroundings of material security, though not luxury. The fathers of Beaumarchais and Mozart were suppliers to the aristocracy, and proud of it. The sons followed in their fathers' footsteps, quickly outstripping their elders in accomplishments and fame. All three boys received haphazard but sufficient educations, mastering several languages each. While not a natural genius, Beaumarchais shared with Mozart a talent for music and was proficient enough to make his way for a time as a music master at Versailles. Like da Ponte, Beaumarchais also showed an early talent for letters. Of the three, only da Ponte received any formal education.

Pierre-Augustin Caron was born in 1732. His French Protestant father had converted to Catholicism eleven years earlier, for Protestants could not join guilds or practice a trade, their marriages weren't recognized, and their children were regarded as illegitimate. Neither Caron, *père* or *fils,* was a good Catholic. Both understood the intolerance that dictated their faith, and the hypocrisy it demanded of them. Beaumarchais's passion for social justice began with this fact of his birth.

The Caron family was an exceptional one: young Pierre-Augustin learned English and music, became an accomplished harpist and flutist, and composed music and plays with his parents and five sisters. At fourteen he was apprenticed to his clock-maker father and by twenty had become the greatest clock maker in France (maybe the world) because of a new regulating mechanism he invented.

Caron purchased a minor royal office. Next he married an older court widow, who left him a title, "de Beaumarchais," after a small wooded estate. By 1759 he was established at court as harp teacher to the four unlovely, unwed daughters of Louis XV. He also entered a business association with an older, world-class royal banker. By 1761 he had made his fortune and entered the nobility by purchasing a royal secretaryship for 55,000 francs. He was no longer Caron de Beaumarchais, but just plain Beaumarchais.

The swiftness of his rise, his ambition, and his talent made him a parvenu to many. When his banker-mentor died in 1770, Beaumarchais was plunged into years of legal warfare which resulted in the seizure of his property and fortune, and prison on three occasions. Beaumarchais fought back with shrewd political skill and true wit.

The first Figaro play, *Le Barbier de Séville,* was written in 1772. It was influenced by an extended visit to Spain several years before, during which Beaumarchais collected folk songs and details about local dress and custom. All these elements were skillfully utilized in his play, which also contained thinly veiled references to Beaumarchais's legal troubles.

It was quickly accepted by the Comédie-Française for production. The day before the scheduled opening, Beaumarchais landed in jail, which caused a two-year postponement. The play opened in 1775 and has remained in the repertory of the Comédie-Française ever since.

There is some evidence that Beaumarchais went to work on a sequel almost immediately and that *Le Mariage de Figaro* was completed in 1777 or 1778. It did not receive its premiere, however, until 1784, after much controversy over its unmistakable political content.

Indeed, the play's third-act courtroom scene, despite its Spanish setting, was a very direct attack on the French legal system. More impossible still, a servant *says* he is going to best his aristocratic master, and then *does*. To be sure, the old commedia dell'arte tradition, upon which the plays of Molière and Beaumarchais are based, often portrayed saucy servants besting their masters; but the masters in those plays were members of the bourgeoisie—lawyers, doctors, merchants—not members of the aristocracy.

Beaumarchais fought his usual tenacious battle for vindication. Numerous private performances and six censors later, permission for public performance finally was granted. The play opened on April 27, 1784. It was a sensation, running for sixty-eight consecutive performances and taking in gross receipts of 347,000 livres, the greatest theatrical success of the century.

Now what about da Ponte, born Emmanuele Conegliano, a Jew, near Venice, in 1749? By his own admission (in his juicy, if self-serving, memoirs published in 1826), he was a rogue and a rascal from the word go.

When Emmanuele was only fourteen, his widower father married a Christian girl of sixteen, after converting himself and his three sons to Catholicism. In the practice of the day, a new family name was taken from the bishop who performed the baptismal ceremonies. Emmanuele was christened Lorenzo da Ponte.

Lorenzo's father then decided that his clever son should study for the priesthood. Ten years later, ordained as the Abbé da Ponte, Lorenzo moved to Venice and embarked on a career of monumental debauchery. He became a friend of Casanova's. Eventually, charged with seducing a married woman, living with her outside the sacraments, and fathering illegitimate children by her, he fled across the border. After sojourns in Gorizia (Austria) and Dresden, he arrived in Vienna in 1782, armed with a letter of introduction to Antonio Salieri. Presented at court, he was appointed court opera poet by Emperor Joseph II. Soon he was introduced to Mozart at the home of Baron Raimund Wetzlar, friend (and at one time landlord) to Wolfgang and his wife. As Mozart himself reported in a letter to his father in May, 1783, "Our poet here now is a certain Abbate da Ponte. He has an enormous amount to do in revising plays for the theater, and he is at present writing an entirely new libretto for Salieri, which will take him two months. He has then promised to write a new libretto for me . . . if he is in league with Salieri, I shall never get anything out of him. But I should certainly love to show that I can write an Italian opera." It should be remembered that at this time, Mozart had written only one opera for Vienna, *The Abduction from the Seraglio,* in German, the year before.

Da Ponte, of course, was *not* in league with Salieri. He collaborated with Mozart on three great triumphs: *Le nozze di Figaro* (1786), *Don Giovanni* (1787), and *Così fan tutte* (1789).

With the death of Joseph II in the winter of 1790, a month after the premiere of *Così fan tutte,* life in Vienna became uncomfortable for da Ponte. Besides a change in court politics, he was under attack for yet-another sex scandal. In mid 1791, he found it convenient to leave Vienna.

Before moving to London, da Ponte visited Trieste, where he fell in love. His consort for the rest of his long life was one Nancy Grabe or Anne Celeste Grahl, depending on which biography you subscribe to. He says he married her, but there is no record of it. She took his name in any case, followed him to London, and bore him four children.

Da Ponte flourished for a time in London as librettist, translator, and poet and later as bookseller and publisher. Finally, close to bankruptcy in 1805, he followed his wife (?) to America, where she was visiting relatives. Settling in Pennsylvania, he made a career as a grocer, distiller, transport agent, and teacher of Latin and Italian.

Eventually he was appointed the first professor of Italian literature at Columbia College (later Columbia University). In 1825, when he was seventy-six years old, the very first season of Italian opera given in New York included his own *Don Giovanni.*

Of course, Mozart was no less peripatetic, with his frequent travels, but his personal life was far more orthodox and domestic. Unlike Beaumarchais's and da Ponte's, Mozart's extramarital liaisons were not the subject of career-threatening scandal.

Mozart's life is too well known to require a detailed recounting; but a few facts surrounding the composition of *Le nozze di Figaro* are in order. As early as 1781, Count Rosenberg, the court opera intendant, had suggested to Mozart that he write an Italian opera. This was a year before the first performance of *The Abduction from the Seraglio* in German.

In his search for a librettist and a suitable story, Mozart made two false starts. First, he turned to Giambattista Varesco, his librettist for *Idomeneo,* the opera seria first performed in Munich in 1781. Their planned collaboration was a sci-fi opera buffa revolving around a mechanical goose. Mozart spent six months working on the first act of *L'oca del Cairo* (The Goose of Cairo) before putting it aside for other projects.

One project that came up was a libretto for an opera buffa submitted by da Ponte, just a few months after meeting Mozart and promising him a text. Mozart began to set *Lo sposo deluso* in early 1784. He completed the overture, two arias, a trio, and a quartet, and he even drew up a proposed cast list, before abandoning the work due to the press of other commitments and a serious illness that summer.

In early 1785, however, a vehicle came along that Mozart couldn't resist. *Le Mariage de Figaro* had been immediately translated into English and German and so found its way to Mozart's desk. Mozart's friend and future collaborator (on *Die Zauberflöte*) Emanuel Schikaneder, the actor/manager, no doubt introduced Mozart to *Le Mariage de Figaro,* or *Die Hochzeit des Figaro,* as it is in German. Schikaneder's company announced a performance of the play for February 3, 1785. Three days before, Joseph II forbade the performances "since this piece contains a great deal that is objectionable." The imperial note still is preserved in the Austrian archives in Vienna.

Da Ponte records in his memoirs that Mozart himself, only days after performances of the play were canceled, brought the subject to him. They decided to take the risk of composing the piece first, "on speculation," and worry about censorship approval and production later.

Da Ponte says the opera was written in six weeks, with Mozart setting the words to music as rapidly as da Ponte could supply them. In truth, the process was more drawn out. Composition probably began in late summer of 1785. On November 2, Mozart wrote his father a brief letter of twelve lines, apologizing for not writing sooner or at greater length "because he is up to his eyes in work on his opera *Le nozze di Figaro,*" as Leopold Mozart, in turn, wrote his daughter. Work on the opera probably continued into the new year, interrupted by the composition of the operatic trifle *Der Schauspieldirektor* in January.

Also, Mozart did not compose the score sequentially, as da Ponte would have supplied the libretto. Scholarly study of autograph scores has revealed that the usual practice of the era was to compose by musical types, once the complete libretto was in hand. The undramatic numbers would come first—recitative, choruses, connective passages—with the lyrical arias last of all, after a prospective cast list had been drawn up.

However it was composed, the problem remained of securing permission for it. Da Ponte took care of this chore, unbeknownst to Mozart, offering the opera to the emperor shortly after the play itself had been banned. Da Ponte records that he assured the emperor that his libretto "omitted or cut anything that might offend good taste or public decency at a performance over which the Soverign Majesty might preside." The emperor replied, "Good! If that be the case, I will rely on your good taste as to the music and on your wisdom as to the morality. Send the score to the copyist." No doubt the truth was not quite so neatly turned as da Ponte described it; still the opera was completed and preferred. Mozart's own catalogue states that he finished the work on April 29, 1786, just two days before the first performance. This must mean, however, that he completed the overture on that date, rather than the body of the work.

Le nozze di Figaro was a triumph at its first performance at the Burgtheater, May 1, 1786. Many pieces were encored, a situation that was repeated at the second and third performances on May 3 and May 8. One duet was sung three times.

Much is made of the fact that *Le nozze di Figaro* initially played only nine times. While true, it must be remembered that May was the tail end of the opera season. By the following fall, a new sensation (an opera by the Italianized Spanish composer Martín y Soler) was on the boards. *Le nozze di Figaro* was staged in Prague, however, where it was a sensation, remaining in the repertory for six months. Prague went *Figaro* crazy and completely lionized Mozart and his wife when they made a month's visit in January, 1787. Here Mozart enjoyed the respect and prestige he never received in Vienna. He was to return to this warm city twice more, each time with a new opera: *Don Giovanni* in 1787 and *La clemenza di Tito* in 1791.

Many critics hold that when da Ponte "omitted or cut anything that might offend good taste or public decency" he emasculated the politics of Beaumarchais's play, and the charge is true. Da Ponte took care to eliminate material he felt would not withstand the scrutiny of official censorship.

Also excised by da Ponte were some of the racier passages, such as the Count's last-act advice to the Countess, disguised as Susanna, that wives should offer "more variety, more liveliness of manner . . . and occasional rebuff" in order to hold their husbands, "reviving the charm of possession with the spice of variety."

Notwithstanding these excisions, da Ponte did a brilliant job of reducing and adapting the play. Acts I and II of the opera follow the play exactly, condensing through the art of versification without eliminating a single incident or nuance of character. Da Ponte keeps all of Beaumarchais's stage directions intact. He even puts in songs where indicated by Beaumarchais, notably Cherubino's song in Act II and the choruses of Count Almaviva's servants who come to sing and dance in honor of Figaro's wedding.

Things are more confusing in Act III of the opera, which combines Acts III and IV of the play. Audiences must pay particularly close attention to follow the plots and reversals. The trial and its climactic revelation—that Marcellina and Dr. Bartolo are Figaro's parents—takes place off-stage and is reported very briefly. The plan of the Countess and Susanna to exchange clothes is revealed only in a recitative for the Countess before her beautiful, lachrymose display piece "Dove sono i bei momenti." There are additions, too. The Count's Act III vengeance aria, "Vedrò, mentr'io sospiro," so important to rounding out his character, is not found in the play at all. Note the music of it, in D major with an orchestration expressing menace and rage. Compare it to the Act I vengeance aria of Dr. Bartolo, "La vendetta," which is blustery comic anger, a buffa showpiece. These are good examples of Mozart's brilliance at musical characterization, rounding out the spaces between the words.

The opera's last act adheres closely to Act V of this play. The Count's apologies to the Countess at the end are brief, perfunctory, and not terribly convincing either in Beaumarchais's or in da Ponte's libretto. It remained, again, for Mozart to fill in the blanks with the psychological profundity of his music.

And what wonderful music! The overture with its great, joyous bursts overwhelming the fussy filigree work in the lower strings and woodwinds. The listener knows immediately that he or she is in for a merry evening and a happy ending.

And what of the economy of the writing? Part of the thanks for the work's blessed directness goes to Beaumarchais and da Ponte, of course, but it was Mozart who ultimately controlled the pace of the work. His sense of timing and theatrical instincts were superb. Look at the first act: no opening chorus, no declamation. In just ten minutes of music containing two *duettini* ("little duets"), one *cavatina* (a one-part solo aria with no repetition of words or phrases, versus the usual three-part *aria de capo*), and one recitative, all the necessary exposition has been revealed and the elaborate plot has been set in motion.

Or listen to the music Mozart wrote for Cherubino's Act I and Act II arias. Compared to the other characters, the love-struck adolescent is unsophisticated and simple. Cherubino's music is graceful, lighthearted, simple, almost like little whistled melodies, perfectly suited to the character and distinct from the musical writing for any other figure in the piece.

Sometimes it seems as if Mozart could spin elegance out of air, and nothing more. Take the Act III *duettino* for the Countess and Susanna. This is the scene in which Susanna sends the Count a note—dictated by the Countess—agreeing to meet him that night. It is brief in the play, made even briefer by da Ponte, who reduced it to four lines. Mozart takes these simple four lines, beginning with "Su l'aria," and exalts them with a ravishing melody.

Da Ponte skillfully adapted and versified the charming, informal vernacular nature of most of the language used by Beaumarchais. There are very few harangues or long speeches. Most of it is a swift dialogue of short lines or short speeches. Mozart respected this, utilizing very few traditional set pieces or big ensembles. Again and again, the "little duets" and trios of the work are constructed of shared dialogue lines, rather than stanzas. They come and go with Apollonian grace and naturalness. Surely Mozart and da Ponte were creating a type of elegant *verismo* a century before that term became associated with reforms in Italian opera.

It is a shame that Beaumarchais never met either da Ponte or Mozart, as they certainly knew of each other by reputation. Beaumarchais would have been well established at court during the time of Mozart's several visits to Paris in 1763, 1766, and 1778. Who knows? Perhaps Beaumarchais heard Mozart play at court or at some great house. As for da Ponte, he crossed pens with Beaumarchais again. The libretto Beaumarchais wrote for Salieri in 1787 was in French. The opera was performed in Paris, where it was one of Salieri's greatest successes. It was even more successful the following year when staged in Vienna, in an Italian translation by da Ponte (the court opera poet, remember). In fact, in his memoirs da Ponte mentions working on the librettos of *Don Giovanni* and *Tarare,* as well as one for Martín y Soler, on the same day! Such were the requisites of the peripatetic career artist of that era, as both Beaumarchais and Mozart knew well.

And so a Frenchman, a German, and an Italian wrote an opera together, and it turned out to be one of the very finest and most enduring of all time. There is no punch line to this musical joke other than the audience's laughter and applause.

VERDI'S *A Masked Ball*

by Karen Monson

Take it as a given: We are all against wanton censorship. But what would you have done had you been one of the Bourbon censors in Naples in 1857, faced with the libretto to Giuseppe Verdi's latest opera, then titled *Una vendetta in domino*?

Even for censors used to having their ways, this was a particularly sticky situation. In the midst of the "Risorgimento," a unification drive, Italians were deeply divided and, some feared, on the verge of revolt. While negotiating concessions from the Congress of Nations in Paris following the Crimean War, the Piedmontese statesman Camillo Cavour (whom Verdi greatly admired) had discussed unification with Daniele Manin, the Venetian hero who had spear-headed the resistance against Austria in 1848. Manin and Cavour aimed to unite Italy's separate states under a Piedmontese banner, with Vittorio Eman-uele of the House of Savoy as king of Italy.

The plan unnerved the Austrians and the French, and the atmosphere was so tense that it should have come as no surprise to the authorities when Felice Orsini, a disciple of Cavour's opponent Giuseppe Mazzini, threw a bomb at the coach that was taking the French Emperor Napoléon III and the Empress Eugénie to the opera to hear Rossini's *Guillaume Tell*. The intended victim escaped unhurt, but many others were killed or severely injured. This act of terrorism took place on January 14, 1858, the very same day upon which, according to most sources, Verdi and Giuseppina Strepponi (with their dog Loulou) arrived in Naples to prepare for the first production of what would become *Un ballo in maschera*.

The coincidence was, of course, miserable luck for the composer whose latest opus hinged on regicide. And it sent the censors, already high-strung and testy, back to their drawing tables to make more emendations on a libretto that, it was to turn out, had already been severely criticized. The directors of the Royal San Carlo theater in Naples well knew that the censors had been having the proverbial field day with the libretto as planned by Verdi and his friend, the lawyer, playwright, and patriot Antonio Somma. But the full extent of his predicament had not been revealed to the composer prior to his arrival in Naples on that fateful January 14. And by the time Verdi realized how bad things were, they were worse.

Vincenzo Torelli, the associate secretary of San Carlo who had commis-sioned the opera of "not less than three acts," wagered that once Verdi got to Naples to oversee *Ballo*'s premiere, he would concede to changes that might, at a distance, have seemed unconscionably drastic. And to a certain extent Torelli was correct. But *Ballo*'s course was not to run smoothly. Even for Verdi, ever the pragmatist ("I respect the power of authority," he wrote), the tug of war required to get the new opera onto a stage—any stage—took on monumental proportions.

The fact that the opera did finally have its first performance on February 17, 1859, at the Apollo in Rome is a tribute to how strongly the composer felt about his newest work. (It would have been uncharacteristic but understandable if, at some point during the struggle, Verdi had simply put *Ballo* on the shelf and turned to other projects, awaiting a better time in which to unmask his tale of witchcraft, infidelity, intrigue, and assassination.) Much has been made of the fact that having presented the three masterpieces of his middle period (*Rigoletto, La traviata,* and *Il trovatore*) within the course of a mere two years (1851–53), Verdi had waited another two before producing *Les Vêpres siciliennes,* then another two before *Simon Boccanegra,* then (with the brief excursion into revising and rewriting *Stiffelio* so that it became *Aroldo*), another two before the premiere of *Ballo.* Now that he was a rich hero, happily tending his country garden and romping with his mistress, was the master sloughing off after he'd turned forty?

The answer, of course, is not at all. But the twenty-first of Verdi's twenty-six operas, unlike most of his earlier works, had problems from the start. In 1857, when he signed the contract with San Carlo, Verdi again felt the urge to return to his dear "Shaspear" (a.k.a. Shakespeare) and, specifically, to the project that had intrigued him even before *Macbeth, King Lear.* He put his friend Somma to work on the libretto, and as had been the case before and would continue to be the case throughout the composer's life, no satisfactory text could be fashioned. The months passed, and the Naples deadline approached. Until the very last minute, Verdi stayed with *Lear,* but when it became evident that the woman who he insisted must sing Cordelia would not be available for Naples, he abandoned the project, again, and scrambled for a subject that would inspire him to meet his obligations to San Carlo.

First he considered *Ruy Blas,* and then he returned to the Spanish play *Il tesoriere del Re don Pedro.* Neither worked. Finally—and, one can guess, not without some hesitation—he set Somma to work on Augustin Eugène Scribe's *Gustave III,* a drama that had already come to operatic life in the forms of *Il Reggente,* by Saverio Mercadante, and *Gustave III, ou Le Bal masqué* (in the original French title of the play) by Daniel Auber. To begin with, Verdi had serious doubts about Scribe. "It is . . . in many ways conventional, like all Scribe's works for music, which I never liked but now find insufferable," the composer wrote. "I repeat, I am in a state of despair because it is now too late to find another subject."

And yet the story of Gustavus III held its appeal. The actual monarch, a bundle of contradictions, was a Francophile, probably homosexual (though he fathered an heir), who managed to turn the anarchy that reigned in Sweden at the time of his ascension to the throne into a liberal society given to fostering the arts. He was his country's most famous playwright before August Strindberg. He promoted Swedish theater. He founded the Swedish Academy, now identified with the Nobel Prize. The Swedes use the word "Gustavian" to signify elegance. Yet Gustavus III was also an able soldier and statesman. And he was assassinated by one Captain Anckarström, a member of a triumvirate of conspirators, who shot the king in the back with a rusty nail. Thoughtless.

It was Scribe who added the love affair with his best friend's wife to the king's history; it was Scribe who placed the assassination at the masked ball; and it was Scribe who added the fortuneteller and thus provided the opportunity for, not one, but two, masked escapades. The play all but begged for operatic settings, and as Verdi wrote: "It is grandiose, it is beautiful, but this one also has the conventional aspects of all operas—a thing I have always disliked and that I now find unbearable."

But despite his complaints to Somma, Verdi received the libretto and wrote the music to what was to become *Ballo* between October and December, 1857, while the censors pored over the story and began their blue-penciling. It can't be said that the composer wasn't warned; some changes had to be made early in the opera's creation. "Poor poets and poor composers!" Verdi lamented when he was told that his king in the new opera would likely have to be demoted to the position of duke (as had already taken place in *Rigoletto*). Then the composer and his collaborator learned that their effort had to be even further removed from fact. Somma wrote, "We are allowed, I am told, all the North, except for Sweden and Norway." Those were too close to the truth. "But what century shall we choose for the action? I don't know how to find one which, as the Censor wishes, justifies the superstition of the sorceress."

The librettist suggested Pomerania in the 12th century, but Verdi wouldn't hear of it. "The 12th century seems too remote for our 'Gustave,'" the composer wrote. "It is such a rough, brutal period, especially in those countries, that it seems to me contradictory to put in it French-style characters like Gustave and Oscar, and such a brilliant story, made according to the customs of our period. We should find some prince or duke or devil, even of the North, who has seen something of the world and caught a whiff of the Court of Louis XIV."

But these were relatively minor problems, even at the time, and they were to turn out to be mere bagatelles. Once Verdi arrived in Naples and discovered the breadth of his difficulty, his tone turned to anger and misery. "I curse the moment I signed this contract," he wrote to a friend in Rome. "I can't understand the reason for the veto on this libretto, which is absolutely the most innocent on earth."

Innocent or not (and it can hardly be seen as innocent, no matter what the composer might have thought at the moment), the libretto had to be changed. Verdi wrote to Somma expressing his defiance:

I'm in a sea of troubles . . . !
They have proposed the following changes (as a special favor to me):
1) change the protagonist to a private gentleman, with no reference to his

being a sovereign of any kind;

2) change his wife into his sister;

3) change the scene of the Witch moving it to a period in which they were believed in;

4) no ball;

5) the murder off stage;

6) cut the scene when the name is chosen by lots;

And on and on and on!

As you can imagine, these changes cannot be accepted . . . what an inferno!"

As we know, Verdi won some of his battles, but the war was not over. To the composer's great disgruntlement, San Carlo hired its own poet to go back to the original *Gustave III* and fashion another libretto more or less from scratch. This turned into *Adelia degli Admiari,* a tale of Guelphs and Ghibellines, which Verdi summarily rejected. Tempers rose to a point at which San Carlo threatened to have Verdi tossed into jail; he did, after all, owe them an opera, and he was not obliging. In practically no time the suit was settled out of court, and a very relieved Verdi was allowed to leave Naples on the promise that he would return the next season to stage *Simon Boccanegra.* So much for *Ballo* in Naples.

The composer had remembered, during those four months of hassle and annoyance, that *Gustave III* had been staged in its original, theatrical version in Rome, so he headed for that city to try to find a house for *Ballo.* Reasonable though his high hopes may have been, he was to meet again with disappointment at the hands of the papal censors, who had their own ideas (some not so different from those of their colleagues in Naples) about how *Ballo* could be made acceptable. Disgusted with the whole procedure and exhausted from the nit-picking that seemed to accompany his new work wherever it went, Verdi traveled on to Sant'Agata, writing to a friend, "I will not do in Rome what I refused to do in Naples."

But tired and resigned to his fate, Verdi relented. He wrote again to Somma, advising changes. The title went from *La vendetta in domino* to *Una festa da ballo in maschera* and then to the version the years have brought to us. Gustave was temporarily changed into the Conte di Göthemburg. Then Verdi went even further to placate his detractors. "The Censors would allow the subject, situations, etc., etc., but the locale should be moved outside of Europe. What would you say to North America at the time of the English domination? If not America, some other place. The Caucasus perhaps?"

Welcome to Boston. Welcome to Riccardo (a.k.a. Gustave), once the Duca di Surrey and then the Conte di Warvick *(sic).* Somma made the changes without much difficulty. Verdi recast a few notes and phrases to suit the rhythms of the new names. Rome wanted the opera badly enough to accommodate the composer at almost every turn. And the censors were, at last, silent.

The opera that had its premiere on February 17, 1859, in Rome showed the composer taking one of the giant steps forward that would henceforth mark his artistic maturity. To distinguish it from its most illustrious predecessors, the great middle-period trilogy, *Ballo* gave its larger orchestra deeper, richer colors, retreating to the relatively simple harmonies and "strummed" accompaniments (*à la* guitar) of its ancestors only rarely, and then for well-planned effect. *Ballo* moved with a new swiftness, an urgency that would characterize the composer's later operas. Critics have complained that the first scene is the weakest and have claimed that Verdi slipped when he wrote the Laughing Song for Sam and Tom. Yet from its very first notes the opera has a sweep that moves uninterrupted until the very end, and when that Laughing Song finally comes along, it seems in perfect place. Most importantly, *Ballo* found Verdi dealing for the first time with noble, mature characters—Riccardo, Renato, and Amelia— and delving into the secrets of true, red-blooded human friendship. (It is interesting to look back at the earlier operas with this in mind. None of them even begins to come to terms with friendship in the manner that Verdi and Somma have portrayed Riccardo and Renato.)

The first-night crowd in Rome saw *Ballo* set in what was alleged to be Boston, of course, and so have audiences around the world for the last 132 years. To be sure, it is easier for American audiences to believe that the action is taking place in far-off Sweden than in colonial Boston, a location of which we all have such well formed mental images. No matter what, we know that the Puritans did not give masked balls. But the fact is that it doesn't really matter a whole lot where *Ballo* is said to take place, or whether the hero is a duke or a king, or whether the weapon is a dagger or a gun, or whether fortunetellers thrived in the Boston/Sweden/Wherever of 1792. The opera lives on because of its own inherent greatness, not because of its setting.

As had happened before in his career (and as would happen again), Verdi had to wait for the second performance of *Ballo* in Rome for his real triumph. The premiere was a disappointment, and the reviews matched. The Roman impresario Jacovacci was ready to despair when he saw the printed notices, but Verdi advised: "You should follow my example. Don't read them, or else let them sing the tune they please, as I have always done. The question boils down to this: either the opera is good or it is bad. If it is bad and the newspapers criticize it harshly, they were right; if it is good, and they refuse to admit it out of petty jealousy or for some other reason, just let them talk and pay no attention."

Ballo proved itself, of course, and it appears to have been after the second performance of this opera that the Italian crowds adopted the now-famous rallying cry "Viva Verdi!" How convenient it was for them not only to praise their favorite composer and fellow patriot but also to lift their voices to the ideal of unification under the man whose name forms an acrostic with that of Verdi, Vittorio Emanuele, Re *d'*Italia.

Within two years of its first performances in Rome, *Un ballo in maschera* had traveled around the Western world, with stops in Paris, London, and New York. Since then, the music of *Ballo* has never stopped.

WAGNER'S *The Mastersingers of Nuremberg*
by Stephanie von Buchau

Richard Wagner began to write *Die Meistersinger von Nürnberg* during the most critical part of his tumultuous life. Financially strapped as always, his monetary affairs were in such disarray that he told a close friend, "I'm done for." This time he meant it. Romantically, his life was a mess. He was still married to his first wife, Minna Planer, but the couple had lived apart since Wagner had become involved with Mathilde Wesendonck. He was also wooing two women with the same last name: Mathilde Maier and Friederike Meyer. Plus, he was beginning to realize that his real interest lay with Cosima von Bülow, daughter of Franz Liszt and wife to conductor Hans von Bülow, Wagner's most ardent supporter.

Tristan und Isolde, the artistic fruit of Wagner's romantic liaison with Mathilde Wesendonck, was finished but unperformed. The four-part *Der Ring des Nibelungen* had been abandoned in despair during *Siegfried*'s second act because the composer saw no hope of ever getting the work performed. Wagner was emotionally at a low point when Otto Wesendonck, who seemed, like many of the people Wagner wronged, to forgive his tormentor, invited the composer to visit Venice.

Wagner, always looking for fresh stimulation and still having a yen for Wesendonck's wife—he later told Eliza Wille that "I shall never stop loving her alone"—joined the couple in November, 1861, in the shimmering city on the Adriatic. There, in the Academy of Fine Arts, Wagner gazed upon Titian's "Assumption of the Virgin." As he puts it in his none-too-reliable autobiography, *My Life:* "The Assumption made a most exalted impression upon me, so that by this inspiration I found my old creative powers awakening within me in their original primordial power. I decided to write *Die Meistersinger.*"

It makes a good story, but *Meistersinger* did not spring full-blown from the head of genius as Wagner would like us to believe. Like his other works, it had its genesis in the murky artistic past. As long ago as 1845 in Marienbad, Wagner had written a prose sketch of a story based on tales of the German mastersingers as reported in Gervinus's *History of German National Literature* (1826). What had appealed to him was its comedy: "I was particularly tickled by the title of 'the Marker' and the function he exercised in mastersinging. Without knowing much about Sachs and his poetic contemporaries, I conceived the idea, during one of my walks, of a droll scene in which the cobbler, in the capacity of artisan-poet, makes the Marker sing, and by application of his hammer to his last, gives him a lesson by way of punishment for his pedantic misdeeds."

He certainly hit on the funniest scene in what was later to become a less than totally comic work. As was typical with Wagner, the initial idea, so slight, so amusing, so deft, became something which the critic Eduard Hanslick—immortalized as Beckmesser, the Marker—criticized thus: "Its greatest fault is in the overelaboration of a small, meager plot which, with neither intricacies nor intrigue, is continually at a standstill and would normally offer barely enough material for a modest two-act operetta."

Although the *Meistersinger* idea had lain dormant while he pursued other artistic avenues, in October of 1861, *before* the fateful trip to Venice, Wagner had actually written to his publisher Schott with the following description of a proposed new work: "The title is *Die Meistersinger von Nürnberg* and the hero is the jovial poet, Hans Sachs." He boasted of a subject rich in pleasant humor, original in plot, and above all, light and easy to produce.

At this time he was going through agonies trying to get *Tristan* performed in Vienna (the premiere eventually went to Munich in 1865), so he knew how difficult his work could be. (*Tristan* itself had originally been proposed as an "easy" opera after the *Ring* seemed unproduceable.) Wagner was constitutionally incapable of thinking small. The "light" comedy that had appealed to him at Marienbad in 1845 now bore a load of fifteen years of artistic and personal disappointments. As he wrote to his estranged wife: "My earlier operas are all over the place; my new works are presenting me with insuperable difficulties. I have pressed on far, far ahead of my time and that which our theaters are capable of . . . I must begin all over again."

In Vienna, after returning from Venice, Wagner read Jacob Grimm's history of the mastersingers and Johann Christoph Wagenseil's *Nuremberg Chronicle* (1697), which contained a thorough listing of the mastersinger's rules and terminology, much of which finds its way into the first act of the opera. In addition, he must have known Johann Deinhardstein's drama *Hans Sachs* (1827), as well as Gustav Albert Lortzing's opera based on that play (1840). Between November 14 and 16 Wagner created a new prose sketch of the comedy, coloring it with his philosophy of art. In *A Communication to My Friends,* written in 1851, Wagner had declared, "I conceive of Hans Sachs as the supreme embodiment of the artistic spirit of the people, setting him against the arid, narrow-minded pedantry of the mastersingers personified by the figure of the Marker."

Biographer Ronald Taylor puts it thus: "Sachs, wise, tolerant, firm, representative of all that is best in his productive environment and his people, is an idealized self-portrait of the mature Wagner, master of his art, the benevolent overseer of the emotional, spiritual, and artistic well-being of the community . . . a man in whom passion, a sense of the tragic, and of other forces whose dominance means destruction, have been brought together in a serene synthesis. . . . Many who find it difficult to stomach the march-like, four-square choruses of praise for German art and the German spirit in *Die Meistersinger* . . . can still find an affectionate smile for this most honestly attractive of Wagner's heroes."

Princess Metternich offered Wagner a small cottage on the estate of the Austrian embassy in Paris where he could work on the *Meistersinger* libretto in peace; but when he arrived, he discovered that as her mother had just died, her increasingly senile father was to be housed there. Instead, Wagner moved into the Hôtel Voltaire and began to write his text. It was finished on January 25, 1862, at which time Wagner wrote to Mathilde Wesendonck, "Steel your heart against Sachs; you will fall in love with him."

Wagner had previously dispatched the prose sketch to Schott with a letter in which he promised the work to German theaters by October of 1862. "The subject permits me to write lucid, transparent, and yet pithy music of the cheerfulest coloring; and yet merely in reading this sketch, you will have found that my characteristic note will be struck just as richly and fully here, most persuasively in the blend of fervor and good humor. . . . I have hit the essential nerve of German life, and in a guise that other countries too will recognize and love as authentic."

The real "characteristic note" was that he underestimated, as usual, the length of time it would take him to write the opera and the length that the work would ultimately obtain. This "simple" comedy stretched eventually into the longest and largest German opera written up to that time, outdistancing even the as yet unperformed *Tristan und Isolde*. To quote the irascible Hanslick again: "There are scenes [in *Meistersinger*] which rank among Wagner's most fortunate musical inspirations, surrounded by long, unrewarding stretches of dull or disagreeable music. . . . Everything is composed in the same monotonous manner and in a slow tempo, Wagner having made the momentous discovery that the *andante* is the specifically German tempo!"

Harsh words, though not entirely without justification. In the meantime, not a note of the music had been written. Finished with the text, Wagner sought another refuge where he could compose in peace. He finally settled on Mainz, where on February 5 he read the text to a large gathering of friends and well-wishers. The composer Peter Cornelius, defying the foul winter weather, made the trip from Vienna specifically for this event, giving a good idea of how loyal Wagner's friends were. The evening's entertainment has been preserved in the memoirs of a young conductor, Wendelin Weissheimer, who described the event as "a brilliant feat of rhetoric," during which Wagner took all the parts, varying his vocal inflections so acutely that he didn't even have to identify the characters who were speaking. The reading was interrupted again and again with loud applause.

Moving from Mainz to nearby Biebrich, Wagner sustained a shattering visit from his wife, Minna. Ill with a heart condition and still troubled by jealousy of Frau Wesendonck (whom she referred to as "that bitch"), Minna produced interminable scenes. Wagner later reported to Cornelius that the visit was "ten days of hell." Despite their inability to get along, Wagner, never one to pay his bills if he could avoid it, faithfully supported Minna until her death. When a local paper accused him of shirking his duty, his wife came to his defense.

By March, Wagner had begun the score, starting, unusually, with the Prelude. In his autobiography, dictated some years later to his second wife, Cosima, he reports how the inspiration for the music came to him. "During a beautiful sunset which transfigured the light as, from the balcony of my apartment, I contemplated a splendid view of 'Mainz the Golden' and the majestic Rhine streaming past it, the prelude to my *Meistersinger,* just as I had once seen it as a distant apparition rising from a mood of despair, now returned suddenly clear and distinct to my soul. I set about putting the prelude on paper and wrote it down precisely as it is in the score today, with all the main themes of the whole drama already definitively formed."

Allow for the usual hyperbole. The Prelude does not contain *all* the main themes of the opera, but three main ones: the sturdy theme of the mastersingers in what Ernest Newman calls "their corporate capacity," Walther's theme of romantic yearning, which later appears in the final section of the Prize Song, and the Guild theme. These three, with other material, are worked into a magnificent polyphonic structure at the end of the Prelude. But there is no thematic mention of Beckmesser or Sachs as personalities apart from the mastersingers guild.

During the composition of *Die Meistersinger,* which occupied Wagner from the Prelude in 1862 until the last page of the score was inscribed, "End of *Meistersinger.* Thursday. 24 October, 1867. 8 pm," two events of monumental importance took place. They involved, as did most of the nonartistic incidents in Wagner's life, money and love. For most of his career, Wagner was financially strapped. He borrowed incessantly from friends, seldom repaying his debts. During the composition of *Meistersinger,* he so harassed publisher Schott for funds that he elicited the exasperated but prophetic reply: "No mere music publisher could satisfy your needs; it would take an enormously rich banker or a reigning prince with millions at his disposal."

By 1864, when the projected Viennese production of *Tristan* was finally scrapped, Wagner owed money (approximately $35,000). He had issued bad checks and had defaulted on dozens of loans. He was forced to flee Vienna, where prison awaited the bad debtor. Yet his elevated style of living was necessary to his artistic concentration. As he told Eliza Wille, striding emotionally about her sitting room: "I must have beauty, brilliance, light. The world owes me what I need. I cannot live in a miserable organist's post like your Master Bach. Is it so outrageous of me to believe that I deserve a modicum of luxury? I, who bring enjoyment to thousands?"

In Stuttgart, in April of 1864, he was at the end of his rope. At that very minute, the Bavarian minister, Franz von Pfistermeister, asked to see him. Thinking it was some creditor pulling a ruse, Wagner refused. The next day the minister returned, and Wagner saw him. It was the turning point of his life. Presenting the astonished composer with a ring, a miniature, and a letter, Pfistermeister announced that King Ludwig II of Bavaria had "resolved to save Wagner from an unjust fate by keeping him forever at his side in friendship." The honor was sweetened with a liberal allowance and assurances from the king that Wagner's works would be performed in Munich, the Bavarian capital.

The handsome homosexual king was more than a little in love with the composer. Despite the gushing letters they exchanged, however, the emotion seems to have been entirely one-sided. Years later, Wagner commented on those letters to Cosima, "The tone isn't good, but then I didn't set it." The king contributed nearly one-tenth of his annual civil list to Wagner's upkeep, which included the Munich establishment of his own "musical company" with Bülow as chief conductor and Cosima as housekeeper, secretary, confidante, and mistress. Bülow's wife had foisted her first child by Wagner, named Isolde, on her compliant husband, who seemed content with the situation; but rumors of her illicit affair began to reach Ludwig's puritanical ears and poisoned his relationship with Wagner.

The second momentous event, then, was Wagner's discovery that Cosima was the ideal woman for whom he had been so assiduously searching. Although he continued, even after their marriage, to seek erotic stimulation from other women, there is no doubt that his affair with Cosima, his "soulmate," was central to Wagner's personal development. Although she was married and twice a mother, Cosima had nurtured a passion for Wagner since adolescence. In 1863, she and the composer took a fateful carriage ride together in Berlin, during which they "gazed mutely into each other's eyes . . . with tears and sobs we sealed the avowal that we belonged to each other alone."

This watery confession was followed by seven years of uncertain cohabitation during which Wagner finished *Meistersinger* and saw it premiered in Munich on June 21, 1868. Cosima eventually shed her husband after he had been subjected to insults in the Bavarian newspapers over the affair he refused to recognize or criticize and after Wagner's wife eventually died of her heart condition, which allowed the lovers to legally join forces. Already parents of three illegitimate children, the composer and his faithful if equivocal sweetheart were finally married in 1870.

While these personal events were taking place, Wagner continued to work steadily on the score of his comedy. On the morning of his forty-ninth birthday he composed the orchestral introduction to Act III, the most thoughtful passage in the opera. In his loneliness, he characterized the melody as one of "extreme resignation. This work will be my consummate masterpiece," he wrote to Mathilde Wesendonck. In September of 1862, a concert in Leipzig offered the first public performance of the *Meistersinger* Prelude. Wagner reported he had never seen a concert so poorly attended, though the Prelude was encored because of loud applause from his supporters.

Later that year, in Vienna, he gave a reading of the *Meistersinger* libretto at a private home. The famous Viennese critic Eduard Hanslick was a guest. Reportedly, he left furious because he recognized himself in the character of Beckmesser, the Marker. (In the original scenario, Beckmesser had been named Viet Hanslich, but cool heads persuaded Wagner that the slur was actionable.) Hanslick later proclaimed innocence of malice, but his subsequent comments on the composer's comedy, though containing some grain of truth, are harshly phrased. On the other hand, though he later took most of it back, he opened his reviews of both the Munich and the Vienna productions with the following encomiums: *"Die Meistersinger* is a remarkable creation, uniquely consistent in method, extremely earnest, novel in structure, rich in imaginative and even brilliant characteristics, often tiring and exasperating, but always unusual." He couldn't say any fairer than that.

In 1864, Liszt, in Munich to try to save his daughter's marriage to Bülow, played excerpts from the score and proclaimed the work "a masterpiece of humor, wit, and charm." By the end of 1865, Wagner's demands on the privy purse of Bavaria and his outrageous behavior with Frau von Bülow had caused the Bavarian ministers to rise en masse against him and forced his removal from Munich. He fled to Switzerland, where he had often found refuge, staying first at a villa on Lake Constance and later at Tribschen, on Lake Lucerne, where Cosima and the children joined him. He continued working feverishly on his score.

In May, while composing the second act, he received a terrifying telegram from the king, announcing that Ludwig wished to abdicate and spend his time living with Wagner in Switzerland. Aside from the fact that this kingly "romance" was one-sided and that Wagner was deeply involved with Cosima, an abdicated king without a civil list to call upon was no use to him. Wagner counseled prudence, suggesting that Ludwig should move the seat of the government to Nuremberg, "the heart of Germany, the old true home of German art, the original German inspiration and splendor, the vigorous, imperial city, preserved like a noble diadem." As biographer Curt von Westernhagen has pointed out, one can almost hear the words set to music.

Finally, early in 1867, Wagner was near completion of the monumental work. At Sachs's final, patriotic monologue, which has become the controversial heart of *Meistersinger* since the era of the Nazis, Wagner suddenly jibbed. Overcome with artistic and political doubts, he decided to end the opera with the Prize Song, but, as Cosima later told the king, she spent a whole day arguing with him until he acceded to her wishes and composed the monologue that night.

The passage in question, beginning "Habt acht! Uns dräuen üble Streich," rises out of the political climate of the late 1860s. Germany, still a nation of individual states, was seeking collective power. Prussia, under Otto von Bismarck, was soon to swallow up the independent states, which was looked upon as a good thing by nationalists demanding a united Germany. When Sachs warns the folk to beware of "false, foreign rule," he is stating the real, natural fear of a divided people, but anti-Teutons hear instead the cry with which Adolf Hitler proclaimed world domination for the German people. What one often forgets is that earlier in that same speech, Sachs reminds Walther, the Junker, that he has won the crown of mastersinger and Eva's hand, not with "spear or sword," but with a poet's sweet song. Sachs's final words are in praise of "holy German art."

The opera finished at last, Wagner returned to Munich to supervise rehearsals for the premiere. He insisted on a realistic re-creation of old Nuremberg for the sets, while the street fight that ends Act II was choreographed by the famous ballerina Lucille Grahn. Bülow, gathering himself for one last heroic effort on behalf of his beloved master, conducted. Truly, no greater tribute to the power of music has ever been witnessed than the agonies that Bülow suffered while Wagner seduced his wife; yet he remained faithful to the genius of the composer he served. When Wagner died and his widow was prostrate with grief, Bülow the saint telegraphed her, "Soeur, il faut vivre."

Friends and former lovers, faithful as always, attended the premiere. After the last rehearsal, Wagner spoke to the assembled artists. He thanked them for their hard work and reminded them that it was their task to demonstrate the eminence and dignity that German art could rise to if all would dedicate themselves to its seriousness. The assembly was visibly moved. The dress rehearsal was held on June 19, with the king in attendance. He wrote Wagner that evening that the performance had exceeded his highest expectations. The composer replied: "I knew it. He understands me! It is impossible that he should not have sensed and clearly recognized, behind the comic wrappings of popular humor, the profound sadness, the lamentation, the cry of distress of the enchained poetry." This is a long way from that "light" comedy that Wagner had envisioned twenty-three years before.

At the official premiere, the king insisted that Wagner share his box. After each act the composer came forward to accept the applause, scandalizing the aristocrats in the audience for whom no mere musician should ever stand before their king. Bülow is supposed to have remarked that the sight was like "Horace at the side of Augustus."

The most successful premiere Wagner had witnessed since his *Rienzi* in 1842, *Die Meistersinger,* despite scathing reviews from important critics such as Hanslick, was launched on its successful worldwide career. Appallingly difficult to perform, with its huge orchestra and chorus, marathon length, three arduous leading roles, and all that deep philosophy mixed with its humor, *Meistersinger* nonetheless represents exactly what Ernest Newman observed, "the dawning of a new day for German art."

GILBERT AND SULLIVAN'S *The Mikado*
by Alfred Glasser

Tradition has it that a Japanese sword hanging as a wall decoration in William S. Gilbert's study fell inexplicably from its place and gave the librettist the idea of writing *The Mikado*. A more likely explanation might be that the mania for all things Japanese that had swept Europe after the opening of Japan to the West (which was responsible for the lethal weapon's being on the wainscoting in the first place) suddenly struck the poet-satirist as a source of innocent merriment. In any case, Gilbert desperately needed an idea. Richard D'Oyly Carte, the businessman of the triumvirate that made theatrical history at the Savoy, had exercised his option to demand a new "opera" (the inaccurate designation of the famous operettas was established at the beginning and still persists) on six months' notice. The Savoy's box-office receipts for *Princess Ida* were dwindling. Time was running out, and Arthur Sullivan was as adamant in rejecting Gilbert's scenario on the humorous effects of a magical lozenge as he had been on the several previous occasions when Gilbert had proposed it.

When the librettist approached the composer with the idea of satirizing the foibles and sacred cows of British society in a thin veneer of Japanese paraphernalia, the impasse was broken. The collaborators then began the familiar procedure that had worked so well for them in the past. Gilbert went home and wrote the libretto. When it was finished down to the last line of spoken dialogue, he delivered it to Sullivan, who wrote melodies to fit Gilbert's ingenious meters. Each had a profound respect for the other's talent; this provided the basis for their work together. (There was no bickering or browbeating, like Verdi's constant demands on Piave for alterations.)

For those interested in such things, Sullivan started with "Three Little Girls from School." He cut himself off from all diversions and worked obsessively at the score. According to his diary, he wrote "The Flowers that Bloom in the Spring" one afternoon between tea and dinner. When the score was completed, the next phase of the tried-and-true routine proceeded.

D'Oyly Carte took charge of the technical aspects of the production—drawing up budgets, paying bills, and running the business side of the enterprise. Sullivan supervised the musical preparation. He was a hard taskmaster. When a singer produced a false note, Sullivan made him repeat it alternately with the correct one until the problem was solved. No abusive language or displays of artistic temperament. He was not without wit on the podium. There is a famous anecdote of a rehearsal in which one of his soloists had just run through a number. Sullivan is reported to have said: "Wonderful tune, my boy! Now would you mind trying mine?"

Gilbert was the stage director of the trio. He dictated every movement and gesture on the stage. He tolerated no deviations. At one of the performances during the initial run of *The Mikado,* which lasted nearly two years, the actor playing Ko-Ko persuaded his Katisha to shove him as they knelt before the Emperor to permit him to turn a somersault. When Gilbert chastised the offender after the performance, the player protested that he had got a laugh. Gilbert replied: "They would also have laughed if you had sat in a pork pie." Gilbert imported geishas from Japan to coach his cast in the proper manipulation of a fan and other niceties of Japanese deportment.

Secrecy was maintained during the rehearsals to protect against unscrupulous impresarios who stole the basic ideas and produced crude imitations. To forestall the ugly practice, D'Oyly Carte sometimes rehearsed two companies and dispatched one to New York immediately after the London opening.

The Mikado was an immediate triumph. Yet more important, it smoothed over a rift between the creative pair that had surfaced just after the premiere of the preceding *Princess Ida.* Sullivan had written to Gilbert: "With *Princess Ida* I have come to the end of my tether—the end of my capability in that class of piece. My tunes are in danger of becoming mere repetitions of my former pieces, my concerted movements are getting to possess a strong family likeness." He went on to say that he felt his music had been too subservient to the text in his efforts to avoid a word of it to be lost. He longed for a chance for his music "to act in its own proper sphere—to intensify the emotional element not only of the actual words but of the situation."

In fact, *The Mikado* reached new levels of artistry. The same playfulness is omnipresent, but there are moments when the music becomes more genuinely operatic and less a parody of opera. The tendency increased as the collaboration continued. The tug of war between composer and librettist is visible in the works. Gilbert obviously won out in *Ruddigore,* which was not an unqualified success. *Yeoman of the Guard* is more like a sentimental Viennese operetta, the kind of piece Sullivan wanted; it fared neither better nor worse than its immediate predecessor. *The Gondoliers* seems to be once again an example of the give-and-take that had prevailed in *The Mikado. The Gondoliers* was a hit and ran for nearly three years. But it was the last of the great collaborations.

Sullivan wanted to try his hand at a serious opera, but Gilbert declined his request. Julian Sturgis, recommended by Gilbert, derived a libretto from Scott's *Ivanhoe.* Sullivan's first and only attempt at "grand" opera premiered at Carte's newly constructed English Opera House (today's Palace Theatre). The work was warmly received and had a run of 160 performances. Certainly it was not a fiasco. However, after nearly a century of hibernation, it seems unlikely that the work will ever be revived.

Haddon Hall was a comic operetta once more, this time with another new librettist, Sidney Grundy. It was not successful.

The partnership was revived to produce *Utopia Limited, or the Flowers of Progress* and *The Grand Duke, or the Statutory Duel.* Neither enjoyed more than a transitory popularity. Nowadays they are revived only by the most fanatical (and alas! usually amateur) Savoyards. Sullivan then tried his hand at librettos by other writers without ever recapturing the old magic.

The Mikado seems to represent a high point in the series of fourteen operettas that Gilbert and Sullivan produced. It preserves its freshness and its ability to provoke laughter after suffering the vicissitudes of professional and amateur productions spanning the complete spectrum from good to bad taste for more than one hundred years.

Gilbert has provided his characters with pseudo-Japanese names that had an arcanely familiar ring to Victorian English ears. Ko-Ko sounds precisely like the wholesome beverage offered to young persons for whom coffee and tea were still taboo. Yum-Yum was the phrase used by many a treacherous nanny to induce a pair of three-year-old lips to part for a spoonful of spinach or castor oil. Peep-Bo is clearly a transparent variant of the name of the negligent shepherdess from Mother Goose. Pitti-Sing perpetuates Victorian baby talk. The syllables were usually intoned by doting adults as they chucked infants under the chin and were universally understood to be the direct translation of "pretty thing." "Pooh," "Bah," "Pish," and "Tush" are orthographic renderings of utterances used by persons of all ages to express scorn or disbelief.

The Mikado's edict making flirtation a crime punishable by decapitation, which is the springboard of the plot, is a direct poke at the prudery of Gilbert's contemporaries, rather than an illustration of Japanese folkways, which Gilbert never bothered to study. Pish-Tush, the haughty nobleman who brings the audience up to date on the status quo of Titipu, is not so much the epitome of oriental inscrutability as he is a model of an Anglo-Saxon politician skilled in the arts of compromise. Although he acknowledges the Mikado's justification in issuing the edict, he also recognizes the objections of those opposing. And with a legalistic archness as Japanese as plum pudding, he has found a loop-hole. By naming a condemned prisoner, Ko-Ko, as Lord High Executioner, he has made it illegal for anyone in Titipu to be executed until Ko-Ko has first cut off his own head. The hilarious list of society offenders drawn up by Ko-Ko to serve as victims always provokes laughter but carries with it a tacit reminder of the old maxim, "Judge not, that ye be not judged." The compiler of the list, as Gilbert has made clear, is a condemned criminal. Yum-Yum and her companions come home from a boarding school despite the Japanese practice of educating girls at home. And after conscious lapses in respect due their elders, they take the adolescent's eternal refuge in their youth. The Mikado's sublime goals turn out to be a hypocritical mask for a sadistic nature. And so it goes.

The language is consummately witty. What could be more delightful than the girls wondering "what on earth the world can be?" Yet what has made The Mikado so durable is its depiction of life the way it is. The tragedy that hovers near the surface of comedy is not obscured by the high spirits. If Katisha did not make us laugh, she would make us cry. There is nothing funny about loneliness; but who can help but laugh at her incongruous arrogance when she tells young Nanki-Poo, "Oh, shallow fool! Come back to joy!"?

Sullivan's music is as witty as Gilbert's text. Handel's lofty recitative style is echoed when he sets the overinflated lines of recitative. The trio for Ko-Ko, Pish-Tush, and Pooh-Bah is a pastiche of the bel canto ensemble with a patter-song finale that Rossini would have cheered. Sullivan's fondness for quoting is well illustrated. There are actual Japanese tunes inserted for authenticity's sake as well as the opening phrase of Bach's *G Minor Organ Fugue* in the accompaniment when the Mikado alludes to that composer as part of the punishment for music-hall singers. There is a humorous parody of the tasteless music-hall ballad in Ko-Ko's "Tit-Willow." And the ascendant chromaticism of the finales of both acts simultaneously raises the spirits and mocks Wagner's famous technique.

The satire is good-natured and universal. No one in the audience can fail to see himself joshed unless he is totally devoid of self-criticism. Young, old, rich, poor—no one is overlooked. The story deals with courtship, love, and the battle of the sexes without ever stooping to questionable taste. The operettas of Gilbert and Sullivan filled a gap for Victorians between the opera and the music hall. Other forms of entertainment have come to share that place, but Gilbert and Sullivan still rule the territory.

GLUCK'S *Orfeo ed Euridice*
by Jonathan Abarbanel

The history of opera shares with almost all other histories a cyclical nature: the reforms of today are the excesses of tomorrow. *Orfeo ed Euridice,* the first and greatest of all so-called reform operas, exemplifies this. It was written in Vienna in 1762 by Christoph Willibald von Gluck, to a libretto by Ranieri de' Calzabigi. It was fresh air, badly needed. It was, too, a child of its times, a seminal work of art which helped usher in the Romantic Era and paved the way for much greater reforms.

The eighteenth century was an age in which the nobility financed the arts, and artists often were identified with the politics of their patrons. The arbiters of public taste were the wealthy and powerful—a much smaller percentage of the people than today—and art was not always above factionalism. Nowhere was this more true than in Vienna, where the sumptuous imperial court was the glory of the Austrian Hapsburgs. There, Gluck settled, in 1748, when well into adulthood. He was German by birth, but he made Vienna his permanent home for most of his life, though he traveled extensively (in an age when even great kings often did not travel). In Vienna, he flourished, for he was as adept at the politics upon which art depended as he was at art itself.

Although he composed a number of instrumental works and a quantity of chapel music, Gluck's fame was built on opera. When he settled in Vienna, he was already an internationally recognized master of Italian opera seria. By 1762, the year of *Orfeo ed Euridice,* his renown was formidable.

He had more than twenty operas to his credit, with productions in London, Vienna, Rome, Naples, Milan, Venice, Turin, Cremona, Hamburg, Copenhagen, Prague, and Paris. He had grown wealthy, married well (a rich merchant's daughter), secured the very highest royal patronage (he was the provisioner of all theatrical and academic music to the imperial court), traveled the Continent several times over, and even had been knighted (Knight of the Golden Spur, Rome, 1756).

Except in France, the Italian tradition of opera seria was dominant everywhere, so Gluck was welcome everywhere. Italian librettists, directors, and singers were found in the major and minor opera houses and court theaters of every nation and principality. And why not? Opera began in Italy and spread from there. Virtually all European nations first were exposed to opera in the Italian fashion and came to accept it as the only fashion.

In the opera seria tradition, there was little staged action; a limited orchestra was present only as accompaniment, with no dramatic functions of its own; little or no use was made of the chorus; all arias were written according to a strict three-part formula (the *aria da capo*); and singers had virtually unlimited authority to embellish. The musical lines and embellishments were exercises in pure technique, with no correlation to the dramatic or emotional sense of the work. It was the age of oratorio, and opera was little more than costumed oratorio.

Opera often was written hastily, in assembly-line fashion. For example, the leading librettist of the day was Pietro Metastasio, an Italian living in Vienna. He provided the words for scores of operas by composers all over Europe: he simply sent them all the same things. Some of his librettos were set to music thirty or more times; some were set to music more than once by the same composer. Gluck set three of his librettos. The words, the story, the drama just did not matter.

Also, most operas were written on demand for some state occasion, public festival, or court celebration. They were only one event out of many decorating joyous (though often solemn) occasions. They were supposed to divert and delight but not take focus themselves. They were generally based on familiar classical myths and invariably had happy endings, more often than not thanks to a deus ex machina—a god descending from the heavens at the end to arbitrarily make all things right. After all, one couldn't permit an opera written for a celebration to have a sad or tragic ending.

As early as 1728, the hackneyed, formularized Italian opera was mocked in *The Beggar's Opera,* the famous satirical English ballad opera by John Gay (upon which the equally famous *Threepenny Opera* is based). Still, it was another thirty-five years before opera seria began to reform itself. The surprise was in the reformer: Christoph Willibald von Gluck! For more than twenty years he had thrived under the system. Why, at the age of forty-eight, would he suddenly make bold changes not only in the direction of his own work but also in the face of an internationally accepted tradition of which he himself was a leading exponent?

In matters of art, "why?" is the question most rarely answered. One thing we do know: Gluck did it for love, not money. *Orfeo ed Euridice* was *not* written on demand. It was composed for no special occasion. It was an act of pure creation, art for art. In all, Gluck composed three Italian reform operas in collaboration with librettist Ranieri de' Calzabigi. *Orfeo* (1762) was followed by *Alceste* (1767) and *Paride ed Elena* (Paris and Helen, 1770). None of the three was written on demand. They were noncommercial, as we might say today, examples of two artists compelled to voice deeply held ideas and deeply felt instincts about art and music.

Call it rebellion, reform, or progress. One leads to the other and often, after sufficient time, come to be regarded as the same thing. It is worth noting, however, that Gluck had reached an estate where he could afford to experiment, without risking livelihood or position. At worst, he would endure a failure; he had endured others. At best, he would become richer and more famous. Reform is not always born in the streets, and necessity is not always the mother of invention. The security of rank and the luxury of position sometimes can be used to good creative advantage, and Gluck did.

What, exactly, were the great reforms? Briefly, Gluck and Calzabigi attempted to fit words to music in a more dramatically effective way. They simplified vocal lines, expanded the use of the orchestra, and purified language so that it might be feelingly sung. Nothing was permitted that inherently wasn't part of the dramatic action.

The first step towards reform was in the libretto. In fact, Calzabigi's text was finished before he met Gluck in Vienna, in 1761. Calzabigi simplified the traditional complexities and absurdities of the mythological plot, attempting to write a story that was believable in its sense of characterization.

Gluck, by necessity, had to eliminate the clutter of embellishment for its own sake and had to make the music supportive of the dramatic narrative being acted out. To this end, mood and coloration became more important, bringing about an expanded use of the orchestra with a function of sustaining and carrying the action. This affected both the style and the quantity of the orchestrations, as well as the complexity of the musical structures. Duets, trios, exchanges of sung dialogue, and choral passages were virtually unknown to opera seria at the time; they were outgrowths of the reform movement. It cannot be emphasized enough that these were striking new concepts to the audiences of 1762.

In an age of media glut, it is difficult for us to imagine the impact a work of art could have in the eighteenth century. Try, if you can, to remember your first reactions upon hearing Stravinsky or Schoenberg or Berg or Elvis Presley or the Rolling Stones or Dylan. You loved it or you loathed it. So it was with *Orfeo ed Euridice,* which stimulated intense controversy, sometimes physical.

It didn't happen right away, and it didn't happen in Vienna, where *Orfeo* was very coolly received. But when it was first performed in Paris in 1774, it touched off the War between the Gluckists and the Piccinnists. The latter were the followers of Niccola Piccinni and were considered to be the musical reactionaries. What hung in the balance of the "war," which went on for five years, was the direction of opera itself: the acceptance or rejection of new ideas. The Gluckists won, with the support of Marie Antoinette, some say.

In the meantime, Gluck and Calzabigi had completed a second opera, *Alceste,* which had been produced in Vienna in 1767 with great success. It was published in 1769 with a dedication (to a noble patron) in which Gluck and Calzabigi stated for the first time their principles of opera reform: "Semplicità, verità e naturalezza." Simplicity, truth, and naturalness. This became the manifesto of reform, a more heretical document to the Piccinnists than the two existing reform operas themselves. Gluck had stumbled on reform first as an artistic entity: an opera. Only later did he consciously define his principles in writing.

Gluck triumphed in Paris, and fittingly so, because the impulses for reform came from Paris. As mentioned before, the French never took to Italian opera with the gung ho enthusiasm of the rest of Europe. The French had a strong national identity, which expressed itself in a taste for opera in the vernacular not paralleled in other European countries. Also, opera in France was largely an outgrowth of ballet, and ballet was to France what opera was to Italy: it was the native art form. Thus, Paris was receptive to ideas deemed anti-Italian, as were Gluck's opera reforms.

Next, the Age of Reason was breaking upon Europe, and it had its birth in France in the ideas of Voltaire, Diderot, Rousseau. All things followed a natural order which was simple and rational. Art was to imitate nature. Ranieri de' Calzabigi had lived in Paris and had absorbed these attitudes. He found an eager receptor in Gluck, and they quickly put their principles into action. It was the beginning of the Romantic Era in art, literature, and music. Rigid formalism as it then existed was to be chucked out.

Finally, the French had developed a musical-theatrical form known as a vaudeville (yes, that's where we got the word). The vaudevilles were light, often satiric plays interspersed with songs. In time, they developed a good deal of sophistication and finally grew into opéra comique. Gluck came into contact with these *pièces-en-vaudeville* in the years directly preceding his work on *Orfeo.* Between 1756 and 1760 he wrote music for nine of them, which were brought to Vienna by his noble patron. Through these, Gluck received his first taste of true theater and strong dramatic structure, as well as the writing of multicharacter scenes.

Increasingly, the songs he wrote for them became more and more intrinsic elements in the storytelling. He was developing a very early form of musical comedy, much like the development of the ballad opera in England, some thirty years earlier. There can be no question that his exposure to works that were essentially theatrical (as opposed to musical) was vital in the development of Gluck's reform thinking.

What Gluck and Calzabigi did not fully reform was the traditional plot of opera seria. Oh, they cleaned it up a bit, but *Orfeo ed Euridice* is still based on a classical myth, perverted with a deus ex machina ending. The real story is something else. It comes to us via the Roman poets, as does a considerable portion of our Greek mythology. Both Ovid and Virgil wrote nearly identical versions of the tale of Orpheus, a mortal who could play and sing music so sweetly and so compellingly that he rivaled the gods.

Orpheus came by his musical abilities honestly: his immortal mother was a Muse, his mortal father was a Thracian prince, and the Thracians were the most musical of all the peoples of Greece. His musical powers were without limit. No one and nothing could resist him when he played. Through his music, Orpheus changed the courses of rivers and moved mountains.

He traveled as a young man, in the years just before the Trojan War, shipping out with Jason and the Argonauts. In fact, he saved the entire enterprise by outsinging the Sirens when the Argo passed near their shore. Orpheus was, perhaps, an antique equivalent of a rock superstar—adored and thronged wherever he went—with all the advantages of an upper-class education and upbringing. He always had a pocketful of obols and more women than he could shake his lyre at. He led an Attic version of the Life of Reilly.

Then he got married.

At this point his life became a living Hell, to make a bad pun, but his story became great. The myth passed onto us by Ovid and Virgil has served as the source of myriad operas, ballets, plays, and films. The addition of Eurydice made Orpheus a lover of heroic dimensions, but the appeal of the tale is not because it is a famous love story. Rather, Eurydice and her death gave the story dramatic action, a purpose, a plot. That plot is in the form of a universally recognized cultural motif: the quest. Orpheus was forced to make a journey which was at once a test of his skills, endurance, wit, and faith and also a search for the most precious of objects, his adored Eurydice.

The literature of psychology and fantasy records that the quest motif is found repeatedly in the myths of all peoples in all cultures. This is the real strength of the "love story" of Orpheus and Eurydice.

The psychological complexity of the relatively simple tale may be seen in the wide variety of treatments it has received. Gluck's opera celebrates the specific love of Orpheus and Eurydice, and also a more universal spirit of love or accord. And of course, he changes the myth to give it a happy ending in which Eurydice is restored to Orpheus. Gluck's romantic approach, however, is not the usual one.

In fact, as recorded by Ovid and Virgil, the story of Orpheus is grim indeed. After losing Eurydice, he forsook the company of men, wandering the earth in despair, careless of all, wasteful of his talents. Finally, he ran into a band of Maenads—wine-crazed female worshippers of Dionysus—who tore him to pieces and ate his raw flesh, throwing away only his head. So much for sweet love stories. Most treatments, particularly in the twentieth century, hone in on the more somber aspects of the tale, dealing with acceptance of death, love, and will, existential undercurrents, and the like.

Another unique approach to the story is that of Offenbach in his *Orphée aux enfers* (Orpheus in the Underworld). In Offenbach's version, Eurydice loathes music and would welcome any escape from it, including death. Pluto obligingly transports her to a good life down below, and everyone is satisfied, especially Orpheus, who is quite happy to be single again. However, Public Opinion—a character in the opera—is scandalized and forces Orpheus to make that famous descent. Jupiter himself, lusting after Eurydice, makes sure that Orpheus looks at her too soon, happily in this case. Everyone ends up single, but content— except Public Opinion.

The Offenbach romp is a deliberate parody of the Gluck work, written nearly a century later in Paris, the city of Gluck's first triumph. That the work had become a fit subject for affectionate parody demonstrates its continued popularity and the acceptance of its once-revolutionary concepts.

HANDEL'S *Orlando*
by Nancy Peponis

Imagine an opera in which the hero does not get the girl—and no one dies. One such exception to the tragic norm is George Frideric Handel's *Orlando,* the twenty-eighth of some forty operas by the composer. Orlando, the hero, is literally mad with love for Angelica, Queen of Cathay. Unfortunately for him, Angelica is secretly involved with Medoro, an African prince. To further complicate matters, Dorinda, a shepherdess, pines not-so-secretly for Medoro. The opera exquisitely contrasts these three loves and comes complete with a happy ending, courtesy of Zoroastro, the magician. Through such wondrous feats as changing a horrid cavern into a temple of Mars, he protects Angelica and Medoro from Orlando's crazed wrath and in the end cures the hero of his insane passion. A wonderful "magic" opera with spectacular effects, *Orlando* is, as Winton Dean has suggested, "musically perhaps the richest of all Handel's operas."

The twentieth century usually associates Handel with the *Messiah* and the medium of the oratorio. Although he wrote magnificent oratorios, Handel was, the *New Grove Dictionary* points out, "by training and inclination primarily a composer for the theater." Handel had composed several operas in Hamburg and Italy before arriving in London in 1710, specifically to compose operas. In 1711, the twenty-six-year-old composer established himself with the successful premiere of his *Rinaldo,* the first Italian opera written especially for London audiences. Over the next four years, Handel would write four new operas.

In 1720, an event occurred that was to turn London, for a short time, into the operatic center of Europe: the founding of the Royal Academy of Music. Under the patronage of George I and members of the aristocracy, the academy was created to provide regular seasons of Italian opera at the King's Theatre in the Haymarket. Handel received the post of music director and proceeded to assemble the finest singers in Europe. His *Radamisto,* the company's second production, opened on April 27, 1720, to great enthusiasm.

Over the next eight years, the academy attracted the best composers and singers to London. The period was immensely successful for Handel as well, seeing the premieres of his *Giulio Cesare, Tamerlano,* and *Rodelinda.* However, the company fell victim to mounting internal conflicts. Handel and his *primo uomo,* the lead castrato Senesino, were bitterly at odds. But more spectacular was the intense feud that raged between the two prima donnas, Francesca Cuzzoni and Faustina Bordoni. The atmosphere became so heated that during one opera the two sopranos burst into a spontaneous hair-pulling match, cheered on by their respective followers. The acrimony eventually took its toll, and opera production was suspended in 1728.

Not one to be deterred by personnel squabbles, Handel formed a five-year partnership in 1729 with the impresario Heidegger to bring opera back to King's Theatre. During this period, sometimes referred to as the "Second Academy," the composer wrote six new operas, including *Orlando.* Featuring Senesino (the hated castrato!) in the title role, *Orlando* premiered on January 27, 1733, and ran for eleven performances, considered a success.

Just as he did for *Ariodante* and *Alcina,* Handel drew the theme for *Orlando* from Ariosto's romantic epic, *Orlando furioso.* The poem, well known to early-eighteenth-century audiences, tells of the hero Orlando, who defends the Christian world against the Moors until he is struck by his irrational love for Angelica. Handel chose to base his libretto specifically on the one written by Carlo Sigismondo Capece and set by Domenico Scarlatti in 1711. It is unknown, though, who revised Capece's libretto, trimming it down from 1,643 lines to the 632 of *Orlando*'s libretto and dropping two characters, while adding that of the magician Zoroastro.

In composing *Orlando,* Handel returned to the world of magic and the supernatural after an eighteen-year absence, since the premiere of his *Amadigi* in 1715. Handel composed only five "magic" operas—the remainder were mostly heroic, with a few exceptions that mocked the opera seria tradition. But these "magic" operas lent themselves particularly well to the visual aspects of Baroque opera. Because the curtain never fell during an opera, the scenery changed in full view of the audience, in this way becoming an integral part of the drama. Theatrical technique was especially advanced in the areas of scenery, lighting, and machinery. The "magic" opera, by its very nature, provided a wonderful excuse for staging the spectacular effects then possible.

(The stage directions that demand Zoroastro to suddenly appear flying through the air in a chariot holding onto Orlando were meant to be taken literally!)

But the "magic" operas allowed for more than elaborate staging. These operas have a different emotional feel than Handel's other operas, and they freed the composer from some of the stiffness inherent in opera seria. The "magic" operas, to quote Dean, "released the vein of romantic fantasy in Handel's imagination," enabling him to create some of his greatest music. Handel most frequently breaks the confines of opera seria in *Orlando*. By including action in arias and duets, he causes a radical modification of musical form.

The hero's madness first appears in the finale to Act II, after Orlando has discovered Angelica's true feelings for Medoro. In a brilliant series of accompanied recitatives, building to a rondo aria, the crazed Orlando believes himself furiously sailing through the underworld. Suddenly, he finds the despised Medoro, in the arms of mythical Proserpine. The rondo violently contrasts Orlando's ravenous need to destroy Medoro with his desire to spare Proserpine from grief. The "mad scene" lasts almost two hundred measures and contains nine changes in meter, including the first notated use of quintuple time, to further underscore Orlando's irrational state. This musical episode transcends the usual opera seria division between "active" recitatives and "reflective" da capo arias.

Dramatically, *Orlando* is an opera of many disparate elements. As Reinhard Strohm has pointed out, Handel "fuses the comic with tragic, the rational, the magical, the pastoral," to create a psychologically intriguing story. The plot marks an unusual alliance between the supernatural and the rational—only through "the constant Zeal of the Magician Zoroastro," the libretto preface explains, can Orlando return to reason and military glory. Orlando's tragic characterization as the undone hero makes a striking contrast to that of Dorinda, who reacts to unrequited love by keeping both feet firmly on the ground. (She is the only character who does not need Zoroastro's magical help.) Her pragmatic language and comical outlook have more in common with the knowing servant of opera buffa than with the typical gentle shepherdess of opera seria. Upon inspection, the dramatic texture of *Orlando* proves to be as varied and fascinating as the music itself—both the libretto and the score illustrate the same avoidance of the predictable, and together they elevate the opera to a masterpiece.

Noted musicologist Winton Dean has written that if Handel's operas are given the study they deserve, "it may be found that Handel's mastery of opera as a fusion of music and drama is scarcely less absolute than that of Monteverdi and Mozart, though it is very differently organized." It is alarming to discover that *none* of Handel's operas, including *Orlando,* was performed between 1754 and 1920. This neglect stems primarily from the downfall of opera seria, whose severe emphasis on the rational caused it to go permanently out of fashion. The disappearance of the castrato voice, a prominent feature of the genre, created additional difficulties in reviving opera seria works. Handel's operas became an unfortunate casualty, dismissed as part of a dry, artificial tradition—a process that began during Handel's own lifetime.

Orlando was the final opera composed by Handel before most of his singers defected to the newly opened Opera of the Nobility, a rival company encouraged by the prince of Wales. But London, hard pressed to support one opera company, could not maintain two. Both Handel's company and the Opera of the Nobility closed in June, 1737, in financial ruin. Although Handel continued to compose for the stage, the response he received grew progressively weaker. His last two operas, *Imeneo* (1740) and *Deidamia* (1741), were dismal failures, due not to the quality of the music or the performers but to the public's indifference.

Handel's audience, as well as his performers, had begun to change. The aristocracy was much less willing to support opera financially. The internationally renowned singers had left England because London could no longer afford their high salaries. Finally, audiences were tired of listening to music in a language that they could not understand. They wanted music in English, a point made as early as 1728 with the wild success of John Gay's *The Beggar's Opera*.

Handel's visit to Dublin in 1741 and 1742 saw the triumphant premiere of the *Messiah* and performances of a number of his other oratorios. The message was not lost on the composer. By the time of *Samson*'s premiere in February, 1743, Handel clearly had the support of the increasingly prosperous middle class for his English oratorios. He was to focus on the oratorio for the remainder of his life.

VERDI'S *Otello*

by Peter P. Jacobi

It began in the summer of 1879.

Giuseppe Verdi, who had said he would compose no more, who felt he deserved permanent respite from a long musical career, visited Milan. He conducted a performance of his *Requiem* as a benefit for victims of a recent flood. The result was not only considerable money for those victims but also a tremendous outpouring of enthusiastic sentiment for Verdi: flowers almost pouring onto the La Scala stage, crowds of people in the streets shouting for the old man.

He felt good about it. The public had not forgotten him.

And so, when a dinner was held some weeks later, a momentous dinner, Verdi was receptive.

A dinner among friends. So Verdi's publisher Giulio Ricordi called it. "I turned the conversation, by chance, on Shakespeare and on Boito," he recalled. Fat chance by chance. Ricordi was trying to get his best meal ticket out of retirement and back to composing. He described the scene later: "At the mention of *Othello,* I saw Verdi fix his eyes on me, with suspicion, but with interest. He had certainly understood; he had certainly reacted."

The following day, conductor and friend Franco Faccio brought Arrigo Boito to see Verdi. Boito, the poet. Boito, the composer. Boito, the librettist. Boito, the salesman, for it was he who explained with ultimately persuasive enthusiasm a grand project: a new opera based on Shakespeare's *Othello,* with libretto by Boito and music by Giuseppe Verdi.

Verdi wasn't at all sure. A new opera? And based on his beloved Shakespeare? He remembered the early failure of *Macbeth* and the toying over decades with a notion to set *King Lear* into opera, a plan that never came to be, at least partially because of the gnawing fear that he couldn't do it justice.

But Verdi was willing to look at whatever verbal sketches Boito might develop. Three days later Boito had sketches. Verdi liked them and urged Boito to set it all to verse. After all, Boito could use the libretto himself, set it to his own music, or collaborate with someone else. Verdi would not commit himself to participate. His main interest, he kept pointing out, was farming, his potatoes and cabbages.

Ricordi, a man of much action behind the scenes, suggested that he and a friend might visit the maestro at his country home, Sant'Agata. Verdi knew full well what Ricordi was up to and hastily replied:

> If you come now with Boito, I shall have to read his libretto. If I think it completely good, you will leave it with me, and I shall find myself, to a certain extent, committed. If I still find it good, but suggest a few modifications which Boito accepts, I am even more committed. If I don't like it, it would be too difficult for me to give my opinion to him in person. No, no! You have already gone too far, and we must stop now before there is any gossip or unpleasantness.

Boito set to work, nevertheless. He had the feeling, as did Ricordi, that somehow the maestro would be won over.

In November, Verdi told Ricordi, "I have just received the chocolate"; they called the story their chocolate project in those early days. Verdi continued to like it, but still he set it aside.

The following summer, after Boito had written an ending for Act III, Ricordi wrote him: "I have the feeling that Verdi has put the Moor to sleep for a bit! An electric shock from your verses would work wonders! Do me the favor then of sending this blessed finale of yours to Busseto."

Boito did. Verdi responded, elaborating on how he visualized that Act III conclusion. And here begins the collaboration. Ricordi, Boito, Faccio had won. Verdi was getting back to work.

The Act III climax, how it should unfold, characterizes the Boito-Verdi collaboration. Two strong personalities were anxious to make their chocolate project work. Two strong personalities respected each other's abilities.

Verdi was still a man at least partially tied to his own successful past, and that meant he wanted to include a big choral scene as the opera moved toward climax. Verdi dreamed up an off-stage revolt by the Turks that could result in an ensemble of tremendous fortissimos. He seemed quite pleased with the concept.

Boito answered with a masterful letter:

> Othello is like a man moving in circles under an incubus, and under the fatal and growing domination of that incubus he thinks, he acts, he suffers and commits his tremendous crime. Now if we invent something which must necessarily excite and distract Othello from this tenacious incubus, we destroy all the sinister enchantment created by Shakespeare and we cannot logically reach the climax of the action. That attack by the Turks is like a fist breaking the window of a room where two persons were on the point of dying of asphyxiation. That intimate atmosphere of death, so carefully built by Shakespeare, is suddenly dispelled. Vital air circulates again in our tragedy and Othello and Desdemona are saved. In order to set them again on the way to death we must enclose them again in the lethal chamber, reconstruct the incubus, patiently reconduct Iago to his prey, and there is only one act left for us to begin the tragedy all over again. In other words: We have found the end of an act, but at the cost of the effect of the final catastrophe.

Verdi bought Boito's argumentation. And so we got instead the intensely dramatic moment of an Othello overcome with anger and hurt, alone on stage, his collapse, and Iago then standing over the Moor in malevolent triumph as the crowd cheers Othello from the outside.

Verdi had good ideas of his own. He knew his Shakespeare and developed certain interpretations. Iago, for instance, received his thoughtful attention. (Interestingly, for most of the five-year period during which *Othello* changed into *Otello,* the opera was referred to as *Iago.*) Verdi visualized the villain clearly and in specifics.

> . . . if I were an actor, and had to play Iago, I would rather have a long, thin face, thin lips, small eyes close to the nose like a monkey, a high, receding forehead, the head well developed at the back. An absent-minded air, nonchalant, indifferent to everything, sceptical, a cutting manner, speaking good and evil lightly as though he were thinking of something else, so that, if anyone were to say to him in reproof: "What you say, what you propose, is monstrous," he could reply: "Really . . . I didn't think so. . . . Let's talk no more of it" . . . . Someone like that could deceive everybody, even, up to a point, his own wife.

How pleased Boito was when he heard the maestro was thinking about the opera; how jubilant he was when Verdi composed. At one point Boito wrote Ricordi not to tell anybody, not even his family, not "even yourself," but the "maestro is writing, indeed he has already written a good part of the opening of the first act and seems to be working with fervor."

Verdi wrote in spurts, separated by bouts of doubt. And all along he would warn his friends not to count on completion. For instance, to the baritone Victor Maurel, whom Verdi had in mind for Iago and who on at least one occasion reminded Verdi of a promise to create the Iago role for him, Verdi answered: "I do not believe I ever promised to write Iago for you. It is not my habit to promise a thing unless I am really sure I can fulfill it. But I may very likely have said that the role of Iago was one which perhaps no one would interpret better than you." He said the work was not finished and that he was not in a hurry to complete it "because I have not given any thought, nor am I giving any thought now, to its being performed."

But through those years Verdi did work, and work hard. The score holds more erasures, more changes than any of his others. And through those years Boito did work, and work hard. He wrote and rewrote and rewrote again (1) to achieve those necessary verbal nuances that could flame Verdi's melodic genius and (2) to make sense of Shakespeare while cutting some thirty-five hundred lines of poetry into about eight hundred.

For a spell it looked as if the chocolate project would not be accomplished. Verdi's purpose was easily set aside: he kept reminding people he didn't want to compose. Thus, a misunderstanding almost turned into disaster.

Actually seeds of the contretemps were planted in 1863. The twenty-year-old Boito, a bit of an artistic firebrand, in a moment of overwrought enthusiasm penned a poem entitled "To Italian Art." It included, amid other pompous verbosity, these lines: "Perhaps the man is already born who, modest and pure, will restore art to its altar stained like a brothel wall."

Verdi had taken offense. That young intellectual Boito, plugging for Wagnerian reform in opera. Verdi told his publisher: "If I too among the others have soiled the altar, as Boito says, let him clean it and I shall be the first to light a candle."

Later Verdi had spoken not too kindly about Boito's opera *Mefistofele*. So, rankling remained that in the tense atmosphere of operatic creation might erupt at any time.

And so it did.

A Neapolitan newspaper misquoted Boito, suggesting he told a reporter that the *Otello* libretto was started against his will but that once he was into it, he gained enthusiasm, so much that he rather regretted not being able to set the poem to music himself.

To Verdi that brought memories of an old wound, of a boisterous Boito bemoaning a besmirched altar of Italian art. He wrote Faccio with restraint and magnanimity.

The worst of it is that Boito's regret that he cannot write the music himself will give rise to the notion that he has no hope of seeing it set suitably by myself. I see clearly all this . . . and therefore beg you, as his oldest and staunchest friend, to tell Boito when he returns to Milan . . . that I give him back his manuscript intact, without a suspicion of resentment or rancor. Moreover, the libretto is my property, and I am ready to make him a present of it if he wishes to set it to music. If he accepts, I shall be happy in the hope of having thus contributed in some small way to the art we both love.

Boito, horrified about the whole business, wrote Verdi a moving, devotional letter. "You alone can set *Othello* to music," he wrote. "If I have been able to divine the inherent powerful musicality of the Shakespearian tragedy . . . and if I have been able to demonstrate it in fact with my libretto, that is because I put myself at the viewpoint of Verdian art." He begged Verdi not to abandon the project. "It is predestined for you. Create it."

Well, I don't know, is what Verdi's answer amounted to; "all this has cast a chill over this *Otello,* and stiffened the hand that had begun to trace out a few bars! What will happen in the future? I don't know!"

Boito, the increasingly diplomatic word smith, pursued correspondence and began to talk specifically about the opera, about an "evil Credo" for Iago. Then he visited Verdi. And before long the old man wrote his colleague: "It seems impossible, and yet it is true!! I am busy, I am writing!!"

The project was saved.

Eventually, finally, the chocolate project was done. In November, 1886, Verdi advised Boito: "It's finished! Greetings to us . . . (and also to Him!!)."

The last year of collaboration was devoted to polishing and orchestrating. During those days of refinement Verdi decided: "Let's come out and call it *Otello.* . . . People speak and write of Iago!" He had gone along with it, first because he was most intrigued by Iago, but later because he hesitated following Rossini in setting an *Otello* to music. Now he concluded, "I'd rather people said: 'He matched himself against a giant and was crushed by him,' than: 'He tried to disguise what he was doing under the title of *Iago.*'"

The premiere at Milan's La Scala took place February 5, 1887, with Franco Faccio conducting a cast headed by Francesco Tamagno (Otello), Victor Maurel (Iago), and Romilda Pantaleoni (Desdemona).

To the moment of the opening curtain, and probably beyond, Verdi was jittery. Faccio's assistant recalled later that Verdi stood on stage, tense and shaken. "Still, maestro?" he asked. Verdi said, "Yes. This is the 25th (Verdi opening night), but for me it would be the same on the 45th."

He needn't have worried.

The event is described by author Blanche Roosevelt. She called Milan "Otellopolis."

By noon of premiere day, she said, streets were no longer streets but human beings run together "like honey." Shouts of "Viva, Verdi!" kept resounding. "Poor Verdi," she commented. "Had he been there, he would certainly have been torn to pieces, as a crowd in its enthusiasm rarely distinguishes between glory and assassination."

She wrote of the audience, from those glittering members up close to the opera fanatics up high.

When it was over, she noted:

> The ovations to Verdi and Boito reached the climax of enthusiasm. Verdi was presented with a silver album filled with the autographs and cards of every citizen in Milan. He was called out 20 times, and at the last recalls hats and handkerchiefs were waved, and the house rose in a body. The emotion was something indescribable, and many wept. Verdi's carriage was dragged by citizens to the hotel. He was toasted and serenaded; and at five in the morning I had not closed my eyes in sleep for the crowds still singing and shrieking "Viva Verdi! Viva Verdi!". Who shall say that this cry will not re-echo all over the world?

As indeed it has.

Surrounded in the hotel room by his closest friends and by his dear wife Giuseppina, Verdi at first surprisingly expressed depression. "I so loved my solitude in Sant' Agata in the company of Otello and Desdemona," he said. "Now the crowd has taken them away from me, leaving me nothing but the remembrance of our secret conversations, our past intimacy."

But the mood changed as the crowds continued to shout. And he smiled, saying, "If I were 30 years younger, I should like to begin a new opera tomorrow, on the condition that Boito wrote the libretto."

He didn't begin "tomorrow," but he did collaborate once more to compose *Falstaff.*

Otello is a wonder.

Boito, who did not read English and therefore worked from a French translation of Shakespeare, managed to evoke all the terror, passion, and poetic grandeur of the original.

Verdi, in his seventy-fourth year, managed to unleash new musical powers. The inventiveness of his melodic imagination was joined by a new authority over orchestra and a matured understanding of how music can enhance drama.

From the thunder of opera's most sweeping storm scene . . .

To the emotional abandon of that haunting love duet . . .

To Iago's shivering Credo, evil in compressed soliloquy . . .

To the shattering Otello-Iago vengeance duet . . .

To Iago's loathsome "Ecco il Leone" (Behold the lion) as he stands above the unconscious Otello . . .

To the lovely "Willow, willow, willow" of Desdemona, followed by her "Ave Maria," her soft goodnight, and a sudden heartrending farewell to Emilia as she senses danger and death . . .

And to the final moments with the reiterated kiss motive.

Otello is what so few artistic creations really are, all unity and a masterpiece.

LEONCAVALLO'S *I pagliacci*

by Roger Dettmer

Fate was hardly kinder to Ruggiero Leoncavallo than it had been to Pietro Mascagni, composer of *Cavalleria rusticana,* the opera that is usually paired with *I pagliacci.* Leoncavallo was born the son of a traveling magistrate in 1858 (five years before Mascagni), was certified early on as a keyboard prodigy, and by age eighteen had graduated from the Naples Conservatory as maestro. He was, however, destined to wait—even longer than Mascagni—for international accolades, in circumstances comparably dire. Whereas the younger composer had supported himself as a provincial teacher and conductor of music until the flash flood of success, Leoncavallo entertained greater ambitions.

Already by 1879 he had arranged for the Bolognese production of his first opera, *Tommaso Chatterton,* only to have its entrepreneur decamp on the eve of the premiere. Leoncavallo, in debt to the upturned points of his mustache, fled from Italy to Egypt, and thence to the Ottoman Empire, where he eked out mere subsistence in the cafés of Turkey and Greece as a pianist. By 1881 he had managed to migrate to northern Europe and settle in Paris. There he frequented salons, played accompaniments and gave piano lessons, in time met the baritone Victor Maurel (already Verdi's first Iago, and subsequently the originator of Falstaff)—all while working on an ambitious operatic trilogy, à la Wagner, called *Crepusculum.* In Paris, Leoncavallo did compose a second opera, *Songe d'une nuit d'été,* based on Shakespeare, which received a private run-through. But research on his tripartite *Crepusculum*—respectively, *I Medici, Girolamo Savonarola,* and *Cesare Borgia,* whereby to glorify the Italian *Rinascimento*—preempted Leoncavallo's creative attention for six years.

Finally, in 1887, he returned to Italy with his scenarios and presented them forthwith to Ricordi. The publishing house accepted them and supplied a modest stipend to support their formal completion and composition. Within a year Leoncavallo had finished *I Medici,* only to have Ricordi renege on the promise of immediate publication and a production. For three further years Leoncavallo waited. When at length *Cavalleria* had its storied first performance, he turned in pique to Sonzogno with the proposal of a short companion opera on a similar theme—carnal passions culminating in a murder, based on an actual case heard by his father fifteen years earlier in Calabria.

Leoncavallo called this *I pagliacci* (The Clowns), as ironic a title as "Rustic Chivalry" for the squalid events of *Cavalleria*. He composed it in five months for a production at Milan's Teatro dal Verme on May 21, 1892, two years and four days after the Rome premiere of Mascagni's *Siciliano*. The occasion was a triumph, a virtual carbon of the clamor attendant upon *Cavalleria*, with the same sad denouement. Leoncavallo right away pulled out *I Medici*, but not even a production by La Scala in 1893 could save the work from failure. A similar pall settled subsequently over a production in Rome of resurrected *Chatterton*, during which period Leoncavallo was dramatizing and composing *his* version of *La Bohème* (1897). An opera based on Henry Murger's *Scènes de la vie de Bohème* had been Leoncavallo's idea originally, but Puccini cribbed it, hired two expert librettists, and beat his colleague to the stage—the Teatro Regio in Turin on February 1, 1896—with twenty months to spare. The rest is history, except to add that Leoncavallo throughout his lifetime wrote his own librettos, and the one for *La Bohème* was dramatically inept. As for the music, after Gustav Mahler conducted Leoncavallo's version commandingly in Vienna (though he despised both it and its meanly meddlesome composer), critic Eduard Hanslick summed up: "No creative force, no personality, no sense of beauty—a caricature of Italian music." As elsewhere, this "other" *Bohème* was withdrawn from the repertory after six performances, nevermore to reappear.

Including *Edipo re* (a *verismo* vehicle for Titta Ruffo, posthumously premiered in Chicago on December 13, 1920), Leoncavallo wrote eighteen operas up to his death in 1919—not including the unfinished *Tormenta* or the pastiche operetta of 1925 called *La maschera nuda,* based on sketches in Leoncavallo's legacy of errata. Yet only *I pagliacci* endures in the repertory, traditionally by now on a double bill, with *Cavalleria* as the fore piece. This worldwide coupling for three-quarters of a century has encouraged scatalogical identification, such as *Cav'n'Pag, Bread and Butter, Ham & Eggs*—to which list let me submit the further alternative of *Cavalliacci.*

The works are as dissimilar in compositional technique as in textual nuance (not to dwell on the shaky ground of taste), with Leoncavallo the more sophisticated musician but less than a vernacular librettist for the lurid events of his *vignetta. Cav'n'Pag* are nonetheless twins under the skin, fraternal if not identical. Adultery, revenge, jealousy, crimes of passion—these are the bedrock of *verismo* opera, whose true colors are black, white, and blood-red. It is, butwise, a blue-collar art form in which style and content are hidebound by sentiment's triumph over reason (even over coherence in the silliest examples), by superstitions, anti-intellectuality, political evasion (except to rake over the distant past for sensational effects), philosophical naïveté, and, at the core, a religion of lip service, habit, and clichés.

This is not to insinuate that *verismo* composers were collectively insincere or as calculating as Leoncavallo when he tailored *I pagliacci* in straw and tatters to make money, to become famous, to expedite his presumptive self-selling as Italy's heir to Wagner. Mascagni, for example, could not manage better or nobler as an artist than *Cavalleria rusticana*. Umberto Giordano somehow summoned an authentic eloquence for the best pages of *Andrea Chénier* (be as it may that his titular hero was a minor poet of *liberté, égalité, fraternité* in real life). Puccini's greatest heroines transcend the genre and were truly beloved by him, from Manon Lescaut to Liù—the latter so wholly that he could not musically transform her rival, the "purple princess" Turandot, into a passionate mortal.

Verismo opera can, often does, cause audience tears to flow past all restraints. On a lesser level of cause and effect, *verismo* can shock or titillate, for intrinsically its appeal is sensual. One is sent out of the theater pleasured rather than purged, without so much as the wry aftertaste of operatic comedy composed preeminently by Rossini and Donizetti, the Kunta Kinte and Chicken George in *verismo* opera's family tree. Indeed, if you tart the tone and bloody-up the endings of most nineteenth-century comic-opera librettos, you find yourself with viable *verismo* texts. Does, for example, the entrance of *I pagliacci* differ in essence from Dulcamara's *"Udite, udite, o rustici"* in *L'elisir d'amore*? One could almost interchange sets, even the principal singers.

By way of concluding, consider at your leisure this observation by Wystan Auden in his essay for a prestereo recording of *Cav'n'Pag* in the earlier 1950s from RCA. Albeit fond of the genre and respectful of its achievements as well as Mascagni's talent, Auden felt the need to write: "It is significant as a warning sign that the concluding line of *Cavalleria rusticana* . . . and the concluding line of *I pagliacci* . . . are spoken, not sung." He could have added, further, that Tosca does not sing but speaks: *"Muori dannato! Muori, muori, muori! . . . E avanti a lui tremava tutta Roma!"* Nor does Gianni Schicchi sing but speaks, rather, an epilogue at the end of an evening's *Il trittico*. Chilling effects, those spoken climaxes in *Cav, Pag,* and *Tosca;* and a charming effect, that spoken solicitation of applause by Schicchi.

However, when music can no longer heighten the expressive substance of a text, then opera transmutes into something other—more "realistic" perhaps, but less than the sublime artifact that three pre-*verismo* centuries of great artists, creative and executive, labored to perfect.

PENDERECKI'S *Paradise Lost*
by Speight Jenkins

Paradise Lost is a poem about the maturing of a man. That he happens to be the first man, who is called Adam, is almost incidental to the larger implications of Milton's epic saga, and though Christopher Fry's fascinating libretto to

Krzysztof Penderecki's new opera telescopes and changes some emphasis in Milton's work, the essential basis of the poem remains.

The wonder of Milton's poem is that pessimism and evil are constantly if narrowly defeated by the forces of optimism and good, a Christian viewpoint by a Christian poet. Yet as Milton wrote *Paradise Lost,* his own world was falling around him. He had believed in the Puritan Revolution which drove Charles I from power and put a military dictatorship in control of England. But after twenty years of Puritan power, with the Parliament bickering and the people sick of the pious, gray government, Milton began his poem with the royalist menace again lurking in the background. As he wrote, the Stuarts came back to England and in 1660 took over the throne in the person of Charles II. Milton feared for his life and indeed barely escaped execution.

In the final five books of *Paradise Lost,* written between 1660 and 1663, the poet really had to struggle to comprehend the ways of God to man. In a sense he was very much the same as his Adam, whose greatest virtue is never to question God no matter how rough the going becomes. After all, Adam could have railed at the Deity for letting the serpent into Eden to tempt Eve. Satan by all rights should have been contained in Hell, its great portals guarded by Sin and Death, but Satan escaped and passed all of God's guards on the way to Eve. Yet Adam never complains, and at no place does one feel that Milton did either. He does regret that men are so puerile and dishonest, but he blames their weak-nesses—which he views as some of Satan in each man—on them, not on God.

Fry, respectful always of his forebear, has in his libretto used almost exclu-sively the language of Milton, but he has made the opera more a study of Adam and Eve than does the poem, which concentrates more on heavenly and Satanic activity. Even so, there are the scene of the Devils, led by Satan, writhing in the boiling lake just after being hurled from heaven, the creation of Adam and later Eve, a few scenes between God and His Son, called Messias, a view of the unholy trinity—Satan, Death, and Sin—and also the major coup de théâtre of the whole poem. When Satan has successfully tempted Eve and returned to Hell, he is met with adulation from his fellow devils. He rises to speak to them and tells what happened. As he completes his tale, he hears, instead of cheers, a chorus of hisses, for all the demons, including Satan himself, have become snakes, writhing on the ground, their shields and spears fallen from nonexis-tent hands. In the opera the event happens at the word "bliss," and the effect should be spectacular. In the poem, of course, there is no speaking by the author in the first person and no chorus, as in the opera, in which Milton himself appears from time to time and a large chorus often praises the wonder of God.

Fry's elimination of Miltonic ideas is fascinating, if only to try to figure out the why of his choices. In Milton the figure of Jesus (or, as he is always called, The Son) is central. Although Jesus is not mentioned in the Biblical account of Adam and Eve (a short story in Genesis, swift and to the point), in Milton it is Jesus whose power and skill at arms drives Satan and his horde from heaven, who early in the poem defends man to His Father before he has sinned, and who constantly seems almost in competition with Satan. At one point Milton, speaking through an Archangel, cautions Adam (and us) not to think of the two as near-equals in war; but the temptation is great, for one seems always to be battling with the other. Indeed, many commentators have found that Milton was not very kind to God, whom he made cold, calculating, and not at all merciful, while showering his affection on the Son. It is also important in the poem that the Archangel Michael's tale of future events includes the Virgin birth and the life of Jesus. Surprisingly, Jesus hardly figures in the opera, with the introduction of Messias (Fry's name for Jesus) coming very late, after the seduction of Eve. Messias does offer himself in exchange for God's mercy toward men and later intercedes with God again for Man, but with far less weight than in Milton.

A second point in the poem not present in the opera is Milton's confusing and complicated astronomical exposition which appears on the surface to be a defense of the Ptolemaic system of the universe, or at the least a placing of earth at the center of a God-created galaxy. Fry obviously left all this out because it needlessly complicates an already complex maze of thought.

The third difference is more subtle: a raising of Eve's status to near-equality with Adam. Though Milton's Eve is sympathetically drawn, she is definitely the weaker sex, an instrument of evil for a few moments but mainly less important than Adam. Taken in a seventeenth-century framework, one can hardly be surprised that the poet created a male-ordered world with God the Father, God the Son, and Satan as central players. For one example of Fry's changes, in the poem when Eve comes to Adam holding the branch of the Tree of Knowledge from which she has already eaten some fruit, he knows exactly what she has done and is confronted with a horrible decision: to stay in Paradise alone or to disobey God out of love for his disobedient wife. He eats the fruit after making a decision to stay at her side, a very romantic choice.

In the libretto his knowledge of what might happen can be found in his second speech: "For with thee / My resolution is to die." But the overall thrust of what they both sing seems more of a gamble than in Milton: the two convince each other that God really won't kill them or hurt them if they do what he forbade them to do. Somehow the gesture is more within a modern concept of two equally intelligent adults than the vision of a man's doing what he does so that his defenseless wife will not be left alone and helpless before God's wrath.

Fry's libretto opens in medias res: after a quote from Milton we find Adam and Eve bickering after having eaten the apple. This focuses audience attention directly on the central characters of the opera, and though there is a quick switch to the flaming lake in which Satan and his fellows lie, Adam and Eve, first seen, remain central. Yet Fry, as did Milton, characterizes the fallen angels individually. Satan, perhaps because of so many opera-house hours with Gounod's *Faust,* seems to have a faint tinge of Mephistopheles's urbanity about him, but has even clearer qualities of leadership. Beelzebub is his chief of staff, ready ever to do as Satan asks, while Moloch takes on the stature of one of

Wagner's giants in the *Ring*. Moloch's words make him big, dumb, and brutal. Belial is a bit cowardly, while Mammon has a predictable interest in gold. All are eager in a very human way to outfox God in easier terrain than in Heaven. And when the corruption of man is suggested, all are enthusiastic. In the libretto there is a moment when Milton as speaker decries the harmony between Devils and the enmity among men of supposedly good conscience. Although the observation could relate to our own—or any—era, in Milton's mouth it represents his sadness at the destruction of the power of Parliament by the smallness of its members' vision.

The first big dramatic scene in the opera is duplicated in the poem. Adam and Eve are found happy in Paradise, and by their comments they let the Devil hear their happiness and that they are forbidden to eat from the Tree of Knowledge. The truncated words of Satan in the opera do not disguise his envy of their joy, and when he is later caught by angels while whispering into Eve's ear, similar operatic scenes dart to mind. So did Mephistopheles entice the flowers to charm Marguerite, and so did Telramund and Ortrud whisper doubts about Lohengrin into the ears of Elsa.

Adam and Eve, along with all heroes in Greek epics, are warned of danger by a higher power, in this case the Archangel Raphael. The operatic warning is a new touch by Fry. In the poem Eve's function is to fix a lunch for Raphael and Adam preparatory to the Archangel's discourse, at Wagnerian-plus length, to Adam on the dangers of Satan. In the opera she has no lunch to fix, and Raphael warns both, succinctly and together. When she decides to go off by herself on her fatal walk in which she meets the disguised Satan, Adam sends her off with a wise warning: "Within ourself the danger lies." To Milton, Satan lives, not outside, but in the very essence of our beings.

The conquest of Eve by Satan, the Devil's short-lived triumph, and Jesus' (or Messias') offering to serve as a Saviour for mankind pass in quick review; and then Fry moves the libretto to the interview with the Archangel Michael, which comprises most of the final two books of Milton's poem. As in the poem, the operatic Adam and Eve summon Michael by prayers of contrition, and as in the poem, the angel first outlines to Adam (not to Eve, who is sent off to take a nap) the murderous assault of one of his yet-to-be-born sons against the other and all the tragedies down to and including the flood. Adam naturally bewails all the horrors, and Michael—without sketching further history as in the poem—tells Adam "learn/obedience to the law of God,/that to obey is best."

Adam muses that if there need be so many laws, so many sins are thereby suggested. And Michael answers, "The law of God . . . thou shalt fulfill/Both by obedience and by love/Though love alone/Fulfill the law." In the poem these words are used by the Archangel to refer to the love of Jesus and His saving power for mankind, and the quote is subtly, vitally different. Milton uses "He" in place of "Thou" and so specifically talks of Jesus, not man. But Adam's reaction in both works is the same. When he hears these words about love, Adam goes into what may well be the crucial point to both Milton and Fry: "Yet full of doubt I stand,/Whether I should repent . . . now/Of sin by me done,/or rejoice/much more that much more good/Thereof shall spring." Even without the knowledge of Christ's coming and Resurrection, Fry's Adam sees that the power of Love will make man's life meaningful and wonders if he has not done well by having eaten the forbidden fruit.

As the Archangel then suggests, when Eve and Adam leave Paradise, they have "a Paradise within . . . happier far," and the two—or at least Adam—is proclaimed an adult, matured through sorrow and tribulation, prepared to seek his future secure in the knowledge of the power of love.

The Making of Paradise Lost
by Gregory Speck

In commemoration of the nation's two-hundredth birthday, Carol Fox and the Lyric Opera of Chicago wanted to offer a special contribution to the Bicentennial celebration. As early as 1972, plans were being formulated for the development of a major new opera to be presented during the 1976 season. The purpose of commissioning the work was to provide an original addition to the permanent opera repertory, not one that might disappear after the American anniversary festivities had subsided, but one that could claim a lasting significance as well as an international appeal. Toward this goal, it was determined that the theme of the opera should be drawn from either the history of the United States or the universal condition of man.

Before any steps could be taken toward the commissioning of a full-scale opera, substantial financial support had to be found. James C. Hemphill, Lyric's faithful Board leader and benefactor of numerous productions—*Madama Butterfly* (1970), *Tosca* (1971), *La Bohème* (1972), *Manon* (1973), *Don Pasquale* (1974), *The Love for Three Oranges* (1976), *Manon Lescaut* (1977), and in cooperation with Mr. and Mrs. Lee A. Freeman, *Un ballo in maschera* (1972), and *Otello* (1975)—once again extended his gracious patronage. Although Mr. Hemphill did not live to see the fruit of his sponsorship, his memory is very much with those who endeavored for the six years it took to realize the production which he made possible.

Miss Fox's aspirations for the occasion demanded a composer of the first order. Benjamin Britten, Gian Carlo Menotti, Hans Werner Henze, Luigi Dallapiccola, and others were considered for the enterprise, but Krzysztof Penderecki, widely regarded as the pre-eminent creator of modern music, seemed the ideal choice to Carol Fox and Bruno Bartoletti, Lyric's artistic director and conductor of the nascent piece, for the enormous task of writing a bold yet serious score. Penderecki's earlier compositions reflected a profound interest in humanitarian causes (*Threnody in Memory of the Victims of Hiroshima,* 1961, and *Dies Irae,* 1967, dedicated to the victims of Auschwitz) as well as in theological subjects (*The Passion According to St. Luke,* 1966, and *Utrenja,* comprising *The Entombment of Christ,* which premiered in 1970 at Altenberg Cathedral, and *The Resurrection of Christ,* 1971, Münster Cathedral). His two operas, *The Devils of Loudun,* based on John Whiting's dramatization of Aldous Huxley's account of witchcraft, exorcism, and sexual hysteria in baroque France, and the unfinished *Ubu Roi,* inspired by the French playwright Alfred Jarry's Dada farce, suggested Penderecki's taste for secular avant-garde literature as a source for his musical creations. Further, his 1972 oratorio *Kosmogonia,* commissioned for the twentyfifth anniversary of the United Nations, expressed the composer's concern for metaphysical speculation in a futuristic world, where man dares to confront and explore the fundamental questions of time, space, and eternity. Certainly Penderecki was a man whose entire oeuvre prepared him for the assignment.

Miss Fox initiated trans-Atlantic telephone conversations with Maestro Penderecki in his native Cracow toward the end of November, 1972. By January, 1973, she had flown to Milan for a meeting with him, and in April of that same year, Mr. Penderecki arrived with his wife Elzbieta in Chicago, where he signed the contract.

Later that spring, Sam Wanamaker, the noted actor and stage director, was engaged as régisseur. Mr. Penderecki had once entertained the notion of writing an opera based on the sweeping Russian saga *Ivan the Terrible,* and Mr. Wanamaker had hoped to direct a new version of Homer's epic poem *The Odyssey.* Thus, when they met in Cracow in June, 1974, their discussions about Lyric's project touched upon monumental works, including such classics of Western literature as Dante's *La divina commedia* and Milton's *Paradise Lost,* both of which explored two subjects that had long intrigued the composer: The Creation and the Apocalypse. For Penderecki, *Paradise Lost* presented the additional opportunity to create a major work for an English libretto, after having previously written scores for Greek, Latin, Italian, French, German, and Russian texts. Subsequent meetings between them took place that year in Salzburg, Madrid, and London. Through Mr. Wanamaker's efforts, the famed British poet and dramatist Christopher Fry was enticed to fashion a libretto after Milton's difficult, powerful verse. By late summer of 1974, Mr. Fry had set about selecting and adapting passages from the immense seventeenth-century masterpiece (nearly twelve thousand lines spanning a dozen separate books), attempting to retain the flavor and style of the Puritan poet's blank verse, while fusing the dignity and grandeur of his vision with the subtlety and lyricism appropriate to an operatic setting.

A working libretto reached both the composer and the Lyric by May, 1975. At that point the celebrated Czech stage designer Josef Svoboda, after months of communication and negotiation, arrived in Chicago for meetings about the scenery for the spectacle. John Butler, at the forefront of contemporary choreographers, was invited to create the dance passages which would dramatize the sections of Milton's magnum opus deleted in Mr. Fry's libretto.

Mr. Penderecki was then teaching composition on a visiting lectureship at the University of Florida in Tallahassee. It was there, in the Sunshine State, that the first notes of *Paradise Lost* were written, with the expectation that they would lead to a *sacra rappresentazione* (a theatrically oriented, allegorically derived musical presentation popularized in the early seventeenth century by Emilio del Cavaliere; its versatile form facilitates performance in concert halls and cathedrals as well as in opera houses). He continued to develop the score in Cracow that summer, and later as visiting professor at Yale during the fall and winter. By February, 1976, however, Maestro Penderecki came to realize that the topic was too vast for the standard oratorio form and that as a full-scale opera it would demand much more time than remained, if the fall 1976 production deadline were to be observed. In order to do justice to a work of the magnitude he had come to envision, he requested an extension, to which Miss Fox agreed, with the provision that the completed score be received in time for a fall 1978 premiere. This respite from the constant drain on his creative energies permitted the composer to gain the distance he needed to refocus his thoughts and acquire fresh insight into the subject. With that in mind, even though only one-third of the score had been completed, he turned his attention to various conducting engagements in Canada, London, and Japan; in retrospect, the composer today avows that this release from the pressure to "create" fostered a necessary regeneration of his productive faculties.

One of Mr. Penderecki's most productive *Paradise Lost* periods came during a summer vacation in a Baltic Sea resort village by the name of Jastrzebia Gora, which translates to "The Hawk's Mountain." Later, in pursuit of the muses on a visit to Rome, he heard an unusual noise. He hurriedly dressed, then ran from his hotel room out into the night, in search of the enchanting sound. On the Piazza Navona he located a group of children twirling "instruments" in the air. The sound they produced was perfect for the children's choir in *Paradise Lost,* he decided, so the "sonars" made their debut on an American opera stage. His most memorable experience in composing the score took place in Israel. Aware that his own conception of how God might speak to Adam was inadequate, Penderecki ventured to Jerusalem, feeling that if there were any place on earth to find the solution to his dilemma, it would surely be in the cradle of occidental religion. One evening he attended a sacred ceremony of the ancient Samaritan sect, which today numbers only a few hundred. The vocal tones that formed their ritual became the basis for certain musical motifs in *Paradise Lost.*

In September, 1977, a working score was at last finished, though polishing and minor rewriting continued through 1978. By this time, Messrs. Wanamaker and Svoboda, who had been contracted on the basis of a 1976 opening, had gone on to other commitments, and Virginio Puecher, who had directed several productions for the company, including *Wozzeck* (1965), *The Angel of Fire* (1966), *Salome,* (1968), and *Les Contes d'Hoffmann* (1976), assumed the responsibilities of régisseur. Later, Miss Fox announced that she had regretfully accepted the resignation of Mr. Puecher as a result of areas of disagreement between him and the composer of the new work. Subsequently, staging was assigned to Igal Perry. Ezio Frigerio, who had designed the successful Lyric productions of *Don Pasquale* (1974) and *Les Contes d'Hoffmann* (1976), became artistic consultant for both the elaborate scenery and the striking wardrobe for all the angels, devils, and other citizens of the heights and depths. During February, 1976, Robert Page, director of the Cleveland Orchestra Chorus, was offered the position of chorus master, which would involve nine months of rehearsal, beginning in March, 1978, with one hundred thirty supporting singers.

When Mr. Penderecki returned to Yale in the fall of 1977, he brought a piano reduction, which his staff of fifteen years had prepared for him in Poland, where he serves as chancellor of the Music Academy at the University of Cracow. B. Schott Söhne of Mainz, Maestro Penderecki's publishers, followed with the orchestral and choral scores, and the scenery, built in Europe, was shipped to Chicago. Ten long moving vans were required to transport Heaven and Hell to the opera house, and the parked procession extended for four blocks along Wacker Drive.

Finally, in August, 1978, Miss Fox convened a meeting at Maestro Bartoletti's villa outside Florence. The entire artistic leadership of *Paradise Lost,* including composer, conductor, stage director, set and costume designer, choreographer, and ballet director, as well as several key members of the cast, arrived to commence the last chapter in the development of their opera. Since the production was conceived in conjunction with Teatro alla Scala, Milan, representatives of Italy's leading opera house were also present to finalize plans for the January 23, 1979, European premiere. Rehearsals for the principal roles began in earnest in Chicago in mid October and required six weeks of intensive work, a record for the company, which celebrated its twenty-fifth anniversary the next year.

Paradise Lost represents not only a milestone in the history of Lyric Opera but also a daring reappraisal of one of the immortal achievements of Western civilization, which rarely, if ever, in the twentieth century, has received the attention it warrants. While other classics of our literary heritage are frequently reborn in theatrical, balletic, cinematic, and operatic interpretations, Milton's greatest contribution to our culture has been left to a silent reverence, a sphinx among our arts and letters, respected but unknown. This foray into our past may even engender a renaissance of those few works of art which have played an integral role in the shaping of our conception of life.

Paradise Lost, in the dimension and scale of its production requirements, as

Carol Fox stated, "is Aïda three times over." Perhaps history repeats itself as well, for that grandest of Italian operas was not actually produced until 1871, also two years after the date for which it was originally planned.

WAGNER'S *Parsifal*
by Stephanie von Buchau

Because Richard Wagner's *Parsifal* is such a complex artistic entity, a program note such as this can only scratch the surface of its many entanglements. To save space, then, I have divided the discussion into arbitrary sections—Genesis and Composition, First Performances, Sources, Religious Mythology, Music and Character, and The Influence of *Parsifal*. These aspects of the opera are all related, but it will be up to the reader to make the connections.

Genesis and Composition

In 1843, when he was just thirty years old, Richard Wagner wrote a choral oratorio called *Das Liebesmahl der Apostel* or *The Love Feast of the Apostles,* i.e., the Last Supper. In 1845, while recuperating from the effects of composing *Tannhäuser,* he visited the spa of Marienbad, where he took for reading material the poems of Wolfram von Eschenbach, who just happened to be a character in *Tannhäuser.*

This medieval epic was called *Parzival,* and it concerned the knights of the Holy Grail. Wagner tells us in *My Life,* "With the book under my arm hid myself in the neighboring wood and seated by a brook, feasted myself on Titurel and Parzival in Wolfram's strange yet intimately appealing poem." The confluence of these two disparate events—the composition of the Christian oratorio and the discovery of Eschenbach's chivalrous *Parzival*—would result, thirty-seven years later, in the creation of Wagner's last work, the opera *Parsifal.*

One can see that questions of religious ethics and mythology—though of a distinctly original cast—concerned Wagner in the intervening years. In 1849 he wrote a sketch for a drama, *Jesus of Nazareth.* In 1854, drawing up the plan for an opera, *Tristan und Isolde,* he suggested including Parsifal in the third act. "Tristan, ill from his wound and unable to die, had become identified in my mind with Amfortas of the Grail legend."

That unwieldy idea dispensed with, in 1856 he sketched a Buddhist drama, *Die Sieger* (The Victors), of all the unrealized Wagnerian projects perhaps the most tantalizing. Finally, in 1857, in Zürich, he made the first attempt at a

Parzival sketch (now lost). He was still spelling it "Parzival" at that time; from now on we will use the final spelling for all references to the title character of Eschenbach's and Wagner's dramas. (In any case, etymology was not Wagner's strong suit. He told Judith Gautier, French poet Théophile Gautier's daughter, that the name Parsifal came from the Arabic "parsi" meaning pure and "fal" meaning fool. Gautier, who was as intelligent as she was beautiful, immediately consulted a scholar who pointed out that there are no such words in Arabic.)

Further prose sketches were written in 1865 and 1877, and the poem (the actual text) was completed in April of 1877. Under the influence of a one-sided romantic involvement with Gautier, Wagner began to compose at white heat. The creative work was done in two years—from August, 1877, to April, 1879. A further thirty months were required, some of them spent in Italy, for the composer to finish the orchestral score. Because he had promised it to his wife, Cosima, as a birthday present, the final page of *Parsifal* is dated 25 December 1881. The actual scoring was not finished until 13 January 1882.

First Performances

Before *Parsifal* was even begun, Wagner had opened his dream theater at Bayreuth with a full performance of *Der Ring des Nibelungen* (1876), an undertaking that lost over $60,000, an enormous sum in those days. No further performances were given at Bayreuth until the premiere of *Parsifal,* 26 July 1882. Wagner subtitled his opera "Bühnenweihfestspiel," which is variously translated as "sacred festival drama" or "stage-consecrating festival play." It was so close to the composer's heart that he was crushed when his patron, Ludwig II of Bavaria, was unable to visit Bayreuth for the premiere.

The stage pictures alternately pleased and annoyed the composer. The magnificent temple of the Grail was based by the Russian painter, Paul von Joukowsky, on the great cathedral at Siena, which Wagner had seen on his Italian sojourn during the scoring of *Parsifal.* It was so successful that it existed at Bayreuth until 1934. The Flowermaidens scene, on the other hand, was marred by garish colors and too realistic action.

Wagner apparently fell in love with one of the comely Flowermaidens and began to loudly "Bravo!" her appearances. The end of Act II was greeted by prolonged applause as the audience wished the artists to take a bow. Wagner came to the front of his box and made a short speech about the inadvisability of "breaking the spell." From this little speech grew the century-old controversy over when, and when not, to applaud at *Parsifal.* It has become the custom to greet the first act with silence and to applaud at the other two; but this was not Wagner's intention. In fact, confused by the Meister's speech, the audience withheld its applause after the third act, until Wagner himself led them on by clapping loudly. "Now I don't know," he complained, "did the audience like it or not?"

On 29 August, the day of the final performance, Wagner slipped into the covered orchestra pit during the third act and took the baton from Hermann

Levi at the twenty-third bar of the Transformation music, conducting the rest of the work himself. Levi, who had had his troubles with Wagner, as we shall see, reported to his father that the final applause beggared description. When silence finally reigned, Wagner began to speak, from the conductor's stand, to the orchestra. He spoke, Levi wrote, "with such warmth and sincerity that everybody began to weep. It was an unforgettable moment."

Although Wagner's contract with Ludwig called for the Royal Opera in Munich to have access to his new works, the composer wished to keep *Parsifal* solely for Bayreuth. "I believe," he wrote to Ludwig, "that anyone who loves me will not grudge my right to keep this one last work of mine from the rough paws of my comrades-in-art and from the cawing of that polymorphous monster, our audiences and the public at large." Ludwig insisted, and a few performances of the opera took place in Munich. Thereafter, the "Bayreuth copyright" was supposed to be in effect, barring other opera houses from performing the work until December, 1913. However, the Metropolitan Opera performed *Parsifal* in 1903, in defiance of the edict, as did Chicago in 1913.

Sources

While the opera *Parsifal* uses Wolfram von Eschenbach as its main source, Wagner needed to do a lot of compressing, rethinking, and collating before he could create a coherent drama out of a sprawling mediaeval epic poem. Anglo-Saxon readers are familiar with the Grail story and its Christian symbolism from Malory's *Le Morte d'Arthur* and Tennyson's *Idylls of the King,* but they are far removed from the French and German originals. In the Anglo-Saxon versions, Gawain and Lancelot are the heroes, and Parsifal is relegated to a supporting role.

The first great artistic treatment of the Parsifal story was written by the French mediaeval poet Chrétien de Troyes (circa 1180). Whatever legends Chrétien created his work from are lost in antiquity. The basic story, however, is fixed in all its subsequent versions. A young knight, Parsifal, is given hospitality at a castle where an old king suffers from an unhealable wound. Because the boy keeps silent—as he has been taught to do—he fails to release the king from his suffering.

Chrétien died before finishing the tale, which Eschenbach completed in the thirteenth century, probably using as his sources old Celtic legends and de-nouncing Chrétien's version as ill-told. The climax of Wolfram's story offered the final inspiration to Wagner, for Parsifal, after wandering in guilt for many years, is granted the grace to refind the mysterious castle and to ask the fateful question: "Uncle, what ails thee?" At that point the old king is cured, and Parsifal is named king in his stead.

As one can see, here is just the bare bones of what Wagner finally wrought. For one thing, the simple asking of a courteous question is hardly enough upon which to base a theatrical climax. For another, though a spear and an object known as "the Grail" are present in Eschenbach's story, they have no religious significance. It was Wagner's leap of faith, if you will, that added the dramatic features which have caused incredible controversy in the ensuing years since the composition of *Parsifal*.

Religious Mythology

As we have seen, the Parsifal of Chrétien and Eschenbach is a character of chivalrous origin. His alteration into the central figure of an opera that has been described (inaccurately) as "a Catholic Mass" comes about because Wagner needed to strengthen and dramatize the original story, to give it resonances, and because his own sense of the religious—while not at all what the sentimental nineteenth century might have suspected—encompassed an ethical framework that becomes the literal subject of the opera *Parsifal*.

In her introduction to Herbert von Karajan's recording of *Parsifal*, Lucy Beckett points out that the specifically Christian framework of *Parsifal* has had unfortunate critical consequences. Wagner was accused of subverting religion in order to make a theatrical show. Nietzsche thought the opera revealed a lapse into sentimental religiosity. Eduard Hanslick, the Viennese critic who was pilloried by Wagner as Beckmesser in *Die Meistersinger,* found the work a "distasteful exploitation of nostalgia for outmoded materialist Catholicism." Thomas Mann thought that the Christian element in the piece was false and that it tricked the audience into elevating a virtuoso exercise in psychopathology, leading eventually to proto-Nazi racial theory. Many listeners simply label *Parsifal* anti-Semitic.

This is not the place, nor do we have the space, to argue these theories. What we can do is try to explain how Wagner used specific Christian symbolism and how his version of it differs from actual (or imagined) Catholic orthodoxy. First we must examine the main Wagnerian alterations of Eschenbach's story: the Christianization of the Grail and the Spear.

The etymology of the word "Grail" is very complicated. It possibly comes from *"sangue réale"* or "holy blood" of the Savior, the words being elided into "Grail." Or it possibly comes from the old French *"graal"* for "cup." (One can see from these two examples how difficult the problem is.) In any case, in Eschenbach, the Grail is not a cup at all; it is a magic stone which has the power to feed and quench the thirst of any number of knights. In other words, like the loaves and the fishes, here is a budding Christian symbol, though Eschenbach seems unaware of its potential. It was a small step for Wagner to associate this magic stone with the sacred chalice used at the Last Supper.

With this same cup, Joseph of Arimathea is supposed to have caught the blood of the dying Christ. Consequently it is a relic of great holiness. In most stories of the Grail, the knights are searching for the object. In *Parsifal,* the old king Titurel has it secure at his castle, Montsalvat, from which the Grail-consecrated knights go forth to do battle with evil.

The Spear, which in Eschenbach is just a spear (prefiguring Freud's witty, "Sometimes a cigar is just a cigar"), in Wagner becomes that Spear with which the Roman soldier Longinus pierced the Savior's side as He hung on the Cross. This Spear is also a sacred relic kept at Montsalvat until Amfortas goes forth one day, carrying it, to do battle with an evil knight who once sought and was refused entry to the brotherhood of the Grail. Klingsor, the evil one, tempts Amfortas with Kundry, and while the knight is dallying in Kundry's arms, Klingsor steals the Spear, wounds Amfortas with it, and retires to his castle in possession of the holy object. When he tries, at the end of Act II, to wound Parsifal in the same manner, the young man, who has just refused Kundry's temptations, simply takes the Spear away from him and destroys his kingdom.

Parsifal's refusal of carnal love is another aspect of the opera which confuses today's sexually liberated listeners. To us it seems like a denial of G.B. Shaw's "life force." In fact, Wagner gained from Schopenhauer, perhaps imperfectly, a sense of sexual love as an all-encompassing "will to life" which, being transcended, brought the transcender power and peace. Far from being a sick sexual repression, transcendence of mind over body is the central precept of most of the world's great religions—eastern as well as Christian. The main ethical preoccupation of *Parsifal* is with a character who grows in knowledge, precisely by denying himself, from a "pure fool" to the "redeemer of the Redeemer."

The charges that Wagner vandalized Christian mythology for stage purposes stem from a basic misunderstanding about Wagner's attitude toward orthodox religion. Fundamental Christian doctrine shows a contempt for the theater that couldn't be further from Wagner's Attic acceptance of theater as a reflection of life. Wagner looked at religion from a philosopher's viewpoint. He once wrote, "It is for art to salvage the nucleus of religion by appropriating its mythical symbols."

As for overt anti-Semitism in *Parsifal,* there is none in the libretto unless one extrapolates it from the fact that Christianity has been historically anti-Semitic. Most of the objections to *Parsifal* rise from a priori knowledge that Wagner himself was a virulent anti-Semite, writing and speaking frequently about the imagined evils of Judaism in music. On the other hand, Wagner's anti-Semitism also seems to have been highly selective. Three of his Bayreuth favorites—Karl Tausig, Hermann Levi, and Samuel Lehrs—were Jews, and Levi conducted the first Bayreuth performances of *Parsifal.*

Levi, the son of a rabbi, was often harangued by the composer about his religion; Wagner even suggested that the conductor be baptized before he led *Parsifal.* The offended Levi departed but was brought back by a penitent letter from Wagner which contained the significant phrase: "Do not lose any of your *faith* [italics mine], but gain the courage to go on with it. Perhaps it will be the turning point in your life, but in any event you are my conductor for *Parsifal.*"

How does one reconcile these contradictory sides of a megalomaniac such as Wagner often seemed to be? Frankly, I don't see any possibility of reconciliation. The best that one can do is try not to be blinded by one's own biases to the point where reaction to the actual music suffers. Even Levi, who had reason to be bitter, pointed out to his disapproving father: "Wagner is not just narrow-mindedly anti-Semitic. . . . The most wonderful thing I have experienced in my life is the privilege of being close to such a man, and I thank God for it every day."

Characters and Music

There are five main characters in the opera, four of them active, one—Gurnemanz—purely receptive. Parsifal suffers from primal guilt on two counts: one, his abrupt departure in search of knightly adventure which caused the death of his mother, Herzeleide; and two, his refusal to understand the actions that take place before him in the temple of the Grail, i.e., his lack of compassion for Amfortas. Clearly, a character with these sins on his conscience is going to have to suffer long trials before he can attain wisdom.

Kundry is an interesting mixture of Christian and Buddhist antecedents. Possibly Wagner equates her with Herodias, the tempter of John the Baptist. (Although that is confusing the issue, because in the final act, it is possible to see Kundry as the Magdalene, Parsifal as Christ, and Gurnemanz as the Baptist. All this proves is that too much reliance on linear logic is anathema to understanding Wagner.) Kundry tells us that she mocked Christ on His way to the Cross and has been cursed to live forever unless she can be redeemed. Her redemption lies in service (the only two words she speaks in the last act are "Dienen, dienen"), and in the refusal of the pure knight (Parsifal) to succumb to her temptations.

Kundry's reincarnation throughout the centuries is a Buddhist concept—Wagner had intended to write his Buddhist drama, *Die Sieger,* after he finished *Parsifal*—but her sexual allure is strictly nineteenth-century European—a century on the edge of Freud's monumental theories. Kundry is a composite of several characters appearing in Eschenbach's poem, and her complexity is such that her arguments in Act II are almost impossible to follow logically. One has to allow the music to fill in the gaps.

Amfortas is a figure based on a Celtic pagan character, the Fisher King, who is mentioned by T.S. Eliot and in Sir Michael Tippett's opera *The Midsummer Marriage.* If we see the Parsifal legend as a pagan one—a kind of fertility rite in which the decline of winter and the awakening of spring are symbolized by the healing of a sick king, we can see how the Christian and the folk elements of the story intermingle. In most legends, the king's wound is in the groin—i.e., the seat of regeneration—but Wagner, perhaps out of Victorian prudishness or perhaps out of the need to connect Amfortas's wound with that of Christ—seems to indicate that the king has been struck in the side.

In Eschenbach, Klingsor is a peripheral figure, a magician who has been unmanned by the husband of a queen with whom Klingsor was committing adultery. Wagner's fresh dramatic idea—to set Klingsor up in primary opposition to Montsalvat and the Grail brotherhood—is a masterful one. Since Klingsor is a knight who once sought entrance to the brotherhood, only to be denied because of his sinful life, we can see him as the Lucifer figure, the fallen angel who failed to live up to God's rules.

Leaving the characters who populate the opera, we come to the miracle itself—Wagner's finest, most craftsmanlike, most organized, most schematic score. The harmonic progress from the third-act Prelude to the radiant A-flat major of the finale involves, as critic David Hamilton points out, "telling metamorphoses of the opera's most important thematic material, including the familiar Dresden Amen representing the Grail itself, the upward fifth of the Pure Fool prophecy, the four ascending notes symbolizing the Holy Spear, and the music of the Love Feast of the Grail that will be familiar to listeners from the opening measures of the opera."

Other felicities involve the use of what biographer Curt von Westernhagen calls "that mysterious, impersonal blend of strings and woodwind, with the addition of the characteristically dry sound of a pianissimo trumpet," for the Last Supper theme; arpeggios in the strings which "create a gentle glow, which Wagner liked to compare to the gold background of the mosaics in St. Mark's"; the structural blocks of the opening Prelude, which Wagner labeled "Love—Faith—Hope?" for the elucidation of Ludwig II, but which are in fact purely musical entities; and the way the composer holds complete mastery over the diatonic harmonies of the Grail brotherhood and the more sensuous chromaticisms of Klingsor's garden.

Nietzsche, who by the time of the *Parsifal* premiere was estranged from his former soul mate, wrote the following after he heard a concert performance of the *Parsifal* Act I Prelude in Monte Carlo in 1887: "From a purely aesthetic aspect, did Wagner ever produce anything better? A sublime and extraordinary feeling, experience, spiritual happening at the heart of the music does Wagner the greatest credit: a synthesis of emotional states which many people would consider incompatible; music imbued with judicial severity, with sublimity, and in an awesome sense of the word, with a cognizance and perception, and with compassion for what is seen and judged. . . . Did ever a painter portray so melancholy a loving gaze as Wagner does with the final accents of his Prelude?"

The Influence of Parsifal

Wagnerisme dominated French literature and music from the 1880s on. Verlaine wrote a sonnet about *Parsifal* which was later quoted in T.S. Eliot's *The Waste Land* (along with four other Wagnerian quotes). Claude Debussy was so strongly under the influence of Wagner when composing *Pelléas et Mélisande* that he wrote to Ernest Chausson, another Wagnerite, that he kept having to tear up pages of his score because "the ghost of old Klingsor [a popular nickname for Wagner] would appear at the turning of one of the bars."

In England, literature was never the same after *Parsifal*. Directly influenced were Virginia Woolf, who had heard the opera at Bayreuth and who wrote a novel called *The Waves* in which one of the characters is named Percival; Joseph Conrad, whose novella *A Smile of Fortune* paraphrases *Parsifal*'s second act, with the seductive Alice Jacobus giving the hero a climactic kiss in her father's romantic garden; and E.M. Forster, another Bayreuth devotee, whose *A Passage to India* not only uses Wagnerian leitmotivs as part of its structural apparatus but also includes an innocent's quest for enlightenment—though the outcome of Emiss Esmoor's quest is hardly Wagnerian.

In music, there is the prime English Wagnerian, Sir Edward Elgar, who loved only one opera—*Parsifal*—and in his choral masterpiece *The Dream of Gerontius* combined Catholic and musical symbolism to express the inexpressible: the passage of the soul to its higher reward after the sufferings of earthly existence.

It would take a whole volume to detail all the Wagnerian resonances in our culture—from music and literature to films by Ken Russell, Eric Rohmer, and Hans Jürgen Syberberg—just as it would take a lengthy book to explore fully all the surrounding philosophical, musical, and religious aspects of this great score. But we need not know more about it than our ears can tell us.

DEBUSSY'S *Pelléas et Mélisande*

by Ernest Ansermet

In trying to understand *Pelléas et Mélisande* the starting point should be Claude Debussy himself, rather than any notion about musical drama, for as a musical drama, this work is the only one of its kind. But when we begin to review what we know about Debussy, we realize how little he explained what he was doing. On the subject of his technique he has said precisely nothing, and about his aesthetic intentions he has spoken only evasively or in epigrams, often bordering on the ironical, although, in his conversation with M. Croche, he has revealed his inclinations, his likes and dislikes, and although a sudden confession may have escaped him, as in this phrase from a letter to a friend: "My music is made to mix with beings and things of good will."

There nevertheless stands out from Debussy's work one essential characteristic: his unfailing ability to express a musical idea in the freshest and most direct terms, without bothering to develop it thematically as the classicists did, and without letting it run away with him as the romantics delighted in doing. This need of direct expression—of expression which is, so to speak, continually in a state of conception—implies a constant fund of sensibility which is seen in a maximum of liberty in melodic behavior and harmonic formation. But it implies also an unceasing expressive fullness which is the reason for Debussy's harmonic refinement and which helps us to understand this moving admission, found in another of his letters: "How much one must invent and then sacrifice in order to reach the bare flesh of emotion"—it is precisely of this that *Pelléas* was to be made.

Such an art is pure lyricism, and this is why it makes an irresistible appeal to an image or to a poetic idea. What, indeed, is musical emotion, if it is not the awakening in us, by a musical (melodic, harmonic, or rhythmic) fact, of a human significance, expressed precisely by this image or by this idea? It is, then, in this significance and in its transcendent radiance that the musical fact finds its raison d'être and the motive for its pursuance. Here, we touch upon the second essential characteristic of Debussy's music: that faculty of linking one fact to another with a logic belonging to the musical idea which has been awakened, and of thus producing a dialectic which, proceeding only from the free expansion of the idea, never becomes a rhetoric. Each of Debussy's works creates its own form—a form that results only from the accomplishment of the movement of an idea born of the musical data.

The first flowers of this art were the *Prélude à l'après-midi d'un faune* and the song cycle *Ariettes oubliées*. It was shortly after producing these works, in 1892, that Debussy made the acquaintance of Maurice Maeterlinck's play *Pelléas et Mélisande* and immediately saw, in its musical setting, the great breadth of design which appealed to his creative vocation. The accomplishment of the design occupied him—in the fullest sense of the term—for ten years, and this means that he lived *Pelléas* in giving it life, the amplitude of the task bringing about a testing and self-disclosure of the full extent of his resources and his powers. Maeterlinck's play is in inspiration "symbolist," by which we understand simply that the situations and conflicts which he presents have a general character which leads us either implicitly or directly or intuitively to our own experiences. The mediaeval atmosphere, the vaguely feudal and Nordic setting from which the characters emerge, only reinforces this generality: it is a means of dating and localizing events which removes any reality from both place and period. The words are the most direct, sometimes the most common expression of the situations, as if to emphasize by their extreme transparency the drama that underlies them. The characters, too, are quite transparent, exclusively occupied with their inner lives, which are revealed to us by their behavior and their speech. "Each one is so well characterized," said Louis Laloy, "that one could give the lie to none of them: they are as they are, and would be incapable of other actions or of conceiving other thoughts; the harm which they do each other springs from their nature: hence the poignant emotion of the work, and its deep pathos." If these few remarks have sufficiently revealed the character of Debussy's art, it will be realized that his music could make of this drama—which is precisely one about "beings of good will"—a poignant work. For in the literary drama the characters appear like figures in a tapestry, the quasifutility of their conversation hardly lending body to their character or warmth to their actions. The music takes up the drama from within, confers on the characters an effective covering of flesh, and infuses into their words an expressive intensity hitherto unsuspected. From this point of view, the musical drama of *Pelléas et Mélisande* is a true re-creation of the literary drama. If Debussy conceived his work as a lyric drama, it is because he wished to make felt in its continuity and unity the pressure of feeling which carries the drama from the beginning to the end. He had the secret of this art from Wagner—the Wagner of *Tristan* and of *Parsifal* —and his creation definitely has certain traces of the style of these works, but differently handled. For Debussy's music aims only at expression; Wagner's music aims at explaining and convincing. In Debussy we find a moderation which in no way excludes vigor, but which is everywhere apparent. Thus, the orchestral pattern is symphonic in style but does not constitute a symphony, so that the melodic elements remain distinct and free. The voice, which together with the instruments contributes to this *melos,* participates in this liberty; it is not bound in the symphony, as with Wagner; it is not subjected to the *melos,* as with the Italians; Debussy can devote himself to giving the words their true musical expression—and this he does with an accuracy and freedom of accent previously unknown in French music and found since then only in Ravel. With this style of singing, which is at once recitative and melody, Debussy unconsciously realized the ideal of the Italian Renaissance, which had been known as *stile rappresentativo*. Since Monteverdi, Moussorgsky alone had discovered its secret, and it is doubtless from him that Debussy learned it. By virtue of the symphonic style, Debussy was able to preserve the *stile rappresentativo* throughout, yet was never prevented from blossoming forth into real melody in the two or three places where he felt the necessity for it. This continuous lyric *melos,* so free and so varied, is unified by a few essential motifs which are themselves expressions of typical traits in the characters: Mélisande's innocent charm, the youthful instability of Pelléas, Golaud's anxious impatience. These are not, properly speaking, "leitmotifs," for they are never raised to the status of "themes" but vary according to the situations in which they appear. The melody ceaselessly springs from these motifs, in the same way as the drama depends upon the characteristic traits that they express.

This work is definitely revealed, then, from the impression of it which we have gained, as a spontaneous creation in the realm of the musical theater; this is why it represents a type of work which is still novel and apparently unique, but which realizes at once that miracle which the musical theater has always tried to produce as its highest ideal: the perfect identification of a musical essence with its poetic substance.

BRITTEN's *Peter Grimes*
by Dorothy Samachson

On June 7, 1945, the Sadler's Wells Theatre presented the world premiere of *Peter Grimes,* an opera by Benjamin Britten. Britten had already achieved an enviable reputation at home and abroad as one of England's most gifted and prolific composers, and his compositions included piano pieces, symphonic works, concertos, chamber music, songs, choral works, and even an operetta, *Paul Bunyan,* to a text by W.H. Auden.

Britten had not, however, essayed an opera. Opera, which has been the graveyard of so many hopeful composers, makes exceptional demands. Native musical talent is, of course, essential; but writing an opera also requires sophisticated craftsmanship, with the ability to combine voices, orchestra, libretto, and dramatic action. Such creation takes time, and a composer needs a certain financial security to enable him to concentrate on the work.

In 1941, when Serge Koussevitzky, the conductor of the Boston Symphony, impressed by Britten's creativity, asked him why he didn't write an opera, Britten's response could be echoed by every other composer: "The construction of a scenario, discussions with a librettist, planning the musical architecture, making preliminary sketches and writing nearly a thousand pages of orchestral score, demands a freedom from other work which is an economic impossibility for most composers." Koussevitzky took the hint, and the Koussevitzky Music Foundation awarded Britten $1,000 and commissioned him to write *Peter Grimes.*

The first performance of *Grimes* was a triumph for the thirty-one-year-old composer and his librettist, Montagu Slater. In his first major work for the lyric theater, Britten demonstrated a genius for delineating character and plot musically, for presenting social and psychological conflict with originality and dramatic assurance, and for the shattering power and beauty of the score. Britten was hailed as the herald of the renaissance of British opera—a role he fulfilled with distinction, composing a total of eleven operas before his premature death in December, 1976.

Some of the initial excitement that greeted *Grimes* might be laid to the euphoria stemming from the allied victory over Nazi Germany only a month before, but in the three decades since that historic premiere, the work has been performed around the world and has been enthusiastically received. It is one of the few twentieth-century operas that have found a permanent place in the repertory. It is a lyrical, romantic work, readily accessible to the ear and the heart. Although solo arias are not as clearly defined as in eighteenth- and nineteenth-century opera, they flow with lovely melody. The choruses are harmonically rich and are illustrative of the text and action. *Grimes,* despite its quintessentially British flavor and atmosphere, continues the great tradition of international grand opera.

In 1941, while living in the United States, Britten read an essay by E.M. Forster that introduced to him the work of George Crabbe, a poet of late-eighteenth- and early-nineteenth-century England. Crabbe, who during his lifetime was considered "one of the most popular and admired of our living poets," had been almost forgotten by later generations. If he is being read again, Forster and Britten can take a large share of the credit.

Crabbe, born in Aldeburgh on the Alde River near the North Sea in 1754, hated his father, his poverty-stricken village, its inhabitants, and his own poverty. Unable to earn a living at various trades and professions (he trained as a surgeon), he ran off to London to become a writer. Under the sponsorship of Edmund Burke, Crabbe achieved notable financial and literary success, with Dr. Johnson one of his admirers. Crabbe then took religious orders and returned to Aldeburgh as curate of the church.

Since his congregation didn't appreciate his efforts to save their souls and improve their characters and since he couldn't conceal his basic dislike and contempt for them, he was soon transferred to another congregation in East Anglia.

But although Crabbe left Aldeburgh, Aldeburgh never left him. Love-hate feelings for his native community colored all his work. His vivid descriptions of the land, sea, and countryside clearly demonstrate his love, while his convictions that poverty and hard work brutalize and degrade human beings are expressed in his harsh depictions of the inhabitants.

The Borough, a somber, ostensibly fictional poetic panorama, divided into twenty-four poems he called "Letters," was published in 1810; it further revealed his attitude toward what he was to call a "venal" village. Letter 22, *Peter Grimes,* was a relentless portrayal of a psychopathic fisherman who was responsible for the deaths of his father and three young apprentices.

Based upon an actual individual, Grimes was a thoroughly detestable sadist of whom Crabbe wrote in the preface, "The mind here exhibited is one untouched by pity, unstung by remorse and uncorrected by shame." In the end, Grimes dies. Shunned by his neighbors, he is accompanied to his fearful death by the ghosts of his victims. But if Crabbe, a stern moralist, was unsparing in his treatment of Grimes, he was equally so of the villagers who, by their indifference and silence, shared responsibility for the deaths of the three children.

Britten's longing for home was deeply stirred, first, by Forster's article that began, "To think of Crabbe is to think of England," and even more by Crabbe's depiction of Suffolk, of which he too was a native. He was especially stimulated by *Grimes* as the theme for an opera. Despite the dangers of trans-Atlantic travel during the war, he managed to get passage to England, where he would share life with his beleaguered countrymen. Once home, he began, with Slater, to develop a plot.

The collaborators were well aware that although a brutal, doltish Grimes might be the central character in a sordid, Grand-Guignol horror play, his fate would not involve a modern audience's sympathy or emotion. They therefore created a Grimes far removed from Crabbe's—stubborn, proud, and inarticulate, who is misunderstood and rejected by his community, not because he is evil, but because he is different.

To fit that characterization into the proper social, historic, and dramatic setting, Grimes's father was omitted, and the number of apprentices was limited to two—one dead before the opera opens. And the action was moved forward to 1830, the period of England's burgeoning Industrial Revolution when such individualistic rebels were appearing in literature and life.

The Borough remains an impoverished backwater, untouched either economically or psychologically by the vast historic changes swirling around it. Its precarious living comes from the sea, as it has for endless generations. It is the sea that gives the village sustenance and life and, with the supreme indifference of nature, takes them away. The sea is an awesome presence throughout the opera. The magnificent orchestral sea interludes connect the scenes of the opera and limn the beauty and terror of this powerful natural force. The interludes also reflect the village's activities, and the storm interlude does more, for it symbolizes the growing turbulence within Peter's tormented spirit as he struggles desperately to achieve his goal.

The sea is an everlasting presence, while the village is an active protagonist. However, a community is composed of individuals, and Britten succeeds brilliantly in capturing separate personalities: the malicious busybody Mrs. Sedley, who is a closet drug addict; Ben Boles, the pious, bigoted Methodist who, when drunk, is as lecherous as less godly men; Mayor Swallow, the self-important bureaucrat who feeds, rather than quiets, the village's prejudices; Auntie, the good-natured innkeeper, and her good-natured but stupid strumpet "nieces."

Then there are Ned Keene, the apothecary, who is fair-minded about Peter; Captain Balstrode, the respected sea captain who is Peter's friend; and Ellen Orford, the heroine, drawn from Letter 21 in Crabbe's *Borough*.

Ellen is a warm, lonely woman whose bleak life has not destroyed her compassion and faith in the human spirit. She shares Peter's pain, and she would share his life, poor as it is. She offers peace, but he cannot accept it.

The tenderness and pity that suffuse her being are movingly expressed in the aria she sings to the little apprentice: "Child, you're not too young to know where roots of sorrow are. Innocent you've learned how near life is to torture." The libretto doesn't tell us how Ellen was widowed, whether she ever had children, what living in the village has done to her, or why she has linked herself to Grimes's difficult nature. The music tells all.

As for Peter, himself, is he truly a Byronic anti-hero? Is he a rebel who defies the village because he has a larger vision of what life can mean, or is he simply a man whose inability to relate is due to his own psychological maladjustment—a maladjustment that deepens because the village refuses to accept him as one of its own?

A Byronic rebel would turn his back on the enmity he confronts and perhaps would leave the stifling environment, but Grimes won't. "I am native, rooted here by familiar field, marsh and sand, ordinary streets. . . . By the shut faces of the Borough clams; and by the kindness of a casual glance." Grimes is tragic because he understands his loss, but doesn't know how to overcome it.

His solutions are mainly those of the petit bourgeois. "These borough gossips listen to money. Only to money." So he will overcome their antipathy with wealth. "The wealthy merchant Grimes will set up household and shop. You will all see it! I'll marry Ellen."

He can't achieve that wealth alone. To bring in a successful catch, he needs help, and he can afford only an apprentice who costs him nothing. But these fantasies are doomed from the beginning. The villagers will believe only the worst of him, as the inquest in the Prologue establishes. The hearing, conducted by Swallow, is an illegal kangaroo court. Peter is innocent of murder, but the village deems him guilty.

If the opera has a villain, it is the cramped, vicious mentality of the villagers. This drives Grimes further and further into his paranoia—the determination to obtain wealth that means respect at any cost. The chorus sings, "We live and let live," which has a bitterly ironic ring, for it soon becomes a posse, revealing itself with "Who holds himself apart/Lets his pride rise/Him who despises us we'll destroy." It is the eternal destructive cry of the small-minded against the outsider reaching a horrifying pitch in music.

The village's concern for the apprentices has a hollow ring. Would it have turned into a vengeful pack of vigilantes if an apprentice had died in the service of one of their own? An apprentice's life had little value. The apprentice system in England dated back to the mediaeval guilds, when youths were apprenticed to craftsmen for seven years to learn a skill.

That system underwent many changes over the centuries, and apprenticeship became a euphemism for cheap labor. It was a loose financial arrangement in which thousands of children were bought and sold out of poorhouses, orphanages, and even from poor parents, and little attention was paid to their suffering. During the nineteenth century, great fortunes were built on the lives of children. Mills and mines were peopled with children as young as six who toiled and died unmourned.

In *Grimes,* only Boles protests the practice. "Is this a Christian country? Are pauper children so enslaved that their bodies go for cash?" But is Boles attacking the purchase of children, or only Grimes for doing the same? Even Balstrode, so sympathetic to Peter, is indifferent to the children's travail when he says, "Something of the sort befits brats conceived outside the sheets." The Age of Enlightenment has not reached the village of Aldeburgh.

The end is foreordained, for the contest is an uneven one. The calm sea takes Grimes into its depths, while the daily life of the village continues as before.

VERDI'S *Rigoletto*

by Speight Jenkins

Is *Rigoletto*'s plot just a good story well told, or does it have an underlying theme that fascinates as much as it horrifies? How many have ever tried to go beneath *Rigoletto*'s surface? Certainly there are many who would not want to do so. Igor Stravinsky belonged to that group. He adored the tunes of Giuseppe

Verdi's first universally popular opera; and as a composer not given to effulgent praise of his fellows, Stravinsky once said that he would give the whole of Wagner's *Ring* for the Duke's fourth-act aria "La donna è mobile." At other times he went on to fault the operas of Verdi's maturity, *Otello* and *Falstaff,* because they lacked (to him) the freshet of spontaneous melody that fills every nook and cranny of *Rigoletto.*

Stravinsky is only one of many who have praised the expertly crafted work. Triumphing over censorship problems (the story originally involved a licentious king of France, an opprobrious theme for the Austrian censors), Verdi adapted the original Victor Hugo play, *Le Roi s'amuse,* into a story involving a dissolute Italian duke. From the first night at Venice's Teatro la Fenice (March 11, 1851), audiences have gone wild over the whole show—music and story. *Rigoletto* has had periods when it was not respected by musicologists and even critics, but it has never fallen out of favor with the public. And *Rigoletto* is one of those peculiar masterpieces of the lyric stage—there are not more than a half dozen of them—that can triumph despite all odds. If the ingenue soprano is over sixty and fat, or if the baritone is either a teen-ager trying to sound and look older or a decrepit has-been with no voice, or if the tenor is the embodiment of one or more of the often-encountered flaws besetting his fraternity, *Rigoletto* still succeeds. It even works, though never well, if the conductor is an incompetent, and that is the highest compliment to Verdi. The public and, to a lesser extent, the critics can always find something that fascinates.

The obvious reason, it must often be stated, is not just Verdi's tunes but the variety and individuality of his construction. The three arias for the Duke explore different facets of both the lyric and the lyric-spinto tenor and can be successful with either; "Caro nome" is a lovely expression of virginity; the baritone's two major scenes are masterpieces of dramatic and musical expression; and the whole opera revels in a variety of duets. But these are interstices in a dramatic outline. One of the best of theatrical operas, *Rigoletto* tells a gripping story in musical terms. In it are no action-crippling operatic conventions, such as Germont's "Di Provenza il mar" in *La traviata.* And in *Rigoletto* the musical action is built toward one of the composer's best coups de théâtre, the quartet in Act IV, an inspired revelation that happens to bring out much of the personalities of the four who are singing.

But a plot is only a plot no matter how musically developed, and there must be a deeper reason for *Rigoletto*'s unusual indestructibility. Something makes the characters more generally interesting than those in *Il trovatore* or *La traviata,* in both of which one charismatic character—Azucena or Violetta—takes up most of our attention. In *Rigoletto* each of the three principals is a distinct personality, and even the lesser characters of Sparafucile, Monterone, and Maddalena are far from ciphers. A major underlying reason for this balanced interest, I would suggest, comes from the plot's preoccupation with one human failing—deception. Everyone in *Rigoletto* is deceived by someone else, and each of the major characters suffers severely from an even worse ailment, self-deception. All of the characters in *Rigoletto,* like many of those in *Don Giovanni,* are living in their own individual universe: they do not communicate, and they do not relate. Unlike the mythic personages of Wagner's *Ring,* no one in *Rigoletto* is lured into sin by a potion or any other magic. Instead, everyone deceives himself without external force. Each person sees what he wants to see—not what is really happening—and only the audience can understand how the characters project their feelings onto others.

Deceptions in *Rigoletto* happen on a greater and on a lesser scale; in each case they work because Verdi's music is uniquely convincing. Rigoletto's basic deception is to Gilda: he is ashamed of being a jester, so he never admits to her what he does. She is therefore totally unprepared to admit that her serious, in fact, grave father, whose manner in Act I, scene 2, is all she knows of him, is a court jester. To emphasize her shock, Verdi, as the scholar Charles Osborne has pointed out, has her see her father dressed in his costume for the first time at the precise moment in Act II when she must tell him that she has yielded to the Duke.

Rigoletto, on a less-successful scale, tries hard to deceive the courtiers about his feeling for his daughter after they have abducted her, and he also tries to deceive her by not telling her what his business is with Sparafucile in the last act. He makes no suggestion to her that he will deal with the murderer to kill her erstwhile lover. The jester, who of course is intensely self-analytical in Act I, scene 2, when he compares his tongue to the assassin's sword, is himself deceived by the courtiers at the end of that act. One wonders how he could, blindfolded, hold the ladder against the wall of his own house, but we somehow accept it. And we do so because of the times we have wanted something not to happen so much that we have deliberately caused it to take place.

Gilda is an innocent girl fighting to find out about life, and it is no small wonder that she moves to deceive her father. First, she does not tell him about the dark, handsome stranger who has seen her in church and followed her home. She deceives him doubly when in the last scene she agrees to go on to Verona, only to return and offer her death for her love. In the same scene she practices another deception, this time on Sparafucile and Maddalena, by representing herself as a beggar asking for some bread and shelter from the storm.

The Duke, who is the shallowest of the three principals, deceives Gilda into believing that he is a student, a harmless deception and one practiced to no ill effect by Almaviva in Rossini's *il barbiere di Siviglia* and in countless other operas. But then he deceives her into thinking that she is the love of his life. Even if in his second-act aria he implies that he really does care for her, the indications are that his line was pretty well memorized and not from the heart. Among the secondary characters, Sparafucile deceives Rigoletto into believing that the sack contains the body of the rich stranger he was supposed to kill, and the courtiers deceive Rigoletto not only when he puts up the ladder for them but also in the Duke's apartment when they lie as to where their master is and with whom.

The self-deception that accompanies all this cleverness is far more insidious and more critical to the poor health of the characters involved. Among the subsidiary characters, the courtiers are deceived about Gilda: convinced that Rigoletto would never have won a woman for a wife, they are sure that the girl is his mistress. Their abduction therefore is based on a fallacy. Their hatred for the jester, however, is such that it is terribly convenient to classify Gilda as his mistress. If one consciously steals another man's daughter and gives her to the biggest rascal in town, it might happen to one's own daughters as well; far safer to see Gilda as a mistress.

Sparafucile, too, practices deception on himself. A man so loyal to the code of the assassin that he will not murder his client still believes that Rigoletto will be fooled that the light body of a "beggar" is the Duke's. He also foolishly believes that a man angry enough to buy the death of another will not check to make sure the right person was killed. But Sparafucile wanted to please his sister.

The Duke is the most clear-headed of the lot, but his basic self-deception lies at the heart of his philandering. He really believes that all women are fickle, and he cannot see the rapaciousness of his own conduct. As a follow-up to this, he believes for only a few seconds at the beginning of Act II that he really loves Gilda. And that is because she has disappeared. What he cannot have, he loves; what he is tired of, he leaves, he tells himself, just before she leaves him.

Gilda's is a straightforward, pure projection. She has wanted a man to love her, a knight in shining armor to take her away from her monastic existence. Now comes a young, handsome student who seems the epitome of love, and she simply gives complete credence to all he says, making him the embodiment of all that is manly and good. And in the best tradition of a projection, she does not and cannot hear the Duke's words when he seduces Maddalena in front of her eyes. Almost surely in the moment of her death she gets satisfaction in taking the pain for the man who she thinks is perfection himself. Gilda does not blindly love him because she is a silly goose; she does so because the Duke is her shadow; he represents everything she wants and hopes for in the world, and she can neither hear nor see him do anything wrong.

Rigoletto's self-deceptions are the saddest. He believes that he was given a perfect daughter whom he can keep virginal and angelic by locking her up; he cannot believe that his angel could love any man, much less the one who is the absolute embodiment to Rigoletto of wickedness. At no point will his mind hear her statements of love for the Duke. He is deceived on a minor scale when he thinks he can—not by his own hand but by money—strike down someone so far above his class and station and live to tell about it. In that he very nearly succeeds. But his fatal deception is that he thinks he can never be hurt by the backlash from his tongue. After Monterone's curse, Rigoletto finally sees himself as a vocal assassin, but earlier he had felt he had license to say anything he chose.

Rigoletto, for all the interest of the other characters, is the most interesting person in the opera. When Verdi first wrote Francesco Maria Piave, his librettist, about Hugo's play, he said, "Triboulet (the Rigoletto character in the play) is a creation worthy of Shakespeare." To Verdi, there was no praise higher. The composer took this character whom he respected and, in G.B. Shaw's words, "burnt his character into music."

A definition of his "character" opens another line of inquiry. In the hands of many modern interpreters of the role—certainly going back to Leonard Warren—Rigoletto may be the only character in the opera who often deceives the audience. The image of a hunchback who is miserably treated, loses his daughter, cannot wreak his vengeance, and finally has to suffer his daughter's death as a consequence of his deeds has won widespread audience favor. The emphasis is on his heartbreak in the line "Marullo, signori" in the big scene in Act II or on the heart-stopping sorrow of the final ethereal duet with Gilda. But this man is basically evil. He keeps his daughter under lock and key and never gives her a chance to live. Although there is no suggestion that his designs are overtly incestuous, there is plenty of justification to see his love for her as the reason for never allowing her even to see, much less to love, another man. And though he talks a big game—denouncing the Duke in an empty palace room— he does not do his dirty work himself but hires someone else to kill his enemy under the most unsavory conditions. Each of these actions can be explained, in that the world treated (and treats) hunchbacks shabbily. Because of a physical flaw, no one would allow Rigoletto to live as a human being. He had to be a jester or nothing. But excuses do not take away the cruelty.

Whatever the truth of a correct insight into Rigoletto, the jester finishes the opera with no understanding of his actions. The self-deception in his character is unchecked. Instead of realizing at the end of Act III that keeping his daughter locked up was an invitation for her to be stolen, he sees the cataclysm as a working out of Monterone's curse. He sees the "rape" (a strange term often used in stories of Rigoletto; when she loved the Duke so much, why would he have to rape her?) of his daughter by the Duke as the same thing. And finally at the end of the opera he cries out, not that he brought about his daughter's death, however inadvertently, but that the curse has finally worked out. The one thing he cannot do is to place any blame on himself, and in that characteristic he is both a part of humanity, eminently recognizable, and an unattractive person.

Rigoletto and all the other characters in Verdi's opera fascinate us not just as songbirds who sing some of the catchiest and most lyrically expressive music ever composed but also as real representatives of life. Like us, they live their lives threading painfully between the Scylla of deception and the Charybdis of self-deception. And if in the end all the characters except the Duke are destroyed, physically, emotionally, or morally, the price is not surprising: deception is a destructive though pervasive failing. And honesty with oneself and with others, almost unpracticed in Rigoletto but intensely prized by Verdi, is rarely painless; it carries with it not destruction but the very seeds of survival.

GOUNOD'S *Roméo et Juliette*
by Speight Jenkins

The names Romeo and Juliet immediately suggest young love and naive passion. The two teen-agers, immortalized by Shakespeare, seem to hover in a charmed world, not free of evil influences, but immune to the coarsening influences of life. Their love, though intensely sexual, always seems pure, and they die with innocence untouched. The desire to create these lovers has burned hotly in the breast of every actor capable of speaking their lines, but the characters have brought despair to many who eagerly sought the roles, principally because Romeo and Juliet never really develop. They begin the drama as teen-agers, and they die as the same teen-agers, with none of the events that crowd into the five days taken up by the play's action really affecting their characters.

The very nature of their love causes great problems. Twenty-five years ago Erich Fromm pointed out in *The Art of Loving* that the state of being "in love" is a passive one, with the man or woman in love seeing the object of his or her affection as a perfect projection of all that he or she idealizes. No matter how many others see the loved one as just an average man or woman, by some wonderful, or at least weird, quirk of human imagination, the loved one is perfect in what he or she does or doesn't do, in what he or she seeks or doesn't seek. How long this euphoria continues depends on many factors, but while it is going on, the lover (in *Romeo and Juliet,* lovers) tends to be unrealistic, involved only in worship of the other. This worship actually contains many elements of narcissism within it, thus making it all the harder to portray on stage, because narcissism suggests introspection and poetry, not dramatic liveliness. Fromm points out additionally that there is a big difference between the "in love" state and loving. The latter state is interesting dramatically because it is active and giving; Romeo and Juliet never have the opportunity to develop a loving relationship, because they are never other than moonstruck.

Although the premiere date of *Romeo and Juliet* is not known, the year of composition, determined by remarks on the play in the press of the time, seems to have been 1594, when Shakespeare was thirty. Called Shakespeare's first great play, it is filled with wonderful poetry. But is it really a great play? Too many times the characters get lost speaking lyrical poetry that does nothing for the action. Moreover, there are excessive puns and much bawdy wit, which, though entertaining, does not increase our understanding of the protagonists or their problems. The weakest point of all is that the tragedy does not occur because of a tragic flaw in either of the two lovers but simply because of bad luck. Events shape Romeo's and Juliet's doom, which, in G.B. Harrison's words, make them pathetic rather than tragic.

Another aspect of the play, not dwelt on by directors in my experience, tends to weaken the play for me: the role of Friar Laurence. Always portrayed as a kind bumbler, trying to right the wrong between the two families ("For this alliance may so happy prove. To turn your household's rancor to pure love"), he sets all the forces in movement by playing at being God. Yet he is never censured by the Prince or by anyone else. Surely his pride deserves some rebuke.

With any and all weaknesses enumerated, however, Shakespeare's incontestably magical poetry cannot be faulted. Moreover, the lack of depth of character, rather than deterring composers, has served as grist for their mills. It was *Othello,* after all, not *Hamlet* that furnished Verdi and Boito their greatest source for opera. And *Othello,* while a great play, has proved much more difficult to perform than the other great tragedies. With a play as philosophically challenging as *Hamlet,* music is confronted with the almost impossible task of enlarging the universe created by the words; in *Romeo and Juliet* all sorts of composers, including Berlioz, Tchaikovsky, Prokofiev, and Gounod, have felt that music could say something unsaid by the verse. For Charles Gounod, the task was to make music widen the scope of the lovers' ecstasy and give their love greater depth.

Working with his familiar librettists Michel Carré and Jules Barbier, with whom he had created *Faust,* Gounod accepted a book that stripped the story to its essentials, making his *Roméo et Juliette* one love duet after another. The opera was composed for the Théâtre Lyrique, which had seen four successes by Gounod in the previous decade, the two most significant having been *Faust* and *Mireille.* Nothing was more popular than the long love duet in the Garden Scene in *Faust,* and that text had brought forth from Gounod exactly the kind of innocent yet passionate music needed for *Roméo.* And in *Roméo,* Gounod had the same soprano who had succeeded so brilliantly in both his other successful operas, Marie Miolan-Carvalho.

Although it can easily be argued that both Berlioz's and Tchaikovsky's scores have more depth than Gounod's, the latter's work swept the opera world. This success was increased fifteen years later when the brothers Jean and Edouard de Reszke, both handsome and colorful figures and the greatest artists of their era, chose often to sing Roméo and Friar Laurent. In London, Paris, and sometimes New York, they were joined by one of the world's most famous divas—Adelina Patti or Nellie Melba—as Juliette. Although the opera was given extensively at the Metropolitan (it has opened that house six times, second only in terms of openings to *Aïda*), some of its most colorful performances took place in Chicago during the pre-Lyric era. The opera opened the Auditorium, with Patti as Juliette on December 10, 1899, while Jean de Reszke once had to use Roméo's sword to stand off a crazed member of the audience there until he was pacified by backstage attendants. It was also the last opera played in the hall before the move to the present home of Lyric Opera, in 1929. In the 1920s, Chicagoans had the opportunity to hear Lucien Muratore, one of the suavest of all tenors, and his wife, Lina Cavalieri, called the most beautiful of all divas, as the two lovers. Not heard in New York from 1947 (Bidú Sayão and Jussi Björling) until 1967, the opera staged a comeback then at the Metropolitan with Mirella Freni as Juliette and Franco Corelli as Roméo. That revival was so successful that the opera enjoyed fifty performances throughout the next few seasons.

Withal, Gounod's opera is not perfect. When the plot was stripped to its bare bones, all of Shakespeare's humor disappeared, and the colorful characters became quite bland. The Nurse, one of the playwright's richest early creations, has only a small role in the opera and gets to sing only a few of her lines. Moreover, the opera has no scene when Capulet meets with violent resistance from Juliette to his order for her to marry Paris. For all her operatic father knows, Juliette has no qualms; she waits to unload her anguish on Friar Laurent. In the play, however, there is a wonderful scene in which Capulet, upon hearing his daughter's refusal to marry, storms at her in a rage. One can imagine what Verdi would have done with that scene; another Aïda-Amonasro duet might well have been the outcome. Overall the opera's most serious problem is a lack of variety. Gounod's music maintains so perfectly the elegant lyricism and heavenly feeling of young untried love that it tends toward repetition. This has undeniably kept the opera from the popularity of the more varied *Faust*. It does, however, give the performers a far greater challenge. They can hold and fascinate an audience by shading and coloring their vocalism so exquisitely that every duet and every page seem a different, subtle variation.

With weaknesses admitted, the strengths of the opera are great indeed. The magic when Roméo first sees Juliette not only catches the spirit of the palmer's episode in the play but also suggests all the wonder of Roméo's imagination at that moment. Juliette is a sudden, blinding manifestation of all he visualized in the ideal woman. And in that rarest of moments, the same is true for Juliette. The only musical response is a duet—short, a little hesitant, but largely in thirds, the musical symbol of togetherness.

Music allows the Roméo to make his apostrophe to the wonder of Juliette a fiery statement of his burgeoning manhood. In the play the poetry is far lovelier, but it is basically only noble words. In the opera the tenor's aria has youth about it, plus a thrill of energy, a feeling of the passion that lurks in Roméo's heart. Gounod carries out the whole Balcony Scene brilliantly, making it far longer than Shakespeare's—146 lines—although no more important.

Another very successful moment in the opera occurred because of French operatic convention. At the end of Act III there had to be an ensemble to end the fight scene. To launch it, Gounod gives the tenor a statement expressing his pain at banishment, which makes him seem older and wiser than Shakespeare's hero, who flees the scene before the Prince comes.

The most striking addition to Juliette in the opera is her Waltz Song. When she first enters, her music characterizes her as a fresh, charming young woman; shortly afterward, her Waltz, replete with grace notes, paints her youth and beauty plain. Those grace notes, indeed, convey much of the youth; slightly off kilter, they make her seem especially young, and the runs and trills only accentuate her freshness. It is one time when a display piece does far more than show off the soprano's technical ability; in the best bel canto tradition the coloratura actually defines the character.

Gounod and his librettists conjured up one effective bit of color unthought of by Shakespeare. In the scene in which Mercutio and Tybalt are killed, the play has the original argument between Tybalt and Roméo. Feeling perhaps that this was too blunt, Gounod added a character, Roméo's page Stephano, who precipitates the battle. Her aria is a gem, a mocking piece quite as effective as, though very different from, Méphistophélès's "Serenade" in *Faust*.

In the play the scene when Romeo and Juliet have their one night together is brief, only forty-two lines. Gounod spins this out into the great duet "Nuit d'hyménée," one of the best of the composer's lyric effusions. The personalities of the two do not change in their night of love; they still seem as innocent as before. Their duet, meltingly sweet as it is, is in every way the converse of the adult passion of Tristan and Isolde in *their* "Night of Love" episode. Gounod's is a classic Romanticization of lovemaking.

Gounod's final success takes place in the last scene, in which he allows the lovers to know the extent of their tragedy. Shakespeare kills off Romeo before Juliet wakes, making Juliet's death all the more lonely. In the opera the poison has not done its work on Roméo when Juliette comes back to life, and the lovers, like Violetta and Alfredo, plan for the happy life they will lead. When Roméo begins to falter and Juliette realizes that something is wrong, for the first time he recalls he has drunk poison. Too weak to stop her, he watches while she stabs herself. The two then die in a duet—their fourth in the opera— singing in perfect unison. That they die singing together may seem unrealistic, but how true to the image of Romeo and Juliet, the Utopian realization of the unsullied perfection that young lovers believe real.

PUCCINI'S *La rondine*
by Roger Dettmer

It is the rueful lot of *La rondine* that even Giacomo Puccini's apologists look askance, speak of it as the runt of his operatic litter. No less an eminence than William James Henderson, writing in the *New York Sun* after the belated American premiere on March 10, 1928, in the old Metropolitan Opera House, concluded that it was "the afternoon off of a genius."

Such judgments almost always exempt *Le villi* and *Edgar* from consideration on the grounds of their being "early works," which is poppycock; Puccini was already twenty-five years old when the first version of *Le villi* had its premiere in 1884. And he had already celebrated his thirtieth birthday when *Edgar* followed in 1889—indeed he was more than halfway through his lifetime when he revised the latter work in 1892. (Consider that Gustav Mahler, Puccini's junior by eighteen months, had already finished both his First Symphony and *Des Knabens Wunderhorn* in 1888, all the while he maintained a full conducting career in opera.) Besides which, surely *Suor Angelica* was Puccini's creative nadir.

On its own, *La rondine* is an entirely professional accomplishment, sometimes authentically charming, by a composer at the peak of his technical powers. In the beginning it offered him an opportunity to earn lots of money— 200,000 Austro-Hungarian kronen, worth at the time between 40,000 and 50,000 U.S. dollars—but subsequently it encountered a series of roadblocks, including Puccini's own musical conscience. The genesis of *La rondine—The Swallow* in English, literally translated—is convoluted, even by the rules of the game in that *circus maximus* called Italian opera.

In 1913, Puccini visited Vienna to supervise the local premiere at the Hofoper an der Ring of *La fanciulla del West* (née Minnie, David Belasco's potboiling *Girl of the Golden West*). On one of his free evenings he attended the Karltheater to hear an operetta by the phenomenally popular Franz Lehár and, by his own account, was approached by the theater's directors, Heinrich Berté and Otto Eibenschütz. They proposed on the spot that he undertake an operetta for them—that is, "setting eight to ten numbers in a book that would be chosen by mutual consent. . . . And, as if he wanted me to accept on the spot, Herr Berté concluded by saying that operetta, too, was a form of art. I thanked him [but] refused definitely. Operetta wasn't for me."

Back home in Torre del Lago, however, Puccini mulled over the offer, no doubt attracted by the promise of 200,000 crowns, and in the end asked a friend in Vienna to make further inquiries. "Did they want the rights only for Vienna or Austria or Germany, or for the whole world? In the latter case there was no point in discussing it. If they wanted the operetta for Vienna alone, then I might consider it." The Viennese wanted everything, of course, but Puccini's emissary argued for his control over "Italy, France, Belgium, England and North America."

In the meantime, a libretto synopsis had crossed the Alps which Puccini considered "at a glance . . . too fragile for me—lacking in any theatrical value. . . . It was the usual slovenly, banal operetta, the usual conflict between Orient and Occident, with balls and other pretexts for dances, and no concern for character or originality. Without interest. I rejected the story out of hand, but the two directors wouldn't give up. With Alfred Willner, the librettist who had written *Der Graf von Luxemburg* and *Eva* for Lehár, they found another story, an original [sic] and modern [sic denuo] plot. The idea of *La rondine* was [Willner's] which he then wrote out with Heinz Reichert."

Working from an outline, Puccini assumed responsibility for "the translation and versification, [and] in March [1914] the first act was ready." But not altogether, whereupon Puccini engaged the Italian playwright Giuseppe Adami, who later wrote librettos for *Il tabarro* and, as co-author, *Turandot*. By this point the composer had received both a contract and a down payment of 40,000 kronen from Vienna, along with a promise from Adami to have the first act ready by May. This Puccini found "charming," and straightaway began to compose.

Before Adami could arrive in Viareggio in August to transform more Viennese prose into Italian verse, for what had become officially a "lyric drama," an assassin's bullet in Sarajevo had set off World War One. In due course, Italy and Austria-Hungary became enemy powers. Yet Puccini continued his work despite the documented fact that texts for Acts II and III gave him compound headaches. In a letter to his librettist he wrote:

> I'm not saying that Act II is ugly, or slipshod, or untheatrical. No, not that. But I do say it isn't beautiful, it isn't well made, it isn't super-theatrical, as it should be. The first act goes very well and the third will go even better [not to be the case, however]. But the second doesn't work. Let us give up Bullier's [a nightclub, in the original and unlaundered meaning of that phrase] and find another setting, more lively, more various . . . I don't know what to suggest . . . but I feel, thanks to that sense that gnaws at my spirit when I'm working, that I don't laugh, I don't enjoy myself, I don't feel any interest. We need something else, dear Peppino . . . We need a second act!

In the long pull they stuck with Bullier's. By November it was Act III that provoked the headaches. "Adamino, believe me, for I can see clearly, *La rondine* is a sad mess!" Yet by February, when Puccini was in Rome for a production of *La fanciulla del West,* he declared that *La rondine* was "well along," adding though that "in the present frightful state of things, with this horrible war, what will happen to the opera?" (Please note, no longer an operetta.)

To the well-publicized fact that Puccini was composing a lighter work, it was publicized even more that this had been commissioned by a theater in one of the enemies' capital cities. As the war escalated, Italian public opinion turned against Puccini—in which context we need to remember that opera composers were national celebrities. His publisher, Tito Ricordi, was even more disturbed by the outcry and urged that Puccini take action to quiet a hostile press stirring up the public.

Thus, in September of 1915, Puccini met with Berté in neutral Switzerland, hoping to reach an agreement that would put a good face on the matter. But Berté insisted stubbornly that any resolution be deferred until the war had ended.

During April following, Puccini wrote to Adami that *La rondine* was completely finished. When he offered it to Casa Ricordi, however, Tito turned down the work as "bad Lehár," angry that Puccini would have composed an operetta—in that place, at that time, the equivalent of a mere musical comedy today. Whereupon Casa musicale Sonzogno, Ricordi's only serious rival, offered to buy all rights from the Viennese, thereby freeing Sonzogno to publish *La rondine*. Puccini asked Ricordi to reconsider but was turned down. Lorenzo Sonzogno acquired the work in December, 1916, and assigned the *prima* to Monte Carlo.

There, on March 27, 1917, the estimable Gino Marinuzzi conducted it. The focal role of Magda, a Parisian demimondaine unmistakably descended from Violetta Valéry, was created by Gilda dalla Rizza, a contemporary of Claudia Muzio, who sang the first performances in Italy of Suor Angelica and Lauretta (following the world premiere of *Il trittico* at the Metropolitan in 1918) and in 1923 was named a leading soprano of Toscanini's select company at La Scala. The role of Ruggero, her provincial swain, modeled unblushingly on Alfredo Germont, was given to Tito Schipa. Ines Maria Ferraris created Lisette, Magda's saucy maid (operettas never had any other kind); her lover, the poet Prunier, was Francesco Dominici.

After the first act at Monte Carlo there were five bows; after the second act, eight; and at the conclusion, eight more. Writing in *L'Action française,* however, Léon Daudet fulminated about "an opera suggested to Puccini by a Viennese editor and a libretto written by another Viennese." He demanded that the producer, Raoul Gunsbourg, be indicted on grounds of consorting with the enemy. Puccini felt an obligation to reply at length (including some self-serving half-truths), until the whole matter ended in a French court, which ultimately absolved Gunsbourg.

If tempers remained high, not so the public's reaction to *La rondine* at subsequent productions—the first one in Italy in June, 1917, at Bologna, the next one six months later at Rome. Leopoldo Mugnone conducted other stagings in Turin, Bergamo, and Milan, while Puccini set to work on revisions. Whereas Prunier had been a baritone in the beginning, he became a tenor, but was changed back to a baritone, before reverting to a tenor in the final version—*those* kinds of revisions.

One consequence of several such changes is the absence of a major role for baritone in *La rondine*. Rambaldo Fernández, a Rothschild among bankers in all but name, who pays Magda's bills in exchange for her amatory favors, is hardly more significant a part than the Baron Douphol in *La traviata*. His functional tour of duty in the first act is followed by just a brief appearance in the second.

La rondine finally did open in Vienna on October 9, 1920—at the rechristened Staatsoper, however, rather than at the Karltheater, with Adami's libretto translated back into German—already a revised version of the music. A subsequent revision was conducted by Vincenzo Bellezza at the Met in 1928, where Lucrezia Bori sang Magda. Her Ruggero was Beniamino Gigli, who had learned the part for Rome a decade earlier on short notice. Edytha Fleischer and Armand Tokatyan were the ancillary lovers, Lisette and Prunier.

Before a revival at the Met for Bori in 1936 (by which time Nino Martini had succeeded Gigli, with Ettore Panizza on the podium in Bellezza's stead), she performed it at Ravinia in 1929, where real champagne was poured in the scene at Bullier's, and in San Francisco in 1934, albeit only a single performance. The next major Magda—at both La Scala and the Rome Opera in 1940—was Mafalda Favero, one of the artists Ottavio Scotto intended to present at Chicago in the storied nonseason of 1947 (along with Maria Callas and Nicola Rossi-Lemeni).

More recently, the role has been recorded by Anna Moffo and Kiri Te Kanawa, although staged performances continue to be few and occasional. Puccini's swallow—"not an early violet" was his verdict, in reference to Verdi's Violetta—never managed to join his dearly beloved heroines in the standard operatic repertory. Productions of *La rondine* are labors of love, sometimes requested by a singer (in the way Renata Tebaldi sometimes made *Adriana Lecouvreur* and *Fedora* the conditions of a return engagement). Mme. Bori had obviously the kind of love affair with audiences that could be translated into clout with management.

To the soprano ideally no weightier than a *lirico spinto,* Magda offers several inducements, not the least a Second Empire gown in the opening act that, just before the curtain fall, she trades for a grisette's get-up, worn throughout the ensuing act in Bullier's. In the last act, on the terrace of a villa overlooking the Côte d'Azur, Magda wears an afternoon frock, with her hair coiffed in yet a different style. Vicissitudes in the libretto enable her to be a worldly-wise hostess in the opening act (taken nonetheless with Ruggero's unspoiled innocence), who masquerades as a working-class girl at Bullier's (where her attraction to, and for, Ruggero combusts into love). Finally, she becomes a self-sacrificing mistress who renounces love rather than marry him under false pretenses.

Magda's further lure for a soprano undoubtedly includes two arias, both in the first act—but without the equivalent of Violetta's "Addio del passato" near the end. In the first, she echoes Prunier's introduction of "the beautiful dream of Doretta," his newest heroine. Challenged to improvise on "Chi il bel sogno di Doretta/poté indovinar?" from her own experience, Magda takes up the tune and triumphantly enlarges on the poet's text. Having recollected her youth, she sings next of a bygone night when a handsome student courted her at Bullier's—"Ore dolci e divine"—and concludes with the words "Potessi rivivere ancora/la gioia d'un'ora! . . . Il profumo squisito/della strana avventura,/amiche, è tutto qui" (If I could live again/the joy of that hour! . . . The exquisite perfume/of that strange adventure,/friends, is all here).

Like "Chi il sogno di Doretta," "Ore dolci e divine" develops into a waltz. A good deal more, too, is in triple time, befitting the original proposal that Puccini create a Viennese operetta (although he begins *La rondine* typically in duple meter, writes Ruggero's unjoined music in 4/4, and ends the opera in that same time signature). A Puccini waltz, however, concedes nothing to the Viennese manner; there are no accents on the second beat of a measure, nor the suggestion of a dotted rhythm. We find instead what Nicholas Slonimsky has called "characteristically Puccinian modalities, chordal parallelisms, and melo-rhythmic sequences."

Very little in *La rondine* is likely to be taken for music by any other composer, even should it be divorced from context, although Puccini repeatedly implies a wish to be straightforward musically rather than sophisticated or subtle. Despite the direction the work took after Puccini's rejection of the first scenario, the sum of it reinforces his determination to fulfill the *spirit* of Viennese musical comedy, if not to honor all the clichés. If one allows that superior craftsmanship of and by itself cannot transform flaxseed into long-stemmed roses, this honorification may be the "tragic flaw" of *La rondine*.

How otherwise to account for a patch of chinoiserie when Prunier reads Magda's palm in the first act or for daubs of orientalism later where nothing in the text remotely invites Far Easternisms?—until, that is, one harkens back to Puccini's initial reaction to the 1913 outline from Vienna—especially his comment about "the usual conflict between Orient and Occident." Several features in *La rondine* point to *Das Land des Lächelns* (The Land of Smiles) as the Lehár confection that Puccini heard in the Karltheater. Yet that work turns out to have been created in 1923, not in 1913—three years *after* the Staatsoper premiere of *La rondine* (which by then was formally a *commedia lirica*).

Even the final form of *La rondine* preserves a number of spoken passages, orchestrally accompanied to be sure, as if to remind everyone of its origins in operetta. It is, furthermore, a "lyric comedy" only to the extent that no one dies before, or at, the final curtain. However, a stunned Ruggero slumps in a chair, dissolved in tears at the contemplated loss of a woman he has just called "my divine lover . . . love of my life." Magda in turn has to lean on Lisette, so physically debilitating is the renunciation of the one true love of *her* life.

"I resume my flight and suffering. . . . Say nothing more, let this grief be mine," she sings. After her final words, a seven-bar coda in slow time fades to a melancholic pianissimo, punctuated by the tolling of a distant bell—not how operettas were supposed to end; or for that matter, operatic *commedie liriche*.

Apart from Magda, the one figure who even approaches dimensionality is Prunier, Lisette's closet lover before the scene in Bullier's, despite his feigned irritation at her chronic outspokenness. By profession, given the words in Adami's libretto, he is a song smith rather than a poet. And he pushes Lisette into a stage appearance between the time Magda and Ruggero declare their mutual love, at second-act curtain fall, and are discovered nesting near Nice at third-act curtain rise. Lisette's audience, however, has hissed her—mercilessly—and this has all but unhinged her reason. She wants her former, uncomplicated life as a lady's maid.

This is purely a plot contrivance, in order to reestablish Lisette in Magda's employ, with "no concern for character or originality," to use Puccini's own words as a weapon against him. At this and similar moments, one feels a tug of war between Puccini the composer and Puccini the business person, understandably eager to pass "Go" and collect 200,000 kronen. Again, in his own words to Adami, *La rondine* "isn't beautiful, isn't well made, isn't super-theatrical," although his later phrase "a sad mess" is extreme and unsupportable. Still, given Puccini's thoroughgoing professionalism as a creator for the lyric theater, it seems an odd lapse that he didn't provide his tenor hero with an excerptible aria.

"Dimmi che vuoi seguirmi alla mia casa" in Act III lasts just over two minutes, builds to no climax, and offers singer and audience no greater vocal challenge than one A—unless Puccini despised the character as a milksop and a mamma's boy (which the text quite cruelly implies). Ruggero's arrival at Magda's in the first act with a letter of introduction (talk about contrivances!) provided opportunity for an aria on the delights of provincial living. Yet Puccini permitted this to get by him. True, Ruggero and Magda spend much of Acts II and III duetting, but Puccini pretty much confined them to a repetition of motifs without supplying any stunning new material.

Whatever *La rondine* left undone—for reasons that haven't survived the time of its creation—it still may be enjoyed for the composer's utter mastery of craft. He knew precisely when to spice the orchestration with percussive pepper, when to add a pinch more of sugar, when to tarten the mixture with a squeeze or two of lime. Whatever staging problems a piano may create when Prunier begins "Doretta's Dream" and again when Magda takes it up, the sound of a piano at this moment is wholly in character, musically as well as dramatically. The *tempo di polka* later in the same act has a thumb print as personal as the one Puccini impressed on his waltzes.

The second act at Bullier's—related more obviously to the Café Momus than to Maxim's or Le Moulin Rouge—includes a choral waltz that does everything except haunt the memory afterwards. What succeeds in sticking are echoes of Puccini's earlier operas. In the act of looking backward as well as sideways, he neglected to look ahead in *La rondine*. Thus, despite the traditionally average length of each act, the whole sounds short of breath, in much the way that Mascagni's *L'amico Fritz* and Giordano's *Fedora* sound truncated, undercomposed.

This is not to say that *La rondine* bubbles any the less—not even *Suor Angelica* at the bottom of his totem pole suggests that Puccini was played out; only that he was hard put to recapture the melodic inspiration of earlier years. He was forever a natural, irrepressible aerator of operatic circumstances, even when the end product turned out to be seltzer water rather than champagne or Asti spumante. And he was clever enough to avoid jeroboam-size projects; rhetoric was no more his forte than metaphysics was. Puccini was attracted to, and served best by, melodramas through which ran a vein of womanly sacrifice; petit-bourgeois tortures were grist for his mill. With a few deft strokes he could outline Lisette or relate Rambaldo to Geronte, created twenty years earlier, even while he fell short of real characterization except in the (recurring) case of Magda.

Magda is solidly in the Puccini tradition, a woman experienced in the backstairs and byways of life, albeit older than he liked best to work with. Verdi would have known instinctively what to do with all of *La rondine,* even if the decision had been to chuck it and work on another project. In the final weighing, Puccini's piece suffers from being so patently patterned on *La traviata* without having stirred the passion, or compassion, that Verdi poured into his work.

Magda indulges herself in a fling, neither more nor less, which cannot weather the bright light of reality. Ruggero's mother blesses their impending nuptials with the proviso that the bride be "pure." Magda has come to care enough for Ruggero that she will not fake virginity (and besides, Rambaldo has invited her through Prunier to recommence their liaison). And so she sends Ruggero home to mother. Two-thirds of a century ago this might have appeared on the surface to be a noble gesture, at least to an Italian Catholic with (Mosco Carner argued) an Oedipal fixation. But it demolished forever any entity Ruggero might have had, and in the process it trivialized the object of Magda's affection to her own considerable disadvantage.

When Magda sings "Lascia ch'io ti parli come una madre al suo figliuolo caro" (Let me speak to you as a mother to her beloved son), her renunciation takes on the faint but unmistakable flavor of Phaedra, abdicating her bed in favor of an unseen Jocasta. Our recourse must be to concentrate instead on the polished surface of a misbegotten work that Puccini tried to animate with all of the spells and incantations at his command. Because he was successful at least as often as not, *La rondine* deserves better than its occluded reputation.

RICHARD STRAUSS'S *Der Rosenkavalier*
by Dorothy Samachson

Richard Strauss was hardly humble about his prodigious talent. He knew his worth, and if he ever had doubts about himself, which is unlikely, he would have been immediately reassured by the plaudits and profits showered on him throughout his career as conductor and composer. Yet Strauss was also honest and modest enough to acknowledge that much of his acclaim as a composer of opera would never have been achieved without Hugo von Hofmannsthal, who wrote the librettos of six of Strauss's operas. In a heartfelt tribute on von Hofmannsthal's fiftieth birthday in 1924, Strauss wrote: "I have deliberately not participated in any literary demonstration in honor of your fiftieth birthday because I cannot escape the feeling that anything I could tell you in words would be banal in comparison with what, as the composer of your wonderful poetry, I have already said to you in music. It was your words which drew from me the finest music that I had to give."

That glowing sentiment will find no argument from opera lovers across the globe who are grateful for the happy chance that united composer and poet in a twenty-five-year artistic partnership, unparalleled by any other duo. Without Hofmannsthal's subtle poetic sensibility as goad to Strauss's musical genius, it is unlikely that *Der Rosenkavalier* or any of the other lyric works they created would ever have reached the stage.

Their historic partnership began after Strauss saw the Max Reinhardt production of Hofmannsthal's hair-raising *Elektra,* his interpretation of Sophocles' classic tragedy about the mythic House of Atreus. Strauss's keen theatrical sense instantly recognized the operatic possibilities in Elektra's obsessed, pathologic hatred of her mother. Elektra, he knew, would make the ideal, blood-soaked companion to his other obsessed pathologic heroine, Salome, now enjoying a very profitable, if scandalous, success.

But to make an opera of the play, Strauss needed a libretto, and Hofmannsthal, the playwright, was the obvious choice for the task. He was available and pleased to accept the invitation from the world-famous composer.

Even before Hofmannsthal put pen to paper on *Elektra,* Strauss, now concentrating his total attention on the composition of operas, saw in Hofmannsthal the ideal librettist he had been seeking, and he unabashedly wooed the poet-playwright: "I would ask you urgently to give me first refusal with anything composable that you write. Your manner has so much in common with mine; we were meant for one another and are certain to do fine things together if you remain faithful to me."

Although Hofmannsthal had no previous experience in setting words to music, he brought such poetic artistry, skill, and psychological insight to the *Elektra* libretto that Strauss realized again that his instinct had been on target and that Hofmannsthal was the right man for him.

Hofmannsthal *was* the right man for Strauss, and he remained faithful during their years together; but the relationship was not quite what Strauss expected. Hofmannsthal was not a malleable unknown, so eager to build a career on Strauss's coattails that he would agree to any project. Ten years younger than the composer, he was as famous for his poetry, essays, and plays as Strauss was for music. A member of a wealthy upper-class family of mixed Austrian, Italian, and Jewish heritage, Hofmannsthal had, like Strauss, first attracted attention while a youth, had gone on to study law, earn a Ph.D., and play a leading role in literary and theatrical circles. He was particularly noted for the exquisite imagery of his language and for his insights into the psyches of the characters he created. A close friend and associate of Reinhardt, who produced many of Hofmannsthal's plays, the two men later founded the Salzburg Festival, where Hofmannsthal's *Jedermann* (Everyman) remains, to this day, a highlight.

His own motivations for taking on the role of librettist were as complex as his personality. He was, of course, flattered by Strauss's blandishments. However, he was not easily seduced. His was an independent artistic sensibility, unable to submerge his ego so completely to a composer that he would write a text on just about any idiotic subject. He could best serve the composer if he were true to himself and as an equal partner.

This independence of thought marked the partnership from the start. What rescued it from foundering was the mutual respect and admiration the two men had for each other's talents. The conviction that "something higher than mere chance" had led them together forged their dependence on each other and overcame the misunderstandings and disagreements caused mainly by the vast differences in their personalities and temperaments.

Strauss was, on the whole, an easygoing, uncomplicated bourgeois, who wanted only to conduct and compose in tranquility, without being troubled by transcendental philosophic questions. He enjoyed domestic life in his beautiful villa, where he spent many evenings playing cards. He was also a clever businessman who kept close track of his considerable earnings, which would have been even larger if Hofmannsthal had been more tractable and productive.

Hofmannsthal, on the other hand, was Strauss's diametric opposite. A highly complex personality, he sought to express his philosophic and metaphysical ideas about love and life in his art.

In an unusually candid letter to Strauss, Hofmannsthal once admitted: "I am a much more bizarre kind of person than you can suspect; what you know is only a small part of me, the surface; the factors which govern me you cannot see. And so I am grateful to you for not prodding me. . . . So please take me as I am and take me kindly." It's unlikely that the confession came as much of a surprise to Strauss.

Despite his personal idiosyncracies, Hofmannsthal was as eager as Strauss to develop a healthy working relationship. He was well aware that he had a great deal to learn about Strauss's music, as well as the art of writing a fine libretto. He acknowledged that it was harder to write a really expert libretto than a competent play, and he devoted much time and serious thought to the vitally important connection between poetic text and plot, as well as the composer's music.

Meanwhile, time inexorably marched on. Hofmannsthal made a couple of false starts for Strauss, but they did not result in a libretto for the increasingly restive Strauss. Then, in the spring of 1909, Hofmannsthal sent Strauss a short note: "I have spent three quiet afternoons drafting the full and entirely original scenario for an opera, full of burlesque situations and characters, with lively action. There are opportunities for lyrical passages, fun, and humor. . . . It contains two big parts, one for baritone and another for a graceful girl dressed up as a man." All was now forgiven, for Hofmannsthal's ribald farce, set in eighteenth-century Vienna of Empress Maria Theresa, was just the comic opera Strauss had been looking for. It also set the pattern for their relationship. The librettist led in the selection of operatic subjects, and the composer followed—sometimes unwillingly—into new dramatic realms.

Even more important, however, was the impact that the comic plot had on

Strauss's music. The revolutionary avant-garde dissonances and monster-sized orchestras of *Salome* and *Elektra,* which had prefigured Schoenberg and Stravinsky, disappeared for all time, and his music took on a warmer, more lyrical coloration.

The farce was intended to last two and a half hours—half the length of Wagner's comic masterpiece *Die Meistersinger.* But as the collaborators fine tuned the ramifications of the plot and gave their characters flesh-and-blood personalities, the work grew, not only in length, but also in thrust and focus. The period-piece comedy of rococo Viennese manners and morals still included its fair share of far-fetched burlesque situations. Baron Ochs von Lerchenau, the lecherous money-hungry nobleman, remained essential to the exuberant farcical complications of the plot; but he was too much the gross buffoon to be the title character in a work that now contained such human understanding and music of ravishing beauty.

Their heroine was now the Marschallin, one of the most extraordinary women to be met in all opera. Thirty-two or -three, this beautiful, sophisticated, and sensual princess has taken her seventeen-year-old distant relative, Octavian, to bed as her latest lover. A wise woman, she knows that the joys she has found with Octavian are short-lived. She foresees the day he will leave her for a younger woman. Time is her enemy, and she reveals her innermost feelings in her first-act soliloquy—one of the most moving expressions of a woman's outlook on love, life, and aging in the entire operatic repertory. In the end she accepts, with grace, the loss of her young lover to a silly girl. It arrives too soon to be painless, but she is not totally bereft, or to be pitied.

Hofmannsthal, who disliked sentimentality, worried that women in the audience might feel too sympathetic to the Marschallin, and he insisted that "the ending should not make us too sorry for the Marschallin." She is too major a figure to inspire pity, and one knows she will find a replacement for Octavian—if not today, then tomorrow. Octavian is a slightly older version of Mozart's Cherubino, who hasn't yet touched a woman, but is preoccupied with thoughts of them. Octavian has discovered his sexuality in the Marschallin's bed, but he remains a boy, full of childish bravado and braggadocio. His sexual experience is limited, but having been introduced to love by the Marschallin, he prides himself on his role as her gallant lover.

Yet with his first glimpse of fifteen-year-old Sophie, he forgets his passionate avowals of love to the Marschallin and falls madly in love. He will protect Sophie against the boorish Ochs and her wealthy parvenu father, who is forcing her into this marriage to help him win entrée into the aristocracy.

Sophie, the fourth principal, is, in Hofmannsthal's words, "very pretty, but she is also very ordinary like dozens of others—that is the whole point of the story: just the fact that Octavian falls for the *very first* little girl to turn up is what unites the whole. The Marschallin remains the dominant figure, between Ochs and Octavian."

Sophie, just out of convent school where she learned nothing, is intrinsically naive, and her conversation with Octavian is mere inane prattle. She is naturally dazzled by her first sight of Octavian, bearing the Silver Rose—the symbol of marriage. But then, how could the two youngsters resist, when Strauss clothed their meeting in such shimmering ecstatic music?

Throughout this, the happiest of their collaborations, Strauss was inspired to compose music that delineated each character with unusual sensitivity and beauty. Instead of an overture, the opera begins with a remarkably graphic orchestral description of sexual passion. It is not Tristan and Isolde, nor was it thus intended; but the lush orchestration leaves very little to the imagination, and it leads brilliantly to the curtain's rise, where the Marschallin and Octavian are relaxing at breakfast after their night's strenuous activities. This charming scene beautifully delineates the personalities of the lovers: quicksilver Octavian—an ardent, impatient, petulant, charming, and handsome boy—and the Marschallin, a mature woman who pampers him, on the one hand, and then scolds him for overstepping the boundaries of polite behavior.

The inventiveness and mutual understanding that Strauss and Hofmannsthal achieved in *Rosenkavalier* did not always come easily. Strauss worked more rapidly than Hofmannsthal and had to learn patience when his poet needed time to think. They accommodated each other's needs and even stepped onto the other's turf.

Strauss recommended changes in Hofmannsthal's script that immeasurably strengthened the dramatic structure, and Hofmannsthal, although no musician, suggested that Strauss fit a sort of waltz into the work. The waltz as such had not yet been invented during the eighteenth century, but that didn't deter the twentieth-century Strauss. He composed a number of enchanting waltzes, designed to limn the various characters. The crude Baron Ochs, ironically, was given one of the loveliest as his theme, further satirizing his coarse behavior and personality. The lilting waltz rhythms were such an integral part of the work that they enjoy worldwide popularity quite apart from the opera.

Hofmannsthal's plot and characters had been partially inspired by Mozart's and Lorenzo da Ponte's *Marriage of Figaro,* as well as by other eighteenth-century French plays (Strauss would always refer to *Rosenkavalier* as his Mozart opera). However, when they realized that their comedy of manners and mores had become a very special treasure, they renamed it *Der Rosenkavalier* and had to seriously think about the production.

They required singers who could not only act but would look their parts, and a director who could create the delicate balance between the exuberant comic convolutions of the plot and the more serious emotional elements of the work.

They wanted Reinhardt. However, the opera-house manager, who was under contract, refused to permit him on stage. The early rehearsals must have been comic, if aggravating, as Reinhardt, in a box seat, had to work through a third person, lest the contractee raise a storm. Eventually, Reinhardt was allowed to prepare the cast, although he never received official recognition for his staging, which was responsible for *Der Rosenkavalier*'s initial enthusiastic reception.

But the two authors were not yet free to see their opera on stage. The censors who kept watch on moral standards were shocked by the opening scene, with the Marschallin and Octavian in bed together. Octavian was moved to the floor, where he knelt near her. Then, some of Hofmannsthal's dialogue was considered too racy for the respectable burghers and was cleaned up—over the partners' objections. Eventually, however, *Der Rosenkavalier* made its debut in the Dresden Opera House, January 20, 1911. Strauss had never enjoyed such a glittering success. From the first glowing notes of the orchestral introduction to the heart-stirring moments of the final exquisite trio, when the Marschallin bravely surrenders Octavian to Sophie, when Octavian achieves a measure of humility and maturity, and when Sophie offers a hint that she will not always remain a silly young thing, the performance was an overwhelming experience.

The heavenly trio and duet worried Hofmannsthal and Strauss. True, *Der Rosenkavalier* explored universal philosophical questions of love, fidelity, renunciation, and aging. Even so, Strauss and Hofmannsthal never lost sight of the humor in the tangled web of relationships among the four characters.

They had composed a comedy, and they didn't want their audiences bathed in sentimental tears when the curtain fell. They therefore reminded the audience that it was indeed a comedy by bringing the Marschallin's impish little Moorish servant out to retrieve Sophie's handkerchief. His saucy wave to the audience as he runs off stage to Strauss's bright orchestral chords as the curtain falls says, in effect: Why the tears? We've all had fun together; the Marschallin is fine, the lovers are together, the villain has been vanquished, and all's well in the world.

RICHARD STRAUSS'S *Salome*
by Dorothy Samachson

For almost two thousand years, the name of Salome has evoked a *frisson* of horror as one of the most notorious women in the Bible—responsible for the gruesome murder of John the Baptist. Of course, Salome was not the only woman in history, legend, or mythology whose sole claim to fame was the evil she did. The list of not-so-gentle members of the gentler sex is hair-raisingly long.

But Salome is separated from the common herd of death-dealing women because the means she used to incite the prophet's death was so uniquely bizarre. Although she did not wield the fatal axe herself, she used an even-grimmer weapon—a dance—to achieve her aim.

The Bible tells of many dances and dancers. However, Salome's was the only one to be rewarded with a death. The idea of using a dance to kill is so perverse that it has perversely contributed to Salome's fascination and kept her image alive. She attracted many great painters, including Leonardo da Vinci, Ghirlandaio, Titian, Rubens, and Dürer, who immortalized her and her dance in their art.

Yet in the Gospels of Matthew (XIV:6–11) and Mark (VI:22–28), which recount the tale of John the Baptist's decapitation, Salome is so minor a character—almost a footnote—that she is not even named; she is identified only as the daughter of Herodias, the wife of the tetrarch Herod Antipas of Judea. Both Gospels give the details of the dance and its dread denouement simply and matter-of-factly. They do not moralize, but both make it clear that Herodias was the guilty one thirsting for John's blood, while the pubescent Salome was a dutiful daughter—a convenient pawn—merely following mother's orders in demanding John's head on a charger as payment for dancing for Herod.

Yet even in the short, understated Gospel recitals, Herod Antipas was hardly an innocent bystander. His demand that only Salome dance for him, as well as the overly generous rewards he offered her, indicate that his desire for the young girl's dance was less aesthetic than lubricious.

Herod Antipas and Herodias were historic figures, whose careers were also chronicled by Josephus, the brilliant renegade Jewish historian who had deserted his people and gone over to the Romans. Although many of his writings were self-serving apologias, his reports did offer valuable details about the period. He identified Herodias's daughter as Salome, and he also reported her two marriages. However, there is no mention at all of her dance anywhere but in the two Gospels. (Theologians and historians have long argued whether there ever was a dance or whether it was simply another apocryphal story that acquired authority over the years.) Still, Salome's dance is so embedded in Christian legend that it remains, for the most part, accepted as historic fact.

The reasons for John's decapitation are found in the political realities of the time. Although he preached the coming of a great leader—Jesus—he was a dangerous political, rather than religious, threat to Herodias and Antipas. His unceasing public attacks on the couple's adulterous marriage threatened their hold on power.

The land seethed with protest over the hated Roman occupation, oppressive taxation, the collusion of the rulers, and their wasteful, luxurious lives. If John also urged the citizenry to withhold taxes in protest, he was an even greater danger—a seditious revolutionary.

Antipas, a son of Herod the Great, had, some time earlier, conceived a great passion for Herodias, his sister-in-law. With her connivance, he had had his own brother done away with, and he took Herodias to his bed and throne, without bothering to divorce his own wife, who had sensibly fled.

Antipas imprisoned John at Herodias's insistence, but the prophet could not be silenced; he continued to inveigh against them. His death was the obvious solution. However, the superstitious Antipas, frightened by the thought of killing a holy man and nervous about his grasp on his throne, which he occupied courtesy of the Romans, refused to order the execution.

It was his inordinate lecherous desire to see his stepdaughter dance, and the oath she extorted from him at her mother's urging, that forced the fatal issue.

For some curious reason, literature didn't pay much attention to Salome and Herodias until the nineteenth century, when Heinrich Heine wrote *Atta Troll,* a long epic poem that retold the story and, in true Romantic style, added supernatural elements to it. The Heine work played an important part in restoring Salome to the attention of other writers, as well as painters.

In the 1860s, J.C. Heywood, an American, wrote a dramatic poem entitled *Salome,* and in 1877, Gustave Flaubert published *Hérodias,* a long story embroidered with historic, political, and religious incident that again emphasized Herodias's responsibility, as well as Herod's libidinous interest in Salome. The Flaubert tale masterfully juxtaposed cool irony, theologic arguments, and vivid voluptuous imagery in its descriptions of Salome's lascivious dance.

Salome also aroused musical interest, and in 1881, Jules Massenet composed his opera *Hérodiade* (Salome's family name), which enjoyed quite a vogue for many years. Its melodramatic plot combined religious piety, Herodias's villainy, and an innocent, self-sacrificing Salome, whose love for John was pure and Christian in spirit as well as deed.

But it remained for Oscar Wilde, the brilliant, controversial fin de siècle Irish poet, playwright, and novelist, to create a new Salome—a Salome of barbaric, poisonous beauty and monstrous pathologic sexual perversion, whom he cloaked in exquisitely perfumed, hypnotically sensuous French that, under its gorgeous mask, revealed a vicious world and its equally vicious denizens. Wilde's Salome was so stunningly depraved and original in concept that she replaced all other Salomes and would inspire Richard Strauss to bring her to sensual, powerfully disturbing musical life as an opera in 1905.

In 1891, the year he wrote *Salome,* Wilde was at the height of his fame in England, the Continent, and the United States, where he had made a successful lecture tour. His prodigious intellect, his irreverent barbed wit, his personal charm, his flamboyant, almost theatrical dress, and his leadership of Decadence, a literary movement that preached the aesthetic ideal of self-indulgence and exploration of new sensations and pleasure in art and life—all were provocative manifestations of his idiosyncratic talents and personality.

Wilde's novel *The Picture of Dorian Gray* shocked England, for its title character represented sybaritic evil. His reckless personal behavior, outspoken contempt for the hypocrisy of Victorian morality, and the increasingly loud whispers about his relationships with various young men seemed designed to outrage. The rather cruel, but funny, caricature of him as Bunthorne, the lily-carrying precious aesthete in the Gilbert and Sullivan operetta *Patience* merely contributed to making him a household name, if a scandalous one.

It was, however, *Salome,* his one-act play, that added fire to the charges of immorality and made a real scandal.

Wilde was, of course, familiar with the story of Salome, the art created around her, and the literature; but it was an exhibit in Paris of paintings of Salome by Gustave Moreau that set him afire with a passion to bring her to new life.

Her exotic oriental mystery obsessed Wilde. He dreamed about her, talked constantly about her, studied paintings of her, and spent days at jewelers, trying to decide which precious gems would best adorn her. He chose to write in French, because French had the musical, poetic texture he wanted. He said his Salome had "refrains whose recurring motifs make it like a piece of music and bind itself together as a ballad." Rarely does an author describe his work so knowingly.

Although strongly affected by Moreau's paintings, Wilde's Salome was a completely original creation—a psychotic monster Freud would have understood. Wilde felt that the accepted version of Salome was so lacking that he was impelled to "heap up dreams and visions at her feet so as to convert her into the cardinal flower of the perverse garden." She was no naive ingenue doing mother's dirty work on command. She was a barbarian, reared in a debauched environment, indifferent to all but herself. Although a virgin, she is consumed by unconsummated lust and is as demented as her equally monstrous mother. The sight of Jochanaan, John's Hebrew name, arouses her latent sexuality, and his rejection of the kiss she demands turns that passion into a vengeful frenzy that cannot be denied. Yet she is also, conversely, almost naively childlike in her responses, her insistence on instant gratification, and her relationship to her mother.

Although *Salome* belonged, stylistically, to the Decadent movement, the play is replete with Symbolist images—the mysterious moon, which looms over the entire work; Herod's superstitious fears, expressed in almost archaic poetic metaphors; the sensuous musical rhythms and repetitions of phrases that pervade the text; and the lush descriptions of the treasures Herod offers Salome—all create an exotic, oriental, and fearsome atmosphere.

The play is in one intermissionless act, culminating with Herod's order to kill Salome during her grotesque passionate paean to John's severed head. Her death was Wilde's invention. When a friend said he shuddered at the play, Wilde responded, "It is only the shudder that counts."

He wrote the play for Sarah Bernhardt, the legendary French actress who was then about fifty years old—an unlikely age to portray an adolescent, but Wilde dismissed questions about her suitability, believing she was the only actress capable of interpreting Salome. Preparations were well under way for a London production when the British censor canceled it. The law at that time forbade the presentation of any Biblical character on stage. Thus, Saint-Saën's *Samson et Dalila,* Massenet's *Hérodiade,* and other dramatic and musical works dealing with Biblical personalities were automatically proscribed.

In the meantime, Wilde commissioned artist Aubrey Beardsley to illustrate the printed play, and the theatrical erotic style of the drawings perfectly complemented the work. The book was eventually published: it was translated into English by Wilde's young lover, Lord Alfred Douglas; but Wilde never saw a professional production of the play during his lifetime.

Wilde's consuming passion for Douglas, an unworthy recipient, led to his doom. Douglas's father, the marquess of Queensberry, as brutally vengeful as Salome and Herodias, hounded Wilde with charges of sodomy and was directly responsible for Wilde's conviction and jail sentence in 1895. Deserted by family, friends, producers, and actors who summarily withdrew his plays for fear of being tarred, Wilde survived a two-year sentence, much of it under harsh conditions. He died in Paris in 1900.

Salome was produced in Paris in 1901, where it was, surprisingly, an abysmal failure. It was in Germany that *Salome* first triumphed on stage, and where Richard Strauss attended a performance in Max Reinhardt's Berlin Theatre in 1903. Like Wilde before him, Strauss caught fire from Salome in Wilde's treatment. She would be his next operatic heroine.

Although Strauss had already won international recognition as composer and conductor, he had failed in his two essays into opera. (His first, *Guntram,* a work about secret mediaeval societies, had been a resounding critical failure. His second, *Feuersnot,* a bawdy earthy comedy based on an old German legend about a town where all fire is extinguished until the heroine surrenders her maidenhead to the hero, was more warmly accepted but was soon banned by the Kaiser on the grounds of indecency and immorality.)

Strauss was avid for success in the lyric theater, and with *Salome,* he immediately knew he had the key. Although his friends Gustav Mahler and Romain Rolland warned him that *Salome* would face censorship problems, he dismissed their objections. His sure instinct for the musical possibilities inherent in the play could not be denied.

It is hard to find two less-compatible individuals than Wilde and Strauss. In his personal life, Strauss was the antithesis of Wilde. He was a devoted husband and father whose home was his castle. Unlike the extravagant, aristocratic Wilde, the bourgeois Strauss was a practical businessman, who knew to a penny what he earned. Nor was he a follower of the Decadent movement; he was more impressed by Nietzsche, whose philosophy had inspired Strauss's tone poem *Also sprach Zarathustra.*

Yet there also existed a darker strain, as Hugo von Hofmannsthal, whose artistic collaboration with Strauss would begin with *Elektra,* noted: "That mastery over the darker, wilder world . . . is a real force in you. Many a time when we have been discussing some new plot, I have been conscious of your desire for an opportunity to exploit this energy . . . which yielded so well in *Salome* and *Elektra,* for something in the furioso vein."

Salome was "furioso." In the music he composed, Strauss ripped away Wilde's perfumed mask and exposed the characters in revolutionary, even brutal, music. Already a master orchestrator in his tone poems, he invented new harmonies and dissonances, cadences and tonal combinations in disturbingly brilliant and innovative orchestral colors that fleshed the characters out in all their febrile, pathologic depravity.

Strauss kept Wilde's one-act format. He was remarkably faithful to the play's text in the German translation, although he cut extraneous characters and many of the religious disputes; he also tightened the dialogue, so that the action and music build implacably to the final terrifying moment of Salome's death.

Strauss also omitted any orchestral overture or prelude. The curtain rises on the set without any warning, and the music moves relentlessly, heightening and deepening Wilde's play with an even-more-ominous brooding atmosphere. Only in *Elektra,* his next opera, did Strauss achieve such musical innovation and hair-raising tension.

Strauss had been warned by Gustav Mahler, Romain Rolland, and other friends that the opera would come under moralistic attack. It began with the soprano engaged to sing Salome. "I'm a decent woman," she complained. Actually, the music was too complex to learn easily. She finally learned the part under protest and Strauss's threats, but she did not perform the dance.

The dance has, throughout the opera's history, created problems. The perfect Salome must have a voice of heroic amplitude, but too often those voices have been encased in bodies of equally heroic amplitude that destroy any illusion of a nubile and sultry oriental princess.

Strauss composed the music for the Dance of the Seven Veils after he had completed all the other music, which was, in itself, rather curious, for the entire opera moves irrevocably toward the dance, which is the breathtaking culmination of the entire work. He insisted that since Salome was a "chaste virgin and an Oriental princess," the dance be performed with "the simplest and most restrained of gestures," yet the music for the dance is of such luscious erotic beauty that his recommendation has rarely been observed, whether performed by a singing Salome or a professional dancer substitute. Too frequently the dance has been patterned after the *danse du ventre* (literally belly dance) and resembles old-fashioned hootchie-kootchie pelvic gyrations.

It is uncertain why the dance has seven veils. They may refer to an old Babylonian myth, or on the other hand, the shedding of one veil after another may have simply been another means of heightening Herod's passion, until Salome stands revealed in all her naked beauty. Occasionally, the dance actually concluded with a glimpse of flesh, which merely added more fuel to the attacks of immorality.

Salome was premiered in Dresden on December 9, 1905, and it created a sensation. Surprisingly, *Salome* wasn't banned in Germany. In Berlin, the performance was permitted on condition that the Star of Bethlehem appear during the final measures. The mind boggles at the thought of the Star while Salome is being crushed to death. The Kaiser, who liked Strauss, warned him that *Salome* would cause him damage. Some damage! The financially astute Strauss later recalled that the "damage" enabled him to build his villa in Garmisch.

However, because of religious objections, Vienna didn't hear *Salome* until

1918. The Metropolitan Opera gave a single performance, and then withdrew it at the behest of a wealthy puritan patron—J.P. Morgan, perhaps?

Salome was the object of vicious critical reviews that condemned it for its very virtues—its harmonic innovations and rich orchestral scoring. But they also condemned the opera for its deleterious effect on the audience's moral standards. Ernest Newman, a distinguished critic, responded to the idiocy with humor: "The hysterical moralists who cry out against *Salome* . . . have a terrified, if rather incoherent, feeling that if women were suddenly to become abnormally morbid, conceive perverse passions for bishops, have those holy men decapitated when their advances were rejected, and then start kissing the severed heads in a blind fury of love and revenge in the middle of the drawing-room, the householder would feel the earth rocking beneath his feet. But women are not going to do these spicy things because they saw Salome on stage."

Today, audiences don't worry that an evening with Salome will drive them to murder. Salome may not be a very nice girl, but she is so gorgeous, musically and dramatically, that few opera lovers would sacrifice the opportunity to meet her in all her fetid beauty simply because she might be a bad example.

HANDEL'S *Samson*
by Thomas Willis

In the essay preceding his 1972 play *The Samson Riddle,* Wolf Mankowitz suggests a sharply contemporary reading for the Old Testament story:

> There is a condition much thought about today and known unamiably as "the male menopause" which is particularly critical in artists and other men committed to the grandiose delusion of Purpose. In the late thirties it tends uneasily to manifest itself, a combination of fatigue, disillusionment and hope for a new, violent, and finally clear revelation. It is a malaise which seeks its resolution in strange countries, women, addictions, and affiliations. Men in their forties, their destinies already deeply committed, struggle to comprehend, twist, turn, and shatter their lives in the attempt to break shackles of iron or gold, only, like Samson, to bend their heads finally to the forbidden question, offer the secret answer to the implacable enemy, suffer the inevitable blindness with deep relief, and go into seclusion to learn patience and await a clearer vision. It seems a unique and highly significant experience at the time, but is, in fact, a common concomitant of the onset of middle age and is, I say, unflatteringly named by psychiatric doctors who have among their drugs many which may or may not deal with endogenous or reactive depression. However, even after taking a pill the writing remains. The Book of

the Judges contains this extraordinarily conceived and amazingly written story of Samson. It has haunted the imaginations and perplexed the intellects of artists through several thousand years of treatments for the male menopause; male delusions have risen and fallen in ruins about it while the story, like all great fables of the floundering of the human spirit in the drift of destiny, remains undamaged and unaltered.

Something of the same point of view must have motivated the aging John Milton in the waning days of the Renaissance, when, blind, lonely, and surrounded by the Philistines of the restored British monarchy, he produced his *Samson Agonistes*. That "Agonistes" comes from the Greek word meaning "to struggle"; it is at the root of the Stravinsky-Balanchine ballet "Agon"; and our English language, mindful of the internal nature of all true human striving, produced "to agonize" and "agony" from it. Mixing the Hebrew and the Hellenic in something like equal proportion, the poet depicted the strong man of Dan as a tragic hero: growing, changing, achieving later insights superior to the earlier ones. As one modern critic has noted, "He breaks through clusters of time-encapsulated beliefs to achieve a new synthesis of understanding. The accomplishment of change is attended by pain, loneliness, and remorse, and it commences with a bitter recognition of failure, loss, and waste. Milton is true to his personal experience, true to his historical experience, true to his national experience. In all those aspects of his life—as a blind poet, as a defeated republican, a solitary reformer—his experience was of tragic loss and of the agonizing discrepancy between his vision and the realities of his world." But though Milton's Samson ultimately loses his life, he regains intellectual control during the process. In the manner of a true Greek tragedy, the poem moves and strengthens us, leading us to the recognition that to change and grow may be difficult almost beyond belief but that the human mind may limit and control failure, may compassionately regard the human condition, and may discard the false and harmonize the inconsistent in its own nature.

This high-minded approach to the legend of the promiscuous, secret-sharing strong man—so often regarded as the susceptible "hunk" of Saint-Saëns's opera and Victor Mature movies—was no doubt considered when George Frideric Handel and his librettist, Newburgh Hamilton, chose Samson as the protagonist for an oratorio in 1741. But there were several other considerations of equal or greater importance. Hamilton's preface to the libretto of the new work mentions two of especial importance: Milton's unimpeachable reputation and the story's suitability for representation in a theater:

> Several pieces of *Milton* having been lately brought on the Stage with Success, particularly his *Penseroso* and *Allegro,* I was of Opinion that nothing of that Divine Poet's wou'd appear in the Theatre with greater Propriety or Applause than his SAMSON AGONISTES. That Poem indeed never was divided by him into Acts or Scenes, nor design'd (as he hints in his Preface) for the Stage; but given only as the Plan of a Tragedy

with Chorus's, after the manner of the Ancients. But as Mr. *Handel* had so happily introduc'd here *Oratorios,* a musical Drama, whose Subject must be Scriptural, and in which the Solemnity of Church-Musick is agreeably united with the most pleasing Airs of the Stage: It would have been an irretrievable Loss to have neglected the Opportunity of that great Master's doing justice to this Work; he having already added new Life and Spirit to some of the finest things in the *English* Language, particularly that inimitable Ode of *Dryden's (Alexander's Feast),* which no Age nor Nation ever excell'd. . . .

In adapting this POEM to the Stage, the Recitative is taken almost wholly from *Milton,* making use only of those Parts in his long Work most necessary to preserve the Spirit of the Subject, and justly connect it. In the Airs and Chorus's which I was oblig'd to add, I have interspersed several Lines, Words, and Expressions borrowed from some of his smaller Poems, to make the whole as much of a piece as possible. . . .

Hamilton sells himself short. His masterly libretto retains the flavor of Milton, to be sure, but it is a new version specifically made for its time, place, and function. Many of these changes had to do with the essentially dramatic nature of the oratorio as Handel conceived it. The chorus, which in Milton impersonated and commented on the action exclusively from the point of view of the Israelites, now depicts both Israelites and Philistines. To increase the possibilities for dramatic interaction, many of the words of Milton's chorus are given to a new character named for another Old Testament figure, Micah. The characters of Delilah, which so aroused Milton's antifeminist wrath, and Harapha, the Philistine giant who challenges Samson, are simplified and made easier to understand. The succession of scenes is altered; a pagan festival begins the action, and an elegy ends it, with a concluding chorus of rejoicing to send everyone home in a happy frame of mind. In between, the dramatic mood fluctuates abruptly as in the operas of the time. In the first act alone, we swing between Samson's recurring despair and unanswered prayers, a vision of God's wrath, confident optimism, pity, self-pity, the anticipation of heavenly bliss, and a lesson in stoical faith. Such a succession of emotional tableaux, so much a part of the Baroque opera's conventional vocabulary, was made to order for a composer of Handel's genius.

Hamilton also provided the composer with a hero more suited to the taste and concerns of the times. His Samson dodges the areas where Milton's wrestles, avoiding the spiritual conflicts, political debates, and frequent passages of moral and self-criticism which were of primary importance to the creator of *Paradise Lost.* Hamilton's shorn warrior has been relieved of almost all responsibility for his plight and is spared the Miltonic "agonizing" struggle for spiritual regeneration. The librettist was right to drop the "Agonistes" from the title, for we are confronted with a hero who is unalterably human and vastly more pitiable, self-pitying, and pitied than Milton's candidate for sainthood. He is also more isolated from his fellow man, more directly exposed to his enemies' scorn, and very little concerned with cosmic struggle and universal concerns. Like Mankowitz's man in mid life, he is not God's archbetrayer; he is a simple, vulnerable man arbitrarily singled out by fate to exemplify pitfalls open to any of us. Inevitably, as in all such encouraging figures, he achieves nobility.

Hamilton takes a further giant step toward the taste and temper of his time. While Samson is the chief figure in the drama, the fate of the Israelite nation is more important to the oratorio's story line. Hamilton's main theme is God's championship of his chosen people, threatened with destruction by the national enemy. It is a threat made more real by the chorus of Philistines and the suspense inherent in Hamilton's hardly Biblical "plot," which answers the question "Will God intervene in time?" Samson's fate and that of his nation are interdependent. When he suffers disgrace, a nation prays for his deliverance. When he needs strength, the people pray for a miracle. After his triumphant death, they mourn him and go on to share his triumph.

To achieve this relationship of hero and nation, Hamilton played fast and loose with his source, omitting political references that would impair portrayal of Israelite unity and strength, and selecting other Miltonic texts which express the identification and interrelationship between hero and nation. In so doing, he reflected the opinion and desires of an important and influential group of writers and thinkers of the period, who were campaigning for a sublimely religious national epic. In these discussions, the nation was always regarded as the epic's central concern, the individual hero being a sort of barometer of national strength. Such an epic would have a Christian framework, partly for Christianity's sake and partly because the epic glorifies a nation and should therefore celebrate the national religion. It was to show a personal, moral God whose mystery was manifested in angelic appearances, yet there must also be free action by men, since blind destiny would make a mockery of the human virtue that the epic is intended to seek. The hero should be virtuous, and he should be passive as well as, or rather than, active. A happy ending is of course required for the virtuous, making a final resounding statement of God's care for His people. Although this prescription was originally directed at poets and preachers, Hamilton shows us in *Samson* how easily it could be adapted to musical drama. It was a recipe that would be followed by Handel throughout the rest of his days as an oratorio composer and on into his canonization as an English musical immortal.

It is entirely possible, however, that none of these lofty concerns were uppermost in Handel's mind when he began *Samson*. In his new biography of Handel, Christopher Hogwood notes the close connection of *Samson* with *Messiah,* which the composer had finished, after only twenty-four days of intense labor, on September 14, 1741. The first act of *Samson* was completed a little more than two weeks later, on September 29, and the whole was complete a month later:

The present-day standing of *Messiah* makes it difficult for us to realize that for Handel its composition was an offbeat venture, unsure in its rewards and probably unrepeatable. It is the only truly "sacred" oratorio he ever wrote, it was the only one performed during his lifetime in a consecrated building, and yet it was intended as a "fine Entertainment." Although quintessentially the work of a theatre composer, it contains no drama in the theatrical sense; there are no warring factions (no Israelites versus Philistines), no named protagonist; the text telescopes prophecy and fulfillment, and the drama is revealed obliquely, by inference and report, almost never by narrative. . . .

Samson was the counterbalance to Messiah and an insurance against any possible criticism it might attract. If Messiah proved too contemplative, Samson was highly charged drama, with firmly-drawn characters and alternating choruses for the Philistines and the Israelites—although Handel makes only modest demands on the chorus. If Messiah were to be declared "sacrilegious" because of its Biblical text, Samson stood on the safer ground of Milton's verse.

Handel's financial difficulties as producer of Italian opera had in fact led to a major crisis in the composer's life. When he returned to London in 1742, after the premiere of Messiah, he was in a state of indecision as to his future in England; and there is some evidence that he considered a move from his adopted homeland. By the New Year of 1743, he had resolved the problem: he would remain where he was and direct his energies to the production of oratorio. A season of six performances in Covent Garden playhouse—the first of the three buildings to be erected on the current Royal Opera House site—was announced, following the subscription plan which had been successful in Dublin. All six were to be devoted to Samson, and in obedience to the law, he applied to the government's inspector of stage plays for permission to produce it. After due inspection of a libretto, permission was granted. The composer also completed an Organ Concerto in A Major (later to be published as Opus 7, No. 2), for performance at the premiere on September 18. The oratorio was an immediate success, and it has remained the most popular of the composer's dramatic oratorios ever since.

Even Horace Walpole, whose attitude concerning the London musical scene was notably acerbic, had to admit that the oratorio was a triumph of the fall season: "Handel has set up an Oratorio against the Operas, and succeeds. He has hired all the goddesses from farces and the singers of Roast Beef from between the acts at both theatres, with a man with one note in his voice and a girl without ever a one; and so they sing, and make brave hallelujahs; and the good company encore the recitative, if it happens to have any cadence like what they call a tune." Roast Beef was a popular ballad of the time; his slighting references to the intermission vaudevilles and musical farces were meant to cut. To his ear, the use of singing actors and actresses without operatic training was as inadmissable as the use of, say, Linda Ronstadt as La Bohème's Mimi. On balance, however, Walpole's criticism of the English voices must be termed unfair. Handel the impresario and Handel the composer were united in the determination to create a new and highly communicative genre of dramatic music, rooted in the language of the audience and making use of the most effective communicators to be found on stage and in the church's choral ensembles. One decision he made and stuck by whenever possible was to trust to native voices singing in their native language, and with the exception of one Signora Avolio, who sang for Handel until the following year, to forgo the stars of Italian opera. With them went the castrato, whose florid soprano and alto virtuosity had been associated with operatic heroes for a century or more. *Samson* is indisputably a tenor, and the casting marks a turning point in the evolution of English oratorio.

The new oratorio sold out for all six subscription nights, and the theater, according to that indefatigable correspondent and chronicler Lady Hertford, "was filled with all the people of quality in town." Moreover, she continued, "They say Handel has exerted himself to make it the finest piece of music he ever composed, and say he has not failed in his attempt."

There was criticism, as there had been earlier with the introduction of *Israel in Egypt,* from the puritan sector of the community. One outspoken correspondent of the *Universal Spectator* wrote: "An *Oratorio* either is an act of *Religion,* or it is not; if it is, I ask if the *Playhouse* is a fit *Temple* to perform it in or a Company of *Players* fit *Ministers* of God's *Word,* for in that Case such they are made. . . . In the other Case, if it is not perform'd as an *Act* of *Religion,* but for *Diversion* and *Amusement* only (and indeed I believe few or none go to an *Oratorio* out of *Devotion*), what a *Prophanation* of God's Name and Word is this, to make so light Use of them? . . . *David* said, *How can we sing the Lord's Song in a strange Land;* but surely he would have thought it much stranger to have heard it sung in a *Playhouse.*" Such opposition may in part be due to the religious revival sparked by the Wesley brothers and William Law, who believed ardently in unadorned, people-centered worship and believed the theater to be responsible for much of the prevailing "licentiousness" and "depravity." The extremist criticism continued for many years, long after the oratorio had been accorded a key position in the mainstream wave of middle-class religious fervor which swept the country and canonized Handel as its musical patron saint.

Neither *Samson* nor its composer was in any difficulty. Even the editor of the *Universal Spectator* felt it necessary to preface his reader's letter with a disclaimer: "The following Letter may to many of my Readers, especially those of a gay and polite Taste, seem too rigid a Censure on a Performance, which is so universally approv'd: However, I could not suppress it, as there is so well-intended a Design and pious Zeal runs through the whole, and nothing derogatory said of Mr. *Handel's* Merit. . . . Of what good Consequences it will produce, I can only say—'*Valeat Quantum valere potest*' [Let it be worth as much as it is worth]."

Samson, Messiah, and the rest of the series, which followed at the rate of one or two a season, rapidly gained a prominent place on the calendars of London's musical public. Observant novelists also took notice. Henry Fielding's heroine in *The History of Amelia* (1751) was so enamored of oratorio that she arrived at the theater early in order to secure good seats and, in the time-hallowed romantic tradition, encountered a handsome stranger:

> Indeed there was only one Person in the House when they came: for *Amelia's* Inclinations, when she gave a loose to them, were pretty eager for this Diversion, she being a great Lover of Music, and particularly of *Mr. Handel's* Compositions. . . . Tho' our Ladies arrived full two Hours before they saw the Back of Mr. *Handel;* yet this Time of Expectation did not hang extremely heavy on their Hands; for besides their own Chat, they had the Company of the Gentleman, whom they found at their first Arrival in the Galery; and who, though plainly, or rather roughly dressed, very luckily for the women happened to be not only well-bred, but a Person of a very lively Conversation. The Gentleman on his part seemed highly charmed with *Amelia,* and in fact was so: for, though he restrained himself entirely within the Rules of Good-Breeding, yet was he in the highest Degree officious to catch at every Opportunity of shewing his Respect, and doing her little Services. He procured her a Book and Wax-Candle, and held the Candle for her himself during the Whole Entertainment. At the End of the Oratorio, he declared he would not leave the Ladies till he had seen them safe into their Chairs or Coach; and at the same time very earnestly entreated that he might have the Honour of waiting on them. (Book 4, chap. 9)

The French poetess Madame Anne-Marie Fiquet du Bocage was particularly taken with Handel's own contribution to the oratorio performances when she visited London in 1750:

> The Oratorio, or pious concert, pleases us highly. *English* words are sung by *Italian* performers, and accompanied by a variety of instruments. HANDEL is the soul of it: when he makes his appearance, two wax lights are carried before him, which are laid upon his organ. Amidst a loud clapping of hands he seats himself, and the whole band of music strikes up at exactly the same moment. At the interludes he plays concertos of his own composition, either alone or accompanied by the orchestra. These are equally admirable for the harmony and the execution. The *Italian* opera, in three acts, gives us much less pleasure.

Not only were the oratorios a part of the scene, they were well on their way to becoming a part of the canon: so great was their reputation that one could safely praise them without comprehending their merit. One Lady Luxborough noted that her steward had been highly entertained at a performance of *Judas Maccabaeus,* and "speaks with such ecstasy of the music, as I confess I cannot conceive any one can feel who understands no more of music than myself; which I take to be his case; But I suppose he sets his judgment true to that of the multitude; for if his ear is not nice enough to distinguish the harmony, it serves to hear what the multitudes say of it."

Hand in hand with acceptance into the canon went the assumption of moral uplift. When she heard *Samson* in 1743, Catherine Talbot could not help thinking that "this kind of entertainment must necessarily have some effect in correcting or moderating at least the levity of the times." Eliza Heywood, finding herself "transported" by a rendering of *Joshua,* declared in her *Epistles for the Ladies* (1749) that such entertainments might "go a great Way in reforming an Age, which seems to be degenerating equally into an Irreverence for the Deity, and a Brutality of Behavior to each other; but as this Depravity of Taste, of Principles, and Manners, has spread itself from *London* even to the remotest Parts of this Island, I should be glad if there were *Oratorios* established in every City and great Town throughout the Kingdom; but even then, to be of general Service, they ought to be given *gratis,* and all Degrees of People allowed to partake of them."

We are all aware that Heywood's hopes of universal coverage were in large part fulfilled, although the selection of the "Entertainments" was somewhat limited—in this country, at least, to the dreary annual repetition of *Messiah* in communities large and small by amateurs of varying abilities and degrees of enthusiasm. In Christopher Hogwood's words: "Handel's standing changed. His sudden elevation to the unique position of a 'classic' was a result of the mobility and social adaptability of oratorio, which, once published, could become the repertory of professional or amateur musicians at any part of the globe. The contrast with operas, limited to the London stage and by the purse-strings of society amateurs, is great—and the spread of oratorio is one of the first signs that 'English music' could at last mean something broader than 'London music.'"

The possibility of producing oratorios with costumes and scenery occurred to at least one audience member long before the composition of *Samson.* The author of the pamphlet *See and Seem Blind,* who had apparently been at one of the oratorio performances in 1732, reported on his experience:

> Away I goes to the *Oratorio,* where I saw indeed the finest Assembly of People I ever beheld in my Life, but to my great Surprize, found this Sacred *Drama* a mere Consort, no Scenary, Dress or Action, so necessary to a *Drama* . . . (I am sorry I am so wicked) but I like one good Opera better than Twenty *Oratorio's:* Were they indeed to make a regular *Drama* out of a good Scripture Story, and perform'd it with proper Decorations, which may be done with as much Reverence in proper Habits, as in their own common Apparel; (I am sure with more Grandeur and Solemnity and at least equal Decency) then I should change my Mind, then would the Stage appear in its full Lustre, and Musick answer its original Design.

It was the Puritan antitheatrical party that submerged this point of view and prevented any tradition of staged oratorios from gaining a foothold during the eighteenth century. Variants of this point of view dominated the nineteenth century. Although a few stagings were attempted, oratorios in England and

America were regarded as the exclusive property of the choral societies. *Messiah* reigned, the nondramatic oratorios predominated in the ancillary repertory, and the swelling choruses often numbered into the hundreds.

A renewed appreciation of Handel's genius in the years following World War I led to a powerful movement in Germany for the stage revivals of both operas and oratorios. Most of these performances were ritualized dance-dramas with musical portions drastically altered in accordance with Wagnerian *Gesamtkunstwerk* principles. Cambridge University started a British amateur tradition of oratorio staging in 1925, and the Falmouth Opera Singers followed with a *Samson* in 1929.

The first fully theatrical performance in England took place in 1958, when the Covent Garden production opened at the Leeds Centenary Music Festival and then came home for further performances. The cast included Jon Vickers (Samson), Elisabeth Lindermeier (Delilah), Joan Sutherland (Israelite Woman), Lauris Elms (Micah), David Kelly (Harapha), and Joseph Rouleau (Manoah); the conductor was Raymond Leppard.

Handel's 1857 biographer, Victor Schoelcher, put the case for staged productions most strongly:

> An oratorio is intended to represent, musically, a certain episode in the Scriptures, and why not, therefore, represent it in reality? Strange contradiction! Devotees permit every dauber to paint the countenance of Christ, to dress him and to exhibit him in the most solemn actions of his life; they do not object when he gives them a face after his own whim, or when he makes him act (as it were) upon the canvas; but when it becomes a question of making Deborah and Samson act in the flesh and blood, they cover their faces in pious horror. Is it because the artists who would play in an oratorio are not of the numbers of the elect? But these are the very artists who actually sing the oratorios. In good truth there seems to be no sufficient reason for such contradictions; it is as if the want of sincerity in religious matters would pass itself off for being truly religious by taking from the oratorio its form, its light and shade—in a word, its physical life.

SAINT-SAËNS'S *Samson et Dalila*
by Alfred Glasser

In the archives of the Paris Conservatory reposes the manuscript of an unpublished *Ode to St. Cecilia* (the patron saint of music and musicians). It is the work of a teen-age composer who stands extraordinarily indebted to the venerable patroness. The mute, meticulously written pages are signed "Camille Saint-Saëns."

The text was ineffably appropriate, for St. Cecilia had lavished upon the young Frenchman all the talents in her gift. As a toddler he could identify notes struck on a piano from an adjoining room; as a preschooler he had mastered the standard piano method of his day; at five he was composing little waltzes and galops. Before he was eleven he gave his first public concert at the Salle Pleyel in his native Paris. According to his memoirs, an audience member asked his mother, "If he plays Beethoven at ten, whose music will he play at twenty?" His mother allegedly replied, "His own!"

But his mother, widowed two months after the birth of her only child, decided against exposing her far-from-sturdy son to the hectic life of a child prodigy. She duly enrolled him at the conservatory, where he distinguished himself in all of his studies—piano and organ as well as composition, the latter subject under the tutelage of Fromental Halévy who regularly canceled classes to write his own operas. Nonetheless, the coveted award that launched the careers of nearly all of France's great composers, the Prix de Rome, was denied Saint-Saëns. That his first attempt in the competition failed is not surprising: he was only seventeen. He drew upon himself considerable public hostility by postponing his second attempt until he was nearly thirty, by which time his high visibility in Parisian musical circles had seriously undermined his amateur status. Again he was rejected. The series of learned panels who annually judged the competition until 1967, when it was discontinued, must have been haunted by this oversight and by a subsequent failure to recognize the talent of another young hopeful named Maurice Ravel.

Notwithstanding this disappointment, Saint-Saëns never had to endure the crippling poverty that plagued the lives of his friends Berlioz and Bizet. His concert fees for appearances as a piano virtuoso supplemented a comfortable salary as a church organist until he could support himself sumptuously from his composing. From the small church of St. Séverin he moved to that of St. Merry in the shadow of the Hôtel de Ville and on to the most prestigious post in all Paris, the Madeleine, where his improvisations and sacred compositions inspired the city's wealthiest and most socially prominent families for twenty years.

From the keyboard dance pieces of the five-year-old Saint-Saëns (reminiscent of Mozart's first minuets—as all Saint-Saëns's biographers unfailingly point out), the composer's style quickly developed. The first performance of his *Symphony No. 1 in E flat* (op. 2) brought a letter of warm congratulations from Gounod to the eighteen-year-old composer. Despite similar successes for his chamber works and other instrumental pieces, Saint-Saëns realized that the theater held the key to lasting success as a composer. The audience for symphonic music was limited, and the impresarios of Paris tended to program only the works of the established masters—Haydn, Mozart, and Beethoven—to the exclusion of contemporary music, especially by French composers. All Paris went to the theater, and it was on the stages of the Opéra, the Opéra-Comique, and the Théâtre Lyrique, where new works were constantly in demand, that a composer could make a name for himself.

But it was not easy for a young composer, however gifted, to gain access to these theaters. The account of Saint-Saëns's decade of tribulations to produce his *Le Timbre d'argent* reads like a horror story. In 1867 Léon Carvalho, the flamboyant director of the Théâtre Lyrique, commissioned Saint-Saëns to set a libretto by the celebrated team of Barbier and Carré, then made him wait two full years after the score was completed before he would even listen to it. There followed two more years' worth of nightmarish revisions before Carvalho went bankrupt and dropped the project. Negotiations with the Opéra, serious enough to induce the composer to invest more time in the indispensable alterations required by the palace of grand opera, eventually came to naught. Next came an interlude with the Opéra-Comique which was terminated by the onset of the Franco-Prussian War. Finally, in 1877, *Le Timbre d'argent* premiered at the original Théâtre Lyrique and lasted through only eighteen performances. It has never been seen or heard since.

Saint-Saëns's first stage work to be produced was *La Princesse jaune,* a one-act fantasy capitalizing on the worldwide enthusiasm for everything Japanese that followed the opening of Japan to the West. The libretto by Louis Gallet was entrusted to Saint-Saëns as a consolation for the Opéra-Comique's share of his *Timbre d'argent* miseries. Librettist and composer turned out to be ideal collaborators who worked together afterwards on four more operas and two highly successful oratorios. Their first effort delighted Gabriel Fauré, but no one else. *La Princesse jaune* opened at the Opéra-Comique on June 12, 1872, and closed after five performances.

In the midst of the aforementioned Sisyphean labors for the theater, the idea came to Saint-Saëns to base a work on the Old Testament story of Samson. His original thinking, perhaps in reaction to his operatic frustrations, was in terms of an oratorio. He discussed the project with Ferdinand Lemaire, who had provided texts for two of his songs ("Souvenances," c. 1858, and "Tristesse," c. 1868). The poet, who incidentally was married to a distant relation of Saint-Saëns, asked a question which brought him immortality: "Why not an opera?" Lemaire promptly delivered a libretto to the composer's specifications and never again in his lifetime produced anything the world has noticed. It is an anomaly of the lyric theater that truly first-rate librettos are most often produced by second-rate poets. They have a gift for suggesting an emotion and leaving its expression to the composer. The titans of poetry write verses with self-contained melodies of vowels and consonants and rhythms that are in themselves a complete expression to which nothing can be added or subtracted. Victor Hugo, France's greatest poet (at least according to André Gide), inspired dozens of librettos, yet never wrote one.

Saint-Saëns proceeded this time with considerably more caution. He began with Dalila's music from the second act. At one of his regular Monday evening soirées, he accompanied a friend in the world's first hearing of the two great arias, "Amour, viens aider!" and "Mon coeur s'ouvre à ta voix"; but his friends did not seem to like them. He repeated the experiment a bit later, with his great friend Augusta Holmes portraying the seductress. Again his friends rejected the music and further discouraged the composer by airing their opinion that no opera director would consider producing an opera based on a Biblical subject. He threw his music into a drawer and turned his mind to other projects. The world came very close to losing a masterpiece.

New Year's Day of 1870 found Saint-Saëns in Weimar on one of his many international concert tours. There he renewed acquaintance with his old friend Franz Liszt, who urged him to finish *Samson* and promised him a world premiere at the Grand Ducal Theatre in Weimar upon its completion. Once back in Paris, although inspired by this encouragement, Saint-Saëns's attention was diverted by the new possibility of staging his *Timbre d'argent* at the Opéra-Comique. The Franco-Prussian War, which annihilated that hope, likewise prevented work on the new opera for the duration of his enlistment in the French army.

Not in the best of health and fearing a recurrence of tuberculosis, which had threatened his life in childhood, Saint-Saëns decided to sit out the rigors of the Parisian winter of 1873 in the tropical warmth of Algeria. There, on a palm-shaded beach, he regained his strength and completed Act III. It was with reluctance that he returned to duty and to Paris in the early spring of 1874. His gloom was delightfully lightened by a surprise prepared for him by Pauline Viardot-Garcia, the great singer who had been his friend since his conservatory days and who had eased his entrée into Parisian musical and social circles. This fascinating woman, whose lack of real beauty did not prevent her from casting a spell over all who met her, had coaxed Gounod out of the cloister to compose *Sapho* for her and had enthralled the great Russian writer Turgenyev in a love affair that spanned many years. For her friend Saint-Saëns she gave a private performance of a complete staging of Act II of *Samson et Dalila* in which she assumed the role of Dalila. Although every important theater manager in Paris responded to her summons, she failed to achieve her goal of finding a producer for her friend's opera. Still, Saint-Saëns was deeply moved to see his work performed with an imposing décor and lavish costumes.

Despite the lack of interest in France, Saint-Saëns still had the offer from Liszt as motivation to complete the opera. Finally, in 1877 the premiere took place in Weimar, in German. Contrary to the general belief, Liszt did not conduct the performance personally; he entrusted the baton to Eduard Lassen, the Swedish composer and conductor who eventually succeeded him as director of the theater. Saint-Saëns himself supervised the final rehearsals. The resounding success in the Ducal Theatre elated the composer but had few international repercussions, since the press scarcely covered the event.

Samson and Dalila did not get to speak French until the spring of 1890: even then it was not Parisian French. The premiere utilizing Lemaire's original libretto took place in the provincial capital of Normandy, Rouen. The success was such that a Paris premiere was arranged for later that year. But not at the Opéra. It was at the Théâtre Lyrique around the corner that Dalila's heart first opened to Samson's voice. The performance was such a triumph that the management of the Opéra made up for past neglect by preparing a sumptuous production. On November 23, 1892, Édouard Colonne, in whose honor the celebrated contemporary orchestra is named, led the first performance of *Samson et Dalila* at the Palais Garnier, where it has been a staple of the repertory ever since.

There are several important reasons behind Saint-Saëns's difficulty in having his opera staged in France. The aversion to Biblical subjects was not new. Jean-Philippe Rameau's eighteenth-century attempt at a Samson opera with a Voltaire libretto never saw the light. The accepted genre for this subject matter was the oratorio. Had either composer attempted an adaptation of a French classic, such as Racine's *Esther,* perhaps the fear of sacrilege could have been avoided; but the Scriptures themselves were shunned. Saint-Saëns also engendered much hostility among the musical establishment by his advocacy of young French composers, bringing upon himself accusations of being avant-garde despite the classical traditions behind his music. Finally there was the snobbish attitude that piano virtuosos are primarily performers and hence incapable of writing serious music. (Subscribers to this belief had no trouble classifying formidable pianists such as Mozart and Beethoven as the exceptions that proved the rule.) Bizet was so aware of this prejudice that he refused to play the piano in public despite an amazing proficiency. The phenomenon persists even today, when many lovers of serious music are embarrassed to confess to a fondness for Rachmaninov.

Samson et Dalila has survived on its own merits. It is a great opera. Despite charges of eclecticism, which beset most of Saint-Saëns's output, the piece has a homogeneity of sound and style throughout; it could have been written by no one else. It is French through and through. Instead of the traditional, extended symphonic overture invented by the Italians and raised to its apogee by Mozart, a simple atmospheric prelude introduces *Samson.* Meyerbeer, who founded the traditions of French grand opera, would not fault it. The importance of the chorus to the total work is another link to this same French tradition. The way in which the ballet sequences contribute to the unfolding of the action is a finesse that Meyerbeer and even Gounod might envy. The Act I dance of the priestesses provides a sensuous atmosphere from which Samson's passion seems to derive. The bacchanal of the final scene is not the conventional submission to the tastes of the Jockey Club members who could not be enticed into the opera house without it. It is an integral part of the action which could not be omitted without mutilating the structure of the drama. The ballet is the dramatization of the pagan way of life as contrasted with the piety of the Israelites. The excesses of the worshippers of Baal are the motivation for Samson's anger and horror, which in turn give him the strength to bring the infamous temple down on himself and his enemies.

The classical ideals of Gluck, court musician to Marie Antoinette, permeate *Samson.* (Saint-Saëns prepared scholarly editions of three Gluck operas: *Ar-*

mida, Orpheus and Eurydice, and *Echo and Narcissus.*) The prelude begins with a simple melodic line suspended over pedal points. It develops into an off-stage chorus lamenting the fate of the Israelites that cannot fail to evoke—without imitating—the opening chorus of nymphs and shepherds mourning Eurydice.

The chorus that officially begins Act I is magnificently contrapuntal, in the tradition of Handel without actually sounding Baroque. It ends with a passage in unison that conveys every syllable of the awesome text with musical power but without musical obfuscation. Samson's first utterance is a concerto-like dialogue between the tenor and the orchestra that benefits from Saint-Saëns's experienced hand at balancing solo and orchestral textures in his great concertos. The scene between Samson and his compatriots closes with a simple phrase and a codetta ascending the scale to a tonic chord.

A Handelian introduction begins the cameo jewel that is the role of Abimélech. An accompanied recitative leads into a duet for bass and brass. Virile, arrogant, mocking, the whole character is expressed in the music of the brief passage. Samson's description of the rising wrath of God the Avenger is set to a chromatic ascent of crystalline simplicity. The brief coda that ends the confrontation allows time for the struggle between Samson and Abimélech to be acted out and concluded before the next scene begins with the arrival of the High Priest.

The entire score is an uninterrupted series of felicities. The scene of the messenger's report and the carrying away of the body of Abimélech is followed by a daybreak which indicates both the physical passing of time and the symbolic dawning of a new era for the Israelites. The musical description is the improvisation of an organist who played Easter morning services from the loft of the Madeleine for twenty years. Dalila's song that ends the act is a classic French *mélodie*. There is no repetition of phrases from the text to extend the melodic line for purposes of vocal display, bel canto style. The musical phrase begins at the beginning of each line of poetry and ends with it: the poetic and musical meters coincide perfectly. The brief episode sung by the Old Hebrew separates the stanzas of the strophic song from the exquisite coda that concludes the aria, the act, and Samson's seduction.

The temptation to proceed practically line by line is strong, but space does not permit such detail. The opera goer needs no help to appreciate the effectiveness of the seduction scene divided by expressions of celestial disapproval. It might be useful, however, to point out that Samson does not follow Dalila into the house immediately. He pauses, and the pause is filled with a fugal interlude as effective as a Lisztian tone poem. The originality of the ballet music of the final scene cannot be overstressed. It is the first significant use of true local color in French music: written on the golden sands of Algeria, where shepherds in sandals and burnooses tended flocks, and camels passed single file, it evokes, at least for Westerners, the Middle East with a vividness that has never been surpassed.

GLASS'S *Satyagraha*
by Thomas Willis

The only training I had from my young days was the training in rhythm, the rhythm in thought, the rhythm in sound! I had come to know that rhythm gives reality to that which is desultory, which is insignificant in itself.

—Rabindranath Tagore

Philip Glass's *Satyagraha* is above all else about *rhythm,* a word which shares a Sanskrit root with "river" and which signifies "flow." Although the opera refers to historical events and to a man who once described himself as "a politician trying to become a saint," it does not treat events chronologically or tell its story in a conventional way. We are asked to consider events in their relationship to time in all its aspects—how they are illuminated by the rhythm of the cosmos, the flow of human history, the life of a single man, and with the aid of music, the microscopic moments that make up a single breath, or heartbeat, or glance.

The first of its seven scenes takes us to the opening chapters of the *Bhagavad-Gita,* the Hindu epic that is at once scripture and commentary on the nature and purpose of action. On the mythic field of justice, the royal armies stand ready to fight. Front and center in this timeless arena stands a pivotal figure in twentieth-century social history, Mohandas K. Gandhi. It is he who invented the word *satyagraha,* combining the Sanskrit words for "truth" and "firmness." "It is soul-force pure and simple," he explained in a publication, "and whenever and to whatever extent there is room for the use of arms or physical force or brute force, to that extent is there so much less possibility for soul force. These are purely antagonistic forces in my view, and I had full realization of this antagonism even at the time of the advent of Satyagraha." English journalists quickly translated it as "passive resistance."

Gandhi has made the journey from the world of history to the world of myth to resolve his doubts. Like the young warrior Arjuna, who has delayed the start of the battle to seek divine advice, he wishes to know whether fighting is right or wrong. At the close of the scene, he takes the Lord Krishna's advice: "Hold pleasure and pain, profit and loss, victory and defeat, to be the same: then brace yourself for the fight."

There is nothing new about operatic conversations between humans and divinities—seventeenth- and early-eighteenth-century operas are full of them. What is interesting here is that *all* of the dialogue is drawn from the *Bhagavad-Gita* and that Glass and his fellow librettist, Constance DeJong, have drawn every word of the opera from the same source. Gandhi and the other on-stage characters are singing the Sanskrit text from the *Gita,* while acting out their roles in history. Text and action are not inseparably bound, but are two parallel narratives running in sequence. As Glass has noted, "this association between specific events and the world of ideas corresponds to the ongoing relation Gandhi formed between his life and the *Gita*."

The melding of history and myth is also suggested in the stage directions for the first scene—"Mythological battlefield/South African plain." The battle in the *Gita* and the racial discrimination against Indians and South Africans at the turn of the century are backdrops for the rest of the opera. The opera's epic frame is dramatized in still another way: The chorus members who impersonate rival mythical armies in the first scene become contemporary policemen and civil-rights workers at the opera's close.

Processions and cycles interact on every possible level. The historical events referred to in the opera took place between 1893, when, as a twenty-three-year-old lawyer, Gandhi first encountered British racial prejudice in South Africa, and 1914, when he left that country following the movement's first major success. The opera places them within the time frame of a single day—from daybreak to star shine.

Each of the opera's three acts has a "figurative counterpart," a wordless figure important to the history of the movement, visible above and to the rear of the action and singing. The first, Count Leo Tolstoy, was the author of one of Gandhi's major philosophic and spiritual resources, *The Kingdom of God Is within You*. Act II takes place in the shadow of Rabindranath Tagore, the poet-educator-philosopher who did much to bring India to world attention during Gandhi's lifetime and whose letters were a source of guidance and comfort to Gandhi throughout his life. As Tolstoy represents Gandhi's past and Tagore his present, so Martin Luther King, Jr., represents Gandhi's future and the future of his movement; King's figure, "in shirtsleeves and at a podium with microphones," is visible through the nonviolent march in Act III.

Even brief descriptions of the historical events in *Satyagraha* resonate strongly with recent history. Anyone involved with the 1960s and 1970s will have no trouble drawing analogies and making comparisons.

Act I, scene 2. The establishment in 1910 of Tolstoy Farm, a cooperative commune where residents would be trained to live a simple, harmonious life and study *satyagraha* principles. "Here all families would live in one place, becoming members of a cooperative commonwealth where residents would be trained to live a new, simple life in harmony with each other. The building of Tolstoy Farm drew everyone into the Satyagraha ideal—'a fight on the behalf of Truth consisting chiefly of self-purification and self-reliance.'"

Act I, scene 3. A public meeting in Johannesburg, attended by some three thousand supporters, which concluded with each of those present swearing before God to resist a proposed, racially restrictive government decree to the death if need be. "A vow would implement for the movement what Gandhi held to be personally true—that a union could be made between the normally separated spiritual and political worlds."

Act II, scene 1. An incident at Durban in 1896 when Gandhi was pursued by a mob of angry Europeans and was saved from injury by the wife of the local superintendent of police, out for a walk. Opening her parasol in a dynamic gesture of humanitarian defiance, she began walking by Gandhi's side. Together, they proceeded to safety.

Act II, scene 2. The founding of the weekly journal *Indian Opinion* in the same year, "to promote greater understanding within the local community, to serve as an organizational force, and to inform the world community about events in South Africa. Every aspect of production was considered in the light of the struggle and the paper reflected the growth of *Satyagraha* principles."

Act II, scene 3. The August 16, 1908, meeting in Johannesburg Park when, following prayer, twenty-three hundred Indians threw their alien registration cards into a flaming cauldron and burst into cheers. "The 'baptism of fire,' as Gandhi called it, was a symbolic indication of the position being taken. Being also of real consequence, the gesture left 2,300 Indians without their legal permits to exist in South Africa."

Act III. "The Newcastle March" of 1913, when five thousand striking miners and Gandhi followers—men, women, and children—marched thirty-six miles to a provincial registration checkpoint and submitted to arrest without violence as a protest against racially discriminatory immigration and tax laws. There were repeated arrests and as many refusals. Finally, the government capitulated and repealed the legislation.

The unfolding and recycling is summarized in the opera's majestic closing moments when principals and chorus praise Gandhi as an "athlete of the spirit, whose ground remains unmoved, whose soul stands firmly upon it" viewing "in the selfsame way comrades and enemies, loving all alike." The soloist's final words place the expanded historical moment in an eternal context:

> The Lord said, "I have passed through many a birth and many have you. I know them all, but you do not. Yet by my creative energy, I consort with nature and come to be in time. For whenever the law of righteousness withers away and lawlessness arises, then do I generate myself upon earth. I come into being age after age and take a visible shape and move a man with men for the protection of good, thrusting the evil back and setting virtue on her seat again."

Within the opera's scenes, the customary connections between action, text, and music are absent. Neither music nor words tells a story. Characters do not develop. The emotions they feel are not expressed. Harmonies do not progress. There are no surging, crested phrases to bring music or action to a climax.

Although its seven major musical patterns may stick in the mind, none is intended to be hummed as you leave the theater. They are designed for multiple repetition, for subtle variations of texture and tone color, for combining in formal hierarchies, or for microscopic lengthening and shortening of their smallest impulses. One declares itself in the simplest of chord progressions;

another beguiles with soft ululations; a third drives with the intensity of a frenzied rock band; a fourth rises through a familiar modal scale while its accompanying bass expands and contracts the harmonic environment. Their pace and texture differ markedly, but there is no obvious relation to text or action specifics.

Although its time-binding processes are innovative, *Satyagraha* never offends our ears. It thrives in the live performance ambience of a Western opera house. Its singers need open bel canto voices with exceptionally secure high registers. Its choristers sometimes depart from the Sanskrit to sing neutral syllables, but they function in familiar, collective ensembles. The orchestra is composed of conventional strings and woodwinds, played in traditional ways; an electronic organ is the only contemporary addition.

The musical motives, melodic fragments, and harmonic sequences are distilled from the language of nineteenth-century opera, motion-picture backgrounds, and once-popular songs. Crafted with remarkable skill, these distillations communicate directly with the opera's subject matter and point of view. In a way difficult to explain, each belongs where it is placed.

Glass did not always work in this way. His musical beginnings were entirely conventional and conservative. Born in Baltimore in 1937, he began flute study at the Peabody Conservatory when he was eight. When he was graduated from the University of Chicago at nineteen, his majors were mathematics and philosophy, but his piano studies were strong enough for admission to Juilliard. His teachers were solid, skillful academics—Vincent Persichetti and William Bergsma. Glass worked with Darius Milhaud at Aspen and, with the aid of a Fulbright grant, joined the class of Nadia Boulanger, the eminent French composition teacher whose generations-long list of American students includes such respectable names as Aaron Copland, Virgil Thomson, Elliott Carter, and Walter Piston. Boulanger stressed composition basics, with emphasis on the French neoclassicists.

An encounter with serialism at Pierre Boulez's *Domaine musical* concerts left Glass unconvinced of the movement's validity, and he seemed, in 1964, ready to join the ranks of the respectable, tradition-oriented American symphonists. As is so often the case, his turnaround resulted from a chance encounter. To earn additional money in Paris, he was playing for recording sessions. At one of these, he met Ravi Shankar, the Indian sitar virtuoso, who was recording music for a counterculture-inspired film, *Chappaqua.* Shankar needed someone to transcribe his raga improvisations into Western notation so that they could be played by conventionally trained performers.

Although he knew relatively little about Indian music, Glass accepted the task. As Shankar and his accompanist, the tabla player Alla Rakha, conducted a crash course in Indian rhythms and scales, Glass worked out ways to put the intricate music on paper. Along the way, he tried to figure out how the music worked. Before long, he had found a way to work for himself.

Then, as now, the basis of action was rhythmic addition and subtraction.

Rhythmic cells are constructed from groups of two and three notes. Repeated over and over, the cells link together in longer units, the units into major divisions. Each division of the hierarchy can remain as is, or it can expand and contract.

During the intervening years, Glass has elaborated and expanded his structural base. Cyclic processes have been added, with longer motives and more elaborate chord groups to increase structural density and expand the tonal canvas. Abrupt transitions have been smoothed out, and more attention has been paid to tone color. The loud amplification, so important to his rock-educated audience, has been toned down on occasion, adding another welcome element of contrast.

As Glass has grown, so have his audiences. In the early years, his listeners for the most part came from New York City's flourishing Soho. Commentators noted his debt to John Cage's liberating ideas, to La Monte Young's use of minimal resources, to Terry Riley's experiments with flexible, participatory scores, and to other cyclic experiments by Steve Reich. With the acquisition of a history, Glass's music acquired a generic name: minimalist. The connection with New York City's minimalist painters—who also employed reductive, repetitive structures and simple, sometimes childlike formal elements—is analytically tenuous, but the popularity of Glass's music with artists, sculptors, vanguard dancers, and other performance artists of that generation remains strong.

Europe discovered the minimalists during the seventies, when many New York City performance groups toured France, Germany, and Holland regularly, playing at state radio stations, art galleries, and concert halls. This reputation was solidified for Glass by the 1976 tour of *Einstein on the Beach,* a collaboration with Robert Wilson. *Satyagraha* was commissioned by the city of Rotterdam soon afterward; the Netherlands Opera premiere followed, with the premiere in Rotterdam, September 5, 1980. It was followed by American performances at Artpark in upstate New York and at the Brooklyn Academy of Music in the summer and fall of 1981. A celebrated production at Stuttgart introduced it to Germany the following year. Glass completed an operatic trilogy with the composition of *Akhnaten* in 1980, having dealt with three major areas of human thought and action: science, politics, and religion.

Controversy has followed Glass and his fellow minimalists from the beginning. Enthusiasts hail the music for its ability to reunite serious music with interested and emotionally committed young audiences. Those less impressed regard it as simple-minded, limited in emotional range, and essentially trivial. In the 1970s New York City–based critics, composers, and commentators drew journalistic and aesthetic battlelines between the "uptown" and "downtown" styles and produced a vitriolic paper storm of pro- and antiminimalist copy. Elsewhere, Glass recalls a 1972 St. Louis headline which read, "Glass Invents New Sonic Torture." *Satyagraha*'s Rotterdam premiere found one critic comparing the opera favorably to *Parsifal,* while another took the opera management to task for making the commission.

There is a demographic and generational division among serious music lovers today. One group asks for traditional opera's stellar singers, emotional intensity, strongly articulated scenes, and variety in melodies, dynamics, and rhythm. The other takes music more meditatively, tuning into its flow without much concern for its drama. Listening to rock has accustomed their ears to repetition, constant dynamic levels, and clearly articulated structures. For them, the meditative attitude and the rocker's strong pulse are equally entrancing and important. As for the dramatic unities, they would probably go along with Merce Cunningham, who used to watch in-flight football to the accompaniment of the headphones' classical-music channel.

Much of the controversy over *Satyagraha* results from such differing expectations.

As for *Satyagraha*'s politics, all art is in a sense political. The subject is certainly no stranger to opera. The ancient Rome of Monteverdi's *L'incoronazione di Poppea* was a thinly veiled reflection of the lives of the Venetian aristocracy. The class system that at once separates and binds Count Almaviva and Figaro is central to Mozart's *Marriage of Figaro* and Rossini's *Barber of Seville*. In *Fidelio,* Beethoven's Leonore crusades against social barbarism. Wagner uses the *Ring*'s Valhalla as a metaphor for all corrupt power centers, embeds the action of *Tristan* in feudal concepts of fealty and fidelity, and treats *Parsifal*'s quest as a journey of acceptance as well as redemption. "Va, pensiero" in Verdi's *Nabucco* reflects the vision of Italy's freedom fighters. And so on.

Politics in its broadest definition deals with the interacting and often conflicting relations between men and women in society. However abstract, ambiguous, or paradoxical a work of art may seem, it reflects its time as well as the views of its creators and supporters. Those who choose to share the experience are equally a part of the action, and the terms and conditions of that interaction can tell us something important about ourselves and the way we respond to others.

VERDI'S *Simon Boccanegra*
by Peter P. Jacobi

Ghita, he called her, his beloved, daughter also of his surrogate father-benefactor, Antonio Barezzi. She seemed quietly to worship him. And the scant accounts suggest that their marriage was idyllic.

But brief, too.

Within four years of vows, she was taken from him, "Through terrible disease, perhaps unknown to the doctors," as her father entered into the family diary. ". . . there died in my arms," he continued, "Margherita in the flower of her years and at the culmination of her good fortune, because married to the excellent youth Giuseppe Verdi, Maestro di Musica. I implore her pure soul eternal peace, while weeping bitterly over this painful loss."

Earlier, Virginia and Romano had been born to Margherita and Giuseppe, only to be taken from them, each child just short of eighteen months. Thus, in a two-year period, from 1838 to 1840, Verdi lost his family, a grief that he exposed directly to his immediate world for a normally brief length of calendar time, a burden that he shared indirectly with a wide world throughout his life and now.

Indirectly, then and now?

Well, *I due Foscari,* in its sensitive father-son relationship, speaks to that awful period when the young Verdi lost so heavily. Father to son, son to father: ties Verdi missed because death cheated him of them. *Luisa Miller, Il trovatore, La traviata, Aïda* echo the man's yearning.

Simon Boccanegra's most admired moment probably is the stunning interplay of emotions and vocal lines in the council-chamber scene. But the opera's most moving sections may well be the recognition scene in which Simon and Amelia discover that they are father and daughter, and the mournful apostrophe to loss which the old patrician, Fiesco, sings in memory of his daughter who died after giving birth to Simon's child, that daughter to whom Boccanegra later is reunited in the just-mentioned scene. At instants such as these the emotional content of Verdi's music seems to overflow.

One should not make too much of reasons behind artistic creation. After all, one can only surmise reasons if the artist has not made them known, through specific comment. Verdi does not speak of motivation. But he makes his feelings so obvious; the music overflows with parental sentiments. Those sentiments contribute to the beauties of *Boccanegra* and undoubtedly help intensify the bond between this special Verdi opera and its devotees.

The composer, however, rarely built his works around a single theme or feeling. In *Simon Boccanegra* the usual ingredient of patriotism is prominent. And conflict. And villainy. And a love affair. And the sort of gloomy calamity that Verdi seemed to consider vital in all but his very early *Un giorno di regno* and in his last, *Falstaff.*

Of musical substance there is plenty. It is, after all, an opera he composed twice, or close to. It is both a middle and a late Verdi work. He wrote it the first time before *Masked Ball,* then he rethought and restructured and rewrote it before *Otello.*

He turned to *Boccanegra* twice because others, like his publisher Ricordi, urged him to. After all, why should a Verdi work languish when the master could make some alterations and thereby give the opera new impetus and vigor? But Verdi turned to it also because he liked the opera. It was his frail child, waiting, needing to be nourished. No matter how much Ricordi or Arrigo Boito, who said he was willing to contribute libretto work (something he was to do with brilliant results in *Otello* and *Falstaff*), no matter how much they wanted action from him, if Verdi hadn't wanted to take such action, he would not have. He could be unmovable. He could be stubborn.

Obviously, he thought loving thoughts about his *Boccanegra*. Long had he harbored views that the opera had been unfairly treated from the start, that it was too good to be disregarded and discarded. He didn't feel that way about all his works. "Dreadful," he termed another of his operas. But *Boccanegra,* no. That had better qualities.

The first time around, in the mid 1850s, Verdi sought something new. He had given his public a series of thunder-and-lightning scores. He had proved repeatedly that no matter what the operatic situation, he could provide the tunes. In *Trovatore* he had proved it beyond all proving; the opera is a parade of melodies. As for chamber opera, the intimate drama set to music, he had tried that also, and rather successfully, in an item called *La traviata.* Why, there had even been obeisance to Meyerbeer in a one-time-only skirmish with grand opera, *I vespri siciliani.*

So what now?

His maturity suggested it was time for maturation of style, the refinement of elements that Verdi had used so vigorously, so easily, and yet sometimes so roughly in the earlier operas. Consider the *Boccanegra* lineage. *I due Foscari* had been composed in a rush, during Verdi's galley years, as he called them. It was a highly flawed opera, but it hinted strongly at how Verdi would come to show through music, rather than stage action, how characters interrelated. *Foscari* held mood, a mood radiated by the characters, characters with problems and emotions approximating real life. In *Rigoletto* he had made an unusual person become like the rest of us through his reactions in crisis and loss. With that opera and *Traviata,* Verdi had told his Italian audience that from here on he wanted to bend music more severely toward dramatic needs, to force melody to serve emotions and events, and that this might mean fewer breaks for applause so that a situation could be more fully exploited in an uninterrupted chunk of music.

In *Simon Boccanegra* all these artistic developments are followed and furthered. Verdi begins to refine his methods, an effort that music historians have dubbed his "middle period." Interestingly, he turned for the story to Antonio Gutierrez, a playwright who had given Verdi material for that final fling at organ-grinder grist, *Trovatore.* Interestingly also, he would have the same sort of story problems that plagued the earlier opera. Dramatically *Trovatore* makes very little sense; things are always happening while the curtain is down, between the acts. Dramatically *Simon Boccanegra* has its confusions, too; things are always happening while the curtain is down, between the acts.

But in this story, Verdi had his themes: filial relationships, patriotism, loyalties, and betrayals, the transcendence of a man beyond his capabilities and stature caused by the needs of people he is meant to rule. The story is based on history. There was a Boccanegra. He faced the problems hinted at in the story. He rose to the occasion. This fourteenth-century doge of Genoa, with a tarnished buccaneer past, turned into a thoughtful leader who labored to bring the warring factions, the patricians and the plebeians, together for the good of the community.

Thus, Verdi had a way to urge his fellow Italians to set aside differences. He had a way to urge the period's politicians to merge efforts, to meld energies for the good of the state. Add the father-daughter angle, and it was more than enough to inspire the man.

Apparently his public didn't think him inspired enough, or at least they didn't understand. The 1857 Venice premiere was not successful. To the audience the story was a jumble. The mood was heavy, shadowy. The music lacked the oomph and the oom-pa-pa that might have filled the gaps and gloom. Verdi noted the reaction to a friend. "*Boccanegra* was almost a greater fiasco in Venice than *Traviata*," he wrote. "I thought I had done something fairly good, but now it seems I was mistaken."

Verdi was disappointed, more so than his restrained letter indicated. He became disgruntled after a revival of the opera two years later at La Scala. Disgruntled but not surprised, because he had complained about the cast and feared the worst, as was his wont even under the best of circumstances. This time Verdi wrote with more passion evident. Ricordi received these sentiments from his favorite composer:

> The fiasco of *Boccanegra* in Milan had to happen, and it did happen. A *Boccanegra* without Boccanegra!! Cut a man's head off, and then recognize him if you can. You are surprised at the public's lack of decorum? I'm not surprised at all. They are always happy if they can contrive to create a scandal!

Considering the subtheme of *Boccanegra,* that of father-child ties, what he says next is revelatory of what whirled in the composer's head:

> When I was 25, I still had illusions, and I believed in their courtesy; a year later my eyes were opened, and I saw whom I had to deal with. People make me laugh when they say, as though reproaching me, that I owe much to this or that audience! It's true: at La Scala, once, they applauded *Nabucco* and *I Lombardi;* but whether because of the music, the singers, orchestra, chorus or production, the entire performances were such that they were not unworthy of applause. Not much more than a year earlier, however, this same audience ill-treated the opera of a poor, sick young man, miserable at the time, with his heart broken by a terrible misfortune.

Verdi referred to the deaths of his wife and children.

> They all knew that, but it did not make them behave courteously. Since that time, I've not seen *Un giorno di regno,* and I've no doubt it's an awful opera, but heaven knows how many others no better were tolerated and even applauded. Oh, if only the public at that time had, not necessarily applauded, but at least suffered my opera in silence. I shouldn't have been able to find words enough to thank them! If they now look graciously upon those operas of mine that have toured the world, then

the score is settled. I don't condemn them: let them be severe. I accept their hisses on condition that I don't have to beg for their applause. We poor gypsies, charlatans, or whatever you want to call us, are forced to sell our labors, our thoughts, and our dreams, for gold. For three lire, the public buys the right to hiss or applaud. Our fate is one of resignation and that's all! But whatever my friends or enemies say, *Boccanegra* is in no way inferior to many other operas of mine which were more fortunate: perhaps this one needed both more care in performance and an audience which really wanted to listen to it. What a sad thing the theatre is!! But, contrary to my usual custom, I've inadvertently gone on chattering uselessly to you. Nevertheless, I'll send it to you, rather than rewrite the letter.

The letter is unusual for the man. He tended toward terseness, introspection. In this one letter he pours out sorrow, bitter memories, a guiding philosophy, and disappointment; it is a verbal melody of sadness. And look at all the exclamation points. He was a bit fevered about events, for sure.

This time that other race of men he distrusted, the critics, treated him well. Critics don't buy enough tickets, however, and so the opera was withdrawn. Verdi moved on to different matters, including that important "middle period" landmark, *A Masked Ball*.

It was 1880 before he got around to *Simon* again, and that, to remind you, was only after a little shove. He gave the score to Boito. Can something be done with the libretto? he asked. "I admit that the table is shaky, but by putting a leg or two in order, I think it can be made to stand upright."

The two men decided to rebuild the table, almost to start over, in fact. The second *Boccanegra* amounts to one of Verdi's most extensive revisions. The new team of Verdi and Boito cut here and added there, added here and cut there, changed words and music just about everywhere. A major addition was the council-chamber scene, presaged in *Foscari* and now deemed one of Verdi's very best big scenes ever. In it all the stray threads are woven together, every personage has his place and his say, and the music glows.

The plot problems remain. But in the pre-*Otello* Verdi there was (and is) so much musical power, so much sweep, so much concern for detail that the listener/viewer tends to overlook the story's weaknesses. Perhaps that's what happened in the theater in 1881 when the new version was introduced. This time, at La Scala, the opera did not fail. Verdi was assured of a proper cast; he could get exactly what and whom he wanted by then: Victor Maurel as Simon, a warm-up for his future assignments as the first Iago and Falstaff; Francesco Tamagno, soon to be the world premiere Otello, as Gabriele; Edouard de Reszke, the legend, as Fiesco. The customary Verdi note to a friend (there seems to be one note to a friend for virtually every opera) exuded a bit more pleasure, a lot less pain:

Even before last night's performance, I could have told you, if I had had time to write, that the broken legs of this old *Boccanegra* seemed to me to have been properly mended. The outcome of last night confirms me in my opinion. So, a very good performance on the part of everybody, and stupendous on the part of the leading man. A splendid success.

Further on he said:

. . . it seems that *Boccanegra* on the fourth night got as much applause as on the others, if not more. And what particularly pleases me is that the theatre was even more crowded than for the second and third performances. . . . Now, if you want to know, I can tell you that *Boccanegra* will be able to tour round the opera houses like its sisters, despite having so sad a subject. It is sad because it has to be sad, but it is interesting. . . .

No, it would not tour the world à la *Traviata* or *Rigoletto* or *Aïda* or *Otello* or several more, but the opera would continue to be performed. It would gain acceptance among those who understood Verdi best and opera most. After all, its orchestration is intricate and subtle, yet powerful and straight to the heart. The melodies are there, not in profusion but in sensitive adjustment to the situations, and they are Verdian, and they are beautiful. The people who people the opera are more than pasteboard; they seem of flesh and the mind; they have personalities as villains and heroes, trappers and trapped, mortals causing trouble and being troubled. Giant among them is Simon, termed by Verdi scholar Charles Osborne "both statesman and dreamer," he "who really bestrides the opera like a colossus," he to whom Verdi gave beauty and eloquence in music, forcefulness and consistency in characterization.

And, oh my, there is atmosphere, somber, yes, but atmosphere. Oozing. Enveloping. As if Verdi were trying to embrace his Ghita and his little ones.

BELLINI'S *La sonnambula*
by Jonathan Abarbanel

Vincenzo Bellini and Felice Romani's *La sonnambula* is, arguably, more important than any other opera ever performed in Chicago. It has the distinction, you see, of being the *first* opera ever performed there, on July 29, 1850. Chicago still was an adolescent city, less than twenty years old, with substantially fewer than one hundred thousand people. The buildings were frame, the sidewalks were boards, and the streets were mostly mud. Like any adolescent, Chicago was growing fast and was known to be a bit raucous. The better sort of people felt that a little grease in the form of culture was just what the city needed to make its cowlick stay down.

One such luminary was J.B. Rice. In 1847 he constructed a large frame building downtown, with a theater on the second floor (not an unusual architectural practice at the time). There, on the evening of July 29, the cream of Chicago society—plus the curious—paid fifty cents for a box seat and twenty-five cents for the gallery to welcome opera to the City in a Garden. The papers reviewed the event favorably, although they weren't too sure what to say about the performance itself. Mainly, they equivocated, saying things such as "Signora Brienta [Elsa Brienti playing Armina] lived up to the reputation which preceded her."

A curious performance it must have been, too. The "company" consisted of four professional singers (including Brienti) who had arrived that afternoon from Milwaukee. All other roles (including two principals) and the chorus were filled by local amateurs. The orchestra was the theater's house band. Nonetheless, that very first Chicago *La sonnambula* was such a hit that a repeat performance was given the next day, in the middle of which Rice's theater caught on fire and burned to the ground. The fire spread to consume more than twenty buildings in one-half square block. Fortunately, no one was hurt, unless you count the seven horses and the cow ("I'm not making this up, you know," as Anna Russell would say). Obviously, opera in Chicago was a hot ticket, a very hot ticket, right from the start.

La sonnambula was a hot ticket right from the start, too. The popularity of this opera once was immense. From the very evening of its premiere, March 6, 1831, at the Teatro Carcano in Milan, *La sonnambula* was a smash hit. In less than a year, it had been staged in London and Paris. Within five years, it had been staged in all the principal cities of Italy plus Budapest, Berlin, Boston, Havana, Mexico City, New York, Philadelphia, Madrid, Prague, and Vienna. In house after house, it was produced *every* season for ten, twenty, even thirty years in a row, right through the 1870s. The Théâtre-Italien in Paris performed it 240 times between 1831 and 1909. The greatest tenors and sopranos coveted the lead roles.

Today, *La sonnambula* is the only example still in the repertory of a once-popular type of opera, the "opera semiseria," or semiserious opera; what we might call a melodrama with a happy ending. Vincenzo Bellini himself wrote only one other "semiseria," his first opera, while still a student at the conservatory in Naples. He much preferred the tragic muse, and he wrote no opera buffa at all. Of his ten operas, *La sonnambula* was number seven, written just after *I Capuleti e i Montecchi* and just before *Norma,* which was written and staged the same year, 1831.

It has been observed that *La sonnambula* enjoyed exaggerated mid-nineteenth-century popularity and suffered from exaggerated twentieth-century neglect, until the bel canto revival of the 1950s and 1960s, inspired by Maria Callas and Joan Sutherland.

The nineteenth-century popularity of Bellini's work is easy to understand: his music is melodious and charming, his vocal lines are elegant and demanding, his operas have lyric and dramatic appeal, his musical craftsmanship is impeccable, and his work is tasteful. What is more, to music lovers of the nineteenth century, Bellini personified the ethereal and elegiac artist of the Romantic Era, with his pale and voluptuous looks, his amorous passions (numerous in life, they rose to mythic numbers in lore), his artistic genius, his moods, his meteoric career, and the wasting disease that killed him six weeks before his thirty-fourth birthday.

Vincenzo Bellini was born in Catania (Sicily) in 1801, the son and grandson of poor but respectable professional musicians. His father, Catania's "maestro di cappella," taught the small boy to play piano before he reached school age. Little Vincenzo played well by five and was composing by six. His grandfather, who lived long enough to see Bellini's success, taught him from the age of seven to eighteen. By that time, young Bellini's sacred compositions were well known in Catania, and his popular songs and instrumental pieces were played in the homes of the local gentry. Bellini's musical education was far more thorough than his studies of the three "r's". His voluminous correspondence reveals only a haphazard mastery of spelling and correct Italian.

By 1819, his family had done all it could for him, but his home town of Catania could offer more: the municipal government provided him with a scholarship to attend the royal conservatory of music in Naples. Within a few years, he was studying with the conservatory director, Niccolo Zingarelli, who introduced Bellini to Haydn and Mozart in addition to studies of the Neapolitan masters.

By early 1825, Bellini was a shooting star about to blaze through the sky. As a graduation showcase, he wrote his first opera. Although performed at the conservatory by students, it was a hit and led to a commission from the Teatro San Carlo. This, too, was a success when performed at a special gala in May, 1826. After some revision, *Bianca e Fernando* became a widely produced opera.

In the meantime, the impresario of La Scala, one Domenico Barbaia (also spelled Barbaja), commissioned the work that laid the foundation of Bellini's career. Moving to Milan, which remained his principal home for six years, Bellini wrote *Il pirata* during the spring and summer of 1827. Its La Scala premiere at the end of October was a career watershed. First, it was greeted with public and critical acclaim. Second, it marked the beginning of Bellini's fruitful collaboration with librettist Felice Romani. Third, it cemented Bellini's relationship with Barbaia. Acclaim speaks for itself; however, a few words are in order about Romani and Barbaia.

Felice Romani (1788–1865) was a well-known poet, critic, and editor who made his home in Turin. An educated man, with a degree from the University of Pisa, Romani wrote his first libretto in 1813 for his friend the composer J.S. Mayr. In short order, Romani became the most successful Italian librettist of the century, with over one hundred composers setting his words to music. Perhaps only Eugène Scribe, in France, rivaled Romani's prolificacy during this period. Romani wrote three librettos for Rossini, four for Donizetti, and seven for Bellini, including all of Bellini's most notable work except *I Puritani*.

Romani was known to knock off up to eight librettos a year. But perhaps "knock off" is a poor choice of words, for Romani was anything but a hack. He was, in fact, as prodigious in the quality of his work as he was in its quantity. He was noted for the elegance of his verse and for his good dramatic sense. Both these qualities drew Bellini to him. Lacking a formal education himself, Bellini nonetheless was a good judge of literature and, especially, of dramatic verse. Bellini also was a much more careful and accomplished prosodist (the fit of the words to music) than any of his contemporaries, including Donizetti and Rossini. The match up of Bellini and Romani which began with *Il pirata* was to be an enduring professional and personal friendship. An established man of letters, Romani also introduced Bellini into the better social circles, an opportunity the status-seeking young Sicilian appreciated.

As for Domenico Barbaia (1778–1841), he not only introduced Bellini to Romani but he also was the most famous impresario of his day. He was noted for his ability to recognize exceptional young talent, and he gave early career boosts to Rossini, Donizetti, Mercadante, and Pacini.

More importantly, Barbaia was in a position to make or break a composer's international career. For a period of years, he held the management contracts for the three royal opera houses of Naples (including Teatro San Carlo), La Scala, La Fenice, a number of secondary Italian houses, plus the Kärntnertor Theater and the Theater an der Wien, both in Vienna. After the successful premiere of *Il pirata* at La Scala in 1827, Barbaia produced it in Vienna in early 1828, launching Bellini's international career. Not surprisingly, Bellini and Romani wrote four more works for Barbaia, including their next opera, *La straniera* (La Scala, 1829, a hit), *I Capuleti e i Montecchi* (La Fenice, 1830, a hit), *Norma* (La Scala, 1831, a hit), and *Beatrice di Tenda* (La Fenice, 1833, a miss).

By 1830, then, the twenty-nine-year-old Bellini was a celebrated international artist. He held a contract to complete a new work for the Teatro Carcano in Milan (a house Barbaia did *not* control, at least for the moment), due for production in the winter of 1831. Over the summer of 1830, Bellini lived at Lake Como, recuperating from the first severe attack of the gastroenteritis that eventually killed him. At Lake Como (where Bellini was the guest of a wealthy industrialist with whose wife he was having a five-year affair), Bellini met with Romani and the great bel canto soprano Giuditta Pasta, who lived across the lake. She was contracted as the prima donna for the new Bellini-Romani collaboration.

The subject they chose—it was a daring choice—was to set Victor Hugo's play *Hernani*. Potent both as a political and as a literary vehicle, *Hernani* had caused a riot at its premiere just months earlier at the Comédie-Française. As Bellini and Romani planned to adapt it, Pasta would play the hero, singing the title role "en travesti."

Distracted by other projects, the authors did no work on *Ernani* (as it was titled in Italian) until late autumn. Finally, Romani completed a number of scenes and Bellini a quantity of music before they abandoned the project in December. They realized—not quite too late—that the stringent Austrian censors never would let such a liberal and political story see the light of day. This was before Italian unification, remember, and Milan was occupied by Austria.

We don't know exactly how or why, but letters reveal that by December 30 they had turned to *La sonnambula,* perhaps for no other reason than the fact that the little melodrama with the happy ending was totally apolitical and innocuous yet full of dramatic situations. The story began life as a short *comédie-en-vaudeville* by Eugène Scribe and Casimir Delavigne, produced in Paris in 1819. On the original theater bill, it would have been a curtain raiser for the principal work of the night. In 1827, the play was turned into a ballet pantomime with music by Louis Joseph Ferdinand Hérold. It was the ballet scenario upon which Romani based his libretto.

It was now January of 1831, and the work was supposed to open on February 20. In the end, it was pushed back to March 6. Bellini normally wrote very slowly and deliberately, often taking six months to complete a work, which was exceptional in an era of opera-on-demand composition and short deadlines. Now, atypically, Bellini had to write under pressure. The fact that he was able to produce a work in which he did not compromise quality is ascribable to two things: first, Bellini's rapid maturation as an artist, coupled with the under-standing he and Romani had of each other's needs; and second, his use of whole segments of music from the unfinished score of *Ernani.*

As has been noted earlier, *La sonnambula* was an immediate success; it quickly spread around the globe. Some may wonder how music written for one set of words could be transposed wholesale into another work. The secret lies in the fact that all Italian composers and librettists of the time used standard verse and compositional forms. The basic musical rhythmic unit was only two-bars long, corresponding to the most common Italian verse form. This made it easier for a composer to draw something from his trunk and place it in a new context. One of the remarkable strengths of Bellini's work was his ability to create extended melody lines from such tiny two-bar "bytes" of material. Writing in 1898, Verdi said of Bellini's work, "there are extremely long melodies as no one else had made before him."

Bellini also was able to integrate music and text much more capably than his contemporaries, so much so that critics of his day often called his music "filosofica." No less an authority on musical drama than Richard Wagner said of Bellini, in 1880, "Bellini's music comes from the heart, and it is intimately bound up with the text."

Bellini was influenced by the folk music of his Sicilian roots and Neapolitan studies, an influence notable in his use of characteristic time signatures such as 6/8, 9/8, and 12/8 time. In *La sonnambula,* listen to the naive and pastoral music of the orchestral introduction in 6/8 time, or the entrance of Alessio from the hills later in the first scene, also in 6/8. A few minutes later, the signing of the marriage contract by Elvino and Amina is done to 12/8 time, a signature that continues through "Prendi, l'anel ti dono," the love duet which is a highlight of the opera. Similar examples are scattered throughout the work.

A final musical trait to notice in *La sonnambula* is Bellini's treatment of recitative. Above all his contemporaries, Bellini began the process of minimizing the difference between recitative and aria, introducing songlike passages into the old *recitativo secco*.

After the 1831 premieres of *La sonnambula* and *Norma,* Bellini made a triumphal return visit to Sicily and Naples in 1832. Most of his remaining three years were spent in Paris, where his last opera, *I Puritani,* was premiered early in 1835, and after which Bellini was made a chevalier of the Légion d'Honneur.

In Paris, Bellini was an acquaintance of Frédéric Chopin, Michele Carafa, Franz Liszt, Heinrich Heine, and Gioacchino Rossini, who took a fatherly interest in the younger composer. Rossini had retired, even though he was only nine years older than Bellini. When Bellini died near Paris on September 23, 1835, following a two-month gastrointestinal inflammation, it was Rossini who arranged his funeral, raised a fund for a monument, wrote the family, supervised the estate, and served as pallbearer (along with Carafa, Cherubini, and Paër). After the funeral at Les Invalides on October 2, Bellini was buried in Père Lachaise (where Rossini also would be buried at his death). His remains were returned to Catania in 1876. Inscribed on his tomb is a line from *La sonnambula:* "Ah! Non credea mirarti si presto estinto, o fiore" (Ah, I did not think to see you extinguished so soon, oh flower).

Bellini's operas lived on to triumph throughout the century. *La sonnambula* even reached Rice's theater in Chicago in 1850. It returned, too, in 1853 to the new brick J.B. Rice's, a fourteen-hundred-seat house with three tiers of boxes. This time, the theater remained standing. Five years later, *La sonnambula* was back at the brand-new McVicker's Theatre. J.B. Rice had gone on to bigger things: he had become mayor of Chicago.

In the twentieth century, *La sonnambula* has been performed in Chicago in 1924, 1926, 1937, and 1988.

OFFENBACH'S *The Tales of Hoffmann*
by Speight Jenkins

Les Contes d'Hoffmann resembles the finest opal—glittering but opaque. The more one tries to categorize any part of it, to explore it, the more elusive it seems. Even its basic composition is in question. With *Simon Boccanegra, Macbeth,* or even *La forza del destino,* there are two versions, but only the last is normally performed. *Hoffmann,* however, makes them all seem simple, because there is a continuing, indeed unresolvable, controversy about the score. No one—or at least no one to my mind with much taste—disputes the quality of Offenbach's musical inspiration, but no one really knows what he wanted the finished product of his opera to be. There was no completed short score, and recent investigators have even shown that gaps existed in the vocal score, particularly in the Venetian scene.

As early as 1851, the composer was drawn to a treatment of the life of the German writer E.T.A. (Ernst Theodor Amadeus) Hoffmann. In that year a play about Hoffmann's loves by Michel Carré and Jules Barbier (who also wrote the libretto for Gounod's *Faust*) made a smash hit in Paris, and Offenbach conducted its incidental music. The play, called *Les Contes d'Hoffmann,* squared off the characters as firm Romantics—good, bad, the best, and the worst, removing all the shades of gray painted by Hoffmann in his writing. That it was such a success is odd, because Hoffmann's work was most admired in France, and the French clearly enjoyed the ambiguous, off-kilter quality of his writing. Théophile Gautier, at about the time of this play, summed up Hoffmann's status in France: "Everybody reads his stories; they appeal to the concierge and the great lady, to the artist and the grocer." The play, however, served its purpose: it inspired Offenbach, who added the Hoffmannlike quicksilver through his music.

At the time Offenbach conducted the incidental music for the play, he was the toast of the Second Empire—the composer of the most extraordinarily successful operettas that the French capital had ever known. Not content with his success, however, Offenbach longed to compose a serious opera, and some twenty years later he made a contract for *Les Contes d'Hoffmann* at the Théâtre de la Gaîté-Lyrique. There was to be no spoken dialogue; the character of Hoffmann was supposed to be a baritone; and the four women in Hoffmann's life were to be sung by one lyric soprano. He began work in 1877, composing with great care. When the Théâtre de la Gaîté-Lyrique went bankrupt, he played the completed portions of the opera for two impresarios: Franz Jauner of the Ringtheater in Vienna and Léon Carvalho of the Opéra-Comique. Both accepted the work, and though Offenbach later is supposed to have said that he would get a better performance in Vienna, he chose the Paris house, because he had for many years wanted an Opéra-Comique success.

He had to recast the roles to suit the voices at the Comique, and Hoffmann was restructured as a tenor. The female role was to be remade for a high lyric coloratura, one Adèle Isaac (a famous Juliette). Offenbach successfully moved up the male part—most tenors would say far too successfully—but had only completed the soprano changes for the doll Olympia before he died. Why Giulietta had originally been composed for a lower voice has remained unclear, but the range of her part has made it nearly impossible to have all four female roles sung by the same artist.

Of course there have been exceptions. At the Metropolitan, Joan Sutherland enacted all the heroines for the new production of 1973, and at the New York City Opera, Beverly Sills sang all four as well. To the question of what type of voice or how many sopranos ideally should sing, there is no answer. In his biography of Offenbach, Alexander Faris has pointed out: "Offenbach did not think of a work as complete until it had been performed before an audience, after which he would revise and finalize it. He regarded the version of the first night as a basis for negotiation with public opinion." And with *Les Contes d'Hoffmann* Offenbach never even had one rehearsal.

A search for what the composer really wanted began shortly after the Second World War. The conductor Antonio de Almeida uncovered a pile of manuscripts in a library in Paris which revealed a lot of music in Offenbach's hand not included in the standard Choudens edition of the opera. He enlisted Fritz Oeser, a musicologist who also prepared an original edition of *Carmen*. Over a number of years the two prepared a score as close as possible to what Offenbach left. A few facts had long been established. Musicologists, for instance, had pointed out that the Barcarolle in Act II, one of the best-known melodies in all of opera, had been taken by Offenbach from his early operetta called *Die Rheinnixen* (in which it had served as the main theme for the overture and for a central chorus of elves). Oeser also found that the main theme of Antonia's mother, the central part of the famous trio in the act set in Munich, came from the overture to an Offenbach work called *Fantasia*. The success of both examples in *Les Contes d'Hoffmann* indicates that Offenbach had an uncanny ability to apply text to music, not, as is normal in opera, the reverse. Even more surprising, the researchers discovered that the septet, sung at the close of the Venetian act, was composed by someone unknown, and Dapertutto's aria "Scintille, diamant," also in the Venetian act, was found to have come from a sixteen-bar passage in the overture of Offenbach's *Voyage to the Moon,* an operetta of the same composition period in the composer's life as *Hoffmann*. The actual construction of the aria, however, was by an unknown hand.

Because the opera is composed of a prologue, three acts, and an epilogue which do not fall in necessary sequence, even the order is variable. Offenbach intended to begin with Olympia, to go to Munich for Antonia, and then to have the Venetian act. His estate, however, left the completion of the opera and its orchestration to Ernest Guiraud, the composer who had done the same favor for Bizet's heirs with *Carmen*. Guiraud's work, first heard in 1881 at the opera's premiere, serves as the basis for the Choudens edition, which is the world's standard edition. This version reverses the second and third tales, placing Antonia last.

Tenor Alfredo Kraus likes it that way. "I think it gives more drama at the end," he has said. "You come from the very light doll scene to Giulietta and then the big drama of Antonia." Plácido Domingo agrees, but for a different reason: "There's no doubt it is much better to have Giulietta as the second tale because this act has a range more difficult than the other acts; dramatically, though, I think it's better to have Antonia second and Giulietta at the end." Domingo points up some possible arguments: "You can look at it as a matter of age.

Hoffmann is twenty when he falls in love with the doll, then about thirty when he has an intense, more mature love with Antonia, then maybe about forty—jaded and bitter—when he falls for Giulietta. On the other hand one could say that Olympia should come first and be followed by Giulietta because a man of twenty-four or twenty-five likes to sow his wild oats. When he's ready to settle down, he tries to do so with Antonia." Just to indicate the complete confusion, there is a version in Paris in which Giulietta is Hoffmann's first love (thus forcing a change in the libretto for the Prologue where the tenor specifically cites Olympia as his first). His frustration with Olympia and Antonia take place because of his giving his reflection to Giulietta. The answer is the usual one for *Hoffmann:* all ways have worked when carried out intelligently with singers who have accepted what the director believes.

Hoffmann himself can be made a drunk, a poet who is a dreamer, a more-than-slightly-demented writer, and numerous other possibilities. However the role itself is characterized, it is a killer—to French opera what Siegfried is to German. Both demand great stamina. Although the opera is not of Wagnerian length, the tenor is almost never off-stage and often stays in the forefront of the vocal action.

A more serious problem is the *tessitura,* or predominant vocal range of the role. Most tenor roles have high notes, some even-more-striking high notes than Hoffmann, but both Italian and non-Wagner German roles usually allow the tenor to pass quickly through the notes at the top of the staff, the area referred to as the passageway or *passaggio* for tenors. It is where the balance of voice between chest and head switches, with the balance moving toward the head as the notes rise in the scale. Although no tenor can make a career without conquering that part of his voice, Hoffmann is one of the few roles that keeps him there for much of the opera. And often, as Kraus points out, the high notes move up little by little from the *passaggio* area, not from below it. This is very tiring.

An ideal example takes place in the scene in Crespel's house in Munich. Hiding behind a drapery, Hoffmann joins in a trio with Antonia's father (Crespel) and his nemesis, this time played by an evil physician, Dr. Miracle. The tenor sings over a full orchestra as well as the two darker voices, the notes remain almost totally in the *passaggio* or just above it, and the whole section, no matter if short, is exhausting. Kraus feels that this passage is a good example of why Hoffmann is not for young singers: "A mature singer has more experience. Young voices are simply not prepared to supply the force needed and not hurt their voices."

Hoffmann himself fits in no easy dramatic category and is difficult to sing because his musical character so often changes. In the first act he seems ever the adolescent, yet his music is anything but light. On one occasion, Hoffmann must make a big point out of only a tiny passage. When he expresses his love for Olympia, the doll, the tenor sings a short, passionate phrase in which he rises to a difficult B natural. Kraus laughed when this was pointed out: "It's such a beautiful moment. It would be nice to continue, but it's good to give the audience a few beautiful things and then stop it. Then, after a while, give them some more. Too many of these moments close together is like too many sweets. As it is, the audience says, 'What a pity we didn't hear more.' Then when they hear the phrase again in Act II, they are happy to remember it."

Earlier, in the Prologue, Offenbach limns the character's ambiguous musical personality. To entertain his student companions, Hoffmann sings the tale of a misshapen dwarf, Kleinzach. Suddenly, Councilor Lindorf, the form of his nemesis who is present in Luther's Tavern, wills him into a reverie. The change is basically a musical one; the tenor can do little to show his metamorphosis. But if he sings the lines as composed, he can catch Hoffmann's elusive spirit—a serious Romantic playing a clown or possibly a clown trying to be a serious Romantic.

In the Venetian act, Hoffmann is asked to change his character, becoming more Italianate. The drinking song is a bravura piece, straightforward in the expression of Hoffmann's passion for Giulietta. Kraus sees it as a bit of "dramatic *joie de vivre*. We have to enjoy this moment and have to sing and laugh." Then Offenbach gives the tenor an aria which is an apostrophe to Giulietta and one of the opera's more troublesome sections. Most tenors, indeed, mark this passage, particularly its beginning, as being the role's most difficult spot. In Faris's biography of the composer, he makes the claim that nowhere else in operatic literature can one find an aria beginning with the interval of a fourth followed by a sixth. Research on my part has not turned up one, but it is almost inconceivable that Offenbach, no matter how original his mind, has penned a unique combination of notes.

With all the ambiguity and complexity, Offenbach had a mastery of the simple phrase. Like Giuseppe Verdi in his day or Irving Berlin in the first half of this century, Offenbach would spin out melodies that demand humming, melodies that can haunt a person for hours if not days. One of these in *Les Contes d'Hoffmann* is the introductory melody for Antonia, the only one of Hoffmann's loves who takes the opera's central focus temporarily away from him. The music is very simple, and the scene appears ordinary; finally there seems to be a major character easy to understand. But the drama quickly becomes bizarre and supernatural. Antonia, committed to music, yet afflicted with an unknown disease that makes any singing at all extremely hazardous to her health, is singing as the act begins. Her song about the turtledove may be, as Faris points out, the only truly sad song Offenbach ever composed, but what an effective piece it is! In only a few bars, Antonia's simplicity is clearly demonstrated. Yet her love for Hoffmann proves to be as ephemeral as that of the other women in his life—a doll who cannot feel, a courtesan whose capacity for feeling has long disappeared, and a singer about whom we learn nothing. True, Antonia seems to be taken from him by demonic forces. When Dr. Miracle, a minor Méphistophélès, makes her sing from her upstairs room as he examines her in absentia, she seems already to have no hope of escape.

Hoffmann's love and his warnings to her give her no strength to withstand Miracle. The game is up when he makes the Mother's portrait come to life. The mother herself died some time before, because Miracle made her sing when the exertion was too much for her. Now from her portrait he brings forth an apparition, resembling Antonia's mother, who encourages the girl to sing. The trio, which has the two women plus Dr. Miracle, combines aria, recitative, and ensemble and is in a sequential pattern. Because the music itself compels Antonia to sing, the melody is of the type that drives its sound into the listener's brain, catchy, insistent, unforgettable.

The tragedy of a girl's being led to death by the forces of evil has seemed straightforward. Finally, something is concrete and clear. Yet when the trio is over and Antonia expires, her death in no way duplicates the realistic demise of a normal nineteenth-century opera heroine, such as Violetta or Mimi. Instead, she leaves us in the midst of a trill. It adds the element of fancy to her death and makes us wonder how much was real. Her character suddenly seems as opaque as all the rest.

In the Epilogue there seem to be some absolute answers. Hoffmann, frustrated by his failures with women, gives over his passion to the Muse: poetry henceforth will be his life. But for how long and with what intensity? The character, as created in the opera, might well prove less than constant. It is yet another question in this marvelously enigmatic, inspired, and rewarding masterpiece by Jacques Offenbach.

ROSSINI'S *Tancredi*
by Alfred Glasser

"I fancied that after hearing my opera they would put me in the madhouse—on the contrary, they were madder than I." The statement is from a bemused Gioacchino Rossini observing the furor that his opera *Tancredi* stirred up in Venice after its premiere at the Teatro la Fenice on February 6, 1813. *Tancredi*'s first-act cavatina "Di tanti palpiti" was sung, hummed, and whistled everywhere, to such an extent that the Venetian authorities passed an ordinance making it a misdemeanor to so much as hum the tune in a court of law, where the well-known words to a cadence ("Tu mi rivedrai, ti rivedrò"—You'll see me again, I'll see you again) could have a chilling effect on a witness. The *Tancredi* mania swiftly swept Europe, and Rossini as swiftly made the transition from struggling young composer to international celebrity.

Young he most certainly was. The premiere of *Tancredi* took place about three weeks before his twenty-first birthday. (Like Frederick in *The Pirates of Penzance*, Rossini was born on February 29.) Yet he was already a veteran composer. He had written his first opera at fourteen, and through the good offices of the Marchese Cavalli he had received his first commission to write a one-act opera buffa, *La cambiale di matrimonio* (The Marriage Market), from the Teatro San Moisè in Venice two years later. Nine of his operas had been staged, with results ranging from fiasco to triumph, by the time he began work on *Tancredi*.

Although he was not making much money (he received a meager 500 francs—about $250—for *Tancredi*), he was enjoying a very colorful life style. In the early years of the nineteenth century, two to three months were deemed adequate for the composition and mounting of an opera; but Rossini did not need that much time. As a result, a marathon of dinner parties would begin upon his arrival and occupy the first two or three weeks of his stay. Then the pressure of an imminent opening night would inspire him to write the music for the singers whose vocal prowess he had ascertained during the informal music making at the parties.

A delightful bit of Rossiniana is this advice on how to compose an overture, which he wrote later in his life to an unknown young composer:

> Wait until the eve of the performance. Nothing stimulates the inspiration more than sheer necessity, the presence of a copyist who is waiting for your work, and the insistence of a frantic impresario who is tearing his hair out by the handful. At my time, all the impresarios in Italy were bald at the age of thirty.

Since Rossini's first Venetian success had been a collaboration with librettist Gaetano Rossi, it was only natural that the team should try again. This time they decided on a full-length opera seria based on a tragedy by Voltaire, *Tancrède*. (Their final collaboration a decade later would involve another Voltaire drama, *Sémiramis*.)

While Voltaire is admired nowadays as the witty satirist of *Candide* and *Micromégas,* he was an immensely successful dramatist during his lifetime. *Tancrède,* which he dedicated to the powerful Madame de Pompadour, was his first play to be produced by the Comédie-Française. It was admired by Byron and was translated into German by Goethe.

Voltaire's *Tancrède*

Voltaire derived the plot for his drama from several sources: from episodes in Ariosto's *Orlando furioso* and from a contemporary novel by Madame de Fontaines. True to his standard formula, Voltaire starts the action at a crucial point and reveals the complicated situations that led to the crisis as the drama unfolds. Ineluctably, the protagonist in the title role is the last to learn the truth.

To begin at the beginning, the Christian knights who controlled Syracuse were torn by internal strife as they struggled to maintain their autonomy from threats posed by the Saracens. At a low point in his conflict with his Christian rival Orbassan, Argire sends his wife and his daughter, Aménaïde, to the safety of the court of the Byzantine emperor. During her sojourn in Constantinople, Aménaïde is wooed by the Saracen knight Solamir and by her fellow Syracusan Tancrède. As Argire's wife lies on her deathbed, Aménaïde and Tancrède swear to her that they will marry. Aménaïde returns to Syracuse; Tancrède stays behind and wins high military honors in the emperor's service. Syracuse is threatened by Solamir at the head of a Saracen army. Aménaïde writes a letter to Tancrède, who has returned to Sicily, asking him to come reign over Syracuse and her heart. Argire, weakened by age, forges an alliance with Orbassan and offers his daughter's hand in marriage to seal it. Aménaïde learns that Tancrède has been condemned to death as a traitor should he ever return and that his lands have been given to Orbassan as her dowry. She stalls for time. At this point, Tancrède reaches Syracuse. Instead of welcoming Tancrède, Aménaïde urges him to flee because she fears for his life. The Saracen army nears Syracuse, prompting Orbassan to insist upon an immediate wedding. When Aménaïde flatly refuses, Orbassan produces her letter, which his men intercepted near the Saracen camp. She had not mentioned Tancrède's name; all assume she intended the letter for Solamir. Aménaïde says nothing, since it would be equally treasonous to write to the outlawed Tancrède. The angry Syracusans clamor for her punishment. Argire is forced to sign his own daughter's death sentence. Tancrède, whom no one recognizes because he left Syracuse as a child, offers to champion Aménaïde's cause in a trial by combat against Orbassan, who is now her accuser. He kills Orbassan in the duel. Aménaïde approaches her champion with further protestations of innocence and with expressions of gratitude; but Tancrède repulses her, because he believes she has been unfaithful. Totally disillusioned, he eagerly grants the Syracusan's request to lead their forces against the Saracens, seeking death in reckless combat. The mortally wounded Tancrède is carried back to Syracuse, where, after learning from Argire that the letter was meant for him, he dies in the arms of Aménaïde, whom he recognizes as his wife.

Rossi's *Tancredi*

Faced with the task of reducing a five-act tragedy of several thousand lines to a two-act libretto of several hundred, Gaetano Rossi acquitted himself with distinction. Naturally, he restored the Italian spellings of Voltaire's gallicized proper names. By omitting a number of Aménaïde's scenes with her father and with her confidante, Rossi more sharply focuses the drama on Tancredi, but sacrifices Voltaire's portrait of a heroically feisty young woman. He follows Voltaire's action faithfully—he even surpasses the original in the moving monologue he provides for Argirio's conflict before signing Aménaïde's death sentence—up to the point where Tancredi goes off to fight the Saracens. To comply with the contemporary taste for happy endings, Rossi has Tancredi return victorious and unscathed. From the lips of his dying victim, Solamir, Tancredi learns of Aménaïde's fidelity. The happy couple is united amidst general rejoicing.

The Tragic Finale

A month after the triumphant premiere in Venice, *Tancredi* was staged with the same cast in not-so-distant Ferrara. Perhaps Rossini realized that the conventional finale weakened his opera. Perhaps the lover of his leading lady, Adelaide Malanotte—the contralto who created the role of Tancredi—felt that a tragic finale would display his beloved's talents to greater advantage.

In any event, the lover, Luigi Lechi, reworked Voltaire's original ending into an exquisitely terse sequence of Italian verses. Rossini rewrote the ending in a revolutionary fashion that flaunted the stylistic conventions of the day, avoiding the coloratura flourishes and elaborate orchestrations that audiences expected. Therefore, it is less than surprising that the new finale was coolly received by the Ferrarese. Subsequent performances reverted to the happy ending, and the tragic finale was seemingly lost until the 1970s, when Rossini's autograph score for it was discovered among the archives of the Lechi family. This finale, along with other authentic variants, is incorporated into a new, critical edition of *Tancredi* prepared by Philip Gossett.

Rossini's *Tancredi*

Tancredi is Rossini's first opera seria of "set" pieces connected by passages of recitative. He still used *recitativo secco* (dry recitative) in which the vocal line is supported by strummed chords from the keyboard. For moments of intense introspection he resorts to *recitativo accompagnato,* where the singer is accompanied by the full orchestra. Some of the set pieces, it is true, interrupt the action for purposes of vocal display; others, however, serve to advance the plot. Ornamentation of the vocal line, according to the usage of the era, was up to the singer. However, Rossini provided completely written-out *colorature* for Giuditta Pasta, when she later interpreted the role. Eventually, he would leave nothing to the singer's initiative but would notate all of his embellishments to make sure that virtuoso display did not obliterate his melodies. And what melodies he wrote! His operas—and *Tancredi* was one of his most celebrated during his lifetime—dominated the operatic world for decades. At the beginning of this century, many of the operas were remembered for their overtures alone; only a few of the comedies remained in the operatic repertory. However, thanks to the efforts of the champions of Rossini's music such as superstar Marilyn Horne and superscholar Philip Gossett, more and more of his operas are being performed. *Tancredi* claims a very special place in the Rossini catalogue, representing as it does a young composer for the first time in complete charge of his style with a youthful and pristine vigor he could never duplicate.

WAGNER'S *Tannhäuser*
by Lilias Wagner Circle

"For my next opera," Richard Wagner wrote in 1844, "I have chosen the beautiful and highly characteristic legend of *Tannhäuser,* who lingered in the Venusberg and then journeyed to Rome in search of atonement. I have made a connection between this legend and the Wartburg Song Contest; the result of this connection is a poem which is rich in dramatic life." *Tannhäuser* premiered in 1845, and again, audiences were puzzled by the unfamiliar style, so it was not instantly successful. It is the first time Wagner used his evolving "song-speech" rather than recitatives and set arias—especially this is noticeable in Tannhäuser's long narrative when he returns, unredeemed, from his pilgrimage in Act III. It was also the first time Wagner fused the themes of lust and piety, using religious ecstasy for theatrical effect, although he had tried out the dramaturgic motif of redemption in his youthful opera *Die Feen.*

The listener who seeks the later genius of the *Ring Cycle* and *Tristan und Isolde* will perceive that genius at work during the stunning first scene of *Tannhäuser.* The orchestra has become an eloquent part of the whole, highlighting the motives, conflicts, and passions of the main characters and explaining their psychological changes. The solemn, peaceful hymn of the pilgrims which opens the opera—and which will reappear several times—is shortly replaced by the ravishing sensual love music of Venus. This dramatic contrast between the sacred and the profane is further enhanced as Tannhäuser returns to earth, awakened by the young shepherd's pure melody, which will soon become part of a brilliant counterpoint to the Venusberg Music and the Pilgrim's Chorus. Wagner's music tells us that Tannhäuser is re-entering gradually, further roused by the very realistic sound of hunting horns. The opening of Act II, with its driving vitality, is reminiscent of Beethoven, who was Wagner's lifelong idol.

As the opera gained popularity and understanding over the next few years, audiences were particularly stirred by the pivotal Wartburg Song Contest in Act II—the scene in which Wagner had taken the greatest risks. "I may triumph," he wrote, "in the knowledge that I was able to hold the attention of an audience unaccustomed to such things, and that my appeal was conceptual and not merely emotional." Wagner expected a sort of "Greek chorus" participation from his congregation / audience, and apparently this scene achieved the desired effect.

This song contest is also a prophecy of the Prize Song sequence in *Die Meistersinger.* Both are based in the premise that art must be performed to survive, and Wagner clearly portrayed his two hero-singers as totally misunderstood by the authorities—a swipe at the critics, who were already having a field day with his music. This was especially the case in England, where British critics continued attacking him even after 1870, when Wagner had attracted a large body of support for his music-drama theories. After hearing *Tannhäuser,* the dean of English critics, Henry Fothergill Chorely, stated that he had "never been so blanked, wearied, insulted even (the word is not too strong) by a work of pretension as by this same *Tannhäuser.*"

While he was still in Dresden, Wagner completed *Lohengrin,* but at the same time, fired up by the revolutionary spirit of 1848, he added the government to his pursuers and so was forced to go into exile. Wagner was not basically a political animal in the sense that he bothered to lobby in court circles, nor was he interested in what king was currently on the throne—except as it affected his messianic goals. Spencer and Millington, in their recently published volume of Wagner's selected letters, suggest, however, that Wagner's actions in the 1848 German uprisings were nevertheless in character. His life during the previous three years had been filled with frustrations. Rebuffed by the court powers at Dresden when he made progressive and sensible suggestions that would improve the lot of the musicians and increase Dresden's standing in the musical sphere, Wagner was a natural ally for the intellectuals who spawned the 1848 German uprisings. Academicians and respected professionals, rather than bomb-throwing anarchists, they were working for relief from the feudal lords and hoping to establish a constitution and a representative form of government.

Wagner stated these aims in a letter to the king of Saxony (whom he considered to be a true Republican), and he delivered an inflammatory speech. The revolution of course failed, but Wagner's highly visible stance forced him to remain outside Germany for eleven years, living mainly off his friends, many of whom were infatuated women. Since *Lohengrin* was produced—and became popular—during those years, he remarked upon his return to Germany that he was probably the only German who had never seen it!

After he completed *Lohengrin* in early 1848, closing the era in German national opera which had begun with *Euryanthe,* Wagner took a break from composition while he formulated his own theory of music as drama. The ideas had of course already been germinating; while he was composing *Tannhäuser,* he had written: "It is not my practice to choose a subject at random, to versify it and then think of suitable music to write for it; no, my method of production is different from that: in the first place I am attracted only by those subjects which reveal themselves to me not only as poetically but, at the same time, as musically significant. And so, even before I set about writing a single line of the text or drafting a scene, I am already thoroughly immersed in the musical aura of my new creation, I have the whole sound and all the characteristic motives in my head so that when the poem is finished and the scenes are all arranged in their proper order the actual opera is already completed, and its detailed musical treatment is more a question of calm and reflective revision, the moment of actual creativity having already passed."

Once Wagner had committed a composition to paper, he seldom revised heavily, especially in later years; and there is only one record of his having made major changes at someone else's bidding. Apparently he was especially depressed in 1860, and in an effort to reestablish himself in Paris, he conducted three concerts there. This attracted the interest of Napoleon III, who ordered a production of *Tannhäuser* (translated into French) to be mounted for the Paris Opéra. Wagner rewrote the Venusberg scene, adding pantomine and attempting to convert it into a French "grand" opera. He also shortened the singing-contest sequence. The Jockey Club of Paris, annoyed because the ballet was early in the performance (instead of in the second act, after they had finished dinner), staged a riot, and the critics joined in; the opera closed after only a few performances.

After Wagner's return to Germany in 1864, he fortunately attracted the patronage of King Ludwig II of Bavaria, who kept Wagner in the lavish style to which he wished to become accustomed. Along the way, Wagner finally found a woman who understood and adored him and was able to provide him with the attention he required. He also betrayed two of his most faithful supporters and friends, Franz Liszt and Hans von Bülow, who nevertheless continued to champion his music, however he treated them personally. He stole von Bülow's wife (who bore Wagner three children before they were finally married); and he disgraced Liszt at the same time, since Cosima von Bülow was Liszt's daughter. Yet evidently, with Cosima, he found some measure of peace, although melancholia and nightmares continued to dog him for the rest of his life.

In order to achieve the results he saw and heard within his inventive, tormented mind he sometimes rehearsed a work fifty or sixty times and then, dissatisfied, set it aside. His single-minded dedication to his ideals about how art should be realized and produced was awesome. Was there a sound he needed in the orchestra? Then he would invent a new instrument (the Wagner tuba). Was there no hall that could contain his mental picture of the gigantic, complex productions his imagination had called forth? Then he would coerce his adoring patron and his long-suffering friends, using whatever methods would work, into paying exorbitant sums to construct the grand Festspielhaus at Bayreuth, which would be the last word in current stage technology. After his death, Cosima would turn it into a Wagner shrine, and his descendants would continue to be active in producing the operas there.

The initial Bayreuth festival in 1876 presented the first full performance of the Ring Cycle, attracting enormous attention all over the civilized world. It was many years before the second festival would be mounted, due to lack of funds, but Wagner built his home there, where he would remain until his death in 1883.

Wagner's operas have always attracted experimental productions. The works can be given very abstract treatment, with suggestions of light and color which enhance the emotional content. The constant struggles between sensual and pure love, and the dichotomy of love and death, which received its ultimate working out in *Tristan und Isolde,* can be set in any age, with the hero becoming a sort of Everyman.

Like Napoleon, Wagner was convinced of his special mission in the world, and without hesitation he set out to accomplish his task. It would be interesting to consider how history might have been changed had Napoleon been a timid commander and had Wagner been content to be a bootlicking conductor. Genius sometimes is best served by a self-centered dedication to the duty that a genius sees as the mission given to him.

Lawrence Gilman summed up Wagner's operas thus: "Nothing quite like them has ever come to us from another mind and hand. They are not musical works, strictly speaking, and they are not drama, and they are something more than a combination of the two, employing both music and drama to make a whole which somehow is greater than its parts."

PUCCINI'S *Tosca*
by Stephanie von Buchau

The most memorable slur cast on opera—at least since Samuel Johnson called it an "irrational entertainment"—is Professor Joseph Kerman's celebrated dismissal of Giacomo Puccini's fifth opera: "*Tosca,* that shabby little shocker," he wrote in the concluding chapter of his 1956 polemic *Opera as Drama.* That this epithet was gleefully seized upon by both those who agreed and those who disagreed only proves the accuracy of Dr. Johnson's earlier sneer.

Of course opera is irrational; in real life nobody sings for ten minutes after drinking poison or sustaining a stab wound. And *Tosca,* with its torture, attempted rape, murder, and suicide, may well be a "shocker," though perhaps "shabby" is going a bit too far. The point is that we like opera because it is irrational, and we love *Tosca* because it is a shocker. Any persons who suggest that they attend Puccini's romantic melodrama in order to have their political consciousness raised need a reality check. If we are honest, one of the reasons we go repeatedly to hear *Tosca,* aside from sizing up a new diva, is to watch Scarpia chase the heroine around the Palazzo Farnese.

Subconsciously, Kerman seems to realize this fact, though he fights against it mightily. In 1956, he could hardly be aware of the turn that operatic entertainment would take in the next three decades. No, I'm not referring to the orgy of naked nuns in Penderecki's *The Devils of Loudun,* but to the real descendants of Puccini's overheated, crowd-pleasing, melodramatic style—popular epic films such as *The Empire Strikes Back, Indiana Jones and the Last Crusade,* and *Batman.* Even in 1956, Kerman intuited the dangerous seduction of mass culture.

He writes, as he readily admits, from a lofty, humorless plane of idealism. In his ideal world, the only popular operas we could hear with complete moral safety are by Mozart and Verdi; Wagner is allowed, but only if you first apply Professor Kerman's ethical sunscreen. Otherwise, our austere, noncaloric operatic diet is to consist of Debussy, Berg, and Stravinsky. Kerman's plans for our aesthetic health are about as much fun as were Surgeon General Koop's plans for our physical health.

Still, Kerman produces a sharp criticism of Puccini's methodology. Aiming at the last few minutes of the opera, he sneers: "Tosca leaps, and the orchestra screams the first thing that comes into its head, 'E lucevan le stelle.'" Now this is not only a witty remark, it is essentially true. If you demand organic unity of leitmotifs, Cavaradossi's lachrymose aria does nothing to explain Tosca's feelings during her suicide. She's never heard "E lucevan le stelle."

However, nobody but university professors (and a few disgruntled composers) goes to the opera demanding dramatic unity and organic leitmotifs, especially if the composer that night is Giacomo Puccini. No, what is really bothering Kerman is the undeniable fact that the Tuscan composer had one eye (at least) on the public and its response. "What matters most," Kerman huffs, "is not Mario's plight, but the effect it could make on the audience. Puccini's faint emotionality *is directed out over the footlights*" (italics mine).

We haven't the space to argue about for whom a composer *should* write his operas, but there is no doubt that Puccini wrote for us, not for Professor Kerman. It won't hurt to quote Debussy, one of Kerman's select few, on another popular composer, Jules Massenet: "His brethren could not easily forgive his power of pleasing, which is a gift . . . the secret envy of many of those purists who can only enjoy the rather labored respect of the cognoscenti."

The point is that Puccini did, and continues to, please. There is no doubt in my mind that this is so precisely because he *did* care about the effect he was having on his listeners. You can have a spirited argument as to whether it is wise to stimulate an audience in the Puccinian manner, just as you can argue whether *Batman* is a dangerously lurid film. But you cannot deny the effect that they have.

Puccini is generally recognized, even by those who dislike him, as a lyricist, capable of writing obvious emotional melodies, catchy and easy to remember. He was also a canny man of the theater; Kerman makes the distinction, not in Puccini's favor, between "drama" and "theatrics." Puccini was drawn to pathetic twists—Mimi's romantic misery and tuberculosis; Cio-cio-san's desertion and suicide; Tosca's mental torture and suicide; Liù's hopeless passion and suicide.

These themes may be exploitative, but then Puccini was a master exploiter. As well ask a shoemaker to bake bread! The method he used for manipulation is the skill for which he is least well known, even among opera cognoscenti. He was a great orchestral craftsman whose skill was comparable to that of Nicholas Rimsky-Korsakov, the nineteenth-century Russian composer who wrote an important treatise on orchestration (which Puccini read) and orchestrated Mussorgsky's *Boris Godunov* and *Khovanshchina*. That it is critically déclassé to admire these orchestrations today does not negate their skill and genuine appeal.

Unlike Verdi, who pretty much lived in his own musical world, Puccini was a voracious reader of contemporary music. He was familiar with all the advances in modern music theater (though naturally he didn't subscribe to all of them) from Italy's verists and the important Russians (including Stravinsky) to Debussy's *Pelléas et Mélisande*. He read, he absorbed, and he learned, but he did not imitate. Thus, after his first two operas, *Le villi* (1883) and *Edgar* (1889), all of Puccini's work bears the unmistakably original stamp of someone consciously stretching the art of orchestration to the utmost limits that Italian lyric theater could bear.

A study of *Tosca* reveals, perhaps to our dismay if we have been carried away by the pulse-elevating surge of the theatrical moment, just how manipulative this composer could be. Every effect in *Tosca* is precisely calculated. It has been crudely suggested that Puccini aimed most of his salvos below the belt—which is, of course, why intellectuals are so offended by his success; Kerman keeps harping on Puccini's lack of taste. Nonetheless, even if you don't care for the direction in which the effect is aimed, only a fool would deny that the target is hit with devastating regularity.

Tosca's orchestration is large and varied. The opera is scored for two piccolos, three flutes, two oboes, English horn, two clarinets, bass clarinet, two bassoons, contrabassoons, four horns, three trumpets, three trombones, bass trombone, timpani (kettledrums), side drum, triangle, cymbals, tam-tam (gong), bass drum, carillon, celeste, bells, harp, and the usual five string sections. Any mature Puccini instrumentation can be studied with profit; just a glimpse at *Tosca*'s bells and woodwinds will give an idea of the richness and dexterity with which Puccini manipulates his orchestra and, by extension, his listeners.

The bells are important because, although *Tosca* is a romantic melodrama rather than a veristic opera, Puccini was striving to achieve a heightened realism in his score. The first act takes place inside the church of Sant'Andrea della Valle, where one would naturally expect to hear bells. And the first bell we hear is the Angelus (in F) which rings, supported by harp, flutes, and strings, while the Sacristan says his prayers. This bell is purely for local color and contributes nothing to the drama but a pregnant pause before Cavaradossi's entrance.

Bells for local color are used again, extensively, in the pastoral introduction to Act III. We hear sheep bells, unnotated, "in the distance," as the Shepherd sings his lament. (The triangle, harp, and celeste add a bell-like sonority to the accompaniment.) Then actual bells are notated, one tolling in the distance (presumably the great bell of St. Peter's) and others, matin bells, on the ramparts of the Castel Sant'Angelo.

Puccini also uses bells dramatically, as a weapon in his armory of scalp-prickling devices. In the finale to Act I, after Scarpia has planted the seed of jealousy in Tosca ("like Iago with the handkerchief"), the police chief remains alone in the church, soliloquizing about his desire for the beautiful singer.

Large bells toll a sinister ostinato, one note to a measure from B-flat to F; they continue right up to the moment that Scarpia blasphemes, "Tosca, you make me forget God!"

This subliminal tolling, reinforced by the on-stage organ and punctuated by cannon shots from the Sant'Angelo prison, where they have discovered Angelotti's absence, creates the most unmistakable erotic tension. The irony is that the soliloquy takes place simultaneously with a religious procession. By the time Scarpia piously joins the chorus in "Te aeternum Patrem omnis terra," the bells of Sant'Andrea are crying lust and hypocrisy.

Puccini is often accused of allowing the strings to overstate the obvious. Doubling the vocal line with sweeping violins may be this composer's besetting sin, but often the string-thick texture we perceive is really the fault of poor conducting. In *Tosca,* at least, the theatricality of Sardou's tawdry but "well-made" play is secured by the original manner in which Puccini employs such unusual sounds as the somber coloration of the bass clarinet. In addition, major melodic material is assigned, not to the strings, but to the flutes, clarinets, and bassoons.

For instance, Tosca's first entrance is announced by eight bars of ravishing flute melody, which is only picked up by the first violins (soaring triple pianissimo e dolcissimo) ten bars later. Her second-act aria "Vissi d'arte" is joined, at the words "with sincere faith," by the flute playing an expressive countermelody, "dolcissimo con grande sentimento," in its middle register, supported by harp arpeggios. Similarly, the clarinet (in A) plays, "lento appassionato," the introduction to "E lucevan le stelle." For sixteen bars the clarinet declaims the melody while Cavaradossi recites in monotone. Only at the words "O sweet kisses" do the violins and cellos begin to double the voice.

Another interesting example of Puccini's precisely calculated sound effects for woodwinds occurs in Act II, when Scarpia commands that Cavaradossi, who has been arrested at his villa, be brought before the police chief. The window in Scarpia's apartment in the Farnese is open, and we can hear from the floor below the cantata that the Queen of Naples has ordered to celebrate General Melas's supposed victory over Bonaparte at the battle of Marengo. Tosca, of course, is singing the solo in the cantata. Into the accompanying flutes, exploiting the sinister quality of their lower registers, creeps an evil little tune, almost jaunty in its baleful way. Three times it is repeated in its original form while Scarpia meaningfully summons a judge and executioner. As Cavaradossi defies Scarpia, the tune continues insistently, now doubled by the clarinet with support from the bassoon and English horn. There is no way that Mario is going to escape the consequence of this situation, as the winds make clear. If you concentrate only on how the baritone and the tenor are singing, you miss (at least consciously) a good portion of Puccini's superior manipulations.

The winds are also used to repeat melodic material that applies to previous events or states of feeling. Essentially, this is the Wagnerian leitmotif method modified by Puccini for his own Italian melodic style, which flows more freely than Wagner's highly organized structures tend to. (The Italian composer also feels free to abandon the leitmotif logic, as we have seen with Professor Kerman's justifiable complaint about the orchestra's screaming the first thing that comes into its head at the end of *Tosca*.)

Don't expect any great psychological revelations from Puccini's repeated motifs: they are usually straightforward, such as the B-flat clarinet singing out the theme from Tosca's "non la sospiri," in which she described her love nest, when Cavaradossi tells Angelotti where he can hide. Another use of the winds for characterization occurs when Scarpia hatches his plot to manipulate Tosca's jealousy by using the Attavanti's fan. The full range of woodwinds plays twitching motifs as the Sacristan stands nervously by, waiting for the blow to fall on his own head. Finally, there is the use of woodwinds to support the vocal line. In "Recondita armonia," much of the tenor's melody is doubled or played in octaves by a combination of flute, oboe, clarinet (in B-flat), even bassoon and English horn.

Yet however attractive the scoring, its main purpose, at least in this opera, is to tighten the thumbscrews on the listener. Puccini may not have been as astute or subtle a psychologist as Mozart, and good taste was not his middle name, but he knew how to use an orchestra—delicately or like a sledge hammer—to shred our nerves. His score to *Tosca* calls for such nonmusical instruments as cannons and rifles, precisely notated, yet the real musical instruments are more sadistic, more chilling, even more explosive than any weaponry could ever be.

The second act of *Tosca* contains at its center the most brutal scene of torture, attempted rape, and murder ever put on stage. Yet people who are squeamish at today's movies sit through *Tosca* with evident enjoyment. Does the music make the torture and murder *more* bearable? I don't think so; if anything, it makes it worse because the abstract nature of music can conjure horrors beyond the puny abilities of a mere stage director. It has also been suggested that most listeners don't really understand *Tosca*'s second act because it is usually given in Italian. This opinion not only sells the audience short; it has been nullified by the advent of supertitles.

My opinion is that we accept the horrors of *Tosca*'s second act—watch a student matinee sometime if you want to see *total* acceptance—because it satisfies our longing for excitement and reconciliation. The events are utterly repellent yet fiercely exciting: when Tosca stabs Scarpia, some primal part of us says, "Take *that*!" This is not bloodthirstiness so much as it is instinctive recognition of the moral dichotomy that makes us human. The ability to encompass and understand both good and evil—*and the difference between them*—is a primary ingredient in any satisfying stage experience, and you may sincerely pity those who think they are above such experiences.

My eighty-year-old grandmother, herself a former singer, once rebuked a prissy critic who complained that the second act of Herbert von Karajan's new *Tosca* recording was too sadistic and brutal. "Young man," she asked, "just what do you think is happening in that act? A parliamentary debate?" If we accept that the subject matter of *Tosca* is raw and violent, then we ought to credit the composer for having the courage to demonstrate that we also find this cathartic violence fascinating.

The sinister coloration of the lower register of the flute and bassoon has already been mentioned. In the Act-II Scarpia-Tosca confrontation, Puccini employs the high register of the woodwinds to evoke the diva's frantic, helpless terror. During the tremendous climax that occurs as Scarpia questions Tosca as to Angelotti's whereabouts, the diva cries, "No, no, ah, ah, ah, I can't take this anymore!" And the entire woodwind section screams with her, the piccolo playing fortissimo at the top of its range, doubled by heart-pounding glissandi on the harp. (This is the kind of effect that Kerman dismisses as "cafe-music banality," but then we all remember Noel Coward's mot: "It is amazing how potent cheap music can be.") Just as Tosca has been goaded beyond endurance by Scarpia, that screaming piccolo shreds *our* nerves. It's a kind of primitive participatory theater experience, and there is not much precedent for it in opera.

When Cavaradossi is brought in from the torture chamber, the bassoon sobs with the violas and is joined by the mournful English horn. After Mario hurls his "Vittoria!" and is dragged away, there is another *tutta forza* climax with the full orchestra—piccolo, flute, oboe, and clarinet in unison with the violins—supporting Tosca's high C. Then, as Scarpia tries to "reassure" her, offering her a glass of Spanish wine, the entire woodwind section insinuates softly, dolce, morbidly, the inequality of the coming struggle. I always have the sneaking suspicion that just as I have never heard a Scarpia I didn't like, Puccini also found the evil Barone the central figure in the opera.

Just from this brief survey, one can see that *Tosca,* like all of Puccini's mature operas, consists of more than just a series of caloric tunes draped over a lurid story line in dubious taste. Puccini was an artisan, and however you rate his inspiration, you have to rate his craftsmanship very near the top of the list.

VERDI'S *La traviata*

by Jonathan Abarbanel

There were successes, great successes, and triumphs: *Luisa Miller* (1849), *Rigoletto* (1851), *Il trovatore* (1853), *La traviata* (1853), *I vespri siciliani* (1855), and *Un ballo in maschera* (1859). There was one coolly received piece, *Simon Boccanegra* (1857). There also was one dismal failure, *Stiffelio* (1850), reworked and offered again in 1857 as *Aroldo* with only moderately better results. This single fiasco notwithstanding, it was a marvelously successful decade by any measure; a creatively fecund ten years. This was Giuseppe Verdi's great Middle Period.

The Middle Period. Biographers proclaim it. Musicologists analyze it. Opera goers can't seem to escape it in notes such as these. During these years, Verdi's work exhibited astonishing growth in its dramatic and musical authority. Verdi developed and expanded the role of the orchestra, deepened his powers of musical characterization, and began to achieve the dramatic unity and truth in each work that came to be called *verismo*.

The Middle Period spanned the creation of the single largest cluster of his most popular operas, works that scholars find linked like a strong chain in musical form and structure. Indeed, it is just such composition-based analysis that gave rise to the declaration of a "Middle Period" and that is used to define it.

But musicology aside, the decade 1849–59 witnessed substantial changes in virtually every aspect of Verdi's public and private life, from politics to family to professional standards in the theaters of his day. Each event, each change significantly influenced the shape and reach of his creative efforts. All these things taken together were Giuseppe Verdi's *real* Middle Period. They were the life behind the music; the basic elements of his craft and inspiration. In the remaining paragraphs of these notes, I shall explore some of these elements with particular reference to *La traviata*.

It is important to keep in mind that *La traviata* was a radically different sort of opera for Verdi and for the genre of opera seria at that time. With very, very few exceptions, all opera seria still used historical or mythological subject matter. Costume epics, stories of royalty and heroes, and period settings still were the norm. Contemporary stories and domestic environments were the province of opera buffa. Now, here was Verdi writing a tragic opera that not only told a contemporary tale but also featured bourgeois characters and an intimate setting of salon and boudoir.

As if that weren't enough, the heroine was a fallen woman. Many of Verdi's followers were shocked that he championed the cause, in effect, of a high-class whore, dignifying her with nobility of motivation and purity of heart. These same followers already were aghast because of earlier Middle Period operas. To the pious public, *Rigoletto* seemed to condone, even to ennoble, suicide; and the now-obscure *Stiffelio* actually made a virtue of divorce in a singular story about a German Protestant clergyman! Can you imagine how Italian audiences took to *that* in 1850?

The Middle Period, then, is marked by a sudden change in the type of stories Verdi told. Why did he change so dramatically? The simple answer is because he could. He was, at last, in a position to call his own shots, to pick and choose his own projects.

By 1849, at the age of thirty-six, Verdi had put the early years of poverty, scrambling, and artistic self-doubts behind him. He was financially secure, was known throughout Europe, and had outdistanced all contemporary rivals as the heir to Rossini and Donizetti. His first lasting success (though his third produced opera) had come only in 1842 with the premiere of *Nabucco* at La Scala. Its manly music—so characteristic of Verdi—and stirring patriotic chorus, "Va, pensiero sull'ali dorate," seized the Milanese, then all Italy, by storm. Despite his lack of formal musical education (the largely self-taught country boy had been rejected as a student by the Royal Conservatory in Milan), Verdi's talents had been recognized, and he shot to prominence.

During the next five years, Verdi composed nine operas. Although his fame and fortune grew, he always called this era his "years in the galley," as he shuttled between the leading opera houses of the peninsula, producing operas on demand for the impresarios. His public came to expect the virile melodies, the grand historical settings, and the thinly veiled patriotic fervor, as the separate dukedoms and kingdoms of Italy struggled to unite as a single nation.

By 1849, Verdi was Steven Spielberg. He had "clout." No longer a galley slave, he could select his own subjects and librettists. Impresarios now could contract with him for an opera, but they dared not dictate what it would be.

Thus, *La traviata* came to pass. It is based, of course, on *La Dame aux camélias* by Dumas, *fils*. The semiautobiographical novel had been a best seller of 1848. Verdi had read it, probably in the original French, and early on mentioned it in several letters as a possible subject for an opera. In 1852, Dumas adapted the work for the stage, and Verdi saw a performance in Paris that February. The play, bringing the titillating high-society demimonde vividly to life, was even more sensational a hit than the book had been. Here was passion, conflict, scandal, and pure love—all the elements Verdi prized in a good story. But more importantly, here, too, were intensity of characterization and realism. This was a story about real people.

Verdi asked Dumas for a copy of the play. Dumas obliged—eight months later! But Verdi hadn't waited; he was off and running. Returning to Italy in March, 1852, he immediately engaged his frequent collaborator, Francesco Maria Piave, to create a libretto, turning the realistic dialogue of the play into verse, tightening the action, and reducing the number of acts from five to three. Verdi had accepted a commission from Teatro la Fenice in Venice for a new work in the spring of 1853. He and Piave corresponded over the summer as to whether their new piece should go to La Fenice. Verdi was concerned about the absence of a soprano in the company to handle the difficult lead role. Verdi's intensity and enthusiasm for the work is evidenced by the fact that he was still struggling with *Il trovatore* that same summer. As during his years in the galley, here he was consumed with overlapping projects. But this time, both were labors by choice. In fact, he had begun to work on *Il trovatore* as a "freelance" project, without a commission or scheduled production. He wasn't worried. He knew he could place his work where he wished. As it fell out, the premiere of *Il trovatore* was delayed until January, 1853, in Rome. *La traviata* was set to open scarcely more than six weeks later.

As noted before, *La traviata* is an intimate, very French love story. Like the

Middle Period operas that preceded it, it is completely devoid of any musical patriotism. The fact that Verdi wrote five such operas in a row—from *Luisa Miller* through *La traviata*—is more coincidence than calculation, but it *did* mean that his work, for the first time, was judged purely on the bases of music and drama, not on nationalistic appeal.

Aside from the exercise of personal clout and artistic inspiration, what else was there about the Middle Period that drew Verdi away from historical spectacle and towards intimate drama? This may seem like a very curious answer, but there was gas.

By 1850, all the major European opera houses had converted to gaslight. When Verdi began his career, theaters still were lit by undimmable candles. Stage and audience were constantly lit at a single, unchangeable level of illumination. Only with gas did it become possible quickly and easily to put the audience in the dark and to light the stage more or less brightly. The impact of this new latitude was profound.

In candle days, one went to the theater to be seen. High society moved from box to box, chatting out loud over recitatives and choruses. By putting them in the dark, the social spectacle during the performance was eliminated. Audience attention was focused and directed away from the now-dim rings of boxes, and towards the stage. Audience composition began to change as social butterflies stopped attending theater, giving way to more serious lovers of art.

As audience manners and concentration improved, playwrights and lyric composers were able to create more demanding dramatic situations: more intimate, more realistic, more intellectually provocative, more unified, more "verismo." The Middle Period operas of Verdi, several of which he regarded as musically and dramatically experimental, represent his expanding into the artistic possiblities offered by the new theater technology.

Other changes quickly followed the introduction of gaslight, all serving to expedite the march towards great stage realism. Most notable among them were the elimination of stage boxes, which actually placed distracting audience members on the stage apron itself, and the trend toward a sunken orchestra pit. Through mid century, the orchestra was at the same level as the audience, throwing up a barrier of motion, tubas, and tall double basses between the audience and the stage. Only after the orchestra position was lowered did the main-floor seats begin to supplant box seats as the best in the house.

While one can see that changing stagecraft undoubtedly had its influence on Verdi (as he himself discussed in his letters), one still searches for a more profound reason for the dramatic changes of his Middle Period. Indeed, such a profound reason existed. For the first time since boyhood, Verdi had a contented and fulfilling private life and a permanent home.

From the age of nineteen on, Verdi had led a gypsy's life, splitting his time between Milan and Busseto, the small district center in Parma near which he had been born (in 1813, the same year as Richard Wagner). Later, after his first operas were produced, he found himself traveling between his rented quarters in Milan, and Venice, Rome, Naples, Florence, Paris, and London. He was a country boy, tied by emotion, familiarity, and dialect to his quiet "paese." Yet here he was, a respected artist, without land and without a home of his own.

Worse still, his life was lonely. Always aloof, Verdi did not mix well in society. He made friends slowly, and he lacked social graces. In time, he acquired great sophistication, but he never lost his direct, honest, gruff temperament. During the years in the galley, he was rumored to have had a number of liaisons but never a permanent attachment. At twenty-three he had been married to Margherita Barezzi, the beautiful daughter of his hometown benefactor. They had known each other for years, and the match appears to have been a true love match. Within two years, the Verdis had a son and daughter. Within four years, children and wife were dead, all within two months of each other in the spring of 1840. Stricken beyond measure, Verdi returned from Milan to Busseto and renounced composing. Fortunately, he was persuaded to change his mind.

In 1848, however, Verdi found his life mate. She was the retired diva Giuseppina Strepponi, known privately as Peppina. Two years younger than Verdi, she had been an early admirer of his work. She was instrumental in pushing his first opera, *Oberto,* and, later, *Nabucco* into production at La Scala. He had known her, then, as early as 1839. Their paths crossed professionally several times during the next ten years, and she sang in several key productions of *Nabucco.* Scholarship does not know for certain when they became lovers, but Verdi biographer George Martin makes a good case for the absence of a relationship until after the successful premiere of *I masnadieri* in London in 1848.

What is known for a fact is that Verdi returned from London to Paris, where Strepponi was living, and they set up house together in Passy, in suburban Paris. They spent the rest of their lives together, until Strepponi's death in 1897. They lived in Passy for more than a year and a half, before moving to Italy in August, 1849 (motivated by the need to escape a cholera epidemic in Paris). When they moved back south of the Alps, Verdi and Strepponi returned to Busseto, only this time Verdi owned the best house in town.

In 1848, Verdi had purchased the Palazzo Cavalli (still standing today and called the Palazzo Orlandi), the most handsome house on the town square. He also purchased a sizeable, somewhat run-down farming estate in a small hamlet nearby: Sant'Agata. He settled his parents on the estate to supervise upgrading of the property and remodeling of the villa. Sant'Agata in time became a model of modern agricultural experimentation—one of Verdi's non-musical passions—and Verdi's lifelong haven: a beautifully landscaped, comfortable, exceedingly private country villa. In the meantime, he and Strepponi lived in town, in their palazzo.

So Verdi launched his Middle Period with a comfortable and satisfying domestic life. He had security, stability, and a protective partner, all of which may have been conducive to greater introspection in his musical and dramatic work. Domestic bliss may have led him to explore domestic subjects for his operas with fresh eyes and new insights.

But life was not completely bliss. There was a problem: Verdi and Strepponi were not married. In a town of two thousand people, and a country town at that, such things were not done. Strepponi was ostracized from any proper social commerce in Busseto. Verdi, naturally aloof even from his fellow Bussetani, took their rejection of Strepponi as a personal insult. It was a particularly tense time for Busseto and for the man already acknowledged as the town's leading citizen. Although relations improved over the years, with Verdi eventually representing the district in the first Chamber of Deputies of the united Italy and also endowing a town hospital, he never fully forgave the town its social slights.

By January, 1853, Sant'Agata was far enough along for Verdi and Strepponi to move in. *La traviata,* just five weeks away from its premiere, thus became the first Verdi opera to be written, at least in part, at Sant'Agata. Art mirrors life, right? Here was Verdi, a prominent man in his community, living on a country estate with a woman who was not his wife, scandalizing society. Exactly the situation in Act II of *La traviata,* with Violetta and Alfredo enjoying a blissful country idyll. Biographers have made much of the coincidence. They should not. The opera was not intended by Verdi to make any type of autobiographical statement. However, it is obvious that he had a profound personal understanding of the emotional crises and social stigmas in the story he was writing.

This understanding, this intense personal feel for *La Dame aux camélias* is, perhaps, why he was able to compose the opera so quickly and straightforwardly. There is less correspondence between Piave and Verdi about *La traviata* than about any of their many other collaborations. Verdi had fewer instructions for Piave, fewer changes. And Verdi had absolutely no doubts about the work. He knew it was dramatically strong and musically effective. He knew he was writing a work every bit as good as *Rigoletto.* Even after the initial failure of the work, he never lost faith in it. *La traviata* seems to have leapt into his head fully formed.

Because of the apparent ease with which the piece came together, there is much we don't know about it. We don't know, for example, why Piave and Verdi changed the names of the characters from the play to the opera. Even more basic, we don't know why they changed the title. "Traviata" means "one who has erred or strayed; a wayward one." At the beginning of Act III, Violetta refers to herself as "traviata," but that is the only direct reference. Perhaps they simply wanted a shorter, more poetic title. Or perhaps they wished to put some distance between their lyric work and the stage play and the novel. Depending on the relative success of the piece, such distance could be useful to Dumas or to Verdi and Piave.

So let us talk about the success of the piece. At first, there wasn't any success. Verdi's doubts about the soprano proved to be well grounded. She sang well enough, but her immense bulk convulsed the audience, literally. Other members of the cast apparently were out and out desultory in their professional enthusiasm. Some critics and members of the audience did not understand this intimate drama, or they were offended by the subject matter. Most curious of all, this very contemporary story was produced as a period piece by La Fenice, with costumes and settings in the style of 1700, not 1850. In fact, *La traviata* was staged that way for years, even though the period setting was against Verdi's expressed intentions. In a letter of January 1, 1853, Verdi described the opera as "a subject from our own time. Another man perhaps would not have composed it because of the costumes, of the period (i.e., the modern period), or a thousand other foolish objections."

Why, then, did Verdi—always a stickler for production according to his wishes—let them get away with it? The answer seems to be time, or the lack of it. Verdi normally spent several weeks in rehearsal, supervising or approving all aspects of music and staging. It was his normal practice, also, to completely orchestrate each opera during the rehearsal period, an enormous task. This time around, however, Verdi's time was short. The premiere of *Il trovatore* had been January 19 in Rome. Verdi returned to Busseto at the end of the month, just in time to move into Sant'Agata. By the time he arrived in Venice, there were only thirteen days until the premiere. This was scarcely time to orchestrate, let alone supervise the production and coach the singers. No doubt La Fenice presented him with a fait accompli with regard to settings and costumes, and Verdi could only go along with it. Too, he might have been persuaded that the historical setting would make the shocking story seem less immediate, less up-to-date, less real, therefore somehow more acceptable to audiences. Didn't work.

After the premiere on March 6, 1853, Verdi wrote at least three letters describing the opening as "a fiasco." He blamed his singers most of all, and he chewed out his baritone, Felice Varesi (who had created Rigoletto). In fact, the opening was greeted with mixed reviews, not pans. But the opera wasn't acclaimed as *Rigoletto* and *Il trovatore* had been. Dare I suggest that Maestro Verdi's ego was showing? Certainly, he knew his work was good, and he continued to have faith in the opera. But perhaps, too, he was looking for an overwhelming validation of his musical and dramatic advances. Even more than that, perhaps he was seeking a validation, indirectly, of his convention-flaunting life style with Strepponi. The validation would come in time, but it wasn't immediate.

Fourteen months later, May 6, 1854, *La traviata* again was given in Venice, with Piave staging it at the Teatro San Benedetto, a smaller but still-important opera house. This time, still with its circa-1700 costumes, the opera was a great success. In 1855 it premiered successfully at the Théâtre-Italien in Paris, and in May, 1856, it opened in London, adored by audiences and damned by the critics for subject matter they considered obscene. No matter, for the opera's triumphal march had begun. In December, 1856, it reached America, first playing at the Academy of Music in New York.

Today, *La traviata* is Verdi's second most popular opera, topped only by *Aïda* in total number of performances. All the great sopranos have sung the role of Violetta Valéry: Marietta Piccolomini (London premiere), Anne Caroline de Lagrange (New York premiere), Marcella Sembrich, Adelina Patti (the finest of Violettas, according to Verdi himself), Nellie Melba, Luisa Tetrazzini, Geraldine Farrar, Lucrezia Bori, Amelita Galli-Curci, Rosa Ponselle, Claudia Muzio, Licia Albanese, Maria Callas, Renata Tebaldi, Joan Sutherland, Montserrat Caballé, Kiri Te Kanawa—and the list will stretch into the future.

Some biographers extend Verdi's Middle Period to 1862 and the composition of *La forza del destino* (for St. Petersburg) and *Hymn of the Nations* (for the London Exhibition of 1862). It is much neater, however, to end the Middle Period in 1859. In that year, two events took place that conveniently cap the decade and also signal the next radical change in Verdi's life. All spring and summer, a war of independence was being fought against the occupying Austrian armies across northern Italy, led by Vittorio Emanuele, king of the Piedmont and soon to be first king of a unified Italian nation. One by one, the various small duchies and states voted to join with Piedmont. Verdi's home state, the duchy of Parma, was one of the first to vote in favor of union. On September 4, 1859, Verdi was elected to represent Parma in its regional assembly and later in its delegation to the king. This launched Verdi's active political career, which lasted until 1865 (though in 1875 the king honored him by declaring him a senator of the kingdom for life). Perhaps more importantly, just a week before the election, on August 29, 1859, Verdi married Giuseppina Strepponi in a quiet private ceremony. The happy ending that *La traviata* couldn't have.

WAGNER'S *Tristan und Isolde*
by Speight Jenkins

Many operas entertain; *Tristan und Isolde* overwhelms. Wagner's opera does so because it speaks directly to the listener's unconscious, and its subjects are nothing less than sex, love, and death.

Because *Tristan* has had such an impact on all that has been composed after—it has often been called the father of twentieth-century music—analyses almost immediately launch into its fascinating musical and dramatic undercurrents. Indeed, if Wagner is clearly the composer about whom the most has been written, *Tristan* of his works has caused the most ink to be spilled. So much thoughtful analysis by some of this century's greatest minds has added to the world's body of knowledge, but it has sometimes frightened away prospective listeners. A person buying an opera ticket is not necessarily expecting a session with an analyst or philosophical speculation, and when threatened with such difficulty, many, no doubt the majority, would much more happily settle for *Rigoletto* or *Carmen*.

So the first point to be made about *Tristan* is that everything that follows is NOT necessary for enjoying the opera. *Tristan*, composed from 1857 to 1859, received its premiere in Munich in 1865; after about twenty or twenty-five years of mystifying audiences, the taste of the public caught up with the music, and the opera became extremely popular—performed everywhere whether singers could handle the notes or not. Then after forty years or so, when it might have had a normal downswing in popularity, Kirsten Flagstad appeared and joined with the already established Lauritz Melchior to put *Tristan* firmly on the gold standard in America. Audiences in New York, Chicago, and San Francisco filled opera houses because they simply reveled in the sound of those wonderful voices in music for which they were created.

And this was perfectly logical, because at the primary level, Wagner created one of the most marvelous of romantic operas, with a goodly number of hits: the Prelude, Isolde's Narrative and Curse, the first-act love duet, the Night of Love section of Act II—which has been called the most sublime twenty minutes composed in the nineteenth century—and of course the Liebestod, almost surely Wagner's most popular excerpt. These popular sections are not enumerated with a trace of condescension. But their thrill is all the greater the more one is immersed in what Elliot Zuckerman in his superb book, *The First Hundred Years of Wagner's Tristan*, calls "Tristanizing."

Much of Wagner's theoretical writing, particularly in the decade prior to the composition of *Tristan*, developed the importance of words in opera and argued that the music stemmed from the text. To this end, so Wagner said, every word must be understood and all ensemble passages—even duets— should be banned so that the audience could hear every single word. Two and two-thirds of the composer's operas actually fulfill this goal: *Das Rheingold, Die Walküre*, and the first two acts of *Siegfried*. But by the time he was deep into the passion of *Die Walküre*, he had become enraptured with a wholly different idea and philosophy—that of Arthur Schopenhauer.

Schopenhauer seemed to answer Wagner's philosophical striving, and the composer quickly moved to incorporate the philosopher's ideas into his own system. This points out one of Wagner's strongest traits: he always took ideas he liked even if they were antipathetic to his own published statements, worked on them, and then proclaimed that they were part of a logical development of his thinking. In the case of Schopenhauer, the philosopher saw music as supreme, far above words. Wagner, whose genius always forced him to make musical over literary decisions, knew that this was right for him. But he couldn't buy the idea outright, so he wrestled with it, not really solving the balance of words and music until about 1870, long after *Tristan*.

But Schopenhauer's more direct influence on *Tristan* came from the core of his depressing philosophy. Wagner wrote in a letter to Liszt: "I have now found a quietus. This is the heartfelt and intense longing for death, for complete unconsciousness, total nonexistence, the disappearance of all dreams—the only final salvation." Wagner's adaptation of this theory and his reason for acceptance of it characteristically revolved around love. But for almost the only time in his operas he was not concerned with man's being saved by the selfless love of a woman but by the transitory nature both of love and of the sexual act. Only in death could the bliss he sought be maintained. Having thus adapted Schopenhauer's thought to suit him, Wagner eagerly embraced the philosopher's description of music's assault "upon the feelings, passions and emotions of the hearer."

This is the very essence of what is loved or hated in Wagner. His music is often called "heavy," a term that in its dictionary meaning as applied to music could mean big voices and a large orchestra. But the word as used by the average opera goer means that Wagner's music, particularly in *Tristan* and the operas that follow it, relentlessly assaults the totality of the listener. From the Prelude's beginning, there is conveyed a frustrating sense of unsatisfied longing. There are technical explanations for what Wagner does—notably an excess of chromaticism and something called the deceptive cadence. But the unsettling feeling to the listener is of *Tristan*'s music moving from point to point, carried on a wave of orchestral and vocal sound, always avoiding a place of rest, a home base. This is the opera's magic, and the relief at the resolution, just at the conclusion of the Liebestod, is indeed a peace that passes all understanding.

The importance of *Tristan*'s special sound fulfills Schopenhauer's dictum about the priority of music over words, because the opera is almost surely the most musical one ever composed. Its music is not just involved with the text; it causes the text to exist. A person who knows the opera cannot, literally cannot, read the libretto without hearing the sounds of Wagner's music in his head. Because the music seems to give the words meaning, *Tristan* is the only opera in which reading the libretto before hearing the music is not a good idea.

The sound comes in part from the chromaticism and the deceptive cadences mentioned above and also from the fabled *Tristan* chord/dissonance that the Germans call the "Ak-kord." This takes place in the first phrase of the Prelude. The combination of notes literally sounds unfulfilled, and it immediately focuses the listener's attention on the crucial musical element in the opera: harmony. The obviousness of the importance of harmony in *Tristan* came home to me several years ago at the Metropolitan. After a particularly fine performance of the opera, I was walking up the aisle, and two young people—both around twenty—were just ahead of me. The man said: "I never heard this before but I can't get over the harmony. Not the tunes. That harmony weaves in and out like a snake." The comment caught the essence of what Wagner did. In order to convey the unfulfilled passion, he consistently manipulated the harmonic effects and stretched the limits of tonality to keep the listener constantly in turmoil. To prove this, one need only play through a piano reduction of the opera. Unlike so many Strauss operas, *Tristan*'s effect has nothing to do with orchestration. The instruments, even though used brilliantly by Wagner, only amplify the line that he had worked out pianistically.

The vital components of the harmony are the leitmotifs. In *Tristan* these signature phrases do not undergo the metamorphoses they do in his later operas, but they are very different from the simple, easy-to-identify motifs of *Das Rheingold*. In *Tristan* for the first time Wagner uses leitmotifs to build the complexities of his characters, stacking one on another and using parts of one with another. Although certain motifs are very clear, the important fact is not picking out one tree but recognizing the interlocking splendor of the forest.

When the sound of *Tristan* is understood, the text can be clarified. In part, this is because Wagner was groping with the infinite and also because he was less than an ideal poet. Had he had a Hugo von Hofmannsthal to convey his thoughts, however, he would not have been the kind of egomaniacal genius it took to create *Tristan*.

Again and again one runs into the word "longing"—*Sehnen* in German—in discussing *Tristan*. It is part of the lovers' nature, and a vision of Tristan and Isolde married and settled in Kareol, Tristan's castle in Brittany, is literally inconceivable. Isolde can no more be a married woman than, in George Bernard Shaw's phrase, could the Count di Luna in *Il trovatore* ever sit down. She is a femme fatale, whose purpose is to represent the impossibility of constant love fulfillment. She and Tristan both seek the realm of peace which the world makes impossible. This gives rise to their "day" and "night" imagery. To them "day" represents the duties and obligations of everyday life; "night" is the goal of bliss, the infinite, the ecstasy of physical love.

The subject of physical love in *Tristan* may be peripheral, but it is vital to make the deeper meanings relevant. For in this opera Wagner did something unique for his century. Instead of idealizing chivalric love as he had through Wolfram's mouth in the earlier *Tannhäuser* and as almost every opera composer did in the nineteenth century, Wagner in *Tristan* glorified and idealized the sexual act itself, something not discussed in Victorian literature or music. The two lovers clearly seek the perpetuity of the ecstasy of orgasm. Isolde, in the midst of the Night of Love section of Act II, dwells on how to remove the "and" between Tristan and Isolde. She longs for a total, continuous communion of their two selves, a way to make their joy never ending. Accustomed in our age to hyperexplicit sex, it is hard to imagine it where everyone is clothed and no one uses four-letter words. But by listening to the music of the second-act duet—shattered at the end just as resolution is about to be accomplished—or in the Liebestod, the clear nature of Wagner's graphic description will become evident.

One technical textual point has often confused the audience. In the first act, Tristan and Isolde drink a love potion and move from acrimonious debate to instant love. Because Wagner composed music that implies the working of the potion on their minds, many see the subsequent drama as the tiresome working out of a chemically induced passion. Nothing could be further from the truth. The crucial factor in the love potion is that both Tristan and Isolde believe it to be a death potion. They think they have only a few minutes to live, and in that time they allow themselves to proclaim exactly what they feel. If we have listened closely to Isolde's anger, we know that she was and is in love with the man who has betrayed her. Tristan later tells us that he always knew he was in love. The potion, substituted by Brangäne, is the classic red herring; it could have been pure water, and the same result would have occurred.

Why Tristan, obviously in love with the woman who cured him, betrayed her by claiming her for his old uncle can possibly be explained by the ethics of knighthood. In love with the Irish princess, Tristan returned home to find that many seemed to think he was now just waiting for his old uncle to die so that he could inherit the kingdom. Marke tells us that he was perfectly happy to will his land to Tristan, but somehow Tristan's chivalric impulse—or was it an unconscious desire for death?—forced him to sell Marke on marriage with Isolde. Although it is dangerous in as symbolic a drama as Wagner's to become literal, Tristan's age—sixteen or seventeen—strengthens the point. In Barbara Tuchman's popular history of the fourteenth century, *A Distant Mirror,* she observes that in the Dark Ages and the Middle Ages life spans were so short that teen-agers were often thrust into mature roles before they had worked out their childishness. To her this explained the often unseemly impetuosity of so many adults of those eras, who acted out as adults what they had never been allowed to do as children. And Tristan at sixteen may well have conceived the whole idea of Isolde's marrying Marke as an impetuous means of showing his own nobility.

The textual basis for the longing for death as the place where the two lovers can both enjoy the kind of union they desire is all through the libretto. Tristan drinks what he thinks is poison cheerfully, calling it "oblivion's kindly draught" and a "balm for endless grief." And in the first ecstasy of their love the two sing a line full of the confusion rampant in *Tristan:* "Escaped from the world, I have won you." By this they mean that only in leaving the world via what they think is a death potion have they won the victory of union that they both long for. In a presentiment of what is coming, Isolde's last words as she quenches the torch in Act II, the signal that will bring Tristan to her, are: "Laughing I fear not to quench the torch, even were it the flame of my existence." The concept of joyfully awaiting death surfaces again in the *Siegfried* love duet, the text of which predates *Tristan.*

In the final act, which contains the most marvelous music in the opera and is the most revealing textually, Tristan longs for a union with Isolde and a return to the land of night where they both belong. In his first monologue he is graphic in his telling Kurwenal that he enjoyed his passage to the realm of night and would have stayed there but he saw Isolde shining in the light of day. Her brightness brought him back to find her and carry her back to the land of night. And in the final delirium, when Tristan rips off his bandages, demanding that his blood pour forth to meet Isolde, he is not at all mad. He is doing exactly what he means to do as he cries, "Let the world pass away as I hasten to her in joy."

Wagner had two particularly relevant comments for any member of a *Tristan* audience. One involves the sea. He asked his listeners to allow themselves to be launched into the sea at the beginning of the Prelude and insofar as possible for the four hours of the opera to lose contact with everyday reality and with the standards governing normal life. This sense of separation necessary to give in to the "endless" melody of *Tristan* is described perfectly in *Nietzsche contra Wagner:* "One walks into the sea, gradually loses one's secure footing and finally surrenders oneself to the elements without reservation. One must *swim.*"

Telling, too, is an oft-quoted remark by Wagner while he was composing *Tristan.* He wrote in a letter: "This *Tristan* is becoming something *dreadful*! . . . Only mediocre performance can save me! Complete good ones are bound to drive people crazy." Every audience, however, hopes that Wagner's pessimism will not be justified. Maybe this time the right soprano and tenor, mezzosoprano, baritone, and bass, most of all a great conductor and orchestra and an inspired director, working within a splendid setting, have come together. Then when the winds and cellos come together on that first *Tristan* sound, the Wagnerian ship can set sail on a triumphant voyage. Chances are madness will not result but instead the greatest fulfillment possible in opera—an intimate involvement with the infinite.

VERDI'S *Il trovatore*
by Stephanie von Buchau

"*Il trovatore,*" writes George Bernard Shaw, "is absolutely devoid of intellectual interest." Having delivered this zinger, Shaw goes on to demonstrate that even a superior intellect such as his is not above being interested by it: "But we must take it or leave it; we must not trifle with it. He who thinks that *Il trovatore* can be performed without taking it with the most tragic solemnity is, for all the purposes of romantic art, a fool."

Shaw then details exactly how *he* would produce the opera. He suggests dressing di Luna in violet velvet and white satin. "No man could sit down in such a tunic and such tights; the vulgar realism of sitting down is ten times more impossible for the Count di Luna than for the Venus of Milo." Shaw goes on to suggest that the scenery be designed in the style of Gustave Doré "at his most romantic. The mountains must make us homesick, even if we are Cockneys who have never seen a mountain bigger or remoter than Primrose Hill."

Tastes change, and today one smiles at the idea of di Luna in violet velvet and white satin (not entirely sure that Shaw wasn't smiling, too), although the Doré idea remains a sound one. Shaw was not, after all, a designer of sets and costumes, but he understood the primary point about romantic melodrama, of which *Il trovatore* is the nineteenth century's most impressive and beloved example. Romantic melodrama may appeal to the senses and instincts rather than to the intellect, but if it is to appeal at all, it must be taken with scrupulous seriousness. As Giuseppe Verdi put it to his librettist, Salvatore Cammarano, "If we cannot do our opera with all the novelty and bizarre quality of the play, we had better give it up."

Il trovatore burns at white heat, with what Charles Osborne admiringly calls "an almost brutal vigor." It is "an opera whose characters," as Eduard Hanslick said, "arrive on stage as if shot from a pistol." Since melodrama, by its very nature, is unbelievable, a successful melodrama, like *Il trovatore,* must have the stamp of sincerity. Ronald Mitchell, in his excellent handbook on opera production, could have been speaking of Verdi's seventeenth opera when he wrote that the born melodramatist considers it his primary job to provide excitement, not to account for it. The undeniable excitement and its seemingly unaccountable motivations are the crux of the continuing "instinct vs. intellect" debate over the worth of *Il trovatore.*

The opera, bar for bar the most popular of Verdi's middle-period works, has had a bad intellectual reputation since its premiere. Contemporary critics, unimpressed by Verdi's distillation of the familiar style, called it "the death of bel canto." Charles Dickens, hearing *Il trovatore* in Naples the year of its premiere, wrote to a friend, "It seemed like rubbish on the whole to me." Finally, Cammarano's libretto has been called preposterous, laughable, and unintelligible. It is none of those things. It can be easily grasped in one read-through, except that most opera lovers would rather go on a diet than open a libretto. With the advent of projected titles in English, the myth of *Il trovatore*'s impenetrable plot is quickly put to rest.

Just to make sure, however, here is the background of the story, which begins twenty years before the opera opens: After her gypsy mother had been burned at the stake by the elder Conte di Luna (father of the opera's baritone) because he thought the old gypsy had cast the evil eye on his eldest son (Manrico, the opera's tenor hero), Azucena carried off the infant Manrico, intending to throw him on the still-smoldering pyre. Instead, in a moment of confusion— more about this later—she threw her own son instead. Since then she has pursued a dream of vengeance while raising the count's son as her own.

Cammarano's lean, well-organized libretto is based on the play *El trovador,* by the Spanish playwright Antonio García Gutiérrez. After it was premiered in Madrid in 1836, the twenty-three-year-old author found himself an overnight celebrity, though he never again equaled this success. A disciple of French dramatist Victor Hugo (whose *Le Roi s'amuse* was the source of Verdi's *Rigoletto*), Gutiérrez was also influenced by a fellow Spaniard, the duke of Rivas, whose play *Don Alvaro* was later turned by the Italian composer into *La forza del destino.*

Gutiérrez's *drama caballeresco* is a play in which the characters care about nothing but their passionate feelings. Sexual desire and jealousy, mother love, and revenge are the sole motivations of the leading quartet, who think nothing of behaving in an extravagant, even irrational manner. Leonora (we'll stick to Verdi's spellings) boldly commits one sin after another—very daring for the time in which the play was produced. She indulges in an illicit sexual relationship; she flees a convent (in the play she has actually taken her vows, but Cammarano avoided the omnipresent Italian censor by having Manrico snatch her from the cloister *before* she commits herself); she makes an immoral bargain with the villain; and she finally commits suicide—all mortal sins in the unforgiving eyes of the Catholic Church.

Azucena has been the butt of operatic jokes for 134 years. (Gilbert and Sullivan parodied the baby switch in *The Gondoliers*.) How, we ask, could any woman "accidentally" throw her own child into a fire instead of the son of her mortal enemy? It may be hard to believe, but it is not impossible. Late at night, in a distraught state, still hearing the cries of her dying mother ("Avenge me!"), Azucena tells us in the *racconto*, "Condotta ell'era in ceppi," exactly how it happened. And we believe her.

Azucena saw a vision of her mother, "barefoot and dishevelled," and with that haunting cry for vengeance still ringing in her ears, blindly thrust the baby into the smoking pyre. She watched the fire devour its tiny victim. The vision faded, and there, beside her—was the count's son! She had murdered her own child. As Julian Budden puts it, "Experienced with this degree of force and dramatic truth, the story of the wrong baby consigned to the flames no longer makes us smile."

Verdi took particular pains that Cammarano not weaken Azucena's psychology in the final act: "Don't make Azucena go mad. Exhausted with fatigue, suffering terror and sleeplessness, she speaks confusedly . . . but she is *not* mad. This woman's two great passions, her love for Manrico and her wild desire to avenge her mother, must be sustained to the end." It is quite clear from this exposition of Azucena's mental state that Verdi did not feel that the murder of the wrong baby motivates the gypsy's actions. Twenty years later, she has accepted her rash and tragic mistake. She has even atoned for her sin by lavishing maternal feelings on the scion of the hated family that deprived her of her mother.

Manrico may be a stock operatic tenor, but he is an exemplary son—loyal, honest, brave, and as devoted to his "mother" as she is to him. Indeed, one of the odder aspects of *Il trovatore*, at least to us, is not why Azucena mixed up the babies but why Manrico, safe at Castellor with his beloved Leonora, throws it all away in a futile effort to rescue his mother from di Luna's clutches. Can you imagine what a modern psychiatrist would make of a groom who abandons his bride at the altar in order to rush to his mother's side?

Since Gutiérrez's play was not performed in Italy, it seems that Giuseppina translated it for Verdi. Once Cammarano got hold of the translation, Verdi had to combat the librettist's essential conservatism. After *Rigoletto,* which had leaped forward to music drama, the composer was ready to apply the same method to the current project. He wrote enthusiastically to Cammarano: "If in an opera there were neither cavatinas, duets, trios, choruses, finales, et cetera, and the whole work consisted of a single number, I should find it all the more right and proper."

This is a bold, visionary statement for any mid-century Italian composer, despite the fact that Wagner was struggling for the same ideal. However, *Il trovatore* remained a conventional "number" opera, in which the despised cavatinas, duets, trios, choruses, and finales are the whole point of the exercise. Verdi obviously realized that the romantic melodrama form was best served by distilling its essence. Budden calls it "an explosion of closed lyrical forms with the orchestra relegated to its traditional role of accompanying the voices." The operative word in that sentence, of course, is "explosion." When Verdi was ready to write a seamless, numberless opera "right and proper," he produced *Falstaff.*

Verdi and Giuseppina spent the winter of 1851–52 in Paris. Despite his tart characterization of the Paris Opéra as "la grande boutique," he loved the cosmopolitan aura of that great city. Although Verdi is often considered a countryman, a farmer, even a social bumpkin, nothing could be further from the truth. He was actually a citizen of the world, with liberal, tolerant ideas about politics, religion, and social intercourse. It was his refusal to "suffer fools gladly" that gave him his reputation for gaucherie.

In Paris he signed a contract for the work that was to become *Les Vêpres siciliennes* (1855); he also investigated the problem of unauthorized versions of his operas being presented at the Théâtre-Italien. So incensed was he by this piracy that he brought suit and, as a consequence, was offered the opportunity to give the French premiere of *Il trovatore* at L'Opéra in 1857.

One of the major myths of nineteenth-century Italian operas concerns the length of time it took to compose them. Rossini supposedly took only two weeks to write *Il barbiere di Siviglia,* and *Il trovatore* was apparently composed between the first and the twenty-ninth of November, 1852. This is the kind of "fact" that delights people with a *Guinness Book of World Records* mentality, but it does disservice to art. We know that many of Mozart's compositions were written down with almost no alterations. Does that make him any more or less a composer than Beethoven, who struggled visibly with every bar? Undoubtedly Verdi was noting ideas—either mentally or on paper—all during the eighteen-month correspondence about the libretto's structure. It is possible, of course, that the simpler, rather formulaic orchestration of *Il trovatore* might have caused less compositional anguish than the more symphonic, asymmetrical scoring of *Otello* or *Falstaff.*

In any case, the opera was finished by December 14, and rehearsals began after Christmas. Originally Verdi had wanted to produce *Il trovatore* in Naples because of Cammarano's connections with the venerable San Carlo—which had seen the premieres of Verdi's *Alzira* (1845) and *Luisa Miller* (1849). But the composer was most concerned that whatever theater took the premiere have the most suitable singers. (Half a century later, Enrico Caruso put a damper on all future *Trovatores* by declaring that all that was needed to make it work was "the four greatest singers in the world.") Verdi finally settled for the Teatro Apollo in Rome, where, oddly, he had the most doubts about the mezzo, Emilia Goggi.

However, the soprano, Rosina Penco, was first-rate, so much so that months later, Verdi tried to avert the disaster that met the first performance of *La traviata* by securing Penco for the role of Violetta. He was overruled by the management of La Fenice, where *Traviata* had its fateful premiere in March of 1853. Verdi also intended Penco to be his original Amelia in *Un ballo in maschera,* giving a good idea of her talents and his appreciation of them. This plan also fell through, though she later sang Amelia at Covent Garden in 1861.

The problem of the mezzo was more serious, but at that point, juggling two world premieres within three months, the composer obviously felt he couldn't afford to hold up the proceedings any longer. Until *Il trovatore* he had made no significant use of a mezzo or contralto in his operas. As Budden points out, "Azucena is the first of a glorious line which includes Ulrica, Eboli, Amneris."

Mezzo or not, *Il trovatore*'s world premiere, January 19, 1853, was a triumph. The critic of *Gazzetta Musicale* reported: "Last night *Il trovatore* was produced in a theater overflowing with people. The music transported us to heaven; and in truth it could not be otherwise, because this is, without exaggeration, heavenly music. . . . The public listened to every number in religious silence and broke into applause at every interval, the end of the third act and the whole of the fourth arousing such enthusiasm that their repetition was demanded." He goes on to call the music "original" and the orchestration "deliciously new."

Francis Toye wryly points out: "No one today would think of describing the orchestration of *Il trovatore* as either new or delicious. It may be—in fact, is—adequate; but the outstanding characteristic of the opera that obliterates all else to us is the expressive passion of the melodies, the reason being, of course, that, whereas composers (including Verdi in his later operas) have brought the art of orchestration to a pitch then undreamed of, nobody has ever surpassed the magnificent collection of [vocal] tunes assembled by Verdi in *Il trovatore.*"

Shaw goes further. Defending the composer from the charges of Wagnerism that attached themselves to his later operas, Shaw makes the astonishing statement—astonishing in view of the riches of *Un ballo in maschera, La forza del destino, Don Carlo, Aïda, Otello,* and *Falstaff*—that "the real secret of the change from the roughness of *Il trovatore* to the elaboration of the last three operas *is the inevitable natural drying-up of Verdi's spontaneity and fertility*" (italics mine). While this may seem an oblique way to *defend* the composer, it makes quite plain the visceral appeal—even to an intellectual like Shaw—of *Trovatore*'s great tunes. (Besides, Shaw wasn't attacking Verdi for the complications of his later operas so much as he was angry with the librettist Boito—because Boito had dared to tamper with Shakespeare.) Shaw further muddies the waters by sneering that the melodies in *Trovatore* are "common" (even though he loves them!), i.e., "Di quella pira" is a bolero, "Stride la vampa" is a waltz.

The genius of Verdi, of course—like that of Bach and Mozart before him—wasto transform the commonplace, the vernacular, the ritual, the formulaic. This is precisely why *Il trovatore* became so popular so quickly. Within two years of its premiere it had circled the globe, inspiring parodies and being played on every barrel organ in Italy. Of course it is vulgar—in the true sense of the word, meaning "of the people." But as Toye eloquently points out, "This vulgarity is the vulgarity of greatness, a by-product of the vitality and passion without which there can be no great art. Is Shakespeare never vulgar? Or Beethoven?"

One of the things that to us makes *Il trovatore* seem "vulgar" (in the negative sense of coarse or trashy) is the accumulation of bad traditions, those unmusical stunts that are handed down as gospel, though they may contradict the composer's intentions. One of these traditions is the interpolated high-Cs in the tenor's two-verse cabaletta "Di quella pira." In the 1909 opera season at New Orleans, a tenor named Léon Escalaïs encored "Di quella pira" (both verses, in French!) four times, singing a total of fifteen high-Cs from the chest. Now if such a stunt comes off, it *can* thrill an audience, but the truth is that Verdi didn't write *any* Cs in this cabaletta. Yet the tradition to add them is so ingrained that if the tenor can't reach C—and a lot of famous tenors have had problems in this area—he transposes the whole aria in order to reach a note that isn't there in the first place. This is worse than vulgarity; it is absurdity.

Budden gives his opinion for *Il trovatore*'s reduced currency in today's world: "The nineteenth century was an age of moral confidence and certainty which found its ideals mirrored in an opera in which no one hesitates for one moment as to what action he or she should take. The present age finds it easier to identify with the torments and uncertainties of Violetta and Don Carlo." Yet that naive moral certainty remains one of *Il trovatore*'s primary charms.

The final word needs to be Italian, because for all its universal appeal, *Il trovatore* is the quintessential Italian opera, its drama propelled by the power of the human voice. So much is this opera a part of the Italian "anima" (soul) that Gianandrea Gavazzeni—the last living link to a noble tradition of Italian conductors which stretches back from Tullio Serafin and Arturo Toscanini to Verdi's onetime friend and rival in love Angelo Mariani—calls it simply, "the Italian *St. Matthew Passion*."

PUCCINI'S *Turandot*
by William Weaver

A gala opening night at La Scala in Milan, for anyone who loves Italian opera, has a special excitement that can be found in no other theater. The statues of Rossini, Bellini, Donizetti, and Verdi that stand in the gold-and-marble foyer are moving reminders of the greatness revealed on that stage; and in the little columned passage between foyer and stalls, the bust of Stendhal reminds the modern visitor that La Scala has welcomed not only great composers but also great spectators. In these surroundings today it is not hard to imagine the atmosphere of expectation, tinged with tragedy, that must have reigned on the night of April 25, 1926, the premiere of Giacomo Puccini's posthumous opera *Turandot*. The Scala audience had been waiting for *Turandot* since 1921, when the first rumors had begun to circulate that the composer was at work on a new opera. After the composer's death, on November 29, 1924, some must have wondered if the opera would ever see the stage at all. But, for almost a year and a half, the delicate task of completing what Puccini had left unfinished had gone on; now the public gathered to pass judgment on the swan song of the world's most popular modern composer of opera.

Turandot's conductor on that opening night was Arturo Toscanini, who—thirty years before—had consolidated the composer's youthful fame, conducting the first performance of his *La Bohème,* at the Teatro Regio in Turin. Although he was to go on conducting Puccini's music for another thirty years, Toscanini must have felt that this performance of *Turandot* was a kind of last farewell to his old friend. All day long, at home, he had remained silent, barely touching his food at dinner. Everything was concentrated on the opera.

The success of the first act, according to the next day's reviews, was complete and enthusiastic. The second act was less warmly received. In the third act, after the scene of Liu's death, Toscanini set down his baton, stopping the orchestra and the artists on the stage. Then—one of the rare occasions on which he addressed the public from the podium—he turned to the audience and said: "Here the opera ends, because at this point the Maestro died."

At the next performances, Toscanini conducted the final few minutes of the opera, prepared from Puccini's notes by the younger composer Franco Alfano, under Toscanini's watchful eye.

The friendship between Puccini and Toscanini had had its ups and downs. Both men were touchy, even irascible (though Puccini's sensitivity was hidden beneath a superficial heartiness); but in the months before the composer's death, they had made up all their differences. The producer of *Turandot,* Giovacchino Forzano, who had also been Puccini's librettist for *Suor Angelica* and *Gianni Schicchi,* in a volume of memoirs published some years ago, tells of his and Toscanini's last visit to the composer. Toscanini was conducting and Forzano was staging a performance of Boito's *Nerone* in Bologna. From Viareggio, where Puccini and Forzano both lived, the producer's wife telephoned to tell him of the composer's fatal illness and of his projected trip to Brussels for a desperate cure (Puccini and his wife were unaware of the gravity of his disease; only his son, Tonio, knew that it was an almost hopeless cancer). Forzano and Toscanini decided to go to Viareggio at once.

"The next morning, with my car, Toscanini and I reached Viareggio. Puccini was expecting us. Toscanini's visits cheered him. He thanked him, and was happy that Toscanini had taken his Chinese creature to heart. He showed him the whole score of *Turandot,* only a little was lacking to complete it; once he was back from Brussels he would finish the opera quickly and he played many passages for us. Unaware of the seriousness of his illness, he joked about the change in his voice. 'You hear my tenor's voice, Arturo?' and, joking, he vocalized. . . . We went back to Bologna. We didn't exchange a word during the whole journey. This was on November 3, 1924."

One of the causes of the brief attrition between Puccini and Toscanini had no doubt been Toscanini's conducting of Ildebrando Pizzetti's *Debora e Jaele* two years before. A member of the younger generation, which was reacting against Puccini, Pizzetti was a composer who represented the opposite of Puccini's attitude towards opera. And no doubt, Puccini also associated him with the younger generation of critics, whose attitude towards Puccini's operas was, covertly or openly, hostile.

So the composer was writing *Turandot* at a moment when he felt the musical world was not with him. Of his latest works, the three one-act operas in *Il trittico,* only *Gianni Schicchi* had been a success. His private life was apparently calm, but it was the exhausted calm after the storm; he and his wife were living together peacefully, but he had paid a high price for that peace. Although he was only in his sixties, he often referred to himself as an old man. *Turandot,* his new opera, was to reassert his vigor, his talent, his vital force.

Always slow and hesitant in the choice of librettos and librettists, this time Puccini was slower than ever. His literary collaborators were an expert team. Renato Simoni, when he first discussed *Turandot* with Puccini in 1920, was forty-five, the drama critic of *Il corriere della sera,* Italy's most important daily paper, and the editor of the literary magazine *Lettura,* which had been edited by another Puccini librettist, Giuseppe Giacosa, until his death. Simoni was also a successful playwright and had even tried his hand at libretto writing. The other librettist of *Turandot,* Giuseppe Adami, was forty-two and had worked with Puccini before, adapting the Italian version of *La rondine* from a German text and writing the libretto of *Il tabarro.* He was also a successful playwright, had written librettos for other composers, and after Puccini's death, was to be his biographer and the first editor of his collected letters.

The crucial meeting between composer and librettists took place in the summer of 1920, at lunch. It was Simoni who first mentioned the eighteenth-century Venetian writer Carlo Gozzi as a possible libretto source, and Puccini apparently hit on Gozzi's *Turandotte,* a play that had already appealed to other composers. Simoni produced a copy of the work, or rather a copy of Andrea Maffei's Italian retranslation of a German adaptation by Schiller. Book in hand, Puccini took the train back to Viareggio and work began. The writing of the text—with Puccini making constant suggestions and, at times, sending prose versions of individual scenes as he visualized them—went on for two years, with frequent interruptions and moments of doubt and regret on the composer's part. Finally, on June 25, 1922, he wrote to his publisher: "Propitious days for me. . . . Simoni and Adami have delivered to me, to my complete satisfaction, the finished libretto of *Turandot*." Of course, there were further changes, but the work of composition went forward. By February 24, 1924, Puccini had completely orchestrated the first two acts; but for the third, he was dissatisfied with the words of the final love duet, the culminating scene of the whole work. His long-suffering librettists were put back to work. On March 13, Puccini wrote to his friend Sybil Seligman in London: "Adami is here to finish the libretto—the last duet, which has come out very well indeed."

But the same letter begins ominously: "I've not been at all well and I've still got a sore throat and an obstinate cough." In the letters that Puccini wrote during the remaining eight months of his life, complaints about his sore throat and complaints about the difficulty of *Turandot*'s last act alternate. When he left for Brussels on November 4, in his baggage there were thirty-six sheets of music paper, scrawled over with notes, sketches for the final duet, false starts, indications of themes, melodies to be developed, with cryptic messages to himself: "find melody," "less silly than the other," and, puzzlingly, "then Tristan."

Franco Alfano was commissioned by the publishers (with the assent of Toscanini and the Puccini heirs) to complete the opera; like everyone else, he naturally and wisely made no attempt to fathom, or still less to carry out, these instructions Puccini had written to himself. Already a successful composer in his own right, Alfano (born in 1876) did not try to "find melody" where Puccini had left none. In fact, in the printed libretto there are some words that have no music; Puccini left no indication of how he would set them, so Alfano sensibly omitted them from the score. The Italian critic Teodoro Celli, who has made a careful examination of the thirty-six pages of notes, writes: "An examination of the material . . . can inspire in us only admiration for what Alfano managed to achieve, not only with an expert's great mastery, but also with extreme respect and loyalty towards Puccini's intentions."

The *Turandot* we hear today is surely not the *Turandot* we would be hearing if Puccini had returned from his journey to Belgium alive. The final duet exists in Alfano's able reconstruction, but it is not the duet the composer himself would have written in the end. We know, from his letters, how he wanted this music to be new and different, to depict in glowing music the transformation of icy Turandot from a figure of legend, almost abstract, into a real and warm human being, a woman in love. Still the opera is a masterpiece, even if a flawed or incomplete one. Unfinished works of great artists have their own fascination.

The Italian music critics, whose reviews appeared in the papers of April 26, 1929, obviously felt that fascination; but at the same time they seem somewhat perplexed by a Puccini who, at times, seems the same, familiar Puccini of the past (Liù's music, after all, is not too different from the music of Mimi and Butterfly), but at other times reveals a dark, exotic side that has only been glimpsed in earlier works. Like critics ever since, the first-night critics disagreed.

Gaetano Cesari, in *Il corriere della sera,* wrote: "In the lyric field, a hard battle is joined between Turandot and Liù, finally won by she who excels in sentiment, namely Liù."

In the equally important Turin daily, *La stampa,* Andrea della Corte took a different view on this question: "Turandot is the best (character)." But della Corte ends his review saying that the opera on the whole is unsuccessful and that Puccini's name will remain in the hands of Mimi and Manon. But on this point, he is opposed by yet another critic, Adriano Lualdi, in *Il secolo,* who also adds a bit of unnecessary chauvinism, in keeping with the political climate of the time: "Giacomo Puccini has given us with *Turandot* the last, unfortunately, and the most meaningful proof of his qualities as a born artist, a born Italian artist."

For the opening night of *Turandot,* music lovers and eminent personalities had gathered from all over Europe. Only one prominent Italian was conspicuously absent: Benito Mussolini. The year before, on the day of Puccini's death, the dictator had issued a typical statement: "This is not the hour in which to discuss the worth and the nobility of his creation. It is certain only that in the history of Italian music and in the history of the Italian spirit, Giacomo Puccini occupies an eminent position. I wish to remind you in this moment that a few months ago this renowned musician requested admission to the National Fascist Party." George Marek, Puccini's biographer, who quotes this statement, was unable to find any proof for Mussolini's assertion. If it had been true, it seems unlikely that the violently antifascist Toscanini would have been so warm towards the composer. In any case, on the night of April 26, it was Toscanini who kept Il Duce out of La Scala, by flatly refusing to play the Fascist anthem "Giovinezza." In discussing the final, triumphant scene of his opera, Puccini had written to his librettists: "Niente retorica"—no bombast. And so the performance began and ended with his own music, and the tin drum of the dictatorship was not heard.

In the space of a few months *Turandot* began its international career: Buenos Aires, New York, Chicago, London, San Francisco. For many years, however, the opera's popularity lagged far behind that of Puccini's earlier works, and to some extent, it still does. But there are clear signs that it is catching up. The cold, enigmatic Chinese princess lacks perhaps the immediate appeal of the Bohemian flower maker and the Japanese child bride, but she still exercises a spell of her own. And, as she captivates poor Prince Calaf, she is—at last— beginning to captivate the international opera audience.
Autumn, 1970

POULENC'S *La Voix humaine*
by Jonathan Abarbanel

It is not surprising that *La Voix humaine* was a success when it premiered at the Opéra-Comique in Paris, February 6, 1959. Quite apart from its qualitative merits, it had almost everything going for it: a stage history, a celebrated composer, an even-more-celebrated librettist (how rare in opera), and a tour de force performance. Also, it was Parisian to the core, and Paris loved it. Its two authors were lifelong men of Paris; its subject was quintessentially Parisian: a beautiful, wronged woman in an intimate, sophisticated drama of "l'amour manqué," with an underlying chord of sentiment.

La Voix humaine the opera is, with only the smallest changes, the complete text of the play of the same name by Jean Cocteau, written in 1928 and produced two years later at the Comédie-Française. In the twenty-nine years between play and opera, it was translated into many languages and performed around the world by the finest actresses, including Ingrid Bergman and Anna Magnani (in a 1950s Italian film version). It remains the most frequently performed of all Cocteau's many works for stage (plays, ballets, operas, and various mixed events).

In 1959, Cocteau had been a dominant force in French arts and letters for fifty years, an aged enfant terrible who first made his mark as a poet while still in his teens, well before World War I. His truly peripatetic genius seems to have had no artistic limits, for he made influential and lasting contributions as a poet, playwright, scenaricist (for ballet), novelist, journalist, propagandist, actor, critic, painter, designer, and—last career of all—film maker. He knew and worked with virtually all the greatest writers, painters, and musicians of this century's first thirty years, beginning with Marcel Proust and Anatole France. Almost single-handedly, he restored modern French drama to a position of esteem, after its long period of nineteenth-century wallowing in bourgeois sentiment. Both Jean Anouilh and François Truffaut generously acknowledge his influence, and Pauline Kael has called Cocteau the "true progenitor" of French New Wave cinema. In 1955, Cocteau was elected to the Académie française.

Despite his achievements, Cocteau was suspect to many; a constant "poseur," self-promoter, and artistic opportunist, he created an exotic persona for himself and relished it. His early successes—especially during the 1920s—were dazzling and constant, but after 1930 his career became one of peaks and valleys, of phoenixlike rebirths. Finally, his absolutely notorious personal life was grist for everyone's mill, whether pro or con. Cocteau was an opium addict for forty years, and his fondness for young men, which bordered on pederasty, was well known. His predilections caused him great despair but also brought him deep artistic inspiration. It's no wonder that one critic, reviewing the 1959 opera premiere, referred to Cocteau as "the old witch doctor."

With his multiplicity of talents, with such an embarrassment of artistic riches, the one thing Cocteau did *not* do was compose music. Therefore, early on he surrounded himself with those who did, including an eighteen-year-old pianist/composer Francis Poulenc.

Poulenc, a pianist of extraordinary suppleness and skill, began composing on his own authority while still a child. All his life he remained largely self-taught as a composer. A few years of piano study with virtuoso Ricardo Viñes and three years of harmony classes with Charles Koechlin were all the formal musical education Poulenc ever received. He never studied counterpoint or orchestration. As his friend Georges Auric commented, "Poulenc has always 'found' the techniques to write the pieces he should write. The others (symphonies, string quartets, etc.) were not right for him."

Shortly after the outbreak of World War I, Poulenc began his piano studies with Viñes, who introduced him to Erik Satie and Jean Cocteau. Cocteau already was the unofficial laureate for the group of young musicians that formed itself around Satie, a musical extension of the Cubist movement in art. With his *Rapsodie nègre* (1917), which caused a sensation in Paris, Poulenc was firmly established as one of "Les Nouveaux Jeunes" in the Satie/Cocteau circle. If Cocteau was an enfant terrible, there can be no mistaking that young Monsieur Poulenc was a *Wunderkind*.

Forty years later, Poulenc had achieved international respect as a composer with numerous works of chamber music and major works such as *Les Biches* (1923), the *Concerto for Organ, Strings, and Timpani* (1938), *Stabat Mater* (1950), and his operas *Les Mamelles de Tirésias* (1944) and *Les Dialogues des Carmélites* (1957 premiere). Above all, Poulenc was known as the outstanding songwriter of the century, a reputation he still enjoys thirty years after his death. He wrote some 137 songs, setting to music texts by nearly all the finest twentieth-century French poets, chief among them being Guillaume Apollinaire and Paul Éluard.

In 1919, Poulenc set three poems of Cocteau's under the title *Cocardes*. These poems are almost nonsense verses, made up of seemingly disjointed and bizarre images, without stanzaic structure. Cocteau had drawn his images from the streets of Paris, the markets and music halls, the street musicians and hawkers. Poulenc, too, was drawn to these real-life sources. It was an article of faith of Cocteau, Poulenc, and their musical circle (the famous Groupe des six: Poulenc, Darius Milhaud, Arthur Honegger, Georges Auric, Germaine Tailleferre, and Louis Durey) that inspiration was to be drawn from what they called "Parisian folklore."

This source of inspiration served Poulenc well all of his life for his mélodies. He was unabashedly a tune smith, with an ear to the streets of Paris and a technical preference for the diatonic. These aspects of his musical personality served him well with *La Voix humaine,* too; for the naturalistic play is filled with disjointed passages, unfinished sentences, and interrupted images, like *Cocardes* and like life itself.

In setting *La Voix humaine,* Poulenc was praised for his prosody: that meticulous, discreet combination of craftsmanship and musical inspiration which permitted him to enhance the text through musical accent and nuance. In a witty remark worthy of Cocteau himself, Poulenc said, "We put words to music; but we must also put to music what is found in the white margin." His success was such that Cocteau himself wrote Poulenc after the opening, "Tu as fixé, mon cher Francis, une fois par toutes, la façon de dire mon texte" (You set once and for all, my dear Francis, the way to speak my text).

Curiously, between *Cocardes* in 1919 and *La Voix humaine* in 1959, Cocteau and Poulenc did not collaborate (with two minor exceptions), though they remained close and good friends. Particularly in the 1920s, biographers record many scenes together: dinners, nights on the town, smoky evenings in favorite bars, and an almost ridiculously impressive shared circle of friends, including princes, counts, dukes, barons, André Gide, Igor Stravinsky, Serge Diaghilev, Vaslav Nijinsky, Pablo Picasso, Georges Braque, Mistinguette, Maurice Chevalier, Claude Debussy, Gertrude Stein, Alice B. Toklas, James Joyce, Paul Claudel, André Breton, Léon-Paul Fargue, Juan Gris, Amedeo Modigliani, Marie Laurencin, Léonide Massine, Ernest Ansermet, Louis Aragon, Marcel Duchamp, Peggy Guggenheim, Edith Piaf, Colette, André Maurois, Cecil Beaton, Jean Marais, Charlie Chaplin, and Coco Chanel!

Some scenes were quite out of the ordinary. Picture the 1920 opening of a Dadaist art gallery, Tristan Tzara presiding, with music provided by a jazz band composed of Georges Auric, Francis Poulenc on piano, and Jean Cocteau playing drum, bass drum, castanets, drinking glasses, mirliton, and klaxon! Picture a private evening with Poulenc in drag as a bathing beauty. Or picture the 1924 scene of Poulenc, Auric, and Cocteau spending long afternoons in the room of a Monte Carlo hotel being introduced to the pleasures of opium smoking by Louis Laloy, a leading music critic of the day.

For Poulenc, opium was a dabble. For Auric, it was a controlled habit, as it was for Laloy. For Cocteau, however, deeply depressed over the recent death at twenty of his lover, Raymond Radiguet, opium became a lifelong addiction, despite a number of cures. Opium deeply affected Cocteau's life and art, though not entirely in negative ways. While it often interfered with his work habits, he was able to incorporate its visions and perspectives into much of his work.

It was just before one of his well-publicized cures (paid for by Coco Chanel) that Cocteau completed *La Voix humaine* in 1928. It was an artistically fallow year, the famous little one-act play being his only significant output. An actual overheard telephone argument between two friends appears to have inspired the framing device for the play's action, complete with numerous interruptions. The Parisian telephone service then, as now, was not the best in the world. However, the psychological and emotional depths must have been drawn from Cocteau's own well. His depth of feeling in this piece, his lack of sarcastic irony and nonsequitur, the anguish and desperation of the abandoned woman, are rare displays in his body of dramatic literature. One of Cocteau's biographers, Francis Steegmuller, believes such a baring of raw nerves and emotions could have been inspired only by a personal experience of a similar kind. Certainly Cocteau, given his penchant for "la tendresse" and infatuations with younger men, could have found himself, like the woman of his play, on the receiving end of such a bittersweet phone call.

Cocteau submitted *La Voix humaine* to the Comédie-Française before entering a clinic for his cure in December, 1928. He did not leave the hospital until

March 19, 1929, on which date he drove to the Comédie-Française to read his play to the Reading Committee and then promptly returned to the clinic for another month (he was well over his addiction, but was working on his great novel *Les Enfants terribles,* and found the clinic a peaceful, congenial place to work). The Comédie-Française, that bastion of theatrical conservatism and classical tradition, had accepted *La Voix humaine* for production at once. For many of his friends, it meant that Cocteau had joined the establishment, selling out to the state-controlled "Maison de Molière." Others saw the acceptance as worthy recognition. Cocteau, a poet and dramatist of genius, finally had moved brilliantly to the forefront of French theater.

Of course, *La Voix humaine* was a conservative play, and intentionally so. Having earned a reputation as an avant-garde or Cubist dramatist, with plays full of devices and stage gimmicks, Cocteau determined to strip them all away to answer his critics who said he could not write a realistic drama. In a preface to a printed edition, Cocteau wrote, "It was therefore essential to use only the simplest means: one act, one room, one character, love, and that banal property of modern plays, the telephone." Critic Edward Lockspeiser observed that the play "brings to life the poetry of unlikely places," in this instance, a lady's boudoir.

La Voix humaine premiered at the Comédie-Française on February 16, 1930, with Berthe Bovy in the role of the Woman. It was an instant success, and has remained popular. In fact, a revival of it was playing at a nearby theater when the world premiere of the opera took place in February, 1959, with Denise Duval on stage and Georges Prêtre conducting. Cocteau himself was stage director and designer of sets and costumes. He even designed the cover of the score, published by Ricordi, with Poulenc receiving top billing.

The possibility of making an opera of the play as a vehicle for Maria Callas had been suggested to Poulenc (perhaps by Cocteau himself, who never was shy about such things) at least two years earlier, after the international success of *Les Dialogues des Carmélites*. Poulenc bit, perhaps because he knew that Hans Werner Henze and at least two other composers also were playing with the idea. But Callas did not interest him (astonishing!); Denise Duval did, the young French soprano who had created the role of Blanche in *Carmélites*. *La Voix humaine* was shaped specifically for her very considerable musical and dramatic talents. Both were needed, for the soprano in this tour de force role is alone on stage for over forty minutes of intense emotion and concentration, with only her symbiotic relationship with the conductor to offer any support whatsoever.

Duval was triumphant. Even those critics (largely from the foreign press) who had quibbles with Poulenc or Cocteau showered praise on Duval, who later recorded the role.

Poulenc's approach to the task of setting the play was what critic Claude Rostand called "musical renunciation" and a "voluntarily subdued score." "Poulenc has written," Rostand noted in a March, 1959, review, "as if he had been intimidated by his text, and he has respected it so much that his music seems little more than a simple and discreet accompaniment, leaving the words in the foreground." Another critic, Peter Dragadze, writing in the April, 1959, *Musical America,* said, "The music is trivial, monotonous, and does not do credit to this important composer."

On the other hand, the April, 1959, *Musical Courier* said the music "is a veritable miracle of emotion." And Elliot Stein, in a 1960 summary of the previous decade for *Opera* magazine, wrote, "Poulenc's 'tragédie lyrique' proved the best new French opera performed in Paris in the last ten years, a work superior to *Les Dialogues des Carmélites,* and a credit to everyone concerned with its production."

Those who didn't care for Poulenc's work missed the point: the text itself was subdued, emotionally colored in pastels, full of psychological subtleties. To have created a score of high drama or intense musical coloration would have been contrary to the mood of the piece. Instead, Poulenc created an exquisite musical atmosphere with a vein of compassion, alloting to his music what Claude Rostand called "a very modest, delicately shaded role."

Poulenc solved most dramaturgical problems with simple devices. The almost-humorous use of a xylophone for the telephone ring and the sudden trumpet and string accents indicative of intrusions on the line are examples, as are the use of disjointed musical phrases contrasted with nostalgic themes to support changes in mood. Perhaps most dramatically effective of all, Poulenc was able to suggest what was being said on the other end of the line, sometimes through a repeated, two-note musical motif in the orchestra, and sometimes by the use of silence, relying on the mime abilities of the singer. Perhaps we should rely, however, on Poulenc's own instruction: "Above all do not analyse my music—love it!"

La Voix humaine played at Piccola Scala (with Duval) less than three weeks after its Paris premiere, and it reached England and America in 1960. There was an English-language broadcast of the opera on CBS-TV in early 1962, and a major revival of it at the Glyndebourne Festival in 1976, as well as numerous other productions.

La Voix humaine was a fitting cap to the long, close friendship of Poulenc and Cocteau, who, during the raucous twenties, had almost been like younger and older brothers. They tried another collaboration in 1961, a similar monologue for soprano and orchestra entitled *La Dame de Monte Carlo,* but it was not a success. Poulenc's intimate personal and professional friend baritone Pierre Bernac observed that it seemed to be too conscious an effort to recapture the spirit of the long-gone twenties and was perceived as being a piece almost cynically out of joint with the times. The days of opium puffing at Monte Carlo, of cruising the boardwalk at Deauville, of being an enfant terrible and a *Wunderkind* were dead. Soon Poulenc and Cocteau were dead, too: Poulenc of a heart attack in January, 1963, aged sixty-four; and Cocteau nine months later (on the same day Edith Piaf died), aged seventy-four.

It is, perhaps, fitting in this case (though not at all usual in opera) to leave the librettist with the last word. After the first performance of *La Voix humaine,* Cocteau wrote, "Thanks to Francis Poulenc and Denise Duval, my play has acquired the mysterious power of the Greek, Chinese, Japanese theatres, where a truth greater than truth transcends life and raises realism to the height of style."

ARGENTO'S *The Voyage of Edgar Allan Poe*
by Charles Nolte

At 4 A.M. on the morning of September 24, 1849, in Richmond, Virginia, the poet Edgar Allan Poe got on a packet steamer bound for Baltimore, Maryland, a tedious trip that normally took about forty-eight hours. There was a saloon on board which served liquor and was a convenient gathering place for passengers. For some inexplicable reason, the ship did not dock in Baltimore until the morning of the twenty-ninth of September, when Poe disembarked. He was expecting to take the train on to Philadelphia, but the train did not depart until the afternoon. Poe found himself with time on his hands. He called on an old friend, Dr. Nathan Brooks, who later observed that Poe was drunk at the time. On leaving Dr. Brooks, Poe apparently disappeared for five days, despite the fact that he was very well known in the city and had many acquaintances there. Baltimore was in the midst of a very corrupt congressional election campaign. There being no voter registration rolls, gangs of rowdies in the pay of various candidates were in the habit of rounding up street derelicts as potential voters, holding them locked up in what appear to have been virtual prisons called "coops" until the actual day of voting, October 3, keeping them happy with liquor, drugs, and plenty of cheap food. When Poe left Dr. Brooks's home, presumably en route to the train station, he was apparently swept up by one of these press gangs. On election day, on the street before a fire-engine house, someone named Joseph Walker recognized both the poet and his condition and was alarmed enough to pencil a quick note to a nearby doctor. "There is a gentleman, rather the worse for wear, at Ryan's 4th ward polls who goes under the cognomen of Edgar A. Poe, and who appears in great distress, and says he is acquainted with you, and I assure you he is in need of immediate assistance." Dr. Snodgrass hurried to Cooth's Tavern, where he found Poe in a terrible condition, as he later testified: "His face was haggard, not to say bloated, and unwashed, his hair unkempt, and his whole physique repulsive." Virtually unconscious, Poe clearly required hospitalization. He was taken to Washington Hospital, where the physician on duty, Dr. J.J. Moran, registered him at 5 P.M. on October third. Poe remained unconscious until around 3 A.M. of the fourth, when he began babbling incoherently to phantom figures apparently circling his bed. Poe's life was coming to an end amid irrational fears, morbid despair, and other evidence of delirium tremens. Dr. Moran's wife was now at the bedside, giving what comfort she could, reading to Poe from the Bible, and even administering a dose of laudanum. Eventually, convinced that he was dying, she left in order to make his shroud. Poe lived through the next three days, moving in and out of consciousness, muttering incoherently, presumably in great mental distress, until Sunday morning, when he became quiet and appeared to rest. At last, gently moving his head, he whispered, "Lord help my poor soul," and died, as he had lived, in tragic misery.

A life of tragic misery, yes, but also of enormous theatricality and of great genius, all of which contribute to Poe's fascination for us and to the suitability of the material for a grand opera. Poe was an extraordinarily romantic character in a very romantic age. His ancestry begins the story. His father, David Poe, left the study of law to become an actor, much against the wishes of his family. What shreds of evidence we have indicate that David Poe was an indifferent actor who played minor roles in various southern cities. He had six siblings, one of whom, Maria Poe, later Mrs. William Clemm, played a large role in Poe's life (and in the opera), as she ultimately became his mother-in-law in addition to being his aunt. Poe lived in the same houses with her (and her daughter) from 1835 virtually until his death.

Poe's mother, Elizabeth, at the early age of ten, had already been noticed by a theater critic as being exceedingly beautiful in roles such as Cupid and Nymph, and by age twelve was already launched on a promising acting career. In 1802 she met the would-be actor and law student David Poe in Baltimore. Despite David's attentions, Elizabeth married one Charles Hopkins, a comedian, who seems to have promptly died, leaving Elizabeth a very young widow in 1805, by which time David Poe had given up all thoughts of the law in favor of a theater career. Local critics noted that "his enunciation seemed to be very distinct, and his voice clear, melodious and variable." But the young man was tubercular as well as excessively shy and awkward. It was said that drink helped him overcome some of his deficiencies.

The young Poe couple made a poor living. A first child was born in 1807, adding to their woes. And in 1809, a second son, Edgar, was born. Mrs. Poe, always the main breadwinner in the family, returned to the stage within three weeks of her confinement. Soon there was a third child. About this time, apparently despondent, David Poe disappears from the story, leaving wife and children to fend for themselves. David Poe died of consumption in 1810, leaving his wife alone in the world, in failing health herself, and with three small infants to care for.

It is worth noting that Poe had an alcoholic father, who was chronically unable to make a satisfactory living, and an extremely beautiful, extremely youthful mother, whom he must clearly have worshiped as a very young boy. Poe remembered his mother later as a small miniature pictured her, describing her thus: "The childish figure, with great, wide-open mysterious eyes, the abundant curling hair confined in the quaint bonnet of a hundred years ago and shadowing the brow in raven masses, the high waist and attenuated arms clasped in an empire robe of flowered design, the tiny but rounded neck and shoulders, the head proudly erect. It is the face of an elf, a sprite, an Undine." But unhappily his Undine was now very ill, in the final stages of tuberculosis, and unable to work. To a very imaginative boy, her symptoms—the damp and flushed cheeks, the consumptive cough stifled by handkerchiefs spotted with blood—must have made a lasting impression. And when she finally died in the winter of 1811, for Edgar, now almost three, the experience was shattering. Now, love and death, two consuming subjects in his later creative life, come together. Doubtless he had seen his mother enact death on the stage many times. Now, seeing her lying in her shroud, candles guttering nearby, was this not yet another performance? A kind of dreamlike sleep? Would she not rise again, to love and protect him? Major themes in the work of Edgar Allan Poe have deep roots in these childhood traumas.

Elizabeth Poe was survived by children who now had to be disposed of. Edgar was taken in by a wealthy merchant, John Allan of Richmond, who became his foster father and the source of lifelong confrontation and anguish.

If the relationship between Edgar Allan Poe and his foster father had not been so bitter, the poet might never have experienced the appalling poverty and degradation that haunted him from the time he left Allan's home until his death a quarter-century later. At seventeen he was admitted to the University of Virginia, where he ran up bills that Allan refused to pay and where he presumably began in earnest his consumption of alcohol, his habit of gambling, and his general nervous eccentricity. When his bills amounted to over $2,500, Allan ordered young Poe home and refused to allow him to return to the university. There were violent quarrels, and ultimately Poe quit Richmond entirely for Boston, then the literary capital of the United States, with Allan's wife, who adored Poe, providing small sums of money. Now attempting to support himself by writing, Poe began the career for which he is justly famous, but at first with such complete lack of success that he was forced to enlist in the army, surely a measure of extreme desperation. For over two years as a soldier, apparently with some spare time on his hands, he spent his days, when his largely clerical military duties permitted, writing poetry and reading. Military records of the time note that he was steady, sober, and intelligent and well worthy of promotion. But Poe knew he was wasting his life, and he attempted a reconciliation with John Allan, only to be angrily rebuffed. Mrs. Allan was now dying, and she begged her husband to allow her "darling boy" to return. Very reluctantly, Allan relented, but the young man arrived too late. Mrs. Allan had expired, her final hope of reconciliation thwarted. Allan even cruelly insisted that the funeral proceed before Poe could arrive. When Poe did arrive hours later, only to find the gentle woman who had been mother to him while he was growing up already in her grave, one can easily imagine his extravagant grief.

Before dying, Mrs. Allan had extracted a promise from her husband to allow the young man to return home. Allan consented, but the rapprochement was barely civil. The foster father gave Poe just enough money to keep alive but remained suspicious of him in the extreme, so much so that Poe was forced to leave home once again. After being robbed by a cousin in a hotel, Poe found refuge in the home of his Aunt Maria, the widow of a Mr. Clemm. Mrs. David Poe, Sr., his paternal grandmother, now old and paralyzed, was also a member of the household. And there was Mrs. Clemm's extraordinarily beautiful daughter, Poe's first cousin Virginia, then a child of seven. This little girl was destined to become Poe's child bride less than five years later.

In those intervening years, the story of Poe is a pitiful tale of his efforts to make a living from his pen. It is also the story of his final break with Allan, disinheritance, an abortive appointment as a cadet to West Point which ended in court-martial, various efforts to publish his growing portfolio of poems and tales, degrees of poverty and poor health, and periods when he lived in the household of his long-suffering aunt, Mrs. Clemm, and her beautiful young daughter, his cousin Virginia.

Poe also fell in love with a girl named Mary Devereaux, but after being refused, took out his rage on the girl's uncle by horsewhipping him. A strange young man! Moving between the cities of Richmond, Baltimore, Philadelphia, and New York, Poe pursued with modest success his literary career, which now included lecturing, magazine editing, and literary criticism. Slowly, he was making a name for himself, though there is continuing evidence of his drinking and possible drug use.

On September 22, 1835, Poe secretly married his Virginia Clemm, then only twelve years old! Needless to say, this rash act infuriated her relatives, which is clearly why the wedding was concluded secretly with only the bride's mother as witness. Henceforth, the child bride and her mother would be part of his permanent household. A year later, on the sixteenth of May, perhaps because he was now anxious to set up his wife and mother-in-law as operators of a boarding house that would bring in needed cash, he remarried Virginia, this time in a public ceremony with many witnesses. The marriage document describes the bride as being twenty-one years old, though in fact she was scarcely thirteen. Now their union was of public record, and plans for the boarding house could go forward.

Meanwhile, Poe continued his literary efforts, editing the *Southern Literary Messenger,* writing a number of poems, including "To Helen" and "Israfel," and many short stories, some of marked morbidity. The poverty of the little family fluctuated between relative and extreme, and family woes mounted. His own ill health continued, perhaps due to stimulants, while it also became clear that his young bride was consumptive. Her frequent hemorrhages must certainly have revived painful memories from his early childhood. These were dark times.

Dark times turned black for Poe as he continually embroiled himself in masochistic controversy with other literary figures, with his employers, and with his friends. One of these friends, Rufus Griswold, became his implacable enemy and is largely responsible for the view of Poe after his death: that of a moral degenerate, "a madman constantly and heavily under the influence of liquor and drugs," an army deserter, a wastrel while at the university which expelled him as a chronic drunkard, a child-molester, and many other half-truths and destructive statements. It is astonishing that Poe, knowing Griswold as he did, committed the horrific error of making this very Griswold, who among other things was a licensed Baptist clergyman, his literary executor. From this position it was all too possible for Griswold, an extremely jealous man of literary pretensions, to "execute" Poe after the latter's death. Two days after Poe died, Griswold published in the *New York Tribune* an account of the poet's death, followed by a narrative of his life which is filled with venomous half-truths, innuendoes, slanders, and calculated deceptions. He speaks of Poe as a man without honor or faith and devoid of moral principles. Unfortunately, it was this view of Poe that prevailed as the genuine one until more accurate biographical material surfaced in the early 1920s. Griswold was indeed in every sense Poe's evil nemesis.

In January, 1845, with Poe and his forlorn little family in dire necessity, his poem "The Raven" was published; it created a sensation. Has any poem in America ever been so popular? And yet, despite the poet's growing fame, his financial woes continued, and he, his mother-in-law, and dying wife lived in virtual destitution. Poe's health, too, was bad, and as his wife sank down into death, he drank heavily. Poor Mrs. Clemm struggled to keep them alive, begging money, even digging for vegetables by night in the fields of neighboring farmers. In the depths of the cold winter of 1847, Virginia died. She was scarcely twenty-four years old.

The final chapters in the sad life of Poe after Virginia's death find him continuing his literary efforts, giving lectures for cash, while at the same time hoping to persuade various affluent widows to marry him, doubtless as a way out of his chronic financial quagmire. This is the period when he wrote "The Bells," "Ulalume," "Annabel Lee," and others of his most important works, many of them reflecting his infatuations with various women. When one of these women refused his advances, he attempted suicide with laudanum. He was clearly approaching a state bordering on insanity. In this pitiful condition, rebuffed by various women he regarded as potential brides, now the center of scandal, he found himself back in Richmond, seeking an engagement with a wealthy widow he had known since childhood, "Elmira." It is at this point that Poe determined to take the packet steamer from Richmond to Baltimore, to undertake what turned out to be the last voyage of Edgar Allan Poe. What happened on that fateful trip and afterward will never be known for certain, but it is clear from the facts here related that Poe was now desperate, sick in mind and body, suffering hallucinations, consumed by morbid longings, and a likely prey for wild, irrational fancies.

These biographical facts are helpful in comprehending the libretto of *The Voyage of Edgar Allan Poe*. Clearly, the more you know about Poe's life, the greater your understanding of the opera's story, the basic reason being that so much of his actual life is reflected phantasmagorically in the opera's text. Revenants from the past come and go: his mother; his foster mother; Mrs. Clemm; his violently antipathetic foster father; his bride, Virginia; his evil nemesis Griswold, determined on destroying Poe's reputation—all appear and reappear in various guises and at various times in the text, contributing to the atmosphere of feverish nightmare.

Thus, the audience experiences episodes from Poe's actual life, but filtered through his warped imagination as he faces dissolution. Chief among these episodes are deathbed scenes involving wife and mother, plus domestic glimpses into the Clemm household, with its odd cast of characters: senile Granny Poe, Edgar's drunken elder brother, and his retarded younger sister.

In addition, woven into this fabric of details from the real world are strands from the world of his imagination. Characters and events from some of his tales and stories are evoked: "King Pest," "The Black Cat," "Imp of the Perverse," "Murders in the Rue Morgue." From this last story, the figure of August Dupin, detective, emerges to play a significant role in the fantastical trial of Poe, which is central to the action of the opera.

Coloring this whole concept are quotations from his poems themselves, particularly those most morbidly lyrical: "Ulalume," "The Bells," "Eldorado," and "Annabel Lee." Echoes and reverberations are virtually endless.

These ghosts from his own past, mingling with creatures of his imagination, ignite degrees of emotional conflict and act as catalysts, triggering present behavior in Poe which in turn reflects his own past behavior, involving alcohol abuse, possible drug use, and much morbid reflection on death and dying and its importance to Poe's artistic credo.

And over all there remains the essential conflict facing the struggling artist: the insuperable problems of just surviving in an inhospitable social climate, where there is an ever-growing accumulation of pressure, complicated by Poe's own masochistic tendency to create ugly rivalries, as in the case of his nemesis Griswold.

It is useful to remember that the location in which these charades and fantastical chimeras take place, reflecting a man who is desperate to make sense of the pain and misery of his existence, is on shipboard, a concentrated space in which the focus can be intense and from which escape is virtually impossible. Moreover, the violence inside Poe's mind is reflected in the violence outside the saloon cabin, where the wind rises to gale proportions and waves lash the hull. Weather, too, has a role to play.

An ironic sidelight is the fact that Poe's mother and father, both itinerant actors, must frequently have found themselves on board just such packet steamers, moving from engagement to engagement. The presence of a theater troupe aboard a vessel of this type must have been commonplace in the 1840s.

Beyond the fact of a literal voyage, there is Poe's metaphysical and spiritual journey, "where the heart must gather the past into hallucination." An extraordinary kaleidoscope of memories results, recalling other expressionistic theater pieces, in particular those of E.T.A. Hoffmann and August Strindberg, and certain poems of decadent romanticism—those of Baudelaire, Mallarmé, and Valéry—as well as several musical works (Debussy's in particular). In many of these works, characters tend to multiply and divide. The illogic of nightmare prevails, a dreamscape wherein anything can happen and everything is possible, where time and space collide. Personages split, scatter, and converge. Griswold is both himself, a minister at Poe's wedding, a doctor in deathbed scenes, and the accusing avenger at Poe's trial.

And what is the object of this kaleidoscope? To make the accused (Poe) face his inner self. It is this land of imagination, of his dreams, memories, and hallucinations, the territory beyond what is clearly expressible, where music plays such an enormous role. We glimpse the borderland separating madness from sanity. Is it indeed true, as Poe argues in the final trial scene of the opera, that madness is merely another and perhaps better kind of "health"? And that the artist, almost by definition, must be insane, or at least not sane in the normal way we view such things? This is indeed much of what the opera is all about.

As Poe's mind verges on the berserk, Griswold becomes what in fact he appears to have been in real life: a coffin worm come to gnaw on Poe's literary corpse. And in the violent whirligig, Poe sees himself the center of a maelstrom, "whirling, whirling, whirling dizzily around, sinking down and down" as his trial proceeds. His plea that perhaps the mad have pleasures that the vulgar sane can never comprehend is the defense that all great artists make in their madness, even if only subconsciously. Perhaps it is true, as Poe himself states at his trial, that the artist must deliberately choose the pain and shadows as others choose the light. Is this not why he can face his ghosts at last, face even his dying bride? "The veins stood out, a milky blue against her marble skin and coal-black eyes." Does he indeed now lust after her death? And does he accept the consequences—her eyes so lifeless and glassy white, her shrunken lips,—as payment for his muse, a necessary fee for creativity?

And ultimately he does indeed require her death a second time, in order that he may discover what lies beyond the grave, that mysterious land "where gold and silver fish swim through the river of silence, and unseen glowing birds drift slowly in the quiet wind in the valley of the many-colored grass, paying homage to the blazing sun." The artist will know all, even if it means that his child bride must die a second death. Is this too great a sum to pay? No. She had to die in order for him to create. This is the ultimate truth which lies at the end of his voyage of self-discovery. His guilt is clear. His muse needed her, violated her, ultimately destroyed her. In his search for the land beyond death, his Eurydice is finally silenced, "her heart a lute suspended." But for what? Accusations pour down upon him with a savage candor. For a tortured cat! Murdered wives!

People buried alive! A raven mocking mankind! She died in order that these dark blooms of his imagination, tales of horror and madness, could live! And so he is accused of being that very imp of the perverse that Griswold, the coffin worm, reveals in his hateful biography.

What then is Poe's final defense before punishment? "Have mercy on my life, for all I touched turned autumn in my hand, my youth a fragile vessel caught upon the waves of a savage sea, my heart a ravaged garden without a single bloom. . . . Pity me. . . . I murdered for my art. I killed all that I most loved, and sacrificed remembered bliss to feed my muse. It had to be. Have mercy on my life."

The opera concludes ambiguously. Was there in fact any such final voyage? It has now been verified that no ship departed from Richmond for Baltimore in that fateful week when Poe died.

My involvement as librettist in this enterprise came about, I believe, because Dominick Argento had seen a play of mine, "A Night at the Black Pig," which dealt with the life of August Strindberg. The play contains similarities with the Poe libretto. Strindberg celebrates his forty-fourth birthday in Berlin, where a congregation of his friends (and some enemies) gathers at the Black Pig Cafe to toast him. They choose to mark the event by enacting scenes from his stormy life. Here, too, in their charades, fact and fancy merge, and characters from his works of imagination mingle with people in his life. Everything grows progressively more drunken and hallucinatory. Remembering that he had seen this play, Dr. Argento asked me to undertake the libretto for his opera about Poe. I welcomed this opportunity, although it was my first experience in writing for the lyric stage. But I had extensive experience as a playwright and theater director.

Research revealed how Poe was virtually worshiped by influential European writers, particularly Baudelaire and Mallarmé. He was far more appreciated in France, for example, than he was in America. Strindberg, as well, was greatly impressed, and as so often in the case of Strindberg, he carried infatuation to the extreme, believing that he himself was Poe's reincarnation, until he discovered that Poe had died six weeks after he, Strindberg, had been born.

As for me personally, to be asked to prepare a libretto for an opera was a challenge of particular appeal, as opera has been a passion of mine practically since childhood, ever since first hearing those fondly remembered mellifluous tones of Milton Cross speaking from Box 44 of the old Metropolitan Opera House on a Saturday afternoon. People scarcely believe me when I tell them today that, yes, I do indeed recall Flagstad's debut as Sieglinde on a broadcast in February, 1935, and that a dim recollection of Rosa Ponselle's Carmen (sic) lurks back somewhere in my memory.

All this, I hasten to add, of someone who cannot sustain a note if life depended on it. Singing (off key) made me yawn when I auditioned to become a member of our high-school choir. They soon discovered where the sour tones were coming from. My vocal career was at an end. I was about thirteen or fourteen. Still, it is a great pleasure to be associated with *The Voyage of Edgar Allan Poe*.

MASSENET'S *Werther*
by Thomas Willis

At first glance it seems so improbable. Jules Massenet, the reigning old pro of the French operatic 1890s, reaching back more than a century to Johann Wolfgang von Goethe's "storm and stress" chronicle of *The Sorrows of Young Werther.*

Massenet—whose string of successes began with an oratorio about Mary Magdalene and ended forty-one years and twenty-eight stage works later with an opera about Cleopatra—deserting the languishing fair sex for a male, and a tenor at that. Neglecting Salome, Esclarmonde, Thaïs, and Cinderella and the exotic climes and places that made for such tantalizing scenery at the Opéra-Comique and the Opéra in favor of a suicidal twenty-three year old who lived in a nearly forgotten but nonetheless real German village thirty-three miles from Frankfurt. Forsaking the glittering, sinuous musical surface which so deftly and economically brought Manon and her scented Parisian boudoir to life to attempt, just this once, a full-bodied emotional characterization of both hero and heroine.

The Massenet biographers suggest that the composer was tricked, or at least beguiled, into *Werther* by his friend and publisher Georges Hartmann. The two had gone to Bayreuth in 1886 for *Parsifal,* a trip that, actually or figuratively, almost every European musician was to make in those years of "Wagnerization." At the time, Massenet was content to admire the ascendant German genius from afar. He had been presented with Henri Murger's *La Vie de bohème* and thought it would make a fine opera libretto. Hartmann, however, had other ideas. The pilgrimage to Bavarian Bayreuth was made via Frankfurt, and the German-born well-educated publisher made certain that they stopped to see the local sights. It was a short trip to Wetzlar, the village where Goethe had written *Werther,* and Massenet's shrewd guide lost no time in taking him to the very house where the autobiographical events in the novel had taken place.

"At the point when Massenet's emotions were at their keenest," writes James Harding in his entertaining 1970 biography of the composer, "Hartmann produced a copy of the book and told him to read it. They went into a nearby tavern filled with noisy students, and, over a couple of bocks, Massenet immersed himself in the letters which tell of the unhappy romance between Werther and Charlotte. At first he was but mildly interested. Then, as he read on, his feelings were aroused by the lovers' fugitive happiness, Charlotte's marriage with Albert, her betrothed, and Werther's despairing suicide. Forgetful of the reek of beer and pipe smoke, he gave in wholeheartedly to the charm of a love story that had entranced generations of romantically minded readers.

"'Such rapturous and ecstatic passion brought tears to my eyes,' Massenet exclaimed. 'What moving scenes, what thrilling moments it could all give rise to! *Werther* it was!' Hartmann was a clever psychologist." Werther and his Charlotte swiftly replaced Murger's Bohemians in Massenet's affections, leaving Mimi and Rodolfo forever in the hands of Puccini. Hartmann continued his campaign, installing his impatient composer in an apartment at Versailles, complete with eighteenth-century paneling and Louis XV furniture. With the aid of Edouard Blau and Paul Millet, two librettists skilled in the theatrical conventions of the time (and Hartmann as kibitzing editor), *Werther* was completed in less than six months.

Finding a stage that would produce it proved unexpectedly difficult. Three years previously, in 1884, *Manon* had brought down the house at the Opéra-Comique and had transformed its creator into the talk of the town. During the intervening seasons, the music had been embraced by the public with a fervor fully the equal of a twentieth-century American musical-comedy hit. *Hérodiade* had been a success at the Théâtre-Italien that same season, introducing Jean de Reszke and his brother Edouard to Parisian audiences. But opera in those days was akin to ballet and drama in its demand for novelty on its own terms.

The director of the Opéra-Comique did not respond to the old-fashioned tale of desire unrequited, with its gloomy lover and determinedly virtuous wife. "I'd hoped you were bringing me another *Manon*," he is quoted as saying. "This depressing subject lacks interest. It's doomed in advance." Negotiations came to an abrupt end the following day when the theater burned to the ground. Massenet turned his attention to another heroine, Esclarmonde, and to the soprano with whom his name was to be linked for several years, the American Sibyl Sanderson.

Werther's time came, oddly enough, at Vienna's German-language Imperial Opera. *Manon* had made its way there in 1890, with immediate acclaim and many repetitions. Did the composer have another work ready for performance? Pleased by the invitation and its openhanded confidence in the composer's ability, Massenet presented *Werther*. Casting was conducted according to his specifications, he was treated with respect by the director and conductor, and he was allowed to supervise minute details of the production. The premiere took place February 16, 1892.

What a strange occasion that opening night must have been. Not entirely novel, of course. Gounod's *Faust* had long since entered the international repertory, and the Germans accepted it with good-natured understanding of its gallic simplifications and alterations. They took pains, of course, to call it *Margarete,* thereby maintaining Goethe inviolate. Ambroise Thomas's *Mignon* and Berlioz's *La Damnation de Faust* had less success, but no lack of Teutonic acceptance. It appears that from the first, German opera goers decided to allow their neighbors a free hand with Goethe, just as the British have done with Shakespeare. Both are secure in the belief that their national geniuses are immune to provincial assault, wherever found.

But where *Faust* had become a classic, *Werther* had been all but forgotten in the more than a century since its completion. The work that transformed Goethe into an international celebrity with its defiance of conventions and its vivid defense of passionate desire was an out-of-date curio by the time Massenet's operatic version appeared. Almost no one was around to object to the dramatic license that allowed the lovers to be united for a conventional death-bed scene in the final act or to note that the ironic contrast of the children's innocent Christmas carols with Werther's final gasp was entirely foreign to both the spirit and the letter of the original author.

In short, the Viennese were more than content with Massenet's treatment of their safely embalmed classic. Max Kalbeck, a major Viennese critic who made the German translation of the French libretto, appraised the new opera in terms which many today would endorse: "This work inclines more toward the new German school than the composer's earlier operas. To be properly correct and stylish, i.e. *Wagnerisch,* Massenet has dispensed with the chorus and ensemble, and even the lovers are allowed to meet only in unison. The only harmony is to be found in the children's Christmas songs and in the two bourgeois tipplers—as though the composer were indicating symbolically that one may accept such folly only in children and drunks." He went on to say that Massenet always followed "the way of too little rather than too much," was neither overblown nor fussy, exotic nor exaggerated, and possessed great skill in calculating stage effects and orchestration.

The years that have elapsed since that first success have seen *Werther*'s fortunes rise and fall. When it arrived at Covent Garden in 1894, George Bernard Shaw wrote:

> Werther is a more congenial subject for Massenet than even Manon was. When he gets away from the artificial and rhetorical into the regions of candid sentiment and the childlike sincerities of love and grief he is charming. Des Grieux, a hero whom we forgive even for cheating at cards, suited him well: Werther suits him still better. . . . He has succeeded in keeping up the interest of a libretto consisting of four acts of a lovelorn tenor who has only two active moments, one when he tries to ravish a kiss from the fair as aforesaid, and the other when he shoots himself behind the scenes.

Gabriel Fauré, who wrote criticism as well as music, was equally captivated by the opera's first act at the French premiere in 1893:

> It takes place almost entirely in an intimate family atmosphere created by fluent and expansive orchestration which remains pleasantly engaging in its simplicity until the moment when, at nightfall, the drama is emphasized with the delightful appearance of Charlotte and Werther by moonlight. At that point the music, blossoming out in gentleness, raises itself to a pitch of the most concentrated, all embracing and enveloping charm.

Here M. Massenet reveals himself constantly and completely with his finest gifts, his most attractive qualities, and an extraordinary sureness of touch.

Still later, Claude Debussy had occasion to appraise Massenet as the music critic of *Revue blanche*. At a time when everyone was imitating Wagner, Debussy noted, Massenet stood against the current:

Massenet was the most genuinely liked of contemporary composers. It was this very affection people had for him which, by the same token, placed him in the special situation which he has not ceased to occupy in the musical world. His colleagues find it hard to forgive him that ability to please which is rightly a gift. To tell the truth, such a gift is not indispensable, particularly in art, and one may assert, among other examples, that Bach never pleased in the meaning of the word when it comes to Massenet. Have you ever heard it said of young milliners that they hummed the *Passion according to Saint Matthew*? I don't think so, yet everyone knows they wake up singing *Manon* or *Werther* in the morning. Let us make no mistake about it, this sort of delightful reputation is secretly envied by more than one of those great purists who have to rely on the somewhat labored respect of cliques to revive their spirits.

For most of Massenet's music, Debussy's ambivalent praise must stand. Above all, Massenet was a man of the musical theater, spiritual and economic (which is to say rich) kin to a Richard Rodgers or Stephen Sondheim in the world of today. Disciplined and routined to an extreme, he rose regularly at 4:30 A.M. to begin the day's work. His early years were spent in the hard-knocks apprenticeship of a journeyman performer, beginning as percussionist in the Opéra orchestra and rising through the ranks of the professionals of his day. Contemporaries tell of his phenomenal grasp of detail, of his determination to see each of his works through until the last moment of the final dress rehearsal, of the skill with which he custom tailored each note of a part to the singer in his mind's ear. Dramatic effects were calculated with the experience gained from a lifetime of association with the flesh, paint, canvas, and wood of the theater of his time. The *Werther* curtain is to rise and fall at precisely indicated points in the score; several rehearsals were needed to get it right at the Paris opening.

This craftsman's skill at orchestration and shaping of the vocal phrase appears in each measure of the *Werther* score. Massenet excelled at the evocative interlude, whose texture and emotional range grazed, but seldom crossed, the line separating subtle inflection from sentimental *kitsch*. In *Werther* the range extends from a suggestive wisp of an opening prelude to a Tchaikovsky forecast of the opera's ending. The voices in the moonlight scene hover on the edge of breathlessness, balancing declamation on the slenderest thread of tone. But as Werther's situation grows more desperate, the musical gestures sharpen and intensify. Accents are displaced. Rhythms become insistent and metaphoric. By the time we reach Werther's Desolation Aria ("J'aurais sur ma poitrine"), the Wagnerian emphasis on a harmonically reinforced climax is apparent. In this opera, Massenet has taken us farther toward innocence and understanding than he dared in any other work. At the age of fifty, he let us glimpse his own "storm and stress."

BERG'S *Wozzeck*
by John W. Freeman

Once in a great while an opera appears, such as *Orfeo ed Euridice* or *Carmen* or *Tristan und Isolde,* that seems to summarize its ancestry, at the same time transcending it with a statement that seems shockingly new. In our century there have been two such, *Pelléas et Mélisande* and *Wozzeck.* People have rallied around them and reviled them—but have not ignored them. Today as when they were new, a production of either is a special event.

What is *Wozzeck* like? The score has been called serialist and avant-garde; it is neither, though these schools are in its debt. Extremely concentrated and learned, it offers a field day for the analyst or theoretician, with its atonality, polytonality, and rich structure. The composer himself gave a detailed lecture on *Wozzeck,* but when it was over, he said, "I beg you to forget all theory and musical aesthetics before you attend the performance." *Wozzeck*'s real character and Alban Berg's purpose in writing it are communicativeness: life is a tragedy to the man who feels. Berg's genius consists not in his skill but in having used it to such a direct and simple end.

The so-called modernism of *Wozzeck* is certainly not novelty in the plot, which combines familiar themes—a love triangle and a man losing his struggle against adversity. No, it is a question of viewpoint. Berg uses his nineteenth-century story and characters in a twentieth-century way, and he does the same with the musical elements that go into his composition. That is why they all emerge transformed.

When Berg began this work in 1917, its viewpoint had been developing since the playwright Georg Büchner's time. An inevitable product of the Industrial Revolution and the atrophying of feudal-aristocratic society, it first surged up in the idealistic socialism that sent many artists of the Romantic Era to the barricades. But where Wagner in the *Ring* postulated sweeping away the old order to make way for a society free to love, Berg was drafted into World War I and, like Jaroslav Hašek, author of *The Good Soldier Schweik,* saw the suffering of military servitude, compounded by Austro-Hungarian exploitation of Central Europe. That is, he saw that the Empire's assault on outside enemies was really its own suicidal struggle within. Disillusion had been expressed increasingly as the Gothic novel gave way to the novel of social protest (Dickens, Balzac, Zola) and as the sentimentalized view of romantic painting gave way to subjective, anguished visions. In all the arts, new terms came to be heard—impressionism, realism, naturalism, expressionism.

An exaggerated statement, psychologists tell us, is more noticed and remembered than a factual one. Expressionist painting, as in the work of Edvard Munch, Emil Nolde, and Ernst Ludwig Kirchner, used starkness and distortion to emphasize the grotesque, the pathetic, and the frightening. On the scientific side, Sigmund Freud was bringing to light the darker elements in human personality. Music, often specifically inspired by literature or painting, followed with Richard Strauss's *Elektra* and Arnold Schoenberg's *Erwartung,* which made the journalistic "verism" of a *Cavalleria rusticana* seem reassuringly folksy. Audiences were shaken, and direct emotional contact was reestablished between them and the composer. "Now," as a psychoanalyst might say after his patient has screamed out some hideous primal recollection, "we can start to talk."

What Alban Berg wanted to talk about with his audience was virtually the history of music, the cultural confessions of a collective past. But this was not his chief concern: his characters were. To portray them vividly, with all the urgency of their plight, Berg distorted them, saw them as the bedeviled Wozzeck saw them. The music contains four distinct ways for the principals to express themselves vocally. Even the most familiar of these, singing melody, seems a little distorted because of the tonal variations from what we would expect in so traditional a melody as Marie's lullaby. Occasionally, straight speech is employed, a device derived from the so-called melodrama of older opera; the gravedigging scene of *Fidelio* is a classic example. In between song and speech, Berg uses two methods developed by Schoenberg. One is *Sprechstimme,* a rhythmic way of speaking that follows written note values and suggests musical pitches without actually sounding them; the other is *Sprechgesang,* in which the suggested pitches are to be half sung and half spoken. Wozzeck's scene with Andrés is the first instance of *Sprechstimme;* Marie's reading of the Bible is the most notable one of *Sprechgesang.*

Although Berg's intent in using distortion was to heighten rather than to caricature, a trenchant irony is often the result. And in every moment the music is part and parcel of both character and situation. When the Doctor expands on his theory, for example (Act 1, scene 4), the composer chooses a musical form, the passacaglia, that experiments with possibilities drawn from a basic melodic idea. As the Doctor goes on about Wozzeck's having a splendid textbook case of idée fixe, it becomes apparent that he is really describing himself. His mania revolves around his theory (passacaglia theme), the idée fixe, upon which bizarre constructions proliferate, with wild squashing or stretching of the theme, extremes of high and low register, until a delusion of grandeur is reached: "Oh, my fame! I shall be immortal!"

Although study of the score is necessary before this structure emerges, its point is felt at once in the theater without noticing the structure. This is what Berg wanted, saying he needed the formal pattern for himself, not for the listener. The opera as a whole, he pointed out, roughly follows an A-B-A pattern like that of ternary song form, with the last act (catastrophe) a parallel to the first (exposition), the second bearing the burden of developments that lead from one to the other. It is impossible to read many of Berg's comments or those of his biographers without coming to realize the composer's own obsession, focused on this matter of form. The first act is relatively cool and clear, a series of character sketches set forth in small, self-contained musical forms (suite, rhapsody, march, lullaby, etc.). The second is more involved, in both senses of the word: cast as a symphony in five movements (scenes), it pursues the vagaries of the characters. The third act is obsessive—no escape: a series of six inventions piling up, each bearing down on one aspect of music (a theme, then a single note, then a rhythm, then a chord, then a tonality, last a continuous triplet pattern).

To draw the scenes into a larger plan, Berg constructed interludes that take their departure from what precedes and lead into what follows, sometimes effecting a complete transformation of mood within a few bars. When signs of impressionism were found in these interludes, the composer rather indignantly disavowed such "vague and groundless sonorities," explaining that his musical conclusions were strictly logical. The intensity of his logic reaches its peak in the interlude before the final scene, which Berg called "the composer's confession, breaking through the framework of the dramatic plot . . . an appeal to the audience, which is here meant to represent humanity itself."

In this outcry over the death of Wozzeck, Berg makes his strongest statement of the two themes most prominently linked with Wozzeck throughout the opera. One is the leitmotif "Wir arme Leut" (Poor folks like us), sung by Wozzeck when the Captain chided him in Act I, scene 1, for his lack of bourgeois morality. The other, following at once, is the theme that took Wozzeck's part in the triple fugue (Act II, scene 2) of his encounter with both Captain and Doctor. Bringing these fragments together in the orchestral peroration creates one of the unforgettable moments in *Wozzeck*, rather like the climax of Act II of *Parsifal* when the hero associates the Magic Garden with Amfortas's wound and the two motifs are heard as one. Berg makes his plea more immediate by basing the interlude—itself an "invention"—on a conventional tonality (D minor), in a score that elsewhere uses fixed tonality only for fleeting points of reference.

Two such brief moments of conventional tonality—a C-major harp glissando leading into the fugue scene, a C-major triad when Wozzeck hands Marie his earnings—were meant to suggest an opposite effect, that of prosaic neutrality. Berg remarked, "How could the objectivity of money be more relevantly expressed than by this chord?" In the scenes where popular music is used—a waltz, a polka, a ländler—Berg's distortions of conventional tonality, though they sound like a drunk's singing out of tune, are carefully worked out according to the rules of harmony. The composer sets his music on a collision course, like two trains on the same track, so that what appears on the surface to be random dissonance will have under it the force and irony of dramatic inevitability.

The simplest effect of all in *Wozzeck* is the full-orchestra crescendo on one note, B natural, after Marie's death (Act III, scene 2). Berg tells us that the scene, a short one, is an invention built on this note, which is first heard in the sustained bass. When Marie is murdered, "all motifs connected with her are sounded precipitately. . . . They pass through her consciousness with lightning speed and in a macabre grimace: the lullaby from Scene 1, suggestions of the scene with the earrings, the Drum Major, the motif of Marie bemoaning her wretched life . . . finally the motif of dreamy fifths, the motif of waiting in vain." Beneath this brief orchestral cataclysm the note B, the "unifying element" of the scene, sounds persistently in the kettledrums. Then it emerges in the full orchestra, suggesting both the pedal point of Marie's fate and the last remnant of Wozzeck's idée fixe, the instrument of her death.

Is the musical form of *Wozzeck* too contrived? The painter Paul Klee said in a lecture in Jena, the year before the premiere of *Wozzeck,* that an artist "does not attach such intense importance to natural form as do many realist critics, because for him these final forms are not the real stuff of the process of natural creation. For he places more value on the powers that do the forming than on the final forms themselves." Still, we might ask, wouldn't heavy structuring overload and sink the opera even more surely than a loose, instinctive approach? Not with Berg: his instincts were so thoroughly channeled along lines of musical form that he could not think, feel, or react in any other way. Instead of putting the cart before the horse, he arranged the drama and let it demonstrate to him what its musical form was. Seen this way, the composition of *Wozzeck* is not a triumph of mind over matter but is as direct a process as choosing the right paints to render colors from nature. Berg was acting on the principle, as Frank Lloyd Wright did in architecture, that form follows function.

Arnold Schoenberg wrote, "I was greatly surprised when this soft-hearted, timid young man had the courage to engage in a venture that seemed to invite misfortune—to set *Wozzeck* to music." Perhaps Schoenberg disapproved because of the humanistic nature of his pupil's project. In art, it has been said, one must choose to be either saint or prophet—to regard the world as a finished product or as organic and growing. Schoenberg, the saint, was motivated by the need to be right. Berg, the prophet (of, among other things, his teacher's dodecaphonic theories), was motivated only by conscience and sensibility, showing us his own vision, rather than absolute truths. He did not settle questions of right and wrong; he posed them. *Wozzeck* continues to disturb and move us with its pinpoint-accurate portrayal of a world, both inner and outer, that we cannot deny is the way Berg shows it. If he never deceives us with the false comfort of resolution, he gives us the greater beauty of what we feel as human truth.

Index

Abbiati, Franco, 110
Abduction from the Seraglio (Mozart), 1–6
Adam, Adolphe Charles, 145, 209
Adami, Giuseppe, 333–34, 415
Adelia (Donizetti), 109
Die Ägyptische Helena (Richard Strauss), 28
Agatina, ossia la virtù premiata (Pavesi), 73, 76
Agolini, Luca, 75
Aïda (Verdi), 6–12, 124, 403
Akhnaten (Glass), 368
Albani, Emma, 152
Alceste (Gluck), 12–17
Alexander Nevsky (Prokofiev), 217
Alfano, Franco, 414, 416
Almaviva, ossia l'inutile precauzione (Rossini), 47
Almeida, Antonio de, 381
Alzira (Verdi), 37
Amato, Pasquale, 173
amore delle tre melarancie, L' (Gozzi), 215–17
Anastasi-Pozzoni, Antonietta, 9
André, Johann, 1
Andrea Chénier (Giordano), 17–22
Anelli, Angelo, 188
Ange de Nisida, L' (Donizetti), 135, 137
Angelo, Tyran de Padoue (Hugo), 167–68
Angiolina, ossia la bontà in trionfo (Rossini), 73
Anna Bolena (Donizetti), 22–27, 108
"Anna Bolena" and the Artistic Maturity of Gaetano Donizetti (Gossett), 25
Apollinaire, Guillaume, 419
Arabella (Richard Strauss), 27–31
Argento, Dominick, *Voyage of Edgar Allan Poe, The,* 423–30
Ariadne auf Naxos (Richard Strauss), 32–35, 160
Arlésienne Suite (Bizet), 66, 68
Artaserse (Gluck), 14
Aschenputtel (Brothers Grimm), 70–71
Ashbrook, William, 135, 262

Atta Troll (Heine), 346
Attila (Verdi), 35–40
Attila, King of the Huns (Werner), 36–37
Auber, Daniel, 108, 145, 273
Auden, W.H., 303, 321
Auric, Georges, 419

Baglioni, Antonio, 79
Baltsa, Agnes, 76
Bandello, Matteo, 60
Barbaia, Domenico, 376–77
Barber of Seville, The (Rossini), 40–49
Barbier, Jules, 134, 181–82, 330, 360, 380
Barbier de Séville, Le (Beaumarchais), 40–42, 266
Barbieri, Fedora, 136
Barbieri-Nini, Marianna, 238
Bardari, Giuseppe, 262
Barezzi, Antonio, 8, 112, 226, 230, 369
Barezzi, Margherita, 400. *See also* Verdi, Margherita
Barrière, Théodore, 51
Bartoletti, Bruno, 307, 310
Basile, Giovanni Battista, 70–71
Bates, Blanche, 243
Beardsley, Aubrey, 347
Beaumarchais, Pierre Augustin Caron de, 40–45, 265–66, 270–71
Beautiful Galatea, The (Suppé), 147
Beckett, Lucy, 314
Beethoven, Ludwig van, *Fidelio,* 138–42
Beggar's Opera, The (Gay), 144, 288, 295
Belasco, David, 171, 243
Belinsky, V.C., 119
Bellezza, Vincenzo, 335
Bellini, Vincenzo, 221; *Capuleti e i Montecchi, I,* 58–64; *sonnambula, La,* 374–79
"Belmont and Constanze," 1
Berg, Alban, 203–4; *Lulu,* 231–37; *Wozzeck,* 435–38
Berg, Smaragda, 233
Berganza, Teresa, 76

439

Bergsma, William, 367
Berlioz, Hector, 65, 108, 131, 330
Bernac, Pierre, 422
Bernard, Paul, 182
Bernhardt, Sarah, 117, 347
Bernstein, Leonard, 138–39, 142
Berté, Heinrich, 333–34
Bettelheim, Bruno, 71
Bhagavad-Gita, 364
Bianca e Fernando (Bellini), 376
Bizet, Georges, 362, 381; *Carmen,* 64–70
Blau, Edouard, 432
Bocage, Anne-Marie Fiquet du, 356
Boccaccio, Giovanni, 70
Boccaccio (Johann Strauss II), 147
Bohème, La (Puccini), 18, 49–54, 258
Boieldieu, François Adrien, 209
Boito, Arrigo, 115, 118, 124–29, 166–69, 231, 296–301, 373
Boleyn, Anne, 22–24
Bonfigli, Lorenzo, 59, 61–62
Bonynge, Richard, 184
Bordoni, Faustina, 293
Bori, Lucrezia, 335–36
Boris Godunov (Mussorgsky), 54–58, 159
Bottesini, Giovanni, 9
Bouilly, J.N., 140
Boulanger, Nadia, 367
Boulez, Pierre, 235, 367
Bourgeois Gentilhomme, Le (Molière), 33–34
Bovy, Berthe, 421
Branca, Emilia, 60
Bretzner, Christoph Friedrich, 1–3
Breuer, Josef, 105
Bride of Lammermoor, The (Scott), 220, 223–24
Britten, Benjamin, *Peter Grimes,* 320–24
Brothers Grimm, 70–71
Büchner, George, 232
Budden, Julian, 6–7, 9–12, 114, 410–11, 413
Bülow, Cosima von, 277, 281–82, 390. *See also* Wagner, Cosima
Bülow, Hans von, 48, 277, 281, 283, 390
Burgess, Anthony, 92–93
Burke, Edmund, 322
Busch, Hans, 6
Butler, John, 308–9

Caballé, Montserrat, 262
Cain, Henri, 98
Caldara, Antonio, 77
Callas, Maria, 26, 225, 241, 375, 421

Calvocoressi, M.D., 54, 202
Calzabigi, Raniero de', 13, 15–16, 287, 289–91
Cammarano, Salvatore, 94, 221–24, 226, 229, 409–10
Campanini, Cleofonte, 215, 219
Campra, André, 186
Capece, Carlo Sigismondo, 293
Capuleti e i Montecchi, I (Bellini), 58–64
Carafa, Michele, 223
Carmen (Bizet), 64–70, 169, 381
Carner, Mosco, 171, 245, 261,
Carnival in Rome (Johann Strauss II), 147
Caron, Pierre-Augustin. *See* Beaumarchais, Pierre Augustin Caron de
Carradori-Allan, Rosalbina, 61–62
Carré, Michel, 134, 181–82, 330, 360, 380
Carte, Richard D'Oyly, 284–85
Caruso, Enrico, 109, 173, 411, 412
Carvalho, Léon, 66, 360, 380
Casanova, 15
Cavalieri, Lina, 5, 330
Cavalleria rusticana (Mascagni), 18–19, 301–2
Cavour, Camillo, 154–55, 272
Celli, Teodoro, 416
Cendrillon (Massenet), 72
Cenerentola, La (Rossini), 70–76
Cerha, Friedrich, 234
Cervantes Saavedra, Miguel de, 96–98
Cesare-Sforza, Francesco, 46–47
Cesari, Gaetano, 416
Chaliapin, Fyodor, 101–2
Chanel, Coco, 420
Charles VI, 77
Charpentier, Gustave, 100
Chénier, André-Marie de, 20–22
Cherepnin, Nikolai, 218
Cherubini, Luigi, 131, 207–8
Chicago Opera Company, 215
Chorely, Henry Fothergill, 389
Chrétien de Troyes, 313–14
Cigna, Gina, 241
Cimarosa, Domenico, 189
Cinderella. *See La Cenerentola*
clemenza di Tito, La (Mozart), 76–82
Cocteau, Jean, 418–23
Coigny, Aimée de, 21
Coini, Jack, 220
Colbran, Isabella, 46
Communication to My Friends, A (Wagner), 211–12, 278
Complete Operas of Verdi, The (Osborne), 7, 117

Comte Ory, Le (Rossini), 144–45
Conegliano, Emmanuele. *See* Ponte, Lorenzo
 da
Conrad, Joseph, 317
Contes d'Hoffmann, Les (Offenbach), 379–84
Corelli, Franco, 331
Cornelius, Peter, 279
Corte, Andrea della, 417
Così fan tutte (Mozart), 1, 82–88
Crabbe, George, 321–22
Crivelli, Giuseppe, 59
Cuzzoni, Francesca, 293

Dame aux camélias, La (Dumas), 398
Dame de Monte Carlo, La (Poulenc), 422
Danchet, Antoine, 186
D'Annunzio, Gabriele, 32
Daudet, Alphonse, 66
Daudet, Léon, 335
Dean, Winton, 292, 294
de Bassini, Achille, 103
de Begnis, Giuseppe, 75–76
Debussy, Claude, 54, 317, 392, 434; *Pelléas et
 Mélisande,* 318–20
Decamerone (Boccaccio), 70
Deinhardstein, Johann, 278
DeJong, Constance, 364
Delavigne, Casimir, 378
Delibes, Léo, *Lakmé,* 207–11
Della Casa, Lisa, 31
Dennis, John, 126
Destinn, Emmy, 173
"Destiny of Opera, The" (Wagner), 177
Diaghilev, Serge, 57
Dialogues des Carmélites, Les (Poulenc),
 421–22
Dickens, Charles, 409
Djamileh (Bizet), 65
Docteur Miracle, Le (Bizet), 64–65
Domingo, Plácido, 381
Dominici, Francesco, 335
Don Carlos (Verdi), 7, 9, 11
Don Giovanni (Mozart), 83, 88–93, 130
Don Pasquale (Donizetti), 93–96, 110, 136
Don Procopio (Bizet), 65
Don Quichotte (Le Lorrain), 98
Don Quixote (Massenet), 96–101
Donizetti, Gaetano, *Anna Bolena,* 22–27; *Don
 Pasquale,* 93–96; *Elixir of Love, The,* 107–
 11; *favorita, La,* 134–38; *Lucia di Lammer-
 moor,* 220–25; *Maria Stuarda,* 261–65
Douglas, Lord Alfred, 348
Dragadze, Peter, 422

Drancht, Paul, 7, 9
Dschinnistan (Liebeskind), 249
Duc d'Albe, Le (Donizetti), 134, 138
due Foscari, I (Verdi), 37, 101–4
due gemelle, Le (Ponchielli), 170
*Dulcamara; or The Little Duck and the Great
 Quack* (Gilbert), 110
Dumas, Alexandre, 181, 253, 398
Duprez, Gilbert-Louis, 225
Dusk of the Gods (Wagner), 175–79
Duval, Denise, 421–23
Duverney, Joseph, 43–44

Eames, Emma, 132
Earth Spirit (Wedekind), 231
Eibenschütz, Otto, 333
Einstein on the Beach (Glass), 368
Elektra (Richard Strauss), 32, 104–6, 160,
 340
Elixir of Love, The (Donizetti), 107–11
Elms, Lauris, 358
Eluard, Paul, 419
"End in Paris, An" (Wagner), 150
Enrico di Borgogna (Donizetti), 108
Entführung aus dem Serail, Die (Mozart), 1–6
Epistles for the Ladies (Heywood), 357
Ernani (Verdi), 102, 111–18, 128
Escalaïs, Léon, 413
Eschenbach, Wolfram von, 212, 311, 313–14,
 316
Escudier, Léon, 154, 237
Étienne, Charles-Guillaume, 72, 75
Eugene Onegin (Tchaikovsky), 118–24
Eugénie (Beaumarchais), 44
Euripides, 16
Everyman (von Hofmannsthal), 32, 340

Faccio, Franco, 296–99
Fair at Sorochintsy, The (Mussorgsky), 201
Falstaff (Verdi), 124–29
fanciulla del West, La (Puccini), 170–75
Fantasia (Offenbach), 381
Fantinitza (Johann Strauss II), 147
Faris, Alexander, 381, 383
Fauré, Gabriel, 180, 360, 433
Faust (Gounod), 129–34, 330
Favero, Mafalda, 336
favorita, La (Donizetti), 110, 134–38
Ferrarese del Bene, Adriana, 84–85
Ferraris, Ines Maria, 335
Ferretti, Jacopo, 73–75
Fidelio (Beethoven), 138–42
Fiedler, Arthur, 219

Fille du régiment, La (Donizetti), 134
Fiorentino, Dante del, 259
Fischer, Karl Ludwig, 3–4
Flagstad, Kirsten, 404
Flaubert, Gustave, 346
Flauto, Vincenzo, 226
Fledermaus, Die (Johann Strauss II), 143–48
Fleischer, Edytha, 335
Flying Dutchman, The (Wagner), 148–53
Forster, E.M., 318, 321
forza del destino, La (Verdi), 9, 153–59
Forzano, Giovacchino, 414
Fox, Carol, 307–8, 310–11
Fra Diavolo (Auber), 145
Franchetti, Baron Alberto, 18, 52, 244
Frau ohne Schatten, Die (Richard Strauss), 159–66
Freeman, Mr. and Mrs. Lee A., 307
Freischütz, Der (Weber), 129, 133
Freni, Mirella, 331
Freud, Sigmund, 105
Frigerio, Ezio, 310
Fry, Christopher, 303–6, 308
Fuchs-Robettin, Hanna, 233–34
Furtwaengler, Wilhelm, 31

Gallet, Louis, 65, 360
Galli, Filippo, 25
Galli-Curci, Amelita, 225
Galli-Marié, Marie, 67
Gandhi, Mohandas K., 364–66
García, Manuel, 69
Garden, Mary, 220
Garibaldi, Giuseppe, 227–28
Gautier, Judith, 312
Gautier, Théophile, 380
Gavazzeni, Gianandrea, 413
Gay, John, 144, 288, 295
Gazzetta, ossia il matrimonio per concorso (Rossini), 73
Gee, Karolynne, 220
Gencer, Leyla, 262
Genée, Richard, 148
Ghiaurov, Nicolai, 101
Ghislanzoni, Antonio, 9, 157–58
Giacosa, Giuseppe, 18, 49, 53, 259, 415
Giesecke, Karl Ludwig, 250
Gigli, Beniamino, 335
Gilbert, William S., 110; *Mikado, The,* 284–87
Gille, Philippe, 256
Gilman, Lawrence, 391
Gioconda, La (Ponchielli), 166–70

Giordano, Umberto, *Andrea Chénier,* 17–22
Giovanna d'Arco (Verdi), 37
Girl of the Golden West, The (Puccini), 170–75
Giulietta e Romeo (Vaccai), 60–61
Glass, Philip, *Satyagraha,* 364–69
Glazunov, Alexander, 203
Gluck, Christoph Willibald, 5–6, 130, 184; *Alceste,* 12–17; *Orfeo ed Euridice,* 287–92
Godunov, Boris, 56–57
Goethe, 130, 161, 247, 431
Goggi, Emilia, 412
Gogol, Nikolai, 55, 204
Goldoni, Carlo, 216
Goldovsky, Boris, 213
Gorrio, Tobia. *See* Boito, Arrigo
Gossec, François-Joseph, 17
Gossett, Philip, 25
Götterdämmerung (Wagner), 175–79
Gounod, Charles, 64, 359; *Faust,* 129–34; *Roméo et Juliette,* 329–32
Gozzi, Carlo, 215–17, 415
Grabe, Nancy, 268
Grahl, Anne Celeste, 268
Grahn, Lucille, 283
Grand'tante, La (Massenet), 99
Grétry, André, 15
Grimm, Jacob, 278
Grisi, Giuditta, 59, 61–63
Grisi, Giulia, 26, 126
Grossi, Eleonora, 9
Grout, Donald, 94
Grundy, Sidney, 285
Guardasoni, Domenico, 78–80
Guasco, Carlo, 113
Guidarini, Anna, 189
Guiraud, Ernest, 66, 68, 147, 381
Gunsbourg, Raoul, 98, 101, 335
Gustave III (Scribe), 273
Gutierrez, Antonio, 371, 409–10
Gye, Frederick, 132
Gypsies, The (Pushkin), 68
Gypsy Baron, The (Johann Strauss II), 148

Haffner, Karl, 148
Halévy, Fromental, 64, 145, 359
Halévy, Ludovic, 66–67
Hamilton, David, 317
Hamilton, Newburgh, 351–53
Hamlet (Thomas), 179–84
Handel, George Frideric, *Orlando,* 292–95; *Samson,* 350–58
Hanslick, Eduard, 117, 143–44, 146–47, 278–79, 282, 302, 314, 409

Harding, James, 431
Harpner, Stefan G., 235
Hartmann, Georges, 431-32
Haydn, Franz Joseph, 86
Heidegger, John James, 293
Heine, Heinrich, 149, 151, 346
Hemphill, James C., 307
Henderson, William James, 132, 332,
Henry, Luigi, 25
Henry IV (Shakespeare), 126-28
Henry V (Shakespeare), 126-28
Hensel, Fanny, 131
Hensel, William, 131
Hernani (Hugo), 112, 377
Hérodiade (Massenet), 346
Hérodias (Flaubert), 346
Hérold, Louis Joseph Ferdinand, 378
Hertz, Daniel, 79
Heywood, Eliza, 357
Heywood, J.C., 346
*Histoires et contes du temps passé, avec des
  moralités* (Perrault), 71
History of German National Literature
  (Gervinus), 277
Hoffmann, E.T.A., 88, 380
Hofmannsthal, Hugo von, 27-30, 32-35,
  104-6, 159-66, 339-44, 348
Hogwood, Christopher, 353, 357
Holmes, Augusta, 361
Horne, Marilyn, 76, 387
Houdon, Jean-Antoine, 17
Hughes, Spike, 49
Hugo, Victor, 112, 117, 154, 167-68, 325, 377

Idoménée (Campra), 186
Idomeneo (Mozart), 4, 184-87
Illica, Luigi, 18-19, 21, 49, 53, 259
Indigo and the Forty Thieves (Johann Strauss
  II), 147
Ingres, Jean Auguste Dominique, 131
Intermezzo (Richard Strauss), 163
Isaac, Adele, 380
Isouard, Nicolo, 72-75
Italian Girl in Algiers, The (Rossini), 187-91

Janáček, Leoš, *Katya Kabanova*, 191-98
Jannetti, Francesco, 135
Jauner, Franz, 380
Jedermann (von Hofmannsthal), 32, 340
Jenůfa (Janáček), 192
Jeritza, Maria, 152, 165
Johnson, Samuel, 391
Jolie Fille de Perth, La (Bizet), 65

Jongleur de Notre Dame, Le (Massenet), 98
Joseph II, 1, 83, 267-68
Joukowsky, Paul von, 312
Joy of Music, The (Bernstein), 138

Kabale und Liebe (Schiller), 228-29
Kalbeck, Max, 433
Kanawa, Kiri Te, 336
Katya Kabanova (Janáček), 191-98
Kelly, David, 358
Kempe, Rudolf, 31
Kerman, Joseph, 391-92, 395
Khovanshchina (Mussorgsky), 55, 198-202
Khovansky, Ivan, 198
Kierkegaard, Søren, 88
Klee, Paul, 438
Koechlin, Charles, 418
Koussevitzky, Serge, 321
Krasner, Louis, 234
Kraus, Alfredo, 381-83
Krauss, Clemens, 31
Krusceniski, Salomea, 242
Küstner, Theodor, 152

Lablache, Luigi, 26
Lady Macbeth of Mtsensk (Shostakovich),
  202-7
Lagrange, Anne Caroline de, 403
Lakmé (Delibes), 207-11
Lanari, Alessandro, 238
Landon, H.C. Robbins, 79
Lang, Paul Henry, 93
Lanner, Joseph, 146
Lassalle, Jean, 132
Lassen, Eduard, 361
Laurent, Adolphe, 99
Lavrovskaya, Elizaveta, 121
Lawrence, Robert, 170
Lechi, Luigi, 387
Legouvé, Ernest, 263
Lehár, Franz, 333
Lehmann, Lotte, 31, 35, 165
Leigh, Mitch, 98
Le Lorrain, Jacques, 98
Lemaire, Ferdinand, 360-61
Leonore (Beethoven), 140-41
Leoncavallo, Ruggiero, 18-19, 52, 244, 258;
  I pagliacci, 301-3
Leopold II, 13, 78, 80
Leppard, Raymond, 358
Leskov, Nikolai, 204-5
Lesseps, Ferdinand de, 7
Leuven, Adolphe de, 67

Levi, Hermann, 312–13, 315
Lewis, D.B. Wyndham, 51
Lewy, Gustav, 148
Liadov, Anatol, 218
Liebestrank, Der (Donizetti), 107–11
Lieutenant Kije (Prokofiev), 217
Life of Rossini (Stendhal), 47, 187
Lind, Jenny, 225
Lindermeire, Elisabeth, 358
Liszt, Franz, 99, 149, 277, 282, 361, 390
Lockspeiser, Edward, 421
Locle, Camille du, 7–9, 66
Loewe, Sophie, 116, 238
Lohengrin (Wagner), 211–15
Lombardi, I (Verdi), 37, 111, 116
Long, John Luther, 243
Lortzing, Gustav Albert, 278
Louis XV, 15, 43
Love for Three Oranges, The (Prokofiev),
    215–20
Lualdi, Adriano, 417
Lucia di Lammermoor (Donizetti), 220–25
Ludwig II, 390
Luisa Miller (Verdi), 225–31
Lulu (Berg), 231–37
Lulu, oder die Zauberflöte (Liebeskind),
    248–49
Luten, C.J., 94
Lyric Opera of Chicago, 307

Macbeth (Verdi), 237–41
Mackerras, Charles, 192
Madama Butterfly (Puccini), 118, 171, 241–46
Maeterlinck, Maurice, 319
Maffei, Andrea, 238
Magic Flute, The (Mozart), 3, 6, 246–52
Mahler, Alma Schindler, 233–34
Mahler, Anna, 234
Mahler, Gustav, 302, 348–49
Maier, Mathilde, 277
Mala vita (Giordano), 18
Malanotte, Adelaide, 387
Malibran, Maria, 63, 263
Man Verdi, The (Walker), 10
Manfredi, Doria, 172
Manin, Daniele, 272
Mann, Thomas, 314
Mann, William, 88, 166
Manon (Massenet), 252–56
Manon Lescaut (Puccini), 52–53, 257–61
Mapleson, Colonel Henry, 132
Marcolini, Marietta, 189, 190
Marek, George, 242, 417

Margarethe (Gounod), 133
Maria Stuarda (Donizetti), 261–65
Mariage de Figaro, Le (Beaumarchais), 40,
    45, 83
Mariani, Angelo, 8, 10
Mariette, Auguste, 7–9
Mariette, Edouard, 7
Marin Faliero (Donizetti), 221
Marinuzzi, Gino, 335
Marnia (Giordano), 18
Marriage, The (Mussorgsky), 55–56
Marriage of Figaro, The (Mozart), 265–71
Martin, George, 400–1
Martini, Nino, 335
Martyrs, Les (Donizetti), 109–10, 134
Mascagni, Pietro, 18–19, 170, 301–2
Masked Ball, A (Verdi), 272–77
Massenet, Jules, 18, 72, 180, 244, 346, 392;
    Don Quixote, 96–101; *Manon*, 252–56;
    Werther, 431–35
Mastersingers of Nuremberg, The (Wagner),
    277–83
matrimonio segreto, Il (Cimarosa), 189
Maupassant, Guy de, 255
Maurel, Victor, 152, 298–99, 301, 373
Mayr, J.S., 376
Mayr, Richard, 165
Mayr, Simone, 107–8, 140
Mazzini, Giuseppe, 227–28, 272
Mazzola, Caterino, 78–79
Medea in Corinto (Mayr), 108
Médecin malgré lui, Le (Gounod), 130
Mefistofele (Boito), 125
Meilhac, Henri, 66–67, 145, 255
Meistersinger, Die (Wagner), 175
Melba, Nellie, 132, 225, 330
Melchior, Lauritz, 404
Mendelssohn, Felix, 131
Mercadante, Saverio, 273
Mérimée, Prosper, 66–68
Merry Wives of Vienna, The (Johann
    Strauss II), 147
Merry Wives of Windsor, The (Shakespeare),
    126–27
Méry, Joseph, 7
Messiah (Handel), 295, 353–54
Metastasio, Pietro, 72, 77–79, 101, 288
Meurice, Paul, 181
Meyer, Friederike, 277
Meyer, Hans, 27
Meyerbeer, Giacomo, 11, 149, 152, 208–9
Meyerhold, Vsevolod, 215–18
Mignon (Thomas), 180

Mikado, The (Sullivan), 284–87
Milhaud, Darius, 367
Miliukova, Antonina, 122
Millet, Paul, 432
Milnes, Sherrill, 180
Milton, John, 303–6, 351–52
Miolan-Carvalho, Maria, 330
Mitchell, Ronald, 409
Mitropoulos, Dimitri, 123
Moberly, R.B., 91
Mocenigo, Nanni, 112–13
Moffo, Anna, 336
Molière, 33–34, 130
Moncada, Gioacchino, 75
Mongini, Pietro, 9
Monteverdi, Claudio, 101
Moreau, Gustave, 347
Mozart, Constanze, 80–81
Mozart, Wolfgang Amadeus, 130; *Abduction from the Seraglio*, 1–6; *clemenza di Tito, La*, 76–93; *Così fan tutte*, 82–88; *Don Giovanni*, 88–93; *Idomeneo*, 184–87; *Magic Flute, The*, 246–52; *Marriage of Figaro, The*, 265–71
Mugnone, Leopoldo, 335
Muratore, Lucien, 330
Murger, Henri, 49–52, 302
Musset, Alfred de, 65, 253
Mussolini, Benito, 417
Mussorgsky, Modest, 159; *Boris Godunov*, 54–58; *Khovanshchina*, 198–202
Muzio, Claudia, 335
Muzio, Emanuele, 37–38, 112
My Life (Wagner), 277, 311

Nabucco (Verdi), 37, 111, 221, 398
Nahowski, Helene, 232, 234
Nerone (Boito), 125
Newman, Ernest, 150–51, 280, 283, 350
Niemetschek, Franz, 79–81
Nietzsche, Friedrich, 142, 314, 317
"Night at the Black Pig, A" (Nolte), 430
Nikolsky, Vladimir, 56
Nilsson, Christine, 183
Ninetta alla corte (Rossini), 73
Nissen, Georg, 79–80
Nolte, Charles, 430
Nonne sanglante, La (Gounod), 130, 133
Nose, The (Shostakovich), 204
Nuremberg Chronicle (Wagenseil), 278

Oeser, Fritz, 68, 381
Oestvig, Karl Aagard, 165

Offenbach, Jacques, 145, 209, 292; *Tales of Hoffmann, The*, 379–84
Oliva, Domenico, 258–59
"On Beethoven" (Wagner), 177
Opera and Drama (Wagner), 175, 177
Operetta: A Theatrical History (Traubner), 144
Orfeo ed Euridice (Gluck), 13, 130, 287–92
Orlandi, Elisa, 25
Orlando (Handel), 292–95
Orphée aux enfers (Offenbach), 145, 292
Orpheus at Eighty (Sheean), 228
Orsini, Felice, 272
Osborne, Charles, 7, 117, 326, 374, 409
Ostrovsky, Nikolai, 191
Otello (Verdi), 103, 295–301

Pacini, Giovanni, 59–60
Paër, Ferdinando, 140
Page, Robert, 310
pagliacci, I (Leoncavallo), 18, 301–3
Paisiello, Giovanni, 42, 47–48
Pandora's Box (Wedekind), 231–32
Panizza, Ettore, 335
Pantaleoni, Romilda, 299
Paradise Lost (Penderecki), 303–11
Parsifal (Wagner), 212, 311–18
Pasdeloup, Jules, 66
Pasha, Ismail, 6–7, 9
Pasta, Giuditta, 25, 377, 387
Patti, Adelina, 225, 330, 403
Paul Bunyan (Britten), 321
Pavesi, Stefano, 73, 76, 94
Pêcheurs de perles, Les (Bizet), 65
Pélissier, Olympe, 41
Pelléas et Mélisande (Debussy), 318–20
Pellegrini, Giulio, 59
Penco, Rosina, 412
Penderecki, Krysztof, *Paradise Lost*, 303–11
Pergin, Marianne, 12
Périchole, La (Offenbach), 145
Perrault, Charles, 71
Perry, Igal, 310
Persichetti, Vincent, 367
Peter "The Great," 198
Peter and the Wolf (Prokofiev), 217
Peter Grimes (Britten), 320–24
Pezzi, Francesco, 108
Pfistermeister, Franz von, 280–81
Phillips, Harvey E., 19
Philtre, Le (Scribe), 108
Piave, Francesco Maria, 8, 36, 102, 112–16, 153–57, 237–38, 398, 401–2

Piccinni, Niccola, 14, 290
Piccolino (Sardou), 147
Piccolomini, Marietta, 403
Pirata, Il (Bellini), 58–59, 376
Pizzetti, Ildebrando, 415
Plançon, Pol, 132
Planer, Minna, 149, 277, 279
Plaschke-von der Osten, Eva, 31
Platonova, Julia, 57
Poe, Edgar Allan, 423–30
Poliuto (Donizetti), 109–10, 134
Pompadour, Madame de, 15
Ponchielli, Amilcare, La Gioconda, 166–70
Ponnelle, Jean-Pierre, 81, 152–53
Pons, Lily, 225
Ponte, Lorenzo da, 78, 82–90, 265–71
Postillon de Longjumeau, Le (Adam), 145
Poulenc, Francis, Voix humaine, La, 417–23
Praga, Marco, 258
Preis, Alexander, 204–5
Prêtre, Georges, 421
Prévost d'Exiles, Antoine-François, 253–55, 257
Prince, Harold, 171
Princess Ida, 284–85
Princesse jaune, La (Saint-Saëns), 360
Prokofiev, Sergei, Love for Three Oranges, The, 215–20
promessi sposi, I (Ponchielli), 170
Puccini: A Critical Biography (Carner), 245
Puccini, Elvira, 172–73, 257, 259–60
Puccini, Giacomo, 18, 118, 302; Bohème, La, 49–54; Girl of the Golden West, The, 170–75; Madama Butterfly, 241–46; Manon Lescaut, 257–61; rondine, La, 332–39; Tosca, 391–96; Turandot, 413–17
Puchberg, Baron, 86
Puecher, Virginio, 309–10
Pushkin, Alexander, 56–57, 68, 118–21
Puzzi-Tose, Giacinta, 263

Raaff, Anton, 184
Radiciotti, Giuseppe, 72
Radiguet, Raymond, 420
Rakha, Alla, 367
Rank, Otto, 88
Ravel, Maurice, 359
Reber, Napoléon-Henri, 99
Redern, Count Wilhelm von, 152
Regina Diaz (Giordano), 18
Reinhardt, Max, 32–33, 340, 343
Reszke, Edouard de, 132, 330, 373, 432,
Reszke, Jean de, 132, 330, 432

Réveillon, Le (Meilhac and Halévy), 145, 147–48
Reyer, Ernest, 66
Rheingold, Das (Wagner), 175–76
Rheinnixen, Die (Offenbach), 381
Rice, J.B., 374
Ricordi, Giulio, 257, 259, 295–96
Ricordi, Tito, 11, 241, 334, 370
Riesemann, Oskar von, 200
Rigoletto (Verdi), 6, 128, 324–28, 396–97
Rimsky-Korsakov, Nicholas, 54–57, 198–202, 392
Rinaldo (Handel), 293
Rizza, Gilda dalla, 335
Robertson, Francis, 167, 169, 170
Rocklitz, Johann, 140
Roeckel, Josef, 140–41
Roi s'amuse, Le (Hugo), 325
Rolland, Romain, 13, 160, 348–9
Romani, Felice, 24–27, 58–61, 72–76, 101–2, 107–8, 222, 374–77
Roméo et Juliette (Gounod), 329–32
rondine, La (Puccini), 332–39
Ronzi-De Begnis, Giuseppina, 63, 262
Roosevelt, Blanche, 300
Rosenkavalier, Der (Richard Strauss), 27–28, 31–33, 339–44
Rossi, Gaetano, 73, 385–86
Rossini, Gioacchino, 11, 59, 116, 144, 221, 264, 379; Barber of Seville, The, 40–49; La Cenerentola, 70–76; Italian Girl in Algiers, The, 187–91; Tancredi, 384–87
Rostand, Claude, 421
Rouleau, Joseph, 358
Roullet, Le Blanc du, 16
Royer, Alphonse, 135
Rubini, Giovanni, 25
Ruffini, Giacomo, 94
Ruffo, Titta, 302
Rumyantsev, Pavel, 121–22
Ruy Blas (Hugo), 154
Rysanek, Leonie, 152, 165, 241

Sachs, Hans, 278
Sadie, Stanley, 248
Sainte-Marie, Constance de, 99
Saint-Saëns, Camille, 68; Samson et Dalila, 358–64
Salieri, Antonio, 45, 78, 80, 86, 267, 271
Salome (Richard Strauss), 106, 160, 344–50
Sammartini, Giovanni Battista, 14
Samson (Handel), 350–58
Samson Agonistes (Milton), 351

Samson et Dalila (Saint-Saëns), 358–64
Sanderson, Sibyl, 100, 432
Santley, Sir Charles, 132
Sapho (Gounod), 130
Sardou, Victorien, 7, 18, 147
Satie, Erik, 419
Satyagraha (Glass), 364–69
Scarlatti, Domenico, 293
Scènes de la vie de Bohème (Murger), 49, 51, 302
Scevola, Luigi, 61,
Schack, Benedict, 249
Schalk, Franz, 165
Schikaneder, Emanuel, 139, 247–49, 251, 268
Schiller, Friedrich, 228–29, 262
Schipa, Tito, 335
Schoelcher, Victor, 358
Schoenberg, Arnold, 231, 436, 438
Schopenhauer, Arthur, 404–5
Schorr, Friedrich, 152
Schröder-Devrient, Wilhelmine, 152
Schutz, Amalia, 63
Scott, Sir Walter, 65, 220, 222–23
Scribe, Eugène, 101, 108, 135, 208, 273–74, 376, 378
Scudo, Pietro, 131
Sembrich, Marcella, 225
Semiramide (Rossini), 264
Seroff, Victor, 219
Serre, Anna del, 262
Sethos: Histoire ou vie tiré des monuments, anecdotes de l'ancien Egypte (Terrasson), 249
1791: Mozart's Last Year (Landon), 79–80
Shakespeare, William, 126–27, 182–83, 237–39, 296, 329–32
Shankar, Ravi, 367
Shaw, George Bernard, 88, 117, 132, 134, 166, 256, 261, 408, 412, 433
Sheean, Vincent, 228
Shilovsky, K.S., 119
Shostakovich, Dmitri, 55; *Lady Macbeth of Mtsensk*, 202–7
Siegfried (Wagner), 176–77
Silja, Anja, 152
Sills, Beverly, 26, 108, 225, 262, 380
Simionato, Giulietta, 136
Simon Boccanegra (Verdi), 369–74
Simoni, Renato, 415
Sinfonia Domestica (Richard Strauss), 163
Singing with Richard Strauss (Lehmann), 165
Slater, Montagu, 321
Slonimsky, Nicholas, 337–38

Solera, Temistocle, 37–38, 102
Somma, Antonio, 272, 274
sonnambula, La (Bellini), 61, 374–79
Sonzogno, Lorenzo, 335
Sophocles, 104
Sorrows of Young Werther, The (Goethe), 431
sposo deluso, Lo (Mozart), 268
Stade, Frederica von, 76
Stadler, Anton, 79
Stanislavsky, Konstantin, 121–22
Stanislavsky on Opera (Stanislavsky and Rumyantsev), 121–22
Stassov, Vladimir, 199
Steber, Eleanor, 31
Steegmuller, Francis, 420
Stein, Elliot, 422
Stein, Erwin, 234
Steller, Francesco, 9
Stendhal, 47–48, 187–90
Stephanie, Gottlieb, 1, 3–4
Sterbini, Cesare, 46
Stiffelio (Verdi), 396–97
Stignani, Ebe, 136
Stoesslova, Kamila, 193
Stoltz, Rosine, 135
Stolz, Teresa, 8, 10, 116
Storchio, Rosina, 241–42
Storm, The (Ostrovsky), 191
straniera, La (Bellini), 59
Stratas, Teresa, 235
Strauss, Eduard, 146
Strauss, Eduard II, 146
Strauss, Johann I, 143, 146
Strauss, Johann II, *Fledermaus, Die,* 143–48
Strauss, Johann III, 146
Strauss, Joseph, 146
Strauss, Pauline de Ahna, 32, 163
Strauss, Richard, *Arabella,* 27–35; *Ariadne auf Naxos,* 32–35; *Elektra,* 104–6; *Frau ohne Schatten, Die,* 159–66; *Rosenkavalier, Der,* 339–50; *Salome,* 344–50
Stravinsky, Igor, 324–25
Strepponi, Giuseppina, 109, 116, 230, 272, 400–3. *See also* Verdi, Giuseppina
Strindberg, August, 430
Strohm, Reinhard, 294
Studies in Hysteria (Breuer and Freud), 105
Sturgis, Julian, 285
Sullivan, Arthur, *Mikado, The,* 284–87
Suppé, Franz von, 147
Süssmayr, Franz, 79–80, 250
Sutherland, Joan, 26, 225, 262, 358, 375, 380
Svoboda, Josef, 308, 309

Tacchinardi-Persiani, Fanny, 225
Tadolini, Eugenia, 38, 239–40
Talbot, Catherine, 357
Tales of Hoffmann, The (Offenbach), 379–84
Tamagno, Francesco, 299, 373
Tamberlick, Enrico, 153–54
Tancredi (Rossini), 384–87
Tannhäuser (Wagner), 388–91
Tarare (Salieri), 45
Taylor, Ronald, 278
Tchaikovsky, Peter Ilyich, 330; *Eugene Onegin,* 118–24
Terrasson, Jean, 249
Tetrazzini, Luisa, 225
Thaïs (Massenet), 100
Thomas, Ambroise, 99; *Hamlet,* 179–84
Tietjens, Therese, 26
Tokatyan, Armand, 335
Tommaso Chatterton (Leoncavallo), 301
Torelli, Vincenzo, 272
Torvaldo e Dorliska (Rossini), 46
Tosca (Puccini), 52, 391–96
Toscanini, Arturo, 11, 53, 125, 173, 414–15, 417
Toye, Francis, 231, 412–13
Traubner, Richard, 143–44, 146–48
traviata, La (Verdi), 396–403
Tristan und Isolde (Wagner), 175, 403–8
trovatore, Il (Verdi), 128, 371, 398, 408–13
Tudor Ring (Donizetti), 24
Turandot (Puccini), 172, 413–17
Turina, Giuditta, 59
Tyson, Alan, 79

Undine (Tchaikovsky), 121
Unger, Caroline, 26
Ursuleac, Viorica, 31
Uses of Enchantment: The Meaning and Importance of Fairy Tales, The (Bettelheim), 71

Vaccaj, Nicola, 60, 63
Vaëz, Gustave, 135
Valentini-Terrani, Lucia, 76
Varesco, Giambattista, 186, 268
Varesi, Felice, 238, 402
Varzar, Nina, 206
Vasselli, Virginia, 109
Verdi, Giuseppe, 109, 221, 243, 325–26, 378; *Aïda,* 6–12; *Attila,* 35–40; *due Foscari, I,* 101–4; *Ernani,* 111–18; *Falstaff,* 124–29; *forza del destino, La,* 153–59; *Luisa Miller,* 225–31; *Macbeth,* 237–41; *Masked Ball, A,*
272–77; *Otello,* 295–301; *Rigoletto,* 324–28; *Simon Boccanegra,* 369–74; *traviata, La,* 396–403; *trovatore, Il,* 408–13
Verdi, Giuseppina, 8–10, 125, 129, 153–56, 300, 410–11. *See also* Strepponi, Giuseppina
Verdi, Margherita, 370. *See also* Barezzi, Margherita
Verni, Andrea, 75–76
Vespasianus, Titus Flavius Sabinus, 76–77
Viardot-Garcia, Pauline, 361
Vickers, Jon, 358
Viñes, Ricardo, 418–19
Visconti, Luchino, 26
Vitarelli, Zenobio, 75
Vittorio Emanuele, 17
Voix humaine, La (Poulenc), 417–23
Voltaire, 385–86
von Meck, Nadezhda, 120–21
Voyage of Edgar Allan Poe, The (Argento), 423–30

Wagenseil, Johann Christoph, 278
Wagner, Cosima, 151, 312. *See also* Bülow, Cosima von
Wagner Nights (Newman), 150
Wagner, Richard, 81, 166–67, 378; *Flying Dutchman, The,* 148–53; *Götterdämmerung,* 175–79; *Lohengrin,* 211–15; *Mastersingers of Nuremberg, The,* 277–83; *Parsifal,* 311–18; *Tannhäuser,* 388–91; *Tristan und Isolde,* 403–8
Waldmann, Maria, 10
Walker, Fran, 10
Walküre, Die (Wagner), 175–77
Walpole, Horace, 354
Walter, Bruno, 248
Wanamaker, Sam, 308–9
Wasserman, Dale, 98
Weaver, William, 159
Weber, Carl Maria von, 129
Wedekind, Benjamin Franklin, 231–33, 236–37
Wedekind, Tilly Newes, 232
Weinstock, Herbert, 107, 135
Weissheimer, Wendelin, 279
Werner, Zacharias, 36
Werther (Massenet), 100, 431–35
Wesendonck, Mathilde, 277, 279
Wesendonck, Otto, 277
West, Edward Sackville, 35
Westernhagen, Curt von, 150, 317
Wetzlar, Baron Raimund, 267

Wilde, Oscar, 346–48
Willermawlaz, Marie-Thérèse, 41
Willnew, Alfred, 333
Wilson, Robert, 368
Wolf, Hugo, 166, 168, 170
Woolf, Virginia, 317
Wozzeck (Berg), 203–4, 232–33, 435–38

Yradier, Sebastián, 68

Zaide (Mozart), 2, 6
Zaira (Bellini), 58–59, 61
Zamboni, Luigi, 46
Zauberflöte, Die (Mozart), 3, 6, 241–46
Zimmerman, Pierre, 65
Zingarelli, Niccolo, 376

PAY 2²⁰
10⁰⁰ – 400 !
Peta
HENRy
BARB
Ricky